탄탄한 영어 실력을 위한 영문법의 시작

마더텅 영문법 3800제

**토익·토플
TEPS
공무원영어
대비**

BASIC 1

발행 초판 1쇄 (2023년 4월 7일) **발행인** 문숙영 **발행처** 마더텅(Mother Tongue Co., Ltd.) **교재 개발 책임** 서은숙
교재 개발 진행 김현수, 최은조, 박상우, 신준기 **문제편 집필** 김은미(대구 달서구) 선생님, 소피아(김규은 경기 분당) 선생님, 고미라(서울 상경중) 선생님, 남현정, 서연서, 이윤정, 이옥현, 양진희, 홍성경, 박상우, 김다영, 박선주, 최은조, 김현수, 신준기, 김현, 김주현, 김혜진, 박혜미, 김다영
교재 검토 김경미(강남 대치) 선생님, 조현정(서울 중계) 선생님, 윤미선(서울 강서) 선생님, 김미경(서울 동작) 선생님, 김미옥(강남 일원) 선생님, 김은미(대구 달서구) 선생님, 이은혜(경기 일산) 선생님, 소피아(김규은 경기 분당) 선생님, 양원석(서울 서초) 선생님, 송수아(충남 보령) 선생님
교정 김현수, 최은조, 박상우, 정은주, 홍지민, 신진실, 도예원, 조수성, 서연서, 이윤정, 윤수경, 양진희, 성은혜, 홍성경, 오정훈, 하은옥, 이은영, 유지원, 김다영 **영문 감수** Kathryn O' Handley **단어장 녹음** 손정은, Janet Lee, 최석환 **녹음 편집** 와이알 미디어
디자인 김연실, 양은선 **삽화** 정제욱, 이혜승, 백승헌, 이유진, 이순웅, 정재환 **인디자인 편집** 고연화, 박경아 **제작** 이주영
주소 서울시 금천구 가마산로 96, 708호(가산동, 대륭테크노타운 8차) **홈페이지** www.toptutor.co.kr **등록번호** 제 1-2423호

* 이 책에 실린 모든 내용에 대한 저작권은 (주)마더텅에 있으므로 적법한 허락 없이는 어떠한 형태나 수단으로도 전재, 복사할 수 없습니다.
* 잘못 만들어진 책은 바꾸어 드립니다.

Problem Solving Skill

차례

CHAPTER 1 | 문장의 기초 Introduction to Sentences

- PSS 1　문장의 종류
- PSS 1-1　명사의 인칭 구분 ········· 5
- PSS 1-2　인칭대명사와 be동사 ········· 6
- PSS 1-3　be동사의 부정문 ········· 7
- PSS 1-4　일반동사의 긍정문/부정문 ········· 8
- PSS 1-5　Yes/No 의문문 ········· 10
- PSS 1-6　부정의문문 ········· 11
- PSS 1-7　의문사로 시작하는 의문문 ········· 13
- PSS 1-8　선택의문문 ········· 14
- PSS 1-9　부가의문문 ········· 16
- PSS 1-10　명령문 ········· 17
- PSS 1-11　Let's로 시작하는 청유문 ········· 18
- PSS 1-12　주의해야 할 부가의문문 ········· 19
- PSS 1-13　감탄문 ········· 20
- PSS 2　품사/문장의 요소/문장의 5형식
- PSS 2-1　영어의 8품사 ········· 21
- PSS 2-2　문장의 요소 ········· 23
- PSS 2-3　문장의 5형식 ········· 25
- PSS 2-4　감각동사+주격 보어(형용사) ········· 26
- PSS 2-5　4형식에서 3형식으로의 전환 ········· 27
- Chapter Review Test ········· 29

CHAPTER 2 | 시제 Tense

- PSS 1　현재시제
- PSS 1-1　일반동사의 3인칭 현재 단수형 I ········· 38
- PSS 1-2　일반동사의 3인칭 현재 단수형 II ········· 39
- PSS 1-3　3인칭 현재 단수형의 '-(e)s' 발음 ········· 40
- PSS 1-4　현재시제의 쓰임 ········· 41
- PSS 2　과거시제
- PSS 2-1　일반동사의 규칙 변화형 I ········· 42
- PSS 2-2　일반동사의 규칙 변화형 II ········· 43
- PSS 2-3　규칙 변화 과거형의 '-(e)d' 발음 ········· 45
- PSS 2-4　일반동사의 불규칙 변화형 ········· 46
- PSS 2-5　과거시제의 쓰임 ········· 51
- PSS 3　미래시제 -will과 be going to ········· 52
- PSS 4　진행시제
- PSS 4-1　동사의 -ing형 I ········· 55
- PSS 4-2　동사의 -ing형 II ········· 56
- PSS 4-3　현재진행시제와 과거진행시제 ········· 57
- PSS 4-4　미래를 나타내는 현재진행시제 ········· 58
- PSS 5　현재완료시제
- PSS 5-1　현재완료시제의 쓰임 ········· 60
- PSS 5-2　현재완료시제와 과거시제의 비교 ········· 61
- Chapter Review Test ········· 63

CHAPTER 3 | 조동사 Modals

- PSS 1　조동사+동사원형 ········· 72
- PSS 2　조동사의 부정형과 축약형 ········· 73
- PSS 3　조동사로 시작하는 의문문 ········· 74
- PSS 4　조동사의 종류
- PSS 4-1　can I ········· 76
- PSS 4-2　can II ········· 77
- PSS 4-3　may ········· 78
- PSS 4-4　May I ~?에 대한 승낙과 거절의 표현 ········· 79
- PSS 4-5　Will[Would] you ~? ········· 80
- PSS 4-6　would like (to) ········· 81
- PSS 4-7　must I ········· 82
- PSS 4-8　must II ········· 83
- PSS 4-9　must not, don't have to ········· 84
- PSS 4-10　should, had better ········· 85
- Chapter Review Test ········· 88

CHAPTER 4 | 수동태 Passive Voice

- PSS 1　격 변화 - 주격과 목적격 ········· 96
- PSS 2　수동태에 많이 쓰이는 불규칙동사 ········· 97
- PSS 3　수동태 문장 만드는 법 ········· 99
- PSS 4　현재시제와 과거시제의 수동태 ········· 100
- PSS 5　「by+목적격」의 생략 ········· 101
- PSS 6　5형식 문장의 수동태 전환 ········· 102
- Chapter Review Test ········· 104

CHAPTER 5 | 명사와 관사 Nouns and Articles

- PSS 1　명사의 종류 ········· 108
- PSS 2　명사의 복수형
- PSS 2-1　명사의 규칙 복수형 I ········· 109
- PSS 2-2　명사의 규칙 복수형 II ········· 110
- PSS 2-3　명사의 불규칙 복수형 ········· 112
- PSS 3　단위명사의 쓰임 ········· 113
- PSS 4　명사의 소유격 ········· 115
- PSS 5　주의해야 할 명사의 수 ········· 118
- PSS 6　부정관사 a(n)의 쓰임 ········· 119
- PSS 7　a(n)의 의미 구별 ········· 120
- PSS 8　정관사 the의 쓰임 ········· 121
- PSS 9　관사를 쓰지 않는 경우 ········· 123
- PSS 10　There is/are ········· 124
- PSS 11　동격 ········· 127
- Chapter Review Test ········· 128

CHAPTER 6 | 대명사 Pronouns

- PSS 1　인칭대명사 ········· 136
- PSS 2　재귀대명사 ········· 138
- PSS 3　비인칭 주어 it ········· 140
- PSS 4　지시대명사 ········· 141
- PSS 5　부정대명사
- PSS 5-1　one ········· 142
- PSS 5-2　another, others, the other(s) ········· 143
- PSS 5-3　each, every ········· 144
- PSS 6　의문대명사
- PSS 6-1　who ········· 144
- PSS 6-2　what, which ········· 145
- PSS 7　so, same, such ········· 147
- Chapter Review Test ········· 148

CHAPTER 7 | 부정사 Infinitives

- PSS 1　명사처럼 쓰이는 to부정사
- PSS 1-1　주어와 보어로 쓰이는 to부정사 ········· 154
- PSS 1-2　목적어로 쓰이는 to부정사 ········· 155
- PSS 2　형용사처럼 쓰이는 to부정사 ········· 157
- PSS 3　부사처럼 쓰이는 to부정사 ········· 158

PSS 4	to가 없는 원형부정사	
PSS 4-1	사역동사(let, have, make)+목적어+원형부정사	160
PSS 4-2	지각동사(hear, see, watch, feel)+목적어+원형부정사	161
Chapter Review Test		163

CHAPTER 8 | 동명사 Gerunds

PSS 1	동명사의 역할	168
PSS 2	동명사를 목적어로 쓰는 동사와 동명사와 to부정사 모두를 목적어로 쓰는 동사	170
PSS 3	동명사의 관용 표현	
PSS 3-1	go+-ing	171
PSS 3-2	How[What] about+-ing?	173
PSS 3-3	그 외 관용 표현	174
Chapter Review Test		176

CHAPTER 9 | 분사 Participles

PSS 1	현재분사와 과거분사의 형태와 개념	182
PSS 2	명사를 수식하는 현재분사와 과거분사	183
PSS 3	동사의 활용에 쓰이는 현재분사와 과거분사	185
PSS 4	현재분사와 동명사의 비교	186
PSS 5	감정을 나타내는 분사	187
Chapter Review Test		190

CHAPTER 10 | 형용사 Adjectives

PSS 1	형용사	194
PSS 2	형용사의 한정적 용법과 서술적 용법	195
PSS 3	-thing, -body(one)+형용사	196
PSS 4	수사	
PSS 4-1	기수와 서수	197
PSS 4-2	정수	199
PSS 4-3	전화번호	200
PSS 4-4	분수와 소수	201
PSS 4-5	시각 I	202
PSS 4-6	시각 II	202
PSS 4-7	연도와 날짜	203
PSS 4-8	금액	204
PSS 4-9	온도	205
PSS 5	관용적인 수사 표현	
PSS 5-1	tens[hundreds, thousands, millions] of+복수 명사	207
PSS 5-2	every+숫자	208
PSS 6	수나 양을 나타내는 형용사	
PSS 6-1	many, much	209
PSS 6-2	(a) few, (a) little	212
PSS 6-3	some, any	213
PSS 6-4	not ~ any = no	214
Chapter Review Test		215

CHAPTER 11 | 부사 Adverbs

PSS 1	부사의 형태	
PSS 1-1	부사의 역할과 형용사를 부사로 만드는 법	222
PSS 1-2	형용사와 형태가 같은 부사	224
PSS 2	빈도부사	
PSS 2-1	빈도부사의 종류와 의미	225
PSS 2-2	빈도부사의 위치	227
PSS 3	too, either	228
PSS 4	well	229
PSS 5	「타동사+부사」	
PSS 5-1	「타동사+부사」의 종류	230
PSS 5-2	「타동사+부사」의 어순	232
PSS 6	의문부사	
PSS 6-1	how, where, when, why	233
PSS 6-2	How+형용사/부사 ~?	234
Chapter Review Test		236

CHAPTER 12 | 비교구문 Comparisons

PSS 1	원급, 비교급, 최상급의 형태	
PSS 1-1	규칙 변화형 I	242
PSS 1-2	규칙 변화형 II	243
PSS 1-3	규칙 변화형 III	244
PSS 1-4	불규칙 변화형	246
PSS 2	원급을 이용한 비교	248
PSS 3	비교급을 이용한 비교	
PSS 3-1	비교급+than	250
PSS 3-2	비교급+and+비교급	252
PSS 3-3	비교급 강조	253
PSS 4	최상급을 이용한 비교	
PSS 4-1	the+최상급	255
PSS 4-2	one of the+최상급+복수 명사	256
Chapter Review Test		258

CHAPTER 13 | 접속사 Conjunctions

PSS 1	and, but	264
PSS 2	and, or	265
PSS 3	so	266
PSS 4	that	267
PSS 5	when, because, if	268
PSS 6	as	270
PSS 7	however, therefore, for example	271
Chapter Review Test		272

CHAPTER 14 | 전치사 & 속담 Prepositions & Proverbs

PSS 1	시간, 때를 나타내는 전치사	
PSS 1-1	at, on, in	278
PSS 1-2	before, after	279
PSS 1-3	for, during	280
PSS 1-4	from, since	281
PSS 2	장소를 나타내는 전치사	
PSS 2-1	at, in, on	283
PSS 2-2	over, under	285
PSS 2-3	in front of, behind, next to	286
PSS 2-4	between, among	287
PSS 3	방향을 나타내는 전치사	
PSS 3-1	into, out of, up, down	289
PSS 3-2	along, across, through, around	291
PSS 3-3	from, to, for	292
PSS 4	도구, 수단을 나타내는 전치사	294
PSS 5	기타 주요 전치사	294
PSS 6	관용표현	
PSS 6-1	형용사와 함께 쓰이는 전치사	296
PSS 6-2	동사와 함께 쓰이는 전치사	297
PSS 7	속담	299
Chapter Review Test		303

CHAPTER 1
문장의 기초

성취도 자기 평가 활용법

구분	평가 기준
Excellent	문법 내용을 모두 이해하고, 문제를 모두 맞힘.
Very good	문법 내용은 충분히 이해했으나 실수로 1~2문제 틀림.
Good	문법 내용이 조금 어려워 3~4문제 틀림.
needs **R**eview	문법 내용 이해가 어렵고, 5문제 이상 틀림, 복습 필요.

PSS 1 문장의 종류	페이지	학습날짜	성취도 자기평가 E V G R	학습체크
PSS 1-1 명사의 인칭 구분	5	/		☐
PSS 1-2 인칭대명사와 be동사	6	/		☐
PSS 1-3 be동사의 부정문	7	/		☐
PSS 1-4 일반동사의 긍정문/부정문	8	/		☐
PSS 1-5 Yes/No 의문문	10	/		☐
PSS 1-6 부정의문문	11	/		☐
PSS 1-7 의문사로 시작하는 의문문	13	/		☐
PSS 1-8 선택의문문	14	/		☐
PSS 1-9 부가의문문	16	/		☐
PSS 1-10 명령문	17	/		☐
PSS 1-11 Let's로 시작하는 청유문	18	/		☐
PSS 1-12 주의해야 할 부가의문문	19	/		☐
PSS 1-13 감탄문	20	/		☐

PSS 2 품사/문장의 요소/문장의 5형식	페이지	학습날짜	성취도 자기평가 E V G R	학습체크
PSS 2-1 영어의 8품사	21	/		☐
PSS 2-2 문장의 요소	23	/		☐
PSS 2-3 문장의 5형식	25	/		☐
PSS 2-4 감각동사+주격 보어(형용사)	26	/		☐
PSS 2-5 4형식에서 3형식으로의 전환	27	/		☐
Chapter Review Test	29	/		☐

문장의 종류

PSS 1-1 명사의 인칭 구분

인칭대명사는 사람, 사물의 이름을 대신하여 쓰는 명사이다. 말하는 사람은 1인칭, 듣는 사람은 2인칭, 그 밖의 사람/사물은 3인칭이라고 한다. 한 명은 단수로 나타내지만, 여러 명은 복수로 나타낸다.

he (3인칭 단수)	she (3인칭 단수)	it (3인칭 단수)
Mike	Jane	a car
Mr. Lee	Ms. Kim	the book
an uncle	an aunt	my school
my father	my mother	this dog
a boy	a girl	that box
the man	the woman	Seoul

we (1인칭 복수)	you (2인칭 복수)	they (3인칭 복수)
you and I	you and Ann	Tom and Sue
Jack and I	you and your friends	these pens
my friends and I	you and Jake	those children
you, my brother and I	you and her sister	teachers

정답 p.0

PRACTICE 1

다음을 인칭대명사(he, she, it, we, you, they)로 바꾸어 쓰세요.

1. your bicycle ➡ _____
2. my friends ➡ _____
3. you and my friend ➡ _____
4. his brother ➡ _____
5. the apples ➡ _____
6. his bag ➡ _____
7. she and I ➡ _____
8. Tom and Jane ➡ _____
9. a tall man ➡ _____
10. you and I ➡ _____
11. that pretty girl ➡ _____
12. you and your teacher ➡ _____
13. computers ➡ _____
14. these children ➡ _____

PSS 1-2 인칭대명사와 be동사

현재형			과거형	
I	am	(= I'm)	I	was
he she it	is	(= he's) (= she's) (= it's)	he she it	was
we you they	are	(= we're) (= you're) (= they're)	we you they	were

cf. it's와 it의 소유격 its는 헷갈리기 쉬우므로 주의해야 한다.
　　It's his book. 그것은 그의 책이다.
　　Its mouth is big. 그것의 입은 크다.

PRACTICE 2

정답 p.0

다음 문장의 빈칸에 am, is, are 중 알맞은 것을 쓰세요.

1 My sister _____ a singer.
2 My pants _____ expensive.
3 That boy _____ a basketball player.
4 My parents _____ teachers.
5 I _____ a student.
6 You _____ my friend.
7 You and your parents _____ kind.
8 Her eyes _____ blue.
9 We _____ Korean.
10 Mary _____ 29 years old.
11 My shoes _____ very clean.
12 I _____ sad to hear that.

PRACTICE 3

정답 p.0

다음 문장의 빈칸에 was, were 중 알맞은 것을 쓰세요.

1 Mr. Kim _____ a police officer.
2 We _____ happy.
3 I _____ very excited.
4 You _____ wonderful.
5 She _____ a little tired.
6 You and I _____ meant to be together.
7 Andy and Mike _____ from New York.
8 The woman _____ beautiful.
9 Two people _____ at a bus stop.
10 My father _____ on the bus.

PSS 1-3 be동사의 부정문

현재형 – am/is/are+not		과거형 – was/were+not	
I am not	(= I'm not)	I was not	(= I wasn't)
he she is not it	(= he's not / he isn't) (= she's not / she isn't) (= it's not / it isn't)	he she was not it	(= he wasn't) (= she wasn't) (= it wasn't)
we you are not they	(= we're not / we aren't) (= you're not / you aren't) (= they're not / they aren't)	we you were not they	(= we weren't) (= you weren't) (= they weren't)

정답 p.0

PRACTICE 4

다음 문장의 밑줄 친 부분을 줄여서 다시 쓰세요.

1 You are not alone.
   ➡ <u>You're not[You aren't]</u> alone.

2 He is at home.
   ➡ _____ at home.

3 I am not happy.
   ➡ _____ happy.

4 She is not angry.
   ➡ _____ angry.

5 We are not thirsty.
   ➡ _____ thirsty.

6 You were not a visitor.
   ➡ _____ a visitor.

7 They are Korean.
   ➡ _____ Korean.

8 It is not warm.
   ➡ _____ warm.

9 I was not in Busan.
   ➡ _____ in Busan.

10 She was not busy.
   ➡ _____ busy.

정답 p.0

PRACTICE 5

다음 문장을 부정문으로 바꾸어 쓰세요.

1 He is my uncle.
   ➡ <u>He is not[He's not/He isn't] my uncle.</u>

2 It was a big deal.
   ➡ _____

3 They are from Australia.
   ➡ _____

4 This towel was wet.
   ➡ _____

5 You were afraid of dogs.
➡ _____

6 The flowers are very pretty.
➡ _____

7 She is from London.
➡ _____

8 We are late.
➡ _____

9 He is a serious person.
➡ _____

10 We were happy with the news.
➡ _____

PSS 1-4 일반동사의 긍정문/부정문

일반동사는 be동사와 조동사를 제외한 모든 동사를 말하며, 주어의 동작이나 상태를 나타낸다.

1. 긍정문

주어+동사원형		주어+동사원형+-(e)s	
I we you they	play like ~ work	he she it	plays likes ~ works

cf. 주어가 he, she, it과 같은 3인칭 단수이고 현재시제일 때는 동사원형에 -(e)s를 붙인다.

2. 부정문

현재형 – do/does+not+동사원형				과거형 – did+not+동사원형			
I	**do not**	(= I don't)		I	**did not**	(= I didn't)	
he she it	**does not**	(= he doesn't) (= she doesn't) (= it doesn't)	play like ~ work	he she it	**did not**	(= he didn't) (= she didn't) (= it didn't)	play like ~ work
we you they	**do not**	(= we don't) (= you don't) (= they don't)		we you they	**did not**	(= we didn't) (= you didn't) (= they didn't)	

PRACTICE 6

다음 문장을 부정문으로 바꾸어 쓰세요.

1. She likes me.
   → She does not[doesn't] like me.
2. It rained a lot.
   → _____
3. They drink coffee.
   → _____
4. I want some ketchup.
   → _____
5. We bought a newspaper.
   → _____
6. It happens very often.
   → _____
7. They work very hard.
   → _____
8. He looks like a good player.
   → _____
9. Mike went to the cinema.
   → _____
10. He watches TV in the morning.
    → _____

PRACTICE 7

우리말과 같은 뜻이 되도록 빈칸에 알맞은 단어를 쓰세요. (단, 부정문의 경우 축약형으로 쓰세요.)

1. 지나는 춤을 추지 않았다. = Jina __didn't__ __dance__ .
2. 그들은 우유를 좋아한다. = They _____ milk.
3. 그는 초콜릿을 만든다. = He _____ chocolate.
4. 내게 거짓말을 하지 마. = _____ _____ to me.
5. 한 소녀가 스마트폰을 산다. = A girl _____ a smartphone.
6. 그것은 꼬리를 가지고 있지 않다. = It _____ _____ a tail.
7. 우리는 우리의 아버지를 사랑한다. = We _____ our father.
8. 그녀는 수영을 잘하지 않는다. = She _____ _____ well.
9. 너는 영어를 공부하지 않았다. = You _____ _____ English.
10. 나는 책을 읽지 않는다. = I _____ _____ books.

PSS 1-5 Yes/No 의문문

의문사로 시작되지 않는 의문문은 Yes나 No로 대답한다.

1. be동사가 있는 의문문

> 「Be동사+주어 ~?」 – Yes, 주어+be동사. / No, 주어+be동사+not.

She is happy. 그녀는 행복하다.

Is she happy? 그녀는 행복하니?
– **Yes**, she is. / **No**, she isn't.
응, 행복해. / 아니, 행복하지 않아.

Is it your dog?
그것은 너의 개니?
– **Yes**, it is. / **No**, it isn't.
응, 내 개야. / 아니, 내 개가 아니야.

Was Sumi late?
수미가 늦었니?
– **Yes**, she was. / **No**, she wasn't.
응, 늦었어. / 아니, 늦지 않았어.

Were they kind? – **Yes**, they were. / **No**, they weren't.
그들은 친절했니?   응, 친절했어. / 아니, 친절하지 않았어.

2. 일반동사가 있는 의문문

> 「Do[Does, Did]+주어+동사원형 ~?」
> – Yes, 주어+do[does, did]. / No, 주어+do[does, did]+not.

You like music. 너는 음악을 좋아한다.

Do you like music? 너는 음악을 좋아하니?
– **Yes**, I do. / **No**, I don't. 응, 좋아해. / 아니, 좋아하지 않아.

Does he love dogs? – **Yes**, he does. / **No**, he doesn't.
그는 개를 좋아하니?   응, 좋아해. / 아니, 좋아하지 않아.

Did they have breakfast? – **Yes**, they did. / **No**, they didn't.
그들은 아침을 먹었니?   응, 먹었어. / 아니, 먹지 않았어.

PRACTICE 8

다음 문장을 의문문으로 바꾸어 쓰세요.

1 Sue is hungry.
➡ _____Is Sue hungry?_____

2 You are in a relationship.
➡ _____

3 Mary likes cats.
➡ _____

4 You live near here.
➡ _____

5 He took photographs.
➡ _____

6 Tom's father was in hospital.
➡ _____

7 They enjoy a rock concert.
➡ _____

8 She has big blue eyes.
➡ _____

9 These books were very interesting.
➡ _____

10 This is the Empire State Building.
➡ _____

PSS 1-6 부정의문문

부정어가 들어가 있는 의문문을 부정의문문이라 하며, 대답은 질문의 긍정/부정 형태와 관계없이 대답의 내용이 긍정이면 Yes, 부정이면 No로 답한다. 이때 Yes, No는 우리말의 '네', '아니오'와는 반대이므로 주의해야 한다.

Don't you know Tom? 너는 Tom을 알지 않니?

- **Yes**, I do. (= Yes, I know Tom.) 아니요, 압니다.
- **No**, I don't. (= No, I don't know Tom.) 네, 모릅니다.

> **Isn't she** American? – **Yes**, she is. / **No**, she isn't.
> 그녀는 미국인이지 않니?   아니, 미국인이야. / 응, 미국인이 아니야.
> **Aren't you** hungry? – **Yes**, I am. / **No**, I'm not.
> 너 배고프지 않니?   아니, 배고파. / 응, 배고프지 않아.
> **Weren't these shoes** dirty? – **Yes**, they were. / **No**, they weren't.
> 이 신발은 더럽지 않았니?   아니, 더러웠어. / 응, 더럽지 않아.
> **Doesn't he** like soccer? – **Yes**, he does. / **No**, he doesn't.
> 그는 축구를 좋아하지 않니?   아니, 좋아해. / 응, 좋아하지 않아.
> **Didn't you** use the Internet? – **Yes**, I did. / **No**, I didn't.
> 너는 인터넷을 사용하지 않았니?   아니, 사용했어. / 응, 사용하지 않았어.

PRACTICE 9

정답 p.0

〈보기〉와 같이 주어진 질문에 대한 알맞은 대답을 빈칸에 쓰세요.

> 보 기
> A: Isn't she an English teacher?
> B: <u>Yes, she is.</u> (She is an English teacher.)

1 A: Isn't he married?
 B: _____ (He isn't married.)

2 A: Don't you speak Spanish?
 B: _____ (We speak Spanish.)

3 A: Does Tim enjoy Korean food?
 B: _____ (Tim enjoys Korean food.)

4 A: Weren't they here?
 B: _____ (They were here.)

5 A: Is your room cold?
 B: _____ (My room isn't cold.)

6 A: Did they draw a picture?
 B: _____ (They didn't draw a picture.)

7 A: Aren't you Becky?
 B: _____ (I'm not Becky.)

8 A: Was Cathy free this morning?
 B: _____ (Cathy was free this morning.)

9 A: Didn't Sena find her watch?
   B: _____ (Sena found her watch.)

10 A: Do you want some bread?
   B: _____ (I don't want any bread.)

PSS 1-7 의문사로 시작하는 의문문

의문사로 시작하는 의문문은 Yes나 No로 대답하지 않는다. be동사가 있는 의문문은 「의문사+be동사+주어 ~?」로, 일반동사가 있는 의문문은 일반적으로 「의문사+do[does, did]+주어+동사원형 ~?」의 어순으로 쓴다.

Who is she?
그녀는 누구니?
– **She is my sister.**
그녀는 내 여동생이야.

What did you do last night?
너는 어젯밤에 무엇을 했니?
– **I watched the movie, *Harry Potter*.**
나는 영화 〈해리포터〉를 봤어.

Where was she yesterday?
그녀는 어제 어디에 있었니?
– **She was at home.**
그녀는 집에 있었어.

When did you go jogging?
너는 언제 조깅하러 갔니?
– **I went jogging this morning.**
오늘 아침에 조깅하러 갔어.

How was your trip?
너의 여행은 어땠니?
– **It was wonderful.**
매우 좋았어.

Why is he absent today?
그는 오늘 왜 결석했니?
– **Because he is ill.**
왜냐하면 그는 아프기 때문이야.

PRACTICE 10

다음 대답을 보고, 괄호 안에 주어진 단어를 바르게 배열하여 의문문을 완성하세요.

1 _____ – My name is Amy.
 (your, is, what, name)

2 _____ – He is my brother.
 (is, who, boy, that)

3 _____ – I'm from Canada.
 (where, from, you, are)

4 _____ – It was great.
 (was, vacation, your, how)

5 _____ – I bought it last year.
 (it, did, you, when, buy)

6 _____ – Because I got a bonus for the best sales record.
 (you, are, so happy, why)

7 _____ – She is a writer.
 (what, do, does, she)

8 _____ – It's just around the corner.
 (the, is, bank, where)

9 _____ – I go to work by bus.
 (how, go, you, do, to work)

10 _____ – It is tomorrow night.
 (the, when, party, is)

PSS 1-8 선택의문문

선택의문문은 둘 중에 하나를 선택하여 대답하는 의문문이므로 Yes나 No로 대답하지 않는다.

Which do you like better, **summer or winter**?	– **I like winter better.**
너는 여름과 겨울 중 어느 것이 더 좋니?	나는 겨울이 더 좋아.
Who cleaned the room, **Tom or Bob**?	– **Tom cleaned it.**
Tom과 Bob 중 누가 그 방을 청소했니?	Tom이 그곳을 청소했어.
Did you go there **by bus or by train**?	– **I went there by train.**
너는 거기에 버스를 타고 갔니, 기차를 타고 갔니?	나는 거기에 기차를 타고 갔어.
Is she **a nurse or a doctor**?	– **She is a doctor.**
그녀는 간호사인가요, 의사인가요?	그녀는 의사예요.

PRACTICE 11

다음 그림을 보고, 빈칸에 알맞은 단어를 쓰세요.

1  2  3  4

5  6  7  8

1   A: _____ do you want, milk _____ juice?
    B: _____, please.

2   A: _____ is your sister, Kate _____ Liza?
    B: _____ is my sister. She is tall.

3   A: Do you have a cat _____ a dog?
    B: I have a _____.

4   A: Is this a pen _____ a pencil?
    B: It's a _____.

5   A: Did you eat oranges _____ apples?
    B: I ate _____.

6   A: _____ do you like better, red _____ blue?
    B: I like _____ better.

7   A: _____ made these sandwiches, Mina _____ Minho?
    B: _____ made them.

8   A: Are you reading a book _____ a newspaper?
    B: I'm reading a _____.

PSS 1-9 부가의문문

상대방에게 확인이나 동의를 구하기 위해 문장 맨 끝에 짧게 덧붙이는 의문문으로 긍정문 뒤에는 부정의 부가의문문이, 부정문 뒤에는 긍정의 부가의문문이 온다. 부가의문문의 주어는 앞의 주어를 받아 그에 맞는 인칭대명사를 써야 한다.

1. 주어+동사의 긍정형, be/do/조동사의 부정형+인칭대명사?

   He **is** a teacher, **isn't he?** 그는 선생님이야, 그렇지 않니?
   You **like** Tom, **don't you?** 너는 Tom을 좋아해, 그렇지 않니?
   Jane **will** meet her friend, **won't she?** Jane은 친구를 만날 거야, 그렇지 않니?

   cf. 부가의문문의 부정형은 반드시 축약형으로 써야 한다.
   She is smart, **isn't she?** (O)   She is smart, is not she? (×)

2. 주어+동사의 부정형, be/do/조동사의 긍정형+인칭대명사?

   The phone **didn't** ring, **did it?** 전화는 울리지 않았어, 그렇지?
   Your brother **can't** drive, **can he?** 네 오빠는 운전을 할 수 없어, 그렇지?
   You **won't** tell anyone, **will you?** 넌 아무에게도 말하지 않을 거야, 그렇지?

PRACTICE 12

정답 p.1

다음 문장의 빈칸에 알맞은 부가의문문을 쓰세요.

1 He can't swim well, _____?

2 The room isn't clean, _____?

3 The trains are never on time, _____?

4 They won't go to the gym, _____?

5 My mother doesn't know him, _____?

6 Computers can work fast, _____?

7 James plays the violin, _____?

8 You like sports, _____?

9 Mrs. Brown didn't sleep well last night, _____?

10 You and Brian are on vacation, _____?

PSS 1-10 명령문

1. 명령문은 주어 없이 동사원형으로 시작하는 문장으로 '~해라'의 뜻을 나타낸다. 명령문이어도 공손하게 지시하는 상황일 경우 please를 붙이기도 한다.
be동사 am, is, are에 대한 동사원형은 be이다.

You are quiet. 너는 조용하다.

Be quiet. 조용히 해라. / **Be** quiet, **please**. [**Please**, **be** quiet.] 조용히 해 주세요.

You are kind to others. ➡ **Be** kind to others.
너는 다른 사람들에게 친절하다. 다른 사람들에게 친절해라.
You keep your promises. ➡ **Keep** your promises.
너는 약속을 지킨다. 약속을 지켜라.

2. 부정명령문은 「Don't+동사원형」의 형태로, '~하지 마라'의 뜻을 나타낸다.

You make a noise. 너는 시끄럽게 한다.

Don't make a noise. 시끄럽게 하지 마라.

You close the door. ➡ **Don't close** the door.
너는 문을 닫는다. 문을 닫지 말아라.

cf. Don't 대신 Never를 사용해 의미가 강조된 부정명령문을 만들 수 있다.
Never talk to strangers. 절대 낯선 사람과 이야기하지 마.

정답 p.1

PRACTICE 13

다음 문장을 괄호 안의 지시에 따라 바꾸어 쓰세요.

1. You wear a helmet. ➡ _____ (긍정명령문으로)
2. You are afraid of snakes. ➡ _____ (부정명령문으로)
3. You take a bus or a taxi. ➡ _____ (긍정명령문으로)
4. You are late again. ➡ _____ (부정명령문으로)
5. You enter my room. ➡ _____ (긍정명령문으로)
6. You make a noise. ➡ _____ (부정명령문으로)
7. You are careful. ➡ _____ (긍정명령문으로)
8. You are upset. ➡ _____ (부정명령문으로)

9 You are ready to go. ➡ _____ (긍정명령문으로)

10 You turn on the TV. ➡ _____ (부정명령문으로)

11 You are prepared for anything. ➡ _____ (긍정명령문으로)

12 You tell her the truth. ➡ _____ (부정명령문으로)

PSS 1-11 Let's로 시작하는 청유문

Let's로 시작하는 청유문은 「Let's+동사원형」의 형태로 권유나 제안을 할 때 쓰며, '~하자'의 뜻을 나타낸다. Let's는 Let us의 줄임말이다. 부정형은 「Let's not+동사원형」으로 '~하지 말자'의 뜻을 나타낸다.

Let's play soccer. 축구하자.
Let's not go. 가지 말자.

cf. 「Let me+동사원형 ~」은 '제가 ~하도록 (허락)해주세요, ~하겠습니다'의 뜻을 나타낸다.
Let me introduce myself. 제 소개를 하겠습니다.
Let me open the door. 제가 문을 열게요.

정답 p.1

PRACTICE 14

우리말과 같은 뜻이 되도록 괄호 안에 주어진 단어를 사용하여 빈칸을 바르게 채우세요.

1 계속 연락합시다. = _____ in touch. (keep)

2 잠시 쉬자. = _____ a break. (take)

3 영화 보러 가자. = _____ to a movie. (go)

4 제가 도와드릴게요. = _____ you. (help)

5 서두르지 말자. = _____ . (hurry)

6 제가 그것에 대해 이야기해 드릴게요. = _____ you about it. (tell)

7 지금부터 영어공부 하자. = _____ English from now on. (study)

8 문을 열지 말자. = _____ the door. (open)

9 여기서 시끄럽게 하지 말자. = _____ a noise here. (make)

10 이 클럽에 가입하자. = _____ this club. (join)

PSS 1-12 주의해야 할 부가의문문

앞 문장의 내용이 긍정형이든 부정형이든 상관없이 명령문의 부가의문문은 항상 will you? 로, Let's로 시작하는 청유문의 부가의문문은 shall we?로 쓴다.

1. 명령문, will you?

Be quiet,		조용히 해, 알겠니?
Close the door,	**will you?**	문을 닫아라, 알겠니?
Don't be late,		늦지 마, 알겠니?
Don't ride a bicycle,		자전거를 타지 마라, 알겠니?

2. Let's ~, shall we?

   | **Let's** go climbing, | **shall we?** | 등산 가자, 어떠니? |
   | **Let's not** watch TV, | | TV 보지 말자, 어떠니? |

정답 p.1

PRACTICE 15

다음 문장의 빈칸에 알맞은 부가의문문을 쓰세요.

1 Let's listen to music, _____?

2 Go to bed early, _____?

3 She played the piano, _____?

4 Don't cry, _____?

5 This bag is so small, _____?

6 You can ride a bicycle, _____?

7 Mr. Lee has a son and two daughters, _____?

8 Let's not play computer games, _____?

9 These stories are interesting, _____?

10 Nami doesn't want hamburgers, _____?

11 Be on time, _____?

12 Tom didn't lose the game, _____?

PSS 1-13 감탄문

how나 what을 사용하여 '정말 ~하구나!'라는 감탄의 의미를 표현할 수 있다. 주어와 동사는 생략이 가능하며 문장의 맨 끝에는 감탄부호(!)를 붙인다.

1. How + 형용사/부사 (+주어+동사)!

   You are very kind. ➡ **How** kind (you are)!
   너는 매우 친절하다.   (너는) 정말 친절하구나!
   That car is very nice. ➡ **How** nice (that car is)!
   저 차는 매우 멋있다.   (저 차는) 정말 멋있구나!

2. What (+a/an) + 형용사 + 명사 (+주어+동사)!

   cf. 감탄의 대상이 되는 명사가 복수일 때는 「What+형용사+복수명사(+주어+동사)!」의 형태로 쓴다.

   She has a really beautiful flower. ➡ **What** a beautiful flower (she has)!
   그녀는 정말 아름다운 꽃을 가지고 있다.   (그녀는) 정말 아름다운 꽃을 가지고 있구나!
   These are very amazing stories. ➡ **What** amazing stories (these are)!
   이것들은 매우 놀라운 이야기들이다.   (이것들은) 정말 놀라운 이야기들이구나!

   cf. 감탄문을 쓸 때는 very, really, so와 같은 강조 표현은 같이 쓰지 않는다.

   How <u>very</u> kind of him! (X)   What a <u>really</u> cute baby she is! (X)

PRACTICE 16

정답 p.1

괄호 안의 단어를 바르게 배열하여 감탄문 문장을 완성하세요.

1 (beautiful, is, garden, this, how)!
➡ How beautiful this garden is!

2 (she, how, is, pretty)!
➡ _____

3 (eyes, big, what, have, you)!
➡ _____

4 (waterfall, huge, what, a)!
➡ _____

5 (he, is, how, handsome)!
➡ _____

6 (fast, move, can, how, the, robots)!
➡ _____

7 (you, what, are, a, liar, big)!
➡ _____

8 (those, are, cute, mascots, what)!
➡ _____

9 (mountain, a, what, high)!
➡ _____

10 (what, museum, nice, a)!
➡ _____

11 (you, dictionary, have, a, what, small)!
➡ _____

12 (I, happy, how, am)!
➡ _____

품사/문장의 요소/문장의 5형식

PSS 2-1 영어의 8품사

명사	명사는 **이름을 나타내는** 말이다. 문장 내에서 **주어, 목적어, 보어**로 쓰인다. **Birds** sing. 새들이 노래한다. (주어) Mary likes **cats**. Mary는 고양이를 좋아한다. (목적어) Tom is a **teacher**. Tom은 선생님이다. (보어)
대명사	대명사는 **명사를 대신하는** 말이다. 명사의 반복을 피하기 위해 쓴다. 문장 내에서 **주어, 목적어, 보어**로 쓰인다. **This** is a yellow book. 이것은 노란 책이다. (주어) Do you know **him**? 너는 그를 아니? (목적어) The farm is **theirs**. 그 농장은 그들의 것이다. (보어)
동사	동사는 **상태나 행동을 나타내는** 말로 '~다'로 해석된다. 동사에는 be동사와 일반동사가 있다. I **am** a student. 나는 학생이다. (be동사) My mother **loves** me. 나의 어머니는 나를 사랑하신다. (일반동사)
형용사	형용사는 명사, 대명사의 **성질, 상태** 등을 나타내거나 보충 설명하는 말이다. 문장 내에서 **수식어** 또는 **보어**로 쓰인다. There is a **tall** tree. 키 큰 나무가 있다. (수식어) I was **sick** yesterday. 나는 어제 아팠다. (보어)
부사	부사는 **시간, 장소, 정도, 빈도, 방법** 등을 나타내는 말이다. 문장 내에서 **형용사, 동사, 다른 부사, 문장 전체**를 수식하는 수식어로 쓰인다. She swims **well**. 그녀는 수영을 잘한다. (수식어 - 동사 수식)
전치사	전치사는 **명사, 대명사의 앞에서 시간, 장소, 방향, 위치를 나타내는** 말이다. There are no classes **on** Saturday. 토요일에는 수업이 없다. (시간) Look at the moon **in** the sky. 하늘에 있는 달을 봐. (장소)
접속사	접속사는 **단어와 단어, 구와 구, 절과 절을 연결하는** 말이다. He is old **but** healthy. 그는 늙었지만 건강하다. (단어 연결) I will clean my room **and** wash the dishes. 나는 내 방을 청소하고, 설거지를 할 것이다. (구 연결) I was tired, **so** I went to bed early. 나는 피곤해서 일찍 잠자리에 들었다. (절 연결)
감탄사	감탄사는 **감정을 표현하는** 말이다. **Wow**, it smells good! 와, 그것은 좋은 냄새가 나!

PRACTICE 17

다음 밑줄 친 단어의 품사를 쓰세요.

1 My team works hard. [   ]
2 Did you make them or buy them? [   ]
3 She looks good today. [   ]
4 I will give you some advice. [   ]
5 Sunflowers are tall. [   ]
6 James opened the door quietly. [   ]
7 Wow! That's amazing! [   ]
8 We took a walk along the river. [   ]
9 My cat was sick yesterday. [   ]
10 Sally saw something strange. [   ]

PRACTICE 18

괄호 안에 주어진 단어 중 알맞은 것을 고르세요.

1 Rock climbing is quite (dangerous, danger).
2 That magic was very (amaze, amazing).
3 I (arrival, arrived) in Los Angeles on Christmas Day.
4 The Internet provides us with a lot of (information, inform).
5 Is Tim a teacher (or, on) an office worker?
6 Let me (introduction, introduce) my best friend.
7 You look (happy, happiness) today.
8 She told us a (scare, scary) story.
9 Exercising makes you (health, healthy).
10 Why is Belle so (busy, business) today?

PSS 2-2 문장의 요소

영어 문장은 네 가지 주요 성분(주어, 동사, 목적어, 보어)과 수식어로 이뤄진다.

1. **주어** – 동작이나 상태의 주체로 우리말 '~은, 는, 이, 가'에 해당한다.

   John played basketball. John은 농구를 했다.

2. **동사** – 상태나 동작을 나타내는 말로 우리말 '~(하)다'에 해당한다.

   He **wrote** a letter to her. 그는 그녀에게 편지를 썼다.
   It **is** cold today. 오늘 (날씨가) 춥다.

3. **목적어** – 동사가 의미하는 동작의 대상이 되는 말로 우리말 '~을, 를'에 해당한다.

   My father wears **glasses**. 나의 아버지는 안경을 쓰신다.

   cf. 전치사의 목적어: 전치사는 목적어를 취할 수 없는 자동사나 형용사가 목적어를 취할 수 있게 해 준다.

   She looks **after** **them**. 그녀는 그들을 돌본다.   I am afraid **of** **bugs**. 나는 벌레를 두려워한다.

4. **보어** – 동사만으로는 문장의 의미를 명확하게 나타낼 수 없기에 그 뜻을 보충해 주는 말로 주어를 설명해주는 것을 주격 보어, 목적어를 설명해주는 것을 목적격 보어라고 한다.

   My dog is **cute**. 나의 개는 귀엽다.
   She became **a teacher**. 그녀는 선생님이 되었다.
   I found the book **difficult**. 나는 그 책이 어렵다는 것을 알았다.
   We saw him **painting**. 우리는 그가 페인트칠하고 있는 것을 보았다.

5. **수식어** – 문장의 주요 성분을 부연 설명하는 역할을 하며 생략해도 문법적인 오류를 일으키지 않는다.

   You walk <u>too fast</u>. 너는 너무 빠르게 걷는다.
   주어 동사 수식어
   Audrey enjoys going shopping <u>with her mother</u>. Audrey는 그녀의 엄마와 쇼핑하러 가는 것을 즐긴다.
   　주어　 　동사　 　목적어　　　수식어

정답 p.2

PRACTICE 19

다음 문장의 주어에는 ○, 동사에는 △표시를 하세요.

1 Her cap is red.
2 They went camping last Saturday.
3 She keeps a diary every day.
4 My favorite food is sushi.
5 Tony sat on the bench.
6 Her family lives in Seoul.

PRACTICE 20

다음 문장의 목적어에 밑줄을 그으세요.

1 My family planted some trees.
2 She heard his voice.
3 I don't know them.
4 We watch TV after dinner.
5 I bought a tablet PC.
6 They play tennis.

PRACTICE 21

다음 문장의 보어에 밑줄을 그으세요.

1 He is Mr. Brown.
2 We felt cold.
3 I find it interesting.
4 She heard the birds sing.
5 The game is exciting.
6 He became a cook.

PRACTICE 22

다음 문장의 수식어에 밑줄을 그으세요.

1 I am so happy.
2 You can meet her next time.
3 It will rain heavily tomorrow.
4 It is a musical about *the Wizard of Oz*.
5 The meeting ends late.
6 In my opinion, you are wrong.

PRACTICE 23

괄호 안에 주어진 단어를 바르게 배열하여 문장을 완성하세요.

1 _____ (he, happy, is)
2 _____ (winter, we, love)
3 _____ (small, are, these shirts)
4 _____ (live, in New York, her parents)
5 _____ (teaches, the teacher, math)
6 _____ (my mother, the dishes, washed)

PSS 2-3 문장의 5형식

1. **목적어를 가지지 않는 문장**

    ① 1형식 The sun shines. 해가 빛난다.
              주어 + 동사

    ② 2형식 He looks happy. 그는 행복해 보인다.
              주어 + 동사 + 주격 보어

2. **목적어를 가지는 문장**

    ① 3형식 Amy likes her co-worker. Amy는 그녀의 동료를 좋아한다.
              주어 + 동사 + 목적어

    ② 4형식 She gave me a book. 그녀는 나에게 책을 주었다.
              주어 + 동사+간접목적어(사람)+직접목적어(사물)

    ③ 5형식 Music makes me happy. 음악은 나를 행복하게 한다.
              주어 + 동사 + 목적어+목적격 보어

   cf. 4형식과 5형식의 구분 방법
   5형식은 목적어와 목적격 보어가 동격이거나 주술 관계를 가지지만, 4형식은 그렇지 않다.
   Mom made me a sweater. (4형식) 엄마께서는 나에게 스웨터를 만들어 주셨다.
         간접목적어 직접목적어
              ≠
   The movie made her a superstar. (5형식) 그 영화는 그녀를 슈퍼스타로 만들었다.
                    목적어 목적격 보어
                       =

정답 p.2

PRACTICE 24

〈보기〉와 같이 주어진 문장의 문장 형식과 밑줄 친 단어에 해당하는 각각의 문장 성분을 쓰세요.

보 기	I cleaned my room. [3형식]
	주어 동사 목적어

1 Birds sing. [형식]

2 The man is strong. [형식]

3 Mary found the article interesting. [형식]

4 I opened the door. [형식]

5 He gave her the ring. [형식]

6 John has a brother. [형식]

7 The movie made me sad. [형식]

8 The baby cried. [형식]

9 He became an engineer. [형식]

10 We sent him a postcard. [형식]

11 Leaves turn red and yellow. [형식]

12 She bought her baby a new toy. [형식]

13 I woke up late in the morning. [형식]

14 I kept my room clean. [형식]

PSS 2-4 감각동사 + 주격 보어(형용사)

look, feel, sound, smell, taste와 같은 감각동사 뒤에는 보어로 형용사가 온다.

주어 +
- look '~하게 보이다'
- feel '~하게 느끼다'
- sound '~하게 들리다'
- smell '~한 냄새가 나다'
- taste '~한 맛이 나다'

\+ 형용사

You **look kind**. 너는 친절해 보인다.
I **feel happy**. 나는 행복하게 느낀다.
That **sounds great**. 그 말은 좋게 들린다.
It **smells good**. 그것은 좋은 냄새가 난다.
The candy **tastes sweet**.
그 사탕은 달콤한 맛이 난다.

cf. 「감각동사 like+명사」 '~처럼 …하다'
The baby **looks like** a small doll. 그 아기는 작은 인형처럼 보인다.
It **sounds like** a great plan. 그것은 훌륭한 계획처럼 들린다.
This candy **tastes like** peaches. 이 사탕은 복숭아 맛이 난다.

PRACTICE 25

〈보기〉에서 알맞은 단어를 골라 빈칸에 쓰세요.

| 보기 | terrible | ghost | sadly | beautiful | beautifully | soap |
| | strangely | strange | delicious | hungry | soft | softly |

1. 너는 아름답게 보인다. ➡ You look _____.
2. 그 파이는 맛있는 냄새가 난다. ➡ The pie smells _____.
3. 이것은 이상하게 들린다. ➡ This sounds _____.
4. 그들은 방을 아름답게 꾸몄다. ➡ They decorated the room _____.
5. 그는 배고프게 느낀다. ➡ He feels _____.
6. 그것은 유령처럼 보인다. ➡ It looks like a _____.
7. 그녀는 슬프게 고개를 가로저었다. ➡ She shook her head _____.
8. 저것은 맛이 형편없다. ➡ That tastes _____.
9. 그녀의 목소리는 부드럽게 들렸다. ➡ Her voice sounded _____.
10. 그녀는 이상하게 차분했고 한편 그는 겁에 질려 있었다. ➡ She was _____ calm while he was panicking.
11. 그 수건들은 비누 같은 냄새가 났다. ➡ The towels smelled like _____.
12. 그는 나를 부드럽게 포옹했다. ➡ He hugged me _____.

PSS 2-5 4형식에서 3형식으로의 전환

두 개의 목적어를 필요로 하는 동사의 4형식 문장을 3형식으로 전환할 때는 간접목적어와 직접목적어의 위치를 바꾸고 간접목적어 앞에 to, for, of 중 해당하는 전치사를 넣는다.

	주어	동사	간접목적어(~에게)	직접목적어(~을)
4형식	He	bought	me	a new computer.

	주어	동사	직접목적어(~을)		간접목적어(~에게)
3형식	He	bought	a new computer	for	me.

1. **to를 쓰는 동사** – give, send, pass, show, teach, tell, write, read

    My parents **gave** me a present. 나의 부모님이 나에게 선물을 주셨다.
    ➡ My parents **gave** a present **to** me.

2. **for를 쓰는 동사** – buy, cook, find, get, make, build

    She **made** us some cookies. 그녀가 우리에게 쿠키를 만들어 주었다.
    ➡ She **made** some cookies **for** us.

3. **of를 쓰는 동사** – ask

    The girl **asked** him a favor. 그 소녀는 그에게 부탁을 하나 했다.
    ➡ The girl **asked** a favor **of** him.

정답 p.3

PRACTICE 26

괄호 안에 주어진 단어 중 알맞은 것을 고르세요.

1 She made a scarf (to, for) me.
2 He gave roses (to, of) the woman.
3 Andy bought the camera (to, for) me.
4 She told the secret (to, for) her friend.
5 May I ask a favor (to, of) you?
6 I showed my heart (to, for) you.
7 Jane sent some books (to, of) her cousin.
8 Mrs. Smith cooked dinner (to, for) us.
9 I got two tickets (to, for) my parents.
10 Mike taught math (to, of) his brothers.

PRACTICE 27

다음 4형식 문장을 3형식으로 바꾸어 쓰세요.

1. Mary told him the news.
   ➡ _____

2. Mr. Kim teaches them English.
   ➡ _____

3. My mother made me a pretty bag.
   ➡ _____

4. Please get me some water.
   ➡ _____

5. Can I ask you some questions?
   ➡ _____

6. She often writes Shelly a letter.
   ➡ _____

7. He found us some books.
   ➡ _____

8. Did you buy her a cake?
   ➡ _____

9. Will you show me your album?
   ➡ _____

10. The Internet gives us a lot of information.
    ➡ _____

11. Please tell me the real reason.
    ➡ _____

12. Will you pass me the salt?
    ➡ _____

13. Vivien sent me some flowers.
    ➡ _____

14. We built the family a new house.
    ➡ _____

15. My husband cooked me spaghetti.
    ➡ _____

16. I read senior citizens newspapers.
    ➡ _____

17. Can I ask you a favor?
    ➡ _____

18. Customers give the waiter a tip.
    ➡ _____

19. I sent you a birthday gift.
    ➡ _____

20. My friend made me a birthday cake.
    ➡ _____

21. Will you give me another chance?
    ➡ _____

22. Can you get me that book?
    ➡ _____

23. He bought us a box of chocolates.
    ➡ _____

24. Olivia teaches students Korean history.
    ➡ _____

25. Evan built his children a small garden.
    ➡ _____

26. Mom often cooks me noodles.
    ➡ _____

27. She often reads her son a fairy tale.
    ➡ _____

28. He showed his father his report card.
    ➡ _____

29. The police officer found me the car key.
    ➡ _____

30. Dominic made his son a big sand castle.
    ➡ _____

Chapter Review Test

CHAPTER 1 문장의 기초

정답 p.3

1 (A)~(E)의 빈칸에 들어갈 말이 나머지 넷과 <u>다른</u> 것은?

(A) This _____ a television.
(B) The Han River _____ in Seoul.
(C) _____ Somi late?
(D) _____ the post office near here?
(E) Minsoo _____ the dishes after dinner.

① (A)   ② (B)   ③ (C)   ④ (D)   ⑤ (E)

2 다음 중 축약형이 <u>잘못된</u> 것의 개수는?

| He's | We're | I amn't | They'r |
| This's | That's | You're | She're |

① 1개   ② 2개   ③ 3개   ④ 4개   ⑤ 5개

3 다음 중 빈칸에 들어갈 수 <u>없는</u> 것은?

_____ is very kind.

① My sister, Jenny   ② She
③ They   ④ Minsu
⑤ Your brother

4 다음 중 어법상 바른 것은?

① Don't shy, will you?
② The movie made me happily.
③ This juice tastes like strawberry.
④ How tall boy you are!
⑤ Does your brother likes to go fishing?

5 다음 문장에서 틀린 곳을 찾아 그 번호를 쓰고, 바르게 고치세요.

Please gives your seat to an elderly or
   ①   ②   ③   ④
disabled person.
   ⑤

➡ _____

6 빈칸을 채워 다음을 부정문으로 바꾸세요.

(1) Amy likes chocolate.
   ➡ Amy _____ _____ chocolate.

(2) He has a brother.
   ➡ He _____ _____ a brother.

(3) I played computer games last night.
   ➡ I _____ _____ computer games last night.

7 다음 중 축약형이 바른 것은?

① I do not - I'd not
② It is - Its
③ I am not - I amn't
④ Jane does not - Jane's not
⑤ They are - They're

8 우리말과 같은 뜻이 되도록 빈칸에 알맞은 단어를 쓰세요.

• 절대 다시는 늦지 마라.
  = Never _____ late again.

9 다음 빈칸에 들어갈 알맞은 부가의문문은?

Jack practices the violin, _____?

① did he
② didn't he
③ doesn't he
④ does he
⑤ doesn't Jack

10 다음 대화의 빈칸에 들어갈 말로 알맞은 것은?

A: _____ like grapes?
B: No, I don't. I don't like fruit.

① Does Cathy
② Does Jack
③ Do you
④ Do they
⑤ Do I

11 다음 밑줄 친 부분이 잘못 쓰인 것은?

① You look lovely today.
② The cookies taste greatly.
③ Don't you feel happy now?
④ That sounds good.
⑤ This soup smells very bad.

12 우리말과 같은 뜻이 되도록 빈칸에 알맞은 단어를 넣어 대화를 완성하세요.

A: We are late for work.
B: _____ take a taxi to work.
 (회사까지 택시타고 가자.)

13 다음 빈칸에 알맞은 be동사를 쓰세요.

Yesterday ⓐ_____ my day off. I was at home because my work ⓑ_____ really tough for a few days. After lunch, I felt bored. So, I went to see a movie. The actors in the movie ⓒ_____ great. They portrayed their roles really well.

14 다음 문장에서 not이 들어갈 가장 적당한 위치는?

My father's hometown ① is ② far ③ from ④ here ⑤.

15 다음 괄호 안의 단어를 바르게 배열한 것은?

My brother (me, a, gave, present).

① gave me a present
② me a present gave
③ a present gave me
④ present gave me a
⑤ gave a present me

16 다음의 빈칸에 들어갈 알맞은 말은?

Jane has dogs, but she _____ cats.

① isn't have
② doesn't has
③ don't have
④ doesn't have
⑤ does have

17 다음 빈칸에 알맞은 현재형 be 동사를 쓰세요.

This ⓐ_____ Jeremy Tucker from 7 PM Live. I ⓑ_____ out here in Nelson Park because two horses have been spotted here. They are said to have escaped from a nearby ranch. One of the horses ⓒ_____ being captured now as I'm speaking. But the other one ⓓ_____ not being cooperative at all. Let's have a closer look.

18 다음 문장에서 생략할 수 있는 부분은?

A: Look at the stars in the sky.
B: How beautiful the stars are!

① How ② beautiful
③ the stars ④ are
⑤ the stars are

19 다음 밑줄 친 부분 중 옳지 않은 것은?

Hi, my name ①is Kate. I ②am from L.A. ③I have a sister. ④She is 28 years old. I like baseball, but she doesn't ⑤likes it.

20 A에 대한 B의 대답을 지시대로 바꾸어 쓰세요. (단, 부정문은 축약형으로 쓸 것.)

A: Didn't you enjoy the movie?
B: (1) 긍정의 대답 → _____
　　(2) 부정의 대답 → _____

21 빈칸을 채워 다음을 의문문으로 바꾸세요.

(1) She reads books in the evening.
→ _____ she _____ books in the evening?

(2) My brother is watching TV.
→ _____ _____ _____ watching TV?

(3) Yumi met him last week.
→ _____ Yumi _____ him last week?

22 다음의 감탄문 중에서 어법에 맞는 것은?

① What beautiful lady she is!
② How nice!
③ How a kind boy!
④ How boring books they are!
⑤ What a very wonderful world!

23 다음 중 어법상 빈칸에 알맞지 않은 것은?

A: Did you _____ him the bag?
B: Yes, I did.

① bring　② give　③ send
④ help　⑤ show

24 다음 주어진 단어를 사용하여 감탄문을 쓰세요.

• 그것은 정말 작은 원숭이구나! (small, monkey)
= _____

조건1. What을 사용할 것.
조건2. 6단어로 영작할 것.
조건3. 문장부호를 꼭 쓸 것.

25 다음 중 평서문을 부정문으로 바르게 고친 것은?

① My friends are angry.
   ➡ My friends don't angry.
② Bob likes action movies.
   ➡ Bob doesn't likes action movies.
③ She was a brave woman.
   ➡ She isn't a brave woman.
④ I had five classes on Tuesday.
   ➡ I didn't have five classes on Tuesday.
⑤ I called Maria yesterday.
   ➡ I didn't called Maria yesterday.

26 빈칸을 채워 다음을 감탄문으로 바꾸세요.

(1) This is a very nice event.
   ➡ What _____ _____ _____ this is!

(2) My puppy is really cute.
   ➡ How _____ my puppy is!

27 다음 빈칸에 들어갈 단어가 순서대로 짝지어진 것은?

- Sally bought a cake _____ him.
- Linda showed her birthday photos _____ him.
- Rachel teaches English _____ us.

① for – to – for
② for – for – to
③ for – to – to
④ to – for – to
⑤ to – for – for

28 의문문으로 고친 것 중 바른 것을 고르세요.

① My brother bought some flowers.
   ➡ Did my brother bought any flowers?
② Susan runs her own business.
   ➡ Does Susan run her own business?
③ You have a cell phone.
   ➡ Does you have a cell phone?
④ They have a big house.
   ➡ Do they has a big house?
⑤ She likes movies.
   ➡ Do she like movies?

29 다음 빈칸에 들어갈 알맞은 문장을 고르세요.

A: _____
B: No, they don't.

① Don't you go to the bookstore?
② Aren't you American?
③ Does Eric ride a bicycle?
④ Do Kevin and Jim play badminton?
⑤ Are you students?

30 질문에 대한 대답이 적절하지 <u>못한</u> 것은?

① Do you walk to work?
   – Yes, I do.
② Didn't you work overtime yesterday?
   – No, I didn't.
③ Are you from India?
   – Yes, I am.
④ Aren't they washing their hands?
   – No, they aren't.
⑤ Is he fourteen years old?
   – No, he is.

31 다음 중 어법상 잘못된 문장을 고르세요.

① Could you pass me the salt?
② Give me those books.
③ Mom got a bicycle to me.
④ She often makes dolls for us.
⑤ Did you write a letter to her?

32 대화의 밑줄 친 부분과 바꾸어 쓸 수 있는 것은?

> A: Did you have fun at the party?
> B: Sure. I met lots of friends there.

① Yes, you did.
② Yes, I did.
③ Yes, we were.
④ No, I didn't.
⑤ No, we didn't.

33 다음 질문의 빈칸에 들어갈 표현이 아닌 것은?

> ㉠ _____ does she usually get up?
> ㉡ _____ are you feeling these days?
> ㉢ _____ did the boys do last night?
> ㉣ _____ will you be coming back?
> ㉤ _____ are you going now?

① What ② Where ③ When
④ Who   ⑤ How

34 다음 표를 설명하는 문장 중에서 어법상 오류 없이 내용과 일치하는 것을 고르세요.

	Tommy	Jane	Somi	Mark
Pilates	😊	😊	😊	😊
Tennis	☹	☹	☹	☹
Golf	😊	😊	☹	☹

① Tommy like tennis.
② Jane do not like tennis.
③ Somi and Mark likes golf.
④ Everyone likes pilates.
⑤ Mark doesn't likes golf.

35 다음 질문에 대한 대답으로 알맞은 것은?

> A: Is Yumi a student or an office worker?
> B: _____

① No, she doesn't.   ② She is a student.
③ Yes, she is.   ④ She isn't young.
⑤ No, she isn't.

36 어법상 어색한 곳을 하나씩 찾아 바르게 고쳐 쓰세요.

> (가) Please let me knowing if you cannot attend the meeting.
> (나) Her voice sounds sweetly.

〈잘못된 곳〉   〈바르게 고친 것〉
(가) _____ ➡ _____
(나) _____ ➡ _____

37 밑줄 친 부분의 쓰임이 잘못된 문장을 고르세요.

① Do they play table tennis?
② Do you have a pet?
③ What does Eric do?
④ Do the company and government work on the project together?
⑤ Does Kevin's parents get up early?

38 다음 중 어법상 틀린 것은?

① Do your best.
② Don't lazy.
③ Be kind to your friends.
④ Switch off the light.
⑤ Go to sleep right now.

39 빈칸에 들어갈 말로 알맞은 것은?

Today is Jenny's birthday, _____?

① aren't you   ② aren't they
③ isn't it   ④ isn't she
⑤ isn't this

40 다음 빈칸에 들어갈 말로 알맞지 않은 것은?

It _____ good.

① sees   ② feels   ③ looks
④ smells ⑤ sounds

41 다음 질문에 대한 알맞은 대답을 빈칸에 쓰세요.

A: Mary played badminton with Emily, didn't she?
B: _____, _____ _____.
She was sick, so she stayed at home.

42 빈칸에 들어갈 단어가 나머지 넷과 다른 하나는?

① _____ a nice car you have!
② _____ a handsome boy he is!
③ _____ a beautiful hat it is!
④ _____ wonderful it is!
⑤ _____ exciting stories these are!

43 다음 빈칸에 들어갈 수 없는 것은?

Susan is _____.

① from Canada   ② runs fast
③ at home   ④ my co-worker
⑤ very kind

44 다음 빈칸에 들어갈 말이 바르게 짝지어진 것은?

A: You can't swim well, _____?
B: No, _____.

① can you   – I'm not
② can't you – you can't
③ can you   – I can't
④ can't you – I can't
⑤ are you   – I can

45 다음 중 어법상 옳은 것을 모두 고른 것은?

ⓐ Be nice to your friends!
ⓑ Doesn't jump here!
ⓒ Let me introduce myself.
ⓓ Jimin looks like happy.
ⓔ My mother makes a cake to me.

① ⓐ,ⓑ ② ⓑ,ⓔ
③ ⓐ,ⓒ ④ ⓑ,ⓒ,ⓓ
⑤ ⓐ,ⓒ,ⓔ

46 밑줄 친 부분의 쓰임이 나머지 넷과 다른 것은?

① You made me angry.
② Rain sometimes makes people sad.
③ Linda made her daughter orange juice.
④ The homework made him tired.
⑤ This music always makes me happy.

47 다음 밑줄 친 부분의 오류를 가장 적절하게 고친 학생은?

너는 가게에서 야채가 필요했어, 그렇지 않니?
You needed vegetables at the store, do you?

① 연수: 앞에 나온 동사가 과거형이니까 뒤에는 did you?로 써야 해.
② 보근: 긍정문 뒤에는 부정의 부가의문문이 오는데 동사가 과거시제이므로 didn't you?를 써야 해.
③ 혜리: 부가의문문은 be동사를 사용해야 해서 are you?를 쓰는 것이 옳아.
④ 민지: 부가의문문은 be동사를 써서 만들지만 부정의 형태를 가져야 해서 aren't you?를 써야 해.
⑤ 영호: 부가의문문은 앞의 동사와 같은 것을 사용해야 해서 need you?를 써야 해.

48 다음 빈칸에 들어갈 be동사가 다른 하나는?

① Today _____ Monday.
② His room _____ clean now.
③ My grandmother _____ a good cook.
④ She _____ always polite and considerate.
⑤ Minji and I _____ college buddies.

49 다음 대화의 빈칸에 들어갈 알맞은 말을 고르세요.

A: Let's have dinner.
B: No, I'll just drink water.
A: Aren't you hungry?
B: _____ But I'm on a diet now.

① No, I'm not. ② Yes, I am.
③ No, I am. ④ Yes, it is.
⑤ Yes, I don't.

50 다음 밑줄 친 부분의 쓰임이 잘못된 것을 고르세요.

① Where is the subway station?
② Where are the books?
③ Where are Mina and Yumi?
④ Where is the zoo?
⑤ Where is my socks?

51 다음 중 빈칸에 들어갈 전치사가 다른 하나는?

① She gave a book _____ me.
② She made a sweater _____ me.
③ She teaches cooking _____ me.
④ She told a funny story _____ me.
⑤ She showed her pictures _____ me.

52 다음 밑줄 친 우리말을 영어로 표현할 때 어색한 문장은?

> A: 정말 멋진 파티야.
> B: Wow, it sure is.

① How nice the party is!
② What a nice party!
③ What nice the party is!
④ It's a really nice party.
⑤ What a nice party it is!

53 다음 밑줄 친 부분의 쓰임이 잘못된 것은?

① It's very sunny today, isn't it?
② You can't play the guitar, can you?
③ Sumi likes dancing, isn't she?
④ You are a driver, aren't you?
⑤ He doesn't study very hard, does he?

54 평서문을 감탄문으로 바꾼 것 중 바른 것을 고르세요.

① You are so handsome.
 ➡ How handsome you are!
② This is a really wonderful gift.
 ➡ What wonderful gift this is!
③ These are very nice pants.
 ➡ What a nice pants these are!
④ Your dog is very smart.
 ➡ How smart is your dog!
⑤ It's a very cloudy day.
 ➡ What cloudy day it is!

55 다음 중 어법상 어색한 문장은?

① The roses smell sweet.
② The music sounds great.
③ It tastes like chicken.
④ The scarf feels soft.
⑤ Jenny looks like wonderful.

56 주어진 문장을 의문문으로 바꾸세요.

(1) You are a police officer.
 ➡ _____

(2) You don't live here.
 ➡ _____

(3) Mary works at a hospital.
 ➡ _____

57 다음 중 문장의 전환이 바르지 않은 것을 고르세요.

① He teaches students English.
 ➡ He teaches English to students.
② Tommy sent me a card.
 ➡ Tommy sent a card to me.
③ They made me some soup.
 ➡ They made some soup to me.
④ He gave me some boxes.
 ➡ He gave some boxes to me.
⑤ My father bought me a new coat.
 ➡ My father bought a new coat for me.

58 어법상 바른 문장은?

① Not talk nonsense.
② My father gave the guitar me.
③ You aren't Korean, aren't you?
④ Do you play the guitar?
⑤ He don't look good today.

CHAPTER 2
시제

성취도 자기 평가 활용법

구분	평가 기준
Excellent	문법 내용을 모두 이해하고, 문제를 모두 맞힘.
Very good	문법 내용은 충분히 이해했으나 실수로 1~2문제 틀림.
Good	문법 내용이 조금 어려워 3~4문제 틀림.
needs **R**eview	문법 내용 이해가 어렵고, 5문제 이상 틀림, 복습 필요.

PSS 1 현재시제	페이지	학습날짜	성취도 자기평가 E V G R	학습체크
PSS 1-1 일반동사의 3인칭 현재 단수형 Ⅰ	38	/		☐
PSS 1-2 일반동사의 3인칭 현재 단수형 Ⅱ	39	/		☐
PSS 1-3 3인칭 현재 단수형의 '-(e)s' 발음	40	/		☐
PSS 1-4 현재시제의 쓰임	41	/		☐

PSS 2 과거시제	페이지	학습날짜	성취도 자기평가 E V G R	학습체크
PSS 2-1 일반동사의 규칙 변화형 Ⅰ	42	/		☐
PSS 2-2 일반동사의 규칙 변화형 Ⅱ	43	/		☐
PSS 2-3 규칙 변화 과거형의 '-(e)d' 발음	45	/		☐
PSS 2-4 일반동사의 불규칙 변화형	46	/		☐
PSS 2-5 과거시제의 쓰임	51	/		☐

| PSS 3 미래시제 — will과 be going to | 52 | / | | ☐ |

PSS 4 진행시제	페이지	학습날짜	성취도 자기평가 E V G R	학습체크
PSS 4-1 동사의 -ing형 Ⅰ	55	/		☐
PSS 4-2 동사의 -ing형 Ⅱ	56	/		☐
PSS 4-3 현재진행시제와 과거진행시제	57	/		☐
PSS 4-4 미래를 나타내는 현재진행시제	58	/		☐

PSS 5 현재완료시제	페이지	학습날짜	성취도 자기평가 E V G R	학습체크
PSS 5-1 현재완료시제의 쓰임	60	/		☐
PSS 5-2 현재완료시제와 과거시제의 비교	61	/		☐
Chapter Review Test	63	/		☐

PSS 1 현재시제

PSS 1-1 일반동사의 3인칭 현재 단수형 I

주어가 3인칭 단수(he/she/it/Mike/Jane/a car)일 때, 일반동사의 현재형은 「동사원형+(e)s」로 나타낸다.

대부분의 경우	-s	get – gets know – knows	like – likes walk – walks
-o, -s, -x, -ch, -sh로 끝나는 경우	-es	do – does mix – mixes finish – finishes	pass – passes watch – watches

PRACTICE 1

정답 p.6

다음 동사의 3인칭 현재 단수형을 쓰세요.

1 stand   – _____
2 reach   – _____
3 impress – _____
4 read   – _____
5 begin   – _____
6 wish   – _____
7 push   – _____
8 spend   – _____
9 send   – _____
10 miss   – _____
11 wake   – _____
12 meet   – _____
13 teach   – _____
14 solve   – _____
15 wear   – _____
16 catch   – _____
17 sound   – _____
18 go   – _____
19 mix   – _____
20 find   – _____
21 pass   – _____
22 finish – _____
23 ride   – _____
24 watch   – _____
25 wash   – _____
26 sit   – _____
27 throw   – _____
28 burn   – _____
29 climb   – _____
30 cross   – _____

PSS 1-2 일반동사의 3인칭 현재 단수형 II

자음+y로 끝나는 경우	y를 i로 바꾸고 -es	copy – copies study – studies	cry – cries try – tries
모음+y로 끝나는 경우	-s	buy – buys pay – pays	enjoy – enjoys say – says

cf. 불규칙 동사 have – has

정답 p.6

PRACTICE 2

다음 동사의 3인칭 현재 단수형을 쓰세요.

1 drink   – _____
2 buy   – _____
3 study   – _____
4 hurry   – _____
5 discuss – _____
6 draw   – _____
7 lay   – _____
8 sell   – _____
9 have   – _____
10 pay   – _____
11 say   – _____
12 cry   – _____
13 copy   – _____
14 put   – _____
15 close   – _____
16 enjoy   – _____
17 touch   – _____
18 try   – _____
19 believe – _____
20 lose   – _____
21 tell   – _____
22 carry   – _____
23 repeat – _____
24 grow   – _____
25 play   – _____
26 make   – _____
27 cost   – _____
28 judge   – _____
29 cheer   – _____
30 use   – _____
31 bring   – _____
32 think   – _____
33 mean   – _____
34 break   – _____
35 show   – _____
36 fly   – _____
37 visit   – _____
38 feel   – _____

39 sing	— _____		**40** turn	— _____
41 harm	— _____		**42** win	— _____
43 fall	— _____		**44** build	— _____
45 stay	— _____		**46** set	— _____
47 see	— _____		**48** envy	— _____
49 dream	— _____		**50** speak	— _____
51 eat	— _____		**52** leave	— _____
53 get	— _____		**54** understand	— _____
55 worry	— _____		**56** keep	— _____
57 give	— _____		**58** laugh	— _____
59 hold	— _____		**60** hear	— _____

PSS 1-3 3인칭 현재 단수형의 '-(e)s' 발음

발음	용법
[s]	[s, ʃ, tʃ]음을 제외한 무성음으로 끝나는 경우 ➡ stops, forgets, cooks, laughs
[z]	[z, dʒ]음을 제외한 유성음으로 끝나는 경우 ➡ lends, hugs, arrives, seems, finds, sings, tells, wears, agrees
[iz]	[s, z, ʃ, tʃ, dʒ]음으로 끝나는 경우 ➡ mixes, loses, touches, changes

PRACTICE 3

〈보기〉와 같이 주어진 단어의 밑줄 친 부분의 발음으로 알맞은 것을 [s], [z], [iz] 중에서 골라 쓰세요.

보 기	wishe<u>s</u> [iz]		trie<u>s</u> [z]		put<u>s</u> [s]	
1 watche<u>s</u> [ ]		**2** call<u>s</u> [ ]		**3** hide<u>s</u> [ ]		
4 hug<u>s</u> [ ]		**5** stay<u>s</u> [ ]		**6** write<u>s</u> [ ]		
7 use<u>s</u> [ ]		**8** set<u>s</u> [ ]		**9** dream<u>s</u> [ ]		
10 pick<u>s</u> [ ]		**11** misse<u>s</u> [ ]		**12** check<u>s</u> [ ]		

13 lives [ ]	14 decorates [ ]	15 judges [ ]
16 orders [ ]	17 seems [ ]	18 beats [ ]
19 attacks [ ]	20 wears [ ]	21 visits [ ]
22 sneezes [ ]	23 impresses [ ]	24 suggests [ ]
25 worries [ ]	26 pushes [ ]	27 meets [ ]
28 places [ ]	29 tells [ ]	30 feels [ ]
31 guesses [ ]	32 camps [ ]	33 teaches [ ]
34 blesses [ ]	35 escapes [ ]	36 touches [ ]
37 runs [ ]	38 raises [ ]	39 brushes [ ]
40 carries [ ]	41 repeats [ ]	42 recycles [ ]
43 thanks [ ]	44 causes [ ]	45 likes [ ]

PSS 1-4 현재시제의 쓰임

1. 현재의 상태

She **is** a teacher.
그녀는 선생님이다.
Alice **looks** happy **now**.
Alice는 지금 행복해 보인다.

2. 습관, 반복적인 일

He **always watches** the news at 9.
그는 항상 9시에 뉴스를 본다.
She **keeps** a diary **every day**.
그녀는 매일 일기를 쓴다.

3. 일반적인 사실, 진리

Three and one **is** four. 3 더하기 1은 4이다.
Water **freezes** at 0°C. 물은 0도에서 언다.

4. 속담, 격언

A rolling stone **gathers** no moss.
구르는 돌에는 이끼가 끼지 않는다.
Time **is** gold. 시간은 금이다.

PRACTICE 4

괄호 안의 단어를 현재시제의 쓰임에 맞게 바꾸어 빈칸에 쓰세요.

1 I _____ a painter. (be)
2 She _____ tennis. (play)
3 Mina usually _____ for work at 8. (leave)
4 You _____ sick. (be)
5 The Earth _____ around the Sun. (go)
6 We _____ from Korea. (be)
7 Minsu _____ football. (like)
8 The weather _____ nice today. (be)
9 You and Mina _____ very happy. (look)
10 My brothers _____ very tall. (be)
11 Bill _____ TV after dinner. (watch)
12 They _____ hungry. (be)
13 My son _____ very hard. (study)
14 Tokyo _____ the capital of Japan. (be)
15 The Sun _____ in the east. (rise)
16 Grandmother always _____ up early. (get)
17 Seoul _____ many beautiful mountains. (have)
18 She _____ a cup of coffee in the morning. (drink)
19 Many hands _____ light work. (make)

PSS 2 과거시제

PSS 2-1 일반동사의 규칙 변화형 I

대부분의 경우	-ed	finish – finish**ed** pass – pass**ed** play – play**ed** walk – walk**ed**
-e로 끝나는 경우	-d	dance – dance**d** like – like**d** move – move**d** save – save**d**

단모음+단자음으로 끝나는 경우	마지막 자음을 하나 더 쓰고 -ed	drop – drop**ped** plan – plan**ned** shop – shop**ped** stop – stop**ped** **cf.** 강세가 앞에 오는 2음절 동사의 경우 enter – enter**ed** visit – visit**ed**

정답 p.7

PRACTICE 5

다음 동사의 과거형을 쓰세요.

1 shop – _____
2 agree – _____
3 call – _____
4 wish – _____
5 invent – _____
6 believe – _____
7 cross – _____
8 rain – _____
9 save – _____
10 work – _____
11 start – _____
12 turn – _____
13 live – _____
14 plan – _____
15 raise – _____
16 happen – _____
17 want – _____
18 move – _____
19 improve – _____
20 love – _____
21 walk – _____
22 jump – _____
23 visit – _____
24 arrive – _____
25 push – _____
26 cover – _____
27 place – _____
28 stop – _____
29 learn – _____
30 open – _____

PSS 2-2 일반동사의 규칙 변화형 II

자음+y로 끝나는 경우	y를 i로 바꾸고 -ed	cry – cr**ied** try – tr**ied**	study – stud**ied** worry – worr**ied**
모음+y로 끝나는 경우	-ed	enjoy – enjoy**ed** play – play**ed**	obey – obey**ed** stay – stay**ed**

PRACTICE 6

다음 동사의 과거형을 쓰세요.

1. close – _____
2. guide – _____
3. worry – _____
4. use – _____
5. repeat – _____
6. wait – _____
7. stay – _____
8. join – _____
9. wonder – _____
10. end – _____
11. study – _____
12. surprise – _____
13. add – _____
14. connect – _____
15. drop – _____
16. play – _____
17. try – _____
18. spoil – _____
19. bake – _____
20. suggest – _____
21. roll – _____
22. tie – _____
23. collect – _____
24. carry – _____
25. enter – _____
26. obey – _____
27. discuss – _____
28. answer – _____
29. touch – _____
30. solve – _____
31. enjoy – _____
32. help – _____
33. marry – _____
34. serve – _____
35. listen – _____
36. waste – _____
37. watch – _____
38. sound – _____
39. share – _____
40. train – _____
41. hurry – _____
42. pour – _____
43. cheer – _____
44. dance – _____
45. return – _____
46. miss – _____
47. lock – _____
48. laugh – _____
49. hate – _____
50. type – _____
51. seem – _____
52. fail – _____
53. look – _____
54. decide – _____
55. practice – _____
56. kick – _____
57. guess – _____
58. change – _____
59. reach – _____
60. swallow – _____

PSS 2-3 규칙 변화 과거형의 '-(e)d' 발음

발음	용법
[t]	[t]음을 제외한 무성음으로 끝나는 경우 ➡ stopped, talked, laughed, missed, pushed, watched
[d]	[d]음을 제외한 유성음으로 끝나는 경우 ➡ lived, harmed, cleaned, called, cheered, raised, enjoyed
[id]	[t, d]음으로 끝나는 경우 ➡ wanted, visited, added, ended

정답 p.7

PRACTICE 7

〈보기〉와 같이 규칙 변화 과거형 동사의 -(e)d의 발음으로 알맞은 것을 [t], [d], [id] 중에서 골라 쓰세요.

보기   cried [d]   picked [t]   visited [id]

1 talked   [   ]   2 stayed   [   ]   3 worked   [   ]
4 called   [   ]   5 looked   [   ]   6 collected [   ]
7 rained   [   ]   8 explained [   ]   9 wanted   [   ]
10 showed   [   ]   11 shouted   [   ]   12 answered [   ]
13 touched   [   ]   14 cleaned   [   ]   15 stopped   [   ]
16 lived   [   ]   17 arrived   [   ]   18 walked   [   ]
19 started   [   ]   20 enjoyed   [   ]   21 helped   [   ]
22 harmed   [   ]   23 learned   [   ]   24 thanked   [   ]
25 played   [   ]   26 asked   [   ]   27 added   [   ]
28 laughed   [   ]   29 kicked   [   ]   30 decided   [   ]
31 spelled   [   ]   32 cheered   [   ]   33 missed   [   ]
34 watched   [   ]   35 ended   [   ]   36 typed   [   ]
37 spoiled   [   ]   38 saved   [   ]   39 attacked [   ]
40 connected [   ]   41 pushed   [   ]   42 turned   [   ]
43 moved   [   ]   44 invented [   ]   45 happened [   ]

PSS 2-4 일반동사의 불규칙 변화형

1. AAA형(원형, 과거형, 과거분사형이 같은 형)

원형	과거형	과거분사형	뜻
cost	cost	cost	비용이 들다
hit	hit	hit	치다
hurt	hurt	hurt	다치다
let	let	let	~하게 하다
put	put	put	놓다
read[ri:d]	read[red]	read[red]	읽다
set	set	set	놓다
shut	shut	shut	닫다
spread	spread	spread	퍼지다

2. ABB형(과거형과 과거분사형이 같은 형)

원형	과거형	과거분사형	뜻
bring	brought	brought	가져오다
build	built	built	짓다
burn	burned / burnt	burned / burnt	타다
buy	bought	bought	사다
catch	caught	caught	잡다
dream	dreamed / dreamt	dreamed / dreamt	꿈꾸다
feed	fed	fed	먹이다
feel	felt	felt	느끼다
fight	fought	fought	싸우다
find	found	found	발견하다
get	got	got(ten)	얻다

원형	과거형	과거분사형	뜻
have	had	had	가지다, 먹다
hear	heard[hə:rd]	heard[hə:rd]	듣다
hold	held	held	지니다
keep	kept	kept	유지하다
lay	laid	laid	놓다, 낳다
lead	led	led	인도하다
leave	left	left	떠나다
lend	lent	lent	빌려주다
lose	lost	lost	잃어버리다
make	made	made	만들다
mean	meant[ment]	meant[ment]	의미하다
meet	met	met	만나다
pay	paid	paid	지불하다
say	said[sed]	said[sed]	말하다
sell	sold	sold	팔다
send	sent	sent	보내다
sit	sat	sat	앉다
sleep	slept	slept	자다
slide	slid	slid	미끄러지다
smell	smelled / smelt	smelled / smelt	냄새 맡다
spend	spent	spent	소비하다
stand	stood	stood	서다
teach	taught	taught	가르치다
tell	told	told	말하다
think	thought	thought	생각하다
understand	understood	understood	이해하다
win	won	won	이기다

3. ABC형(원형, 과거형, 과거분사형이 다른 형)

원형	과거형	과거분사형	뜻
be	was / were	been	~이다, 있다
bear	bore	borne/born	낳다, 견디다
begin	began	begun	시작하다
bite	bit	bitten	물다
blow	blew	blown	불다
break	broke	broken	깨뜨리다
choose	chose	chosen	선택하다
do	did	done	하다
draw	drew	drawn	그리다
drink	drank	drunk	마시다
drive	drove	driven	운전하다
eat	ate	eaten	먹다
fall	fell	fallen	떨어지다
forget	forgot	forgotten	잊다
fly	flew	flown	날다
give	gave	given	주다
go	went	gone	가다
grow	grew	grown	자라다
know	knew	known	알다
ride	rode	ridden	타다
ring	rang	rung	울리다
rise [raɪz]	rose [róuz]	risen [rízn]	오르다
see	saw	seen	보다
sing	sang	sung	노래하다
show	showed	shown	보여주다
speak	spoke	spoken	말하다
swim	swam	swum	수영하다

원형	과거형	과거분사형	뜻
take	took	taken	가지고 가다
throw	threw	thrown	던지다
wake	woke	woken	깨다
wear	wore	worn	입다
write	wrote	written	쓰다

4. ABA형(원형과 과거분사형이 같은 형)

원형	과거형	과거분사형	뜻
become	became	become	되다
come	came	come	오다
run	ran	run	달리다

정답 p.7

PRACTICE 8

다음 동사의 과거형과 과거분사형을 쓰세요.

1 set   — _____ — _____
2 hold   — _____ — _____
3 become — _____ — _____
4 smell — _____ — _____
5 bear — _____ — _____
6 break — _____ — _____
7 cost — _____ — _____
8 mean — _____ — _____
9 stay — _____ — _____
10 dream — _____ — _____
11 run — _____ — _____
12 blow — _____ — _____
13 feed — _____ — _____
14 drive — _____ — _____
15 put — _____ — _____
16 understand — _____ — _____
17 come — _____ — _____
18 choose — _____ — _____
19 drink — _____ — _____
20 draw — _____ — _____
21 read — _____ — _____
22 shop — _____ — _____
23 fight — _____ — _____
24 stand — _____ — _____
25 wear — _____ — _____
26 bite — _____ — _____
27 sing — _____ — _____
28 let — _____ — _____

29 win – ___ – ___	30 hit – ___ – ___
31 tell – ___ – ___	32 write – ___ – ___
33 sell – ___ – ___	34 slide – ___ – ___
35 take – ___ – ___	36 wake – ___ – ___
37 fly – ___ – ___	38 carry – ___ – ___
39 try – ___ – ___	40 swim – ___ – ___
41 feel – ___ – ___	42 show – ___ – ___
43 burn – ___ – ___	44 keep – ___ – ___
45 forget – ___ – ___	46 ring – ___ – ___
47 send – ___ – ___	48 hear – ___ – ___
49 build – ___ – ___	50 hurt – ___ – ___
51 rise – ___ – ___	52 catch – ___ – ___
53 bring – ___ – ___	54 spread – ___ – ___
55 lend – ___ – ___	56 grow – ___ – ___
57 begin – ___ – ___	58 throw – ___ – ___
59 buy – ___ – ___	60 enjoy – ___ – ___
61 sit – ___ – ___	62 be – ___ – ___
63 play – ___ – ___	64 find – ___ – ___
65 go – ___ – ___	66 give – ___ – ___
67 plan – ___ – ___	68 eat – ___ – ___
69 ride – ___ – ___	70 know – ___ – ___
71 spend – ___ – ___	72 close – ___ – ___
73 speak – ___ – ___	74 get – ___ – ___
75 teach – ___ – ___	76 see – ___ – ___
77 lead – ___ – ___	78 study – ___ – ___
79 make – ___ – ___	80 have – ___ – ___
81 fall – ___ – ___	82 say – ___ – ___
83 lose – ___ – ___	84 leave – ___ – ___
85 sleep – ___ – ___	86 do – ___ – ___
87 meet – ___ – ___	88 think – ___ – ___
89 lay – ___ – ___	90 pay – ___ – ___

PSS 2-5 과거시제의 쓰임

과거시제는 과거에 이미 끝난 동작이나 상태, 역사적 사실을 나타낼 때 쓰인다.

It **was** sunny **yesterday**.
어제는 화창했다.
We **went** to the movies **last weekend**.
우리는 지난 주말에 영화관에 갔다.
The Korean War **broke** out **in 1950**.
한국전쟁은 1950년에 일어났다.

I **went** to the beach **yesterday**.

정답 p.8

PRACTICE 9

괄호 안에 주어진 단어 중 알맞은 것을 고르세요.

1 It (is, was) cold yesterday, but it is warm today.
2 I (am, was) now ready to answer your questions.
3 The man is rich now, but he (isn't, wasn't) rich 5 years ago.
4 My cat (was, were) sick yesterday afternoon.
5 Barbara and I (are, were) at a restaurant last night.
6 They (are, were) in Japan last weekend.
7 We (aren't, weren't) good at snowboarding last winter.
8 Ms. Kim (is, was) a teacher. She teaches us English.
9 You were a driver two years ago, but you (are, were) an engineer now.
10 I stopped by your office yesterday, but you (aren't, weren't) there.

정답 p.8

PRACTICE 10

괄호 안의 단어를 알맞은 형태로 바꾸어 빈칸에 쓰세요.

1 Yesterday was his birthday. We _____ a T-shirt for him. (buy)
2 I usually _____ breakfast, but this morning I skipped it. (eat)

3   He _____ to bed early because he was very tired. (go)
4   My grandma _____ glasses when she reads a book. (wear)
5   My father _____ the house in 2001. (build)
6   It _____ to rain last night. (begin)
7   Seho _____ this novel a month ago. (read)
8   She _____ her lost wallet yesterday. (find)
9   They _____ the picture an hour ago. (finish)
10 Namsu always _____ the violin when he stays home. (practice)

PSS 3 미래시제 – will과 be going to
Problem Solving Skill

I **will** carry it for you.

I**'m going to** play soccer after school.

will이나 be going to를 사용하여 미래시제를 표현할 수 있다.

주어	will / be going to	동사원형
I	will am going to	be at home.
He / She / It	will is going to	
We / You / They	will are going to	

1. 미래에 대한 추측이나 의지를 나타낼 때 – will '~일 것이다, ~할 것이다'

   It **will** rain **next Sunday**. 다음 주 일요일에는 비가 올 것이다.
   I**'ll** show you my album. 네게 내 사진첩을 보여줄게.

   cf. 추측을 나타낼 경우 be going to로도 쓸 수 있다.
   It **is going to** rain **next Sunday**. 다음 주 일요일에는 비가 올 것이다.

2. 미래의 계획이나 예정을 나타낼 때 – be going to '~하려고 하다'

   He **is going to** have a date with Jane **tomorrow**.
   그는 내일 Jane과 데이트를 하려고 한다.
   What **are** they **going to** do **this weekend**? – They**'re going to** have a party.
   그들은 이번 주말에 무엇을 하려고 하니?   그들은 파티를 열 거야.

정답 p.8

PRACTICE 11

〈보기〉와 같이 짝지어진 두 문장의 의미가 같도록 빈칸을 채우세요.

| 보 기 | It will snow this afternoon.
= It is going to snow this afternoon. |

1 Jack will get the job.
   = Jack _____ the job.

2 They will go to the museum.
   = They _____ to the museum.

3 We will get there tomorrow morning.
   = We _____ there tomorrow morning.

4 He will visit his grandparents.
   = He _____ his grandparents.

5 She will make dinner for us.
   = She _____ dinner for us.

6 You and Eric will paint the room together.
   = You and Eric _____ the room together.

PRACTICE 12

괄호 안에 주어진 말 중 알맞은 것을 고르세요.

1 I'm going to (spend, spends) the weekend just relaxing.
2 (Is, Will) he going to play tennis?
3 Sales (are, will) rise next year.
4 He (went, will go) to the market yesterday.
5 They will (make, makes) time for their family.
6 (Are, Will) you be there tonight?
7 Mary will (be, is) a singer someday.
8 Ted always (get, gets) up at six.
9 Tom (stayed, will stay) up all night last night.
10 How long (will, are) you going to stay there?

PRACTICE 13

그림을 보고, 〈보기〉에서 알맞은 동사를 골라 B의 대답을 완성하세요.

보기	travel buy study paint have

1 A: What are you going to do this Saturday?   B: I _____ my house.
2 A: What will he do during his next vacation?   B: He _____ to Egypt.
3 A: What is Kelly going to do today?   B: She _____ at the library.
4 A: What will you do this weekend?   B: We _____ a party.
5 A: What are they going to do?   B: They _____ some flowers.

진행시제

PSS 4-1 동사의 -ing형 I

대부분의 경우	-ing	call – call**ing** start – start**ing**	sing – sing**ing** teach – teach**ing**
자음+e로 끝나는 경우	e를 빼고 -ing	come – com**ing** make – mak**ing**	give – giv**ing** ride – rid**ing**

정답 p.8

PRACTICE 14

다음 동사의 -ing형을 쓰세요.

1 live   – _____
2 leave   – _____
3 sleep   – _____
4 hold   – _____
5 draw   – _____
6 play   – _____
7 carry   – _____
8 believe – _____
9 write   – _____
10 say   – _____
11 buy   – _____
12 spend   – _____
13 lose   – _____
14 wake   – _____
15 check   – _____
16 bring   – _____
17 look   – _____
18 dive   – _____
19 join   – _____
20 smoke   – _____
21 do   – _____
22 blow   – _____
23 make   – _____
24 choose – _____
25 add   – _____
26 sell   – _____
27 give   – _____
28 have   – _____
29 take   – _____
30 meet   – _____

PSS 4-2 동사의 -ing형 Ⅱ

-ie로 끝나는 경우	ie를 y로 바꾸고 -ing	lie – l**y**ing	tie – t**y**ing
단모음+단자음으로 끝나는 경우	마지막 자음을 하나 더 쓰고 -ing	run – run**n**ing put – put**t**ing ***cf.*** 강세가 앞에 오는 2음절 동사의 경우 enter – ente**r**ing	get – get**t**ing begin – begin**n**ing visit – visi**t**ing

PRACTICE 15

다음 동사의 -ing형을 쓰세요.

1. get   – _____
2. lie   – _____
3. change   – _____
4. open   – _____
5. park   – _____
6. push   – _____
7. read   – _____
8. wear   – _____
9. put   – _____
10. call   – _____
11. find   – _____
12. bike   – _____
13. burn   – _____
14. set   – _____
15. come   – _____
16. respect   – _____
17. win   – _____
18. see   – _____
19. close   – _____
20. begin   – _____
21. tie   – _____
22. grow   – _____
23. keep   – _____
24. drink   – _____
25. swim   – _____
26. help   – _____
27. climb   – _____
28. enter   – _____
29. sing   – _____
30. go   – _____
31. jump   – _____
32. shop   – _____
33. lend   – _____
34. catch   – _____
35. collect   – _____
36. send   – _____

37	stay – _____		38	ride – _____
39	fall – _____		40	fly – _____
41	teach – _____		42	dream – _____
43	sit – _____		44	drive – _____
45	plant – _____		46	turn – _____
47	stand – _____		48	start – _____
49	float – _____		50	break – _____
51	tell – _____		52	eat – _____
53	speak – _____		54	run – _____
55	arrive – _____		56	build – _____
57	ask – _____		58	camp – _____
59	cheer – _____		60	walk – _____

PSS 4-3 현재진행시제와 과거진행시제

<Now>

<Last night>

He **is watching** television **now**.　　He **was working** last night.

1. 현재진행 – 「am / is / are + -ing」
   '~하고 있다'

   Ted **is listening** to pop songs.
   Ted는 대중 가요를 듣고 있다.
   Insu and Suji **are having** lunch together.
   인수와 수지는 함께 점심을 먹고 있다.

2. 과거진행 – 「was / were + -ing」
   '~하고 있었다'

   Ted **was listening** to pop songs.
   Ted는 대중 가요를 듣고 있었다.
   Insu and Suji **were having** lunch together.
   인수와 수지는 함께 점심을 먹고 있었다.

PRACTICE 16

〈보기〉와 같이 주어진 문장을 진행시제의 문장으로 바꾸어 쓰세요.

| 보 기 | Tom reads a book.
➡ Tom is reading a book. |

1 It snows.
➡ _____

2 I clean my room.
➡ _____

3 Sumi makes a card.
➡ _____

4 He wears blue jeans.
➡ _____

5 It flew over the tree.
➡ _____

6 We enjoyed the holiday.
➡ _____

7 They do their best.
➡ _____

8 My grandparents smiled at us.
➡ _____

9 A man stood in front of the door.
➡ _____

10 I played basketball with my friends.
➡ _____

PSS 4-4 미래를 나타내는 현재진행시제

1. 현재진행형으로 가까운 미래의 계획을 나타낼 수 있다. 주로 왕래발착을 나타내는 동사인 go, come, start, leave, arrive와 함께 쓰이지만, 다른 동사들도 미래를 나타내는 부사나 부사구와 함께 현재진행형으로 미래를 나타낼 수 있다.

    We **are going** camping **this weekend**. 우리는 이번 주말에 캠핑을 갈 것이다.
    He **is coming** here **soon**. 그는 곧 여기로 올 것이다.
    I'**m leaving tomorrow morning**. 나는 내일 아침에 떠날 것이다.

2. '진행'을 나타내는 현재진행형과 '미래'를 나타내는 현재진행형의 비교

    What **are** you **doing now**?   - I'**m reading** a book.
    너는 지금 무엇을 하고 있니?   나는 책을 읽고 있어.
    What **are** you **doing tomorrow**?   - I'**m studying** in the library **tomorrow**.
    너는 내일 무엇을 할 거니?   나는 내일 도서관에서 공부할 거야.
                           (= I'**m going to study** in the library **tomorrow**.)

PRACTICE 17

괄호 안의 단어를 이용하여 현재진행형으로 B의 대답을 완성하세요.

1. A: What is Junho doing tomorrow morning?
   B: He ___is cleaning the house___ tomorrow morning. (clean, the house)

2. A: What are you doing this evening?
   B: I _____ this evening. (read, a book)

3. A: What is Liza doing next vacation?
   B: She _____ next vacation. (visit, her aunt)

4. A: What are they doing next Saturday?
   B: They _____ next Saturday. (eat out, with their family)

5. A: What are you doing this Sunday?
   B: We _____ this Sunday. (go, to church)

PRACTICE 18

그림을 보고, 〈보기〉에서 알맞은 동사를 골라 B의 대답을 완성하세요.

보기 read   climb   go   write   paint

1. A: What is Nari doing now? B: She _____ a letter to her friend.
2. A: What did you do yesterday? B: We _____ to the movies.
3. A: What are you going to do tomorrow? B: I _____ the mountain.
4. A: What will Jinho do at home? B: He _____ a picture.
5. A: What was she doing at 7 a.m.? B: She _____ a newspaper.

현재완료시제

PSS 5-1 현재완료시제의 쓰임

현재완료시제는 「have/has+과거분사」의 형태로 과거에 일어난 일을 현재와 연관지어 나타낼 때 쓴다.

주어	have/has	과거분사
I/You/We/They	have have not (= haven't)	been ill since last week.
He/She/It	has has not (= hasn't)	

He began to live in London six years ago. He lives in London now.
그는 6년 전에 런던에서 살기 시작했다. 그는 지금 런던에 산다.
➡ He **has lived** in London for six years. 그는 6년째 런던에서 살고 있다.

Have you ever **been** to Canada? – Yes, I have. / No, I haven't.
너는 캐나다에 가본 적이 있니?   응, 가봤어. / 아니, 가보지 않았어.

PRACTICE 19

정답 p.9

괄호 안의 단어를 현재완료시제로 바꾸어 빈칸에 쓰세요.

1 They ___have built___ the bridge since last year. (build)
2 She _____ a sports car for four months. (drive)
3 I _____ anything about him. (not, hear)
4 _____ Bill _____ Cathy? (meet)
5 Hana _____ a bicycle since last week. (have)
6 _____ you ever _____ New York? (visit)
7 My brother and I _____ the sunrise. (not, see)
8 Ms. Song _____ math for a long time. (teach)
9 _____ you _____ in the library before? (study)

PRACTICE 20

다음 밑줄 친 부분을 현재완료시제가 되도록 어법에 맞게 고쳐 쓰세요.

1. Sujin have played the violin since 2020.
   ➡ _has played_

2. Has she watch a soccer game before?
   ➡ _____

3. They haven't leaved the building yet.
   ➡ _____

4. I have feeded a lost dog for 2 weeks.
   ➡ _____

5. Seyeon had the cell phone since last year.
   ➡ _____

6. The smell still hasn't went away.
   ➡ _____

7. She has founded her lost keys in the room.
   ➡ _____

8. How long have he been in that seat?
   ➡ _____

9. I never read Harry Potter in my life.
   ➡ _____

10. Seungjun has grew 20cm since last year.
    ➡ _____

PSS 5-2 현재완료시제와 과거시제의 비교

현재완료	과거
과거 ──▶ 현재	과거 · 현재
1. 과거부터 현재까지 계속되는 동작이나 상태를 나타낸다. Steve **has stayed** in Japan for two months. Steve는 두 달 동안 일본에 있었다. (현재 일본에 계속 있다는 의미)	1. 과거에 이미 끝난 동작이나 상태를 나타낸다. Steve **stayed** in Japan for two months. Steve는 두 달 동안 일본에 있었다. (현재 일본에 있지 않다는 의미)
2. 기간을 나타내는 부사(구)와 함께 쓸 수 있다. since는 '과거의 어느 시점부터 (현재까지)'란 뜻을 가지며 주로 현재완료시제와 잘 쓰인다. She **has played** the piano **since last year**. 그녀는 작년부터 피아노를 쳤다.	2. yesterday, last+명사, ago, 'in+과거 연도'와 같은 명백한 과거 시점을 나타내는 부사(구)와 함께 쓸 수 있다. She **played** the piano **a few days ago**. 그녀는 며칠 전에 피아노를 쳤다. **cf.** 의문사 when은 현재완료시제와 함께 쓰일 수 없다. **When did** you **clean** your room? 너는 방을 언제 청소했니?

PRACTICE 21

괄호 안에 주어진 표현 중 알맞은 것을 고르세요.

1. (Have, Did) you ever seen that movie?
2. He (lived, has lived) in Seoul since 2000.
3. Last night he (brushed, has brushed) his teeth.
4. When (did, has) he go there?
5. He (left, has left) Korea last year.
6. They (have been, are) married for ten years.
7. I have (know, known) her for a long time.
8. Mina has (plays, played) the violin for five years.
9. She (met, has met) her friends last night.
10. He (has, was) been sick for the last few days.
11. We (have studied, studied) English since 2001.
12. Sally (watched, has watched) the movie a week ago.
13. My uncle (has worked, worked) in a bank since this summer.
14. He (went, has gone) to work by car yesterday.
15. The party (ended, has ended) at midnight.
16. It (rained, has rained) since last night.
17. We (had, have had) his birthday party last weekend.
18. She has (listens, listened) to music for an hour.
19. He (threw, has thrown) away the bottles a moment ago.
20. They have (make, made) carpets for 50 years.
21. (Have, Did) you finish the project?
22. She (won, has won) her first gold medal in 2002.
23. We (have visited, visited) New York 2 years ago.
24. The actor (played, has played) the role since last year.
25. It (has snowed, snowed) heavily two hours ago.
26. (Have, Did) you ever been to London?
27. I (have been, was) with Suji last Friday.

Chapter Review Test

정답 p.9

CHAPTER **2**
시제

1 다음 중 밑줄 친 부분이 어색한 것을 고르세요.

I ① have a friend named Ashton. He was a very hard-working guy when he ② was a student. He ③ majored in world history in college. Now, he ④ teach history in high school. He is very popular among the students. Students ⑤ love him because he is very humorous.

2 다음 글 전체의 시제와 일치하지 않는 동사 3개를 찾아 바르게 고쳐 쓰세요.

Yesterday, my family had my mom's birthday party. I prepared a birthday cake, and my sister decorates our house with balloons. My dad bought some roses for my mom. My grandparents also come to celebrate mom's birthday. We sing a birthday song together and my mom cut the cake.

ⓐ _____ ➡ _____
ⓑ _____ ➡ _____
ⓒ _____ ➡ _____

3 다음 밑줄 친 부분 중 어법상 바른 것은?

① Does it snow heavily yesterday?
② He is moving to Seoul next month.
③ She had the house since last year.
④ I have already finish my work.
⑤ The woman was walking by the post office now.

4 다음 글에서 어법상 틀린 곳을 찾아 바르게 고쳐 쓰세요.

David liked to grow tropical plants. He builded a small greenhouse for himself. It cost a lot of money.

_____ ➡ _____

5 빈칸에 들어갈 말로 알맞지 않은 것은?

_____ go to the library.

① We   ② Women   ③ Sue and John
④ People   ⑤ My aunt

6 다음 문장을 〈보기〉와 같이 바꾸어 쓰세요.

보기 | I have lunch at noon.
➡ He has lunch at noon.

• I do the cooking in the evening.
➡ She _____ the cooking in the evening.

7 주어진 우리말을 영어로 가장 바르게 영작한 학생은?

우리는 탁구를 치고 있는 중이었다.

① 수혁 : We were playing table tennis.
② 서진 : We are going to play table tennis.
③ 민주 : We are playing table tennis.
④ 승준 : We played table tennis.
⑤ 윤서 : We was playing table tennis.

CHAPTER 2 _ 시제   63

8 다음 대화의 빈칸에 공통으로 들어갈 단어를 쓰세요.

> A: How _____ the weather there yesterday?
> B: It _____ cloudy.

9 다음 우리말을 참조하여 빈칸에 알맞은 말을 쓰세요. (단, 주어진 동사를 사용하고, 필요한 경우 동사의 형태를 변형할 것)

> He _____ _____ the town tomorrow.
> 그는 내일 그 도시를 떠날 것이다. (be, leave)

10 괄호 안의 단어를 현재시제로 바꾸어 빈칸에 쓰세요.

> Homemade food ⓐ _____ (have) a lot of benefits. It ⓑ _____ (bring) a family together. Cooking at home ⓒ _____ (help) to improve your cooking skills. Also, you can eat healthier ingredients. Not only that, it ⓓ _____ (save) you money.

11 빈칸에 들어갈 수 있는 것을 두 개 고르면?

동사원형	과거형	과거분사형
ride	r☐de	ridden
draw	drew	dr☐wn
bear	b☐re	b☐rn
begin	beg☐n	begun

① a ② e ③ i
④ o ⑤ u

12 다음 밑줄 친 부분 중 어법상 옳은 것은?

> I ① take the TOEFL exam yesterday. However, I didn't do ② very good. So, I checked the official website ③ to see the next exam date. The next test will be ④ in November 27th. Until then, I'm going to ⑤ studying for the test, specifically for the speaking portion of the test.

13 다음 빈칸에 들어갈 수 없는 말은?

> Where did you go _____ ?

① last winter ② yesterday
③ this afternoon ④ three days ago
⑤ next Saturday

14 다음 밑줄 친 부분 중 어법상 어색한 것은?

① I am a graduate student.
② He will be ninety years old next year.
③ We was making a chair.
④ She is very kind.
⑤ They are my friends.

15 다음 질문에 대한 대답으로 알맞은 것은?

> A: What are you going to do?
> B: _____

① Yes, I am.
② I'm going to do my laundry.
③ I'm good at swimming.
④ Yes, I have to go now.
⑤ I went home.

16 다음 밑줄 친 부분의 쓰임이 다른 하나는?

① I'm going to the zoo now.
② I'm going to write a letter.
③ I'm going to have a party tonight.
④ I'm going to make a plan.
⑤ I'm going to go to London.

17 다음 대화의 빈칸에 들어갈 단어로 알맞게 짝지어진 것은?

A: _____ he and his family visited here?
B: Yes, they _____.

① Has – have
② Has – has
③ Has – had
④ Have – has
⑤ Have – have

18 다음 밑줄 친 동사의 형태가 잘못된 것은?

① Mary takes a bus.
② She plaies the violin with her mother.
③ Your father has a nice car.
④ He studies English very hard.
⑤ Mike gets up early in the morning.

19 다음 빈칸에 들어갈 말로 알맞은 것을 모두 고르세요.

Alice _____ shopping next weekend.

① go
② want
③ will go
④ is going
⑤ went

20 다음 빈칸에 들어갈 알맞은 말을 고르세요.

• Susan moved here five years ago. She still lives here.
= Susan _____ here for five years.

① lives
② was living
③ lived
④ has lived
⑤ have lived

21 다음 중 어법상 옳은 문장의 개수는?

ⓐ This's your cell phone.
ⓑ She will makes it in time.
ⓒ He read the book last week.
ⓓ Mr. and Mrs. Cheney are my good neighbors.
ⓔ Jane and I am talking about the movie.

① 1개
② 2개
③ 3개
④ 4개
⑤ 5개

22 밑줄 친 동사의 알맞은 형태를 고르세요.

A few years ago, her father make kites for her.

① makes
② made
③ making
④ has made
⑤ is making

23 다음 문장을 〈보기〉와 같이 바꾸어 쓰세요.

보기 | Do you clean your room?
➡ Are you cleaning your room?

Does she water the plant?
➡ _____

24 다음 문장을 〈보기〉와 같이 바꾸어 쓰세요.

보기	He listens to music. ➡ He is listening to music.

(1) Yumi sings a song.
➡ _____

(2) Mike swims in the pool.
➡ _____

25 다음 중 밑줄 친 부분의 쓰임이 나머지 넷과 다른 하나는?

① My dad is going fishing tomorrow.
② Mr. Smith is coming soon.
③ Are you meeting Alex next week?
④ We are having a barbecue this Friday.
⑤ What are you doing now?

26 다음 문장의 밑줄 친 부분과 쓰임이 같은 문장으로 짝지어진 것은?

What are we going to do there?

ⓐ I am going to clean my room. ⓑ He is going to a concert with Evan. ⓒ We are going to go to Jeju-do for a family trip. ⓓ She is going to the art gallery. ⓔ Jina is going to wear a new dress.

① ⓐ, ⓑ   ② ⓐ, ⓒ, ⓔ   ③ ⓐ, ⓓ, ⓔ
④ ⓑ, ⓓ   ⑤ ⓑ, ⓓ, ⓔ

27 빈칸에 공통으로 들어갈 kid의 알맞은 형태를 고르세요.

A: Did you hear? The temperature will drop below zero tomorrow. B: What? You must be _____. It's still the middle of fall. A: I know. But I'm not _____. The forecast said so. B: The weather is getting crazier every year.

① kid   ② kids   ③ to kid
④ kidding   ⑤ do kid

28 아래의 그림을 보고 주어진 물음에 답하세요.

(1) What is Bomi doing?
➡ _____

(2) What are Peter and John doing?
➡ _____

29 우리말과 같은 뜻이 되도록 주어진 단어를 바르게 배열하세요. (단, 필요시 어형을 바꿀 것)

• 그는 과학자가 될 것이다.
  = _____
  (he, scientist, will, a, is)

30 다음 문장을 괄호 안의 조건대로 옮긴 것 중 잘못된 것은?

> She plays the piano.

① (현재완료로) → She has played the piano.
② (현재진행형으로) → She is playing the piano.
③ (미래시제로) → She will plays the piano.
④ (과거시제로) → She played the piano.
⑤ (과거진행형으로) → She was playing the piano.

31 괄호 안에 주어진 단어를 사용하여 빈칸에 알맞은 말을 쓰세요.

> A: Lisa! What are you doing?
> B: I _____ _____ my hands. (wash)
> A: Where is your father?
> B: He is in the living room. He _____ _____ a newspaper. (read)

32 다음 중 어법상 어색한 문장을 모두 고르세요.

① How are you doing?
② I go to Mt. Halla last week.
③ It was great.
④ I made new friends.
⑤ She's name is Sumin.

33 다음 중 동사의 변화형이 잘못된 것을 고르세요.

① feel – felt – felt
② know – knew – known
③ give – gave – given
④ make – made – maden
⑤ come – came – come

34 다음 밑줄 친 부분의 쓰임이 다른 것은?

① Many people are carrying umbrellas.
② Some young people are walking in the rain.
③ We are living at the beginning of the 21st century.
④ Steve and Cathy are visiting the museum.
⑤ My hobby is reading books.

35 〈보기〉를 참고하여 빈칸에 알맞은 단어를 쓰세요.

> 보기 | Open daily 9:30 a.m.

→ It _____ at 9:30 a.m. every day.

36 다음 세미의 일정표를 보고 be going to를 이용하여 질문에 알맞은 답을 쓰세요.

Tuesday	buy some books
Wednesday	make cookies
Thursday	go swimming
Friday	go to the movies

> Q: What is Semi going to do on Thursday?
> A: She _____.

37 다음 빈칸에 순서대로 들어갈 be동사의 알맞은 형태는?

- I _____ 33 years old last year.
- I _____ 34 years old now.
- I _____ 35 years old next year.

① am – was – will be
② was – am – will be
③ will be – was – am
④ am – will be – was
⑤ was – will be – am

38 다음 문장에서 잘못된 두 군데를 찾아 바르게 고쳐 쓰세요.

He get up early and go jogging every morning.

_____ ➡ _____

_____ ➡ _____

39 다음 중 현재진행형으로 고친 문장이 바르지 않은 것은?

① He makes his bed.
  ➡ He is making his bed.
② She lies on the floor.
  ➡ She is lieing on the floor.
③ The meeting begins.
  ➡ The meeting is beginning.
④ I do exercises.
  ➡ I am doing exercises.
⑤ He plays the piano.
  ➡ He is playing the piano.

40 다음 ⓐ~ⓒ에 들어갈 말을 알맞게 짝지은 것은?

On Sunday morning, Bora __ⓐ__ taking a walk. Then, she saw two foreigners. They __ⓑ__ Bora for help. They were __ⓒ__ for a bus stop. Bora showed them the way to the bus stop.

	ⓐ	ⓑ	ⓒ
①	was	asked	look
②	was	ask	looking
③	was	asked	looking
④	were	asked	looking
⑤	were	ask	look

41 빈칸에 들어갈 알맞은 말은?

Who am I _____ to, please?

① talk   ② talks   ③ can talk
④ talking   ⑤ will talk

42 다음 중 밑줄 친 부분의 쓰임이 잘못된 것은?

① We cleaned our house.
② He washed his clothes.
③ I made some food for my parents.
④ We had dinner together.
⑤ My sister came back home at eight.

43 다음 중 어법상 올바른 문장을 고르세요.

① I will a good designer.
② I will visited my grandmother tomorrow.
③ Cathy is having lunch now.
④ Mr. Park was busy tomorrow.
⑤ He was playing not basketball this morning.

PSS 4-3 may

추측	'~일지도 모른다'라는 뜻으로 약한 추측을 나타낸다. She **may** go out. 그녀는 외출할지도 모른다. She **may not** go out. 그녀는 외출하지 않을지도 모른다.
허가	'~해도 좋다'라는 뜻이며, 이때의 may를 부정형인 may not으로 쓰면 '~해서는 안 된다'라는 금지의 뜻을 가진다. You **may** sit here. 너는 여기에 앉아도 좋다. You **may not** sit here. 너는 여기에 앉아서는 안 된다. **May** I sit here? 제가 여기에 앉아도 될까요?

PRACTICE 7

밑줄 친 부분이 추측과 허가 중 어떤 의미를 지니는지 구분하여 쓰세요.

1 Hi, <u>may</u> I help you? [   ]
2 You <u>may</u> use my pencil. [   ]
3 She <u>may</u> not be sick. [   ]
4 It <u>may</u> be true. [   ]
5 They <u>may</u> be busy. [   ]
6 <u>May</u> I ask a question? [   ]
7 Hello, <u>may</u> I speak to Mr. Smith? [   ]
8 She <u>may</u> not want to see us. [   ]
9 The bus <u>may</u> come in five minutes. [   ]
10 Jenny <u>may</u> be thirsty. [   ]
11 You <u>may</u> bring it back tomorrow. [   ]
12 She <u>may</u> be 42 years old. [   ]
13 <u>May</u> I borrow the car? [   ]
14 You <u>may</u> have a seat. [   ]

PSS 4-2 can II

허가	'~해도 된다'라는 뜻이며, 이때의 can을 부정형인 cannot[can't]으로 쓰면 '~해서는 안 된다'라는 금지의 뜻을 가진다. You **can** open the window. 너는 창문을 열어도 된다. He **can't** open the window. 그는 창문을 열어서는 안 된다. **Can I** open the window? 내가 창문을 열어도 될까? **Could I** open the window? 제가 창문을 열어도 될까요? *cf.* Could I ~?는 Can I ~?보다 정중한 표현으로 이때의 could는 can의 과거형이 아니다.
요청	Can you ~? 또는 Could you ~?의 형태로 쓰이며, '~해주겠니?'라는 뜻을 가진다. **Can you** send these postcards for me? 네가 나 대신 이 엽서들을 보내주겠니? **Could you** send these postcards for me? 당신이 저 대신 이 엽서들을 보내주시겠어요? *cf.* Could you ~?는 Can you ~?보다 정중한 표현으로 이때의 could는 can의 과거형이 아니다.

PRACTICE 6

다음 문장의 빈칸에 can, could, can't 중 알맞은 것을 넣으세요.

1 You look thirsty. You _____ drink juice there.

2 You _____ go out alone at night. It's dangerous.

3 Jane, _____ I borrow your pen?

4 _____ you come down a little?

5 Hello, _____ I speak to Tom, please?

6 She loves him, but she _____ marry him.

7 _____ you give me a hand?

8 You _____ park here. Please move your car.

9 _____ you do me a favor?

10 You _____ come too, if you want.

PSS 4 조동사의 종류

PSS 4-1 can I

He **can** swim.

능력

1. '~할 수 있다'의 뜻으로 능력을 나타낼 때는 be able to로 바꾸어 쓸 수 있다.

   I **can** drive a car. 나는 차를 운전할 수 있다.
   = I **am able to** drive a car.
   She **can't** drive a car. 그녀는 차를 운전할 수 없다.
   = She **isn't able to** drive a car.
   Can you drive a car? 너는 차를 운전할 수 있니?
   = **Are** you **able to** drive a car?

2. can의 과거형은 could로 '~할 수 있었다'의 뜻을 나타낸다.

   Mark **couldn't** drive a car. Mark는 차를 운전할 수 없었다.
   = Mark **wasn't able to** drive a car.

PRACTICE 5

〈보기〉와 같이 밑줄 친 부분을 be able to를 이용하여 바꾸어 쓰세요.

> 보기 Jenny <u>couldn't</u> say a word for a while.
> → Jenny <u>wasn't able to</u> say a word for a while.

1. She <u>can</u> take a picture well.
   → She _____ take a picture well.

2. I <u>can't</u> understand the situation.
   → I _____ understand the situation.

3. <u>Can</u> you make it at six?
   → _____ you _____ make it at six?

4. He <u>could</u> get a new bike on Christmas Day.
   → He _____ get a new bike on Christmas Day.

5. We <u>couldn't</u> find an exit in that store.
   → We _____ find an exit in that store.

6. <u>Can</u> you find this word in a dictionary?
   → _____ you _____ find this word in a dictionary?

PRACTICE 3

〈보기〉와 같이 주어진 문장을 의문문으로 바꾸어 쓰세요.

> 보 기
> You can change a ten-dollar bill.
> ➡ Can you change a ten-dollar bill?

1 They will get there by subway.
➡ _____

2 We should take a bus.
➡ _____

3 He can play the violin.
➡ _____

4 Jenny will move to London.
➡ _____

5 I should buy this shirt.
➡ _____

6 Minsu can cook Chinese food.
➡ _____

7 The movie will start at 11:20.
➡ _____

8 This elephant can draw pictures.
➡ _____

PRACTICE 4

우리말과 같은 뜻이 되도록 괄호 안에 주어진 단어를 바르게 배열하세요.

1 너는 젓가락을 사용할 수 있니?
= _____
(chopsticks, use, you, can)

2 커피 좀 마실래요?
= _____
(like, some coffee, you, would)

3 내가 민수를 저녁식사에 초대해야 해?
= _____
(invite, should, Minsu, to dinner, I)

4 당신의 전화기를 써도 될까요?
= _____
(I, your phone, may, use)

5 제 가방을 들어 주시겠어요?
= _____
(my bag, could, you, carry)

6 나와 함께 거기에 갈래?
= _____
(will, go there, you, with me)

7 이 병들을 재활용해야 합니까?
= _____
(I, recycle, must, these bottles)

8 Bill과 통화할 수 있을까요?
= _____
(speak, Bill, may, I, to)

PRACTICE 2

정답 p.12

〈보기〉와 같이 주어진 문장의 조동사에 not을 붙여 부정문으로 바꾸어 쓰세요.

> 보기
> Alex could sleep well last night.
> ➡ Alex could not[couldn't] sleep well last night.

1 Jane will use your desk.
➡ _____

2 You must take this ball.
➡ _____

3 She can play the guitar.
➡ _____

4 He should break the promise.
➡ _____

5 It might be true.
➡ _____

6 Minsu could dance last night.
➡ _____

7 I knew she would come here.
➡ _____

8 You may like the movie.
➡ _____

9 You had better stay here.
➡ _____

조동사로 시작하는 의문문

「조동사+주어+동사원형 ~?」의 어순으로 의문문을 만든다.

You can speak English. 너는 영어를 말할 수 있다.

Can you speak English? 너는 영어를 말할 수 있니?

– **Yes**, I can. / **No**, I can't.
응, 할 수 있어. / 아니, 할 수 없어.

Will he be at home? – **Yes**, he will. / **No**, he won't.
그가 집에 있을까?   응, 있을 거야. / 아니, 없을 거야.

Should I leave here? – **Yes**, you should. / **No**, you shouldn't.
내가 여기를 떠나야 하니?   응, 그래야 해. / 아니, 그래서는 안 돼.

PRACTICE 1

괄호 안에 주어진 단어 중 알맞은 것을 고르세요.

1. You should (watch, watched) the ball.
2. Minho can (swim, swims) in the sea.
3. He will (can, be able to) stay with us.
4. You had better (see, saw) a doctor.
5. She always (leave, leaves) for work early.
6. He may (come, comes) to class.
7. We must (be, been) ready for the rainy weather.
8. Seho really (want, wants) something to eat.
9. I could (wash, washed) my dirty hands in that place.
10. She thought she would (have, has) a cup of coffee.
11. Tony often (write, writes) letters to your sister.
12. That dog might (bite, bitten) you.

조동사의 부정형과 축약형

조동사+not	축약형	예문
cannot	can't	She **cannot[can't]** drive. 그녀는 운전을 하지 못한다.
could not	couldn't	I **couldn't** find him. 나는 그를 찾을 수 없었다.
may not	—	You **may not** be right. 네가 옳지 않을지도 모른다.
might not	mightn't	We **mightn't** win the match. 우리가 그 시합에서 이기지 못할지도 모른다.
will not	won't	They **won't** meet him. 그들은 그를 만나지 않을 것이다. = They**'ll not** meet him.
would not	wouldn't	She said she **wouldn't** be late. 그녀는 늦지 않을 거라고 말했다.
must not	mustn't	He **mustn't** be late. 그는 늦어서는 안 된다.
should not	shouldn't	We **shouldn't** break off the branches. 우리는 나뭇가지를 꺾어서는 안 된다.
had better not	—	You **had better not** go there. 너는 그곳에 가지 않는 게 낫다. = You**'d better not** go there.

조동사

다른 동사와 함께 쓰여 능력, 허가, 요청, 추측, 제안, 의무, 충고의 의미를 더하는 동사로 주어의 인칭과 수에 관계없이 항상 형태가 같다. 조동사는 항상 뒤에 동사원형을 취한다.

He can park here.
그는 여기에 주차를 할 수 있다.

He could park here.
그는 여기에 주차를 할 수 있었다.

He may park here.
그가 여기에 주차를 할지도 모른다.

He will park here.
그는 여기에 주차를 할 것이다.

He might park here.
그가 여기에 주차를 할지도 모른다.

He said he would park here.
그는 여기에 주차를 할 거라고 말했다.

He must park here.
그는 여기에 주차를 해야 한다.

He should park here.
그는 여기에 주차를 해야 한다.

He parks here.
그는 여기에 주차를 한다.

He had better park here.
그는 여기에 주차를 하는 것이 낫다.

 **조동사 + 동사원형**

주어	조동사	동사원형
I He/She/It We/You/They	can could may might will would must should had better	be park come ~ do make

cf. 조동사는 겹쳐 쓰지 않는다.
He will can buy the ticket. (×)   He will buy the ticket. (○)

72 | 마더텅 영문법 3800제 1 – BASIC

CHAPTER 3
조동사

성취도 자기 평가 활용법

구분	평가 기준
(E)xcellent	문법 내용을 모두 이해하고, 문제를 모두 맞힘.
(V)ery good	문법 내용은 충분히 이해했으나 실수로 1~2문제 틀림.
(G)ood	문법 내용이 조금 어려워 3~4문제 틀림.
needs (R)eview	문법 내용 이해가 어렵고, 5문제 이상 틀림. 복습 필요.

Problem Solving Skill	페이지	학습날짜	성취도 자기평가 E V G R	학습체크
PSS 1 조동사+동사원형	72	/		☐
PSS 2 조동사의 부정형과 축약형	73	/		☐
PSS 3 조동사로 시작하는 의문문	74	/		☐
PSS 4 조동사의 종류	페이지	학습날짜	성취도 자기평가 E V G R	학습체크
PSS 4-1 can Ⅰ	76	/		☐
PSS 4-2 can Ⅱ	77	/		☐
PSS 4-3 may	78	/		☐
PSS 4-4 May I ~?에 대한 승낙과 거절의 표현	79	/		☐
PSS 4-5 Will[Would] you ~?	80	/		☐
PSS 4-6 would like (to)	81	/		☐
PSS 4-7 must Ⅰ	82	/		☐
PSS 4-8 must Ⅱ	83	/		☐
PSS 4-9 must not, don't have to	84	/		☐
PSS 4-10 should, had better	85	/		☐
Chapter Review Test	88	/		☐

51 다음 글의 밑줄 친 부분 중 쓰임이 어색한 것은?

Hi Lauren,
I'm wondering if you ① could do me a favor. I have a doctor's appointment on Monday ② at 1 P.M. So, I ③ will not be in the office. Could you please take care of my incoming calls until I ④ am back at the office? I ⑤ was happy to take you to lunch on Tuesday to show my appreciation. Thank you.

52 다음 중 어법상 어색한 문장은?

① I will call you tonight.
② When will she leave for New York?
③ Will you going to visit Paris this summer?
④ I am going to play tennis after work.
⑤ She is going to take a dance lesson on Tuesday.

53 다음 표는 친구들이 내일 할 일을 정리한 것입니다. 〈보기〉와 같이 빈칸을 완성하세요.

이름	할 일
Jaemin	listen to music
Mina and Suji	play the guitar
Jieun	make spaghetti

보 기 | Jaemin is going to listen to music.

(1) Mina and Suji _____.

(2) Jieun _____.

54 다음 괄호 속의 동사를 문맥에 맞게 고친 것은?

㉠ They (study) Chinese since last year.
㉡ Tony (visit) his parents last weekend.
㉢ She (teach) English in this school for the past 3 years.

	㉠	㉡	㉢
①	studied	visited	taught
②	studied	has visited	taught
③	have studied	visited	has taught
④	have studied	has visited	has taught
⑤	have studied	visited	is teaching

55 다음 대화의 빈칸에 들어갈 단어가 바르게 짝지어진 것은?

A: Where _____ Nami last winter vacation?
B: She _____ in Busan with her cousins.

① were – was
② was – were
③ were – were
④ was – was
⑤ are – am

56 대화의 빈칸에 들어갈 말로 적절한 것은?

A: _____
B: I am planning to visit my grandparents this Saturday.

① How will you visit your grandparents?
② Do you visit your grandparents every week?
③ What are you visiting your grandparents for?
④ Why did you plan to visit your grandparents?
⑤ What are you planning to do this Saturday?

44 다음 빈칸에 들어갈 알맞은 말은?

> A: You look tired, Susan.
> B: I didn't sleep well last night.
> A: What happened?
> B: _____

① I will stay up all night.
② A man is walking down the hall.
③ He looks tired.
④ I am going to go fishing.
⑤ My baby sister cried all night.

45 다음 문장에서 틀린 곳을 올바르게 고치지 않은 것은?

① Minsu sing very well. → Minsu sings very well.
② She have a lovely cat. → She has a lovely cat.
③ He need little help. → He needs little help.
④ John play the violin. → John plays the violin.
⑤ He fly to many countries. → He flys to many countries.

46 밑줄 친 단어를 알맞은 형태로 바꾸어 쓰세요.

> A: What time did you eat lunch yesterday?
> B: I eat lunch at 12:30.

➡ _____

47 다음 중 빈칸에 go를 쓸 수 없는 문장은?

① Minji will _____ to Busan.
② I sometimes _____ to Jane's house.
③ What time does he _____ to work?
④ Minho _____ hiking with his friends.
⑤ My parents _____ to bed early every night.

48 다음 글을 읽고 어법상 어색한 문장을 고르세요.

> ① Mike is going to busy next week. ② He is planning to wash his car on Monday. ③ He is going to borrow some books in the library on Wednesday. ④ He will play basketball with his friends on Friday. ⑤ He will go swimming on Saturday.

49 다음 문장의 내용을 잘못 파악한 것은?

> A. I have worked as a lawyer for 2 years.
> B. Sunny and her aunt have just had lunch.
> C. Kate and Mina have lived in Seoul since they were babies.
> D. Jiah has gone to Australia with her family.
> E. Junho has liked this animation since he was seven years old.

① A. I started to work as a lawyer 2 years ago and I am still a lawyer.
② B. Sunny and her aunt are eating lunch now.
③ C. Kate and Mina still live in Seoul now.
④ D. Jiah and her family live in Australia. They are not here now.
⑤ E. Junho liked this animation and he still likes it.

50 다음 중 어법상 옳은 문장은?

① We were playing soccer now.
② Sue and Mary are talking about him.
③ They learned an important lesson tomorrow.
④ He will finish his presentation a few minutes ago.
⑤ We're going to have a workshop last week.

PSS 4-4 May I ~?에 대한 승낙과 거절의 표현

승낙	거절
Yes, you may. 응, 그래도 돼. Yes, you can. 응, 그래도 돼. Sure. 그럼. Of course. 물론이지. Why not? 왜 안 되겠니? Okay. 알았어.	No, you may not. 아니, 안 돼. No, you must not. 아니, 절대 안 돼. Sorry, you can't. 미안하지만, 안 돼. I'm afraid not. 그럴 수는 없을 것 같아.

정답 p.13

PRACTICE 8

빈칸에 알맞은 단어를 넣어 대화를 완성하세요.

1 A: May I sit here?
   B: Yes, you _____.

2 A: May I have some coffee?
   B: Sure, why _____?

3 A: May I go out?
   B: I'm sorry, but _____ can't.

4 A: May I take your message?
   B: Of _____.

5 A: May I use your computer?
   B: I am afraid _____.

6 A: May I try this shirt on?
   B: _____.

7 A: May I come in?
   B: No, you _____ not.

8 A: May I have a sandwich for dinner?
   B: _____ not?

PSS 4-5 Will[Would] you ~?

요청

Will you ~?나 Would you ~?의 형태로 쓰이며, '~해줄래요?'라는 뜻을 가진다. Will you ~?보다는 Would you ~?가 보다 정중한 표현이다.

Will you please be quiet? 좀 조용히 해줄래요?
Would you please be quiet?
좀 조용히 해주시겠어요?
Will you close the window? 창문을 닫아 줄래요?
Would you close the window?
창문을 닫아 주시겠어요?

PRACTICE 9

정답 p.13

우리말과 같은 뜻이 되도록 괄호 안에 주어진 단어를 바르게 배열하세요.

1 여기서 머무를래요? (you, will, stay, here)
= _____

2 저 좀 도와주시겠습니까? (help, you, would, me)
= _____

3 라디오 좀 꺼 주시겠어요? (would, the radio, you, turn off)
= _____

4 저한테 편지 좀 보내줄래요? (you, send, will, a letter, me)
= _____

5 내일 아침 7시에 깨워줄래요? (will, at 7 a.m. tomorrow, you, wake me up)
= _____

6 당신의 전화번호를 말씀해주시겠습니까? (you, me, would, tell, your phone number)
= _____

7 당신의 신분증을 보여주시겠습니까? (you, would, me, show, your ID card)
= _____

PSS 4-6 would like (to)

would like+(대)명사	would like to+동사원형
would like는 '~을 원하다'라는 뜻으로 want와 같은 의미이다. **Would you like** some ice cream? 너는 아이스크림을 좀 원하니? = **Do you want** some ice cream?	would like to는 '~하고 싶다'라는 뜻으로 want to와 같은 의미이다. **I'd like to** go to sleep. 나는 자고 싶다. = I **want to** go to sleep.

정답 p.13

PRACTICE 10

빈칸에 would like 또는 would like to를 넣어 대화를 완성하세요.

1. A: I _____ two hamburgers and a small coke.
   B: OK. For here or to go?

2. A: _____ you _____ join our team?
   B: Yes, I'd love to.

3. A: Which color would you like to try on?
   B: I _____ try on the blue one.

4. A: What would you like to do tonight?
   B: I _____ watch TV tonight.

5. A: _____ you _____ some bread?
   B: No, thank you.

6. A: Where _____ you _____ go?
   B: I _____ visit the Louvre Museum.

정답 p.13

PRACTICE 11

우리말과 같은 뜻이 되도록 괄호 안에 주어진 말 중 알맞은 것을 고르세요.

1. 이것을 입어 봐도 될까요?
   = (Could, Would) I try this on?

2 Tom은 마지막 문제를 풀지 못했다.
= Tom (can, could) not solve the last problem.

3 너는 기타를 칠 수 있니?
= (Can, May) you play the guitar?

4 Sarah는 내일까지 그 일을 끝낼 것이다.
= Sarah (will, would) finish the work by tomorrow.

5 더러운 물은 우리를 병에 걸리게 할지도 모른다.
= Dirty water (would like to, may) make us sick.

6 주스 좀 더 드시겠어요?
= (Will, Would) you like more juice?

7 그것에 대해 말해 줄래요?
= (May, Will) you tell me about it?

8 회의 후에 내게 전화해주겠니?
= (Can, May) you call me after the meeting?

PSS 4-7 must I

의무	'~해야 한다'라는 뜻으로 의무를 나타낸다. You **must** get there by 10. 너는 10시까지 그곳에 도착해야 한다. I **must** wait for Becky. 나는 Becky를 기다려야 한다.
강한 추측	'~임에 틀림없다'라는 뜻으로 강한 추측을 나타낸다. That restaurant **must** be very good. 그 음식점은 아주 훌륭할 것임에 틀림없다. He **must** be at home. 그는 집에 있을 것임에 틀림없다.

PRACTICE 12

정답 p.14

밑줄 친 부분이 의무와 강한 추측 중 어떤 의미를 지니는지 구분하여 쓰세요.

1 Cars go very fast on this street. We <u>must</u> be careful. [   ]

2 She hasn't eaten anything all day. She <u>must</u> be hungry. [   ]

3 Soldiers <u>must</u> wear uniforms. They cannot wear casual clothes. [   ]

4 I have a meeting tomorrow. I <u>must</u> prepare my presentation. [   ]

5 Sorry. I <u>must</u> have the wrong number. [   ]

6 The baby is crying. She <u>must</u> be sleepy. [   ]

7 Don't say anything about it. You <u>must</u> keep it secret. [   ]

8 There is a fire. We must call the fire station. [   ]

9 Nari wears pink every day. She must like that color. [   ]

10 Minho looks young. He must be a student. [   ]

11 I can't go out. I must help Mom at home. [   ]

12 He stayed up all night. He must be tired. [   ]

PSS 4-8 must Ⅱ

의무	현재	must가 '~해야 한다'는 뜻의 의무를 나타낼 때는 have[has] to로 바꾸어 쓸 수 있다. We **must** go to Seoul now. 우리는 지금 서울에 가야 한다. = We **have to** go to Seoul now. She **must** go to Seoul now. 그녀는 지금 서울에 가야 한다. = She **has to** go to Seoul now.
	과거	must는 쓸 수 없고 had to로 쓴다. We **had to** go to Seoul yesterday. 우리는 어제 서울에 가야 했다.

cf. have to는 조동사가 아니므로 의문문에서 주어 앞으로 이동하지 않고, 「Do[Does/Did]+주어+have to ~?」의 어순으로 의문문을 만든다.
  Do we have to go to the party? 우리는 파티에 가야 하니?
  Does he have to get up early tomorrow? 그는 내일 일찍 일어나야 하니?
  Did she have to pay a fine? 그녀는 벌금을 내야 했니?

정답 p.14

PRACTICE 13

〈보기〉와 같이 짝지어진 두 문장의 의미가 같도록 빈칸을 채우세요.

보 기	They must get some sleep. = They <u>have to</u> get some sleep.

1 People must follow the law.
  = People _____ follow the law.

2 Jeff must pass his driving test.
  = Jeff _____ pass his driving test.

3 She must get up early.
  = She _____ get up early.

4 I must be in good shape.
  = I _____ be in good shape.

5 You must do your best.
  = You _____ do your best.

6 We must wait for the train.
  = We _____ wait for the train.

PRACTICE 14

빈칸에 have[has] to 또는 had to를 넣어 문장을 완성하세요.

1 It was late. We _____ take a taxi.
2 He is very hungry. He _____ eat some food.
3 It is very cold outside. You _____ wear a coat.
4 We missed the bus last night. We _____ walk home.
5 I _____ sleep now. I want to get up early tomorrow.
6 Bob's room isn't clean. He _____ clean it right now.
7 I broke my glasses. I _____ buy a new pair last week.
8 Tomorrow is Parents' Day. We _____ buy carnations now.
9 I met Ted. I _____ borrow the book from him yesterday.
10 She broke her arm. She _____ go to the hospital an hour ago.

PSS 4-9 must not, don't have to

must not	'~해서는 안 된다'라는 뜻으로 금지를 나타낸다. You **must not** park your car in front of the entrance. 당신은 그 입구 앞에 당신의 차를 주차해서는 안 된다. She **must not** go out now. 그녀는 지금 외출해서는 안 된다.
don't have to	'~할 필요가 없다'라는 뜻으로 불필요를 나타낸다. They **don't have to** hurry. 그들은 서두를 필요가 없다. Jinsu **doesn't have to** move to Suwon. 진수는 수원으로 이사할 필요가 없다.

PRACTICE 15

그림을 보고, must not 또는 don't[doesn't] have to를 넣어 문장을 완성하세요.

1

2

3

1 Sujin _____ get up early. She doesn't work today.

2 You _____ drink and drive.

3 Here's the elevator. You _____ climb the stairs.

4 Don't make a noise. We _____ wake the baby.

5 You _____ bring food in this room. It should be kept clean.

6 You _____ call Mr. Kim. I already called him.

PSS 4-10 should, had better

should	'~해야 한다'의 뜻으로 의무나 당연을 나타낸다. I **should** call her tonight. 나는 오늘 밤에 그녀에게 전화해야 한다. He **should not** sit here. 그는 여기에 앉지 말아야 한다.
had better	'~하는 게 낫다'의 뜻으로 강한 충고나 권유를 나타낸다. You **had better** go to the dentist. 너는 치과 의사에게 가는 게 낫다. We**'d better not** take a bus. 우리는 버스를 타지 않는 게 낫다.

PRACTICE 16

〈보기〉에서 알맞은 단어를 골라 should나 had better를 사용하여 문장을 완성하세요.

보 기	wear make walk go play stay put throw change steal

1. 너는 학급 친구들에게 좋은 인상을 주어야 한다.
   = You _____ a good impression on your classmates.

2. 나는 감기에 걸렸다. 나는 이 코트를 입는 게 낫겠다.
   = I got a cold. I _____ on this coat.

3. 너는 창문 밖으로 쓰레기를 던져서는 안 된다.
   = You _____ waste out of the window.

4. 네 눈을 보호하기 위해서 선글라스를 끼는 게 좋겠다.
   = You _____ sunglasses to protect your eyes.

5. 너는 컴퓨터 게임을 너무 많이 해서는 안 된다.
   = You _____ computer games too much.

6. 비가 많이 내리고 있다. 우리는 나가지 않는 게 좋겠다.
   = It's raining heavily. We _____ outside.

7. 너는 옷을 갈아입어야 한다.
   = You _____ your clothes.

8. 너는 역까지 걸어가지 않는 게 좋겠다. 그곳은 여기에서 매우 멀다.
   = You _____ to the station. It's very far from here.

9. 너는 다른 사람의 아이디어를 훔쳐서는 안 된다.
   = You _____ others' ideas.

10. 그녀는 햇볕 속에 너무 오래 나가있지 않는 게 좋겠다.
    = She _____ out in the sun for too long.

PRACTICE 17

우리말과 같은 뜻이 되도록 괄호 안에 주어진 말 중 알맞은 것을 고르세요.

1. 그가 또다시 거짓말을 하고 있음에 틀림없다.
   = He (must, can) be telling a lie again.

2. 너는 그것에 대해 걱정할 필요가 없다.
   = You (don't have to, must not) worry about that.

3 나무가 없다면, 우리는 깨끗한 공기를 얻을 수 없다.
= Without trees, we (should not, cannot) get clean air.

4 소금 좀 건네주시겠어요?
= (Would, Should) you pass me the salt?

5 지난밤 나는 보름달을 볼 수 있었다.
= Last night I (should, could) see the full moon.

6 그녀는 거실에 있을지도 모른다.
= She (may, must) be in the living room.

7 비가 올지도 모른다. 우산을 챙기는 게 좋겠다.
= It (may, had better) rain. You (can, had better) take an umbrella.

8 나는 매일 나의 강아지를 산책시켜야 한다.
= I (have to, will) walk my dog every day.

9 뭐 마실 것 좀 드릴까요?
= (Will, Would) you like something to drink?

10 영화 보는 동안 시끄럽게 해서는 안 된다.
= You (don't have to, should not) make a noise during the movie.

11 오늘 밤에 여기서 묵어도 될까요?
= (Can, Will) I stay here tonight?

12 우리는 건강을 위해 운동을 시작해야 한다.
= We (should, had to) start exercising for our health.

13 너는 곧장 가서는 안 된다.
= You (don't have to, must not) go straight.

14 나는 너무 늦게까지 깨어 있지 않는 게 낫겠다.
= I (must, had better) not stay up too late.

15 상자를 열어주시겠어요?
= (Could, May) you open the box?

16 너는 노는 데 많은 시간을 보내서는 안 된다.
= You (don't have to, should not) spend a lot of time playing.

17 그들은 신발을 벗어야 했다.
= They (must, had to) take off their shoes.

18 그는 설거지를 하지 않을 것이다.
= He (will, must) not wash the dishes.

Chapter Review Test

CHAPTER 3 조동사

정답 p.14

1 빈칸에 들어갈 동사의 알맞은 형태는?

He may _____ interested in music.

① be ② is ③ been
④ were ⑤ was

2 다음 밑줄 친 부분과 바꾸어 쓸 수 있는 말을 고르세요.

You <u>must</u> take care of your little sister.

① have to ② has to ③ can
④ are going to ⑤ had better

3 다음 밑줄 친 표현과 바꿔 쓸 수 있는 말을 세 단어로 쓰세요.

- 그녀는 인터넷에서 무엇이든 살 수 있습니다.
 = She <u>can</u> buy anything on the Internet.

= She _____ _____ _____ buy anything on the Internet.

4 다음 밑줄 친 부분이 어떤 조동사와 함께 축약된 것인지를 고르세요.

<u>I'd</u> like to buy a nice car.

① I did ② I had ③ I would
④ I should ⑤ I could

5 다음 질문에 대한 대답으로 알맞은 것은?

A: Can John run fast?
B: _____

① Yes, he can't. ② Yes, he cans.
③ Sure, he can't. ④ No, John can.
⑤ No, he can't.

6 다음 우리말과 같은 뜻이 되도록 빈칸에 알맞은 말을 쓰세요.

- 우리는 다음 달의 계획을 세우는 게 좋겠다.
 = We _____ _____ make plans for next month.

7 다음 문장에서 어법상 틀린 부분을 찾아 바르게 고쳐 쓰세요.

(1) You will are a good teacher.
_____ ➡ _____

(2) Can I borrowing your umbrella?
_____ ➡ _____

8 빈칸에 들어갈 말로 알맞은 것을 고르세요.

We can get anything with money. But we _____ get health with it.

① do ② should ③ shouldn't
④ can ⑤ can't

9 다음 빈칸에 들어갈 말로 알맞은 것을 고르세요.

A: May I park my car here?
B: _____ There's a sign that says, 'No parking.'

① Yes, you may.   ② Yes, you should.
③ No, you could not.   ④ No, you must not.
⑤ No, you don't have to.

10 우리말과 같은 뜻이 되도록 주어진 단어들을 바르게 배열하세요.

• 제가 지금 집에 가야만 하나요?
= _____
(have, I, home, do, go, to, now)

11 다음 두 문장이 같은 뜻이 되도록 빈칸에 들어갈 알맞은 말을 쓰세요.

• Humans can change the world.
= Humans _____ _____ _____ change the world.

12 다음 빈칸에 들어갈 가장 적절한 말을 고르세요.

A: Look out the window. People are holding their umbrellas.
B: It _____ be raining outside now.

① will   ② had to   ③ had better
④ must   ⑤ should

13 다음 우리말과 같은 의미가 되도록 조건에 맞게 영작하세요.

그는 내일 그의 친구들을 만날 것인가?
조건1 – meet 동사를 포함시킬 것.
조건2 – 6단어로 쓸 것.
조건3 – 문장 부호를 반드시 삽입할 것.

➡ _____

14 도서관 이용 수칙에 대한 안내문을 다음과 같이 작성하려고 할 때, 빈칸에 들어갈 말로 어색한 것은?

You _____ in the library.

① must not run
② have to be quiet
③ must set your phone to vibration mode
④ don't have to study hard
⑤ should not talk loudly

15 다음 그림 표지판과 같은 뜻이 되도록 빈칸을 채울 때 알맞지 않은 것은?

You _____ take a picture here.

① cannot   ② must not
③ don't have to   ④ should not
⑤ may not

16 조동사 will과 괄호 안의 단어를 사용하여 아래 두 문장을 우리말에 맞게 쓰세요. (단, 필요시 단어를 변형 및 추가하세요.)

(1) 그녀는 대중가요를 듣지 않을 것이다.
(pop songs, to, she, listen)
➡ _____

(2) 도서관에서 조용히 해 주실래요?
(the, quiet, library, are, in, you)
➡ _____

17 다음 두 문장의 뜻이 같도록 빈칸에 들어갈 알맞은 단어를 고르세요.

- I would like to know about your country.
  = I _____ to know about your country.

① have   ② plan   ③ want
④ think   ⑤ begin

18 다음 밑줄 친 부분의 쓰임이 어색한 것은?

① It may not rain this afternoon.
② Can you bring me an umbrella?
③ He won't arrive here in time.
④ You should make a noise in the library.
⑤ You must turn off your cell phone in the theater.

19 다음 글의 빈칸에 들어갈 말로 알맞은 것은?

If you fall asleep with the window open, you _____ catch a cold.

① may   ② must not   ③ had better
④ cannot   ⑤ have to

20 다음 중 밑줄 친 can의 쓰임이 같은 것끼리 묶인 것은?

ⓐ Can I borrow your book?
ⓑ He can understand Spanish well.
ⓒ Can you play the guitar?
ⓓ Can I help you?
ⓔ Come on. You can do it.

① (ⓐ),(ⓑⓒⓓⓔ)   ② (ⓐⓑ),(ⓒⓓⓔ)
③ (ⓐⓓ),(ⓑⓒⓔ)   ④ (ⓐⓒⓓ),(ⓑⓔ)
⑤ (ⓐⓑⓒⓔ),(ⓓ)

21 다음 질문에 대한 대답으로 알맞은 것은?

A: Can I have some hamburgers?
B: _____

① Sure, here you are.
② I don't like hamburgers.
③ I like spaghetti very much.
④ No, thanks. I'm full.
⑤ Wow! It's delicious.

22 다음 대화의 빈칸에 들어갈 단어로 알맞게 짝지어진 것은?

A: Mom, _____ I play baseball with my friends?
B: No! You _____ finish your homework first.

① can – can   ② should – will
③ may – must   ④ may – can
⑤ must – will

23 다음 중 문장의 전환이 옳지 않은 것은?

① She can make delicious *bulgogi*. (의문문)
→ Can she make delicious *bulgogi*?
② The story may be true. (부정문)
→ The story may not be true.
③ Robert has to wear glasses. (의문문)
→ Has Robert to wear glasses?
④ We should recycle cans and bottles. (의문문)
→ Should we recycle cans and bottles?
⑤ He will move to Incheon. (부정문)
→ He won't move to Incheon.

24 다음 질문에 대한 대답으로 알맞지 않은 것은?

> A: Can you join our club?
> B: _____

① I'm afraid not.   ② I'm sorry, I can't.
③ Sure.   ④ Yes, you can.
⑤ Of course.

25 다음 중 어법상 어색한 문장은?

① They will not stay at home.
② He is going to go to the museum next Sunday.
③ She had better to go home now.
④ Can he play soccer?
⑤ David can swim well.

26 주어진 문장을 must를 이용하여 금지를 나타내는 말로 바꾸어 쓰세요.

> • You have to carry a balloon here.
> → _____

27 밑줄 친 may의 쓰임이 다른 하나는?

① It may be fine tomorrow.
② She may win the contest.
③ It may be difficult for you.
④ May I take your order?
⑤ She may come, or she may not.

28 우리말과 같은 뜻이 되도록 괄호 안에 주어진 단어를 활용하여 5단어로 영작하세요.

> • 너는 바이올린을 연주할 수 있니?
> = _____
> (the violin, play)

29 다음 두 문장의 뜻이 같도록 빈칸에 알맞은 말을 쓰세요.

> • Do you want to go for a walk?
> = Would you _____ _____ go for a walk?

30 다음 빈칸에 공통으로 들어갈 알맞은 말은?

> • You _____ wear a swimming cap.
> • You _____ be kind to other people.

① are   ② would like   ③ were
④ weren't   ⑤ should

31 다음 대화의 빈칸에 들어갈 표현으로 어색한 것을 고르세요.

> A: May I go to the movies tonight?
> B: _____

① Yes, you may.   ② Yes, you can.
③ Yes, I would.   ④ No, you can't.
⑤ No, you should not.

32 다음 대화의 빈칸에 들어갈 알맞은 말은?

> A: I'm going to the post office. Will you come with me?
> B: _____ I have to do my homework.

① I'm sorry, I can't.   ② Sure.
③ Of course.   ④ Yes, I will.
⑤ Why not?

33 다음 주어진 문장들 중 어법상 옳은 것의 개수는?

> • Birds can fly with their wings.
> • This work may easy for you.
> • You have not to bring your library card.
> • You shouldn't talk or eat loudly here.
> • He musts practice English every day.

① 1개   ② 2개   ③ 3개
④ 4개   ⑤ 5개

34 다음 중 밑줄 친 부분의 쓰임이 어색한 것을 고르세요.

① You cannot sit here.
② Study hard, or you willn't succeed in life.
③ Junsu doesn't like his name.
④ You don't have to go to the bank.
⑤ He couldn't find the book.

35 밑줄 친 부분이 어법상 잘못된 것은?

① He had to help his mother.
② Mr. Brown have to stay home today.
③ My parents had to visit my grandparents.
④ I have to see a doctor.
⑤ We have to throw trash in a trash can.

36 우리말과 같은 뜻이 되도록 할 때 빈칸에 들어갈 알맞은 말은?

> • 상호는 그곳에서 수영을 하고 놀 수 있었다.
> = Sangho _____ swim and play there.

① could   ② can   ③ couldn't
④ cannot   ⑤ should

37 다음 빈칸에 공통으로 들어갈 알맞은 단어는?

> • _____ I help you?
> – Yes. I'm looking for a shirt.
> • _____ I speak to Alex?
> – This is Alex speaking. Who's calling, please?

① Would   ② Should   ③ Must
④ Do   ⑤ May

38 다음 대화의 빈칸에 들어갈 알맞은 것은?

A: It's very cold here, isn't it?
B: Yes, it is.
A: _____
B: No problem.

① Will you close the door?
② Why are you closing the door?
③ Must you close the door?
④ May you close the door?
⑤ Do I have to close the door?

39 빈칸에 들어갈 말들이 바르게 짝지어진 것은?

Bob: Will you _____ to the movies tonight?
Sarah: Sounds good.
Bob: What time shall we _____?
Sarah: How about six?
Bob: OK. Let's meet at six.

① to go – meet   ② going – meeting
③ go   – meet   ④ go   – meeting
⑤ to go – to meet

40 다음 빈칸에 공통으로 들어갈 알맞은 말은?

• I _____ go home now.
• You _____ get there before dark.
• She _____ buy a new book.

① must   ② have to   ③ has to
④ need   ⑤ do

41 다음 밑줄 친 우리말을 영어로 바르게 옮긴 것은?

A: Why didn't you come to my house?
B: <u>나는 내 방을 청소해야 했어.</u>

① I must clean up my room.
② I did must clean up my room.
③ I have to clean up my room.
④ I had to clean up my room.
⑤ I had had to clean up my room.

42 다음 대화를 읽고 빈칸에 들어갈 알맞은 말을 고르세요.

A: You look sick. What's the matter?
B: I have a toothache.
A: That's too bad. I think you _____ see a dentist.

① will   ② have   ③ has to
④ should   ⑤ able to

43 괄호 안의 단어를 알맞게 배열하여 문장을 완성하세요.

Mom: _____ (better, go, bed, you, to, had) early tonight. You don't want to be late for school, do you?
Mary: I know. Would you wake me up at 6?

44 다음 단어들로 문장을 만들 때 다섯 번째로 올 단어는?

for, to, would, lunch, what, you, like, eat ?

① for　　　② to　　　③ like
④ eat　　　⑤ lunch

45 다음 중 밑줄 친 may의 쓰임이 다른 하나는?

① She may be angry about your lie.
② You may not lie to your friends.
③ He may be sick. He doesn't look well.
④ It snows a lot. She may be late.
⑤ People may see squirrels here.

46 다음과 같이 말하는 아이에게 해줄 수 있는 충고로 적절하지 않은 것을 고르세요.

I want to be healthy. What should I do?

① You should exercise every day.
② You should not eat junk food.
③ You should skip meals.
④ You shouldn't go to bed late.
⑤ You should eat a lot of vegetables.

47 다음 중 표현이 바른 문장은?

① You have better see a doctor.
② She can a nice teacher.
③ I'd like to drinking some ice tea.
④ You may change the rules.
⑤ You must not be talk on the phone here.

48 다음 빈칸에 들어갈 말이 알맞게 짝지어진 것은?

A: May I take a picture here? This painting is very beautiful.
B: No, you ＿＿＿＿＿. You ＿＿＿＿＿ take a picture in this museum.

① may　　　－ can
② must not － must
③ must　　 － may not
④ can　　　－ may not
⑤ may not － cannot

49 짝지어진 두 문장의 의미가 같지 않은 것은?

① May I speak to Minhee?
　= Can I speak to Minhee?
② You must not make noise here.
　= You don't have to make noise here.
③ You must come home early tomorrow.
　= You have to come home early tomorrow.
④ Can you wash the dishes for me?
　= Could you wash the dishes for me?
⑤ He is able to read and write in French.
　= He can read and write in French.

CHAPTER 4
수동태

성취도 자기 평가 활용법

구분	평가 기준
Excellent	문법 내용을 모두 이해하고, 문제를 모두 맞힘.
Very good	문법 내용은 충분히 이해했으나 실수로 1~2문제 틀림.
Good	문법 내용이 조금 어려워 3~4문제 틀림.
needs **R**eview	문법 내용 이해가 어렵고, 5문제 이상 틀림, 복습 필요.

태(voice)는 주어와 동사의 관계를 나타낸다.

① 능동태(active voice)는 주어가 동사의 동작을 하는 경우에 쓴다.

She opened the door. 그녀는 문을 열었다.
주어 — 동사
└ 능동관계 ┘

② 수동태(passive voice)는 주어가 동사의 동작을 받을 때 쓴다.

The door was opened by her. 문은 그녀에 의해 열어졌다.
주어 — 동사
└ 수동관계 ┘

Problem Solving Skill	페이지	학습날짜	성취도 자기평가 E V G R	학습체크
PSS 1 격 변화 - 주격과 목적격	96	/		☐
PSS 2 수동태에 많이 쓰이는 불규칙동사	97	/		☐
PSS 3 수동태 문장 만드는 법	99	/		☐
PSS 4 현재시제와 과거시제의 수동태	100	/		☐
PSS 5 「by+목적격」의 생략	101	/		☐
PSS 6 5형식 문장의 수동태 전환	102	/		☐
Chapter Review Test	104	/		☐

격 변화 – 주격과 목적격

주격(~은, 는)	I	you	he	she	it	we	they
목적격(~을, 를)	me	you	him	her	it	us	them

인칭대명사만이 격 변화가 있고, 명사(Tom/this book/my parents)는 주격과 목적격의 형태가 같다.

I love you. You love **me**. 나는 너를 사랑한다. 너는 나를 사랑한다.
Tom loves you. You love **Tom**. Tom은 너를 사랑한다. 너는 Tom을 사랑한다.

정답 p.16

PRACTICE 1

주어진 단어를 알맞은 형태로 바꾸어 빈칸에 쓰세요.

1 he
   ① My dog likes _____.
   ② _____ likes my dog.

2 they
   ① _____ visited their aunt.
   ② Their aunt visited _____.

3 Sumi
   ① They invited _____.
   ② _____ invited them.

4 it
   ① _____ changed him.
   ② He changed _____.

5 we
   ① _____ called her.
   ② She called _____.

6 my family
   ① Mr. Kim knows _____.
   ② _____ knows Mr. Kim.

7 I
   ① _____ met her.
   ② She met _____.

8 you
   ① _____ can understand them.
   ② They can understand _____.

9 the bird
   ① _____ is looking at me.
   ② I'm looking at _____.

10 she
    ① I told _____ about it.
    ② _____ told me about it.

11 your brother
    ① _____ taught me.
    ② I taught _____.

12 their parents
    ① _____ help them.
    ② They help _____.

수동태에 많이 쓰이는 불규칙동사

원형	과거형	과거분사형	원형	과거형	과거분사형
be	was/were	been	lose	lost	lost
bear	bore	borne/born	make	made	made
bite	bit	bitten	read	read	read
blow	blew	blown	ride	rode	ridden
break	broke	broken	say	said	said
bring	brought	brought	see	saw	seen
build	built	built	set	set	set
buy	bought	bought	sell	sold	sold
catch	caught	caught	send	sent	sent
do	did	done	sing	sang	sung
draw	drew	drawn	speak	spoke	spoken
drink	drank	drunk	spend	spent	spent
eat	ate	eaten	steal	stole	stolen
find	found	found	take	took	taken
fly	flew	flown	teach	taught	taught
forget	forgot	forgotten	tell	told	told
get	got	got(ten)	think	thought	thought
give	gave	given	throw	threw	thrown
hold	held	held	understand	understood	understood
keep	kept	kept	wake	woke	woken
know	knew	known	wear	wore	worn
lay	laid	laid	write	wrote	written

정답 p.16

PRACTICE 2

다음 동사의 과거형과 과거분사형을 쓰세요.

1 throw – _____ – _____

2 cook – _____ – _____

3 make – _____ – _____

4 bring – _____ – _____

#	Verb				#	Verb			
5	begin	–	___	– ___	6	call	–	___	– ___
7	invent	–	___	– ___	8	hold	–	___	– ___
9	wear	–	___	– ___	10	blow	–	___	– ___
11	read	–	___	– ___	12	build	–	___	– ___
13	fly	–	___	– ___	14	kill	–	___	– ___
15	lose	–	___	– ___	16	wake	–	___	– ___
17	take	–	___	– ___	18	clean	–	___	– ___
19	bear	–	___	– ___	20	say	–	___	– ___
21	answer	–	___	– ___	22	find	–	___	– ___
23	catch	–	___	– ___	24	know	–	___	– ___
25	invite	–	___	– ___	26	steal	–	___	– ___
27	think	–	___	– ___	28	write	–	___	– ___
29	ride	–	___	– ___	30	open	–	___	– ___
31	spend	–	___	– ___	32	be	–	___	– ___
33	buy	–	___	– ___	34	stop	–	___	– ___
35	use	–	___	– ___	36	speak	–	___	– ___
37	bite	–	___	– ___	38	put	–	___	– ___
39	get	–	___	– ___	40	do	–	___	– ___
41	collect	–	___	– ___	42	lay	–	___	– ___
43	understand	–	___	– ___	44	drink	–	___	– ___
45	break	–	___	– ___	46	keep	–	___	– ___
47	sell	–	___	– ___	48	forget	–	___	– ___
49	carry	–	___	– ___	50	eat	–	___	– ___
51	send	–	___	– ___	52	see	–	___	– ___
53	sing	–	___	– ___	54	set	–	___	– ___
55	try	–	___	– ___	56	draw	–	___	– ___
57	give	–	___	– ___	58	tell	–	___	– ___
59	drop	–	___	– ___	60	teach	–	___	– ___

수동태 문장 만드는 법

주어가 동작을 행하는 형식의 문장을 능동태, 주어가 동작의 대상이 되는 형식의 문장을 수동태라고 한다. 능동태 문장은 '~가 …을 하다'로, 수동태 문장은 '~가 …되어지다'로 해석한다.

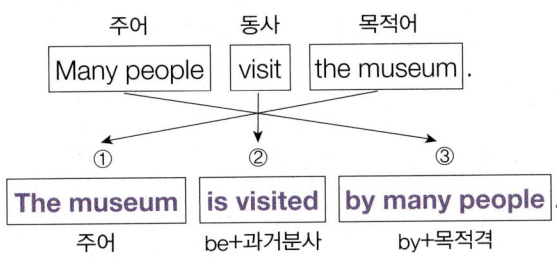

① 능동태의 목적어를 수동태의 주어로 한다.
   the museum ➡ The museum
② 능동태의 동사를 「be동사+과거분사」의 형태로 바꾼다.
   이때, be동사는 바뀐 주어의 인칭과 수, 원래 능동태 문장의 동사의 시제에 일치시킨다.
   visit ➡ is visited
③ 능동태의 주어를 「by+목적격」의 형태로 바꾼다.
   Many people ➡ by many people

My parents love me. 나의 부모님은 나를 사랑하신다.
➡ I **am loved by** my parents. 나는 나의 부모님에 의해 사랑 받는다.
Ann always locks the doors. Ann은 항상 문을 잠근다.
➡ The doors **are** always **locked by** Ann. 문은 항상 Ann에 의해 잠긴다.

PRACTICE 3

다음 문장의 밑줄 친 부분을 주어로 하는 수동태 문장으로 바꾸어 써 보세요.

1 David writes a letter.
   ➡ _____

2 I send an e-mail.
   ➡ _____

3 Chickens lay eggs.
   ➡ _____

4 I collect foreign coins.
➡ _____

5 My mother cooks the steaks.
➡ _____

6 Their father teaches them.
➡ _____

7 My brother reads the book.
➡ _____

8 Most people use this expression.
➡ _____

9 The principal calls them.
➡ _____

10 She makes these bags.
➡ _____

11 She paints those pictures.
➡ _____

12 The teacher answers the questions.
➡ _____

13 Jacob picks up the trash in the river.
➡ _____

현재시제와 과거시제의 수동태

현재시제의 수동태는 「am/is/are+과거분사」의 형태로, 과거시제의 수동태는 「was/were+과거분사」의 형태로 쓴다.

I **clean** my room. ➡ My room **is cleaned** by me.
나는 내 방을 청소한다.   내 방은 나에 의해 청소된다.

I **cleaned** my room. ➡ My room **was cleaned** by me.
나는 내 방을 청소했다.   내 방은 나에 의해 청소되었다.

PRACTICE 4

다음 문장을 수동태로 바꿀 때, 빈칸에 알맞은 말을 쓰세요.

1. She opened the boxes. ➡ The boxes _____ by her.
2. Ms. Song plays the piano. ➡ The piano _____ by Ms. Song.
3. Giho broke my glasses. ➡ My glasses _____ by Giho.
4. Mina uses the computer. ➡ The computer _____ by Mina.
5. My mother washes the dishes. ➡ The dishes _____ by my mother.
6. The dog bit my sister. ➡ My sister _____ by the dog.
7. The students sing this song. ➡ This song _____ by the students.
8. Bell invented the telephone. ➡ The telephone _____ by Bell.
9. My grandfather grows potatoes. ➡ Potatoes _____ by my grandfather.
10. The president delivered the speech. ➡ The speech _____ by the president.

「by + 목적격」의 생략

능동태의 주어가 people 또는 you, we, they로 일반 사람을 나타낼 경우 「by+목적격」을 대체로 생략한다. 또 행위자가 분명하지 않거나 나타낼 필요가 없을 때에도 생략할 수 있다.

People speak English all over the world. 사람들은 전 세계적으로 영어를 쓴다.
➡ English **is spoken** all over the world. 영어는 전 세계적으로 쓰인다.
Someone broke the vase. 누군가가 꽃병을 깨뜨렸다.
➡ The vase **was broken** (**by someone**). 꽃병이 (누군가에 의해) 깨졌다.

PRACTICE 5

다음 능동태 문장을 수동태 문장으로 바꾸어 쓰세요.

1. We write a lot of letters.
   ➡ _____

2. People buy groceries here.
   ➡ _____

3 You wear shorts in summer.
➡ _____

4 They killed my son during the war.
➡ _____

5 We use smartphones every day.
➡ _____

6 Someone stole my bicycle.
➡ _____

7 People forgot the memories.
➡ _____

8 Someone made this wine in 1970.
➡ _____

9 We sell fresh fruit in the store.
➡ _____

10 They built these buildings 20 years ago.
➡ _____

PSS 6 — 5형식 문장의 수동태 전환

The movie makes them sad. 그 영화는 그들을 슬프게 만든다.
➡ They **are made sad** by the movie. 그들은 그 영화에 의해 슬퍼진다.

A refrigerator keeps food fresh. 냉장고는 음식을 신선하게 유지시킨다.
➡ Food **is kept fresh** by a refrigerator. 음식은 냉장고에 의해 신선하게 유지된다.

PRACTICE 6

다음 능동태 문장을 수동태 문장으로 바꾸어 쓰세요.

1 Some readers find the story interesting.
➡ _____

2 We elected him president.
➡ _____

3 People call a lion the king of the jungle.
➡ _____

4 Good paintings make people happy.
➡ _____

5 Mira found the rabbit dead.
➡ _____

6 My parents called me a princess.
➡ _____

PRACTICE 7

다음 능동태 문장을 수동태 문장으로 바꾸어 쓰세요.

1 Her children respect her.
➡ _____

2 He made his sister angry.
➡ _____

3 The teacher helped us.
➡ _____

4 They keep their village clean.
➡ _____

5 Andre Kim designed those dresses.
➡ _____

6 Ms. Smith finished this work.
➡ _____

7 We speak many languages in Switzerland.
➡ _____

8 A lot of teenagers watch TV programs.
➡ _____

9 We call Mozart and Beethoven great musicians.
➡ _____

10 The company published the magazine in 1997.
➡ _____

Chapter Review Test

정답 p.18

CHAPTER 4
수동태

1 다음 우리말과 같은 뜻이 되도록 빈칸에 들어갈 알맞은 말을 고르세요.

- 꿀은 일벌에 의해 만들어진다.
  = Honey _____ by worker bees.

① makes   ② made
③ is made   ④ are made
⑤ is making

2 두 문장이 같은 뜻이 되도록 빈칸에 들어갈 알맞은 단어를 쓰세요.

- They often invite us for dinner.
  = _____ are often _____ for dinner by them.

3 다음 문장에서 생략해도 되는 부분을 찾아 쓰세요.

English is spoken by people all over the world.

➡ _____

4 다음 밑줄 친 단어를 알맞은 형태로 바꾼 것을 고르세요.

The World Cup is <u>hold</u> every four years.

① hold   ② held
③ holding   ④ holds
⑤ holded

5 다음 두 문장이 같은 뜻이 되도록 빈칸에 들어갈 알맞은 말을 고르세요.

- Peter broke the window.
  = The window _____ by Peter.

① breaks   ② broke   ③ broken
④ is broken   ⑤ was broken

6 다음 문장에서 밑줄 친 단어를 바르게 고친 것을 고르세요.

A long time ago, *gimchi* was <u>calling</u> 'Dimchae'.

① called   ② calls   ③ be called
④ is calling   ⑤ call

7 두 사람의 대화를 보고 (A), (B)에 들어갈 문장을 바르게 쓴 것은?

G: 진수야, 뭐하고 있니?
B: 영어 문제집을 풀고 있는 중인데, 이 문제의 답을 모르겠어.
G: 'This table is made of wood.'의 부정문은 ___(A)___ 이고, 의문문은 ___(B)___ 야.

① (A) This table is not made of wood.
   (B) Is this table make of wood?
② (A) This table is not make of wood.
   (B) Does this table made of wood?
③ (A) This table is not made of wood.
   (B) Is this table made of wood?
④ (A) This table is not made of wood.
   (B) Does this table made of wood?
⑤ (A) This table is not make of wood.
   (B) Is this table made of wood?

8 다음 주어진 문장의 밑줄 친 부분을 바르게 고쳐 쓰세요.

> *Romeo and Juliet* <u>wrote</u> by Shakespeare.

➡ _____

9 다음 두 문장이 같은 뜻이 되도록 빈칸에 알맞은 말을 쓰세요.

> • The music makes me happy.
> = I _____ _____
>   _____ by the music.

10 다음 중 어법상 바르지 <u>않은</u> 문장은?

① Vegetables are sold in markets.
② Those potatoes are grown by my mom.
③ My bicycle was fix by Tom.
④ These were drawn by Picasso.
⑤ The school was founded in 1976.

11 다음 두 문장이 같은 뜻이 되도록 빈칸에 들어갈 알맞은 말을 쓰세요.

> • She washed my dog.
> = My dog _____ _____
>   _____ _____.

12 다음을 수동태 문장으로 바르게 바꾼 것은?

> The Wright brothers invented the airplane.

① The airplane invented the Wright brothers.
② The airplane was invented the Wright brothers.
③ The airplane is invented by the Wright brothers.
④ The airplane was invented by the Wright brothers.
⑤ The airplane were invented by the Wright brothers.

13 〈보기〉의 단어를 사용하여 주어진 우리말을 영작하세요. (단, 필요시 어법에 맞게 형태를 바꾸어야 함)

(1)

| 보 기 | teach, Mr. Kim, be, English, by |

영어는 김 선생님에 의해 가르쳐진다.
➡ _____

(2)

| 보 기 | be, her handbag, by, steal, the thief |

그녀의 핸드백은 도둑에 의해 도난당했다.
➡ _____

14 다음을 수동태 문장으로 바르게 바꾼 것은?

> People call her Big Mouth.

① Big Mouth is called by her.
② Big Mouth was called by her.
③ People are called by Big Mouth.
④ She is called Big Mouth.
⑤ She was called Big Mouth.

15 우리말 뜻에 맞게 영작한 문장으로 어법상 옳지 않은 것은?

① 이 옷은 유명한 디자이너에 의해 디자인되었다.
  This cloth was designed by a famous designer.
② 김 선생님께서 우리에게 강의해주시고 있다.
  Mr. Kim is giving us a lecture.
③ 나는 밤에 밖에 나가는 것이 허락되지 않는다.
  I am not allowed to go out at night.
④ 그들은 우리에게 음식을 주었고 우리는 그들에게 감사했다.
  They gave us food and we were grateful to them.
⑤ 거울은 조심스럽게 다루어져야 한다.
  Mirrors should handle carefully.

16 우리말과 같은 뜻이 되도록 주어진 단어를 바르게 배열하세요. (단, 필요시 어형을 바꿀 것)

- 그 집은 나의 할아버지에 의해 지어졌다.
  = _____
  (my, the, be, build, grandfather, house, by)

17 다음 두 문장이 같은 뜻이 되도록 빈칸에 들어갈 알맞은 말을 쓰세요.

- Many people visit the museum.
  = The museum _____ _____ by many people.

18 다음 대화의 빈칸에 들어갈 알맞은 말은?

A: This is a very good picture.
B: I think so, too. It _____ in Paris.

① takes ② is taken ③ was taken
④ took   ⑤ taken

19 다음 문장에서 어색한 부분을 찾아 그 번호를 쓰고, 바르게 고치세요.

①My bicycle ②is ③stolen ④a week ago by ⑤somebody.

→ _____

20 다음 중 어법상 바르지 않은 문장은?

① The office is cleaned once a week.
② Rice is grown in Asia.
③ He was bite by my dog.
④ English is spoken all over the world.
⑤ The letter was sent by her.

21 다음 중 어법상 옳은 문장의 개수를 고르세요.

- These flowers were planted by my father.
- Some cookies were maden by her.
- The baby was left alone.
- The cartoons were drawing by us.
- French is not spoken in this country.

① 1   ② 2
③ 3   ④ 4
⑤ 5

22 주어진 두 문장의 내용이 같도록 빈칸에 적절한 표현을 쓰세요.

(1) Jake bought the wallet.
  = The wallet _____.

(2) The desk was broken by my brother.
  = My brother _____.

CHAPTER 5
명사와 관사

성취도 자기 평가 활용법

구분	평가 기준
Excellent	문법 내용을 모두 이해하고, 문제를 모두 맞힘.
Very good	문법 내용은 충분히 이해했으나 실수로 1~2문제 틀림.
Good	문법 내용이 조금 어려워 3~4문제 틀림.
needs **R**eview	문법 내용 이해가 어렵고, 5문제 이상 틀림, 복습 필요.

Problem Solving Skill	페이지	학습날짜	성취도 자기평가 E V G R	학습체크
PSS 1 명사의 종류	108	/		☐
PSS 2 명사의 복수형	페이지	학습날짜	성취도 자기평가 E V G R	학습체크
PSS 2-1 명사의 규칙 복수형 I	109	/		☐
PSS 2-2 명사의 규칙 복수형 II	110	/		☐
PSS 2-3 명사의 불규칙 복수형	112	/		☐
PSS 3 단위명사의 쓰임	113	/		☐
PSS 4 명사의 소유격	115	/		☐
PSS 5 주의해야 할 명사의 수	118	/		☐
PSS 6 부정관사 a(n)의 쓰임	119	/		☐
PSS 7 a(n)의 의미 구별	120	/		☐
PSS 8 정관사 the의 쓰임	121	/		☐
PSS 9 관사를 쓰지 않는 경우	123	/		☐
PSS 10 There is/are	124	/		☐
PSS 11 동격	127	/		☐
Chapter Review Test	128	/		☐

명사의 종류

셀 수 있는 명사	a(n)을 붙이거나 복수형으로 쓸 수 있다. 1. 보통명사 – 사람이나 사물을 나타낸다. 　car, banana, father, egg, flower, girl, city, job, sister, house, bird 2. 집합명사 – 사람이나 사물이 모여 집합체를 나타낸다. 　class, family, audience, band, team, club
셀 수 없는 명사	a(n)을 붙일 수 없고 복수형으로도 쓸 수 없다. 1. 고유명사 – 사람의 이름, 지명과 같이 고유한 이름을 말하며 첫 글자를 항상 대문자로 표기한다. 　Mike, Microsoft, Mt. Everest, the Nile, America 2. 추상명사 – 형태 없이 단순히 개념이나 감정을 나타낸다. 　hope, life, kindness, beauty, truth, freedom, love, peace, advice 3. 물질명사 – 물이나 공기처럼 일정한 형태가 없는 것을 말한다. 　paper, sugar, gas, snow, hair, water, bread, butter, rice, flour, air

PRACTICE 1

다음 중 단어의 성격이 나머지 넷과 다른 것을 고르세요.

1	① eye	② newspaper	③ coffee	④ coin	⑤ book
2	① subway	② Becky	③ village	④ tree	⑤ kite
3	① group	② audience	③ band	④ team	⑤ dictionary
4	① England	② Busan	③ Niagara Falls	④ club	⑤ China
5	① wealth	② dish	③ kindness	④ pity	⑤ science
6	① class	② rain	③ meat	④ fire	⑤ iron
7	① pleasure	② luck	③ health	④ life	⑤ family
8	① paper	② Mt. Halla	③ cheese	④ money	⑤ hair
9	① animal	② lesson	③ smoke	④ girl	⑤ job
10	① information	② happiness	③ hope	④ snow	⑤ truth

PRACTICE 2

괄호 안에 주어진 표현 중 알맞은 것을 고르세요.

1   (A water, Water) always changes its form.
2   We brought (a child, child) with us.
3   Her (family, families) is now in New York.
4   I put (sugar, a sugar) in my coffee.
5   (A Korea, Korea) has four seasons.
6   (A friendship, Friendship) is very important to me.
7   My favorite (class, classes) is music.
8   We want to enjoy (a freedom, freedom).
9   (A Mike, Mike) has a nice car.
10 She drew (a flower, flower) on the paper.
11 Spread (butter, a butter) inside the bread.
12 (A love, Love) can change the world.

명사의 복수형

PSS 2-1 명사의 규칙 복수형 I

대부분의 경우	-s	map – map**s** pencil – pencil**s**	star – star**s** sport – sport**s**
-s, -x, -ch, -sh로 끝나는 경우	-es	bus – bus**es** church – church**es**	box – box**es** dish – dish**es**
자음+o로 끝나는 경우	-es	potato – potato**es** *cf.* piano – piano**s** mosquito – mosquito**(e)s**	tomato – tomato**es** photo – photo**s**
모음+o로 끝나는 경우	-s	radio – radio**s** video – video**s**	audio – audio**s** zoo – zoo**s**

PRACTICE 3

다음 명사의 복수형을 쓰세요.

1. egg ➡ _____
2. bus ➡ _____
3. address ➡ _____
4. star ➡ _____
5. day ➡ _____
6. present ➡ _____
7. photo ➡ _____
8. umbrella ➡ _____
9. sport ➡ _____
10. cup ➡ _____
11. beach ➡ _____
12. friend ➡ _____
13. cat ➡ _____
14. problem ➡ _____
15. tomato ➡ _____
16. shirt ➡ _____
17. box ➡ _____
18. map ➡ _____
19. zoo ➡ _____
20. bath ➡ _____
21. cookie ➡ _____
22. boat ➡ _____
23. flower ➡ _____
24. watch ➡ _____
25. radio ➡ _____
26. mosquito ➡ _____
27. passport ➡ _____
28. test ➡ _____
29. brush ➡ _____
30. potato ➡ _____

PSS 2-2 명사의 규칙 복수형 II

자음+y로 끝나는 경우	y를 i로 바꾸고 -es	city – cities candy – candies	baby – babies country – countries
모음+y로 끝나는 경우	-s	boy – boys monkey – monkeys	day – days toy – toys
-f, -fe로 끝나는 경우	f/fe를 v로 바꾸고 -es	leaf – leaves knife – knives *cf.* roof – roofs	wolf – wolves wife – wives safe – safes

PRACTICE 4

다음 명사의 복수형을 쓰세요.

1. candy ➡ _____
2. song ➡ _____
3. day ➡ _____
4. idea ➡ _____
5. knife ➡ _____
6. body ➡ _____
7. cow ➡ _____
8. class ➡ _____
9. shelf ➡ _____
10. factory ➡ _____
11. wife ➡ _____
12. lady ➡ _____
13. building ➡ _____
14. animal ➡ _____
15. mistake ➡ _____
16. door ➡ _____
17. family ➡ _____
18. safe ➡ _____
19. pencil ➡ _____
20. story ➡ _____
21. dish ➡ _____
22. picture ➡ _____
23. audio ➡ _____
24. doll ➡ _____
25. toy ➡ _____
26. key ➡ _____
27. wolf ➡ _____
28. fox ➡ _____
29. boy ➡ _____
30. sandwich ➡ _____
31. ship ➡ _____
32. video ➡ _____
33. monkey ➡ _____
34. leaf ➡ _____
35. letter ➡ _____
36. banana ➡ _____
37. piano ➡ _____
38. computer ➡ _____
39. baby ➡ _____
40. note ➡ _____
41. town ➡ _____
42. party ➡ _____
43. blouse ➡ _____
44. question ➡ _____
45. pig ➡ _____
46. doughnut ➡ _____
47. card ➡ _____
48. holiday ➡ _____
49. city ➡ _____
50. farmer ➡ _____
51. headache ➡ _____
52. bottle ➡ _____
53. house ➡ _____
54. country ➡ _____
55. poster ➡ _____
56. roof ➡ _____
57. block ➡ _____
58. diary ➡ _____
59. church ➡ _____
60. self ➡ _____

PSS 2-3 명사의 불규칙 복수형

1. 단수형과 복수형이 같은 명사

    deer – deer   fish – fish   sheep – sheep

    cf. fish의 복수형은 같은 종류의 물고기가 여럿 있을 때는 fish, 서로 다른 종류의 물고기가 여럿 있을 때는 fishes로 쓴다.

2. 그 밖의 명사의 불규칙 복수형

    foot – feet   tooth – teeth   goose – geese
    man – men   woman – women   mouse – mice
    child – children   ox – oxen

정답 p.20

PRACTICE 5

다음 명사의 복수형을 쓰세요.

1. duck ➡ _____
2. hobby ➡ _____
3. ox ➡ _____
4. festival ➡ _____
5. scarf ➡ _____
6. deer ➡ _____
7. room ➡ _____
8. student ➡ _____
9. sheep ➡ _____
10. man ➡ _____
11. candle ➡ _____
12. month ➡ _____
13. mouse ➡ _____
14. foot ➡ _____
15. team ➡ _____
16. subject ➡ _____
17. snowman ➡ _____
18. neighbor ➡ _____
19. goose ➡ _____
20. hour ➡ _____
21. fish ➡ _____
22. woman ➡ _____
23. sweater ➡ _____
24. bag ➡ _____
25. child ➡ _____
26. seat ➡ _____
27. bench ➡ _____
28. habit ➡ _____
29. tooth ➡ _____
30. thief ➡ _____

PRACTICE 6

〈보기〉와 같이 괄호 안의 명사를 알맞은 형태로 바꾸어 빈칸에 쓰세요. (단, 빈칸 하나당 한 개의 단어를 쓸 것.)

| 보 기 | He has ten <u>geese</u> on his farm. (goose) |

1 We need two _____ for cutting the meat. (knife)
2 _____ eat everything around the house. (mouse)
3 There is a _____ in the city. (church)
4 Some _____ are making snowmen outside. (child)
5 I need a _____ of my own. (room)
6 My _____ are about nine inches long. (foot)
7 The _____ change colors in autumn. (leaf)
8 The _____ in the fishbowl are goldfish. (fish)
9 I want to make good movies about _____. (woman)
10 My grandfather raises a lot of _____. (sheep)
11 Two _____ are pulling the wagon. (ox)
12 How do _____ protect themselves? (deer)
13 Don't forget to brush your _____. (tooth)
14 Place two _____ of cheese on each of the four plates. (slice)

PSS 3 단위명사의 쓰임
Problem Solving Skill

a piece of cheese

two cups of coffee

a glass of water

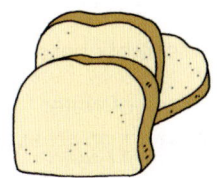
three slices of bread

1. 셀 수 없는 물질명사의 경우, 그 모양이나 담는 그릇을 나타내는 말을 이용하여 수량을 나타낸다. 복수형으로 쓰일 때에는 물질명사는 그대로 두고 단위를 나타내는 명사에 -(e)s를 붙인다.

a piece of	bread[cake, cheese, pizza, paper, chalk] advice[information, news] / furniture ***cf.*** advice, information, news는 추상명사이고, furniture는 의미상으로는 집합명사에 가깝지만 수량 표현 시 piece를 사용한다.
a cup of	coffee[tea]
a glass of	water[milk, juice, beer]
a slice of	bread[meat, cheese, pizza]
a pound of	sugar[meat]
a bottle of	beer[ink, juice, milk]

Do you want **a slice of pizza**? 피자 한 조각을 원하니?
Please give me **two pieces of paper**. 제게 종이 두 장을 주세요.
I'd like **three glasses of grape juice**. 포도 주스 세 잔을 원해요.

2. 두 개의 짝으로 이루어져 복수형으로 쓰는 명사인 glasses(안경), scissors, pants, jeans의 수량을 나타낼 때에는 a pair of, two pairs of …의 형태를 이용한다.

He bought **a new pair of pants**. 그는 새 바지 한 벌을 샀다.

PRACTICE 7

정답 p.20

〈보기〉와 같이 주어진 말을 알맞은 형태로 바꾸어 빈칸에 쓰세요.

| 보 기 | a piece of cake ➡ three <u>pieces of cake</u> |

1 a glass of milk   ➡ two _____
2 a piece of furniture   ➡ six _____
3 a bottle of juice   ➡ three _____
4 a piece of chalk   ➡ ten _____
5 a glass of water   ➡ some _____
6 a slice of bread   ➡ four _____
7 a pair of scissors   ➡ two _____
8 a pound of sugar   ➡ three _____
9 a cup of tea   ➡ five _____
10 a piece of news   ➡ four _____

11 a slice of pizza ➡ eight _____
12 a pair of socks ➡ seven _____
13 a piece of paper ➡ ten _____
14 a bottle of ink ➡ two _____
15 a pound of flour ➡ six _____

정답 p.20

PRACTICE 8

〈보기〉에 주어진 단어를 알맞게 활용하여 빈칸에 쓰세요.

| 보 기 | pair   glass   cup   bottle   piece   slice   pound |

1 Do you have a _____ of scissors?
2 He bought a _____ of jeans today.
3 They ate a _____ of cake after dinner.
4 Five _____ of bread are on the table.
5 I drink a _____ of milk every morning.
6 Mr. Kim drinks four _____ of coffee every day.
7 He got a new _____ of glasses.
8 We ate two _____ of meat.
9 Mike carried three _____ of beer with him.
10 He gave a _____ of chalk to his teacher.

명사의 소유격

1. 사람이나 동물을 나타내는 명사는 '(s)를 이용하여 소유격을 만든다.

   ① 단수 명사+'s
      Sora's brother 소라의 남동생
      an elephant's nose 코끼리의 코
   ② -s로 끝나는 복수 명사+'
      the boys' bags 그 소년들의 가방들

Andy's umbrella

CHAPTER 5 _ 명사와 관사   115

③ -s로 끝나지 않는 복수 명사+'s
a women's university 여자대학교

2. 무생물을 나타내는 명사는 of를 이용하여 소유격을 만든다.
the window of this room 이 방의 창문
employees of our company 우리 회사의 직원들
the legs of the chair

3. 명사가 반복되거나 공공건물, 집, 상점 등의 명사가 소유격 뒤에 오면 그 명사는 생략이 가능하다.
This camera is Sumi's (camera). 이 카메라는 수미의 것이다.
I stayed at my uncle's (house). 나는 삼촌 댁에 머물렀다.

PRACTICE 9

정답 p.20

괄호 안의 단어와 어퍼스트로피(')를 사용하여 문장을 완성하세요.

1 Where is ___Kelly's house___ ? (Kelly, house)
2 My son graduated from a _____. (boys, middle school)
3 Tomorrow is _____. (Ted, birthday)
4 What is your _____? (dog, name)
5 It is a famous _____. (women, university)
6 The store sells _____. (women, apparel)
7 He is _____. (Mr. Kim, son)
8 It is my _____. (parents, photo album)
9 We should respect other _____. (people, ideas)
10 Is there a _____ around here? (children, bookstore)
11 I have to clean out the _____. (dogs, houses)
12 _____ is best known for its seafood dishes. (Ana and Hailey, restaurant)
13 What is _____? (Andy, job)
14 _____ is amazing. (Richard, voice)

PRACTICE 10

괄호 안의 단어와 of를 사용하여 문장을 완성하세요.

1. Seoul is ___the capital of Korea___. (Korea, the capital)
2. Here is _____. (this city, the end)
3. Can you open _____? (the door, the room)
4. A dog has a good _____. (smell, sense)
5. _____ had a special party. (the people, the village)
6. What is _____? (the color, your shoes)
7. Here is _____. (the classes, the list)
8. We put candles in _____. (the middle, the table)
9. _____ looks very promising. (the future, the company)
10. We remember _____. (the mountain, the name)

PRACTICE 11

〈보기〉와 같이 짝지어진 두 문장의 의미가 같도록 빈칸을 채우세요.

보기	This is my father's car. = This <u>car</u> is <u>my father's</u>.

1. That is Mira's umbrella.
   = That _____ is _____.
2. It is my daughter's voice.
   = The _____ is _____.
3. This is her brother's puppy.
   = This _____ is _____.
4. Which is Mr. Felini's house?
   = Which _____ is _____?
5. These are Peter's books.
   = These _____ are _____.
6. That is a robot's arm.
   = That _____ is _____.
7. It is Mr. Smith's painting.
   = The _____ is _____.
8. This is Yumi's room.
   = This _____ is _____.
9. That is my friend's jacket.
   = That _____ is _____.
10. Those are the children's toys.
    = Those _____ are _____.

주의해야 할 명사의 수

숫자와 명사가 하이픈(-)으로 연결되어 뒤에 오는 명사를 꾸며주는 형용사처럼 쓰일 때는 「숫자+단수 명사」의 형태를 취한다.

a **fifty**-**year**-old man 50세의 남자
a **two**-**week** vacation 2주일의 방학
two **four**-**leaf** clovers 네 잎 클로버 2장

This house has **three stories**. 이 집은 3층이다.
= This is a **three-story** house. 이것은 3층짜리 집이다.
I have two brothers. They are **four years old**. 나는 남동생 2명이 있다. 그들은 4살이다.
= I have two **four-year-old** brothers. 나에게는 4살짜리 남동생 2명이 있다.

PRACTICE 12

정답 p.21

〈보기〉와 같이 짝지어진 두 문장의 의미가 같도록 빈칸을 채우세요.

| 보 기 | Tom is six years old.
= Tom is a <u>six-year-old</u> boy. |

1 This clover has four leaves.
 = This is a _____ clover.

2 Our vacation is five weeks.
 = We have a _____ vacation.

3 This book has one hundred pages.
 = This is a _____ book.

4 She has a son. He is three years old.
 = She has a _____ son.

5 Those buildings have ten stories.
 = Those are _____ buildings.

6 Ethan and Luke are twin brothers. They are eight years old.
 = Ethan and Luke are _____ twin brothers.

7 They planned a trip. It was two months.
 = They planned a _____ trip.

8 I saw three fish. They were two meters long.

= I saw three _____ fish.

9 I have a bill. It is five dollars.

= I have a _____ bill.

10 The break is ten minutes.

= There is a _____ break.

부정관사 a(n)의 쓰임

She had **a** banana and **an** apple.

셀 수 있는 단수 명사 앞에 a(n)를 쓴다.
a(n)는 많은 것들 중 막연한 하나를 나타내며,
대부분의 경우 해석하지 않는다.

첫소리가 자음인 단어 앞에는 a	첫소리가 모음인 단어 앞에는 an
1. a+명사 　**a** pencil, **a** desk, **a** house, **a** taxi, **a** farmer	1. an+명사 　**an** artist, **an** engineer, **an** umbrella, **an** egg
2. a+형용사+명사 　**a** special day, **a** new student	2. an+형용사+명사 　**an** interesting story, **an** old book
cf. 철자가 모음이지만 발음이 자음으로 시작하는 경우에는 a를 쓴다. 　**a** uniform, **a** university	**cf.** 철자가 자음이지만 발음이 모음으로 시작하는 경우에는 an을 쓴다. 　**an** hour, **an** honest boy

정답 p.21

PRACTICE 13

다음 문장의 빈칸에 a나 an 중 알맞은 것을 쓰세요.

1 She is _____ English teacher.

2 A computer is _____ useful tool.

3 I want to be _____ animal doctor.

4 The student didn't wear _____ uniform.

5 I met _____ European during my travels.

6 Jinho lent me _____ umbrella.

7 My mother found _____ old dress in her box.

8 He saw _____ picture on the wall.

9 He looks like _____ honest person.

10 I decided to go to _____ university abroad.

11 Mike is _____ elementary school student.

12 She had _____ busy day yesterday.

13 The book has _____ interesting story in it.

14 John drove for _____ hour.

15 I will open _____ hospital for sick people.

16 Do you have _____ idea about this?

17 We had _____ wonderful time last weekend.

18 I'm staying here for _____ year.

19 Wait _____ minute, please.

20 We learned _____ important lesson from this story.

PSS 7 a(n)의 의미 구별

용법	예문
one 하나의	**A** year has twelve months. 1년은 열두 달이다.
per ~마다	I go to the gym twice **a** week. 나는 일주일에 두 번 체육관에 간다.
종족 전체를 대표	**A** cow is a useful animal. 소는 유용한 동물이다.

PRACTICE 14

밑줄 친 a(n)의 용법과 같은 것을 〈보기〉에서 골라 그 번호를 쓰세요.

> 보기
> ① He has <u>a</u> son and two daughters.
> ② I met him once <u>a</u> month.
> ③ <u>A</u> fish cannot live without water.

1 They were running for <u>an</u> hour. [   ]
2 <u>A</u> crane has long legs. [   ]
3 She has only three classes <u>a</u> week. [   ]
4 We need eleven players for <u>a</u> team. [   ]
5 I usually study eight hours <u>a</u> day. [   ]
6 <u>A</u> snake sleeps during the winter. [   ]
7 <u>An</u> elephant has a long nose. [   ]
8 Rome wasn't built in <u>a</u> day. [   ]
9 Minsu visits his grandparents twice <u>a</u> year. [   ]

정관사 the의 쓰임

He is reading **a** book.　　She is reading a book. **The** book is interesting.

특정한 것을 가리킬 때 the를 쓰며, 단수 명사와 복수 명사 앞에 모두 쓰인다.

용법	예문
앞에 나온 명사가 다시 반복될 때	I have **a doll**. **The doll** is very cute. 나에게는 인형이 있다. 그 인형은 매우 귀엽다.
문맥이나 상황으로 보아 무엇을 가리키는지 알 수 있을 때	Would you please open **the** window? 그 창문 좀 열어주실래요?

용법	예문
구나 절에 의해 수식을 받아 가리키는 대상이 분명할 때	**The** key **on the table** isn't mine. 탁자 위의 열쇠는 내 것이 아니다.
일반적으로 유일한 것을 말할 때	**The Earth** goes around **the Sun**. 지구는 태양 주위를 돈다.
서수, 최상급, last, only, same, very 앞	She lives on **the third** floor. 그녀는 3층에 산다.
악기 이름 앞	She can play **the piano**. 그녀는 피아노를 칠 수 있다.
종족 전체를 대표	**The dog** is a friendly animal. 개는 다정한 동물이다.

PRACTICE 15

정답 p.21

밑줄 친 the의 용법과 같은 것을 〈보기〉에서 골라 그 번호를 쓰세요.

> 보 기
> ① They took a trip. <u>The</u> trip was great.
> ② Please pass me <u>the</u> salt.
> ③ <u>The</u> rooms in the house are small.
> ④ <u>The</u> sky is clear and blue.
> ⑤ It is <u>the</u> tallest building in Korea.
> ⑥ I play <u>the</u> violin every day.
> ⑦ <u>The</u> chicken cannot fly.

1 Can you imagine a trip to <u>the</u> Moon? [   ]

2 A bee is one of <u>the</u> most useful insects to people. [   ]

3 <u>The</u> Jindo dog is very faithful. [   ]

4 Paris is <u>the</u> capital of France. [   ]

5 Minho practiced <u>the</u> piano. [   ]

6 It was a book about space. I liked <u>the</u> book. [   ]

7 Excuse me. Where is <u>the</u> post office? [   ]

PRACTICE 16

괄호 안에 주어진 단어 중 알맞은 것을 고르세요.

1. He is learning to play (a, the) violin.
2. It's (a, the) third Sunday in June.
3. Look at (a, the) traffic light.
4. They spend 9 hours (a, the) day at school.
5. (A, The) Sun rises in the east.
6. (A, The) week has seven days.
7. She walks for (an, the) hour in the morning.
8. I bought (a, the) same car as yours.
9. She needs 25 hours in (a, the) day.
10. (A, The) bathrooms of the station are clean.
11. She pointed at (the, a) hole in the door.
12. They got on (a, the) last airplane.
13. A boy is playing at the beach. (A, The) boy looks happy.

관사를 쓰지 않는 경우

1. 식사, 운동, 질병 이름 앞에

   I had **breakfast**. 나는 아침을 먹었다.
   We are playing **baseball**. 우리는 야구를 하고 있다.
   My grandmother had **cancer**. 나의 할머니는 암에 걸리셨다.

2. 건물, 기구가 본래의 목적으로 쓰일 때

   go to **school** (공부하러) 학교에 가다
   go to **church** (예배 드리러) 교회에 가다
   go to **bed** 잠자리에 들다

   cf. I went to the school. – 여기서의 school은 '학교 건물'을 의미하며, 정규 수업을 받기 위해서가 아니라 다른 목적으로 학교에 간 상황을 나타낸다.
   I went to **the** school to see my son's English teacher.
   나는 나의 아들의 영어 선생님을 뵈러 학교에 갔다.

PRACTICE 17

다음 문장의 빈칸에 a(n)나 the 중 알맞은 것을 쓰고, 필요 없는 곳에는 ×표 하세요.

1 I got _____ F on the test.
2 She has _____ breakfast at seven thirty.
3 Sally is _____ tallest woman in her office.
4 Students go to _____ school from Monday to Friday.
5 He often plays _____ tennis.
6 I went to _____ school to pick up my daughter.
7 He is playing _____ guitar.
8 My cousin is _____ dentist.
9 He died of _____ cancer.
10 My parents go to _____ church every Sunday.
11 Mike wears _____ same shirt every day.
12 Shall we meet after _____ lunch?
13 I come here three times _____ month.
14 Go to _____ bed early tonight.
15 Will you close _____ door?

PSS 10 — There is/are
Problem Solving Skill

There is/are는 '~가 있다'의 뜻으로 there is 뒤에는 단수 명사가 오고, there are 뒤에는 복수 명사가 온다.

| There is+단수 명사 | **There is a book** on the desk.
책상 위에 책 한 권이 있다.
Is there a book on the desk?
책상 위에 책 한 권이 있니?
– Yes, there is. / No, there isn't.
응, 있어. / 아니, 없어.
There was a book on the desk.
책상 위에 책 한 권이 있었다. |

cf. 셀 수 없는 명사는 단수 취급하므로 there is를 쓴다.
There is some **milk** in the bottle. 병 안에 약간의 우유가 있다.

There are+복수 명사

There are books on the desk.
책상 위에 책들이 있다.
Are there books on the desk?
책상 위에 책들이 있니?
– Yes, there are. / No, there aren't.
응, 있어. / 아니, 없어.
There were books on the desk.
책상 위에 책들이 있었다.

cf. '~가 몇 개 있니?'의 표현으로는 How many ~ are there?를 쓴다.
How many festivals are there in Korea?
한국에는 몇 개의 축제가 있니?

'~가 얼마나 있니?'의 표현으로는 How much ~ is there?를 쓴다.
How much money is there in your pocket?
네 주머니 속에 돈이 얼마나 있니?

정답 p.22

PRACTICE 18

다음 문장의 빈칸에 is 또는 are를 넣어 문장을 완성하세요.

1 There _____ another key in my bag.
2 _____ there a lot of seats in the theater?
3 There _____ some money in my pocket.
4 _____ there apples in the box?
5 _____ there a soccer game today?
6 There _____ many famous buildings in the city.
7 There _____ some children in the park.
8 _____ there any sugar in the bowl?
9 There _____ three toys in his room.
10 There _____ water in my ears.

PRACTICE 19

그림을 보고, 빈칸에 알맞은 말을 쓰세요.

1. Is there an orange on the table? – Yes, _____.

2. _____ an accident yesterday? – Yes, there was.

3. How many desks _____ in the classroom? – There are 35 desks.

4. Were there a lot of people in the park? – No, _____.

5. _____ students are there on the playground?
   – _____ five students on the playground.

6. _____ there many stores on the street? – Yes, _____.

7. How many armchairs are there in the room? – _____ 2 armchairs.

8. _____ there a dog on the sofa? – Yes, _____.

9. _____ milk is there in your mug?
   – _____ about 200ml of milk in my mug.

동격

명사나 대명사를 보충 설명하기 위해 그 뒤에 콤마(,)를 덧붙여 다른 명사(구)를 쓸 수 있는데 이런 관계를 동격이라 한다.

This is **my friend, Mariah**.
이 사람은 내 친구인 Mariah입니다.

I like **Junwoo, the boy in the blue shirt**.
난 파란 셔츠를 입고 있는 소년인 준우를 좋아해.

Jason, the most popular guy in my team, talked to me.
우리 팀에서 가장 인기가 많은 남자인 Jason이 나에게 말을 걸었다.

The Moon, a satellite of the Earth, goes around the Earth.
지구의 위성인 달은 지구의 주위를 돈다.

정답 p.22

PRACTICE 20

밑줄 친 부분이 동격을 나타내면 ○, 동격을 나타내지 않으면 ×를 쓰세요.

1 After dark, the children returned to their home. [   ]
2 Yesterday was a hot, humid and airless day. [   ]
3 My favorite writer is Shakespeare, the writer of *Romeo and Juliet*. [   ]
4 My sister entered London University, a top medical school. [   ]
5 They came soon, and solved the problem. [   ]
6 My mom cooked a big American bird, turkey. [   ]
7 If you work hard, you will succeed. [   ]
8 We visited Abuja, the capital of Nigeria. [   ]
9 She was tired, hungry and sleepy. [   ]
10 He didn't say anything to me, so I know nothing about the plan. [   ]
11 My favorite place, the English building, is on 4th Street. [   ]
12 When he came into the room, I didn't recognize him. [   ]
13 I'd like to introduce my sister, Suji. [   ]
14 After I ran for an hour, I took a break for ten minutes. [   ]

Chapter Review Test

CHAPTER 5 명사와 관사

정답 p.22

1 다음 빈칸에 들어갈 수 <u>없는</u> 단어는?

> This is a _____.

① computer ② water
③ picture ④ book
⑤ desk

2 다음 빈칸에 들어갈 단어로 알맞은 것은?

> There are many _____.

① butter ② baby
③ sheep ④ man
⑤ child

3 다음 빈칸에 들어갈 말로 알맞은 것은?

> This is _____ umbrella.

① a ② an
③ lots of ④ many
⑤ much

4 다음 중 셀 수 없는 명사를 <u>모두</u> 고르세요.

보기	air	tooth	furniture
	money	milk	doll

➡ _____

5 다음 글의 밑줄 친 부분과 쓰임이 같은 것은?

> My sister<u>'s</u> job is a writer. She writes children's books. She's a good story-teller.

① He<u>'s</u> my English teacher.
② John<u>'s</u> dad wakes him up.
③ Where<u>'s</u> her bag?
④ What<u>'s</u> your favorite kind of music?
⑤ It<u>'s</u> twenty minutes' walk to the station.

6 다음 대화의 빈칸에 들어갈 알맞은 말을 고르세요.

> A: Is there a book on the desk?
> B: Yes, _____.

① it isn't ② it is
③ there are ④ there isn't
⑤ there is

7 다음 빈칸에 들어갈 수 <u>없는</u> 단어는?

> I have five _____.

① candies ② milk
③ mice ④ deer
⑤ fish

8 다음 문장에서 어법상 <u>잘못된</u> 것을 고르세요.

> ①There ②is five ③beds and two ④desks ⑤in the room.

9 다음 밑줄 친 부분을 바르게 고쳐 쓰세요.

- There are a lot of ⓐ deers in the park.
- My ⓑ foot are about seven inches long.
- ⓒ Man are cooking in the kitchen.

ⓐ _____ ⓑ _____ ⓒ _____

10 다음 밑줄 친 부분의 쓰임이 바른 것을 고르세요.

① It takes an hour.
② This is an spoon.
③ That is a interesting story.
④ He is a office worker.
⑤ I have to buy an uniform.

11 짝지어진 두 문장이 같은 뜻이 되도록 빈칸에 알맞은 말을 쓰세요.

(1) This jacket is Jane's.
   = This is _____ _____.

(2) The building is my father's.
   = It is my _____ _____.

(3) That is my friend's cell phone.
   = That cell phone is _____ _____.

12 다음 문장 중에서 어법상 올바른 것은?

① Gooses can make great pets.
② She saves many people's lifes.
③ How many child are there in the picture?
④ There are three cookies on the plate.
⑤ What are the coolest hobbys?

13 다음 빈칸에 들어갈 알맞은 말을 쓰세요.

- There ⓐ _____ many beautiful fish in the lake.
  호수에 많은 아름다운 물고기들이 있다.
- ⓑ _____ there any salt in the bowl?
  그릇에 소금이 있나요?
- There ⓒ _____ some juice in the glass.
  유리잔에 약간의 주스가 있다.

ⓐ _____ ⓑ _____ ⓒ _____

14 다음 그림을 묘사한 것 중 어법이 올바르지 않은 것을 세 개 고르세요.

① There are four desks in the office.
② There are two copiers in the office.
③ There is two plants in the office.
④ There is a women in the office.
⑤ There are three window in the office.

15 다음 밑줄 친 문장 중 어법상 틀린 문장을 찾아 올바르게 고쳐 쓰세요.

ⓐ I am playing the basketball with my friends. I am a member of the basketball club. ⓑ I'm the tallest man on our team. ⓒ We practice after work twice a week. We will have an amateur match soon. I am doing my best.

➡ _____

16 다음 주어진 두 문장을 하나의 문장으로 바르게 만든 것은?

- She made me chocolate cake.
- Chocolate cake is my favorite dessert.

① She made, chocolate cake, my favorite dessert, me.
② She made my favorite dessert, me, chocolate cake.
③ She made me my favorite dessert's chocolate cake.
④ She made me chocolate cake of my favorite dessert.
⑤ She made me my favorite dessert, chocolate cake.

17 밑줄 친 부분의 쓰임이 잘못된 것은?

① There are a book and two pencils.
② There is a gym in my apartment building.
③ There are seven days in a week.
④ There is not enough water.
⑤ There are a lot of juice in the bottle.

18 다음 중 밑줄 친 a[an]의 의미가 다른 하나를 고르세요.

① We eat out twice a month.
② I brush my teeth three times a day.
③ It took an hour to fix it.
④ He goes shopping twice a week.
⑤ They meet together once a year.

19 다음 중 어법상 어색한 문장을 고르세요.

① My hobby is taking pictures.
② My hobby is listening to music.
③ My hobby is watching movies.
④ My hobby is playing guitar.
⑤ My hobby is collecting stamps.

20 빈칸에 들어갈 단어가 나머지 넷과 다른 하나는?

① There _____ a girl next to a baby.
② There _____ some people in the park.
③ _____ there many books in the library?
④ There _____ pencils on my desk.
⑤ There _____ pretty birds on the tree.

21 빈칸에 들어갈 단어가 바르게 짝지어진 것은?

- I found your post _____ useful read.
- Mr. Lee is _____ office worker.

① a – a   ② an – an   ③ a – an
④ an – a   ⑤ the – a

22 빈칸에 들어갈 단어가 순서대로 바르게 짝지어진 것은?

- There _____ some shoes on the shelves.
- There _____ jeans on the bed.
- There _____ a clock on the wall.

① is – is – are   ② are – is – is
③ is – are – is   ④ are – are – is
⑤ are – is – are

23 다음 대화의 밑줄 친 부분 중 틀린 것을 고르세요.

A: How ① many ② childrens do you ③ have?
B: I have three ④ sons and two ⑤ daughters.

24 다음 빈칸에 들어갈 알맞은 말을 고르세요.

There are _____ in the field.

① three sheep　　② two mouses
③ four wolfs　　④ three benches
⑤ five foxs

25 다음 지문을 읽고, ⓐ, ⓑ, ⓒ에 들어갈 알맞은 관사를 골라 쓰세요.

Minsu always gets up at 6 o'clock. As soon as he wakes up, he watches the morning news to decide whether or not to bring ⓐ (a / an) umbrella. Then, he has breakfast and takes a shower. It usually takes ⓑ (a / an) hour to get to his workplace. His company has ⓒ (a / an) uniform, so he has to change his clothes after he arrives at work.

ⓐ: _____　ⓑ: _____　ⓒ: _____

26 다음 중 어법상 바르게 쓰인 문장은?

① We had nice dinner.
② I will see you at the noon.
③ My father is a very fat.
④ Do you play piano?
⑤ Is she a teacher, too?

27 밑줄 친 우리말을 영어로 바르게 옮긴 것끼리 짝지어진 것은?

We bought 피자 세 조각 and 콜라 두 병.

① three slice of pizza　– two bottle of coke
② three slices of pizza　– two bottles of coke
③ three pieces of pizza – two bottle of coke
④ three piece of pizzas – two bottle of cokes
⑤ three slices of pizzas – two bottles of cokes

28 다음 두 문장의 뜻이 같도록 빈칸에 들어갈 알맞은 말을 고르세요.

• Korea has many old buildings.
 = _____ many old buildings in Korea.

① Here is　　② It is
③ They are　④ There is
⑤ There are

29 다음 글에서 틀린 부분을 고르세요.

Jessica has ① small ears, a small nose, and ② a big mouth. She also has ③ big blue eyes, ④ long legs, and ⑤ red hairs.

30 우리말과 같은 뜻이 되도록 빈칸에 알맞은 단어를 쓰세요.

A: Is this pen yours?
B: No. It's my _____ pen.
　(아니요. 그건 제 삼촌의 펜이에요.)

31 다음 중 밑줄 친 부분의 쓰임이 바른 것을 고르세요.

① She likes to wear an uniform.
② My son is an middle school student.
③ Your father is an taxi driver.
④ He's an engineer.
⑤ Are you an nurse?

32 다음 우리말과 같은 뜻이 되도록 빈칸에 들어갈 알맞은 말을 쓰세요.

- 나의 가족은 지구를 위해 좋은 일을 하려고 노력한다.
  = My family tries to do good things for _____.

33 다음 괄호 안의 말을 이용하여 알맞은 문장을 쓰세요.

A: (1) _____
   _____
   (how)
B: There are four books on the desk.
A: Whose books are they?
B: (2) _____
   (Jane)

34 다음 문장의 밑줄 친 a와 쓰임이 같은 것을 고르세요.

I watch TV several times a week.

① We studied for an hour.
② A dog is a useful animal.
③ There is a park in my town.
④ I write a letter to my parents twice a month.
⑤ It is a wonderful day.

35 다음 그림을 보고 There is/are를 이용하여 주어진 단어를 가지고 문장을 만드세요.

| 보 기 | There is a chair in front of the desk. |

(1) _____
   (cat, on the bed)
(2) _____
   (ball, on the floor)

36 다음 중 어법상 옳은 문장을 고르세요.

① I'd like to buy a pairs of shoes.
② Can I drink two glass of water?
③ She ate a slice of cheese.
④ My mother bought two bottle of juices.
⑤ He needs three pieces of papers.

37 빈칸에 들어갈 단어가 바르게 짝지어진 것은?

- We work eight hours _____ day.
- March is _____ third month of the year.

① a – the   ② the – a
③ a – a   ④ the – the
⑤ an – the

38 다음 중 어법상 옳은 문장을 고르세요.

① Is John student?
② Suji is a newspaper reporter.
③ Today is a second day of the festival.
④ My wife is from a Busan.
⑤ She looks a very honest.

39 다음 중 어법상 바르지 <u>않은</u> 문장을 고르세요.

① The boy's name is James.
② I like your sister's bag.
③ This is Mr. Kim's daughter.
④ The door's color is yellow.
⑤ It's Yongsu's dog.

40 다음 밑줄 친 부분의 쓰임이 <u>어색한</u> 것은?

① The sun sets in <u>the</u> west.
② Could you open <u>the</u> door?
③ You can play <u>the</u> soccer after school.
④ She is <u>the</u> youngest winner of the contest.
⑤ Look at <u>the</u> Chinese boy.

41 다음 중 밑줄 친 부분의 쓰임이 <u>잘못된</u> 것을 고르세요.

We went ① <u>sightseeing</u> in New York. There ② <u>was</u> many famous ③ <u>buildings</u> such as the Empire State Building. There ④ <u>were</u> plays and performances on Broadway, ⑤ <u>too</u>.

42 다음 중 어법상 올바른 문장을 고르세요.

① I'm wearing glass.
② What kind of pant do you want?
③ She wants to buy red shoes.
④ Miki likes these jean.
⑤ Did you find your scissor?

43 다음을 읽고 <u>틀린</u> 부분을 찾아서 바르게 고쳐 쓰세요.

Sora always goes to the school at eight o'clock. She usually has six classes a day. She has ten-minutes breaks between classes. She has the lunch at twelve o'clock.

(1) _____ ➡ _____
(2) _____ ➡ _____
(3) _____ ➡ _____

44 다음 빈칸에 들어갈 수 <u>없는</u> 것은?

Andy is looking for a pair of _____.

① jeans   ② shoes   ③ scissors
④ notebooks   ⑤ glasses

45 다음 빈칸에 들어갈 단어로 알맞지 <u>않은</u> 것은?

A: Can I help you?
B: Yes, I'd like _____. How much is it?
A: It is 2 dollars and 40 cents.

① sugar   ② bread
③ cheese   ④ coffee
⑤ tomatoes

46 다음 두 문장을 〈보기〉처럼 하나의 문장으로 바꿔 쓰세요.

보기
- J. K. Rowling is a famous writer.
- She wrote the *Harry Potter* series.
➡ J. K. Rowling, a famous writer, wrote the *Harry Potter* series.

- Sungmin is the leader of our volunteer club.
- He is kind to everyone.
➡ _____

47 빈칸에 들어갈 말이 바르게 짝지어진 것은?

A: How many oranges _____ in the basket?
B: _____ only one orange in the basket.

① is there – There are
② are there – There is
③ are they – They are
④ is there – They are
⑤ are there – This is

48 다음 중 보기의 밑줄 친 부분과 쓰임이 다른 것은?

보기 | My brother's name is Minsu.

① What is your teacher's name?
② Tom's mom likes us.
③ I want to write children's books.
④ He is my father's friend.
⑤ She's having dinner with us.

49 다음 밑줄 친 부분의 뜻이 나머지와 다른 하나는?

① Are there many children in the playground?
② They go there with my brother.
③ There are eight buildings on this street.
④ Is there a desk in your room?
⑤ There is an elephant in the zoo.

50 다음 대화의 빈칸에 들어갈 알맞은 말을 고르세요.

A: There's _____.
B: Really? Where?
A: Over there. It's under the oak tree.
B: Keep it. It will bring you good luck.

① a four leaf clovers
② four leaves clover
③ a four-leaf clover
④ four-leaves clovers
⑤ a four leaves clovers

51 다음 중 어법상 바르지 않은 것을 고르세요.

When I have some ①questions or ②problems, I ask my sister for some ③help. She always gives me good ④advices and helpful ⑤information.

52 다음 중 밑줄 친 부분의 쓰임이 나머지와 다른 것은?

① He saw Beyoncé, his favorite singer.
② We, human beings, should love each other.
③ She bought a skirt, a blouse and a jacket.
④ Do you like *bibimbap*, a Korean dish?
⑤ Miss Lala, my English teacher, is very kind to me.

CHAPTER 6
대명사

구분	평가 기준
Excellent	문법 내용을 모두 이해하고, 문제를 모두 맞힘.
Very good	문법 내용은 충분히 이해했으나 실수로 1~2문제 틀림.
Good	문법 내용이 조금 어려워 3~4문제 틀림.
needs Review	분법 내봉 이해가 어렵고, 5문제 이상 틀림, 복습 필요.

성취도 자기 평가 활용법

Problem Solving Skill	페이지	학습날짜	성취도 자기평가 E V G R	학습체크
PSS 1 인칭대명사	136	/		☐
PSS 2 재귀대명사	138	/		☐
PSS 3 비인칭 주어 it	140	/		☐
PSS 4 지시대명사	141	/		☐
PSS 5 부정대명사	**페이지**	**학습날짜**	**성취도 자기평가 E V G R**	**학습체크**
PSS 5-1 one	142	/		☐
PSS 5-2 another, others, the other(s)	143	/		☐
PSS 5-3 each, every	144	/		☐
PSS 6 의문대명사	**페이지**	**학습날짜**	**성취도 자기평가 E V G R**	**학습체크**
PSS 6-1 who	144	/		☐
PSS 6-2 what, which	145	/		☐
PSS 7 so, same, such	147	/		☐
Chapter Review Test	148	/		☐

인칭대명사

수	인칭	주격 (~은, 는, 이, 가)	소유격 (~의)	목적격 (~을, 를, 에게)	소유대명사 (~의 것)
단수	1	I	my	me	mine
	2	you	your	you	yours
	3	he	his	him	his
	3	she	her	her	hers
		it	its	it	—
복수	1	we	our	us	ours
	2	you	your	you	yours
	3	they	their	them	theirs

1. **주격과 목적격** – 주격 대명사는 주어로, 목적격 대명사는 목적어로 쓰인다.

    Sumi likes **milk**. ➡ **She** likes **it**.
    수미는 우유를 좋아한다. 그녀는 그것을 좋아한다.
    Minho likes **books**. ➡ **He** likes **them**.
    민호는 책을 좋아한다. 그는 그것들을 좋아한다.
    Sumi and Minho like **their house**. ➡ **They** like **it**.
    수미와 민호는 그들의 집을 좋아한다. 그들은 그것을 좋아한다.

2. **소유격과 소유대명사** – 소유격 뒤에는 명사가 오지만, 소유대명사 뒤에는 명사가 오지 않는다.

    This is **my dog**. ➡ This dog is **mine**.
    이것은 나의 개이다. 이 개는 나의 것이다.
    That is **our car**. ➡ That car is **ours**.
    저것은 우리의 차이다. 저 차는 우리의 것이다.
    These are **your shoes**. ➡ These shoes are **yours**.
    이것들은 너의 신발이다. 이 신발은 너의 것이다.

3. **전치사 뒤에는 주로 목적격 인칭대명사가 온다.**

    Babies are curious about everything **around them**.
    아기들은 그들 주변의 모든 것에 대하여 궁금해한다.

PRACTICE 1

〈보기〉와 같이 밑줄 친 부분을 알맞은 인칭대명사로 바꾸어 쓰세요.

> 보 기   I don't want grapes. ➡ I don't want them.

1 That is his room.
  ➡ That room is _____.

2 The cat is brown.
  ➡ _____ is brown.

3 That is my present.
  ➡ That present is _____.

4 This is my grandparents' farm.
  ➡ This farm is _____.

5 The girl works at a bakery.
  ➡ _____ works at a bakery.

6 Is this her photo album?
  ➡ Is this photo album _____?

7 My brother and I got there by bus.
  ➡ _____ got there by bus.

8 Semin rested with his family.
  ➡ _____ rested with his family.

9 The dog's tail is very long.
  ➡ _____ tail is very long.

10 She welcomed my brother and me.
  ➡ She welcomed _____.

11 Minsu's and my hometown isn't far.
  ➡ _____ hometown isn't far.

12 TV helps me learn a lot of things.
  ➡ _____ helps me learn a lot of things.

13 Inho showed his new shirt to Susan.
  ➡ Inho showed his new shirt to _____.

14 You should wash your hands very often.
  ➡ You should wash _____ very often.

15 Tom and his friends' journey was very tough.
  ➡ _____ journey was very tough.

16 Those are your glasses.
  ➡ Those glasses are _____.

PRACTICE 2

괄호 안에 주어진 단어를 알맞은 형태로 바꾸어 빈칸에 쓰세요.

1 What's _____ name? (you)

2 We made some food for _____. (they)

3 This prize is _____. (he)

4 Please help _____ with my English. (I)

5 Mike just returned from _____ trip. (he)

6 Our culture is similar to _____. (you)

7 I often play tennis in _____ free time. (I)

8 _____ room is full of books. (she)

9 It is because of _____. (he)

10 This room is _____ . (we)
11 _____ is my notebook. (it)
12 The video camera is _____ . (they)
13 She gave _____ a lot of food. (we)
14 He may give _____ some advice. (you)
15 Food is very important for _____ lives. (we)
16 I made _____ a cold drink. (she)
17 I don't like _____ color. (it)
18 That old book isn't _____ . (I)
19 This yellow blouse is _____ . (she)
20 They usually wear shoes in _____ homes. (they)

PSS 2 재귀대명사
Problem Solving Skill

단수	복수
I ➡ myself	we ➡ ourselves
you ➡ yourself	you ➡ yourselves
he ➡ himself	
she ➡ herself	they ➡ themselves
it ➡ itself	

She is looking at **herself** in the mirror.

1. 재귀 용법 – 문장의 주어와 목적어가 같을 때 동사 또는 전치사의 목적어로 재귀대명사를 쓴다.

   He loves **himself**. 그는 그 자신을 사랑한다.
   They enjoyed **themselves** at the party. 그들은 파티에서 신나게 즐겼다.
   You should be proud of **yourself**. 너는 스스로를 자랑스러워해야 한다.

2. 강조 용법 – 주어나 목적어, 보어를 강조할 때 강조되는 말 바로 뒤나 문장 맨 끝에 재귀대명사를 쓴다. 이 때의 재귀대명사는 생략이 가능하다.

   My father (**himself**) designed that building. 아버지가 직접 그 건물을 설계하셨다.
   = **My father** designed that building (**himself**).

PRACTICE 3

괄호 안에 주어진 단어 중 알맞은 것을 고르세요.

1 I feel proud of (me, myself).
2 They (yourselves, themselves) got very tired.
3 The cat cleaned (itself, themselves).
4 Let me introduce (myself, ourselves).
5 Namsu (him, himself) sent an e-mail to me.
6 Did you make the salad (you, yourself)?
7 He thought to (myself, himself), 'No way.'
8 The weather (it, itself) doesn't matter.
9 Sometimes Susan talks to (yourself, herself).
10 Many people enjoyed (ourselves, themselves) in the park.
11 I was angry with (myself, himself).
12 We enjoyed (yourselves, ourselves) during the trip.
13 Help (you, yourself) to some *bibimbap*.
14 Mike likes (himself, itself) in a cap.
15 A lot of people don't know about (itself, themselves).

PRACTICE 4

밑줄 친 부분을 생략할 수 있으면 ○표, 생략할 수 없으면 ×표 하세요.

1 I decided to go there myself. [   ]
2 You wanted nothing for yourself. [   ]
3 She paid for herself at the restaurant. [   ]
4 Computers themselves help us study alone. [   ]
5 Mike's father likes playing football himself. [   ]
6 The dinner itself was really delicious. [   ]
7 Can you imagine yourself in ten years? [   ]
8 History repeats itself. [   ]
9 She caught a cold herself. [   ]
10 I said to myself, "Is it true?" [   ]

비인칭 주어 it

비인칭 주어 it은 시간, 날짜, 요일, 계절, 날씨, 거리, 명암을 나타낼 때 쓰인다. 이 때의 it은 가리키는 대상이 없고, 특별한 의미를 갖지 않으므로 해석하지 않는다.

① 시간 : What time is **it**? – **It** is eight o'clock. 지금 몇 시니? – 8시야.
② 날짜 : What date is **it** today? – **It**'s May 24th. 오늘은 며칠이니? – 5월 24일이야.
③ 요일 : What day is **it** today? – **It** is Friday. 오늘은 무슨 요일이니? – 금요일이야.
④ 계절 : **It** is winter now. 지금은 겨울이다.
⑤ 날씨 : **It** was cold yesterday. 어제는 추웠다.
⑥ 거리 : How far is **it** from here to the museum? 여기서 박물관까지 얼마나 머니?
　　　　 – **It** is about three miles. 약 3마일이야.
⑦ 명암 : **It**'s dark outside. 밖이 어둡다.

cf. 대명사 it은 '그것'이라고 해석한다.
　　There is **a pencil** on the desk. **It** (= The pencil) is hers.
　　책상 위에 연필이 한 자루 있다. 그것은 그녀의 것이다.

PRACTICE 5

다음 문장의 밑줄 친 it의 용법이 〈보기〉의 A와 같으면 A를, B와 같으면 B를 쓰세요.

> 보기　　A. <u>It</u> is Saturday.
> 　　　　B. I'll bring <u>it</u> tomorrow.

1　What does <u>it</u> mean? [　　]　　2　<u>It</u>'s three thirty. [　　]
3　<u>It</u> was a summer day. [　　]　　4　What a huge turtle <u>it</u> is! [　　]
5　<u>It</u> takes ten minutes by bus. [　　]　　6　<u>It</u> is Wednesday. [　　]
7　<u>It</u> is still spring. [　　]　　8　<u>It</u> is hot today. [　　]
9　<u>It</u> helps me save time. [　　]　　10　<u>It</u> is November 9th. [　　]
11　<u>It</u> is getting dark. [　　]　　12　<u>It</u> is my brother's umbrella. [　　]
13　What time is <u>it</u> now? [　　]　　14　<u>It</u> is between the bank and the store. [　　]
15　<u>It</u> isn't your fault. [　　]　　16　How many miles is <u>it</u> from Seoul to Daegu? [　　]

지시대명사

1. this / these – 가까이에 있는 사람이나 사물을 가리킬 때 쓰인다.

   This is my bag. 이것은 나의 가방이다.
   These are my bags. 이것들은 나의 가방이다.

2. that / those – 멀리 있는 사람이나 사물을 가리킬 때 쓰인다.

   That is my watch. 저것은 내 시계이다.
   Those are my watches. 저것들은 내 시계이다.

cf. this/these와 that/those는 지시형용사로서 명사 앞에 쓰여 명사를 꾸며주기도 한다.
   This cake is very delicious. 이 케이크는 매우 맛있다.
   Those notebooks are mine. 저 공책들은 내 것이다.

3. 누군가를 소개할 때나 전화상에서 전화를 건 사람과 받는 사람을 가리킬 때는 this를 쓴다.

   Tim, **this** is Jane. Jane, **this** is Tim. Tim, 얘는 Jane이야. Jane, 얘는 Tim이야.
   Hello, **this** is Sumi. Is **this** Mike? 여보세요. 나 수미인데, Mike니?

정답 p.26

PRACTICE 6

그림을 보고, 빈칸에 this/these 또는 that/those를 넣어 문장을 완성하세요.

1

2

3

4

1 _____ is my dog, Sandy.

2 Who is _____ girl?

3 Are _____ pine trees?

4 _____ is Mary speaking. Who's calling, please?

5 How about _____ shoes?

6 _____ is my house.

7 Are _____ your glasses on the table?

8 _____ are my family's pictures.

 **부정대명사**

PSS 5-1 one

1. 앞에서 언급한 명사와 종류는 같지만, 특정하지 않은 막연한 대상에 대해 말할 때는 **one**을 쓴다.

   My computer is too old. I want a new **one**. (one = computer)
   내 컴퓨터는 너무 오래됐다. 나는 새것을 원한다.

   cf. 앞에서 언급한 특정한 명사를 가리킬 때는 it을 쓴다.
   My computer is too old. I don't like **it**. (it = my computer)
   내 컴퓨터는 너무 오래됐다. 나는 그것을 좋아하지 않는다.

2. 앞에서 언급한 명사가 복수형일 때는 one 대신 **ones**를 쓴다.

   My shoes are too old. I want new **ones**. (ones = shoes)
   내 신발은 너무 낡았다. 나는 새것들을 원한다.

PRACTICE 7

다음 문장의 빈칸에 one, ones 또는 it을 넣어 문장을 완성하세요.

1 She bought some postcards. I want to buy the same _____.

2 Don't throw paper away. We can use _____ again.

3 Where is an umbrella? – There is _____ in my room.

4 I went to London. _____ is a very beautiful city.

5 I lost my bag. I need a new _____.

6 I don't like yellow roses. I will buy red _____.

PSS 5-2 another, others, the other(s)

일부를 뺀 나머지에 대해 말할 때는 another, others, the other(s)를 사용할 수 있다. 특정한 것을 가리킬 때는 the를 붙인다.

1. another '또 다른 하나'

   I don't like this color. Can you show me **another**?
   나는 이 색깔을 좋아하지 않아요. 저에게 또 다른 것을 보여줄래요?

2. One ~ the other … '하나는 ~, 다른 사람[것]〈나머지 하나〉은 …'

   She has two flowers. **One** is a rose and **the other** is a lily.
   그녀는 두 송이의 꽃을 가지고 있다. 하나는 장미이고 다른 하나는 백합이다.

3. Some ~ others … '몇몇은 ~, 다른 사람[것]들〈나머지 일부〉은 …'

   Some students like English. **Others** don't like it.
   몇몇 학생들은 영어를 좋아한다. 다른 학생들은 그것을 좋아하지 않는다.
   = Some students like English. Other students don't like it.

   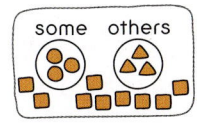

4. Some ~ the others … '몇몇은 ~, 다른 사람[것]들〈나머지 전부〉은 …'

   Some cats are white. **The others** are brown.
   몇몇 고양이들은 털이 하얗다. 다른 고양이들은 털이 갈색이다.
   = Some cats are white. The other cats are brown.

   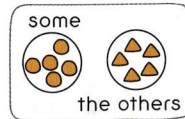

   cf. another와 other는 「another+단수 명사」와 「other+복수 명사」의 형태로 명사를 수식하는 형용사로도 쓰인다.
   Can you show me **another** shirt? 저에게 또 다른 셔츠를 보여줄래요?
   Can you show me **other** shirts? 저에게 다른 셔츠들을 보여줄래요?

정답 p.26

PRACTICE 8

괄호 안에 주어진 표현 중 알맞은 것을 고르세요.

1 Some people are honest, but (other, others) are dishonest.

2 He wants to read (another, other) book.

3 She has a lot of fruits. (Some, They) of them are oranges, and the others are apples.

4 Ingyu's mother made two doughnuts. One is Ingyu's, and (another, the other) is hers.

5 They did well in some courses, but they didn't do well in (other, others) courses.

6 This is (another, other) good example.
7 I have two brothers. One is tall, and (another, the other) is short.
8 Some of the dresses are clean, but (other, the others) are not.
9 There are two coats. (It, One) is blue, and the other is black.
10 This pen is broken. Do you have (another, other)?

PSS 5-3 each, every

1. each – '각자, 각기, 각각의'의 뜻으로 단수 명사를 수식하고 단수 취급한다. each는 대명사, 부사로도 쓰인다.

   Each box weighs 200 pounds. 각각의 상자는 무게가 200파운드이다. (형용사)
   Each has his own opinion. 각자 자기만의 의견을 가지고 있다. (대명사)
   I gave them five cards **each**. 나는 그들에게 각각 카드 다섯 장씩 주었다. (부사)

2. every – '모든'의 뜻으로 단수 명사를 수식하고 단수 취급한다.

   I want to make **every** child happy. 나는 모든 아이들을 행복하게 만들고 싶다.
   every people (X)   every children (X)

   cf. everyone, everybody, everything도 단수 취급한다.
      Everyone likes watching movies. 모든 사람들이 영화를 보는 것을 좋아한다.

정답 p.26

PRACTICE 9

괄호 안에 주어진 단어 중 알맞은 것을 고르세요.

1 What will each (men, man) have for lunch?
2 He wrapped each (present, presents).
3 Every dog (has, have) his day.
4 Everything (is, are) going to be all right.
5 The number of people living alone grows each (years, year).

PSS 6 의문대명사

PSS 6-1 who

사람의 이름이나 관계 등을 물을 때 쓴다.

1. 주격
   Who is she?   – She is **my aunt**.
   그녀는 누구니?   그녀는 우리 이모야.

2. 소유격

   Whose car is this?   – It's **my father's**.
   이것은 누구의 차니?   그것은 우리 아빠의 것이야.

   cf. 「whose+명사」에서 whose는 who의 소유격으로 '누구의'라는 의미를 나타내지만, whose가 명사 없이 단독으로 쓰일 경우에는 소유대명사로서 '누구의 것'이라는 의미이다.
   Whose is this car? 이 차는 누구의 것이니?

3. 목적격

   Whom did you meet yesterday?   – I met **Minho**.
   너는 어제 누구를 만났니?   나는 민호를 만났어.

   cf. 구어체에서는 whom보다 who를 쓰는 경향이 많다.

정답 p.26

PRACTICE 10

다음 문장의 빈칸에 who, whose, whom 중 알맞은 것을 쓰세요. (단, who와 whom이 모두 가능할 경우에는 whom을 쓸 것)

1 _____ did they help?
2 _____ wrote the book?
3 _____ is this watch?
4 _____ is your favorite singer?
5 _____ did he visit?
6 _____ does she talk to?
7 _____ book is that?
8 _____ is her favorite author?
9 _____ are those clothes?
10 _____ makes you sad?

PSS 6-2   what, which

1. what – 동물이나 사물, 그리고 사람의 직업이나 신분을 물을 때 쓴다.

   What did Mary buy?   – She bought **some clothes**.
   Mary가 무엇을 샀니?   그녀는 옷을 몇 벌 샀어.

   What does your father do?   – He is **a teacher**.
   너의 아버지는 무엇을 하시니?   그는 선생님이셔.

   cf. what은 「what+명사」의 형태로 명사를 수식하는 의문형용사로도 쓰인다.
   What food do you like? 너는 어떤 음식을 좋아하니?

CHAPTER 6 _ 대명사 | 145

> 2. **which** – 동물이나 사물을 가리킬 때 쓴다. 단, 제한된 선택의 범위 내에서 '어느 것'인지를 물을 때 쓴다.
>
> **Which** is cheaper, meat **or** fish? 고기와 생선 중 어느 것이 더 값이 싸니?
> **Which** do you want, tea **or** coffee? 차와 커피 중 어느 것을 원하니?
>
> ***cf.*** which는 「which+명사」의 형태로 명사를 수식하는 의문형용사로도 쓰인다.
> **Which season** do you like, summer **or** winter? 여름과 겨울 중 어느 계절을 좋아하니?

PRACTICE 11

괄호 안에 주어진 단어 중 알맞은 것을 고르세요.

1 (What, Who) is your favorite song?
2 (Whom, Whose) did he meet last night?
3 (Who, Whose) violin is this?
4 (What, Who) is this baby in the photo?
5 (What, Who) size do you wear?
6 (Who, Whose) book did you borrow?
7 (What, Which) is bigger, Canada or Australia?
8 (What, Which) pet do you like better, a dog or a cat?

PRACTICE 12

다음 질문에 알맞은 응답을 찾아 그 기호를 쓰세요.

[A]
1 Which team is stronger? [   ]   ⓐ It's mine.
2 Whose book is that? [   ]   ⓑ How about five o'clock?
3 Who is this man? [   ]   ⓒ He is my father.
4 What time shall we make it? [   ]   ⓓ The Spanish team is stronger.

[B]
5 Who's calling, please? [   ]   ⓔ I'm hanging out with Tom.
6 What did you get at Christmas? [   ]   ⓕ This is Susan.
7 Whom are you hanging out with? [   ]   ⓖ A subway, of course.
8 Which is faster, a taxi or a subway? [   ]   ⓗ A backpack.

so, same, such

so	'그렇게'라는 뜻으로 think, suppose, believe, expect, hope, say, tell의 목적어로 쓰이며 앞에 나온 긍정의 문장을 대신한다. She will be safe. – I hope **so**. 그녀는 안전할 것이다. – 나도 그러길 바란다.
same	'같은'이라는 뜻으로 항상 정관사 the와 함께 쓴다. The prices are **the same**. 그 가격들은 같다. **cf.** A is/are the same as B 'A는 B와 같다' 　The password **is the same as** the username. 　비밀번호는 사용자 명과 동일하다. **same**은 형용사로도 쓰인다. Can we meet up at **the same** time tomorrow? 우리가 내일 같은 시간에 만날 수 있을까? **cf.** the same ~ as … '…와 같은 ~' 　I bought **the same** umbrella **as** Jenny. 나는 Jenny와 같은 우산을 샀다. 　Do you like **the same** music **as** Kevin? 너는 Kevin과 같은 음악을 좋아하니?
such	'그러한 것'이라는 뜻으로 앞에 나온 단어, 구, 절을 받는다. **Such** was his answer. 그의 대답은 그러했다. **cf.** such as ~ '~와 같은 그런' 　I like team sports **such as** soccer. 나는 축구와 같은 그런 단체 운동을 좋아한다.

정답 p.27

PRACTICE 13

우리말과 일치하도록 괄호 안에 주어진 단어를 바르게 배열하세요.

1 그녀는 부지런하다. – 나는 그렇게 생각하지 않아.
= She is diligent. – _____ (I, so, think, don't)

2 그것들은 같아 보이지 않는다.
= _____ (don't, look, they, the, same)

3 그는 너와 같은 의견을 가지고 있다.
= _____ (has, the, as, same, he, you, opinion)

4 나는 노란색과 같은 밝은 색을 좋아한다.
= _____ (such, I, like, yellow, as, bright, colors)

5 이 신발들은 사이즈가 같다.
= _____ (shoes, these, the, same, are, size)

Chapter Review Test

CHAPTER 6
대명사

1 다음 대화의 빈칸에 들어갈 알맞은 단어는?

> *Jane*: Do you like pop songs, Ted?
> *Ted*: Yes, I like _____ very much.

① this   ② that   ③ it
④ they   ⑤ them

2 빈칸에 공통으로 들어갈 알맞은 단어를 쓰세요.

> • Look at _____ picture.
>   – Wow, it's beautiful.
> • May I speak to Nick, please?
>   – Oh, _____ is Nick.

3 다음 대화의 빈칸에 들어갈 알맞은 단어는?

> *A*: _____ camera is this?
> *B*: It's my father's.

① What   ② Who   ③ Whose
④ Which   ⑤ When

4 다음 빈칸에 알맞은 말을 쓰세요.

> Dorothy likes watching movies. She is going to watch two different movies this week. (1) _____ is science fiction and (2) _____ is horror.

5 다음 빈칸에 들어갈 말이 차례대로 짝지어진 것은?

> Hi, everyone! My name is Codi. __(A)__ am from Canada. My family and I like to travel abroad. __(B)__ favorite country is Korea. __(C)__ has many beautiful places to visit such as Gyeongbokgung Palace.

  (A)   (B)   (C)
① I   – Their – It
② We   – Their – It
③ I   – Our   – He
④ I   – Our   – It
⑤ We   – My   – He

6 다음 빈칸에 들어갈 알맞은 단어는?

> _____ is that tall man?

① Who   ② What   ③ Which
④ When   ⑤ Where

7 다음 대화의 빈칸에 들어갈 알맞은 단어를 쓰세요.

> *A*: _____ do you want, a chocolate cake or a cheesecake?
> *B*: A chocolate cake.

8 다음 빈칸 ⓐ~ⓓ에 들어가지 않는 것은?

- I don't like the red one. Show me _____ⓐ_____.
- There are 30 strawberries in the basket. _____ⓑ_____ of them are rotten.
- Yumi has two dogs. _____ⓒ_____ is black, and _____ⓓ_____ is white.

① some ② one ③ the other
④ the others ⑤ another

9 빈칸에 공통으로 들어갈 알맞은 단어는?

- _____ time is it?
- _____'s the weather like?

① How ② What ③ Who
④ Which ⑤ When

10 우리말을 영어로 표현할 때 ⓐ에 들어갈 단어는?

- 소라는 진희와 똑같은 가방을 가지고 있다.
  = Sora _____ _____ _____ⓐ_____ _____ _____ Jinhee.

① same ② the ③ has
④ bag ⑤ as

11 다음의 빈칸 어디에도 들어갈 수 없는 것을 고르세요.

- This house is _____.
- This house belongs to _____.
- _____ own this house.

① mine ② you ③ he
④ us ⑤ theirs

12 주어진 두 문장을 한 문장으로 바꿀 때 바르게 쓰인 것을 고르세요.

Seho is a curator. I am a curator, too.

① He is a curator.
② You are curators.
③ We are curators.
④ They are curators.
⑤ She and I are curators.

13 다음 빈칸에 공통으로 들어갈 알맞은 단어는?

- _____ a wonderful day!
- _____ do you do on weekends?

① Which ② Where ③ How
④ Who ⑤ What

14 다음 대화의 밑줄 친 부분을 두 단어로 바꾸어 쓰세요.

A: Whose watch is this?
B: It is mine.

➡ _____

15 빈칸에 공통으로 들어갈 단어를 쓰세요.

- _____ is six o'clock in the morning.
- _____ takes 10 minutes to get there.
- _____ is rainy today.

16 다음 우리말과 같은 뜻이 되도록 빈칸에 들어갈 알맞은 단어를 쓰세요.

- 그는 그 자신을 자랑스럽게 여겼다.
  = He felt proud of _____.

17 다음 대화에서 밑줄 친 부분의 어법이 틀린 것은?

A: I don't have a pen. I have to buy ①one.
B: I have two pens. You can use the red one.
A: Thank you. Where is ②it?
B: Oh, I put ③one in my pencil case, but I can't find ④it.
A: Oh, then never mind. I can borrow ⑤one from Paul.

18 다음 빈칸에 들어갈 단어가 순서대로 바르게 짝지어진 것은?

- _____'s your favorite book?
- _____'s your favorite writer?

① What – Who
② Who – When
③ When – Why
④ What – What
⑤ Who – What

19 다음 중 어법상 어색한 문장은?

① Helen and Jack love their son.
② What is your favorite season?
③ This is our house.
④ I have a pig. It's tail is short.
⑤ These are my pictures.

20 다음 빈칸에 공통으로 들어갈 재귀대명사를 쓰세요.

- She looked at _____ in the mirror.
- My mom made this cake _____.
- She said to _____, "It will be okay."

21 다음 중 보기의 밑줄 친 it과 쓰임이 같은 문장은?

보기 | It's fall here. It's getting cold.

ⓐ It's raining now.
ⓑ She bought it for my birthday.
ⓒ How far is it from here to the library?
ⓓ It's my favorite food.
ⓔ It's five o'clock.

① ⓐⓑ   ② ⓐⓑⓒ   ③ ⓐⓒⓔ
④ ⓑⓓⓔ   ⑤ ⓒⓓⓔ

22 다음 글에서 밑줄 친 ⓐ를 괄호 안의 단어를 이용하여 영어로 바르게 옮겨 쓰세요.

The penguin and the *ostrich are birds. ⓐ하지만, 펭귄은 타조와 같지 않다. Its neck and legs are very short. It can't run fast, but can swim well.

*ostrich 타조

➡ But, the penguin is _____
_____.
(same, as)

23 다음 중 밑줄 친 부분이 틀린 것은?

A: How do you like these beautiful fish?
B: ①They are good, but I can't hold them in ②my arms. I like pets with fur.
A: Then how about ③this hamster?
B: Oh, ④its perfect! It has fur, and I can hold ⑤it!

24 다음 대화에서 우리말과 같은 뜻이 되도록 빈칸에 들어갈 알맞은 말을 쓰세요.

> A: Hello, may I speak to Mr. Brown?
> B: Who's calling, please?
> A: _____ _____ John.
> (저는 John이에요.)

25 다음 글의 빈칸에 들어갈 단어가 순서대로 바르게 짝지어진 것은?

> _____ people buy all their needs on the Internet. _____ people don't want to buy them on the Internet.

① Some – Others
② Some – Other
③ One – The others
④ One – Others
⑤ One – Another

26 다음 대화에서 밑줄 친 부분 대신에 쓸 수 있는 단어는?

> A: Can I help you?
> B: Yes, please. Do you have a backpack?
> A: Yes, we do. What color do you want?
> B: A yellow backpack.

① this   ② that   ③ one
④ it   ⑤ else

27 다음 대화의 빈칸에 들어갈 가장 알맞은 문장을 고르세요.

> A: _____
> B: He is a fashion designer.

① What does he do?
② What does he like?
③ How is he?
④ How is he doing?
⑤ What will he do?

28 다음 중 밑줄 친 부분을 생략할 수 없는 것을 고르세요.

① Let me introduce myself.
② I myself went there.
③ Did you cook this meal yourself?
④ John would like to make music himself.
⑤ The cute girl was Sujin herself.

29 다음 글에서 빈칸에 들어가기 적절한 단어는?

> Everyone in this club _____ a musical instrument.

① play   ② plays
③ playing   ④ were playing
⑤ are playing

30 다음 밑줄 친 우리말을 괄호 안의 단어를 이용하여 영어로 바르게 옮겨 쓰세요.

> *Reporter*: You're a famous painter. 모든 사람이 당신의 그림을 좋아하나요?
> *Monet*: Of course. My paintings make people happy.

➡ _____
(everybody)

31 다음 밑줄 친 It의 쓰임이 나머지와 다른 하나는?

① It takes 15 minutes on foot.
② It is eight thirty.
③ It's March 17th.
④ It's a very big clock.
⑤ It's Tuesday today.

32 괄호 안의 단어를 우리말에 맞게 배열하여 문장을 완성하세요.

> • 너는 어떤 계절을 가장 좋아하니?
> = _____
>   (season, you, most, the, which, do, like)

33 다음 대화의 빈칸에 들어갈 알맞은 단어는?

> A: How do I get to Gyeongbokgung?
> B: You can take the subway.
> A: _____ line?
> B: Line 3.

① Who　　② Which　　③ How
④ Where　　⑤ Whose

34 다음 빈칸에 알맞은 것은?

> A: She is good at science. I think she will be a great scientist someday.
> B: I think _____, too.

① so　　② same　　③ as
④ such　　⑤ either

35 다음 밑줄 친 부분을 소유대명사로 바꾼 것 중 잘못된 것은?

① That is his computer.
　= That computer is his.
② This is her hat.
　= This hat is hers.
③ Those are their bags.
　= Those bags are theirs.
④ This is our car.
　= This car is us.
⑤ This is your laptop case.
　= This laptop case is yours.

36 다음 중 어법상 바르지 않은 것을 모두 고르세요.

① Every baby is cute.
② Cut each apple with a knife.
③ He loves every children.
④ Each class is about 35 minutes.
⑤ Everything look beautiful.

37 다음 글의 빈칸에 들어갈 단어가 순서대로 바르게 짝지어진 것은?

> I have two sons. _____ is a teacher, and _____ is a pilot.

① One　– the other　② One　– other
③ Some – other　　　④ Some – the other
⑤ Some – the others

38 다음 밑줄 친 부분을 대명사로 바꾼 것 중 잘못된 것을 고르세요.

① She met Mr. Han. (➡ him)
② I know Sally. (➡ her)
③ He studies Spanish and French. (➡ it)
④ We helped Jason and Cathy. (➡ them)
⑤ They visited Mrs. Lopez. (➡ her)

39 다음 빈칸에 들어갈 단어가 순서대로 짝지어진 것은?

> • I don't like sweets _____ as chocolate.
> • They stayed at the _____ hotel.

① such　– so　　② such – same
③ so　　– such　④ so　　– same
⑤ same – such

CHAPTER 7
부정사

성취도 자기 평가 활용법

구분	평가 기준
Excellent	문법 내용을 모두 이해하고, 문제를 모두 맞힘.
Very good	문법 내용은 충분히 이해했으나 실수로 1~2문제 틀림.
Good	문법 내용이 조금 어려워 3~4문제 틀림.
needs **R**eview	문법 내용 이해가 어렵고, 5문제 이상 틀림, 복습 필요.

PSS 1 명사처럼 쓰이는 to부정사	페이지	학습날짜	성취도 자기평가 E V G R	학습체크
PSS 1-1 주어와 보어로 쓰이는 to부정사	154	/		☐
PSS 1-2 목적어로 쓰이는 to부정사	155	/		☐
PSS 2 형용사처럼 쓰이는 to부정사	157	/		☐
PSS 3 부사처럼 쓰이는 to부정사	158	/		☐
PSS 4 to가 없는 원형부정사	페이지	학습날짜	성취도 자기평가 E V G R	학습체크
PSS 4-1 사역동사(let, have, make)+목적어+원형부정사	160	/		☐
PSS 4-2 지각동사(hear, see, watch, feel)+목적어+원형부정사	161	/		☐
Chapter Review Test	163	/		☐

명사처럼 쓰이는 to부정사

PSS 1-1 주어와 보어로 쓰이는 to부정사

「to+동사원형」의 형태로 동사의 의미나 성질을 가지면서 동시에 명사, 형용사, 부사의 역할을 하는 것을 to부정사라고 한다. to부정사가 명사처럼 쓰일 때는 문장 안에서 주어, 목적어, 보어의 역할을 하며 '~하는 것'으로 풀이된다.

> swim '수영하다' ➡ to swim '수영하는 것'
> play the guitar '기타를 치다' ➡ to play the guitar '기타를 치는 것'
> study English '영어를 공부하다' ➡ to study English '영어를 공부하는 것'

1. **주어**
   To use chopsticks isn't easy. = **It** isn't easy **to use** chopsticks.
   젓가락을 사용하는 것은 쉽지 않다.
   To play the piano is a lot of fun. = **It** is a lot of fun **to play** the piano.
   피아노를 치는 것은 아주 재미있다.
   cf. to부정사가 주어인 경우에는 주어 자리에 it을 쓰고 to부정사를 뒤로 보낼 수 있다. to부정사로 시작하는 문장보다 「It ~ to부정사」 구문이 보다 자연스러운 문장이다. 이때 쓰인 it을 가주어라고 하고, to부정사구를 진주어라고 한다.

2. **보어**
   My hobby is **to read** books. 나의 취미는 책을 읽는 것이다.
   My goal is **to lose** five kilograms. 나의 목표는 5킬로그램을 감량하는 것이다.

PRACTICE 1

〈보기〉와 같이 주어진 문장을 바꾸어 쓰세요.

> 보기   To send an e-mail is simple. ➡ It is simple to send an e-mail.
> To find your house was difficult. ➡ It was difficult <u>to find your house</u>.

1. To visit a historic place is interesting.
   ➡ It is interesting _____.

2. To raise cows is a farmer's work.
   ➡ _____ to raise cows.

3. To make good friends is helpful to your life.
   ➡ It is helpful to your life _____.

4 To stay here for a week was my plan.
➡ _____ to stay here for a week.

5 To get enough sleep is good for your health.
➡ It is good for your health _____.

6 To get lost in these woods was very dangerous.
➡ _____ to get lost in these woods.

정답 p.29

PRACTICE 2

주어진 동사를 동사원형 또는 to부정사 중 알맞은 형태를 골라 빈칸에 쓰세요.

1 go
(1) I want _____ to Disneyland.
(2) Who should I _____ to Disneyland with?

2 learn
(1) Her plan is _____ how to swim.
(2) We all _____ by experience.

3 visit
(1) My hope is _____ New York.
(2) I _____ my grandparents' house every weekend.

PSS 1-2 목적어로 쓰이는 to부정사

1. to부정사를 목적어로 쓰는 동사들은 다음과 같다.

begin	decide	expect	hope	like	love
need	plan	start	try	want	would like

+ to부정사

I **hope to be** a famous musician. 나는 유명한 음악가가 되기를 바란다.
I **like to study** the stars. 나는 별을 연구하는 것을 좋아한다.
We **decided to give** Jim a birthday party. 우리는 Jim에게 생일 파티를 열어주기로 결정했다.

2. 「의문사+to부정사」는 문장 안에서 주로 목적어 역할을 한다.
I don't know **how to drive** a car. 나는 차를 운전하는 방법을 모른다.
We haven't decided **when to meet**. 우리는 언제 만날지 결정하지 않았다.
Do you know **what to do** in an emergency? 너는 응급상황에 무엇을 해야 하는지 아니?
I'm not sure **where to visit** in Spain. 나는 스페인에서 어디를 방문해야 할지 모르겠다.

PRACTICE 3

〈보기〉에서 알맞은 동사를 골라 to부정사의 형태로 바꾸어 빈칸에 쓰세요.

| 보 기 | buy   meet   watch   live   come   start |

1 We planned _____ jogging next week.
2 Ingyu needs _____ a book.
3 I want _____ in a peaceful world.
4 I hope _____ the president.
5 She loves _____ the stars in the sky.
6 Would you like _____ to dinner?

PRACTICE 4

우리말과 같은 뜻이 되도록 괄호 안에 주어진 단어를 바르게 배열하세요.

1 비가 오기 시작했다.
    = Rain _____. (fall, to, began)
2 그들은 그 호텔에서 머무르기를 기대했다.
    = They _____ at the hotel. (to, stay, expected)
3 나는 이 기계를 어떻게 쓰는지 모른다.
    = I have no idea _____ this machine. (use, to, how)
4 그의 친구들은 그를 그곳에서 만나기로 결정했다.
    = His friends _____ there. (meet, to, decided, him)
5 나는 토마토를 재배하기 시작했다.
    = I _____. (tomatoes, grow, started, to)
6 너는 나에게 마트에서 무엇을 살지 말해줄 수 있니?
    = Can you tell me _____ at the market? (to, what, buy)
7 그녀는 매일 일기를 쓰려고 노력한다.
    = She _____ a diary every day. (keep, tries, to)
8 저에게 시청에 가는 방법을 알려주시겠어요?
    = Could you tell me _____ to City Hall? (get, how, to)

형용사처럼 쓰이는 to부정사

to부정사가 명사나 대명사를 뒤에서 꾸며주는 형용사의 역할을 할 때는 '~할, ~해야 할'로 풀이된다.

She has many interesting **books to read**. 그녀는 읽을 많은 재미있는 책을 가지고 있다.

They looked for **something to eat**. 그들은 먹을 것을 찾았다.

cf. 형용사는 보통 수식하는 명사 앞에 쓰이지만, to부정사는 명사 뒤에서 수식한다.

I need **cold water**. 나는 차가운 물이 필요하다.

I need **water to drink**. 나는 마실 물이 필요하다.

Could you give me **a chair to sit on**? 앉을 의자를 저에게 주실 수 있나요?

정답 p.29

PRACTICE 5

괄호 안에 주어진 말 중 알맞은 것을 고르세요.

1 I have a lot of (to do chores, chores to do).
2 It was your (turn to introduce, introduce to turn) your family.
3 The museum is a good (place to visit, visit to place).
4 We had no (to talk chance, chance to talk) together.
5 My family doesn't have any (time to exercise, to exercise time).
6 He wanted a (sail to ship, ship to sail).
7 She is asking for (something to put on, to put on something).
8 It's (time say to, time to say) good-bye.
9 People need clean (air to breathe, to breathe air).
10 Is there (anything to read, to read anything) here?

정답 p.30

PRACTICE 6

우리말과 일치하도록 괄호 안에 주어진 단어를 활용하여 빈칸에 알맞은 말을 쓰세요.

1 돌아갈 시간이다.
   = It is _____. (go back, time)

2 우리는 먹을 것을 살 필요가 있다.
= We need to buy _____. (eat, something)

3 경주는 방문하기에 멋진 도시였다.
= Gyeongju was a nice _____. (city, visit)

4 아버지는 입을 셔츠를 찾지 못했다.
= My father didn't find a _____. (shirt, wear)

5 인호는 다음 주 금요일에 치를 시험이 있다.
= Inho has a _____ next Friday. (take, test)

6 그녀는 지불해야 할 치과 의사의 청구서를 받았다.
= She got the dentist's _____. (bill, pay)

PSS 3 부사처럼 쓰이는 to부정사

to부정사는 부사처럼 동사, 형용사 등을 꾸며주는 역할을 한다.

1. 목적 '~하기 위해서'

   He **used** science **to help** many people. 그는 많은 사람들을 돕기 위해서 과학을 이용했다.
   I **went** to the store **to buy** a backpack. 나는 배낭을 사기 위해서 가게에 갔다.

2. 형용사 수식 '~하기에'

   This problem is **difficult to solve**. 이 문제는 풀기에 어렵다.
   The books are **hard to understand**. 그 책들은 이해하기에 어렵다.

3. 감정의 원인 '~하니, ~하게 되어'

   | glad | happy | pleased | sad | sorry | surprised |

   I'm **glad to see** you. 나는 당신을 보니 기쁘다.
   He was **surprised to learn** that she was deaf. 그는 그녀가 귀가 멀었다는 것을 알게 되어 놀랐다.

4. 결과 '~해서 (결국) …하다'

   My grandfather **lived to be** 80 years old. 나의 할아버지는 80세까지 사셨다.
   She **grew up to be** a doctor. 그녀는 자라서 결국 의사가 되었다.

PRACTICE 7

〈보기〉에서 알맞은 표현을 골라 to부정사의 형태로 바꾸어 빈칸에 쓰세요.

보 기	make cookies	play soccer	be 100 years old
	watch with children	be a famous painter	hear the bad news
	find a new cure	understand without a dictionary	

1 He grew up _____.

2 I am sorry _____.

3 She used flour _____.

4 The old man lived _____.

5 The doctors are happy _____.

6 The movie is not good _____.

7 The word isn't easy _____.

8 How many players do you need _____?

PRACTICE 8

다음 문장을 밑줄 친 to부정사의 사용에 유의하여 우리말로 해석하세요.

1 What do you want to buy?
   ➡ _____

2 It is important to set goals.
   ➡ _____

3 It's time to get up.
   ➡ _____

4 We cut down trees to make paper.
   ➡ _____

5 What can we do to lose weight?
   ➡ _____

6 His novel was easy to read.
   ➡ _____

7 To see is to believe.
   ➡ _____

8 She lived to be 80 years old.
   ➡ _____

to가 없는 원형부정사

PSS 4-1 사역동사(let, have, make) + 목적어 + 원형부정사

Let me introduce my friend to you.

She helps her mom (to) wash the dishes.

원형부정사는 to부정사와 형태상으로 비교해 볼 때 to 없이 동사원형만으로 이루어져 있다. 사역동사의 목적격 보어로 쓰인다.

사역동사 + 목적어 + 원형부정사 '~가 …하게 하다'

- **Let** **me** **show** you an example. 내가 네게 하나의 예를 보여줄게.
- The teacher **had** **students** **clean** their classroom. 선생님은 학생들이 그들의 교실을 청소하게 했다.
- She **makes** **her son** **keep** a diary every day. 그녀는 그녀의 아들이 매일 일기를 쓰게 한다.

cf. 준사역동사인 help는 목적격 보어로 원형부정사 대신 to부정사를 쓰기도 한다.
I **helped** him **(to) do** his homework. 나는 그가 그의 숙제를 하는 것을 도와주었다.

정답 p.30

PRACTICE 9

〈보기〉와 같이 우리말과 같은 뜻이 되도록 주어진 단어를 순서대로 배열하세요.

| 보 기 | 나의 학창 시절에 대해 이야기해 줄게.
= <u>Let me tell you</u> about my school days. (tell, you, me, let) |

1. 내가 네 가방을 들어줄게.
   = _____ your bag. (hold, let, me)

2. 꽃은 사람들을 기분 좋게 만든다.
   = Flowers _____. (good, make, people, feel)

3. 컴퓨터는 우리가 다른 이들과 대화하도록 도울 수 있다.
   = Computers can _____. (others, us, help, with, chat)

4 화학 약품은 잡초를 죽게 한다.
  = Chemicals _____. (weeds, die, make)

5 그들은 내가 여름 내내 머물도록 해줄 것이다.
  = They'll _____ for the whole summer. (me, let, stay)

6 나는 내 여동생이 매일 책을 읽게 했다.
  = I _____ every day. (read, my, books, had, sister)

PSS 4-2 지각동사(hear, see, watch, feel)＋목적어＋원형부정사

I **heard** Mary **sing**.

He **saw** them **cross** the road.

지각동사의 목적격 보어로 원형부정사가 쓰인다.

지각동사 ＋ 목적어 ＋ 원형부정사 '~가 …하는 것을 듣다/보다/느끼다'

- I **heard** her **play** the violin. 나는 그녀가 바이올린을 연주하는 것을 들었다.
- They **saw** Jack **go** out. 그들은 Jack이 외출하는 것을 보았다.
- She **watched** him **steal** the bag. 그녀는 그가 가방을 훔치는 것을 목격했다.
- We **felt** the house **shake**. 우리는 집이 흔들리는 것을 느꼈다.

cf. 동작이 진행 중임을 강조할 때는 지각동사의 목적격 보어로 현재분사(-ing)를 쓰기도 한다.
  I **heard** her **playing** the violin. 나는 그녀가 바이올린을 연주하고 있는 것을 들었다.

정답 p.30

PRACTICE 10

괄호 안에 주어진 표현 중 알맞은 것을 고르세요.

1 She helped us (solving, to solve) this problem.

2 They saw him (play, to play) football.

3 We felt the storm (comes, coming).

4 Tim watched his brother (cross, crosses) the street.

5 Let me (show, to show) you something.

6 Mr. Smith made his wife (cleans, clean) the room.

7 I saw the girl (sells, selling) flowers.

8 I had my daughter (run, to run) an errand.

9 She heard him (calling, called) her name.

10 Could you let me (know, knowing) the deadline for this project?

PRACTICE 11

〈보기〉에서 알맞은 단어를 골라 빈칸에 쓰세요.

보 기	run wait go shout bring swim

1 They watched me _____ out.

2 He had his son _____ a glass of water.

3 They heard her _____ .

4 The man made us _____ for an hour.

5 I saw the dog _____ after me.

6 Her parents didn't let her _____ in the sea.

PRACTICE 12

괄호 안에 주어진 표현 중 알맞은 것을 고르세요.

1 Let me (write, to write) it down.

2 Have you ever learned how (swim, to swim)?

3 Did you let him (go, to go) home?

4 He made his son (study, to study) abroad.

5 Mr. Han had Linda (wait, to wait) for him.

6 Have you ever seen a chicken (fly, to fly)?

7 I can't hear him (talk, to talk).

8 Please tell me how (using, to use) this.

9 Can I help you (find, finding) the website?

10 I saw a blind man (to walk, walking).

11 I could feel someone (to look, looking) at me.

12 She showed me how (getting, to get) to the station.

Chapter Review Test

CHAPTER 7 부정사

1 다음 빈칸에 들어갈 말로 알맞은 것은?

> I hope to hear from you soon and _____ some volunteer work there.

① done ② doing
③ to do ④ to doing
⑤ is doing

2 밑줄 친 부분 중 잘못 쓰인 것을 고르세요.

> ① My hobby is ② go for a ③ walk ④ in the park ⑤ every morning.

3 다음 주어진 단어를 우리말에 맞게 배열한 문장은?

> • 그들은 그에게 무엇을 사주길 원하니?
> = What (want, they, do, buy, to) for him?

① What they want to do buy for him?
② What to want buy do they for him?
③ What they want buy to do for him?
④ What do they want to buy for him?
⑤ What buy they want do to for him?

4 다음 중 어법상 어색한 문장을 고르세요.

① We want to live in a world with no war.
② He went to the store to buy a present.
③ I love go shopping.
④ She likes to wear a skirt.
⑤ They hope to see her.

5 다음 우리말과 같은 뜻이 되도록 빈칸에 들어갈 알맞은 말을 쓰세요.

> • 당신은 할 일이 많은가요?
> = Do you have much work _____ _____?

6 다음 주어진 문장의 밑줄 친 부분과 쓰임이 같은 것은?

> <u>It</u> is difficult to remove this stain.

① <u>It</u> is dark outside.
② <u>It</u> is October 5th.
③ <u>It</u> is used to make cookies.
④ <u>It</u> is not mine. It's Jinu's.
⑤ <u>It</u> is easy to get there by bus.

7 다음 밑줄 친 부분의 쓰임이 잘못된 것을 고르세요.

> A: This room <u>is</u>① very <u>cold</u>②.
> B: <u>Let</u>③ me <u>closes</u>④ the <u>window</u>⑤.

8 다음 주어진 문장에서 잘못된 부분을 찾아 바르게 고쳐 쓰세요.

> We decided inviting you to the party.

→ _____

9 다음 그림을 보고 빈칸에 들어갈 알맞은 말을 써서 대화를 완성하세요.

(1)
Q: Do you know _____ _____ _____ a bike?
A: No, I don't.

(2)
Q: Do you know _____ _____ _____ to the library?
A: Sure. Go straight and turn right. It's on your left.

(1) 자전거를 타는 방법
➡ _____ _____ _____ a bike

(2) 도서관에 가는 방법
➡ _____ _____ _____ to the library

10 다음 빈칸에 들어갈 말로 알맞은 것은?

Mira is happy _____ her friends again.

① see   ② sees   ③ to seeing
④ to see   ⑤ will see

11 다음 빈칸에 들어갈 동사의 알맞은 형태를 고르세요.

He made me _____ the house.

① paint   ② paints   ③ painted
④ to paint   ⑤ painting

12 다음 주어진 문장의 밑줄 친 부분과 쓰임이 다른 하나는?

To see is to believe.

① It was not easy to read this book.
② To travel abroad is great.
③ To take exercise is a good habit.
④ It is helpful to keep a diary in English.
⑤ People use computers to save time.

13 빈칸에 들어갈 알맞은 말을 두 개 고르세요.

• 나는 그녀가 수영장에서 수영하는 것을 보았다.
= I saw her _____ in the pool.

① swim   ② swims   ③ swam
④ swimming   ⑤ to swim

14 주어진 문장의 밑줄 친 부분과 용법이 같은 것은?

We went there to help him.

① Kids love to play with toys.
② I cut down these trees to make a boat.
③ I want something to eat.
④ He started to run fast.
⑤ To read a book is very interesting.

15 다음 빈칸에 들어갈 수 없는 것은?

We _____ to make our club mascot.

① needed   ② enjoyed   ③ planned
④ wanted   ⑤ decided

16 다음 중 빈칸에 to를 쓸 수 있는 것은?

① I heard my mother _____ call my name.
② My sister helped me _____ win the race.
③ She didn't let him _____ go out and play.
④ We felt the ground _____ shake.
⑤ Jenny watched me _____ play baseball.

17 다음 주어진 문장의 밑줄 친 부분과 쓰임이 다른 하나를 고르세요.

> They have no chance to talk together.

① We like to play cards.
② Please give me something to drink.
③ They have no money to buy a house.
④ Sumi has many friends to help her.
⑤ He doesn't have any time to exercise.

18 다음 주어진 문장의 밑줄 친 부분과 쓰임이 같은 것을 고르세요.

> She plans to visit her grandparents.

① Ann went to the library to borrow some books.
② She gives some dessert to her friend.
③ Jack invited Maria to the party at his home.
④ A dog moves its tail from side to side.
⑤ I took a bus to go there.

19 다음 우리말과 같은 뜻이 되도록 주어진 말을 알맞게 배열하세요.

> • 밤에 혼자 길을 걸어가는 것은 위험하다.
> (to walk, it, alone, at night, is, dangerous)

➡ _____

20 다음 빈칸에 들어갈 알맞은 말을 고르세요.

> She will learn _____ this winter.

① what to ski   ② how to ski
③ way to ski   ④ where to ski
⑤ when to ski

21 다음 중 어법상 옳은 것은?

① Let me to show you my new shoes.
② Scott didn't want going to the party.
③ Mike heard a dog to bark late at night.
④ I decided to staying in Canada for a while.
⑤ The book helps me understand math well.

22 다음 밑줄 친 부분의 쓰임이 나머지와 다른 하나를 고르세요.

① She likes to change clothes every morning.
② I want to help poor children in the world.
③ How many players do you need to play soccer?
④ They went there to take part in the recycling campaign.
⑤ Many people went to the park and enjoyed the sun.

23 다음 문장의 밑줄 친 우리말을 영작한 것으로 어법상 옳지 <u>않은</u> 것은?

> I'll buy him a new smartphone <u>그의 생일을 축하하기 위해서</u>.

① to celebrate his birthday
② in order to celebrate his birthday
③ in order he to celebrate his birthday
④ so that I can celebrate his birthday
⑤ in order that I can celebrate his birthday

24 다음 빈칸에 공통으로 들어갈 말을 고르세요.

> • We are going _____ go fishing this weekend.
> • You have _____ see a doctor today.
> • She tries _____ take a walk every day.
> • Tom decided _____ take piano lessons on Sundays.

① with   ② from   ③ to
④ in   ⑤ into

25 다음 문장의 밑줄 친 부분과 바꾸어 쓸 수 있는 것은?

> Could you let me know <u>how to produce a map</u>?

① how producing
② how I produced
③ how I should produce
④ how it is produced
⑤ how it has to produce

26 밑줄 친 부분과 쓰임이 같은 것은?

> Dear Premium Store shopper,
> Thank you for being a loyal customer of Premium Store. Our store takes great pride in our attentive staff and our quality products. We strive <u>to ensure</u> that you are satisfied with your shopping experience here. Please answer three short questions to get a chance to win a $200 gift card. The questionnaire link is attached at the bottom of this email. As always, thank you for your loyalty to our store.
> Sincerely,
> Sue Marrie, Owner and General Manager

① Mark hopes <u>to be</u> on a tv show someday.
② I went to the theater <u>to watch</u> a movie.
③ Zack asked me <u>to help</u> him with his work.
④ It is difficult <u>to learn</u> a new language as an adult.
⑤ I want <u>to buy</u> new shoes for the winter.

27 다음 그림을 보고 Jim이 지난주에 한 일의 목적을 괄호 안의 단어를 이용하여 빈칸을 완성하세요.

(1) Jim went to the library _____. (borrow)

(2) Jim went to the post office _____. (send)

CHAPTER 8
동명사

성취도 자기 평가 활용법

구분	평가 기준
Excellent	문법 내용을 모두 이해하고, 문제를 모두 맞힘.
Very good	문법 내용은 충분히 이해했으나 실수로 1~2문제 틀림.
Good	문법 내용이 조금 어려워 3~4문제 틀림.
needs **R**eview	문법 내용 이해가 어렵고, 5문제 이상 틀림. 복습 필요.

Problem Solving Skill	페이지	학습날짜	성취도 자기평가 E V G R	학습체크
PSS 1 동명사의 역할	168	/		☐
PSS 2 동명사를 목적어로 쓰는 동사와 동명사와 to부정사 모두를 목적어로 쓰는 동사	170	/		☐
PSS 3 동명사의 관용 표현	페이지	학습날짜	성취도 자기평가 E V G R	학습체크
PSS 3-1 go+-ing	171	/		☐
PSS 3-2 How[What] about+-ing?	173	/		☐
PSS 3-3 그 외 관용 표현	174	/		☐
Chapter Review Test	176	/		☐

동명사의 역할

「동사원형+-ing」의 형태로 동사의 의미나 성질을 가지면서 명사 역할을 하는 것을 동명사라고 한다.

> cook '요리하다' ➡ cooking '요리하는 것'
> sing a song '노래를 부르다' ➡ singing a song '노래를 부르는 것'
> ride a horse '말을 타다' ➡ riding a horse '말을 타는 것'

동명사는 문장에서 주어, 목적어, 보어의 역할을 한다.

1. 주어
   Sending an e-mail is fast. 이메일을 보내는 것은 빠르다.
   Seeing is believing. 보는 것이 믿는 것이다.

   cf. 동명사 주어는 단수 취급한다.
   Raising pets is good for children. 애완동물들을 키우는 것은 아이들에게 좋다.

2. 보어
   Her hobby is **collecting** stamps. 그녀의 취미는 우표를 수집하는 것이다.
   My favorite activity is **drawing** pictures. 내가 가장 좋아하는 활동은 그림을 그리는 것이다.

3. 타동사의 목적어
   We **enjoyed talking** about Korea and America. 우리는 한국과 미국에 대해 이야기하는 것을 즐겼다.
   I think we should **start exercising**. 나는 우리가 운동하는 것을 시작해야 한다고 생각한다.

4. 전치사의 목적어
   I learned a lot **about farming**. 나는 농사짓는 것에 대해 많이 배웠다.
   Thank you **for inviting** me. 나를 초대해줘서 고마워.

PRACTICE 1

정답 p.32

〈보기〉에서 알맞은 동사를 골라 동명사의 형태로 바꾸어 빈칸에 쓰세요.

보기	take	draw	play	become	come
	buy	keep	exercise	join	read

1 Have you finished _____ that magazine?

2 Her good habit is _____ a diary every day.

3 _____ regularly is good for our health.

4 Thank you for _____ to see me.

5 Hana is good at _____ the piano.

6 Do you mind _____ the subway?

7 I like _____ cartoons.

8 They talked about _____ a book club.

9 My dream is _____ a teacher.

10 _____ a book through the Internet is easy.

정답 p.32

PRACTICE 2

밑줄 친 동명사의 쓰임과 같은 것을 〈보기〉에서 골라 그 번호를 쓰세요.

| 보 기 | ① Talking with him is boring.
② Our goal is winning a prize.
③ She finished writing the report.
④ Cats are good at climbing. |
|---|---|

1 Riding a bicycle is fun. [   ]

2 I love studying wild flowers and plants. [   ]

3 Recycling paper is a good idea. [   ]

4 I'm sorry for being late. [   ]

5 Her job is selling flowers. [   ]

6 They didn't practice dancing. [   ]

7 His hobby is listening to classical music. [   ]

8 She really enjoys helping others. [   ]

9 Are you interested in working with children? [   ]

10 Flying the model airplane is a lot of fun. [   ]

11 We need clean water for drinking. [   ]

12 Mike's plan is studying abroad. [   ]

동명사를 목적어로 쓰는 동사와 동명사와 to부정사 모두를 목적어로 쓰는 동사

1. 동명사만을 목적어로 쓰는 동사들

   | enjoy   finish   give up |
   | mind   practice   stop | + -ing

   He **enjoys visiting** other countries. 그는 다른 나라를 방문하는 것을 즐긴다.
   My mother **finished cleaning** the kitchen. 나의 어머니는 부엌을 청소하는 것을 끝내셨다.
   I don't **mind waiting**. 나는 기다리는 것을 꺼려하지 않는다.
   Jack **stopped eating**. Jack은 먹는 것을 멈추었다.
   cf. Jack stopped **to eat**. Jack은 먹기 위해서 멈추었다.
     여기서 to eat은 '~하기 위해서'라는 뜻의 목적을 나타내는 to부정사의 부사적 용법으로 쓰였다.

2. 동명사와 to부정사 모두를 목적어로 쓰는 동사들

   | begin   start   continue |
   | like   love   prefer   hate | + -ing / to부정사

   It **started raining**. = It **started to rain**. 비가 내리기 시작했다.
   She **loves reading** a book. = She **loves to read** a book. 그녀는 책을 읽는 것을 좋아한다.

PRACTICE 3

정답 p.32

괄호 안의 단어를 알맞은 형태로 바꾸어 빈칸에 쓰세요. (단, 답이 두 개인 경우 둘 다 쓰세요.)

1 He loves _____ abroad. (travel)

2 I don't mind _____ the door. (open)

3 They continue _____ English. (study)

4 We would like _____ a movie. (watch)

5 Kitty kept _____ for her brother. (wait)

6 We decided _____ to the beach. (go)

7 He will not give up _____ it. (try)

8 The baby started _____ asleep. (fall)

9 Did people finish _____ their dinner? (eat)

10 I hope _____ Jejudo some day. (visit)

11 I enjoy _____ for a walk. (go)

12 I must have a cold. I can't stop _____. (sneeze)

13 Jim expected _____ in New York. (stay)

14 I would like _____ with you. (exercise)

15 Linda began _____ the dishes. (wash)

16 People need _____ the rules. (obey)

17 I hate _____ the dentist. (see)

18 I practice _____ every day. (sing)

19 Cathy likes _____ with children. (play)

20 He wants _____ a car. (drive)

21 I prefer _____ online. (shop)

22 I plan _____ for New York tomorrow. (leave)

PSS 3 동명사의 관용 표현

PSS 3-1 go + -ing

go -ing는 '~하러 가다'라는 의미를 나타낸다.

- go shopping '쇼핑하러 가다'
- go surfing '서핑하러 가다'
- go swimming '수영하러 가다'
- go skating '스케이트 타러 가다'
- go skiing '스키 타러 가다'
- go fishing '낚시하러 가다'
- go camping '야영하러 가다'
- go hiking '하이킹하러 가다'

Let's **go swimming**.

PRACTICE 4

> 보 기   그는 어제 야영하러 갔다.
> = He <u>went camping</u> yesterday. (camp)

1 내일 나는 수영하러 갈 것이다.
= Tomorrow, I'll _____. (swim)

2 우리는 지난 겨울에 스케이트를 타러 갔다.
= We _____ last winter. (skate)

3 그는 딸과 낚시하러 갈 것이다.
= He will _____ with his daughter. (fish)

4 Alex는 여름마다 서핑하러 간다.
= Alex _____ every summer. (surf)

5 그들은 새 상점에 쇼핑하러 갔다.
= They _____ at a new store. (shop)

6 많은 사람들이 그 산에 스키를 타러 간다.
= A lot of people _____ on the mountain. (ski)

7 Paul은 친구와 함께 배를 타러 갔다.
= Paul _____ with his friend. (sail)

8 John은 하이킹 가는 것을 좋아한다.
= John loves to _____. (hike)

9 우리는 저녁식사 후에 드라이브를 하러 갈 것이다.
= We will _____ after dinner. (drive)

10 우리는 Kelly의 파티에 춤추러 갔다.
= We _____ at Kelly's party. (dance)

11 나미는 승마하러 갈 계획을 세웠다.
= Nami planned to _____. (ride)

12 그 남자들은 함께 사냥하러 갔다.
= The men _____ together. (hunt)

13 그녀는 아침에 조깅하러 갔다.
= She _____ in the morning. (jog)

PSS 3-2 How[What] about + -ing?

How about taking some pictures?

How[What] about -ing?는 '~하는 것이 어떠니?'라는 의미를 나타낸다.

How about writing a letter to her? 그녀에게 편지를 쓰는 것이 어떠니?
= **What about writing** a letter to her?
How about using the Internet? 인터넷을 사용하는 것이 어떠니?
= **What about using** the Internet?
How about going shopping? 쇼핑하러 가는 것이 어떠니?
= **What about going** shopping?

cf. How[What] about -ing?는 「Let's+동사원형」으로 바꾸어 쓸 수 있다.
How[What] about going on a picnic? ➡ **Let's go** on a picnic.
소풍 가는 것이 어떠니?   소풍 가자.

정답 p.33

PRACTICE 5

〈보기〉에서 알맞은 동사를 골라 동명사의 형태로 바꾸어 빈칸에 쓰세요.

| 보기 | try | eat | play | stay | do | go | visit | write | take | talk |

1 How about _____ at Minsu's house?
2 How about _____ Mt. Halla?
3 What about _____ a picture?
4 How about _____ to the movie theater?
5 What about _____ a letter to your mom?
6 What about _____ about your family?

7 How about _____ on this skirt?
8 How about _____ your homework?
9 What about _____ basketball?
10 How about _____ pizza for lunch?

PRACTICE 6

정답 p.33

〈보기〉와 같이 주어진 문장을 바꾸어 쓰세요.

| 보 기 | Let's go by bus.
➡ How[What] about going by bus? |

1 Let's help each other. ➡ _____
2 Let's get some rest. ➡ _____
3 Let's keep the promise. ➡ _____
4 Let's have lunch together. ➡ _____
5 Let's go out for some fresh air. ➡ _____
6 Let's drink a cup of coffee. ➡ _____
7 Let's study Spanish. ➡ _____
8 Let's read the newspaper. ➡ _____
9 Let's buy some fruit. ➡ _____
10 Let's sit down on the bench. ➡ _____

PSS 3-3 그 외 관용 표현

1. keep[stop] … from ~ing '…가 ~하는 것을 막다[방지하다]'

   Heavy snow **kept[stopped]** him **from visiting** his hometown.
   폭설이 그가 그의 고향 마을을 방문하는 것을 막았다.

2. spend … ~ing '~하는 데 …를 소비하다'

   My children **spend** too much time **playing** computer games.
   나의 자녀들은 컴퓨터 게임을 하는 데 너무 많은 시간을 소비한다.

PRACTICE 7

〈보기〉와 같이 우리말과 같은 뜻이 되도록 괄호 안의 단어를 알맞은 형태로 바꾸어 빈칸에 쓰세요.

보 기	그는 파티를 여는 데 많은 돈을 쓴다. = He <u>spends</u> a lot of money <u>having</u> a party. (spend, have)

1 빗소리는 그녀가 자는 것을 방해했다.
 = The noise of rain _____ her _____ _____. (stop, from, sleep)

2 그녀는 그 옷을 사는 데 300달러를 썼다.
 = She _____ $300 _____ the dress. (spend, buy)

3 폭설로 나는 외출하지 못했다.
 = The heavy snow _____ me _____ _____ _____.
   (keep, from, go out)

4 Mary는 그녀의 친구들과 이야기하는 데 시간을 보내고 있는 중이다.
 = Mary _____ _____ time _____ with her friends. (spend, talk)

5 그들은 외식하는 데 50달러를 썼다.
 = They _____ $50 _____ _____. (spend, eat out)

6 우리는 그가 떠나는 것을 막을 수 없었다.
 = We couldn't _____ him _____ _____. (keep, from, leave)

7 그는 그 두 소년이 싸우지 못하게 막았다.
 = He _____ the two boys _____ _____. (stop, from, fight)

8 나는 눈물이 나오는 것을 막을 수 없었다.
 = I couldn't _____ tears _____ _____ _____. (keep, from, come out)

9 그녀는 가족들과 이야기하는 데 많은 시간을 보내지 않는다.
 = She doesn't _____ much time _____ with her family. (spend, talk)

10 나는 그 개가 누구도 물지 못하게 막았다.
 = I _____ the dog _____ _____ anyone. (stop, from, bite)

11 공을 차는 것은 대부분의 아이들이 뚱뚱해지는 것을 방지할 수 있다.
 = Kicking a ball can _____ most children _____ _____ fat.
   (keep, from, become)

12 나는 매일 두 시간을 내 휴대폰을 사용하는 데 보낸다.
 = I _____ two hours _____ my cell phone every day. (spend, use)

Chapter Review Test

정답 p.33

CHAPTER 8
동명사

1 밑줄 친 ⓐ~ⓔ중 바르게 쓰인 표현의 개수는?

> Jerry likes ⓐtravelling to foreign countries. He plans ⓑto visit France this summer. He thinks talking with people from different countries ⓒare exciting. So, he has been practicing ⓓspeak French these days. Also, he will go shopping and ⓔtries some cheese when he is there.

① 1개　② 2개　③ 3개　④ 4개　⑤ 5개

2 다음 우리말과 같은 뜻이 되도록 빈칸에 알맞은 단어를 쓰세요.

> • Nami는 일주일에 한 번씩 수영을 하러 간다.
> = Nami goes _____ once a week.

3 다음 빈칸에 알맞지 않은 것을 고르세요.

> Julie _____ reading books.

① began　② wanted　③ loved
④ liked　⑤ hated

4 다음 중 밑줄 친 부분이 바르게 쓰인 것을 고르세요.

① She kept to draw cartoons.
② Protect nature is important.
③ Thank you for help me.
④ Have you finished writing letters?
⑤ How about play the violin?

5 다음 빈칸에 공통으로 들어갈 단어는?

> • She is good at _____.
> • The singer stopped _____ suddenly.

① sing　　　　② to sing
③ sang　　　　④ sings
⑤ singing

6 다음 빈칸에 들어갈 말이 순서대로 바르게 짝지어진 것은?

> • We expected _____ to a rock concert.
> • Susan enjoys _____ care of animals.

① go – take
② to go – taking
③ to go – to take
④ going – taking
⑤ going – to take

7 다음 대화를 읽고, 밑줄 친 우리말을 조건에 맞게 영작하세요.

> A: I'm nervous about the test tomorrow.
> B: 음악을 듣는 것은 어때? It will make you feel better.
> A: Okay, I'll give it a try.

> 조건
> 1. How로 시작하는 의문문으로 쓸 것.
> 2. 5단어로 작성할 것.
> 3. 동명사를 사용할 것.

➡ _____

8 밑줄 친 ⓐ~ⓔ 중 어법상 알맞은 것은?

> Nowadays I have trouble ⓐstudy Chinese characters. My grandmother is Chinese, so we talk in Chinese. I feel confident that I am good at speaking and ⓑlisten to Chinese. However, writing Chinese ⓒare another story. I spend so much time ⓓlearning Chinese characters, but there's no progress. I hope that my Chinese writing skills will improve. If you have any ideas to help me study more efficiently, please let me ⓔknowing.

① ⓐ ② ⓑ ③ ⓒ ④ ⓓ ⑤ ⓔ

9 주어진 문장의 밑줄 친 watch를 알맞은 형태로 바꾼 것은?

> What about watch the movie *King and I* with Mom?

① watch ② watched ③ watching
④ to watch ⑤ watches

10 다음 빈칸에 들어갈 단어가 순서대로 바르게 짝 지어진 것은?

> • The noise kept me from _____.
> • He spends much time _____ with his family.

① sleep – talk
② sleeping – talk
③ sleep – talking
④ slept – talked
⑤ sleeping – talking

11 주어진 문장에서 밑줄 친 go를 알맞은 형태로 고쳐 쓰세요.

> Keep go on this street, and you will get to the subway station.

➡ _____

12 다음 중 어법상 어색한 문장을 고르세요.

① I started exercising.
② They take a walk on weekends.
③ He gave up to climb a tree.
④ Mary likes talking with me.
⑤ We should drink 8 glasses of water a day.

13 다음 우리말과 같은 뜻이 되도록 빈칸에 들어갈 알맞은 말을 고르세요.

> • 그녀는 일하던 것을 멈추고 그에게 그 소식을 말해주었다.
> = She stopped _____ and told him the news.

① work ② working ③ to work
④ was working ⑤ has worked

14 다음 글에서 어법상 틀린 부분을 두 개 골라 바르게 고쳐 쓰세요.

> Paul is a disabled man. But he doesn't give up learn many things. He can play the violin and swim very well. He continues overcome his limitations.
> *disabled: 장애를 가진

(1) _____ ➡ _____
(2) _____ ➡ _____

15 다음 빈칸 (A), (B)에 들어갈 말을 바르게 짝지은 것은?

> I sometimes dream about _____(A)_____ high in the sky. I hope to go to the moon someday. So I want _____(B)_____ an astronaut.

　　(A)　　　　　(B)
① to fly　　　　to become
② flying　　　　to become
③ to fly　　　　becoming
④ flying　　　　becoming
⑤ flying　　　　become

16 다음 빈칸에 들어갈 말이 순서대로 짝지어진 것은?

> • She practices _____ the piano every day.
> • Let's _____ a helping hand to elderly people.

① playing – giving　　② play　　– give
③ playing – give　　　④ to play – give
⑤ to play – giving

17 다음 빈칸에 들어갈 말로 알맞은 것을 모두 고르세요.

> One of my good habits is _____.

① to get up early in the morning
② ate a healthy breakfast
③ recycled paper, glass, and cans
④ keeping a diary every day
⑤ do enough exercise

18 다음 중 문법적으로 옳지 않은 것은?

> Saying no to others ①are difficult. It feels like you're a bad person when you refuse to do something. So, most people ②usually say yes when asked to do a favor. But sometimes, it's not easy ③doing favors for others. That's why you have to learn ④to say no. It will make your life ⑤much easier.

19 다음 밑줄 친 부분이 잘못 쓰인 것을 고르세요.

① We hope to visit Jejudo someday.
② My sister likes cleaning rooms.
③ What about playing soccer?
④ He wanted to go to the mountain.
⑤ I planned staying with you.

20 다음 중 밑줄 친 부분과 쓰임이 다른 것은?

> We finished cleaning the room.

① I stopped walking on the street.
② A woman is carrying a box.
③ Yunha loves reading books.
④ He spent a lot of time riding a bicycle.
⑤ Swimming is good for you.

21 다음 빈칸에 들어갈 말이 차례로 연결된 것은?

In every English class, we spend a lot of time _____ something good about ourselves. We really enjoy _____ this because we can focus on _____ our strengths.

*strength: 장점, 강점

① writing – to do – see
② to write – doing – seeing
③ writing – doing – seeing
④ to write – to do – to see
⑤ writing – do – seeing

22 다음 밑줄 친 부분의 쓰임이 다른 하나는?

① <u>Living</u> in the mountain must be fun.
② <u>Eating</u> too much is bad for your health.
③ His dream was <u>becoming</u> a famous singer.
④ I think <u>getting</u> up early gives me more energy.
⑤ <u>Watching</u> too much TV is not good for children.

23 다음 두 문장의 의미가 같지 <u>않은</u> 것은?

① How about going to a movie tonight?
= Let's go to a movie tonight.
② My hobby is riding a bicycle.
= I like riding a bicycle in my free time.
③ I hate to get up early.
= I hate getting up early.
④ She likes watching soccer games on TV.
= She likes to watch soccer games on TV.
⑤ He stopped picking up the trash.
= He stopped to pick up the trash.

24 다음 대화의 밑줄 친 부분 중 어법상 바른 것을 고르세요.

A: What does Giho ① <u>wants to do</u> this Saturday?
B: He ② <u>want to</u> ③ <u>go fishing</u>.
A: What ④ <u>does Sora going to do</u>?
B: She is going ⑤ <u>to went in-line skating</u>.

25 (A), (B)의 각 네모 안에서 어법상 바른 어휘를 골라 쓰세요.

Trees are useful to both nature and all human beings. They get rid of bad gas in the air and make the air cleaner. They can also keep rivers (A) from / to overflowing because they hold water and let it go little by little. If there are no trees, we will have floods. Therefore, we have to spend more time (B) to plant / planting trees.

(A) _____
(B) _____

26 다음 중 (a)와 (b)의 빈칸에 차례로 들어갈 말로 알맞은 것은?

- We _____(a)_____ to meet again.
- Susan _____(b)_____ practicing the piano.

    (a)   (b)
① expected – enjoys
② planned   – decided
③ kept   – stopped
④ hope   – wants
⑤ gave up   – finished

27 다음 빈칸에 들어갈 말로 알맞게 짝지어진 것은?

- My dad loves _____ pictures.
- He finished _____ the story.

① taking – reading
② to take – to read
③ taking – to read
④ take – to read
⑤ took – reading

28 다음 주어진 단어를 이용하여 우리말에 맞게 빈칸을 채우세요. (단, 필요시 형태를 변화시킬 것)

- 그는 매일 운동하는 것을 포기했다.
  (give up, exercise)

→ He _____ every day.

29 다음 대화의 밑줄 친 ⓐ~ⓔ 중에서 쓰임이 다른 것 두 개를 고르세요.

A: Hello. Who's ⓐcalling?
B: This is Kate. Can I speak to James?
A: Speaking. What's up?
B: My computer is not ⓑworking again. Do you mind ⓒcoming over to fix it?
A: Sorry, I can't. I'm ⓓgoing out to pick up my sister. How about tomorrow?
B: Okay. How about ⓔmeeting at 3?
A: Great. I'll see you tomorrow.

① ⓐ ② ⓑ ③ ⓒ ④ ⓓ ⑤ ⓔ

30 어법상 바르지 <u>않은</u> 것을 <u>두 개</u> 고르세요.

① She finished painting the walls.
② They practiced to play the guitar.
③ Sally began to walk along the beach.
④ We spent lots of time changing the rules.
⑤ Taking pictures are very interesting.

31 다음 중 어법상 올바른 것으로 짝지어진 것은?

I play with my dog, Jackie, after I finish _____(A)_____ my room every Sunday morning. He always wants _____(B)_____ with me. And I spend lots of time _____(C)_____ on Sunday afternoon.

	(A)	(B)	(C)
①	cleaning	playing	to read
②	cleaning	to play	reading
③	to clean	playing	reading
④	to clean	to play	to read
⑤	to clean	playing	to read

32 다음 중 밑줄 친 부분의 쓰임이 다른 하나는?

① I apologize for <u>being</u> late.
② He is <u>worrying</u> about the exam.
③ <u>Making</u> cookies is a lot of fun.
④ <u>Taking</u> the stairs can be good exercise.
⑤ Are you tired of <u>eating</u> the same food every day?

CHAPTER 9
분사

성취도 자기 평가 활용법

구분	평가 기준
(E)xcellent	문법 내용을 모두 이해하고, 문제를 모두 맞힘.
(V)ery good	문법 내용은 충분히 이해했으나 실수로 1~2문제 틀림.
(G)ood	문법 내용이 조금 어려워 3~4문제 틀림.
needs (R)eview	문법 내용 이해가 어렵고, 5문제 이상 틀림. 복습 필요.

Problem Solving Skill	페이지	학습날짜	성취도 자기평가 E V G R	학습체크
PSS 1 현재분사와 과거분사의 형태와 개념	182	/		☐
PSS 2 명사를 수식하는 현재분사와 과거분사	183	/		☐
PSS 3 동사의 활용에 쓰이는 현재분사와 과거분사	185	/		☐
PSS 4 현재분사와 동명사의 비교	186	/		☐
PSS 5 감정을 나타내는 분사	187	/		☐
Chapter Review Test	190	/		☐

현재분사와 과거분사의 형태와 개념

falling leaves
떨어지고 있는 나뭇잎

fallen leaves
떨어진 나뭇잎

「동사원형+-ing/-ed」의 형태로 동사를 형용사처럼 쓸 수 있게 변형한 것을 분사라고 한다.

현재분사(-ing)	과거분사(-ed)
a **boring** speech 지루하게 하는 연설 (능동)	a **bored** audience 지루해진 청중 (수동)
a **burning** building 불에 타고 있는 건물 (진행)	a **burned** building 불에 탄 건물 (완료)

PRACTICE 1

정답 p.35

〈보기〉와 같이 우리말과 같은 뜻이 되도록 괄호 안의 단어를 알맞은 형태로 바꾸어 빈칸에 쓰세요.

보 기	날아가는 새 = a <u>flying</u> bird (fly)

1 죽어가는 나무들
　= _____ trees (die)

2 실종된 어린이들
　= _____ children (lose)

3 울리는 전화
　= a _____ telephone (ring)

4 잊혀진 이야기
　= a _____ story (forget)

5 잠자고 있는 고양이
　= a _____ cat (sleep)

6 이름
　= a _____ name (give)

7 갓 구워진 빵
　= freshly _____ bread (bake)

8 구르는 돌
　= a _____ stone (roll)

9 중고차
　= a _____ car (use)

10 떠오르는 태양
　= the _____ Sun (rise)

11 미소 짓는 아기
　= a _____ baby (smile)

12 깨진 창문
　= a _____ window (break)

명사를 수식하는 현재분사와 과거분사

분사가 홀로 명사를 꾸며줄 때는 명사 앞에 위치하고, 구를 이루어 명사를 꾸며줄 때는 명사 뒤에 위치한다. '능동'이나 '진행'의 의미일 때는 현재분사를 쓰고, '수동'이나 '완료'의 의미일 때는 과거분사를 쓴다.

현재분사	능동	She has an **interesting book**. 그녀는 흥미로운 책을 가지고 있다.
	진행	He knows **that girl standing** at the gate. 그는 정문에 서 있는 저 소녀를 안다.
과거분사	수동	Jessica is **the actress loved** by a lot of people. Jessica는 많은 사람들에게 사랑받는 여배우이다.
	완료	There are a lot of **closed stores**. 문을 닫은 상점들이 많다.

PRACTICE 2

그림을 보고, 괄호 안의 단어를 알맞은 형태로 바꾸어 빈칸에 쓰세요.

1

2

3

1 She carried the _____ chair. (break)

2 Look at the kites _____ in the sky. (fly)

3 The _____ girl is so beautiful. (dance)

4 There are two candles _____ on the table. (burn)

5 Tom bought a _____ bicycle at a garage sale. (use)

6 I want to live in the house _____ of red brick. (build)

PRACTICE 3

정답 p.35

괄호 안에 주어진 단어 중 알맞은 것을 고르세요.

1 That (singing, sung) bird is a sparrow.

2 He told her the (surprising, surprised) news.

3 The boy (picking, picked) up trash is my son.

4 The money (spending, spent) for Christmas is too much.

5 You are like a (walking, walked) dictionary.

6 This is the (borrowing, borrowed) pen.

7 We took the (dying, died) dog to the pet hospital to save him.

8 This is a book (writing, written) in English.

9 He is the very person (bearing, born) in Europe.

10 Do you know the man (crossing, crossed) the street?

11 Water (coming, come) from factories is dirty.

12 She found her (losing, lost) daughter.

13 Look at the girl (listening, listened) to music.

14 Show me the picture (painting, painted) by Yumi.

15 Isn't it a (finishing, finished) product?

16 I'll keep my fingers (crossing, crossed) for you.

동사의 활용에 쓰이는 현재분사와 과거분사

현재분사	진행형	be동사와 현재분사가 결합하여 진행형을 만든다. I **am cleaning** this room. 나는 이 방을 청소하고 있다. He **was writing** some letters. 그는 몇 통의 편지를 쓰고 있었다.
과거분사	완료형	have/has와 과거분사가 결합하여 완료형을 만든다. I **have cleaned** this room. 나는 이 방을 청소했다. He **has written** some letters. 그는 몇 통의 편지를 썼다.
	수동태	be동사와 과거분사가 결합하여 수동태를 만든다. This room **was cleaned** by me. 이 방은 나에 의해 청소되었다. Some letters **were written** by him. 몇 통의 편지가 그에 의해 쓰여졌다.

정답 p.36

PRACTICE 4

괄호 안에 주어진 단어 중 알맞은 것을 고르세요.

1. The radio was (breaking, broken) by my brother.
2. I have never (being, been) on an airplane.
3. We are (living, lived) together.
4. Two trees were (planting, planted) in her garden.
5. He is (eating, eaten) lunch.
6. I was (practicing, practiced) the piano.
7. The street is (calling, called) Chester Street.
8. Her bag is (stealing, stolen).
9. Has she (working, worked) for this company?
10. I have (making, made) a lot of friends.
11. Some houses were (flooding, flooded) by rain.
12. Have you ever (riding, ridden) a horse?
13. Children are (making, made) snowmen.
14. I have (doing, done) this work.
15. Some girls were (walking, walked) in the rain.

현재분사와 동명사의 비교

현재분사	동명사
1. 「be동사+현재분사」는 '~하는 중이다'의 뜻으로 진행을 나타낸다. She is **taking** pictures. 그녀는 사진을 찍고 있는 중이다.	1. 「be동사+동명사」는 '~하는 것이다'의 뜻으로 이때 동명사는 주격 보어의 역할을 한다. Her hobby is **taking** pictures. 그녀의 취미는 사진을 찍는 것이다.
2. 「현재분사+명사」는 '~하고 있는'의 뜻으로 명사를 꾸며주며, 현재의 상태나 현재 진행중인 동작을 나타낸다. a **sleeping** baby 자고 있는 아기	2. 「동명사+명사」는 명사의 용도나 목적을 나타낸다. a **sleeping** bag 침낭

PRACTICE 5

정답 p.36

밑줄 친 부분이 현재분사와 동명사 중 어느 것인지 구분하여 쓰세요.

1 Christmas is <u>coming</u> soon. [   ]
2 Take a seat in the <u>waiting</u> room. [   ]
3 They told us an <u>interesting</u> story. [   ]
4 Bring me some <u>shopping</u> bags. [   ]
5 His job is <u>making</u> bread. [   ]
6 All <u>living</u> things need air. [   ]
7 My hobby is <u>collecting</u> foreign coins. [   ]
8 The leaves are <u>changing</u> colors. [   ]
9 My goal is <u>running</u> my own business. [   ]
10 He bought a pair of <u>running</u> shoes. [   ]
11 My mother was <u>waiting</u> for me. [   ]
12 His problem is not <u>keeping</u> an appointment. [   ]

감정을 나타내는 분사

The game is **exciting**.
Many people are **excited** about the game.

감정을 일으키는 -ing

The film was **moving**.
그 영화는 감동적이었다.
His job is **boring**.
그의 일은 지루하다.
The news was **surprising**.
그 소식은 놀라웠다.
Science is very **interesting**.
과학은 매우 흥미진진하다.
It was **disappointing** news to me.
그것은 나에게 실망스러운 소식이었다.
The movie was pretty **shocking**.
그 영화는 꽤 충격적이었다.

감정을 느끼는 -ed

Many people were **moved** by the film.
많은 사람들이 그 영화에 감동 받았다.
He is **bored** with his job.
그는 그의 일에 지루해 한다.
We were **surprised** at the news.
우리는 그 소식에 놀랐다.
Ted is **interested** in science.
Ted는 과학에 흥미를 가지고 있다.
I was **disappointed** at the news.
나는 그 소식에 실망했다.
She was **shocked** by the movie.
그녀는 그 영화에 충격을 받았다.

※ 그 외 감정을 나타내는 동사의 분사형

amazing '놀라운'	amazed '놀란'
depressing '우울하게 하는'	depressed '우울한'
pleasing '기쁘게 하는'	pleased '기쁜'
satisfying '만족스럽게 하는'	satisfied '만족스러운'
tiring '지치게 하는'	tired '지친'
frustrating '좌절감을 주는'	frustrated '좌절감을 느끼는'
confusing '혼란스럽게 하는'	confused '혼란스러워 하는'
worrying '걱정스러운'	worried '걱정하는'
annoying '짜증스러운'	annoyed '짜증이 난'

PRACTICE 6

〈보기〉와 같이 주어진 단어를 분사 형태로 바꾸어 빈칸에 쓰세요.

| 보 기 | bore
① The TV program will be boring.
② He was bored with reading. |

1 interest
① I heard some _____ stories this morning.
② I'm _____ in farming.

2 please
① They will be very _____ with the news.
② The design of this sofa is _____.

3 shock
① His death was _____ to us.
② My family was _____ at the news.

4 move
① Kate was _____ by his letter.
② His words are _____.

5 excite
① Surfing is really _____.
② Sujin is very _____ about this picnic.

6 disappoint
① His novel was _____.
② David was _____ because he lost the game.

PRACTICE 7

그림을 보고, 괄호 안의 단어를 알맞은 형태로 바꾸어 빈칸에 쓰세요.

1

2

3

1 He has studied all day. He feels _____. (tire)
2 I was very _____ by her present. (surprise)
3 Superman has _____ powers. (amaze)
4 Mary got a _____ result. (satisfy)
5 I'm _____. I've lost my wallet. (depress)
6 Her story is so _____. (bore)

정답 p.36

PRACTICE 8

괄호 안에 주어진 단어 중 알맞은 것을 고르세요.

1 You can see an (interesting, interested) musical here.
2 He always looks (tiring, tired).
3 She did (amazed, amazing) things.
4 Don't be (surprised, surprising) at the result.
5 I was (moving, moved) by his behavior.
6 How (shocked, shocking) the accident was!
7 All of the dishes are (satisfying, satisfied).
8 The performance was (disappointing, disappointed).
9 I couldn't find the place because of this (confused, confusing) map.
10 He went outside because he felt (bored, boring).
11 My sister was (pleased, pleasing) with her new bike.
12 This is a (frustrated, frustrating) time for Mr. Brown.

Chapter Review Test

정답 p.37   CHAPTER **9** 분사

1 우리말과 같은 뜻이 되도록 빈칸에 들어갈 알맞은 단어를 고르세요.

> • 깨진 창문 좀 봐.
> = Look at the _____ window.

① break   ② broken   ③ breaking
④ broke   ⑤ breaks

2 다음 빈칸에 공통으로 들어갈 알맞은 말을 고르세요.

> • My cell phone is _____ .
> • I heard the phone _____ .

① ring   ② rang   ③ rung
④ to ring   ⑤ ringing

3 다음 대화의 빈칸에 들어갈 수 <u>없는</u> 것은?

> A: You like sports, don't you?
> B: Yes, I think they're _____ .

① enjoyable   ② fun   ③ boring
④ interesting   ⑤ exciting

4 다음 밑줄 친 부분의 쓰임이 나머지 넷과 <u>다른</u> 것은?

① Seeing is <u>believing</u>.
② They are <u>talking</u> about pop music.
③ <u>Climbing</u> a mountain is their favorite activity.
④ My goal is <u>speaking</u> English fluently.
⑤ The topic is <u>keeping</u> pets at home.

5 다음 빈칸에 들어갈 말이 순서대로 바르게 짝지어진 것은?

> • I saw a girl _____ glasses.
> • We enjoyed _____ at the full moon.

① to wear – looking
② wear – to look
③ wearing – looking
④ wearing – to look
⑤ wear – looked

6 다음 대화에서 밑줄 친 surprise의 알맞은 형태는?

> A: You know what? Plants like music.
> B: Really? That's very <u>surprise</u>.

① surprise   ② surprising   ③ to surprise
④ surprised   ⑤ for surprising

7 다음 글의 빈칸에 들어갈 말이 알맞게 짝지어진 것은?

> My friends and I went camping. The weather was _____ . After setting up the tent, we saw a strange shadow. We thought it was a deer and chased after it. However, we couldn't find anything. We were _____ .

① amazed – disappointing
② amazing – disappointed
③ amazing – disappointing
④ amazed – disappointed
⑤ amaze – disappointed

8 다음 빈칸에 들어갈 단어의 알맞은 형태를 고르세요.

> She is _____ in helping others.

① interest
② interested
③ interesting
④ interests
⑤ will be interested

9 다음 주어진 문장의 밑줄 친 부분과 쓰임이 같은 것은?

> Keeping a diary is very helpful, isn't it?

① Jenny is collecting stamps.
② The dog is running.
③ What are you doing?
④ I like studying wild flowers.
⑤ Tom is looking for his book.

10 두 문장이 같은 뜻이 되도록 빈칸에 알맞은 단어를 쓰세요.

> • I like the boy. He's standing near the window.
> = I like the boy _____ near the window.

11 다음 중 밑줄 친 부분의 쓰임이 나머지 넷과 다른 것을 고르세요.

① Eating too much is bad for health.
② I enjoy learning different languages.
③ My hobby is listening to music.
④ Does he like playing tennis?
⑤ Look at the girls dancing on the stage.

12 다음 문장의 밑줄 친 단어를 문맥에 맞게 고쳐 쓰세요.

> She was please because her son won first prize in the contest.

➡ _____

13 다음 중 밑줄 친 부분의 표현이 어색한 것을 고르세요.

① The news was shocking.
② We were surprised.
③ The game is exciting.
④ He feels tiring.
⑤ This movie is interesting.

14 다음 중 밑줄 친 부분의 쓰임이 같은 것끼리 묶인 것은?

> ⓐ What are you drawing?
> ⓑ Drawing national flags is difficult.
> ⓒ I am drawing a cake and candles.
> ⓓ His hobby is drawing cartoons.
> ⓔ She is drawing a dinosaur.

① (ⓐⓑ), (ⓒⓓⓔ)
② (ⓐⓔ), (ⓑⓒⓓ)
③ (ⓐⓒⓔ), (ⓑⓓ)
④ (ⓐⓒⓓ), (ⓑⓔ)
⑤ (ⓐⓑⓒⓓ), (ⓔ)

15 다음 빈칸에 들어갈 단어가 순서대로 바르게 짝지어진 것은?

> • _____ babies are so cute.
> • Look at those _____ leaves.

① Slept – falling   ② Slept – fallen
③ Sleeping – fell   ④ Sleeping – fall
⑤ Sleeping – fallen

16 밑줄 친 부분의 쓰임이 다른 하나는?

① I don't like being hesitant.
② Her job is taking care of babies.
③ Susan is good at cooking spicy food.
④ Being honest is the key to a good friendship.
⑤ Those two companies are competing against each other.

17 괄호 안에 주어진 단어를 알맞은 형태로 바꾸어 대화를 완성하세요.

> A: What are you reading now?
> B: I'm reading a novel _____ in English. (write)

18 다음 중 밑줄 친 부분의 표현이 어색한 것을 고르세요.

① It's a very worrying situation.
② When I failed the test, I felt frustrated.
③ He was surprised when his aunt visited him.
④ The rainy season makes people feel depressing.
⑤ People showing up late for a meeting are annoying.

19 다음 빈칸에 공통으로 들어갈 알맞은 말은?

> • I want to buy a _____ car.
> • He has _____ his car for 10 years.

① using   ② used   ③ use
④ be using   ⑤ be used

20 다음 주어진 단어를 바르게 배열하여 문장을 완성하세요.

(1) 벤치에 앉아 있는 소녀는 나의 여동생이다.
= _____
_____
(my sister, sitting, the girl, is, on the bench)

(2) 나무 밑에 주차되어 있는 저 멋진 스포츠카를 봐.
= _____
_____
(under, look, sports car, the tree, nice, at, that, parked)

21 어법상 맞는 표현으로만 짝지어진 것은?

> Jihun loves ⓐ cooking. He likes ⓑ cook for his family. One day, he invited all his family members to dinner and served them some delicious meat ⓒ roasting with garlic and onions. Everybody felt ⓓ surprising with his food. Jihun also felt ⓔ satisfied to see his family members smile.

① ⓐⓔ   ② ⓐⓒⓔ   ③ ⓐⓑⓒ
④ ⓑⓒⓓⓔ   ⑤ ⓑⓓⓔ

CHAPTER 10
형용사

성취도 자기 평가 활용법

구분	평가 기준
(E)xcellent	문법 내용을 모두 이해하고, 문제를 모두 맞힘.
(V)ery good	문법 내용은 충분히 이해했으나 실수로 1~2문제 틀림.
(G)ood	문법 내용이 조금 어려워 3~4문제 틀림.
needs (R)eview	문법 내용 이해가 어렵고, 5문제 이상 틀림. 복습 필요.

Problem Solving Skill	페이지	학습날짜	성취도 자기평가 E V G R	학습체크
PSS 1 형용사	194	/		☐
PSS 2 형용사의 한정적 용법과 서술적 용법	195	/		☐
PSS 3 -thing, -body(one)+형용사	196	/		☐
PSS 4 수사	페이지	학습날짜	성취도 자기평가 E V G R	학습체크
PSS 4-1 기수와 서수	197	/		☐
PSS 4-2 정수	199	/		☐
PSS 4-3 전화번호	200	/		☐
PSS 4-4 분수와 소수	201	/		☐
PSS 4-5 시각 I	202	/		☐
PSS 4-6 시각 II	202	/		☐
PSS 4-7 연도와 날짜	203	/		☐
PSS 4-8 금액	204	/		☐
PSS 4-9 온도	205	/		☐
PSS 5 관용적인 수사 표현	페이지	학습날짜	성취도 자기평가 E V G R	학습체크
PSS 5-1 tens[hundreds, thousands, millions] of+복수 명사	207	/		☐
PSS 5-2 every+숫자	208	/		☐
PSS 6 수나 양을 나타내는 형용사	페이지	학습날짜	성취도 자기평가 E V G R	학습체크
PSS 6-1 many, much	209	/		☐
PSS 6-2 (a) few, (a) little	212	/		☐
PSS 6-3 some, any	213	/		☐
PSS 6-4 not ~ any = no	214	/		☐
Chapter Review Test	215	/		☐

 # 형용사

> 형용사는 명사나 대명사를 꾸며주는 말로 사람이나 사물의 성질, 상태를 나타낸다. 이때 명사의 앞이나 뒤에서 꾸며주기도 하고, 주격 보어나 목적격 보어로도 쓰인다.
>
> There is a **tall tree** in the field. 들판에 키가 큰 나무가 있다.
> We help **poor children**. 우리는 가난한 아이들을 돕는다.
> It is **cold** in winter. 겨울에는 춥다.
> I want to be **rich** and **famous**. 나는 부유하고 유명해지고 싶다.
> I found **this story interesting**. 나는 이 이야기가 흥미롭다는 것을 알았다.

PRACTICE 1

〈보기〉와 같이 우리말과 같은 뜻이 되도록 괄호 안에 주어진 단어 중 알맞은 것을 고르세요.

보 기	그녀는 친절한 소녀이다. = She is a (**kind**, kindness) girl.

1 그는 특별한 재능을 가지고 있다.
  = He has a (special, specially) talent.

2 이 유리 조각들을 조심해라.
  = Be (care, careful) with these pieces of glass.

3 그들은 멋진 시간을 보냈다.
  = They had a (wonder, wonderful) time.

4 불은 매우 위험하다.
  = Fire is very (danger, dangerous).

5 그것은 도움이 될 것이다.
  = It's going to be (help, helpful).

6 아침식사 준비는 됐니?
  = Are you (ready, readily) for breakfast?

7 너는 좋은 책을 가지고 있니?
  = Do you have (good, well) books?

8 배고프지, 안 그러니?
  = You're (hunger, hungry), aren't you?

9 나는 어제 아팠다.
  = I was (sick, sickness) yesterday.

10 Jane은 그 편지에 대해 궁금해했다.
  = Jane was (curious, curiously) about the letter.

형용사의 한정적 용법과 서술적 용법

한정적 용법	형용사가 수식어로 쓰여 (대)명사 앞 또는 뒤에서 꾸며주는 경우를 가리킨다. He is a **nice boy**. 그는 다정한 소년이다. We saw **something strange**. 우리는 이상한 무언가를 보았다.
서술적 용법	형용사가 보어로 쓰여 주어나 목적어의 상태나 모습을 설명하는 경우를 가리킨다. **My sister** is **pretty**. 나의 여동생은 예쁘다. → 형용사 pretty가 주어인 My sister의 상태를 설명한다. The news made **me happy**. 그 소식은 나를 행복하게 만들었다. → 형용사 happy가 목적어 me의 상태를 설명한다.

PRACTICE 2

밑줄 친 부분의 용법이 〈보기〉의 A와 같으면 A를, B와 같으면 B를 쓰세요.

> 보기
> A. You did a <u>good</u> job!
> B. I'm not <u>good</u> at math.

1. This subject is very <u>difficult</u>. [ ]
   I like <u>difficult</u> puzzles. [ ]

2. It is a <u>beautiful</u> necklace. [ ]
   The weather is <u>beautiful</u> today. [ ]

3. The market was very <u>crowded</u>. [ ]
   I don't like <u>crowded</u> places. [ ]

4. I'm a <u>perfect</u> person. [ ]
   She didn't think he was <u>perfect</u>. [ ]

5. I have a <u>good</u> memory. [ ]
   This coffee tastes <u>good</u>. [ ]

6. They are in <u>different</u> classes. [ ]
   Minsu is <u>different</u> from his brother. [ ]

7. The cake is so <u>sweet</u>. [ ]
   He wants something <u>sweet</u>. [ ]

8. What a <u>huge</u> place it is! [ ]
   They found the palace really <u>huge</u>. [ ]

9. She can make <u>delicious</u> food. [ ]
   That sandwich looks <u>delicious</u>. [ ]

10. This movie has nothing <u>exciting</u> in it. [ ]
    The game was <u>exciting</u>. [ ]

-thing, -body(one) + 형용사

-thing, -body(one)로 끝나는 대명사를 꾸미는 형용사는 항상 뒤에 위치한다.

Let's do **something good** for others. 다른 사람들을 위해 좋은 무언가를 하자.
Do you have **anything hot** to drink? 마실 뜨거운 것이 있나요?
There was **nothing interesting** on TV. TV에는 재미있는 것이 아무 것도 없었다.
There wasn't **anybody famous** at the party. 파티에는 어떤 유명한 사람도 없었다.

cf. something, anything, nothing의 형태가 아닌 단독으로 thing만 쓰일 때는 형용사가 thing 앞에 위치한다.
He learned many **new things**. 그는 많은 새로운 것들을 배웠다.

PRACTICE 3

정답 p.38

괄호 안에 주어진 말 중 알맞은 것을 고르세요.

1 She wants (something sweet, sweet something).
2 Do you have (anything else, else anything)?
3 (Delicious everything, Everything delicious) is sold out.
4 Would you like (cold something, something cold) to drink?
5 Can you send (anything interesting, interesting anything) to me?
6 He believes that he is (nobody special, special nobody).
7 We discovered (important something, something important).
8 I don't like (anything slow, slow anything).
9 There is (wrong nothing, nothing wrong) between us.
10 They bought (everything necessary, necessary everything) for their trip.
11 He needs (useful something, something useful).
12 Have you ever met (famous anyone, anyone famous)?
13 You should not put (anything sharp, sharp anything) in your suitcase.
14 You will learn a (new thing, thing new) today.
15 The bride should wear (something old, old something) on her wedding day.
16 There was (nothing cheap, cheap nothing) in the mall.

 **4 수사**

PSS 4-1 기수와 서수

기수는 '개수'를 나타내는 말이고, 서수는 '순서'를 나타내는 말이다. 대개 기수 뒤에 -th를 붙이면 서수가 된다.

(*는 주의)

기수	서수	기수	서수
one (1)	first (1st) *	fifteen (15)	fifteenth (15th)
two (2)	second (2nd) *	nineteen (19)	nineteenth (19th)
three (3)	third (3rd) *	twenty (20)	twentieth (20th) *
four (4)	fourth (4th)	twenty-one (21)	twenty-first (21st) *
five (5)	fifth (5th) *	twenty-two (22)	twenty-second (22nd) *
six (6)	sixth (6th)	twenty-three (23)	twenty-third (23rd) *
seven (7)	seventh (7th)	thirty (30)	thirtieth (30th) *
eight (8)	eighth (8th) *	forty (40)	fortieth (40th) *
nine (9)	ninth (9th) *	ninety (90)	ninetieth (90th) *
ten (10)	tenth (10th)	a[one] hundred (100)	one hundredth (100th)
eleven (11)	eleventh (11th)	a[one] thousand (1,000)	one thousandth (1,000th)
twelve (12)	twelfth (12th) *	a[one] million	one millionth
thirteen (13)	thirteenth (13th)	a[one] billion	one billionth

정답 p.38

PRACTICE 4

다음 빈칸에 알맞은 말을 쓰세요.

	숫자	기수	서수		숫자	기수	서수
1	1	one	first	**2**	2		
3	3			**4**	4		
5	5			**6**	6		

7	7			**8**	8		
9	9			**10**	10		
11	11			**12**	12		
13	13			**14**	14		
15	15			**16**	16		
17	17			**18**	18		
19	19			**20**	20		
21	21			**22**	22		
23	30			**24**	40		
25	50			**26**	55		
27	60			**28**	70		
29	80			**30**	90		
31	100			**32**	1,000		
33	1,000,000			**34**	1,000,000,000		

PRACTICE 5

정답 p.38

괄호 안의 숫자를 서수 형태로 바꾸어 빈칸에 쓰세요.

1 Their _____ son is very clever. (2)

2 Today is my daughter's _____ birthday. (9)

3 This is his _____ trip abroad. (12)

4 I remember the _____ day of work. (1)

5 May _____ is Parents' Day. (8)

6 Can you explain the _____ line? (40)

7 I'm a _____ grade student at middle school. (3)

8 I was born on November _____. (30)

9 You are the _____ person in the line. (5)

10 There were great changes in the _____ century. (20)

PSS 4-2 정수

정수는 세 자리씩 끊어서 천 단위로 읽으며, hundred 뒤의 and는 생략 가능하다.

279 ➡ two hundred (and) seventy-nine
3,000 ➡ three thousand
5,473,584 ➡ five million, four hundred (and) seventy-three thousand, five hundred (and) eighty-four

정답 p.38

PRACTICE 6

다음 숫자를 영어로 읽을 때의 표기법을 쓰세요.

1 4,256   ➡ _____
2 36   ➡ _____
3 57,403   ➡ _____
4 1,052   ➡ _____
5 530   ➡ _____
6 8,826   ➡ _____
7 72   ➡ _____
8 601   ➡ _____
9 75,419   ➡ _____
10 12,000,000 ➡ _____
11 5,500   ➡ _____
12 713   ➡ _____
13 223,600   ➡ _____
14 411   ➡ _____
15 2,780   ➡ _____
16 131   ➡ _____
17 6,238   ➡ _____
18 256   ➡ _____
19 99   ➡ _____
20 302   ➡ _____

PSS 4-3 전화번호

1. 전화번호는 한 자리씩 읽는데, 같은 숫자가 나란히 나오는 경우에는 double을 이용하기도 한다. 0은 o[ou]라고 읽는 것이 보통이지만, zero라고도 읽는다.

    935-7304 ➡ nine three five, seven three o four
    703-2269 ➡ seven o three, two two[double two] six nine

2. 지역번호는 area code를 붙여 읽는다. 맨 첫 자리가 0인 경우에는 주로 zero라고 읽는다.

    (02) 828-2932 ➡ **area code zero** two, eight two eight, two nine three two

3. 휴대폰 앞 자리의 경우, 주로 zero라고 읽는다.

    010-1234-5678 ➡ **zero** one **zero**, one two three four, five six seven eight

PRACTICE 7

정답 p.39

다음 전화번호를 숫자 표기는 영어 표기로, 영어 표기는 아라비아 숫자로 바꿔 쓰세요.

1. 846-0236 ➡ _____
2. 306-4400 ➡ _____
3. (02) 428-5597 ➡ _____
4. 319-2713 ➡ _____
5. 018-2818-3710 ➡ _____
6. 274-5515 ➡ _____
7. (031) 865-8438 ➡ _____
8. 119 ➡ _____
9. 2060-4362 ➡ _____
10. 963-5908 ➡ _____
11. zero one nine, one seven nine two, o o one two ➡ _____
12. area code zero six four, double four o, double three one eight ➡ _____
13. five nine four, three three eight six ➡ _____
14. area code zero four two, seven five four, three eight nine two ➡ _____
15. two nine six, four three double o ➡ _____
16. one, six double seven, eight two o, double three double two ➡ _____

17 one one four ➡ _____

18 six four six, five nine five eight ➡ _____

19 area code zero five one, seven double five, double o eight one ➡ _____

20 zero one zero, five three five, seven five eight seven ➡ _____

PSS 4-4 분수와 소수

1. 분수 – 분자는 기수로 분모는 서수로 읽으며, 분자를 먼저 읽고 분모를 나중에 읽는다. 분자가 2 이상인 경우에는 분모에 -s를 붙인다.

   1/5 ➡ a fifth 또는 one-fifth   1/8 ➡ an eighth 또는 one eighth
   3/8 ➡ three-eighth**s**   3 2/5 ➡ three and two-fifth**s**
   cf. 1/2 ➡ a half 또는 one-half   1/4 ➡ a quarter 또는 one-quarter

2. 소수 – 소수점까지는 기수로 읽고, 소수점은 point로, 소수점 이하는 하나씩 따로 읽는다. 소수에서는 0을 보통 zero로 읽는다.

   3.14 ➡ three **point** one four
   0.01 ➡ zero **point** zero one 또는 **point** zero one
   cf. 소수점 앞의 수가 0인 경우에는 zero를 생략하고 point부터 읽기도 한다.

정답 p.39

PRACTICE 8

다음 분수나 소수를 숫자 표기는 영어 표기로, 영어 표기는 아라비아 숫자로 바꿔 쓰세요.

1 3/4 ➡ _____   **2** 1/4 ➡ _____
3 2.5 ➡ _____   **4** 0.31 ➡ _____
5 2.09 ➡ _____ **6** 20 1/3 ➡ _____
7 2/7 ➡ _____   **8** 2/9 ➡ _____
9 1 1/2 ➡ _____ **10** 5 3/10 ➡ _____
11 0.99 ➡ _____ **12** 1.272 ➡ _____
13 seven-fifteenths ➡ _____   **14** four-elevenths ➡ _____
15 three and six-sevenths ➡ _____   **16** six and one-fifth ➡ _____
17 point six ➡ _____   **18** thirty-four point nine ➡ _____
19 three point one two six ➡ _____   **20** five and five-sixths ➡ _____

PSS 4-5 시각 I

일반적으로 읽는 방법 – 시간과 분을 끊어서 읽는다.

8:05 ➡ eight-(o)-five   8:07 ➡ eight-(o)-seven
8:15 ➡ eight fifteen   8:30 ➡ eight thirty
8:43 ➡ eight forty-three   8:50 ➡ eight fifty
8:55 ➡ eight fifty-five   9:00 ➡ nine (o'clock)

cf. o'clock은 '~시 00분'의 의미로, 정각이 아닐 경우에는 o'clock을 쓰지 않는다.

PRACTICE 9

정답 p.39

다음 시각을 영어로 읽을 때의 표기법을 쓰세요.

1 9:20 ➡ _____   2 3:05 ➡ _____
3 8:25 ➡ _____   4 5:00 ➡ _____
5 10:30 ➡ _____   6 1:37 ➡ _____
7 6:15 ➡ _____   8 11:00 ➡ _____
9 12:08 ➡ _____   10 4:50 ➡ _____

PSS 4-6 시각 II

'~을 지나서'를 뜻하는 after[past]와 '~ 전에'를 뜻하는 to를 사용하여 읽기도 한다. 일반적으로 past는 (a) quarter나 half와 주로 쓰이는데, (a) quarter는 '15분'을, half는 '30분'을 나타낸다.

8:05 ➡ five **after** eight   8:10 ➡ ten **after** eight
8:15 ➡ **(a) quarter after** eight 또는 **(a) quarter past** eight
8:20 ➡ twenty **after** eight   8:25 ➡ twenty-five **after** eight
8:30 ➡ **half past** eight   8:35 ➡ twenty-five **to** nine
8:40 ➡ twenty **to** nine   8:45 ➡ **(a) quarter to** nine
8:50 ➡ ten **to** nine   8:55 ➡ five **to** nine

PRACTICE 10

다음 시각을 after[past] 또는 to를 사용하여 영어로 읽을 때의 표기법을 쓰세요.

1 9:45 ➡ _____
2 1:15 ➡ _____
3 11:55 ➡ _____
4 4:20 ➡ _____
5 7:15 ➡ _____
6 7:35 ➡ _____
7 8:50 ➡ _____
8 3:10 ➡ _____
9 5:45 ➡ _____
10 1:55 ➡ _____
11 3:15 ➡ _____
12 5:50 ➡ _____
13 3:30 ➡ _____
14 6:05 ➡ _____
15 2:25 ➡ _____
16 11:30 ➡ _____
17 9:10 ➡ _____
18 4:40 ➡ _____
19 10:20 ➡ _____
20 7:30 ➡ _____

PSS 4-7 연도와 날짜

1. **연도** – 보통 두 자리씩 끊어서 읽는다.

    1988년 ➡ nineteen eighty-eight
    1700년 ➡ seventeen hundred
    654년 ➡ six (hundred and) fifty-four

    cf. 2002년 ➡ two thousand (and) two

2. **날짜** – 서수를 이용하여 읽는다. 연도와 날짜를 함께 읽을 때에는 월과 일을 먼저 읽고, 연도를 나중에 읽는다.

    9월 5일 ➡ September (the) fifth 또는 the fifth of September
    1997년 7월 3일 ➡ July (the) third, nineteen ninety-seven
    　　　　　　　또는 the third of July, nineteen ninety-seven

    cf. 월을 나타내는 말

1월 January	2월 February	3월 March	4월 April
5월 May	6월 June	7월 July	8월 August
9월 September	10월 October	11월 November	12월 December

PRACTICE 11

다음 연도나 날짜를 영어로 읽을 때의 표기법을 쓰세요.

1 10월 13일 ➡ _____
2 2020년   ➡ _____
3 1592년   ➡ _____
4 2월 20일 ➡ _____
5 452년   ➡ _____
6 7월 1일   ➡ _____
7 1980년   ➡ _____
8 3월 31일 ➡ _____
9 1910년   ➡ _____
10 12월 15일 ➡ _____
11 4월 8일   ➡ _____
12 9월 26일 ➡ _____
13 1999년   ➡ _____
14 5월 5일   ➡ _____
15 2000년   ➡ _____
16 11월 10일 ➡ _____
17 1238년   ➡ _____
18 6월 17일 ➡ _____
19 1600년   ➡ _____
20 1970년   ➡ _____

PSS 4-8 금액

미화는 dollar와 cent를 이용하여 읽고, 원화는 won을 이용하여 읽는다.

$7.35 ➡ seven dollars (and) thirty-five cents
₩900 ➡ nine hundred won

cf. $1 = 100¢ (cents)
cf. dollar나 cent는 복수일 경우 -s를 붙이지만, won은 붙이지 않는다.

PRACTICE 12

다음 금액을 영어로 읽을 때의 표기법을 쓰세요.

1. $1.25 ➡ _____
2. ₩5,200 ➡ _____
3. $10.10 ➡ _____
4. ₩12,000 ➡ _____
5. ₩1,850 ➡ _____
6. $0.75 ➡ _____
7. $12.30 ➡ _____
8. ₩400 ➡ _____
9. $3.50 ➡ _____
10. ₩4,900 ➡ _____

PSS 4-9 온도

섭씨는 Celsius를 이용하여 나타내고 화씨는 Fahrenheit를 이용하여 나타낸다.

35℃ ➡ thirty-five **degrees** Celsius
95℉ ➡ ninety-five **degrees** Fahrenheit

cf. 전 세계적으로 지배적인 온도 단위는 섭씨이지만, 미국에서는 주로 화씨를 사용한다. 화씨는 1724년 독일의 물리학자 Gabriel Fahrenheit가 제안한 온도 측정 단위로 물의 어는 점이 32도, 끓는점이 212도가 되어 180단계로 구분된다. 섭씨 35도(35℃)는 화씨 95도(95℉)이다.

PRACTICE 13

다음 온도를 영어로 읽을 때의 표기법을 쓰세요.

1. 23℃ ➡ _____
2. 50℉ ➡ _____
3. 150℃ ➡ _____
4. 75℉ ➡ _____
5. 350℉ ➡ _____

6 275℃   ➡ _____
7 180℃   ➡ _____
8 116.6°F ➡ _____
9 273.15℃ ➡ _____
10 420°F   ➡ _____

PRACTICE 14

정답 p.40

우리말과 같은 뜻이 되도록 괄호 안에 주어진 동사를 알맞은 형태로 쓰고, 숫자를 영어로 바르게 바꿔 쓰세요.

1 설탕 1/4컵을 넣어라. (add)
   = _____ _____ _____ of a cup of sugar.

2 세종대왕은 1443년에 한글을 발명했다. (invent)
   = King Sejong _____ Hangul in _____ _____-_____.

3 이 셔츠는 4,900원이다. (cost)
   = This shirt _____ _____ _____ _____ _____ won.

4 그녀는 그녀의 오래된 신발을 $18.90에 팔았다. (sell)
   = She _____ her old shoes for _____ _____ and _____ _____.

5 나는 3월 1일 뉴욕에 도착하였다. (arrive)
   = I _____ in New York on _____ _____ of _____.

6 식품 가격이 80.7% 증가했다. (rise)
   = Food prices _____ by _____ _____ _____ percent.

7 Elena는 총 투표수의 4/5를 받았다. (receive)
   = Elena _____ _____-_____ of the vote.

8 나는 보통 아침 7시 15분에 일어난다. (get up)
   = I usually _____ _____ at a _____ _____ _____ in the morning.

9 Evelyn은 2000년 11월 4일에 태어났다. (be born)
   = Evelyn _____ _____ _____ on the _____, _____ _____.

10 그는 동전 4,774개를 수집했다. (collect)
   = He _____ _____ _____, _____ _____ and _____-_____ coins.

11 물은 100℃에서 끓기 시작한다. (start)
   = Water _____ to boil at _____ _____ degrees _____.

12 그의 사무실 전화번호는 (02) 767-4367이다. (be)

= His office number _____ _____ _____ _____ _____, seven six seven, _____ _____ _____ _____.

13 기온이 86°F에 도달했다. (reach)

= The air temperature _____ _____-_____ _____ Fahrenheit.

14 Logan의 새로운 핸드폰 번호는 010-275-9981이다. (be)

= Logan's new cell phone number _____ _____ _____ _____, two seven five, _____ _____ _____ one.

15 나의 할머니는 1,229,900원을 모으셨다. (save)

= My grandmother _____ one _____, _____ _____ and _____-_____ _____, _____ _____ won.

PSS 5 관용적인 수사 표현

PSS 5-1 tens[hundreds, thousands, millions] of + 복수 명사

막연히 큰 수를 나타낼 때는 숫자의 단위를 복수형으로 쓴다.

tens[dozens] of '수십의'   hundreds of '수백의'
thousands of '수천의'   millions of '수백만의'

I have collected **tens of coins**. 나는 수십 개의 동전을 수집했다.
Thousands of people watched the TV program. 수천 명의 사람들이 그 TV 프로그램을 보았다.

cf. 막연한 숫자가 아니라 정해진 수를 나타낼 때는 「기수+hundred, thousand, million」을 쓴다.
two thousand people 2000명의 사람들

정답 p.40

PRACTICE 15

〈보기〉와 같이 우리말과 같은 뜻이 되도록 빈칸에 알맞은 말을 쓰세요.

| 보 기 | 수백 명의 기자들이 파리에 모였다.
= <u>Hundreds of</u> reporters gathered in Paris. |

1 매년 우리는 수백만 그루의 나무를 벤다.

= Every year we cut down _____ trees.

2 그는 수십 통의 편지를 가지고 있다.

= He has _____ letters.

3 이 사원은 400년 전에 세워졌다.

= This temple was built _____ years ago.

4 수백 명의 사람들이 그 뉴스를 보고 있었다.

= _____ people were watching the news.

5 나는 500장의 우표를 수집했다.

= I've collected _____ stamps.

6 수천 명의 사람들이 그 도시에 산다.

= _____ people live in the city.

7 수백만의 어린이들이 이 책을 읽는다.

= _____ children read this book.

8 나는 어제 수십 권의 책을 기부했다.

= I donated _____ books yesterday.

9 극장에는 1000개의 좌석이 있다.

= There are _____ seats in the theater.

10 3백만 명의 노동자들이 거리로 나왔다.

= _____ workers went out to the street.

PSS 5-2 every + 숫자

「every+기수+복수 명사」와 「every+서수+단수 명사」는 '매 ~, ~마다'의 의미를 나타낸다.

He goes to the gym **every two days**. 그는 이틀마다 체육관에 간다.
= He goes to the gym **every second day**.
I meet her **every three weeks**. 나는 그녀를 3주마다 만난다.
= I meet her **every third week**.

정답 p.40

PRACTICE 16

짝지어진 두 문장의 의미가 같도록 빈칸에 알맞은 말을 쓰세요.

1 I call her every fifth day.

= I call her _____.

2 I read a book every second week.

= I read a book _____.

3 We practice soccer every third day.

= We practice soccer _____.

4 My family eats out every four weeks.

= My family eats out _____.

5 They change their car every tenth year.

= They change their car _____.

6 She goes shopping every seventh day.

= She goes shopping _____.

7 I go to the hospital every fifteenth day.

= I go to the hospital _____.

8 The World Cup is held every fourth year.

= The World Cup is held _____.

9 He had swimming lessons every two days.

= He had swimming lessons _____.

10 Tony goes to the theater every nine days.

= Tony goes to the theater _____.

PSS 6 수나 양을 나타내는 형용사
Problem Solving Skill

PSS 6-1 many, much

many	셀 수 있는 명사 앞에 쓰여 '많은, 다수의'의 의미를 나타낸다. There are **many books** in the library. 도서관에 많은 책들이 있다. How **many hours** did you watch TV? 너는 얼마나 많은 시간동안 TV를 봤니?
much	셀 수 없는 명사 앞에 쓰여 '많은, 다량의'의 의미를 나타낸다. I don't have **much money**. 나는 돈이 많지 않다. How **much milk** do you drink every day? 너는 매일 얼마나 많은 우유를 마시니? ***cf.*** much는 주로 부정문과 의문문에서 쓰이지만, too much와 so much는 긍정문에도 쓰인다. There was **so much** trash in the park. 공원에 아주 많은 쓰레기들이 있었다.

a lot of [lots of]	셀 수 있는 명사와 셀 수 없는 명사 앞에 모두 쓰이며 '많은'의 의미를 나타낸다. a lot of[lots of] 뒤에 복수 명사가 오면 many가, 단수 명사가 오면 much가 대신할 수 있다. I saw **a lot of[lots of]** animals in the zoo. 나는 동물원에서 많은 동물들을 보았다. = I saw **many** animals in the zoo. We don't have **a lot of[lots of]** food. 우리는 많은 음식을 가지고 있지 않다. = We don't have **much** food.

PRACTICE 17

정답 p.41

〈보기〉와 같이 빈칸에 many나 much 중 알맞은 것을 쓰고, 괄호 안에 주어진 단어의 알맞은 형태를 쓰세요.

보 기	There are <u>many stores</u> on that street. (store) I didn't have <u>much money</u>. (money)

1 She has _____. (flower)
2 Do you need _____? (water)
3 She used _____. (dish)
4 I joined _____. (club)
5 She made too _____. (soup)
6 I had _____ last night. (dream)
7 He can make _____. (kite)
8 There isn't _____ in the bottle. (juice)
9 She saw _____. (planet)
10 There are _____ in the world. (job)
11 Do you have _____ in summer? (rain)
12 He visited _____ in London. (place)
13 She didn't get _____. (sleep)
14 I have _____. (Korean friend)
15 How _____ is Kate taking? (course)
16 Did the idea give her _____? (pleasure)

17 We don't have _____ in winter. (snow)

18 There are _____ . (sports activity)

19 There are _____ . (interesting site)

20 Do you have _____ in a trip to China? (interest)

21 She doesn't have _____ with dogs. (experience)

22 Thanks to his efforts, _____ live better lives. (people)

정답 p.41

PRACTICE 18

빈칸에 many와 much 중 밑줄 친 부분을 대신할 수 있는 말을 쓰고, 괄호 안에 주어진 단어의 알맞은 형태를 쓰세요.

1 I saw lots of (rock). ➡ many rocks

2 Did you spend lots of (time) with her? ➡ _____

3 We have a lot of (apple pie). ➡ _____

4 There are lots of (school) here. ➡ _____

5 Do you save a lot of (money)? ➡ _____

6 Ted took a lot of (picture). ➡ _____

7 It doesn't need a lot of (courage). ➡ _____

8 There are a lot of (animal). ➡ _____

9 Susan doesn't drink a lot of (coffee). ➡ _____

10 He told me a lot of (thing) about you. ➡ _____

11 There were lots of (insect) here. ➡ _____

12 They didn't have lots of (fun). ➡ _____

13 We can see lots of (child) there. ➡ _____

14 A lot of (people) came to the party. ➡ _____

15 The car doesn't need a lot of (oil). ➡ _____

16 He asked David a lot of (question). ➡ _____

17 The book doesn't have a lot of (information). ➡ _____

18 People came from a lot of (different country). ➡ _____

19 The players should follow lots of (rule). ➡ _____

20 I didn't get lots of (sleep) last night. ➡ _____

CHAPTER 10 _ 형용사

PSS 6-2 (a) few, (a) little

a few, few	셀 수 있는 명사 앞에 쓰이며, a few는 '약간의', few는 '거의 없는'의 의미를 나타낸다. I have **a few friends** in America. 나는 미국에 친구가 몇 명 있다. (긍정적 의미) He has **few friends** in America. 그는 미국에 친구가 거의 없다. (부정적 의미)
a little, little	셀 수 없는 명사 앞에 쓰이며, a little은 '약간의', little은 '거의 없는'의 의미를 나타낸다. There is **a little water** in the glass. 유리잔에 물이 약간 있다. (긍정적 의미) There is **little water** in the glass. 유리잔에 물이 거의 없다. (부정적 의미)

정답 p.41

PRACTICE 19

우리말과 같은 뜻이 되도록 빈칸에 a few, a little, few, little 중 알맞은 것을 쓰세요.

1 Bill은 프랑스 단어를 거의 모른다.
= Bill knows _____ French words.

2 남은 음식이 거의 없다.
= There is _____ food left.

3 몇 명의 직원들이 그것에 동의했다.
= _____ employees agreed to that.

4 우리는 그것에 관해 거의 문제가 없었다.
= We had _____ trouble with it.

5 오직 몇 명의 사람들만이 그들의 음악을 좋아한다.
= Only _____ people like their music.

6 Jane은 사촌이 거의 없다.
= Jane has _____ cousins.

7 상자 안에 공기가 거의 없다.
= There is _____ air in the box.

8 나는 스페인어를 조금 한다.
= I speak _____ Spanish.

9 남은 시간이 거의 없다.
= There is _____ time left.

10 몇 년 전에 나는 Milo를 만났다.
= _____ years ago, I met Milo.

11 물 조금만 주세요.
= _____ water, please.

12 약간의 작업이 완료되어야 한다.
= _____ work needs to be done.

13 우리는 몇 개의 유명한 그림을 보았다.
= We saw _____ famous paintings.

14 우리는 그 경기에서 운이 거의 없었다.
= We had _____ luck in the game.

15 며칠 뒤에 그는 이곳으로 돌아올지도 모른다.
= In _____ days, he may come back here.

16 그 차이를 이해하는 사람은 거의 없다.
= _____ people understand the difference.

PSS 6-3 some, any

some	셀 수 있는 명사와 셀 수 없는 명사 앞에 모두 쓰인다. 일반적으로 긍정문에 쓰이며 '약간의'의 의미를 나타낸다. He wants to buy **some** milk. 그는 약간의 우유를 사기를 원한다. I have **some** postcards. 나는 약간의 엽서를 가지고 있다. *cf.* Yes의 대답을 기대하는 권유나 부탁을 나타내는 의문문에는 some을 쓴다. **Would** you like **some** juice? 주스 좀 드실래요?
any	셀 수 있는 명사와 셀 수 없는 명사 앞에 모두 쓰인다. 일반적으로 부정문과 의문문에 쓰이며 '약간의'의 의미를 나타낸다. He **doesn't** want to buy **any** milk. 그는 약간의 우유도 사기를 원하지 않는다. **Do** you have **any** postcards? 너는 엽서를 좀 가지고 있니?

정답 p.41

PRACTICE 20

우리말 해석과 같은 뜻이 되도록 다음 문장의 빈칸에 some이나 any 중 알맞은 것을 쓰세요.

1 그들은 그에게 약간의 좋은 책들을 주었다.
   = They gave him _____ good books.

2 나는 약이 좀 필요하다.
   = I need _____ medicine.

3 나는 지금 조금의 시간도 없다.
   = I don't have _____ time now.

4 그녀는 어떤 사진도 찍지 않았다.
   = She didn't take _____ pictures.

5 여기 약간의 쿠키와 주스가 있어요.
   = Here are _____ cookies and juice.

6 나는 어떤 남자 형제들도 없다.
   = I don't have _____ brothers.

7 너는 어떤 생각이라도 있니?
   = Do you have _____ ideas?

8 오늘 밤을 위한 어떤 계획이라도 있니?
   = Do you have _____ plans for tonight?

9 우리는 토요일에 어떤 수업도 없다.
   = We don't have _____ classes on Saturday.

10 커피 좀 드시겠어요?
   = Would you like _____ coffee?

11 나는 약간의 종이와 연필이 필요하다.
   = I need _____ paper and pencils.

12 너는 휴식을 좀 취해야 한다.
   = You should get _____ rest.

13 그는 오늘 돈을 하나도 쓰지 않았다.
   = He didn't spend _____ money today.

14 이 공원에 어떤 동물이라도 있나요?
   = Are there _____ animals in this park?

15 아이스크림을 좀 드시겠습니까?
   = Would you like to have _____ ice cream?

16 그녀는 그녀의 지갑에 약간의 동전을 넣었다.
   = She put _____ coins in her wallet.

PSS 6-4 not ~ any = no

not ~ any는 no로 바꾸어 쓸 수 있으며 '조금도[아무(것)도] ~ 없는'의 의미를 나타낸다.

There are**n't any** children in the park. 공원에는 아이들이 아무도 없다.
= There are **no** children in the park.
He does**n't** know **anything** about it. 그는 그것에 관해 조금도 모른다.
= He knows **nothing** about it.

PRACTICE 21

정답 p.41

〈보기〉와 같이 짝지어진 두 문장의 의미가 같도록 빈칸을 채우세요.

보 기	I don't have any time.
	= I have <u>no</u> time.

1 There aren't any seats now.
 = There are _____ seats now.

2 They didn't see anybody.
 = They saw _____ .

3 I don't have anything to say.
 = I have _____ to say.

4 There isn't anyone in the room.
 = There is _____ _____ in the room.

5 My car isn't anywhere around here.
 = My car is _____ around here.

6 You don't need any special ways.
 = You need _____ special ways.

7 I couldn't see anybody in this house.
 = I could see _____ in this house.

8 There isn't anything wrong.
 = There is _____ wrong.

9 I cannot go anywhere without the shoes.
 = I can go _____ without the shoes.

10 We won't have any chance to talk together.
 = We will have _____ chance to talk together.

Chapter Review Test

정답 p.41

CHAPTER 10
형용사

1 다음 중 짝지어진 단어의 성격이 나머지 넷과 <u>다른</u> 것은?

① happiness - happy
② beauty - beautiful
③ sadness - sad
④ friend - friendly
⑤ pretty - prettily

2 다음 빈칸에 들어갈 수 <u>없는</u> 것은?

Jack is a _____ boy.

① nice
② smart
③ very
④ handsome
⑤ famous

3 다음 중 서수의 철자 표기가 바르지 <u>않은</u> 것을 고르세요.

① ninth
② third
③ hundredth
④ twelveth
⑤ eighth

4 다음 빈칸에 들어갈 수 <u>없는</u> 것은?

There are _____ grapes in the basket.

① a lot of
② much
③ many
④ lots of
⑤ some

5 다음 밑줄 친 nice의 쓰임이 다른 하나는?

① He is a <u>nice</u> boy.
② We had a <u>nice</u> holiday.
③ That is a <u>nice</u> picture.
④ The man is really <u>nice</u> and kind.
⑤ This is a <u>nice</u> movie.

6 〈보기〉와 같이 다음 두 문장이 같은 뜻이 되도록 빈칸에 알맞은 말을 쓰세요.

| 보 기 | This story is really interesting.
= This is a really interesting story. |

• The girl is very pretty.
 = She is _____.

7 다음 짝지어진 단어가 바르게 쓰이지 <u>않은</u> 것은?

① one – first
② two – second
③ four – forth
④ fifteen – fifteenth
⑤ twenty – twentieth

8 다음 연도를 영어로 읽은 것 중 <u>잘못된</u> 것을 고르세요.

① 1981년 = nineteen eighty-one
② 2005년 = two thousand five
③ 1800년 = eighteen hundred
④ 1871년 = one eight seven one
⑤ 723년 = seven twenty-three

9 다음 우리말과 같은 뜻이 되도록 빈칸에 알맞은 단어를 쓰세요.

• 9월은 한 해의 아홉 번째 달이다.
 = September is the _____ month of the year.

10 다음 숫자를 영어로 읽은 것 중 옳지 않은 것은?

① 25 = twenty-five
② 345 = three hundred and forty-five
③ 1,251 = one two hundred fifty-one
④ 20,000 = twenty thousand
⑤ 32,903 = thirty-two thousand, nine hundred and three

11 다음 문장의 밑줄 친 부분과 바꾸어 쓸 수 있는 단어를 고르세요.

> She doesn't drink a lot of coffee.

① many
② much
③ few
④ little
⑤ a few

12 다음 중 시간 표현이 잘못된 것은?

① 9:15 = a quarter past nine
② 7:50 = seven fifty
③ 10:30 = half to eleven
④ 11:00 = eleven o'clock
⑤ 1:10 = ten to one

13 다음 밑줄 친 부분을 영어로 바르게 옮긴 것은?

> A: Can you come to my birthday party?
> B: Of course. When is it?
> A: It's 7월 23일.

① July twenty-three
② July twenty-third
③ July twentieth-third
④ June twenty-three
⑤ June twenty-third

14 다음 밑줄 친 부분을 영어로 바르게 읽은 것은?

> Friday, August 31

① thirty-one
② three-one
③ thirty-first
④ third-first
⑤ three and one

15 다음 문장과 바꾸어 쓸 수 있는 표현을 고르세요.

> It's a quarter to eleven.

① It's ten fifteen.
② It's eleven forty-five.
③ It's ten forty-five.
④ It's twelve fifteen.
⑤ It's eleven fifteen.

16 다음 대화를 읽고 괄호 안의 마지막 말을 바르게 배열하여 쓰세요.

> A: I skipped breakfast this morning.
> B: Oh, I guess you are very hungry now.
> A: Of course.
>   (I, delicious, something, for, want, lunch)

➡ _____

17 주어진 우리말과 같은 뜻이 되도록 빈칸에 알맞은 말을 쓰세요.

> • 수백 명의 사람들이 그 행사에 참가했다.
>   = _____ _____ people joined the event.

18 다음 두 문장이 같은 뜻이 되도록 괄호 안의 숫자를 알맞은 형태로 쓰세요..

- It is good to go to the dentist every
  ⓐ ___(6)___ month.
  = It is good to go to the dentist every
  ⓑ ___(6)___ months.

ⓐ: _____ ⓑ: _____

19 다음 문장의 밑줄 친 부분과 바꾸어 쓸 수 있는 단어를 고르세요.

You can see a lot of animals in the zoo.

① some   ② any
③ many   ④ much
⑤ one

20 다음 우리말과 뜻이 같도록 문장에서 틀린 부분을 바르게 고쳐 쓰세요.

- 미국의 아버지날은 6월 세 번째 일요일이다.
  = Father's Day is the three Sunday in June in America.

➡ _____

21 다음 글에서 틀린 곳을 찾아 그 번호를 쓰고, 바르게 고치세요.

We will ①make a cheesecake. So we ②need cheese and ③butter. But we ④don't need ⑤some apples.

( ) _____ ➡ _____

22 밑줄 친 부분의 쓰임이 어법상 어색한 것은?

① She drank a lot of milk.
② There are many rules at school.
③ A lots of people go skiing in winter.
④ Can I have some chicken?
⑤ He has two tomatoes for lunch.

23 다음 시각을 나타내는 표현 중에서 같은 시각이 아닌 것을 고르세요.

① It is five thirty. = It is half past five.
② It is six forty-five. = It is fifteen to six.
③ It is nine fifteen. = It is a quarter past nine.
④ It is eight fifty-five. = It is five to nine.
⑤ It is three twenty. = It is twenty after three.

24 다음 두 문장이 같은 뜻이 되도록 빈칸에 들어갈 알맞은 단어를 쓰세요.

- They don't have any money.
  = They have _____ money.

25 다음 우리말과 같은 뜻이 되도록 빈칸에 알맞은 단어를 쓰세요.

- 내 아들은 내년에 2학년이 될 것이다.
  = My son will be in the _____ grade next year.

26 다음 중 어법상 어색한 문장은?

① This soup smells delicious.
② Peter's jokes sounded silly.
③ Her apple jam tastes sweet.
④ You look lovely in that dress.
⑤ My mom's blanket feels softly.

27 다음 밑줄 친 부분의 쓰임이 잘못된 것은?

① They played some games.
② I want some more food.
③ Please give me some water.
④ He has some friends in Japan.
⑤ We don't need some special ideas.

28 다음 글의 빈칸에 들어갈 가장 알맞은 말은?

Minji studied hard last night, but now she can't remember _____.

① somebody ② nobody
③ anyone   ④ nothing
⑤ anything

29 다음을 영어로 읽은 것 중 옳지 않은 것은?

① 847-6637
= eight four seven, double six three seven
② 6시 45분
= a quarter to seven
③ 2006년 11월 19일
= November nineteenth, two thousand six
④ $2.39
= two dollar and thirty-nine cent
⑤ 120°F
= one hundred twenty degrees Fahrenheit

30 다음 중 분수 표현이 바른 것은?

① 1/5 = one-five   ② 3/5 = third-fifths
③ 4/7 = four-sevenths ④ 5/6 = five-sixth
⑤ 3 1/8 = three and one-eight

31 다음 빈칸에 들어갈 알맞은 말로 짝지어진 것은?

- Nathan was a (A) _____ doctor before becoming a writer.
- The party was a great (B) _____.

	(A)	(B)
①	success	successful
②	success	successfully
③	successful	successfully
④	successful	success
⑤	succeed	success

32 다음 괄호 안에 주어진 단어를 바르게 배열하세요.

A: What time is it?
B: _____
(quarter, to, four, it's, a)

33 다음 빈칸에 들어갈 단어가 순서대로 짝지어진 것은?

A: Excuse me, do you have _____ problems?
B: Yes, I have _____ problems. Could you help me?

① any – any
② any – some
③ no – some
④ some – any
⑤ some – one

34 빈칸에 들어갈 단어로 알맞은 것은?

• It's two thirty.
= It's half _____ two.

① to
② past
③ until
④ from
⑤ before

35 다음 밑줄 친 우리말과 같은 뜻이 되도록 빈칸에 들어갈 알맞은 표현을 고르세요.

A: What are you going to do this weekend?
B: 특별한 일 없어. What's up?
A: I'm going to watch the soccer game with Mina. Why don't you come?

① I don't know.
② Special nothing.
③ Nothing special.
④ I have something special.
⑤ I don't have nothing.

36 다음 중 어법상 어색한 것을 고르세요.

① He has a few friends.
② He has many friends.
③ He has a lot of friends.
④ He has a little friends.
⑤ He has lots of friends.

37 다음 문장의 밑줄 친 sound와 의미가 같은 것을 고르세요.

The young man has a sound mind.

① The church bell sounded at eleven o'clock.
② That sounds very interesting.
③ The violin can make various sounds.
④ He is sound in body and spirit.
⑤ We heard the strange sound from the next room.

38 밑줄 친 부분이 바른 것은?

① I put a little soups in the bowl.
② I drink much coffees every day.
③ I put lots of sugar in my tea.
④ How many book do you have?
⑤ I got a little moneys from my grandmother.

39 두 문장의 의미가 같도록 빈칸에 알맞은 말을 쓰세요.

• I don't have any houses.
= I _____ _____ _____.

40 다음 빈칸에 들어갈 말이 순서대로 짝지어진 것은?

- There are _____ books in the library.
- There is too _____ sand in the playground.

① few – many
② many – few
③ many – much
④ much – many
⑤ few – few

41 다음 중 빈칸에 들어갈 말이 밑줄 친 부분과 같은 것은?

The first Korean bobsled team had to overcome <u>many</u> difficulties.

① Does Jerry drink _____ milk?
② There isn't _____ water on this island.
③ There are _____ cafeterias here.
④ I have so _____ money.
⑤ People throw away too _____ trash in the sea.

42 다음 ⓐ~ⓓ 중 어법상 잘못된 두 개의 문장을 골라 바르게 고쳐 쓰세요. (반드시 완전한 영어 문장으로 답하세요.)

ⓐ There are a lot of children in the playground.
ⓑ There are much pencils on the desk.
ⓒ There's too many garbage in the park.
ⓓ They don't have a lot of time to wait for you.

(1) _____
(2) _____

43 다음 ⓐ~ⓒ에 들어갈 말이 알맞게 짝지어진 것은?

- I got __ⓐ__ advice from him.
- His dogs deliver __ⓑ__ things to the neighborhood.
- We have __ⓒ__ snow in winter.

　　　ⓐ　　　ⓑ　　　ⓒ
① some – many – few
② any – much – little
③ some – many – little
④ any – many – few
⑤ some – much – little

44 다음 글을 읽고 **틀린** 부분 **세 곳**을 찾아 바르게 고쳐 쓰세요.

My friend Bob loves soccer. He goes to the soccer stadium every two week. He likes to watch soccer games there. Yesterday, Bob and I went to the stadium. About five hundreds people were watching the game. About three-forth of them cheered for the home team.

(1) _____ ➡ _____
(2) _____ ➡ _____
(3) _____ ➡ _____

CHAPTER 11
부사

성취도 자기 평가 활용법

구분	평가 기준
Excellent	문법 내용을 모두 이해하고, 문제를 모두 맞힘.
Very good	문법 내용은 충분히 이해했으나 실수로 1~2문제 틀림.
Good	문법 내용이 조금 어려워 3~4문제 틀림.
needs **R**eview	문법 내용 이해가 어렵고, 5문제 이상 틀림, 복습 필요.

PSS 1 부사의 형태	페이지	학습날짜	성취도 자기평가 Ⓔ Ⓥ Ⓖ Ⓡ	학습체크
PSS 1-1 부사의 역할과 형용사를 부사로 만드는 법	222	/		☐
PSS 1-2 형용사와 형태가 같은 부사	224	/		☐

PSS 2 빈도부사	페이지	학습날짜	성취도 자기평가 Ⓔ Ⓥ Ⓖ Ⓡ	학습체크
PSS 2-1 빈도부사의 종류와 의미	225	/		☐
PSS 2-2 빈도부사의 위치	227	/		☐
PSS 3 too, either	228	/		☐
PSS 4 well	229	/		☐

PSS 5 「타동사+부사」	페이지	학습날짜	성취도 자기평가 Ⓔ Ⓥ Ⓖ Ⓡ	학습체크
PSS 5-1 「타동사+부사」의 종류	230	/		☐
PSS 5-2 「타동사+부사」의 어순	232	/		☐

PSS 6 의문부사	페이지	학습날짜	성취도 자기평가 Ⓔ Ⓥ Ⓖ Ⓡ	학습체크
PSS 6-1 how, where, when, why	233	/		☐
PSS 6-2 How+형용사/부사 ~?	234	/		☐
Chapter Review Test	236	/		☐

부사의 형태

PSS 1-1 부사의 역할과 형용사를 부사로 만드는 법

부사는 '천천히, 매우'처럼 행동이나 일의 상태, 특징을 설명하는 말이다. 부사는 명사를 제외한 동사, 형용사, 다른 부사, 문장 전체를 수식한다.

동사 수식	The car **moved slowly**. 그 차는 느리게 움직였다.
형용사 수식	He is a **very brave** man. 그는 매우 용감한 남자이다.
다른 부사 수식	She studied **really hard**. 그녀는 정말로 열심히 공부했다.
문장 전체 수식	**Luckily, his son passed the exam**. 운 좋게도, 그의 아들은 시험에 통과했다.

형용사를 부사로 만드는 법은 다음과 같다.

대부분의 경우	-ly	quick 빠른 – quick**ly** 빠르게 kind 친절한 – kind**ly** 친절하게 clear 맑은 – clear**ly** 맑게 nice 멋진, 훌륭한 – nice**ly** 멋지게, 훌륭하게
자음+y로 끝나는 경우	y를 i로 바꾸고 -ly	easy 쉬운 – eas**ily** 쉽게 happy 행복한 – happ**ily** 행복하게 lucky 운이 좋은 – luck**ily** 운 좋게 angry 화난 – angr**ily** 화내어

PRACTICE 1

정답 p.44

다음 밑줄 친 우리말에 유의하여 괄호 안에 들어갈 알맞은 말을 고르세요.

1 그녀는 매우 <u>친절한</u> 간호사이다.
  ➡ She is a very (kind / kindly) nurse.

2 우리는 <u>기쁘게</u> 우리의 선물 상자를 열었다.
  ➡ We (glad / gladly) opened our gift box.

3 그녀의 목소리는 매우 <u>크다</u>.
  ➡ Her voice is very (loud / loudly).

4 그는 그의 새로운 스마트폰을 자랑스럽게 보여주었다.
  ➡ He (proud / proudly) showed his (new / newly) smartphone.

5 그녀는 몹시 아팠다.
  ➡ She was (terribly / terrible) sick.

6 문이 조용히 열렸고 그녀가 들어왔다.
  ➡ The door opened (quiet / quietly) and she came in.

7 운 좋게도, 나는 그 경기를 쉽게 이길 수 있었다
  ➡ (Luckily / Lucky), I could win the game (easily / easy).

8 나는 그의 이야기를 주의 깊게 들었다.
  ➡ I listened (careful / carefully) to his story.

9 그것은 아름다운 꽃이다.
  ➡ That is a (beautifully / beautiful) flower.

10 갑자기, 비가 심하게 내리기 시작했다.
  ➡ (Suddenly / Sudden), it started to rain (heavy / heavily).

정답 p.44

PRACTICE 2

다음 형용사의 부사형을 쓰세요.

1	nice	➡ _____	2	beautiful	➡ _____
3	happy	➡ _____	4	clear	➡ _____
5	different	➡ _____	6	kind	➡ _____
7	careful	➡ _____	8	heavy	➡ _____
9	usual	➡ _____	10	real	➡ _____
11	quick	➡ _____	12	glad	➡ _____
13	lucky	➡ _____	14	surprising	➡ _____
15	pretty	➡ _____	16	strong	➡ _____
17	dangerous	➡ _____	18	noisy	➡ _____
19	loud	➡ _____	20	easy	➡ _____
21	new	➡ _____	22	regular	➡ _____
23	slow	➡ _____	24	sad	➡ _____
25	brave	➡ _____	26	great	➡ _____
27	special	➡ _____	28	quiet	➡ _____
29	similar	➡ _____	30	bad	➡ _____

PRACTICE 3

〈보기〉와 같이 우리말과 같은 뜻이 되도록 괄호 안에 주어진 단어 중 알맞은 것을 고르세요.

> **보 기** 너는 조심해서 길을 건너야 한다. = You should cross the streets (careful, **carefully**).

1. Susan은 그 소식에 행복하지 않았다. = Susan didn't feel (happy, happily) at the news.
2. 나는 대개 직장에 걸어간다. = I (usual, usually) walk to work.
3. 그녀의 음식은 아주 맛있었다. = Her food tasted (great, greatly).
4. 나는 너의 파티를 정말로 즐겼어. = I (real, really) enjoyed your party.
5. 시험은 쉽지 않을 거야. = The test won't be (easy, easily).
6. 하늘은 갑자기 어두워졌다. = The sky (sudden, suddenly) went dark.
7. 지하철은 안전하고 빠르다. = The subway is (safe, safely) and fast.
8. 차는 우리의 삶을 놀랍게 변화시켰다. = Cars changed our lives (surprising, surprisingly).
9. 이것은 중요한 정보이다. = This is (important, importantly) information.
10. 그는 문을 조용히 열었다. = He opened the door (quiet, quietly).
11. 그는 슬프게 고개를 저었다. = He shook his head (sad, sadly).
12. 군인들은 용감하게 적에 맞서 싸웠다. = The soldiers (bravely, brave) fought against the enemy.

PSS 1-2 형용사와 형태가 같은 부사

1. **late** '늦은, 늦게'

   I was **late** for the meeting this morning. (형용사) 나는 오늘 아침에 회의에 늦었다.
   She got up **late** this morning. (부사) 그녀는 오늘 아침에 늦게 일어났다.

2. **early** '이른, 일찍'

   The **early** bird catches the worm. (형용사) 일찍 일어나는 새가 벌레를 잡는다.
   He gets up **early** in the morning. (부사) 그는 아침에 일찍 일어난다.

3. **hard** '어려운, 열심히'

   English is **hard** for me. (형용사) 영어는 나에게 어렵다.
   I'm working **hard**. (부사) 나는 열심히 일하고 있다.

   cf. 그 외 형용사와 부사의 형태가 같은 단어들
   fast 빠른, 빨리   long 긴, 길게   low 낮은, 낮게   high 높은, 높게   daily 매일의, 매일
   pretty 귀여운, 꽤

PRACTICE 4

밑줄 친 부분의 쓰임이 〈보기〉의 A와 같으면 A를, B와 같으면 B를 쓰세요.

보 기	A. I don't eat fast food.
	B. The train goes very fast.

1. I'm late again. [ ]
   Don't go out too late. [ ]

2. The hospital opens early. [ ]
   It is too early now. [ ]

3. Everybody wants to live long. [ ]
   There's a long line. [ ]

4. The students studied very hard. [ ]
   It is hard to work on the farm. [ ]

5. We sell them at a low price. [ ]
   The bird is flying low. [ ]

6. He often drives fast. [ ]
   I'm a fast runner. [ ]

7. A bottle of milk comes daily. [ ]
   It's a daily paper. [ ]

8. I have a high fever. [ ]
   The kite is flying high. [ ]

PSS 2 빈도부사

PSS 2-1 빈도부사의 종류와 의미

빈도부사란 어떤 일의 빈도, 즉 횟수나 정도를 나타내는 부사를 말한다.

always '항상'   **usually** '보통, 대개'   **often** '자주, 종종'
sometimes '때때로'   **never** '결코 ~ 아닌'

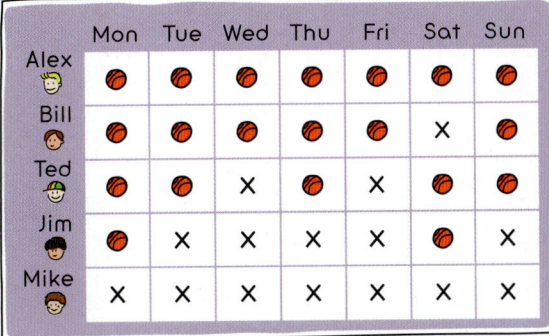

Alex **always** plays basketball.
Alex는 항상 농구를 한다.
Bill **usually** plays basketball.
Bill은 대개 농구를 한다.
Ted **often** plays basketball.
Ted는 종종 농구를 한다.
Jim **sometimes** plays basketball.
Jim은 때때로 농구를 한다.
Mike **never** plays basketball.
Mike는 결코 농구를 하지 않는다.

PRACTICE 5

우리말과 같은 뜻이 되도록 〈보기〉에서 알맞은 빈도부사를 골라 빈칸에 쓰세요.

보 기	always usually often sometimes never

1 Paul은 절대로 아침을 먹지 않는다.
   = Paul _____ eats breakfast.

2 물은 항상 그 형태가 변한다.
   = Water _____ changes its form.

3 나는 종종 영화관에 간다.
   = I _____ go to the movies.

4 나는 네 친절을 결코 잊지 않을 것이다.
   = I'll _____ forget your kindness.

5 Jenny는 대개 하루에 다섯 번의 수업이 있다.
   = Jenny _____ has five classes a day.

6 그의 어머니는 그에게 자주 전화한다.
   = His mother _____ calls him.

7 나는 때때로 꽃을 산다.
   = I _____ buy flowers.

8 Helen은 항상 여기에 있니?
   = Is Helen _____ here?

9 그녀는 대개 매우 신중하다.
   = She is _____ very careful.

10 이곳에는 때때로 비가 내린다.
    = It _____ rains here.

11 그들은 여러 가지 방법으로 항상 나를 돕는다.
    = They _____ help me in many ways.

12 나는 태국에 한 번도 가보지 않았다.
    = I've _____ been to Thailand.

13 그는 보통 주말에 영화를 본다.
    = He _____ watches movies on weekends.

14 나는 때때로 밤에 우유를 마신다.
    = I _____ drink milk at night.

PSS 2-2 빈도부사의 위치

1. be동사/조동사+빈도부사

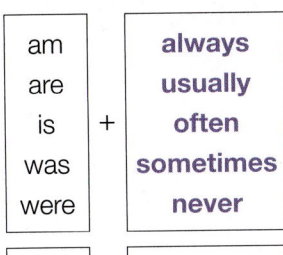

Mike **is always** kind. Mike는 항상 친절하다.
They **were usually** busy. 그들은 대개 바빴다.
Mistakes **are often** the best teachers. 실수는 종종 최고의 스승이다.
Ann **was sometimes** very sick. Ann은 때때로 매우 아팠다.
I**'m never** late for work. 나는 절대로 회사에 지각하지 않는다.

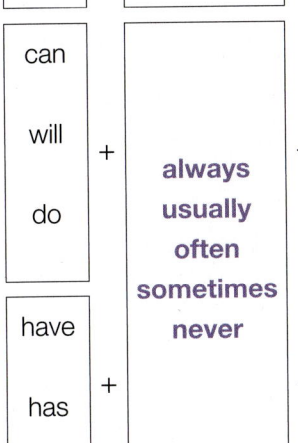

You **can always depend** on me.
너는 항상 나를 믿어도 된다.
He**'ll usually stay** there.
그는 대개 그곳에 머물 것이다.
I **don**'t **often eat** vegetables.
나는 야채를 자주 먹지 않는다.
I **have always been** a writer.
나는 항상 작가였었다.
He **has never ridden** a horse.
그는 결코 말을 타본 적이 없다.

2. 빈도부사+일반동사

always usually often sometimes never	+	go work enjoy take use

He **always goes** to bed at 10. 그는 항상 10시에 잠자리에 든다.
I **usually work** 8 hours a day. 나는 대개 하루에 8시간 일한다.
She **often enjoys** Italian food. 그녀는 종종 이탈리아 음식을 즐겨 먹는다.
They **sometimes take** a taxi. 그들은 때때로 택시를 탄다.
We **never use** plastic bags. 우리는 절대로 비닐 봉지를 사용하지 않는다.

정답 p.44

PRACTICE 6

〈보기〉와 같이 괄호 안의 빈도부사를 알맞은 곳에 넣어 문장을 다시 쓰세요.

보 기	They go to church on Sundays. (always) ➡ They always go to church on Sundays.

1 Mrs. Kim is kind. (always)
➡ _____

2 Do you surf the Internet? (often)
➡ _____

3 Shelly tries to smile. (always)
➡ _____

4 I have taken an airplane. (never)
➡ _____

5 This street is crowded. (sometimes)
➡ _____

6 Tom is at home after 8 o'clock. (never)
➡ _____

7 It is foggy in London. (often)
➡ _____

8 He has made mistakes. (often)
➡ _____

9 He finishes his work on time. (never)
➡ _____

10 I go to the French restaurant. (often)
➡ _____

11 My work starts at 8:30. (usually)
➡ _____

12 What do you do on weekends? (usually)
➡ _____

13 She has been nice to others. (always)
➡ _____

14 She walks to her office. (sometimes)
➡ _____

15 The newspaper is delivered at 7. (usually)
➡ _____

16 You can count on me. (always)
➡ _____

PSS 3 too, either
Problem Solving Skill

too와 either는 '또한, 역시'의 뜻으로 too(=as well)는 긍정문에서, either는 부정문에서 쓰인다.

Cathy **likes** music. John **likes** music, **too**.
Cathy는 음악을 좋아한다. John도 역시 음악을 좋아한다.

Giho **doesn't like** coffee. Mary **doesn't like** coffee, **either**.
기호는 커피를 좋아하지 않는다. Mary도 역시 커피를 좋아하지 않는다.

cf. '너무, 매우'의 의미를 갖는 too는 형용사나 부사 앞에 위치한다.
I have **too much** homework. 나는 숙제가 너무 많다.

PRACTICE 7

다음 문장의 빈칸에 too나 either 중 알맞은 것을 쓰세요.

1 A: He couldn't eat any more.   B: I couldn't eat any more, _____.
2 A: She failed her test.   B: I failed my test, _____.
3 A: I didn't go to the meeting.   B: She didn't go to the meeting, _____.
4 A: I studied math.   B: David studied math, _____.
5 A: I'm thirty years old.   B: I'm thirty years old, _____.
6 A: I don't have a dog.   B: John doesn't have a dog, _____.
7 A: Mike joined the club.   B: I joined the club, _____.
8 A: I won't stay at home.   B: They won't stay at home, _____.
9 A: He cannot swim.   B: I can't swim, _____.
10 A: We didn't sleep all night.   B: They didn't sleep all night, _____.
11 A: We could find the way.   B: They could find the way, _____.
12 A: Nice to meet you.   B: Nice to meet you, _____.
13 A: I don't like the dish.   B: They don't like the dish, _____.
14 A: I'm from Seoul.   B: I'm from Seoul, _____.
15 A: I don't have a pen.   B: She doesn't have a pen, _____.
16 A: I'm ready to go.   B: Your dad is ready to go, _____.
17 A: I can't hear you very well.   B: I can't hear you very well, _____.
18 A: He likes horror movies.   B: I like horror movies, _____.

 well

> good은 명사를 수식하거나 보어 역할을 하는 형용사이고, well은 동사를 수식하는 부사이다.
>
> She is a **good swimmer**. 그녀는 훌륭한 수영 선수이다.
> She **is good** at swimming. 그녀는 수영을 잘한다.
> She **swims well**. 그녀는 수영을 잘한다.
>
> *cf.* well은 '건강한, 몸이 좋은'의 의미를 갖는 형용사로도 쓰인다.
> I don't **feel well**. 나는 몸이 좋지 않다.

PRACTICE 8

정답 p.45

다음 문장의 빈칸에 good이나 well 중 알맞은 것을 쓰세요.

1 I couldn't sleep _____ last night.
2 It's _____ to see you.
3 Some foreigners eat gimchi _____.
4 The reading club was _____ for us.
5 I hope you get _____ soon.
6 We don't know them _____.
7 This is a _____ place to talk.
8 I'm a _____ painter.
9 His English is very _____.
10 You did _____ on the test.
11 Seho speaks French very _____.
12 My exam results were _____.
13 Your jacket looks _____ on you.
14 I can't read _____ without my glasses.

「타동사 + 부사」
Problem Solving Skill

PSS 5-1 「타동사 + 부사」의 종류

동사는 목적어를 필요로 하는가에 따라 자동사(목적어 불필요)와 타동사(목적어 필요)로 분류할 수 있다.

The door opened quickly. 그 문은 빠르게 열렸다.
주어   자동사   수식어

He opened the door. 그는 문을 열었다.
주어   타동사   목적어

「타동사+부사」가 만나면 원래 동사와는 다른 새로운 의미를 나타내게 된다.

turn은 '(~을) 돌리다'라는 뜻인데, turn과 on이 만나면 '(전기, TV 등을) 켜다'라는 새로운 의미가 된다.

She turned on the light. 그녀는 불을 켰다.
주어 타동사 부사 목적어

1. turn on '켜다' ↔ turn off '끄다'

She **turned on** the light. 그녀는 불을 켰다.

He **turned off** the light. 그는 불을 껐다.

2. put on '입다' ↔ take off '벗다'

Liza **put on** her glasses.
Liza는 그녀의 안경을 썼다.

Bob **took off** his jacket.
Bob은 그의 재킷을 벗었다.

3. try on '입어보다'
   May I **try on** these shoes? 제가 이 신발을 신어봐도 될까요?

4. pick up '줍다, 집어 들다, ~를 (차에) 태우러 가다'
   I can **pick up** food with chopsticks. 나는 젓가락으로 음식을 집어들 수 있다.

5. throw away '버리다'
   Some people **threw away** trash on the street. 몇 명의 사람들이 길거리에 쓰레기를 버렸다.

6. bring back '돌려주다'
   I will **bring back** your umbrella. 나는 네 우산을 돌려줄 것이다.

정답 p.45

PRACTICE 9

〈보기〉에서 알맞은 부사를 골라 빈칸에 쓰세요.

보기	on off up away back

1. Put _____ your coat to stay warm.
2. Turn _____ your phone in the theater.
3. My brother tried _____ his new suit.
4. I saw people throw _____ their garbage.
5. His uncle will pick _____ John at the station.
6. Did you bring _____ the book to Jim?
7. You should take _____ your shoes here.
8. Why don't you try _____ this shirt?
9. I brought _____ the money.
10. I turned _____ your computer to find the file.

PSS 5-2 「타동사 + 부사」의 어순

1. 목적어가 명사인 경우, 「타동사+부사+명사」 또는 「타동사+명사+부사」의 어순 둘 다 가능하다.

   I **turned on** the TV. = I **turned** the TV **on**. 나는 TV를 켰다.
   He **turned off** the TV. = He **turned** the TV **off**. 그는 TV를 껐다.

2. 목적어가 대명사인 경우, 「타동사+대명사+부사」의 어순만 가능하다.

   I **turned** it **on**. (○)   I **turned on** it. (×) 나는 그것을 켰다.
   He **turned** it **off**. (○)   He **turned off** it. (×) 그는 그것을 껐다.
   He **put** them **on**. (○)   He **put on** them. (×) 그는 그것들을 입었다.
   I can **pick** her **up**. (○)   I can **pick up** her. (×) 나는 그녀를 태우러 갈 수 있다.

   cf. 「자동사+전치사」의 경우와 혼동해서는 안 된다.

   Listen to this music. (○)   **Listen** this music **to**. (×) 이 음악을 들어라.

PRACTICE 10

정답 p.45

괄호 안에 주어진 말 중 알맞은 것을 고르세요.

1 Can you (turn on the radio, turn on it)?

2 Will you (try on them, try them on)?

3 Please (turn off it, turn off the alarm).

4 They (picked up Bob, picked up him).

5 Nancy (threw away her hat, threw away it).

6 Ralph (took off it, took his raincoat off).

7 I'm going to (bring back them, bring them back).

8 She (put on her necklace, put on it).

9 I couldn't (turn it on, turn on it).

10 Don't (throw away them, throw them away).

11 Meredith didn't (give up him, give him up).

12 The old lady couldn't even (write her name down, write down it).

의문부사

PSS 6-1 how, where, when, why

1. 방법을 모를 때 – how(어떻게)로 묻는다.

   How does he go to the library? — He goes to the library **by bus**.
   그는 도서관에 어떻게 가니? 그는 버스를 타고 도서관에 가.

2. 장소를 모를 때 – where(어디에)로 묻는다.

   Where does he go by bus? — He goes **to the library** by bus.
   그는 버스를 타고 어디를 가니? 그는 버스를 타고 도서관에 가.

3. 때를 모를 때 – when(언제)으로 묻는다.

   When does he go to the library? — He goes to the library **in the morning**.
   그는 언제 도서관에 가니? 그는 아침에 도서관에 가.

4. 원인/이유를 모를 때 – why(왜)로 묻는다.

   Why does he go to the library? — **Because he wants to study in a quiet place.**
   그는 왜 도서관에 가니? 그는 조용한 곳에서 공부하기를 원하기 때문이야.

정답 p.45

PRACTICE 11

괄호 안의 단어를 바르게 배열하여 의문문을 완성하세요.

1 A: _____ B: It's under the desk.
   (my, where, bag, is)

2 A: _____ B: I love it.
   (do, food, like, how, you, this)

3   A: _____   B: December 12th.
      (her, when, birthday, is)

4   A: _____   B: Because I had a few questions.
      (call, you, why, me, did)

5   A: _____   B: It's sunny.
      (how, Seoul, the, in, is, weather)

6   A: _____   B: At about 3 o'clock.
      (did, work, finish, when, the, Minsu)

7   A: _____   B: Because it's so long.
      (book, like, the, why, he, doesn't)

8   A: _____   B: To Europe.
      (are, travel, where, going, you, to)

9   A: _____   B: At the restaurant.
      (you, did, lunch, eat, where)

10 A: _____   B: Because I was late for work.
      (why, running, you, were)

PSS 6-2 How + 형용사/부사 ~?

'얼마나 ~하니?'라는 뜻으로 횟수, 기간, 거리, 나이, 금액 등의 정도를 물을 때 쓰인다.

How often does he come here?	– **Twice a month**.
그는 얼마나 자주 여기에 오니?	한 달에 두 번.
How long does it take to come here?	– It takes **about fifteen minutes**.
여기로 오는 데 얼마나 걸리니?	15분 정도 걸려.
How far is it from here to the station?	– It is **about three kilometers**.
여기에서 역까지는 얼마나 머니?	약 3km 정도야.
How old is she?	– She is **26 years old**.
그녀는 몇 살이니?	그녀는 26살이야.
How tall are you?	– I'm **165 centimeters**.
네 키는 얼마니?	나는 165cm야.
How much is this skirt?	– It is **ten dollars**.
이 치마는 얼마인가요?	10달러예요.
How many sisters do you have?	– I have **two sisters**.
너는 누나가 몇 명이나 있니?	나는 누나가 두 명 있어.

PRACTICE 12

〈보기〉와 같이 빈칸에 알맞은 단어를 넣어 대화를 완성하세요.

> 보기 A: How <u>often</u> do you go to the movies?
> B: About twice a year.

1 A: How _____ will you stay in this hotel?   B: Two weeks.
2 A: How _____ is your sister?   B: She's twenty years old.
3 A: How _____ is this notebook?   B: It's two thousand won.
4 A: How _____ do you take the bus?   B: Every day.
5 A: How _____ is it from here to the museum?   B: It is two blocks away.
6 A: How _____ is that scarf?   B: It's twelve dollars.
7 A: How _____ is your father?   B: He is 180 centimeters.
8 A: How _____ shoes do you have?   B: I have four pairs of shoes.
9 A: How _____ pets do you have?   B: I have a dog and a cat.
10 A: How _____ do you play the piano a day?   B: Half an hour.
11 A: How _____ is this table?   B: About ten years old.
12 A: How _____ does it take to get to your home?   B: About 10 minutes on foot.
13 A: How _____ is it from Seoul to Busan?   B: It is about 325km.
14 A: How _____ is this building?   B: It has 27 stories.
15 A: How _____ do you get a haircut?   B: Once a month.

PRACTICE 13

다음 질문에 알맞은 응답을 찾아 그 기호를 쓰세요.

1 When do you leave? [   ]
2 Why can't you come here? [   ]
3 How often do you brush your teeth? [   ]
4 Where did you find it? [   ]
5 How old is your dog? [   ]

ⓐ Three times a day.
ⓑ It is three years old.
ⓒ Because I have to see a doctor.
ⓓ In three days.
ⓔ Behind the sofa.

Chapter Review Test

정답 p.46

CHAPTER 11 부사

1 다음 문장에서 usually가 들어갈 알맞은 위치는?

I ① dream ② about ③ flying ④ in the sky ⑤.

2 다음 대화의 빈칸에 들어갈 알맞은 단어는?

A: _____ do you go to work?
B: I go to work by bus.

① How   ② What   ③ When
④ Why   ⑤ Where

3 다음 글의 밑줄 친 ⓐ~ⓔ 중 어법상 옳은 것은?

I am a basketball coach. When my son was young, he went to the basketball court ⓐ <u>many time</u> to watch a game. I think that is why he wants to be a basketball player when he grows up. His friends like ⓑ <u>play</u> basketball, too. After school, we often play basketball. It feels so nice to ⓒ <u>drink a water</u> after we sweat a lot. However, his friend, Tom, ⓓ <u>never plays</u> basketball. One day, I asked him, "Tom, do you want to play basketball with us?" He answered, "I'm sorry, but I don't ⓔ <u>have the time</u>."

① ⓐ   ② ⓑ   ③ ⓒ   ④ ⓓ   ⑤ ⓔ

4 다음의 빈칸에 공통으로 들어갈 알맞은 단어는?

- He tried _____ another shirt.
- She showed me how to turn _____ the light.

① by   ② at   ③ to   ④ on   ⑤ off

5 다음 대화의 빈칸에 들어갈 알맞은 단어는?

A: _____ did you go during summer vacation?
B: I went to Paris.

① How   ② What   ③ Why
④ When   ⑤ Where

6 다음 빈칸에 들어갈 말이 바르게 짝지어진 것은?

- Make sure you don't take flash photos in the museum. You should not bring any food into the museum, _____.
- Andy and Kate are really good dancers. They can sing well, _____.

① too – either   ② either – too
③ either – also   ④ also – either
⑤ too – also

7 다음 두 문장이 같은 뜻이 되도록 빈칸에 들어갈 알맞은 단어를 쓰세요.

- My mom is a good cook.
  = My mom cooks _____.

8 다음 글의 밑줄 친 (A)를 6단어로 영작하세요.

My brother has trouble sleeping. So, (A) <u>그는 밤에 커피를 절대로 마시지 않는다</u>.

➡ _____

9 다음 짝지어진 두 단어의 관계가 〈보기〉와 같은 것은?

보기	nice – nicely

① friend – friendly
② careful – carefully
③ elder – elderly
④ week – weekly
⑤ luck – luckily

10 다음 대화의 빈칸에 들어갈 알맞은 말은?

A: _____ is this blue T-shirt?
B: It is 25 dollars.

① How old
② How far
③ How many
④ How much
⑤ How long

11 다음 빈칸에 들어갈 말이 알맞게 짝지어진 것은?

A: _____ don't we go for a bike ride this weekend?
B: Sounds great!
A: _____ are we going to ride our bikes?
B: Let's go to the Grand Park.

① How – Where
② Where – What
③ Why – What
④ Why – When
⑤ Why – Where

12 다음 빈칸에 공통으로 들어갈 알맞은 단어는?

- I turned _____ my computer.
- He took _____ his glasses.

① on
② off
③ to
④ back
⑤ away

13 다음 중 어법상 잘못된 문장을 고르세요.

① She sometimes goes to bed early.
② Mike never works out at the gym.
③ I usually go for a walk in the evening.
④ I often visit my grandparents on Sunday.
⑤ He always is busy in the morning.

14 다음 대화를 읽고, 괄호 안의 단어를 이용하여 빈칸에 의문부사로 시작하는 문장을 쓰세요. (단, 시제에 주의하세요.)

A: Hi, good to see you again.
B: Me, too. Where have you been during summer vacation?
A: I've been to Hawaii.
B: Oh, really? (1) _____? (go, there)
A: I went there to visit my uncle.
B: I see. (2) _____? (stay, there)
A: I stayed there for a week.

(1) _____
(2) _____

15 다음 대화 중 어색한 것은?

① A: How do you like the Beatles' songs?
   B: I love them. I listen to 'Yesterday' every day.
② A: When did you go to bed last night?
   B: I went to bed at about 10 p.m.
③ A: I didn't bring my wallet.
   B: I didn't bring mine, too. We are in trouble.
④ A: Where do your grandparents live now?
   B: They live in Sejong now.
⑤ A: Why does Mina always drink green tea?
   B: Because she likes its taste.

16 다음 대화의 빈칸에 들어갈 알맞은 표현은?

> A: _____ do you go to the shopping mall?
> B: I go there three times a month.

① How often
② How far
③ How long
④ How much
⑤ How many

17 다음 글의 밑줄 친 부분 중 어법상 틀린 것은?

> I got up early in the morning. Birds were singing. I ① looked around the lake. I breathed ② deeply. The fresh air ③ woke me up. I finished my breakfast and packed my stuff. I ④ picked a map up at the front desk and ⑤ looked it at. I decided where to go and started the second day of my journey.

18 다음 대화 중 어색한 것은?

① A: How much are these jeans?
　B: They're 70,000 won.
② A: How long does it take to get there by plane?
　B: It is 530km.
③ A: How old is your brother?
　B: He is 19 years old.
④ A: How often do you take a shower?
　B: Twice a week.
⑤ A: How many pets do you have in your house?
　B: I have three dogs and two cats.

19 다음 대화의 밑줄 친 부분과 바꾸어 쓸 수 있는 단어는?

> A: What time shall we meet?
> B: How about seven?
> A: No problem.

① Where
② How
③ What
④ Who
⑤ When

20 다음 두 문장이 같은 뜻이 되도록 빈칸에 알맞은 단어를 쓰세요.

> • My friend also gave me some cookies.
> = My friend gave me some cookies, _____.

21 다음 글의 ⓐ~ⓔ 중 어법상 바른 것은?

> This is my family. We love music. I play ⓐ violin and my dad plays the guitar. Mom and my sister ⓑ plays the piano. Our family ⓒ goes often to a concert. I ⓓ feel great when I am at the concert. I hope ⓔ having a concert with my family one day.

① ⓐ　② ⓑ　③ ⓒ　④ ⓓ　⑤ ⓔ

22 다음 빈칸에 공통으로 들어갈 의문부사를 쓰세요.

> • _____ long does it take?
> – It only takes half an hour.
> • _____ can I get there?
> – You can get there by subway.

23 다음 대화의 빈칸에 들어갈 말로 알맞지 <u>않은</u> 것은?

A: How often do you go to the movies?
B: _____

① Sometimes.　　② Never.
③ An hour.　　　④ Twice a week.
⑤ Three times a month.

24 다음 질문에 대한 대답으로 가장 알맞은 것은?

A: How can I get to Busan?
B: _____

① Sure, I will get you a map.
② It won't take too long.
③ Yes, you can get anything.
④ I went to Busan a month ago.
⑤ You can go there by train.

25 다음 밑줄 친 부분의 쓰임이 바르지 <u>못한</u> 것은?

① The bus arrived very <u>lately</u> in the morning.
② She always studies very <u>hard</u>.
③ Thank you <u>so</u> much.
④ You have to carry it <u>carefully</u>.
⑤ You should get up <u>early</u>.

26 다음 대화의 빈칸에 들어갈 단어로 알맞은 것은?

A: _____ does she live?
B: She lives in New York.

① When　　② Where　　③ What
④ Which　　⑤ Why

27 다음 정민이의 주간 계획표를 보고 각 문장에 들어가기에 적합한 단어를 〈보기〉에서 골라 쓰세요. (단, 각 단어는 반드시 한 번씩만 쓸 것.)

Jungmin's weekly plan
go swimming every morning
eat pizza once a week
play tennis three times a week
go to the library five times a week
go to bed before 10

보 기	never, often, sometimes, always, usually

(1) Jungmin _____ plays tennis.
(2) Jungmin _____ goes to the library.
(3) Jungmin _____ eats pizza.
(4) Jungmin _____ goes to bed after 10 o'clock.
(5) Jungmin _____ goes swimming in the morning.

28 다음 중 단어의 관계가 〈보기〉와 같은 것은?

보 기	sad – sadly

① play – player
② noisy – noisily
③ talk – talkative
④ catch – caught
⑤ friend – friendly

29 다음 밑줄 친 부분이 의미하는 것은?

> A: Why do some people want to watch horror movies? I don't like watching scary things.
> B: I don't, either. But I've heard that some people get excited by scary movies.

① I like to watch horror movies.
② I don't like watching horror movies.
③ I understand why people watch horror movies.
④ I don't understand why people watch horror movies.
⑤ I don't like to see scary things, but I like horror movies.

30 다음 두 문장이 같은 뜻이 되도록 빈칸에 주어진 철자로 시작하는 알맞은 단어를 쓰세요.

> • It was lucky that Mary met James on the street.
> = L_____, Mary met James on the street.

31 다음 대화의 빈칸에 들어갈 알맞은 단어는?

> A: What time shall we meet?
> B: At twenty to four.
> A: Good. And _____ shall we meet?
> B: Let's meet in front of the train station.

① what   ② who   ③ where
④ which ⑤ how

32 다음 밑줄 친 부분 중 어법상 잘못된 것은?

① They were shouting loudly.
② You have to think carefully.
③ Jane can sing very well.
④ The family lived happily.
⑤ I can run fastly.

33 다음 빈칸 (A), (B)에 들어갈 말로 알맞게 짝지어진 것은?

> Hi! I'm Minho. I started to learn how to play the piano recently. It's not _____(A)_____ but I'm not going to quit it. I hope I can play my favorite song _____(B)_____ by the end of this year.

	(A)	(B)
①	ease	beautiful
②	easily	beauty
③	easily	beautifully
④	easy	beautifully
⑤	easy	beauty

34 다음 직원들이 직장에 가는 방법을 나타낸 표와 내용이 다른 것은?

	MON	TUE	WED	THU	FRI
James	bus	bus	bus	bus	bus
Susan	bike	bike	bike	bus	bike
Mike	subway	bus	subway	bus	subway
Kate	bike	subway	subway	bike	subway
Lucy	subway	bike	subway	bus	bike

① James always goes to work by bus.
② Susan usually goes to work by bike.
③ Mike sometimes goes to work by bus.
④ Kate often goes to work by subway.
⑤ Lucy never goes to work by bus.

CHAPTER 12
비교구문

성취도 자기 평가 활용법

구분	평가 기준
Excellent	문법 내용을 모두 이해하고, 문제를 모두 맞힘.
Very good	문법 내용은 충분히 이해했으나 실수로 1~2문제 틀림.
Good	문법 내용이 조금 어려워 3~4문제 틀림.
needs **R**eview	문법 내용 이해가 어렵고, 5문제 이상 틀림. 복습 필요.

	페이지	학습날짜	성취도 자기평가 E V G R	학습체크
PSS 1 원급, 비교급, 최상급의 형태				
PSS 1-1 규칙 변화형 Ⅰ	242	/		☐
PSS 1-2 규칙 변화형 Ⅱ	243	/		☐
PSS 1-3 규칙 변화형 Ⅲ	244	/		☐
PSS 1-4 불규칙 변화형	246	/		☐
PSS 2 원급을 이용한 비교	248	/		☐
	페이지	학습날짜	성취도 자기평가 E V G R	학습체크
PSS 3 비교급을 이용한 비교				
PSS 3-1 비교급+than	250	/		☐
PSS 3-2 비교급+and+비교급	252	/		☐
PSS 3-3 비교급 강조	253	/		☐
	페이지	학습날짜	성취도 자기평가 E V G R	학습체크
PSS 4 최상급을 이용한 비교				
PSS 4-1 the+최상급	255	/		☐
PSS 4-2 one of the+최상급+복수 명사	256	/		☐
Chapter Review Test	258	/		☐

원급, 비교급, 최상급의 형태

PSS 1-1 규칙 변화형 I

원급은 형용사나 부사의 원형, 비교급은 원급에 -er을 붙인 형태, 최상급은 원급에 -est를 붙인 형태를 말한다.

대부분의 경우	원급에 -er/-est	tall – taller – tallest 키가 큰 – 키가 더 큰 – 키가 가장 큰 old – older – oldest 나이 든 – 더 나이 든 – 가장 나이 든 hard – harder – hardest 열심히 – 더 열심히 – 가장 열심히
-e로 끝나는 경우	원급에 -r/-st	nice – nicer – nicest 멋있는 – 더 멋있는 – 가장 멋있는 large – larger – largest 큰 – 더 큰 – 가장 큰 wise – wiser – wisest 현명한 – 더 현명한 – 가장 현명한

정답 p.48

PRACTICE 1

다음 형용사나 부사의 비교급과 최상급을 쓰세요.

1 kind – _____ – _____
2 large – _____ – _____
3 tall   – _____ – _____
4 loud – _____ – _____
5 safe – _____ – _____
6 weak – _____ – _____
7 great – _____ – _____
8 soft – _____ – _____
9 low   – _____ – _____
10 huge – _____ – _____
11 smart – _____ – _____
12 cheap – _____ – _____
13 nice – _____ – _____
14 strong – _____ – _____
15 clean – _____ – _____
16 fast – _____ – _____
17 poor – _____ – _____
18 brave – _____ – _____
19 sweet – _____ – _____
20 fresh – _____ – _____

PSS 1-2 규칙 변화형 II

단모음+단자음으로 끝나는 경우	마지막 자음을 하나 더 쓰고 -er/-est	fat – fat**ter** – fat**test** 뚱뚱한 – 더 뚱뚱한 – 가장 뚱뚱한 hot – hot**ter** – hot**test** 더운 – 더 더운 – 가장 더운 big – big**ger** – big**gest** 큰 – 더 큰 – 가장 큰
자음+y로 끝나는 경우	y를 i로 바꾸고 -er/-est	pretty – prett**ier** – prett**iest** 예쁜 – 더 예쁜 – 가장 예쁜 happy – happ**ier** – happ**iest** 행복한 – 더 행복한 – 가장 행복한 easy – eas**ier** – eas**iest** 쉬운 – 더 쉬운 – 가장 쉬운

정답 p.48

PRACTICE 2

다음 형용사나 부사의 비교급과 최상급을 쓰세요.

1 hot   – _____ – _____
2 light   – _____ – _____
3 mild   – _____ – _____
4 noisy   – _____ – _____
5 heavy   – _____ – _____
6 fat   – _____ – _____
7 wise   – _____ – _____
8 sunny   – _____ – _____
9 dirty   – _____ – _____
10 cool   – _____ – _____
11 warm   – _____ – _____
12 happy   – _____ – _____
13 hungry – _____ – _____
14 big   – _____ – _____
15 wet   – _____ – _____
16 tasty   – _____ – _____
17 strict – _____ – _____
18 ugly   – _____ – _____
19 pretty – _____ – _____
20 hard   – _____ – _____

PSS 1-3 규칙 변화형 Ⅲ

다음의 경우에는 원급 앞에 more, most를 붙여 비교급과 최상급을 만든다.

대부분의 2음절 이상의 형용사(단, -y로 끝나는 형용사는 제외)	useful – **more** useful – **most** useful
	유용한 – 더 유용한 – 가장 유용한
	hopeless – **more** hopeless – **most** hopeless
	가망 없는 – 더 가망 없는 – 가장 가망 없는
	foolish – **more** foolish – **most** foolish
	어리석은 – 더 어리석은 – 가장 어리석은
	famous – **more** famous – **most** famous
	유명한 – 더 유명한 – 가장 유명한
	patient – **more** patient – **most** patient
	인내심 있는 – 더 인내심 있는 – 가장 인내심 있는
	popular – **more** popular – **most** popular
	인기 있는 – 더 인기 있는 – 가장 인기 있는
	difficult – **more** difficult – **most** difficult
	어려운 – 더 어려운 – 가장 어려운
	important – **more** important – **most** important
	중요한 – 더 중요한 – 가장 중요한
	expensive – **more** expensive – **most** expensive
	비싼 – 더 비싼 – 가장 비싼
	cf. 음절이란 모음을 포함한 소리의 단위를 말한다.
	    useful – use / ful 2음절
	    important – im / por / tant 3음절

분사 형태의 형용사	interesting – **more** interesting – **most** interesting 흥미로운 – 더 흥미로운 – 가장 흥미로운 tired – **more** tired – **most** tired 피곤한 – 더 피곤한 – 가장 피곤한 excited – **more** excited – **most** excited 흥미진진한 – 더 흥미진진한 – 가장 흥미진진한
「형용사+ly」의 형태의 부사	quickly – **more** quickly – **most** quickly 빨리 – 더 빨리 – 가장 빨리 easily – **more** easily – **most** easily 쉽게 – 더 쉽게 – 가장 쉽게 seriously – **more** seriously – **most** seriously 심각하게 – 더 심각하게 – 가장 심각하게

PRACTICE 3

다음 형용사나 부사의 비교급과 최상급을 쓰세요.

1. busy — _____ — _____
2. interesting — _____ — _____
3. beautiful — _____ — _____
4. bright — _____ — _____
5. seriously — _____ — _____
6. careful — _____ — _____
7. friendly — _____ — _____
8. important — _____ — _____
9. glad — _____ — _____
10. expensive — _____ — _____
11. lovely — _____ — _____
12. quickly — _____ — _____
13. useful — _____ — _____
14. quiet — _____ — _____
15. exciting — _____ — _____
16. special — _____ — _____
17. soon — _____ — _____
18. difficult — _____ — _____
19. close — _____ — _____
20. helpful — _____ — _____
21. popular — _____ — _____
22. easy — _____ — _____
23. colorful — _____ — _____
24. tough — _____ — _____
25. curious — _____ — _____
26. delicious — _____ — _____
27. near — _____ — _____
28. dangerous — _____ — _____
29. diligent — _____ — _____
30. lucky — _____ — _____

PSS 1-4 불규칙 변화형

원급		비교급	최상급
good '좋은' well '건강한, 잘'		better	best
bad '나쁜' badly '나쁘게' ill '병든'		worse	worst
many '수가 많은' much '양이 많은'		more	most
little '양이 적은'		less	least
old	'나이 든, 낡은'	older	oldest
	'연상의, 손위의'	elder	eldest
late	〈시간〉 '늦은'	later	latest
	〈순서〉 '나중인'	latter	last
far	〈거리〉 '먼'	farther/further	farthest/furthest
	〈정도〉 '더욱, 한층'	further	furthest

PRACTICE 4

정답 p.48

다음 형용사나 부사의 비교급과 최상급을 쓰세요.

1. dark — _____ — _____
2. old(나이 든) — _____ — _____
3. boring — _____ — _____
4. slow — _____ — _____
5. terrible — _____ — _____
6. tired — _____ — _____
7. various — _____ — _____
8. small — _____ — _____
9. badly — _____ — _____
10. wonderful — _____ — _____

11 well – _____ – _____
12 costly – _____ – _____
13 similar – _____ – _____
14 late(늦은) – _____ – _____
15 rich – _____ – _____
16 far(더욱, 한층) – _____ – _____
17 cute – _____ – _____
18 young – _____ – _____
19 far(먼) – _____ – _____
20 famous – _____ – _____
21 thin – _____ – _____
22 faithful – _____ – _____
23 slim – _____ – _____
24 ill – _____ – _____
25 patient – _____ – _____
26 thick – _____ – _____
27 useless – _____ – _____
28 handsome – _____ – _____
29 thirsty – _____ – _____
30 bad – _____ – _____
31 heavily – _____ – _____
32 deep – _____ – _____
33 angry – _____ – _____
34 late(나중인) – _____ – _____
35 old(손위의) – _____ – _____
36 cold – _____ – _____
37 much – _____ – _____
38 different – _____ – _____
39 foolish – _____ – _____
40 little – _____ – _____
41 easily – _____ – _____
42 peaceful – _____ – _____
43 many – _____ – _____
44 generous – _____ – _____

45 high	– _____	– _____
46 crowded	– _____	– _____
47 funny	– _____	– _____
48 comfortable	– _____	– _____
49 good	– _____	– _____
50 hopeless	– _____	– _____
51 long	– _____	– _____

원급을 이용한 비교

Sena is **as tall as** Namsu.
세나는 남수만큼 키가 크다.

He isn't **as old as** her.
그는 그녀만큼 나이가 많지 않다.

1. 「as+원급+as」 '~만큼 …한'

   Sally is **as beautiful as** Ann. Sally는 Ann만큼 아름답다.
   This book is **as thick as** that one. 이 책은 저 책만큼 두껍다.
   I want to run **as fast as** lightning. 나는 번개만큼 빨리 달리고 싶다.
   I can sing **as well as** he can. 나는 그가 할 수 있는 만큼 노래를 잘할 수 있다.

   cf. 「as+원급+as」 뒤에 오는 「주어+동사」는 목적격의 형태로도 쓸 수 있다.
   I can sing **as well as he can**. = I can sing **as well as him**.

2. 「not as[so]+원급+as」 '~만큼 …하지 않은'

   Paul isn't **as[so] strong as** I am. Paul은 나만큼 강하지 않다. (→ I'm stronger than Paul.)
   You aren't **as[so] young as** he is. 너는 그만큼 어리지 않다. (→ He is younger than you.)
   His car doesn't look **as[so] nice as** mine. 그의 차는 내 것만큼 멋져 보이지 않는다.

PRACTICE 5

우리말과 같은 뜻이 되도록 〈보기〉에서 알맞은 단어를 골라 원급 비교 문장을 완성하세요.

보 기	loud　angry　cold　well　simple　interesting　tall　small　clever　slow

1   소민이는 그녀의 언니만큼 피아노를 잘 치지 못한다.
　　= Somin doesn't play the piano _____ her sister.

2   극장은 나의 집만큼이나 작았다.
　　= The theater was _____ my home.

3   Jane은 그녀의 오빠만큼 키가 크지 않다.
　　= Jane is _____ her brother.

4   과학은 역사만큼이나 흥미롭다.
　　= Science is _____ history.

5   그녀는 그녀의 남편만큼 화나지는 않았다.
　　= She was _____ her husband.

6   개는 고양이만큼이나 영리하다.
　　= A dog is _____ a cat.

7   늦은 밤에 택시는 지하철만큼이나 느리지 않다.
　　= A taxi is _____ a subway late at night.

8   이번 겨울은 작년 겨울만큼이나 춥다.
　　= This winter is _____ last winter was.

9   핫도그를 만드는 것은 토스트를 만드는 것만큼이나 간단하다.
　　= Cooking hot dogs is _____ making toast.

10   내 목소리는 네 목소리만큼 크지 않다.
　　= My voice is _____ yours.

PRACTICE 6

〈보기〉와 같이 괄호 안의 단어와 'as ~ as' 구문을 사용하여 두 문장을 한 문장으로 연결하세요.

보 기	• John is 168 cm tall. Susan is 168 cm tall, too. 　➡ John <u>is as tall as</u> Susan. (tall) • This shirt is a large size. That one is an X-large size. 　➡ This shirt <u>isn't as[so] large as</u> that one. (large)

1   Nari is 23 years old. Minho is 24 years old.
　➡ Nari _____ Minho. (old)

2 This scarf is 30 dollars. That one is 30 dollars, too.
→ This scarf _____ that one. (expensive)

3 His pencil is 9 cm. Your pencil is 10 cm.
→ His pencil _____ yours. (long)

4 This building is ten stories high. That building is ten stories high, too.
→ This building _____ that building. (high)

5 I clean my room twice a week. Sangmin cleans his room every day.
→ I _____ Sangmin. (often)

6 This building is huge. That building is also huge.
→ This building _____ that one. (huge)

7 The train can go 120 km/h. The car can go 150 km/h.
→ The train _____ the car. (fast)

8 David is honest. His father is honest, too.
→ David _____ his father. (honest)

9 This book is 6cm thick. That one is 8cm thick.
→ This book _____ that one. (thick)

10 This fruit doesn't look fresh. That one looks fresh.
→ This fruit _____ that one. (fresh)

PSS 3 비교급을 이용한 비교

PSS 3-1 비교급 + than

David's dog is **bigger than** Liza's.
David의 개는 Liza의 것보다 더 크다.

The blue shirt is **more expensive than** the yellow one. 파란 셔츠가 노란 셔츠보다 더 비싸다.

> 「-er than」 또는 「more+원급+than」 '~보다 더 …한' / 「less+원급+than」 '~보다 덜 …한'
>
> Nari studies math **harder than** he does. 나리는 그보다 수학을 더 열심히 공부한다.
> My mother gets up **earlier than** I do. 엄마는 나보다 더 일찍 일어나신다.
> Two heads are **better than** one. 혼자보다 두 사람의 머리가 낫다.
> This story is **more interesting than** that one. 이 이야기는 저 이야기보다 더 흥미롭다.
> Diet Coke is **less popular than** the original one. 다이어트 콜라는 일반 콜라보다 덜 인기 있다.
>
> ***cf.*** than 뒤의 「주어+동사」는 목적격의 형태로도 쓸 수 있다.
> Nari studies math harder **than he does**. = Nari studies math harder **than him**.

정답 p.49

PRACTICE 7

괄호 안의 단어를 사용하여 비교급 문장을 완성하세요.

1 Seoul is _____larger than_____ Busan. (large)
2 My book is _____ yours. (heavy)
3 His English is _____ hers. (good)
4 Next week will be _____ this week. (cool)
5 Sally is _____ her sister. (careful)
6 I am _____ Minho. (young)
7 The movie was _____ the play. (interesting)
8 Your garden is _____ Mr. Kim's. (beautiful)
9 I work _____ Miss Ford. (quickly)
10 It is _____ before. (bright)
11 Your shoes are _____ mine. (new)
12 This house is _____ that one. (modern)
13 My teacher's voice is _____ our voices. (high)
14 Cooking is _____ eating. (difficult)
15 Bees are _____ butterflies to humans. (useful)
16 The library is usually _____ the cafeteria. (quiet)
17 Pigs are _____ dogs. (intelligent)
18 A bad excuse is _____ no excuse. (bad)

PRACTICE 8

괄호 안에 주어진 말 중 알맞은 것을 고르세요.

1. Paris is (beautiful, **more beautiful**) than London.
2. Andy is as (**kind**, kinder) as Mary.
3. China is (small, **smaller**) than Canada.
4. You didn't eat as (**much**, more) food as I did.
5. This actor is as (**popular**, more popular) as his father.
6. Your computer is (slow, **slower**) than mine.
7. My father is as (**busy**, busier) as my mother.
8. Sora eats (little, **less**) than I do.
9. I bought a (cheap, **cheaper**) jacket than Namsu's.
10. This dog is as (**cute**, cuter) as mine.
11. Mike looks (old, **older**) than his older brother.
12. We traveled (far, **farther**) than they did.
13. He goes to the theater as (**often**, more often) as I do.
14. Today's test was (easy, **easier**) than yesterday's.
15. Tim's room is (clean, **cleaner**) than his sister's.
16. Simba wanted to be as (**brave**, braver) as his father.
17. A cell phone can be (dirty, **dirtier**) than a public restroom.

PSS 3-2 비교급 + and + 비교급

「비교급+and+비교급」 또는 「more and more+원급」은 '점점 더 ~한'의 뜻으로 주로 get, become, grow, turn과 같이 '~되다'의 의미를 갖는 동사와 함께 쓰인다.

It's getting cold. 날씨가 추워지고 있다.
➡ It's getting **colder and colder**. 날씨가 점점 더 추워지고 있다.

Robots are getting **better and better**. 로봇들은 점점 더 향상되고 있다.
The sky is growing **darker and darker**. 하늘이 점점 더 어두워지고 있다.
Companies are turning **more and more eco-friendly**.
기업들은 점점 더 친환경적으로 변하고 있다.

PRACTICE 9

〈보기〉와 같이 괄호 안의 단어를 사용하여 '비교급+and+비교급' 문장을 완성하세요.

보 기	It is getting <u>darker and darker</u>. (dark)

1. He became _____. (poor)
2. The boy is becoming _____. (handsome)
3. The leaves are turning _____. (red)
4. The movie is getting _____. (boring)
5. Her dancing is getting _____. (good)
6. Mark's sickness is getting _____. (bad)
7. The hall became _____. (quiet)
8. My cat is growing _____. (fat)
9. It is raining _____. (heavily)
10. Computers are becoming _____. (cheap)
11. Her face turned _____. (white)
12. It's getting _____. (warm)

PSS 3-3 비교급 강조

다음의 부사는 비교급 앞에서 '훨씬, 더욱'의 뜻으로 쓰여 비교급을 강조한다.

부사	비교급
even	larger
much	bigger
still	+ better
far	more famous
a lot	more important

This sweater is **still better** than that one. 이 스웨터는 저것보다 훨씬 더 좋다.
That camera is **much more expensive** than mine. 저 카메라는 내 것보다 훨씬 더 비싸다.
He works **a lot harder** than others. 그는 다른 사람들보다 훨씬 더 열심히 일한다.

cf. very는 '매우'의 뜻으로 형용사나 부사의 원급을 수식한다.
He sings **very** well. (○)   He sings **very** better. (×)

PRACTICE 10

〈보기〉와 같이 괄호 안의 단어를 알맞은 형태로 바꾸어 빈칸에 쓰세요.

| 보 기 | My house is <u>much bigger</u> than yours. (much, big) |

1. Love is _____ than money. (far, important)
2. Her Korean is _____ than her sister's. (a lot, good)
3. My school has _____ rules than his. (much, strict)
4. Nami studied _____ than he did. (even, hard)
5. My brother was _____ to me than they were. (much, helpful)
6. My diary is _____ than his. (still, thin)
7. Tigers are _____ than lions. (even, strong)
8. E-mail is _____ than air mail. (far, convenient)
9. This way is _____ than that one. (still, safe)
10. London has _____ rain than Rome. (a lot, much)

PRACTICE 11

밑줄 친 부분의 쓰임이 바르면 ○표, 바르지 않으면 ×표 하세요.

1. This box is <u>still</u> larger than that one. [ ]
2. She got up <u>even</u> late this morning. [ ]
3. The hospital is <u>a lot</u> farther than the drugstore. [ ]
4. My sister is <u>very</u> happier than I am. [ ]
5. The women looked <u>a lot</u> weak. [ ]
6. I have a headache. I need <u>far</u> fresher air. [ ]
7. Ted is a <u>very</u> brave boy. [ ]
8. The Nile is <u>much</u> longer than the Han River. [ ]
9. They are looking for a <u>very</u> cheap desk. [ ]
10. The *Harry Potter* series is <u>much</u> exciting. [ ]
11. Dolphins are <u>very</u> cleverer than sharks. [ ]
12. He is <u>far</u> curious about the woman. [ ]
13. The soup is <u>very</u> more delicious than the salad. [ ]
14. My brother is <u>even</u> older than me. [ ]
15. He is <u>still</u> kinder than she is. [ ]

최상급을 이용한 비교

PSS 4-1 the + 최상급

The red pencil is **the shortest** of the three.
빨간 연필이 셋 중에서 가장 짧다.

My son is **the tallest** in my family.
나의 아들은 우리 식구 중에서 가장 크다.

「the+최상급+(명사)+of+복수명사/시간, 기간」 '~중에서 가장 …한'

    Summer is **the hottest** season **of the four**. 여름은 사계절 중 가장 더운 계절이다.
    This was **the funniest** movie **of the year**. 이것은 그 해 (나온) 영화 중 가장 재미있는 영화였다.

「the+최상급+(명사)+in+장소, 범위」 '~에서 가장 …한'

    What is **the fastest** animal **in the world**? 세계에서 가장 빠른 동물은 무엇입니까?
    The dress is **the most expensive** thing **in the clothing shop**.
    그 원피스는 그 옷 가게에서 가장 비싼 것이다.

cf. 「the+최상급+명사」의 형태로 쓰는 것이 일반적이지만, 앞뒤 문맥상으로 그 내용을 미루어 짐작할 수 있는 경우에는 뒤의 명사를 생략할 수 있다.
    Mary is **the tallest** (girl) **of her friends**.
    Mary는 그녀의 친구들 중에서 가장 키가 크다(가장 키가 큰 소녀이다).

정답 p.50

PRACTICE 12

괄호 안의 단어를 사용하여 최상급 문장을 완성하세요.

1 Today is _____the coldest_____ day of the year. (cold)

2 He is _____ person in the group. (important)

3 Insu is _____ of his brothers. (young)

4 It was _____ day of his life. (happy)

5 It was _____ choice of my life. (bad)

6 My bag is _____ of them all. (heavy)

7 That room is _____ in this house. (bright)

8 We visited _____ people in the village. (poor)

9 What is _____ mountain in the world? (high)

10 Michael Jackson is _____ singer of pop music. (good)

11 He did _____ work in the team. (little)

12 A cheetah is _____ of all animals. (fast)

13 His picture is _____ of them all. (interesting)

14 It's _____ news. (late)

15 This is _____ tree in the garden. (thick)

PSS 4-2　one of the + 최상급 + 복수 명사

「one of the+최상급+복수 명사」 '가장 ~한 것들 중의 하나'

This is **one of the longest bridges** in the world.
이것은 세계에서 가장 긴 다리들 중 하나이다.
He is **one of the best players** in the team.
그는 그 팀에서 가장 훌륭한 선수들 중 한 명이다.
Tom Cruise is **one of the most famous actors**.
Tom Cruise는 가장 유명한 배우들 중 한 명이다.

정답 p.51

PRACTICE 13

〈보기〉와 같이 괄호 안의 단어를 바꾸어 문장을 완성하세요.

| 보 기 | Soccer is <u>one of the most popular sports</u>. (popular, sport) |

1 The World Cup is _____. (exciting, festival)

2 It is _____ in this city. (nice, restaurant)

3 Kate got _____ in her class. (high, score)

4 Venice is _____ in Italy. (beautiful, city)

5 The dinosaur was _____. (big, animal)

6 Andy is _____ in the country. (handsome, actor)

7 This is _____. (pleasant, present)

8 The necklace is _____ in the store. (expensive, thing)

9 Minsu is _____ in his class. (strong, boy)

10 A dog is _____. (faithful, animal)

정답 p.51

PRACTICE 14

그림을 보고, 빈칸에 알맞은 사람의 이름을 쓰세요.

1 _____ is as tall as John.

2 John is taller than _____.

3 Ted is not as old as _____.

4 _____ is younger than Ted.

5 _____ is the oldest of the three.

John 25   Cathy 21   Ted 22

정답 p.51

PRACTICE 15

괄호 안에 주어진 단어 중 알맞은 것을 고르세요.

1 That pig is the (fatter, fattest) of them all.

2 It is the (brighter, brightest) star in the sky.

3 Elephants are (smarter, smartest) than dogs.

4 This problem is as (difficult, most difficult) as that one.

5 This drink isn't as (cool, cooler) as that one.

6 She didn't spend as (much, more) money as her friends did.

7 He is one of the loveliest (baby, babies).

8 A queen bee is the (big, biggest) of all the bees.

9 Yumi is even (quiet, quieter) than her sister.

10 Bob was one of the happiest (men, man) at the party.

11 The potato is very (healthy, healthiest) food.

12 His illness became (very, even) worse than before.

13 Snowboarding is one of the most exciting (sports, sport).

14 She became (much, more) and more famous.

15 His house is (much, very) smaller than my house.

Chapter Review Test

정답 p.52 **CHAPTER 12** 비교구문

1 빈칸 ⓐ, ⓑ에 들어갈 말이 순서대로 알맞게 짝지어진 것은?

> Do you know what the ⓐ _____ country in the world is? It is indisputably Russia. Russia's land area takes up about 11% of the world's land area. It is almost two times ⓑ _____ than the second in rank, China, which covers about 6%.

① most large – larger
② most large – more large
③ largest – larger
④ largest - largest
⑤ largest – more large

2 다음 중 빈칸에 알맞지 <u>않은</u> 것은?

> A is more _____ than B.

① famous   ② funny   ③ difficult
④ useful   ⑤ interesting

3 다음 우리말과 같은 뜻이 되도록 빈칸에 들어갈 알맞은 단어를 고르세요.

> • 수미는 민수만큼이나 영어를 잘 구사한다.
> = Sumi speaks English as _____ as Minsu.

① so   ② good   ③ much
④ better   ⑤ well

4 우리말과 같은 뜻이 되도록 괄호 안의 단어를 활용하여 빈칸을 완성하세요..

> • 그는 가장 유명한 음악가들 중 한 명이다.
> = He is _____.
> (famous, musician)

5 다음 내용의 밑줄 친 ①~⑤ 중 어법상 어색한 것은?

> Cats and dogs are the ①<u>most</u> popular pets ②<u>in</u> the world. Cats are ③<u>quieter</u> than dogs. Cats like to stay inside, ④<u>but</u> dogs like to go outside. However, dogs are ⑤<u>more brave</u> than cats. Dogs can protect your house and family.

6 다음 우리말과 같은 뜻이 되도록 주어진 단어를 바르게 배열하여 문장을 완성하세요.

> • 개들은 곰들만큼 크지 않다.
> = _____
> (dogs, big, not, as, bears, so, are)

7 다음 우리말과 같은 뜻이 되도록 빈칸에 알맞은 말을 쓰세요.

(1) 그녀는 나의 할머니만큼 나이 들었다.
   = She is ___ _____ ___ my grandmother.

(2) 나는 너만큼 일찍 일어난다.
   = I get up ___ _____ ___ you.

8 다음 우리말과 같은 뜻이 되도록 빈칸에 알맞은 단어를 쓰세요.

• 고래는 세상에서 가장 무거운 동물들 중 하나이다.
= The whale is one of the heaviest _____ _____ the world.

9 다음 우리말과 같은 뜻이 되도록 빈칸에 알맞은 말을 고르세요.

• 그녀는 큰 집들보다 작은 집들을 더 좋아한다.
= She likes _____.

① better small houses than big houses
② better than small houses
③ small houses than big houses
④ small houses better than big houses
⑤ small houses better

10 다음 문장과 같은 의미가 되도록 주어진 단어를 알맞은 형태로 바꾸어 쓰세요.

Playing tennis is easier than playing the piano.
= Playing the piano is _____ playing tennis. (difficult)

11 다음 중 밑줄 친 부분이 어법상 어색한 것은?

① She is the beautifulest woman in the world.
② My younger brother is the shortest of his friends.
③ It was the greatest moment of my life.
④ Seho is the best singer in my group.
⑤ Antarctica is the coldest place on Earth.

12 다음 메뉴판에 대한 설명으로 틀린 것은?

Shrimp burger : $5.15
Beef burger : $6.50
Chicken burger : $5.49
Cheese burger : $3.99

① Cheese burger is cheaper than Shrimp burger.
② Chicken burger is more expensive than Shrimp burger.
③ Beef burger is the most expensive of all.
④ Shrimp burger is the cheapest burger on the menu.
⑤ Shrimp burger is less expensive than Beef burger.

13 다음 표와 일치하도록 괄호 안의 단어를 알맞은 형태로 바꿔 빈칸을 채우세요.

이름	나이	키	몸무게
Yuri	27	158cm	47kg
Sangmin	25	175cm	62kg
Jiyeon	26	170cm	60kg

(1) Jiyeon is _____ than Yuri. (tall)
(2) Sangmin is _____ than Jiyeon. (young)
(3) Yuri is _____ of the three. (old)
(4) Sangmin is _____ of the three. (heavy)

14 우리말과 같은 뜻이 되도록 괄호 안의 단어를 알맞은 형태로 바꾸어 빈칸에 쓰세요.

• 낮이 점점 더 길어지고 있다.
= The daytime is getting _____ _____. (long)

15 직장인에게 인기 있는 스포츠에 관한 조사 결과에 대해 옳은 것은?

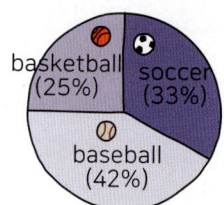

① Soccer is the least popular sport among office workers.
② Basketball is more popular than baseball.
③ Soccer is less popular than basketball.
④ Baseball is as popular as soccer.
⑤ Basketball is less popular than soccer.

16 다음 중 밑줄 친 부분이 바르게 쓰인 것을 모두 고르세요.

① Susan is very taller than Jenny.
② Korea can become a stronger country.
③ It is getting more and more dark.
④ This book is the heavier than that one.
⑤ A cheetah is still faster than a zebra.

17 다음 중 어법상 옳은 문장을 고르세요.

① You are the bestest at math.
② That was one of the funniest activity.
③ Sam is the most strongest of the three.
④ This test was the difficultest test of my life.
⑤ What is the most expensive thing that you have?

18 빈칸에 들어갈 단어가 순서대로 바르게 짝지어진 것은?

• The Nile River is a lot _____ than the Han River.
• The Nile River is the _____ river in the world.

① long – longer
② long – longest
③ longer – longer
④ longer – longest
⑤ longest – longest

19 우리말 뜻과 같은 뜻이 되도록 다음 괄호 안의 단어들을 알맞은 형태로 바꿔 빈칸에 쓰세요.

(1) 당신의 가방 안에서 가장 비싼 것이 무엇인가요?
 = What is _____ thing in your bag? (expensive)

(2) 세계에서 가장 큰 나라는 무엇인가요?
 = What is _____ country in the world? (large)

(3) 이것은 모든 것들 중에서 가장 맛있는 케이크입니다.
 = This is _____ cake of all. (delicious)

20 주어진 우리말과 같은 뜻이 되도록 빈칸에 알맞은 단어를 쓰세요.

• 이 매장에서 가장 싼 것은 무엇인가요?
 = What is _____ _____ thing in this shop?

21 다음 질문에 대한 대답으로 적절하지 않은 것은?

> A: Which color do you like better, pink or blue?
> B: _____

① Pink is better than blue.
② Blue is darker than pink.
③ Blue.
④ I like blue better than pink.
⑤ I like pink better.

22 다음 밑줄 친 비교급의 형태가 잘못된 것은?

① Mike gets up earlier than I do.
② My dad goes to bed latter than I do.
③ New York is bigger than Seoul.
④ I play basketball better than soccer.
⑤ Mina reads faster than her sister.

23 다음 중 어법상 옳은 문장을 고르세요.

① I'll watch the most interesting movie all movies.
② Daegu is more hot than Seoul.
③ Your legs are long as mine.
④ Jack is one of the funny guys in the office.
⑤ Who sings better than you in your family?

24 다음 중 어법상 어색한 것을 고르세요.

① Mr. Han looks even nicer than before.
② She is a lot taller than him.
③ He is far older than her.
④ Jenny is still happier than her friends.
⑤ My car is very bigger than your brother's.

25 다음 표와 일치하지 않는 내용을 고르세요.

	Sena	Yumi
Get up	5:30 a.m.	6:00 a.m.
Go to bed	9:00 p.m.	10:00 p.m.

① Sena gets up earlier than Yumi.
② Sena sleeps more than Yumi.
③ Sena goes to bed earlier than Yumi.
④ Yumi sleeps longer than Sena.
⑤ Yumi goes to bed later than Sena.

26 우리말과 같은 뜻이 되도록 괄호 안의 단어를 알맞은 형태로 바꾸어 빈칸에 쓰세요.

(1) 너는 다음번에는 더 잘 할 것이다.
 = You will do _____ next time. (well)
(2) 너는 어제보다 더 좋아 보인다.
 = You look _____ than yesterday. (good)

27 다음 표에 대한 설명으로 옳은 것은?

Portable charger	A	B	C
capacity	20,000mAh	10,000mAh	20,000mAh
price	26,000won	11,000won	22,000won

① C is more expensive than A.
② B's capacity is as big as A's.
③ B is the most expensive of the three.
④ C's capacity is bigger than B's.
⑤ A is as expensive as B.

28 다음 문장 중 어법상 표현이 틀린 것을 모두 고르세요.

① The building is as tall as others in the city.
② Russia is the biggest country in the world.
③ The Han river is not longer than the Mississippi.
④ I get up early than my dad.
⑤ The restaurant has one of the most cheap steak in the town.

29 다음 글에서 틀린 곳이 몇 군데인지 고르세요.

I went to the shopping mall this afternoon with my parents. On the second floor, I went into a store and saw the most pretty skirt in the entire mall. I wanted to buy it but my mom said, "Don't you have many other prettier skirts at home?" I said, "Mom! It's on sale. It's very cheaper than other skirts in the store!"

① 1   ② 2   ③ 3   ④ 4   ⑤ 5

30 두 문장의 의미가 다른 하나는?

① I am older than my brother.
= My brother is not older than me.
② Giraffes are taller than horses.
= Horses are not as tall as giraffes.
③ America is smaller than Russia.
= Russia is larger than America.
④ My fan makes cooler air than yours.
= Your fan makes less cool air than mine.
⑤ My room is not cleaner than your room.
= Your room is as clean as my room.

31 어법상 옳은 문장을 고르세요.

① I think Suzy is the prettiest singer in Korea.
② They are one of the best team this year.
③ That chair is the most comfortable than this chair.
④ His score is the highest at his friends'.
⑤ My hair is longer than you.

CHAPTER 13
접속사

성취도 자기 평가 활용법

구분	평가 기준
Excellent	문법 내용을 모두 이해하고, 문제를 모두 맞힘.
Very good	문법 내용은 충분히 이해했으나 실수로 1~2문제 틀림.
Good	문법 내용이 조금 어려워 3~4문제 틀림.
needs Review	문법 내용 이해가 어렵고, 5문제 이상 틀림, 복습 필요.

Problem Solving Skill	페이지	학습날짜	성취도 자기평가 E V G R	학습체크
PSS 1 and, but	264	/		☐
PSS 2 and, or	265	/		☐
PSS 3 so	266	/		☐
PSS 4 that	267	/		☐
PSS 5 when, because, if	268	/		☐
PSS 6 as	270	/		☐
PSS 7 however, therefore, for example	271	/		☐
Chapter Review Test	272	/		☐

접속사

단어와 단어, 구와 구, 절과 절을 연결하는 역할을 한다. 구(phrase)는 '주어+동사'가 포함되지 않은 2개 이상의 단어 조합을 가리킨다. 절(clause)은 '주어+동사'가 포함된 단어 조합을 가리킨다.

[단어+단어] **She and** I like music. 그녀와 나는 음악을 좋아한다.
[구+구] We can go there **by subway or by bus**. 우리는 지하철이나 버스로 그곳에 갈 수 있다.
[절+절] **He has no money, so he can't buy the car**. 그는 돈이 없어서 그는 그 차를 살 수 없다.

PSS 1 and, but

and는 서로 비슷하거나 대등한 내용을 연결하고, but은 반대 혹은 대조되는 내용을 연결한다.

He is old **and** unhealthy. 그는 늙고 건강하지 않다.
He is old **but** healthy. 그는 늙었지만 건강하다.

He likes her **and** she likes him. 그는 그녀를 좋아하고 그녀는 그를 좋아한다.
He likes her **but** she doesn't like him. 그는 그녀를 좋아하지만 그녀는 그를 좋아하지 않는다.

PRACTICE 1

정답 p.54

괄호 안에 주어진 접속사 중 알맞은 것을 고르세요.

1 I have a brother (and, but) I don't have a sister.
2 There are cats (and, but) dogs in the garden.
3 She has dark brown eyes (and, but) short black hair.
4 The soup is a little cold (and, but) very tasty.
5 Jason (and, but) I live in the same house.
6 I like fish a lot (and, but) Susan doesn't like them.
7 We played games (and, but) sang songs after lunch.
8 My teacher is kind (and, but) strict.
9 They drink a lot of milk (and, but) they don't drink coffee.
10 The sky is cloudy (and, but) dark.
11 He is lazy (and, but) smart.
12 I learned speaking (and, but) reading from him.

PSS 2 and, or

1. **and**는 둘 다를, **or**는 둘 중 하나를 선택하여 말할 때 쓰인다.

   He **and** I have to take care of the child. 그와 내가 그 아이를 돌보아야 한다.
   He **or** I have to take care of the child. 그 또는 내가 그 아이를 돌보아야 한다.

   I will clean my room **and** wash the dishes. 나는 내 방을 청소하고 설거지를 할 것이다.
   I will clean my room **or** wash the dishes. 나는 내 방을 청소하거나 설거지를 할 것이다.

2. **and**와 **or**가 각각 명령문 뒤에 쓰이면 **and**는 앞 내용에 대해 '그러면'의 뜻을, **or**는 '그렇지 않으면'의 뜻을 나타낸다.

   Study harder, and you'll pass the exam. 더 열심히 공부해라, 그러면 너는 시험에 합격할 것이다.
   = If you study harder, you'll pass the exam. 만약 네가 더 열심히 공부하면, 너는 시험에 합격할 것이다.

   Hurry up, or you can't get there in time. 서둘러라, 그렇지 않으면 시간 내에 거기에 도착할 수 없다.
   = If you don't hurry up, you can't get there in time.
   만약 네가 서두르지 않으면, 너는 시간 내에 거기에 도착할 수 없다.

정답 p.54

PRACTICE 2

괄호 안에 주어진 접속사 중 알맞은 것을 고르세요.

1. Run fast, (and, or) you'll be late.
2. I can swim (but, or) she can't swim.
3. Work hard, (and, or) you will succeed.
4. Eat more, (and, or) you'll be hungry later.
5. Come here two (and, or) three times a month.
6. Put this coat on, (and, or) you'll get warm.
7. She will be a writer (but, or) a reporter.
8. He is playing the guitar (and, or) his brother is singing.
9. Don't watch TV too close, (and, or) your eyesight will go bad.
10. Don't throw trash (but, or) cans away.
11. Take a map with you, (and, or) you won't be lost.
12. My mother may be in the living room (and, or) in the kitchen.

PRACTICE 3

〈보기〉와 같이 다음 문장을 괄호 안의 지시에 따라 명령문으로 바꾸어 쓰세요.

> 보 기
> If you take a taxi, you won't be late for work.
> = Take a taxi, and you won't be late for work. (and 사용)
> = Take a taxi, or you will be late for work. (or 사용)

1 If you turn right, you'll see the post office.
   = _____ (and 사용)

2 If you put salt on your hamburger, it will taste good.
   = _____ (or 사용)

3 If you call him, he will help you.
   = _____ (and 사용)

4 If you take the medicine, you'll feel better.
   = _____ (or 사용)

5 If you eat all your dinner, you can have some ice cream.
   = _____ (and 사용)

6 If you go now, you can avoid traffic jams.
   = _____ (or 사용)

7 If you wait a moment, I'll come and open the door.
   = _____ (and 사용)

8 If you get up early, you will see the sunrise.
   = _____ (or 사용)

 SO

> so는 '그래서, 그러므로'라는 뜻으로 so 앞의 절은 원인을, 뒤의 절은 결과를 나타낸다.
> I was tired, **so** I went to bed very early. 나는 피곤해서 매우 일찍 잠자리에 들었다.
> Sumi didn't have breakfast, **so** she is hungry. 수미는 아침식사를 하지 않아서 배가 고프다.

PRACTICE 4

괄호 안에 주어진 접속사 중 알맞은 것을 고르세요.

1 We tried hard, (but, so) we didn't win.

2 She bought a pair of glasses, (but, or) she didn't wear them.
3 There are no classes on Saturday (and, but) Sunday.
4 It is summer, (but, so) the weather is hot.
5 I studied hard, (or, so) I passed the test.
6 My friend (and, but) I go to the same university.
7 She needed some help, (but, so) I helped her.
8 Are you Japanese (and, or) Chinese?
9 I got up late, (or, so) I had to hurry up.
10 Are you good with computers (or, so) other machines?

 **that**

Ann | thought / believed / knew / said / hopes / wishes | that Tim loved her.

타동사의 목적어절을 이끄는 that은 '~라는 것'으로 해석할 수 있으며 생략이 가능하다.

I think (**that**) he is right. 나는 그가 옳다고 생각한다.
I believed (**that**) she would come. 나는 그녀가 올 거라고 믿었다.
I know (**that**) the Earth is round. 나는 지구가 둥글다는 것을 안다.

정답 p.54

PRACTICE 5

〈보기〉와 같이 목적어절을 이끄는 접속사 that이 들어갈 자리에 √표 하세요.

보 기   I know √ she is smart.

1 Minji believes there is a God.
2 The doctor says I have a cold.
3 I don't think it is a nice restaurant.
4 They wish they weren't late.
5 Do you believe she is kind?
6 Kate thinks there is no one at home now.
7 I wish I could meet your family soon.
8 Sumi hopes she can speak English well.
9 Did you know the dolphin is very clever?
10 People say only the strongest man survives.

PRACTICE 6

우리말과 일치하도록 괄호 안에 주어진 단어를 바르게 배열하세요.

1 나는 그것이 멋진 건물이라고 생각한다.
= I think _____. (is, a nice building, that, it)

2 그녀는 우리가 이틀 동안 거기에 머물 거라는 것을 알고 있다.
= She knows _____. (for two days, we, there, will, that, stay)

3 나는 날씨가 좋기를 바란다.
= I wish _____. (that, be, fine, would, the weather)

4 Jim은 세상에서 Mary가 가장 예쁜 소녀라고 믿는다.
= Jim believes _____ in the world. (that, is, Mary, the prettiest girl)

5 나는 그가 시험을 잘 볼 수 있기를 바랐다.
= I hoped _____. (well, he, do, could, on his test, that)

PSS 5 — when, because, if
Problem Solving Skill

시간, 원인, 조건을 나타내는 접속사 when, because, if는 부사절을 이끄는 대표적인 접속사이다. 부사절이 주절 앞에 위치할 경우에는 부사절의 맨 뒤에 콤마(,)를 써서 주절과 부사절의 경계를 구분해 준다.

1. when '~할 때' (시간)

   When it rains, I don't go out. 비가 올 때, 나는 밖에 나가지 않는다.

   cf. when은 '언제'라는 의미의 의문부사로도 쓰이므로 구분해야 한다.
   「When+동사+주어 ~?」 '언제 ~하니?'
   When do you go to work? 너는 언제 직장에 가니?

2. because[since] '~때문에' (원인/이유)

   I didn't go out **because** it rained. 비가 왔기 때문에, 나는 밖에 나가지 않았다.

   cf. because of 다음에는 명사(구)를 쓴다.
   Because of the rain, I didn't go to the party. 비 때문에 나는 파티에 가지 않았다.

3. if '만약 ~라면' (조건)

   If it rains, I will not go out. 만약 비가 온다면, 나는 밖에 나가지 않을 것이다.

   cf. 부사절이 시간과 조건의 의미일 때, 현재시제가 미래시제 역할을 한다.
   If I **am** late, don't wait for me. (○) 만약 내가 늦으면, 나를 기다리지 말아라.
   If I will be late, don't wait for me. (×)

PRACTICE 7

〈보기〉와 같이 괄호 안의 접속사를 사용하여 두 문장을 한 문장으로 연결하세요.

보 기	I feel good. I sing a song. (when)
	➡ When I feel good, I sing a song.
	➡ I sing a song when I feel good.

1 It snows. We will go skiing. (if)
➡ _____
➡ _____

2 She got up late. She took a taxi. (because)
➡ _____
➡ _____

3 I took a walk. I met my best friend. (when)
➡ _____
➡ _____

4 There are no traffic lights. This road is dangerous. (because)
➡ _____
➡ _____

5 It rains hard. My uncle usually listens to music. (when)
➡ _____
➡ _____

6 You go to the supermarket. Buy some milk for me. (if)
➡ _____
➡ _____

7 I was tired. I went home early. (because)
➡ _____
➡ _____

8 He heard the news. He cried. (when)
➡ _____
➡ _____

9 You ask Ms. Han about the problem. You'll get the answer. (if)
➡ _____
➡ _____

10 I didn't dress warmly. I have a cold. (because)
➡ _____
➡ _____

as

as	~처럼, ~대로	Do **as** I say, not **as** I do. 내가 하는 대로가 아니라 말하는 대로 해라. I have to work on math **as** my teacher said. 나는 선생님이 말씀하신 대로 수학을 열심히 해야 한다.
	~함에 따라, ~할수록	**As** I help poor people more often, I feel happier. 가난한 사람을 더 자주 도울수록, 나는 더 행복하다. **As** she grew older, she became interested in arts. 그녀는 나이가 듦에 따라, 예술에 관심을 가지게 되었다.
	~때문에	**As** she did well on the test, she was happy. 그녀는 시험을 잘 봤기 때문에 기뻤다. **As** he broke his arm, he was in the hospital. 그는 팔이 부러졌기 때문에 입원했다.

PRACTICE 8

정답 p.55

밑줄 친 as의 의미가 〈보기〉의 (A)와 같으면 A, (B)와 같으면 B, (C)와 같으면 C를 쓰세요.

> 보기
> (A) As the days get long, the nights get short.
> (B) As I said before, it's all about me.
> (C) As the book was so sad, he was crying.

1. As time goes by, we get older. [   ]
2. As he is honest, he is trusted by everyone. [   ]
3. Do in Rome as the Romans do. [   ]
4. As my mom is sick, I feel sad. [   ]
5. I went jogging as the doctor ordered. [   ]
6. As it snowed heavily, I stayed at home. [   ]
7. We will go to China as I planned. [   ]
8. It became colder as it grew darker. [   ]
9. As Tom grows up, he gets brighter. [   ]
10. We have to hurry as we are late. [   ]

however, therefore, for example

두 문장 간의 논리적인 관계를 알려주는 부사에는 however, therefore, for example이 있다.

1. **however** '그러나, 하지만' (역접, 대조)

   David drives carefully. **However**, he had an accident this morning.
   David는 주의 깊게 운전한다. 그러나 그는 오늘 아침에 사고를 당했다.

2. **therefore** '그러므로, 그리하여' (인과)

   He studied hard. **Therefore**, he got a good mark in this exam.
   그는 열심히 공부했다. 그리하여 그는 이번 시험에서 좋은 점수를 받았다.

3. **for example** '예를 들어' (예시)

   Becky loves Italian food. **For example**, she enjoys pasta, pizza and so on.
   Becky는 이탈리아 음식을 좋아한다. 예를 들어 그녀는 파스타, 피자 등을 즐긴다.

정답 p.55

PRACTICE 9

괄호 안에 주어진 말 중 알맞은 것을 고르세요.

1. It is sunny. (However, Therefore), it is a little cold.
2. She was very tired. (Therefore, For example), she went to bed early.
3. We didn't have any money. (Therefore, For example), we had to walk home.
4. Barbara is kind. (However, For example), she always smiles and helps her neighbors.
5. Jenny's test was difficult. (However, For example), she did very well.
6. I don't throw away used things. (However, Therefore), my room is full of old things.
7. He bought a new computer. (However, Therefore), it didn't help him with his work.
8. Many people like roses. (However, Therefore), I bought some for her.
9. You can shop on the Internet. (However, For example), you can order books and clothes on it.
10. He likes sports. (However, For example), he plays tennis, soccer, and many other sports on weekends.
11. I was very tired. (However, Therefore), I stayed up all night preparing my presentation for the meeting.
12. I need some clothes. (However, For example), I want a white T-shirt and a blue skirt.

Chapter Review Test

정답 p.56　　CHAPTER **13**　접속사

1 다음 문장이 어법에 맞고 의미가 자연스럽게 통하도록 빈칸에 공통으로 들어갈 단어를 고르면?

- Wake up now, _____ you can eat breakfast.
- Eat more vegetables, _____ you will be healthy.

① as　　② and　　③ but
④ or　　⑤ that

2 다음 글의 빈칸에 들어갈 알맞은 단어는?

My friends and I visited a home for the aged last Saturday. We cleaned their rooms and washed their clothes. It was hard work, _____ we felt proud of ourselves.

① and　　② or　　③ but
④ therefore　　⑤ because

3 다음 빈칸에 and가 들어가기에 <u>어색한</u> 것을 고르세요.

① He studied hard _____ got an A on the test.
② She _____ I have to water the plants.
③ Run fast, _____ you'll be late.
④ This is a picture of me _____ my brother, Sean.
⑤ He is tall _____ has curly hair.

4 다음 문장에서 that이 들어갈 알맞은 위치는?

I ① think ② we ③ will ④ be ⑤ very good friends.

5 다음 대화의 빈칸에 들어갈 접속사가 순서대로 바르게 짝지어진 것은?

A: You look tired. Let's get some rest.
B: _____ we must hurry up. The museum closes at 5 o'clock.
A: Why don't we take a bus _____ a taxi?
B: Yes, let's do that.

① And – so　　② And – or
③ So – or　　④ But – or
⑤ But – so

6 다음 우리말과 같은 뜻이 되도록 올바르게 영작한 것은?

- 너무 더웠기 때문에 그는 자켓을 벗었다.

① He took off his jacket if it was too hot.
② He took off his jacket when it was too hot.
③ He took off his jacket as it was too hot.
④ He took off his jacket, so it was too hot.
⑤ He took off his jacket because of it was too hot.

7 빈칸에 공통으로 들어갈 알맞은 단어는?

- I drink a lot of water _____ I have a cold.
- _____ does the train arrive?

① when ② what ③ where
④ how ⑤ who

8 다음 빈칸에 공통으로 들어갈 알맞은 단어는?

- I respect King Sejong _____ he invented Hangeul, the Korean alphabet.
- He is hungry _____ he didn't have breakfast.

① so ② but ③ when
④ then ⑤ because

9 다음 대화의 빈칸에 공통으로 들어갈 알맞은 단어는?

A: Why did you go to bed _____ early yesterday?
B: I was feeling tired, _____ I went to bed early.

① but ② and ③ so
④ very ⑤ that

10 다음 중 밑줄 친 부분의 쓰임이 어색한 것은?

① Hurry up, or you'll miss the train.
② Just do your best, and you'll do better.
③ Take a taxi, and you can get there in time.
④ Get up now, or you won't be late for school.
⑤ Work hard, and you will succeed.

11 다음 글의 빈칸에 들어갈 알맞은 단어는?

A dirty environment is harmful to our body. _____, we should care more about our environment.

① Or ② But ③ Therefore
④ However ⑤ For example

12 다음 밑줄 친 부분의 쓰임이 나머지와 다른 것은?

① They know that Jiho is honest.
② I think that Betty would like *gimchi*.
③ I know that boy standing under the tree.
④ Do you believe that he is telling the truth?
⑤ She hopes that she sings well in the contest.

13 다음 글의 빈칸에 들어갈 수 없는 것은?

We played a baseball game _____ the Dragon team last Tuesday. We lost the game. _____, we weren't disappointed _____ we did our best. We know that sometimes we learn more _____ losing than winning. We won't stop trying, _____ will go on to win next time.

① however ② with
③ and ④ because of
⑤ from

14 다음 중 어법상 어색한 것은?

① I'm very tall, but my sister isn't.
② We can go there by subway or by taxi.
③ We had dinner and watched a movie.
④ She is not beautiful, but she is kindly.
⑤ I go to work, but Kate doesn't.

15 다음 빈칸에 들어갈 알맞은 단어를 고르세요.

British people would feel upset _____ you stick out your tongue to them because, in England, it means "I don't respect you."

① or ② if ③ what
④ so ⑤ that

16 다음 두 문장을 한 문장으로 연결할 때 빈칸에 들어갈 알맞은 단어를 쓰세요.

- I called Katie. Katie was feeding a street cat then.
  ➡ Katie was feeding a street cat _____ I called her.

17 다음 빈칸에 들어갈 가장 알맞은 단어를 고르세요.

The subway system in Seoul is very well-organized, so you can go anywhere you want. _____, visitors to Seoul usually travel by subway.

① Therefore ② However ③ But
④ Anyway   ⑤ Because

18 다음 글의 빈칸에 들어갈 알맞은 말은?

Sumi is good at foreign languages. _____, she can speak English, Chinese and Japanese well.

① If   ② That
③ However   ④ For example
⑤ Then

19 우리말과 같은 뜻이 되도록 주어진 단어를 바르게 배열하여 문장을 완성하세요.

- 나는 그가 거짓말을 했다고 믿지 않는다.
  = _____
  (lie, believe, a, I, not, do, told, he, that)

20 다음 표를 보고 문장을 완성하세요. (단, 빈칸 하나당 한 단어만 쓸 것.)

likes	Minwoo	Dana
dogs	☺	☺
computer games	☺	☹

(1) Minwoo and Dana _____ _____.
(2) Minwoo likes computer games, _____ Dana _____ _____ computer games.

21 주어진 문장의 밑줄 친 as와 용법이 같은 것은?

Please do that <u>as</u> I asked.

① <u>As</u> time went by, she missed him more.
② <u>As</u> she grew older, she got smarter.
③ The air grows colder <u>as</u> we go up.
④ I'm talking to you <u>as</u> a friend.
⑤ When in Rome, do <u>as</u> the Romans do.

22 다음 빈칸에 알맞은 동사의 형태는?

If you _____, will you buy some food for me?

① goes shopping
② went shopping
③ go shopping
④ will go shopping
⑤ did go shopping

23 다음 빈칸에 들어갈 알맞은 접속사를 쓰세요.

- I caught a cold, so I couldn't go camping.
= I couldn't go camping _____ I caught a cold.

24 다음 빈칸에 ⓐ~ⓒ 들어갈 말이 순서대로 알맞게 짝지어진 것은?

The Fitness Gym for Busy People
Do you want to get in shape ___ⓐ___ be healthy? Come ___ⓑ___ join the Fitness Gym! We have many programs from group yoga to cycling. Visit our gym in person ___ⓒ___ call 808-524-8425 for more information.

    ⓐ   ⓑ   ⓒ
① and – or – and
② and – and – or
③ or – and – and
④ but – and – or
⑤ and – but – or

25 밑줄 친 when의 쓰임이 나머지 넷과 다른 것은?

① She was ill when I was young.
② I was hungry when I got home.
③ Tony, when do you usually have dinner?
④ What do you do first when you get up?
⑤ When it gets cold, people wear heavy coats.

26 다음 중 빈칸에 들어갈 말이 다른 하나는?

① He cried _____ the movie was so sad.
② I didn't like him _____ he was so rude.
③ I am tired _____ I went to bed late last night.
④ I don't have time to watch TV _____ my busy schedule.
⑤ She wore a raincoat _____ it rained a lot.

27 다음 밑줄 친 부분과 쓰임이 다른 것은?

Do you know that he is good at singing?

① Did you believe that he would come back?
② I hope that I will go skiing this winter.
③ I know that man in the picture.
④ She believed that it was true.
⑤ He thinks that she will do better next time.

28 다음 중 밑줄 친 because와 다른 의미로 사용된 것은?

> Eric was angry because his sister drew on his book.

① Since my computer didn't work, I had to borrow my friend's.
② As Tony speaks little Korean, I talk with him in English.
③ I climb the mountain on Sundays since it makes me healthy.
④ It is common to lose muscle mass as we get older.
⑤ As he always comes late, no one expects him to come early.

29 다음 빈칸 ⓐ, ⓑ에 들어갈 말이 알맞게 짝지어 진 것은?

> Before the invention of the telephone, communicating directly with others over a long distance was impossible. The telephone, _____ⓐ_____, made that possible. It had a great impact on society. It was especially useful in business because it reduced the time it took to send messages. _____ⓑ_____, business growth accelerated and society developed quickly.

	ⓐ	ⓑ
①	for example	Therefore
②	when	As
③	therefore	Because
④	however	Therefore
⑤	for example	When

30 다음 중 어법상 옳은 문장을 고르세요.

① If you will clean your room, you will feel better afterwards.
② They go on a field trip as it didn't rain.
③ He wasn't late for school because of he got up early.
④ I want to be in good shape, but I work out every morning.
⑤ Hurry up, or you'll miss the bus.

31 because를 사용하여 다음 두 문장을 한 문장으로 쓰세요.

> • I couldn't sleep at all. It was noisy outside.
> = _____
> _____
> _____

32 다음 중 어법상 옳은 것을 〈보기〉에서 모두 고른 것은?

> 보 기
> ⓐ I'll call you when she will come back.
> ⓑ She was very ill when she was seven.
> ⓒ I think you can do it.
> ⓓ I was very sick yesterday, so I went to the hospital.
> ⓔ He was tired because he gets up early.

① ⓐ, ⓑ   ② ⓐ, ⓒ   ③ ⓑ, ⓒ
④ ⓑ, ⓒ, ⓓ   ⑤ ⓒ, ⓓ, ⓔ

CHAPTER 14
전치사 & 속담

성취도 자기 평가 활용법

구분	평가 기준
(E)xcellent	문법 내용을 모두 이해하고, 문제를 모두 맞힘.
(V)ery good	문법 내용은 충분히 이해했으나 실수로 1~2문제 틀림.
(G)ood	문법 내용이 조금 어려워 3~4문제 틀림.
needs (R)eview	문법 내용 이해하기 어렵고, 5문제 이상 틀림, 복습 필요.

	페이지	학습날짜	성취도 자기평가 E V G R	학습체크
PSS 1 시간, 때를 나타내는 전치사				
PSS 1-1 at, on, in	278	/		☐
PSS 1-2 before, after	279	/		☐
PSS 1-3 for, during	280	/		☐
PSS 1-4 from, since	281	/		☐
PSS 2 장소를 나타내는 전치사	페이지	학습날짜	성취도 자기평가 E V G R	학습체크
PSS 2-1 at, in, on	283	/		☐
PSS 2-2 over, under	285	/		☐
PSS 2-3 in front of, behind, next to	286	/		☐
PSS 2-4 between, among	287	/		☐
PSS 3 방향을 나타내는 전치사	페이지	학습날짜	성취도 자기평가 E V G R	학습체크
PSS 3-1 into, out of, up, down	289	/		☐
PSS 3-2 along, across, through, around	291	/		☐
PSS 3-3 from, to, for	292	/		☐
PSS 4 도구, 수단을 나타내는 전치사	294	/		☐
PSS 5 기타 주요 전치사	294			☐
PSS 6 관용표현	페이지	학습날짜	성취도 자기평가 E V G R	학습체크
PSS 6-1 형용사와 함께 쓰이는 전치사	296	/		☐
PSS 6-2 동사와 함께 쓰이는 전치사	297	/		☐
PSS 7 속담	299	/		☐
Chapter Review Test	303	/		☐

전치사

1. 전치사는 명사 앞에 쓰여 그 명사와 다른 어구와의 관계를 밝혀주는 말이다.
   a cell phone **on** the desk 책상 위의 휴대폰   stay **at** home 집에 머물다

2. 전치사 뒤에는 (대)명사, 동명사가 올 수 있다.
   I'm afraid **of** **bugs[them]**. 나는 벌레들을[그것들을] 두려워 한다.
   I'm good **at** **singing**. 나는 노래 부르기를 잘한다.

3. 전치사 뒤에 오는 대명사는 주로 목적격을 쓴다.
   I'm looking **for** **him**. 나는 그를 찾고 있는 중이다.

 시간, 때를 나타내는 전치사

PSS 1-1 at, on, in

at	1. 구체적인 시각 – **at** nine 9시에 2. 특정한 시점 　**at** noon 정오에　　**at** that time 그때에 　**at** night 밤에　　　**at** the end of this year 올 연말에 　**at** midnight 자정에　**at** this time tomorrow 내일 이맘때에 　**at** dawn 새벽에　　**at** the beginning of the 21st century 21세기 초에 　**at** lunchtime 점심시간에
on	1. 날짜 – **on** May 5th 5월 5일에　**on** the 18th of August, 1992 1992년 8월 18일에 2. 요일 – **on** Monday 월요일에 3. 특정한 날, 특정한 날의 아침·점심·저녁 　**on** my birthday 내 생일에　　　**on** Thanksgiving Day 추수감사절에 　**on** Christmas morning 크리스마스 아침에　**on** Saturday afternoon 토요일 오후에
in	1. 월, 연도 – **in** November 11월에　　**in** 2010 2010년에 2. 계절 – **in** (the) spring 봄에 3. 세기 – **in** the 21st century 21세기에 4. 아침·점심·저녁 – **in** the morning[afternoon, evening] 아침[점심, 저녁]에

The TV show begins **at nine o'clock**. 그 TV쇼는 9시에 시작한다.
We're going to move **at the beginning of this month**. 우리는 이번 달 초에 이사할 것이다.

There are no classes **on Saturday and Sunday**. 토요일과 일요일에는 수업이 없다.
Koreans eat *songpyeon* **on Chuseok**. 한국인들은 추석에 송편을 먹는다.

In summer it's hot and humid. 여름에는 날씨가 덥고 습하다.
Sumi gets up late **in the morning**. 수미는 아침에 늦게 일어난다.

정답 p.58

PRACTICE 1

다음 문장의 빈칸에 at, on, in 중 알맞은 전치사를 쓰세요.

1. He has breakfast _____ 7:30.
2. I'll invite them for dinner _____ Saturday.
3. I heard someone shouting _____ midnight.
4. Will you send Jiyeon a card _____ her birthday?
5. What time do you get up _____ the morning?
6. My grandfather died _____ 1998.
7. We eat rice-cake soup _____ New Year's Day.
8. Shall we meet here _____ this time tomorrow?
9. I was very sick _____ that time.
10. I left here _____ July 15th.

PSS 1-2 before, after

before dinner

at dinner

after dinner

before	~ 전에	She watched TV **before** dinner. 그녀는 저녁식사 전에 TV를 보았다. She watched TV **before** 7 o'clock. 그녀는 7시 이전에 TV를 보았다.
after	~ 후에	She kept a diary **after** dinner. 그녀는 저녁식사 후에 일기를 썼다. She kept a diary **after** 7 o'clock. 그녀는 7시 이후에 일기를 썼다.

PRACTICE 2

〈보기〉에 주어진 표현과 before나 after를 사용하여 우리말과 같은 뜻이 되도록 문장을 완성하세요.

보 기	lunch school the meeting twelve six work

1 회의가 끝난 후에, 그는 휴식을 취했다.
   = _____, he took a break.

2 Jenny는 6시 전에 아침 식사를 한다.
   = Jenny has breakfast _____.

3 점심을 먹기 전에, 미나는 바이올린을 연습한다.
   = _____, Mina practices the violin.

4 퇴근 후에, 우리는 그 불쌍한 아이들을 돕는다.
   = _____, we help the poor children.

5 12시 전에, 모든 것이 팔렸다.
   = _____, everything was sold out.

6 그들은 방과 후에 배드민턴을 친다.
   = They play badminton _____.

PSS 1-3 for, during

for	~ 동안	구체적인 시간의 길이를 나타내는 말과 함께 쓰인다. We stayed there **for** a month. 우리는 한 달 동안 그곳에 머물렀다. I waited **for** 30 minutes outside her house. 나는 30분 동안 그녀의 집 밖에서 기다렸다.
during		특정 기간을 나타내는 말과 함께 쓰인다. We stayed there **during** summer vacation. 우리는 여름방학 동안 그곳에 머물렀다. Nobody spoke **during** the presentation. 그 발표 동안 아무도 말하지 않았다.

PRACTICE 3

다음 문장의 빈칸에 for와 during 중 알맞은 전치사를 쓰세요.

1 She played the piano _____ three hours.

2 I fell asleep _____ the meeting.

3 My father went away _____ a few weeks.

4 Cathy traveled _____ her holidays.

5 Don't speak _____ mealtime.

6 Sujin took swimming lessons _____ four years.

7 Stay out of the sun _____ these hours.

8 What are you doing _____ the winter?

PSS 1-4 from, since

from	~부터	시작된 시점만 나타내며 완료형 이외의 시제들과 함께 쓰인다. They **stayed** there **from** yesterday. 그들은 어제부터 그곳에 머물렀다. *cf.* from A to B 'A에서 B까지' They stayed there **from** yesterday **to** this morning. 그들은 어제부터 오늘 아침까지 그곳에 머물렀다.
since	~ 이래로 ~ 이후로	과거에 시작된 일이 현재까지 지속되는 것을 나타내며 완료형 시제와 함께 쓰인다. They **have stayed** there **since** yesterday. 그들은 어제 이후로 그곳에 머물고 있다.

정답 p.58

PRACTICE 4

괄호 안에 주어진 전치사 중 알맞은 것을 고르세요.

1 I've studied (from, since) this morning.

2 They have been married (from, since) 1990.

3 The store opens (from, since) 10 o'clock.

4 I have played tennis (from, since) last month.

5 (From, Since) this morning, she cleaned all day.

6 She worked for the company (from, since) last year.

PRACTICE 5

〈보기〉와 같이 괄호 안에 주어진 단어와 'from ~ to …'를 사용하여 문장을 완성하세요.

| 보 기 | He usually works from Monday to Friday. (Monday, Friday) |

1 I study in the library _____. (eight, four)
2 _____, she's not at home. (morning, afternoon)
3 The building was repaired _____. (March, June)
4 Lunchtime is _____. (12:00, 12:40)
5 You need a jacket _____. (late fall, early spring)
6 The house was built _____. (2003, 2005)

PRACTICE 6

괄호 안에 주어진 전치사 중 알맞은 것을 고르세요.

1 I don't work so late (at, on) night.
2 What do you do (in, on) Sunday afternoons?
3 (Since, After) shopping, they were tired and hungry.
4 I have been busy (since, at) last weekend.
5 (At, In) 1492, Columbus sailed west.
6 My friend called me (at, in) 9.
7 She usually takes a walk (before, since) sunset.
8 Mom has been ill (from, since) last Thursday.
9 He painted the house (during, for) a week.
10 My father sleeps from 11 p.m. (at, to) 7 a.m.
11 Lunchtime starts (at, on) twelve thirty.
12 I couldn't go to work (from, since) Tuesday to Thursday.
13 Spring begins (in, on) March.
14 The food will be served (from, since) 11 o'clock.
15 We came back home (after, at) a long trip.

장소를 나타내는 전치사

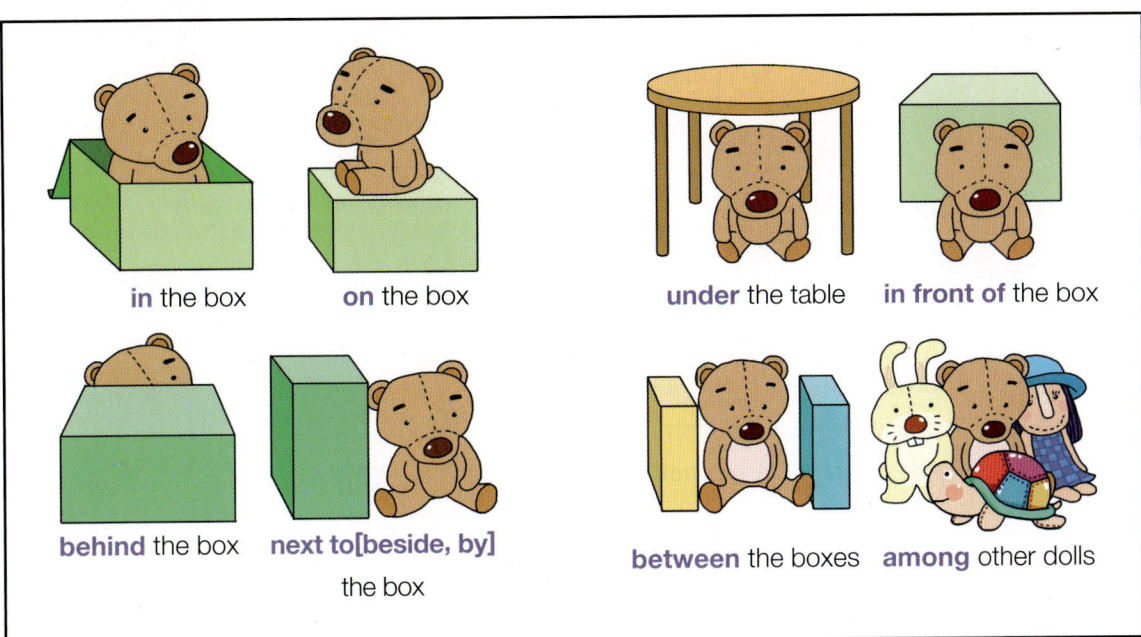

PSS 2-1 at, in, on

at	**1. 하나의 지점을 나타낼 때** at home 집에 　　　　　　at the bus stop 버스 정류장에 at the corner 모퉁이에 　　　at the door 문에 **2. 건물의 용도에 맞는 일을 하고 있을 때** at school 학교에 　　　　　at work 직장에 at university 대학에 　　　　at the airport 공항에 **3. 행사나 모임을 말할 때** at sports events 스포츠 행사에 　at the wedding 결혼식에 at the concert 콘서트에 　　　at the party 파티에
in	**1. 마을, 도시, 국가와 같은 비교적 넓은 장소일 때** in a small town 작은 마을에 　in Seoul 서울에 in America 미국에 　　　　in the world 세계에 **2. 건물, 탈것, 용기 등의 내부를 말할 때** in the building 건물 안에 　　in a car 차 안에 in a box 상자 안에 　　　　in the pocket 호주머니 안에 **3. 우주, 하늘을 말할 때** in space 우주에 　　　　　in the sky 하늘에

CHAPTER 14 _ 전치사 & 속담

	1. 표면상에 맞닿은 것을 말할 때	
on	**on** the wall 벽에	**on** the ground 땅에
	on an island 섬에	**on** the Earth 지구 상에
	on the Moon 달에	**on** the third floor 3층에
	2. 교통수단, 통신수단을 말할 때	
	on a subway 지하철을 타고	**on** a train 기차를 타고
	on foot 걸어서	**on** the Internet 인터넷 상에서
	on TV TV에서	**on** channel 11 11번 채널에서
	3. 길을 말할 때	
	on the road 도로에서	**on** Chester Street Chester 가에서

I stayed **at home** yesterday. 나는 어제 집에 있었다.
Minho takes Chinese lessons **at school**. 민호는 학교에서 중국어 수업을 받는다.
There were a lot of people **at the concert**. 그 콘서트에는 많은 사람들이 있었다.

New York is the biggest city **in America**. 뉴욕은 미국에서 가장 큰 도시이다.
Sora found an interesting story **in the book**. 소라는 그 책에서 흥미로운 이야기를 발견했다.
Look at the stars **in the sky**. 하늘에 있는 별들을 봐.

Peter saw a beautiful picture **on the wall**. Peter는 벽에 있는 아름다운 그림을 보았다.
They came here **on the subway**. 그들은 지하철을 타고 이곳에 왔다.
There is a bank **on 5th Street**. 5번가에 은행이 하나 있다.

PRACTICE 7

다음 문장의 빈칸에 at, in, on 중 알맞은 전치사를 쓰세요.

1 You should turn right _____ the next corner.
2 There are many stores _____ the mall.
3 Did they go home _____ a train?
4 Jane stayed _____ home all day.
5 We're living _____ the Earth.
6 Paris is one of the oldest cities _____ Europe.
7 Who are you going to dance with _____ the party?

8   She takes a lot of lessons _____ school.

9   My car won't work so I have to travel _____ foot.

10 I studied hard _____ university.

11 Mom listens to the news _____ the radio.

12 We met foreigners _____ the street.

13 Mary keeps her socks _____ a drawer.

14 I dropped my cup _____ the floor.

15 We have copiers _____ our office.

16 How many planets are there _____ space?

17 He was talking loudly _____ the phone _____ the subway.

18 The groom sang a lovely song for his bride _____ the wedding.

19 _____ Canada, milk comes _____ bags, not _____ cartons.

20 The popular organic restaurant is _____ Green Street.

21 There are offices _____ the first and second floor.

22 Storm clouds are hanging low _____ the sky.

PSS 2-2 over, under

over '~ 위에' ↔ under '~ 아래에' – 기준이 되는 사물의 표면과 접촉해 있지 않은 상태를 나타낸다.

Birds are flying **over** the tree.
새들이 나무 위를 날아가고 있다.

Tom and Ann are standing **under** the tree.
Tom과 Ann은 나무 아래에 서 있다.

PRACTICE 8

그림을 보고, 빈칸에 over나 under 중 알맞은 전치사를 쓰세요.

1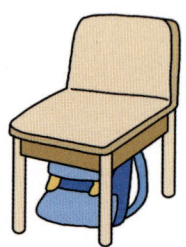
2
3
4
5
6

1 My bag is _____ the chair.
2 A plane is flying _____ the city.
3 The ball is passing _____ his head.
4 There is a key _____ the sofa.
5 There is a rainbow _____ the mountain.
6 A boat is passing _____ the bridge.

PSS 2-3 in front of, behind, next to

in front of '~ 앞에' / behind[in back of] '~ 뒤에' / next to[beside, by] '~ 옆에'

There is a bus stop **in front of** the station. 역 앞에 버스 정류장이 있다.
There is a department store **behind** the station. 역 뒤에 백화점이 있다.
= There is a department store **in back of** the station.
There is a toyshop **next to** the station. 역 옆에 장난감 가게가 있다.
= There is a toyshop **beside** the station.
= There is a toyshop **by** the station.

cf. behind 대신 in back of, next to 대신 beside나 by도 같은 뜻으로 쓸 수 있다.

PRACTICE 9

그림을 보고, 빈칸에 알맞은 말을 쓰세요.

1. Yumi is sitting _____ Jiyeon.
2. Yunsu is sitting next to _____.
3. Sangmin is sitting _____ Inho.
4. Changho is sitting behind _____.
5. Jinho is sitting _____ Sujin.
6. _____ is sitting in front of Hana.
7. _____ is sitting by Seho.
8. Sujin is sitting _____ Changho.

PSS 2-4 between, among

1. between '~ 사이에' (둘 사이)

   Jeff was standing **between** two children.
   Jeff는 두 아이들 사이에 서 있었다.

   cf. between은 between A and B의 형태로도 사용된다.
   I was standing **between** Mina **and** Inho.
   나는 미나와 인호 사이에 서 있었다.

2. among '~ 사이에' (셋 이상일 때)

   Kelly was standing **among** five children.
   Kelly는 다섯 명의 아이들 사이에 서 있었다.

PRACTICE 10

다음 문장의 빈칸에 between이나 among 중 알맞은 전치사를 쓰세요.

1. There is a ten-minute break _____ classes.
2. Do you know the difference _____ the twins?
3. Her postcard was _____ dozens of letters.
4. There is a house _____ three trees.
5. You should hold chopsticks _____ your fingers.
6. The star is shining the brightest _____ many other stars.
7. Sumi is popular _____ her co-workers.
8. It's _____ the bank and the hotel.

PRACTICE 11

괄호 안에 주어진 말 중 알맞은 것을 고르세요.

1. Do you live (at, in) a big city?
2. There is a store (among, between) the station and the post office.
3. The bus stopped (at, on) a small village.
4. His family lives next (to, by) my house.
5. There are many plants (under, over) the sea.
6. There are five floors (in, on) the building.
7. Draw a line (at, on) the ground.
8. What time is it (at, in) Korea?
9. The cat was sitting (over, on) the roof.
10. She threw the ball (over, between) the wall.
11. There is an interesting program (at, on) channel 7.
12. The drummer is (behind, at) the singer.
13. I want to live (between, in) a nice house.
14. Jack is the most popular (between, among) the four men.
15. Let's meet (in front of, on) the station at 3.

PSS 3 방향을 나타내는 전치사

PSS 3-1 into, out of, up, down

1. into '~ 안으로' ↔ out of '~ 밖으로'

He put his hands **into** his pockets.
그는 손을 호주머니 안으로 넣었다.

He took his hands **out of** his pockets.
그는 손을 호주머니 밖으로 꺼냈다.

2. up '~위로' ↔ down '~아래로'

They climbed **up** a mountain.
그들은 산 위로 올라갔다.

They climbed **down** a mountain.
그들은 산 아래로 내려갔다.

PRACTICE 12

정답 p.59

그림을 보고, 〈보기〉에서 알맞은 전치사를 골라 빈칸에 쓰세요.

1

2

3

4

5

6

| 보 기 | into   out of   up   down |

1 We walked _____ the hill.

2 I put the card _____ an envelope.

3 Go _____ the steps.

4 A famous actress came _____ the car.

5 They went _____ the gift shop.

6 Salmon swim _____ the stream.

PSS 3-2 along, across, through, around

1. along '~을 따라서', across '~을 가로질러'

He ran **along** the road.
그는 길을 따라 달려갔다.

He ran **across** the road.
그는 길을 가로질러 달려갔다.

2. through '~을 통하여', around '~ 주위에'

We drove **through** the city.
우리는 그 도시를 통과하여 운전했다.

We drove **around** the city.
우리는 그 도시 주변을 운전했다.

PRACTICE 13

그림을 보고, 〈보기〉에서 알맞은 전치사를 골라 빈칸에 쓰세요.

1
2
3
4
5
6

보 기	along across through around

1   The Earth goes _____ the Sun.
2   People go _____ the road when the light is green.
3   The thief came into the house _____ the window.
4   There are a lot of tall buildings _____ the museum.
5   We took a walk _____ the river.
6   The train is passing _____ a tunnel.

PSS 3-3 from, to, for

from	~로부터	출발 지점을 나타낸다. Paul came **from** London. Paul은 런던에서 왔다.
to	~에, ~으로	go, come 같은 동사와 함께 쓰여 도착 지점을 나타낸다. Paul went **to** London. Paul은 런던으로 갔다. Paul came **from** London **to** Seoul by airplane. Paul은 비행기를 타고 런던에서 서울로 왔다.
for	~을 향하여	start, leave 같은 동사와 함께 쓰여 방향을 나타낸다. Paul left **for** London. Paul은 런던을 향해 떠났다.

PRACTICE 14

우리말 해석과 같은 뜻이 되도록 다음 문장의 빈칸에 from, to, for 중 알맞은 전치사를 쓰세요.

1 We went _____ the town.   ➡ 우리는 시내로 갔다.

2 This bus leaves _____ Busan.   ➡ 이 버스는 부산을 향해 떠난다.

3 Can you come _____ my house tomorrow?   ➡ 너 내일 우리 집으로 올 수 있니?

4 Are those tourists _____ Canada?   ➡ 저 관광객들은 캐나다 출신이니?

5 They started _____ Africa.   ➡ 그들은 아프리카를 향해 출발했다.

6 We moved _____ a restaurant _____ a coffee shop.   ➡ 우리는 식당에서 커피숍으로 옮겨갔다.

7 How far is the hospital _____ your house?   ➡ 그 병원은 네 집에서 얼마나 머니?

8 We are heading _____ the nearest river.   ➡ 우리는 가장 가까운 강으로 향하고 있다.

PRACTICE 15

괄호 안에 주어진 전치사 중 알맞은 것을 고르세요.

1 A lot of foreigners come (at, to) Korea.

2 The airplane started (for, to) China.

3 We did the dishes (after, since) dinner.

4 The Moon goes (around, through) the Earth.

5 A man walked (between, into) a restaurant.

6 Tears ran (down, into) her cheeks.

7 Kitty stayed at my home (during, for) five days.

8 A boy ran (across, over) the street.

9 I was born (in, on) 1993.

10 There is a bakery (among, by) the gift shop.

11 Monkeys climbed (between, up) a tree.

12 The astronaut landed (in, on) the Moon.

13 I will meet Mike (at, on) 3:30.

14 The boat went (above, along) the river.

15 The children jumped (among, into) the water.

도구, 수단을 나타내는 전치사

1. 도구와 함께 쓰이는 전치사 with '~을 가지고'

    She wrote a letter **with a pencil**. 그녀는 연필을 가지고 편지를 썼다.

2. 교통수단과 함께 쓰이는 전치사 by '~을 타고'

    Mina goes to work **by bus**. 미나는 버스를 타고 회사에 간다.

    cf. Giho goes to work **on foot**. 기호는 걸어서 회사에 간다.

3. 일반적 수단과 함께 쓰이는 전치사 by '~을 통해'

    He got well **by taking the medicine**. 그는 그 약을 먹고 몸이 좋아졌다.

PRACTICE 16

정답 p.60

〈보기〉에서 알맞은 전치사를 골라 빈칸에 쓰세요.

보기	with by on

1 We can go to the Moon _____ spacecraft.
2 It takes about ten minutes _____ foot.
3 I cut the picture into pieces _____ the scissors.
4 We went there _____ plane.
5 You can improve your English _____ writing more.
6 You can save money _____ this coupon.
7 He makes money _____ selling clothes.

기타 주요 전치사

1. like '~처럼, ~같이'

    He ran **like** the wind. 그는 바람처럼 달렸다.

    She looks **like** a middle-aged woman. 그녀는 중년 여성 같이 보인다.

2. without '~ 없이'

   People can't live **without** water. 사람들은 물 없이 살 수 없다.
   He can't see **without** his glasses. 그는 그의 안경 없이 볼 수 없다.

3. about '~에 대해'

   We learned **about** Greece. 우리는 그리스에 대해 배웠다.
   Can you tell us **about** her? 그녀에 대해 말해줄 수 있니?

정답 p.60

PRACTICE 17

다음 문장의 빈칸에 like나 without, about 중 알맞은 전치사를 쓰세요.

1 I like coffee _____ cream.
2 I'll write _____ my family.
3 She looks _____ a teacher.
4 I've never seen a nice car _____ yours.
5 Let's talk _____ the issue.
6 Don't go out _____ an umbrella.
7 My brother can swim _____ a fish.
8 _____ enough money, you can't travel.

정답 p.60

PRACTICE 18

괄호 안에 주어진 전치사 중 알맞은 것을 고르세요.

1 My dad goes to work (by, with) bicycle.
2 The dog looked (like, without) a lion.
3 Paint a picture (by, with) the brush.
4 You can't enter (with, without) your ID card.
5 It'll take a long time to go there (by, on) foot.
6 I couldn't succeed (from, without) your advice.
7 David drew a picture (by, with) his crayons.
8 I always go home (by, with) bus.
9 Tim went to the theater (by, with) subway.
10 You can gargle (by, with) salt water.

PSS 6 관용 표현

PSS 6-1 형용사와 함께 쓰이는 전치사

1. **be afraid of** '~을 두려워하다'
   I'm **afraid of** the dark. 나는 어둠을 두려워한다.

2. **be absent from** '~에 결석하다'
   Mike **was absent from** school. Mike는 학교에 결석했다.

3. **be curious about** '~에 대해 궁금해하다'
   We **were curious about** the story. 우리는 그 이야기에 대해 궁금해했다.

4. **be different from** '~와 다르다'
   Graduate school **is different from** university. 대학원은 대학교와 다르다.

5. **be good at** '~을 잘하다'
   She **is good at** singing. 그녀는 노래하는 것을 잘한다.

6. **be good for** '~에 좋다, 유익하다'
   This event may **be good for** children. 이 행사는 어린이들에게 유익할지도 모른다.

7. **be bad for** '~에 나쁘다, 해롭다'
   This game may **be bad for** children. 이 게임은 어린이들에게 해로울지도 모른다.

8. **be famous for** '~으로 유명하다'
   This village **is famous for** its traditional houses. 이 마을은 전통 가옥들로 유명하다.

9. **be full of** '~으로 가득하다'
   His pocket **is full of** coins. 그의 주머니는 동전들로 가득하다.

10. **be interested in** '~에 흥미[관심]가 있다'
    Barbara **is interested in** plants. Barbara는 식물에 관심이 있다.

11. **be late for** '~에 늦다'
    She **is** never **late for** her job. 그녀는 그녀의 직장에 절대 늦지 않는다.

12. **be proud of** '~을 자랑스러워하다'
    He **is proud of** himself. 그는 그 자신을 자랑스러워한다.

13. **be ready for** '~을 위한 준비가 되다'
    We **are ready for** the test. 우리는 시험 볼 준비가 되어있다.

14. **be sorry for[about]** '~에 대해 미안해하다'
    He **was sorry for[about]** making the mistake. 그는 그 실수를 저지른 것에 대해 미안해했다.

PRACTICE 19

다음 문장의 빈칸에 알맞은 전치사를 쓰세요.

1. Ann is interested _____ Korean food.
2. Exercise is good _____ your health.
3. Paris is famous _____ the Eiffel Tower.
4. My brother is curious _____ jazz music.
5. Don't be late _____ dinner.
6. Her room is full _____ books.
7. My idea is different _____ yours.
8. He is afraid _____ insects.
9. My father is good _____ cooking.
10. Are you ready _____ the test?
11. I've never been absent _____ this class.
12. I am sorry _____ being late.
13. She was proud _____ her work.
14. Too much sugar is bad _____ your teeth.

PSS 6-2 동사와 함께 쓰이는 전치사

1. **buy … for ~** '~에게 …를 사주다'
   She wants to **buy** a hat **for** him. 그녀는 그에게 모자를 사주고 싶어한다.

2. **give … to ~** '~에게 …를 주다'
   He **gave** his old textbooks **to** his brother. 그는 그의 옛 교과서들을 그의 남동생에게 주었다.

3. **look at** '~을 보다'
   I **looked at** the posters. 나는 그 포스터들을 보았다.

4. **look for** '~을 찾다'
   Ted is **looking for** the bus stop. Ted는 버스 정류장을 찾고 있다.

5. **thank ~ for …** '~에게 …에 대해 고맙게 여기다'
   Thank you **for** your help. 너의 도움에 대해 고마워. (도와줘서 고마워.)

6. **wait for** '~을 기다리다'
   We were **waiting for** the sunrise. 우리는 일출을 기다리고 있었다.

PRACTICE 20

괄호 안에 주어진 전치사 중 알맞은 것을 고르세요.

1. Look (at, to) the beautiful birds.
2. You must wait (for, to) the green light.
3. Thank you (for, with) sending me a card.
4. His mother bought a computer (for, to) him.
5. Can you give this book (of, to) Giho?
6. The baby looked (for, on) her mother.
7. My family is now (at, on) Jeju Island.
8. He always goes skiing (at, in) winter.
9. We must not throw trash (into, out of) the river.
10. (After, In) lunch, they cleaned up their picnic area.
11. Koreans cannot live (by, without) gimchi.
12. My family took a trip (of, to) Italy.
13. I will arrive (on, in) July 8th.
14. He became popular (from, since) that time.
15. Susan took her present (into, out of) the box.
16. It rained (during, for) several days.
17. People will watch the singer (in, on) TV.
18. My sister goes to bed late (in, on) Fridays.
19. Summer comes (after, before) autumn.
20. The market opens (at, for) 10 a.m.
21. He has already left (for, to) his hometown.
22. I'm not good (at, in) math.
23. Summer vacation starts (at, in) July.
24. I couldn't find him (during, for) class.
25. She washes her hair (by, with) soap.
26. I met him (at, in) this time yesterday.
27. The room was full (with, of) treasures.
28. They went to the waterfall (by, on) boat.
29. He studies drama (at, in) New York.
30. There was no one (around, through) the beach.

속담

1. **Walls have ears.**
   벽에도 귀가 있다. (낮말은 새가 듣고 밤말은 쥐가 듣는다.)

2. **No pain, no gain.**
   고통 없이는 얻는 것도 없다.

3. **Even a worm will turn.**
   벌레도 돌아설 것이다. (지렁이도 밟으면 꿈틀한다.)

4. **Look before you leap.**
   잘 보고 뛰어라. (돌다리도 두드려보고 건너라.)

5. **Every dog has his day.**
   모든 개도 그의 날이 있다. (쥐구멍에도 볕들 날 있다.)

6. **More haste, less speed.**
   급할수록 천천히 (급할수록 돌아가라.)

7. **All roads lead to Rome.**
   모든 길은 로마로 통한다. (많은 길을 통해 같은 목표에 도달한다.)

8. **Practice makes perfect.**
   훈련이 완벽을 만든다.

9. **Fine clothes make the man.**
   좋은 옷이 사람을 만든다. (옷이 날개다.)

10. **Small drops make a shower.**
    작은 물방울이 소나기를 만든다. (티끌 모아 태산이다.)

11. **Go home and kick the dog.**
    집에 가서 개를 발로 차다. (종로에서 뺨 맞고 한강 가서 눈 흘긴다.)

12. **A barking dog never bites.**
    짖는 개는 절대 물지 않는다. (빈 수레가 요란하다.)

13. **Don't cry over spilt milk.**
    엎질러진 우유 때문에 울지 마라. (이미 엎질러진 물이다.)

14. **Out of sight, out of mind.**
    눈에서 멀어지면 마음에서도 멀어진다.

A monkey sometimes falls from the tree.

15. **Habit is (a) second nature.**
    습관은 제2의 천성이다. (세 살 버릇 여든까지 간다.)

16. **Honesty is the best policy.**
    정직이 최선의 방책이다.

17. **So many men, so many minds.**
    너무나 많은 사람들, 너무나 많은 생각들 (각인각색)

18. **A good medicine tastes bitter.**
    몸에 좋은 약은 입에 쓰다.

19. **Kill two birds with one stone.**
    한 개의 돌멩이로 두 마리의 새를 죽인다. (일석이조)

Kill two birds with one stone.

20. **Two heads are better than one.**
    두 사람이 한 사람보다 낫다. (백지장도 맞들면 낫다.)

21. **The early bird catches the worm.**
    일찍 일어나는 새가 벌레를 잡는다.

22. **Experience is the best teacher.**
    경험이 최고의 스승이다.

23. **There is no smoke without fire.**
    불 없이 연기가 날 리 없다. (아니 땐 굴뚝에 연기 나랴.)

24. **Too many cooks spoil the broth.**
    요리사가 너무 많으면 수프를 망친다. (사공이 많으면 배가 산으로 올라간다.)

25. **Don't judge a book by its cover.**
    책의 표지로 그 책을 판단하지 말라. (겉모습보다는 내면이 중요하다.)

26. **When in Rome, do as the Romans do.**
    로마에 있을 때는 로마인들이 하는 것처럼 해라. (로마에서는 로마법을 따르라.)

27. **A bad workman always blames his tools.**
    서투른 일꾼이 항상 연장을 탓한다.

28. **A monkey sometimes falls from the tree.**
    원숭이도 나무에서 떨어질 때가 있다.

29. **Don't put off today's work until tomorrow.**
    오늘의 일을 내일로 미루지 말라.

30. **A journey of 1000 miles begins with a single step.**
    1000마일 여행도 한 걸음으로 시작한다. (천리 길도 한 걸음부터.)

PRACTICE 21

다음 우리말에 맞는 속담을 〈보기〉에서 골라 그 번호를 쓰고 전체 문장을 빈칸에 쓰세요.

보 기	
	① Two heads are better than one.
	② Small drops make a shower.
	③ A good medicine tastes bitter.
	④ Even a worm will turn.
	⑤ A journey of 1000 miles begins with a single step.
	⑥ Don't judge a book by its cover.
	⑦ Fine clothes make the man.
	⑧ Too many cooks spoil the broth.
	⑨ Go home and kick the dog.
	⑩ Walls have ears.

1 낮말은 새가 듣고 밤말은 쥐가 듣는다.   ➡ [⑩] Walls have ears.

2 옷이 날개다.   ➡ [   ] _____

3 겉모습보다는 내면이 중요하다.   ➡ [   ] _____

4 종로에서 뺨 맞고 한강 가서 눈 흘긴다.   ➡ [   ] _____

5 지렁이도 밟으면 꿈틀한다.   ➡ [   ] _____

6 티끌 모아 태산이다.   ➡ [   ] _____

7 몸에 좋은 약은 입에 쓰다.   ➡ [   ] _____

8 백지장도 맞들면 낫다.   ➡ [   ] _____

9 사공이 많으면 배가 산으로 올라간다.   ➡ [   ] _____

10 천리 길도 한 걸음부터.   ➡ [   ] _____

PRACTICE 22

빈칸에 알맞은 단어를 넣으세요.

1 A bad workman always _____. 서투른 일꾼이 항상 연장을 탓한다.
2 Experience is _____ teacher. 경험이 최고의 스승이다.
3 _____ catches the worm. 일찍 일어나는 새가 벌레를 잡는다.
4 _____ makes _____. 훈련이 완벽을 만든다.
5 There is no smoke _____. 아니 땐 굴뚝에 연기 나랴.
6 So many _____, so many _____. 각인각색
7 Every _____ has his _____. 쥐구멍에도 볕들 날 있다.
8 When in Rome, do _____. 로마에서는 로마법을 따르라.
9 No _____, no _____. 고통 없이는 얻는 것도 없다.
10 Out of _____, out of _____. 눈에서 멀어지면 마음에서도 멀어진다.
11 A _____ dog never _____. 짖는 개는 절대 물지 않는다. (빈 수레가 요란하다.)
12 Habit is a _____. 습관은 제2의 천성이다. (세 살 버릇 여든까지 간다.)
13 _____ is the best _____. 정직이 최선의 방책이다.
14 Look before you _____. 잘 보고 뛰어라. (돌다리도 두드려보고 건너라.)
15 More _____, less _____. 급할수록 돌아가라.

PRACTICE 23

아래의 속담에 들어갈 알맞은 전치사를 〈보기〉에서 골라 쓰세요.

보 기	until	with	from	to	over

1 A journey of 1000 miles begins _____ a single step.
2 All roads lead _____ Rome.
3 Don't put off today's work _____ tomorrow.
4 Kill two birds _____ one stone.
5 A monkey sometimes falls _____ the tree.
6 Don't cry _____ spilt milk.

Chapter Review Test

정답 p.61   CHAPTER 14
전치사 & 속담

1 다음 빈칸에 들어갈 알맞은 단어를 고르세요.

> Yujin plays computer games _____ Saturdays.

① in   ② to   ③ on
④ at   ⑤ for

2 다음 빈칸에 들어갈 알맞은 단어를 고르세요.

> Our summer vacation begins _____ July.

① on   ② at   ③ in
④ to   ⑤ for

3 다음 빈칸에 들어갈 알맞은 전치사를 쓰세요.

> A: When is your birthday?
> B: It is _____ the 27th of September.

4 다음 우리말과 같은 뜻이 되도록 빈칸에 들어갈 알맞은 말을 고르세요.

> • 나는 잠시 동안 그와 이야기하기를 원했다.
>   = I wanted to talk with him _____ .

① on a minute   ② by a minute
③ at a minute   ④ for a minute
⑤ in a minute

5 다음 우리말과 같은 뜻이 되도록 빈칸에 들어갈 알맞은 전치사를 쓰세요.

(1) 문 뒤에 있는 저 아이는 누구니?
　= Who is that child _____ the door?

(2) 너는 대도시에서 살기를 원하니?
　= Do you want to live _____ a big city?

6 다음 대화의 빈칸에 들어갈 알맞은 단어는?

> A: Can you cut this apple _____ a knife?
> B: Of course.

① to   ② at   ③ on
④ with   ⑤ by

7 다음 우리말과 같은 뜻이 되도록 빈칸에 들어갈 알맞은 전치사를 쓰세요.

> • Kate는 노래를 잘한다.
>   = Kate is good _____ singing.

8 다음 빈칸에 공통으로 들어갈 말로 알맞은 것은?

> • It opens _____ 9 a.m. to 6 p.m.
> • My name is Mina. I am _____ Jinju.
> • He's going to come back _____ France this Friday.

① to   ② at   ③ from
④ of   ⑤ on

9 다음 우리말과 같은 뜻이 되도록 빈칸에 들어갈 알맞은 전치사를 고르세요.

> • 어머니는 저녁 식사 후에 설거지를 하신다.
> = My mother does the dishes _____ dinner.

① before   ② after   ③ at
④ during   ⑤ for

10 빈칸에 들어갈 알맞은 단어는?

> We have to be ready _____ the rainy season.

① to   ② with   ③ for
④ at   ⑤ from

11 빈칸에 들어갈 단어가 순서대로 바르게 연결된 것은?

> • My uncle grows tomatoes and potatoes _____ his farm.
> • Look _____ the wonderful rocks in the picture.

① on – at
② on – with
③ at – on
④ with – to
⑤ for – at

12 다음 빈칸에 들어갈 말이 알맞게 짝지어진 것은?

> • I was late _____ work again.
> • He went bungee jumping _____ fear.
> • He will stay at his grandparents' _____ a month.

① to   – without – for
② for – without – during
③ to   – on   – for
④ for – without – for
⑤ to   – on   – during

13 다음 그림에 대한 설명으로 올바르지 <u>않은</u> 것은?

① There is a dog under the desk.
② There is a clock next to the desk.
③ There are backpacks beside the desk.
④ There are a few books and a clock on the desk.
⑤ There are a calendar and a picture on the wall.

14 빈칸에 공통으로 들어갈 알맞은 전치사를 쓰세요.

- What's _____ channel 9 at 8 p.m.?
- My favorite drama is now _____ TV.

15 다음 우리말 해석과 일치하도록 〈보기〉의 단어를 활용하고, 어법상 필요한 단어를 추가하여 문장을 완성하세요. (필요시 단어의 형태를 바꿀 것)

| 보 기 | feel / sorry / her |

내가 그 소식을 들었을 때, 나는 그녀에 대해 안쓰럽게 느꼈다.
= When I heard the news, _____ _____ _____ _____ _____.

16 빈칸에 공통으로 들어갈 알맞은 전치사는?

- The weather changes very often _____ fall.
- There are many people _____ the building.

① at ② to ③ for
④ of ⑤ in

17 다음 지도를 보고 빈칸에 들어갈 알맞은 말로 짝지어진 것을 고르세요.

Start here.

A: How can I get to the bakery?
B: Go straight and turn right. It's _____ the post office.
A: Sorry, I don't understand. Could you tell me again?
B: Go straight and turn right. It's _____ the post office and the bank.

① next to   – by
② in front of – next to
③ next to   – between
④ in front of – among
⑤ next to   – in front of

18 빈칸에 들어갈 단어가 순서대로 바르게 연결된 것은?

- A little bear was walking _____ the forest.
- My father works _____ Computer Plus Company.

① around – to   ② around – on
③ across – as   ④ around – for
⑤ across – on

19 다음 중 밑줄 친 부분이 잘못 쓰인 것은?

① There are no classes in Saturday and Sunday.
② We usually eat breakfast at 8:40.
③ Our office hours are from 9 a.m. to 5 p.m.
④ I sent him a card on his birthday.
⑤ Where did you go during the vacation?

20 다음 빈칸에 들어갈 말이 알맞게 짝지어진 것은?

> I will get my year-end bonus soon. I've made some plans to spend this bonus money. I will spend 30% of it ⓐ_____ myself and my family. Also, I will spend another 30% on blue chip stocks _____ⓑ_____ Apple and Coca-Cola. And the rest of the money will go into my savings account. I will save it _____ⓒ_____ future purposes.

	ⓐ	ⓑ	ⓒ
①	on	like	in
②	in	to	for
③	on	like	for
④	on	in	with
⑤	with	in	like

21 우리말과 같은 뜻이 되도록 빈칸에 들어갈 알맞은 전치사를 쓰세요.

> A: Excuse me. Where is the Hanil Building?
> B: It's _____ the street from the drugstore.
> (약국 길 건너편에 있어요.)

22 다음 빈칸에 들어갈 전치사를 순서대로 바르게 나열한 것은?

> • There are a lot of shops _____ my town.
> • The first class begins _____ 8:30 every day.
> • What do Koreans usually do _____ special holidays?

① on – at – in   ② for – at – in
③ at – in – on   ④ in – at – on
⑤ in – for – to

23 다음 상황을 공통으로 가리키는 속담을 고르세요.

> • Whenever I jog, I like listening to a podcast in English. That way, I can stay fit while I improve my English language skills.
> • On the way back home, Kevin will drop by the dry cleaner as well as fill up his gas tank.
> • Sera went to London on a business trip. While there, she visited her relatives as well.

① No pain, no gain.
② More haste, less speed.
③ All roads lead to Rome.
④ Kill two birds with one stone.
⑤ Two heads are better than one.

24 다음 문장의 빈칸에 들어갈 알맞은 단어는?

> _____ the way home, Seho came across his old friend.

① To   ② In   ③ On   ④ By   ⑤ For

25 다음 대화의 빈칸에 쓰일 수 없는 말은?

> A: Excuse me, may I ask you something?
> B: Sure, go ahead.
> A: I'm looking for Times Square. Do you know how I can get there?
> B: Oh, it's very close from here. Here, look at this map. We're here now. So, just go straight for three blocks and turn right at the bank.
> A: Is it _____ the bank?
> B: That's right.

① next to   ② close to   ③ in front of
④ looking for   ⑤ across from

26 다음 빈칸에 들어갈 말이 나머지와 다른 것은?

① They went there _____ taxi.
② He goes to work _____ car.
③ He explored the city _____ foot.
④ She always comes home _____ bicycle.
⑤ I go to my grandma's house _____ train.

27 빈칸에 들어갈 단어가 순서대로 바르게 연결된 것은?

> We sometimes go _____ the shopping mall _____ a subway.

① to – by   ② to – on   ③ with – for
④ for – by   ⑤ on – at

28 다음 빈칸에 공통으로 들어갈 단어로 알맞은 것은?

> • I want to be a painter _____ Picasso.
> • He acts _____ a comedian in class. He is funny.

① for   ② like   ③ from
④ on   ⑤ at

29 다음 ①~⑤ 중 어법상 옳은 것은?

> Yesterday, I ①take a walk after dinner. I was walking ②on the river when I found three dogs. They were sleeping ③under a tree. The smallest one ④between them was shaking with cold. I brought them home, so they have been with me ⑤from yesterday.

30 다음 밑줄 친 단어의 뜻이 나머지 넷과 다른 하나는?

① The Turtle Ship looks like a turtle.
② How do you like this place?
③ Mina wants to be a famous singer like him.
④ Does he swim like a fish?
⑤ I have never seen a nice picture like that.

31 주어진 우리말과 같은 뜻이 되도록 빈칸에 공통으로 들어갈 알맞은 전치사를 쓰세요.

• 아니 땐 굴뚝에 연기 나랴.
  = There is no smoke _____ fire.
• 우리는 우주선 없이 달에 갈 수 없다.
  = We can't go to the Moon _____ spaceships.

32 〈보기〉 중 다음 글의 빈칸에 들어가는 것끼리 짝지어진 것은?

Some good bacteria live inside some foods. For example, *gimchi* is full _____ good bacteria. So *gimchi* is good _____ your body.

보기 | ⓐ of ⓑ on ⓒ by ⓓ about ⓔ for

① ⓐ, ⓒ   ② ⓒ, ⓔ   ③ ⓑ, ⓒ
④ ⓑ, ⓓ   ⑤ ⓐ, ⓔ

33 다음 문장의 빈칸과 들어갈 말이 같은 것은?

• She read a book _____ flowers.
• Kids are curious _____ everything around them.

① Look _____ the picture on the wall.
② She is afraid _____ bees.
③ The city is famous _____ its buildings.
④ I am interested _____ playing the piano.
⑤ I'm going to write _____ animals.

34 우리말과 일치하도록 주어진 말을 알맞게 배열하세요.

우리의 관습은 너희의 것과 상당히 다르다.
(are / yours / customs / different / our / quite / from)

➡ _____

35 다음 글의 밑줄 친 부분과 쓰임이 다른 것은?

Take a look at this. It's a bagel. It looks <u>like</u> a doughnut. It came from Poland. However, now it is the favorite breakfast of New York.

① The paper smells <u>like</u> a flower.
② Let's make two rooms <u>like</u> this.
③ My parents treat me <u>like</u> a child.
④ They <u>like</u> riding a bicycle very much.
⑤ What's the weather <u>like</u> in your country?

36 다음 ①~⑤ 중 어법상 옳지 않은 것은?

Amy went to Paris during her holiday. She arrived ①<u>at</u> the hotel. The next day, she visited the Versailles Palace ②<u>by</u> car. She walked ③<u>into</u> the palace. She found that there were a lot of mirrors. She looked ④<u>on</u> those mirrors with a smile. She was answered with the same smiles ⑤<u>from</u> the mirrors.

37 다음 중 빈칸에 on이 들어갈 수 없는 것을 고르세요.

① Koreans wear *hanbok* _____ Chuseok.
② Look at the beautiful kites _____ the sky.
③ What do you do _____ Sundays?
④ We enjoyed ourselves _____ the beach.
⑤ I'm _____ a diet now.

38 다음 문장의 빈칸에 들어갈 알맞은 전치사를 쓰세요.

(1) I bought some flowers _____ her.

(2) Can you tell me _____ Korean history?

39 다음 글에 알맞은 속담을 고르세요.

In India, people eat with their right hands. So it is important to wash your hands before a meal. In France, people may think you're rude if you speak with your mouth full at table. In Italy, it is not polite to place your hands under the table during a meal. So before you go to other countries, you had better know about their etiquette.

① Don't cry over spilt milk.
② Practice makes perfect.
③ When in Rome, do as the Romans do.
④ Fine clothes make the man.
⑤ Go home and kick the dog.

40 빈칸에 들어갈 단어가 순서대로 바르게 연결된 것은?

• The bus stops _____ Gwanghwamun.
• She made a circle _____ her thumb and forefinger.
• There is a department store _____ 5th Street.

① at – with – on
② in – on – to
③ at – to – with
④ in – with – on
⑤ at – on – in

41 주어진 우리말과 같은 뜻이 되도록 빈칸에 들어갈 알맞은 전치사를 쓰세요.

• 나는 티셔츠를 찾고 있다.
 = I'm looking _____ a T-shirt.
• 당신은 이 사진을 보고 있나요?
 = Are you looking _____ this picture?

42 빈칸에 공통으로 들어갈 알맞은 전치사를 쓰세요.

• We always have lunch _____ noon.
• I'm going to Paris _____ the end of this year.

43 우리말과 같은 뜻이 되도록 빈칸에 알맞은 전치사를 쓰세요.

• 나는 3개월 동안 고모 댁에 머물렀다.
= I stayed at my aunt's _____ 3 months.

44 Jason의 방을 보고 엄마가 남긴 메모입니다. 그림을 보고 빈칸에 알맞은 말을 쓰세요.

Dear Jason,
Look at your room. Your pants are
(1)_____ the table. Your sock is
(2)_____ the table. Look at the box.
It's (3)_____ your bed.
Please, don't forget to clean your room!
　　　　　　　　　　　　　　　　　Mom

45 빈칸에 들어갈 전치사가 순서대로 짝지어진 것은?

Minji was absent _____ work today. She was very sick because she got a bad cold. Her husband made her hot soup. It was good _____ her headache and sore throat.

① at – for　　② in – to
③ with – by　④ from – of
⑤ from – for

46 다음 글과 어울리는 속담을 고르세요.

Seho wants to get a new bag, but he has no way to earn money. So, he walks to school instead of taking a bus these days. In this way, he can save about 30,000 won a month. Moreover, he decides not to spend money on fun things. By doing so, he will be able to buy a new bag in about three months.

① Every dog has his day.
② Look before you leap.
③ Too many cooks spoil the broth.
④ Small drops make a shower.
⑤ Don't put off today's work until tomorrow.

47 주어진 문장의 밑줄 친 for와 의미가 같은 것을 고르세요.

What food do you want for dessert?

① He is always late for school.
② We ate steak for dinner.
③ She is looking for her bag.
④ I planned to stay here for two weeks.
⑤ Thank you for your letter.

48 빈칸에 공통으로 들어갈 알맞은 단어는?

• Mr. Brown and his family live next _____ my house.
• How about writing a letter _____ her?
• You should go _____ see a doctor.

① for　　② with　　③ to
④ in　　⑤ by

49 다음 글의 주제와 어울리는 속담을 고르세요.

One day, Thomas was invited to a dinner party by his neighbor. He wore his old suit and went there. But the neighbor said that Thomas couldn't come to the party in such an old suit. Soon after, Thomas went back to the party in his new suit and the neighbor welcomed him. But Thomas didn't enter his house and gave him his new suit, saying "Enjoy your party with my new suit. You invite not me but my suit."

① A barking dog never bites.
② Honesty is the best policy.
③ Don't judge a book by its cover.
④ Even a worm will turn.
⑤ Go home and kick the dog.

50 ①~⑤ 중 들어갈 말이 나머지 넷과 다른 것은?

Many children ① the world are ② danger now. They are suffering ③ hunger and disease. They need your help. You can donate money for them. You can start from 3,000 won a month! Your small help can make a big change ④ their lives. Save your money for children ⑤ need.

51 다음 빈칸에 들어갈 알맞은 말을 쓰세요.

Boryeong is famous for its global Mud Festival. It is one of the most famous festivals (1)_____ Korea. It takes place at mud flat. It usually starts very early (2)_____ the morning. It lasts (3)_____ eleven days.

*mud: 진흙

52 다음 빈칸에 들어갈 말이 차례대로 짝지어진 것은?

- We should not sleep _____ class.
- She exercises _____ 30 minutes a day.

① for – to   ② to – for   ③ to – during
④ during – for   ⑤ for – during

53 아래의 전치사 중 필요한 것을 선택하여 다음 〈보기〉와 같이 괄호 안의 단어를 가지고 그림을 묘사하세요.

| 보 기 | There is a table in the room. (table) |

on, between, over, behind, under, next to, in front of

(1) _____ (books)
(2) _____ (dog)

54 다음을 읽고 틀린 부분 세 가지를 찾아 바르게 고쳐 쓰세요.

On weekends, Maria's family goes camping. They go there by foot. They usually stay in a cabin. They like to spend time on nature. On sunny days, Maria and her sister, Anna go in the forest to pick wild fruits.

(1) _____ ➡ _____
(2) _____ ➡ _____
(3) _____ ➡ _____

55 다음 ⓐ~ⓓ에 들어갈 말이 알맞게 짝지어진 것은?

- She gave a chocolate ___ⓐ___ her mother.
- I'd like to do volunteer work ___ⓑ___ a hospital.
- There was a lost dog ___ⓒ___ the street.
- He painted the wall ___ⓓ___ a brown crayon.

	ⓐ	ⓑ	ⓒ	ⓓ
①	to	on	in	with
②	for	in	in	by
③	to	at	on	with
④	for	at	over	by
⑤	to	in	at	with

56 다음 빈칸에 들어갈 말과 같은 말이 들어갈 수 있는 문장을 고르세요.

The bridge has been built _____ the river.

① Can you come _____ my room in an hour?
② I picked up a strawberry and put it _____ my mouth.
③ She is _____ the Philippines.
④ The birds are flying _____ the river.
⑤ We make wonderful movies _____ our digital cameras.

57 다음 ⓐ~ⓒ에 들어갈 말이 알맞게 짝지어진 것은?

Jessie's family stayed ___ⓐ___ a *hanok* guesthouse last night. She slept ___ⓑ___ *ondol* instead of in a bed. After breakfast, they went to Gyeongbokgung ___ⓒ___ bus. Jessie and her brother took lots of pictures with a camera.

	ⓐ	ⓑ	ⓒ
①	at	on	from
②	in	in	on
③	at	over	on
④	at	on	by
⑤	on	on	by

영어의 8품사

품사	설명	예문
명사	**사람, 사물, 동물의 이름**을 나타내는 말 → 주어, 목적어, 보어 예) Jane, Mr. Brown, desk, chair, computer, bag, dog, bird	This computer looks new. 이 컴퓨터는 새것처럼 보인다. I have a dog. 나는 개가 한 마리 있다.
대명사	명사를 **대신**하는 말 → 주어, 목적어, 보어 예) I, my, you, he, she, it, them, we, myself, yourself, ourselves	Look at the dog! It is cute. 개 좀 봐! 그것은 귀여워. I'm proud of myself. 나는 내 자신이 자랑스럽다.

동사	**행위, 동작, 상태를 묘사**하며 '~다'로 해석되는 말 → 서술어
	- 일반동사: 주로 움직임을 나타내며 '~하다'라고 해석
	  예) walk, run, eat, study, play, make, buy, love, like
	- be동사: 상태나 위치를 주로 묘사하며 '~이다'라고 해석
	  예) am, are, is, was, were
		We eat dinner at 7.
		우리는 7시에 저녁을 먹는다.
		She loves her daughter.
		그녀는 그녀의 딸을 사랑한다.
		I am an artist.
		나는 예술가이다.

형용사	**명사**를 꾸미거나 보충 설명하는 말 → 수식어, 보어 **생김새, 색깔, 크기, 성격, 특징**을 묘사하는 말 예) pretty, beautiful, red, tall, big, small, nice, kind, easy, difficult	She has big eyes. 그녀는 큰 눈을 가지고 있다. He is a kind boy. 그는 친절한 소년이다. The book is easy. 그 책은 쉽다.
부사	**형용사, 동사, 다른 부사, 문장 전체**를 자세히 설명하여 문장의 의미를 더욱 풍부하게 하는 말 → 수식어 **시간, 장소, 정도, 빈도**를 묘사하는 말 예) now, here, very, well, always, early, really, happily, sadly	What are you doing now? 지금 뭐 하고 있어? Your sister is very pretty. 네 언니는 무척 예쁘다. We really enjoyed the party. 우리는 정말 그 파티를 즐겼다.

접속사	**단어와 단어, 구와 구, 절과 절**을 이어주는 말
	- 등위접속사: **같은 종류**의 말을 연결
	  예) and, but, or, so
	- 종속접속사: **명사절, 부사절, 형용사절**을 주절에 연결
	  예) because, when, as, if
		She is old and wise.
		그녀는 나이가 있고 지혜롭다.
		I slept early, because I was tired.
		나는 피곤했기 때문에 일찍 잤다.

전치사	명사 앞에서 **시간, 장소, 방향, 위치**를 나타내는 말 예) at, on, in, before, after, under, from, to, for, with, between, in front of	I sleep at 11 p.m. 나는 밤 11시에 잔다. Your pen is under the chair. 네 펜은 의자 밑에 있다. Let's meet in front of the building. 건물 앞에서 만나자.
감탄사	**감정**을 표현하는 말 예) Oh, Wow, Well	Wow, you got a new phone! 와, 너 새로운 전화기를 샀구나!

필수문법용어 : 문장의 구성 단위와 성분

		예문
단어	의미를 지니는 **말의 최소 단위** 명사, 대명사, 동사, 형용사, 부사, 전치사, 접속사, 감탄사로 나눌 수 있음	He lied to all of us. 그는 우리 모두에게 거짓말을 했다.
구	완결된 의미를 가지고 있는 두 단어 이상의 모음으로 **주어와 동사를 포함하지 않음** - 명사구 → 주어, 목적어, 보어 - 형용사구 → 명사 수식 - 부사구 → 동사, 형용사, 다른 부사, 문장 전체 수식	There is a pencil on the desk. 책상 위에 연필이 있다. Thank you for helping me. 나를 도와주어서 고마워.
절	완결된 의미를 가지고 있는 두 단어 이상의 모음으로 **주어와 동사를 반드시 포함** - 대등절: 등위접속사로 연결된 대등한 절 - 종속절: 주절에 종속접속사로 연결되어 명사, 형용사, 부사의 역할을 함	She got very angry, but she tried not to show it. 그녀는 매우 화가 났지만, 그것을 보이려고 하지 않았다. Please let me know if he is kind. 그가 친절한지 아닌지 내게 알려 줘.
주어	동작이나 상태의 **주체**를 가리키는 말	She arrived at her office. 그녀는 그녀의 사무실에 도착했다.
동사	주어의 **동작이나 상태**를 나타내는 말	He is a nurse. 그는 간호사이다. They call her an angel. 그들은 그녀를 천사라 부른다.
목적어	동작이나 상태의 **대상**을 가리키는 말	I put this rabbit in the hat. 나는 모자에 이 토끼를 넣는다.
보어	주어나 목적어를 **보충 설명**해 주는 말	I want to become a teacher. 나는 선생님이 되고 싶다. He forced me to hurry. 그는 내가 서두르도록 강요했다.
수식어	문장의 주요 성분을 **부연 설명**하는 역할 생략해도 문법적인 오류를 일으키지 않음	You look pretty tired. 너 꽤 피곤해 보여.

탄탄한 영어 실력을 위한 영문법의 시작

토익·토플
TEPS
공무원영어
대비

마더텅
영문법 3800제
정답과 해설

BASIC 1

CHAPTER 1 문장의 기초
Introduction to Sentences

본문 _ p.5

PRACTICE 1

1	it	2	they	3	you
4	he	5	they	6	it
7	we	8	they	9	he
10	we	11	she	12	you
13	they	14	they		

PRACTICE 2

1	is	2	are	3	is
4	are	5	am	6	are
7	are	8	are	9	are
10	is	11	are	12	am

PRACTICE 3

1	was	2	were	3	was
4	were	5	was	6	were
7	were	8	was	9	were
10	was				

PRACTICE 4

2 He's
3 I'm not
4 She's not[She isn't]
5 We're not[We aren't]
6 You weren't
7 They're
8 It's not[It isn't]
9 I wasn't
10 She wasn't

PRACTICE 5

2 It was not[wasn't] a big deal.
3 They are not[They're not/They aren't] from Australia.
4 This towel was not[wasn't] wet.
5 You were not[weren't] afraid of dogs.
6 The flowers are not[aren't] very pretty.
7 She is not[She's not/She isn't] from London.
8 We are not[We're not/We aren't] late.
9 He is not[He's not/He isn't] a serious person.
10 We were not[weren't] happy with the news.

PRACTICE 6

2 It did not[didn't] rain a lot.
3 They do not[don't] drink coffee.
4 I do not[don't] want any ketchup.
5 We did not[didn't] buy a newspaper.
6 It does not[doesn't] happen very often.
7 They do not[don't] work very hard.
8 He does not[doesn't] look like a good player.
9 Mike did not[didn't] go to the cinema.
10 He does not[doesn't] watch TV in the morning.

PRACTICE 7

2	like	3	makes
4	Don't lie	5	buys
6	doesn't have	7	love
8	doesn't swim	9	didn't study
10	don't read		

PRACTICE 8

2 Are you in a relationship?
3 Does Mary like cats?
4 Do you live near here?
5 Did he take photographs?
6 Was Tom's father in hospital?
7 Do they enjoy a rock concert?
8 Does she have big blue eyes?
9 Were these books very interesting?
10 Is this the Empire State Building?

> 2, 6, 9, 10 be동사가 있는 의문문의 경우 be동사를 문장의 맨 앞으로 옮겨서 「be동사+주어 ~?」의 형태로 만든다.
> 3, 4, 5, 7, 8 일반동사가 있는 의문문의 경우 「Do[Does, Did]+주어+동사원형 ~?」의 형태로 만든다. 주어가 3인칭 단수일 경우 문장의 시제가 현재면 Does를, 과거면 Did를 사용한다.

PRACTICE 9

1	No, he isn't.	2	Yes, we do.
3	Yes, he does.	4	Yes, they were.
5	No, it isn't.	6	No, they didn't.
7	No, I'm not.	8	Yes, she was.
9	Yes, she did.	10	No, I don't.

PRACTICE 10

1 What is your name?

CHAPTER 1

2 Who is that boy?
3 Where are you from?
4 How was your vacation?
5 When did you buy it?
6 Why are you so happy?
7 What does she do?
8 Where is the bank?
9 How do you go to work?
10 When is the party?

PRACTICE 11

1 Which, or, Milk
2 Who, or, Liza
3 or, dog
4 or, pencil
5 or, oranges
6 Which, or, blue
7 Who, or, Mina
8 or, newspaper

PRACTICE 12

1 can he
2 is it
3 are they
4 will they
5 does she
6 can't they
7 doesn't he
8 don't you
9 did she
10 aren't you

PRACTICE 13

1 Wear a helmet.
2 Don't be afraid of snakes.
3 Take a bus or a taxi.
4 Don't be late again.
5 Enter my room.
6 Don't make a noise.
7 Be careful.
8 Don't be upset.
9 Be ready to go.
10 Don't turn on the TV.
11 Be prepared for anything.
12 Don't tell her the truth.

2, 4, 6, 8, 10, 12 의미가 강조된 부정명령문을 만들기 위해 Don't 대신 Never를 쓰는 것도 가능하다.

PRACTICE 14

1 Let's keep
2 Let's take
3 Let's go
4 Let me help
5 Let's not hurry
6 Let me tell
7 Let's study
8 Let's not open
9 Let's not make
10 Let's join

PRACTICE 15

1 shall we
2 will you
3 didn't she
4 will you
5 isn't it
6 can't you
7 doesn't he
8 shall we
9 aren't they
10 does she
11 will you
12 did he

1, 8 Let's로 시작하는 청유문의 부가의문문은 'shall we?'로 쓴다.
2, 4, 11 명령문의 부가의문문은 'will you?'로 쓴다.
3, 5, 6, 7, 9 긍정문 뒤에는 부정의 부가의문문이 온다. 「주어+동사의 긍정형, be/do/조동사의 부정형+인칭대명사?」 형태로 쓴다. 3번은 문장의 시제가 과거이므로 didn't를, 7번은 주어가 3인칭 단수이므로 doesn't를 사용한다.
10, 12 부정문 뒤에는 긍정의 부가의문문이 온다. 「주어+동사의 부정형, be/do/조동사의 긍정형+인칭대명사?」 형태로 쓴다. 10번은 주어가 3인칭 단수이므로 does를, 12번은 문장의 시제가 과거이므로 did를 사용한다.

PRACTICE 16

2 How pretty she is!
3 What big eyes you have!
4 What a huge waterfall!
5 How handsome he is!
6 How fast the robots can move!
7 What a big liar you are!
8 What cute mascots those are!
9 What a high mountain!
10 What a nice museum!
11 What a small dictionary you have!
12 How happy I am!

PRACTICE 17

1 부사
2 접속사
3 동사
4 대명사
5 형용사
6 명사
7 감탄사
8 전치사
9 동사
10 형용사

PRACTICE 18

1 dangerous
2 amazing

3	arrived	4	information
5	or	6	introduce
7	happy	8	scary
9	healthy	10	busy

PRACTICE 19

1 Her cap is red.
2 They went camping last Saturday.
3 She keeps a diary every day.
4 My favorite food is sushi.
5 Tony sat on the bench.
6 Her family lives in Seoul.

PRACTICE 20

1	some trees	2	his voice
3	them	4	TV
5	a tablet PC	6	tennis

PRACTICE 21

1	Mr. Brown	2	cold
3	interesting	4	sing
5	exciting	6	a cook

PRACTICE 22

1 so
2 next time
3 heavily tomorrow
4 about *the Wizard of Oz*
5 late
6 In my opinion

PRACTICE 23

1 He is happy.
2 We love winter.
3 These shirts are small.
4 Her parents live in New York.
5 The teacher teaches math.
6 My mother washed the dishes.

PRACTICE 24

1 [1형식] 주어 동사
2 [2형식] 주어 동사 주격 보어
3 [5형식] 주어 동사 목적어 목적격 보어
4 [3형식] 주어 동사 목적어
5 [4형식] 주어 동사 간접목적어 직접목적어
6 [3형식] 주어 동사 목적어
7 [5형식] 주어 동사 목적어 목적격 보어
8 [1형식] 주어 동사
9 [2형식] 주어 동사 주격 보어
10 [4형식] 주어 동사 간접목적어 직접목적어
11 [2형식] 주어 동사 주격 보어
12 [4형식] 주어 동사 간접목적어 직접목적어
13 [1형식] 주어 동사
14 [5형식] 주어 동사 목적어 목적격 보어

1 [1형식: S는 V한다. 새들이 노래한다.] 문장의 주어(Birds)와 동작을 나타내는 동사(sing)만 있는 문장이므로 1형식이다.
2 [2형식: S는 C하게 V한다. 그 남자는 강하다.] 주어(The man)의 상태를 설명해주는 형용사(strong)가 주격보어 자리에 있으므로 2형식이다. 참고로 be동사는 1,2형식만 가능하다.
3 [5형식: S는 O를 O.C하도록(하게) V한다. Mary는 그 기사가 흥미롭다고 생각했다.] 타동사(found) 뒤에 목적어(the article)가 나오고 그 목적어를 설명해주는 형용사(interesting)가 목적격 보어 자리에 나왔으므로 5형식이 적절하다. 5형식에서 find(found)는 '생각하다' think로 해석된다.
4 [3형식: S는 O를 V한다. 나는 그 문을 열었다.] 타동사(opened) 뒤에 동사의 대상이 되는 명사(the door)가 나왔으므로 3형식이다.
5 [4형식: S는 I.O에게 D.O를 V한다. 그는 그녀에게 반지를 주었다.] 타동사(gave) 뒤에 명사 her과 the ring이 나란히 나왔으므로 4형식이다. 첫 번째 명사(her)는 간접목적어(~에게), 두 번째 명사(the ring)는 직접목적어(~을,를)에 해당된다.
6 [3형식: S는 O를 V한다. John은 남동생이 있다.] 타동사 has 뒤에 동사의 대상이 되는 명사(a brother)가 목적어 자리에 나왔으므로 3형식이다.
7 [5형식: S는 O를 O.C하도록(하게) V한다. 그 영화는 나를 슬프게 만들었다.] 동사(made)의 대상이 되는 목적어(me)와 목적어의 상태를 설명해주는 형용사(sad)가 그 뒤에 나왔으므로 5형식 문장이다.
8 [1형식: S는 V한다. 그 아기는 울었다.] 문장의 주어(The baby)와 주어의 동작을 나타내는 동사(cried)만 있는 문장이므로 1형식이다.
9 [2형식: S는 C하게 V한다. 그는 기술자가 되었다.] 자동사 became이 나오고, 문장의 주어(He)와 주격보어 자리에 나온 명사(an engineer)가 가리키는 대상이 같으므로 2형식이다.
10 [4형식: S는 I.O에게 D.O를 V한다. 우리는 그에게 엽서를 보냈다.] 타동사(sent) 뒤에 명사 him과 a postcard가 나란히 나왔으므로 4형식이다. 첫 번째 명사(him)는 간접목적어(~에게), 두 번째 명사(a postcard)는 직접목적어(~을,를)에 해당된다.
11 [2형식: S는 C하게 V한다. 나뭇잎들은 빨갛고 노랗게 된다.] 주어(Leaves)의 상태를 설명해주는 형용사(red and yellow)가 주격보어 자리에 나왔으므로 2형식 문장이다. 동사 turn은 자동사, 타동사 둘 다 가능하며, 2형식에서 자동사로 쓰인 경우 '~되다, ~해지다'로 해석한다.
12 [4형식: S는 I.O에게 D.O를 V한다. 그녀는 그녀의 아기에게 새 장난감을 사주었다.] 타동사(bought) 뒤에 명사 her baby와 a new toy가 나란히 나왔으므로 4형식이다. 첫 번째 명사(her baby)는 간접목적어(~에게), 두 번째 명사(a new toy)는 직접목적

CHAPTER 1

어(~을,를)에 해당된다.
13 [1형식: S는 V한다. 나는 아침에 늦게 일어났다.] 주어(I)와 동사(woke up)만 있어도 '나는 일어났다'로 완전한 문장이다. late in the morning은 동사를 꾸며 주고 있으므로 부사구에 해당된다.
14 [5형식: S는 O를 O.C하도록(하게) V한다. 나는 나의 방을 깨끗하게 유지했다.] 타동사(kept) 뒤에 목적어(my room)와 목적어의 상태를 보충 설명해주는 형용사(clean)가 나왔으므로 5형식 문장이다.

PRACTICE 25

1	beautiful	2	delicious
3	strange	4	beautifully
5	hungry	6	ghost
7	sadly	8	terrible
9	soft	10	strangely
11	soap	12	softly

1, 2, 3, 5, 8, 9 감각동사 look, smell, sound, feel, taste는 보어로 형용사만을 가진다. 우리말 해석이 부사처럼 되어 영어로도 부사를 쓸 것 같지만 보어로 형용사만 쓸 수 있음에 유의해야 한다.
4 빈칸이 없다고 가정할 때 They decorated the room.(그들은 방을 꾸몄다.)은 문장 구성 요소 중 빠진 것이 없이 완전하다. 따라서 빈칸에는 문장의 필수 구성 요소가 아닌 부사 beautifully(아름답게)가 들어가는 것이 적절하다.
6 look like 뒤에는 명사가 오므로 ghost가 적절하다.
look like+명사: ~처럼 보이다
7 빈칸이 없다고 가정할 때 She shook her head.(그녀는 고개를 가로저었다.)는 문장 구성 요소 중 빠진 것이 없이 완전하다. 따라서 빈칸에는 문장의 필수 구성 요소가 아닌 부사 sadly(슬프게)가 들어가는 것이 적절하다.
10 빈칸이 없다고 가정할 때 She was calm while he was panicking.(그녀는 차분했고 한편 그는 겁에 질려 있었다.)은 문장 구성 요소 중 빠진 것이 없이 완전하다. 따라서 빈칸에는 문장의 필수 구성 요소가 아닌 부사 strangely(이상하게)가 들어가는 것이 적절하다.
11 감각동사(smell) 뒤에 전치사(like)가 나올 경우 명사가 온다.
smell like+명사: ~같은 냄새가 나다
12 He hugged me.(그는 나를 포옹했다.) 자체로 완전한 문장이다. 따라서 빈칸에는 부사 softly(부드럽게)가 들어가는 것이 적절하다.

PRACTICE 26

1	for	2	to	3	for
4	to	5	of	6	to
7	to	8	for	9	for
10	to				

PRACTICE 27

1 Mary told the news to him.
2 Mr. Kim teaches English to them.
3 My mother made a pretty bag for me.
4 Please get some water for me.
5 Can I ask some questions of you?
6 She often writes a letter to Shelly.
7 He found some books for us.
8 Did you buy a cake for her?
9 Will you show your album to me?
10 The Internet gives a lot of information to us.
11 Please tell the real reason to me.
12 Will you pass the salt to me?
13 Vivien sent some flowers to me.
14 We built a new house for the family.
15 My husband cooked spaghetti for me.
16 I read newspapers to senior citizens.
17 Can I ask a favor of you?
18 Customers give a tip to the waiter.
19 I sent a birthday gift to you.
20 My friend made a birthday cake for me.
21 Will you give another chance to me?
22 Can you get that book for me?
23 He bought a box of chocolates for us.
24 Olivia teaches Korean history to students.
25 Evan built a small garden for his children.
26 Mom often cooks noodles for me.
27 She often reads a fairy tale to her son.
28 He showed his report card to his father.
29 The police officer found the car key for me.
30 Dominic made a big sand castle for his son.

Chapter Review Test 정답 본문_ p.29

1 ⑤ 2 ④ 3 ③ 4 ③ 5 ① gives → give
6 (1) doesn't like (2) doesn't have (3) didn't play 7 ⑤ 8 be 9 ③ 10 ③ 11 ②
12 Let's 13 ⓐ was ⓑ was ⓒ were 14 ②
15 ① 16 ④ 17 ⓐ is ⓑ am ⓒ is ⓓ is 18 ⑤
19 ⑤ 20 (1) Yes, I did. (2) No, I didn't.
21 (1) Does, read (2) Is my brother (3) Did, meet
22 ② 23 ④ 24 What a small monkey it is!
25 ④ 26 (1) a nice event (2) cute 27 ③
28 ② 29 ④ 30 ⑤ 31 ③ 32 ② 33 ④
34 ④ 35 ② 36 (가): knowing → know
(나): sweetly → sweet 37 ⑤ 38 ② 39 ③

40 ①		**41** No, she didn't		**42** ④		**43** ②		
44 ③		**45** ③		**46** ③		**47** ②		**48** ⑤
49 ②		**50** ⑤		**51** ②		**52** ④		**53** ③
54 ①		**55** ⑤		**56** (1) Are you a police officer? (2) Don't you live here? (3) Does Mary work at a hospital? **57** ③ **58** ④						

Chapter Review Test 해설

1. (A), (B), (C), (D)에는 be동사 is[Is]가 들어가지만, (E)에는 일반동사 does[washes]가 들어간다.

2. I amn't → I'm not, They'r → They're, This's → This is, She're → She's

3. 주어가 3인칭 단수일 때 is를 쓴다. They는 3인칭 복수이므로 are를 써야 한다.
   cf. My sister, Jenny는 동격을 나타낸다. 나의 여동생인 Jenny

4. ③ taste like(~와 같은 맛이 나다) 뒤에는 명사가 오므로 어법상 적절하다. strawberry가 셀 수 있는 명사여서 like 뒤에 a strawberry[strawberries]가 와야 하는 것이 아닌가 생각할 수 있다. taste like a strawberry[strawberries]는 「딸기 '과일' 같은 맛이 나다」라는 뜻이고 taste like strawberry는 「딸기 '맛'과 같은 맛이 나다」라는 표현으로 둘 다 어법상 맞다. 주스의 맛을 표현하는 이 문장에서는 관사 없이 쓰는 것이 더 적절하다.
   ① Don't shy → Don't be shy
   ② happily → happy
   ④ tall boy → tall
   ⑤ likes → like

5. 명령문은 주어 없이 동사원형으로 시작하므로 gives를 give로 고쳐야 한다.

6. (1),(2) 일반동사 현재의 부정문「do[does]+not+동사원형」
   (3) 일반동사 과거의 부정문「did+not+동사원형」

7. ① I'd not → I don't
   ② Its → It's
   ③ I amn't → I'm not
   ④ Jane's not → Jane doesn't

8. 부정명령문은「Never+동사원형」의 어순으로 나타낼 수 있다. late는 형용사이므로 be동사와 함께 써야 하고 be동사의 원형은 be이다.

9. 긍정문(practices) 뒤에는 부정(doesn't)의 부가의문문이 와야 하며, 주어 Jack의 인칭대명사는 he로 받는다.

10. I(나는 ~.)를 주어로 대답하였으므로 Do you(너는 ~하니?)로 묻는 의문문이 되어야 한다.

11. ② The cookies taste great. 감각동사(taste) 뒤에는 보어로 형용사가 온다.
    cf. greatly 매우(부사)

12. 「Let's+동사원형」'~하자'

13. 어제 있었던 일을 서술하는 지문이므로 과거 시제를 써서 주어가 3인칭 단수(ⓐ Yesterday, ⓑ my work)일 때는 was, 3인칭 복수(ⓒ The actors)일 때는 were를 쓴다.

14. be동사의 부정문은 be동사(is) 뒤에 not을 쓴다.

15. 4형식「주어+동사+간접목적어(사람)+직접목적어(사물)」 나의 남동생은 나에게 선물을 주었다.

16. 일반동사 현재의 부정문은「do[does]+not+동사원형」의 어순이며, 주어(she)가 3인칭 단수이므로 does not을 쓴다.

17. 주어가 3인칭 단수(ⓐ This, ⓒ One, ⓓ the other one)일 때는 is, 1인칭 단수(I)일 때는 am을 쓴다. 빈칸 ⓒ에서 'One of+복수명사'에서 One에 수 일치시키는 것에 주의해야 한다.

18. 감탄문에서 주어(the stars)와 동사(are)는 함께 생략이 가능하다.

19. 일반동사 현재형의 부정문 ⑤「do/does+not+동사원형」

20. 부정의문문에 대한 대답은 일반의문문과 마찬가지로 Yes 뒤에는 긍정형으로, No 뒤에는 부정형으로 대답한다.

21. (1),(3) 일반동사가 있는 의문문「Do[Does, Did]+주어+동사원형 ~?」
    (2) be동사가 있는 의문문「Be동사+주어 ~?」

22. 감탄문의 어순「How+형용사/부사(+주어+동사)!」또는「What(+a/an)+형용사+명사(+주어+동사)!」

23. ④ help는「주어+동사+간접목적어(사람)+직접목적어(사물)」의 어순인 4형식 동사로 쓰이지 않는다.

24. 감탄문의 어순「What(+a/an)+형용사+명사(+주어+동사)!」

25. ① be동사의 부정문은 be동사 다음에 not을 쓴다. (are not/aren't)
    ② 주어가 3인칭 단수인 일반동사의 부정문은「does+not+동사원형」이므로 like를 쓴다.
    ③ be동사 과거의 부정문은 be동사의 과거형 다음에 not을 쓴다. (was not/wasn't)
    ⑤ 일반동사 과거의 부정문은「did+not+동사원형」이

26 므로 call을 쓴다.
감탄문의 어순 「What(+a/an)+형용사+명사(+주어+동사)!」 또는 「How+형용사/부사(+주어+동사)!」

27 3형식 문장에서 buy는 간접목적어(사람) 앞에 전치사 for를 쓰며, show와 teach는 전치사 to를 쓴다.

28 ① Did my brother buy any flowers?
③ Do you have a cell phone?
④ Do they have a big house?
⑤ Does she like movies?

29 인칭대명사 they로 받을 수 있는 주어는 Kevin and Jim이다.

30 ⑤ Yes, he is. 또는 No, he isn't.

31 ③ Mom got a bicycle for me.

32 일반동사 과거 의문문에 대해 긍정으로 답했으므로 「Yes, 주어+did.」와 바꿔 쓸 수 있으며, 뒷 문장으로 보아 주어는 I이다.

33 ㉠ 그녀가 주로 언제 일어나냐고 묻는 것이므로 의문사 When이 적절하다.
㉡ 요즘 기분이 어떻냐고 묻는 것이므로 의문사 How가 적절하다.
㉢ 그 소년들이 어젯밤 무엇을 했냐고 묻는 것이므로 의문사 What이 적절하다.
㉣ 언제 돌아올 것이냐고 묻는 것이므로 의문사 When이 적절하다.
㉤ 지금 어디를 가고 있냐고 묻는 것이므로 의문사 Where가 적절하다.

34 ① 주어가 3인칭 단수(Tommy)이고 테니스를 싫어하므로 doesn't like가 와야 한다.
② 주어가 3인칭 단수(Jane)이므로 does가 와야 한다.
③ 주어가 복수(Somi and Mark)이고 골프를 싫어하므로 don't like가 와야 한다.
⑤ 3인칭 단수(Mark)의 일반 동사 현재의 부정문은 「doesn't+동사원형」이다. 따라서 doesn't 뒤에 동사원형 like가 와야 한다.

35 선택의문문은 Yes나 No로 대답하지 않고 질문에서 언급한 내용 둘 중에 하나를 선택하여 대답한다.

36 (가): 「Let me+동사원형~」은 '제가 ~하도록 해주세요'의 뜻을 나타낸다. Let me know는 '알려주세요'라는 의미이다.
(나): 감각동사 sound(~하게 들리다)의 주격 보어 자리에는 형용사만 올 수 있다.

37 ⑤ Do Kevin's parents get up early?

38 부정명령문은 「Don't+동사원형」의 어순으로 쓰는데 lazy는 형용사이므로 앞에 be를 써야 한다.

39 긍정문(is) 뒤에는 부정(isn't)의 부가의문문이 와야 하며, 주어 Today의 인칭대명사는 it으로 받는다.

40 「주어+동사+주격 보어」의 어순인 2형식 문장이므로, 빈칸에는 감각동사(feel, look, smell, sound, taste)를 써야 한다.

41 didn't she?로 물어봤기 때문에 시제는 과거이며, '그녀가 아파서 집에 있었다.'라고 말하고 있기 때문에 부정의 대답을 써야 한다.

42 ④ How ①②③⑤ What

43 be동사 다음에는 명사, 형용사, 전치사구만 쓸 수 있다.

44 부정문(can't) 뒤에는 긍정(can)의 부가의문문이 와야 하며, 조동사로 묻는 의문문은 조동사로 대답한다.

45 ⓑ 부정명령문 「Don't+동사원형」
ⓓ 「look+형용사」 '~하게 보이다'
「look like+명사」 '~처럼 보이다'
ⓔ make+직접목적어+for+간접목적어

46 ③ 4형식 「주어+동사+간접목적어(사람)+직접목적어(사물)」
①②④⑤ 5형식 「주어+동사+목적어+목적격 보어」

47 긍정문 뒤에는 부정의 부가의문문이 오는데, 이때 시제는 앞에 나온 동사와 일치해야 하므로 didn't you?로 고쳐야 한다.

48 ⑤ 주어 Minji and I는 복수이므로 be동사 are를 써야 한다.
①②③④ 주어가 3인칭 단수이므로 be동사 is를 써야 한다.

49 부정의문문에 대한 대답은 일반의문문과 마찬가지로 Yes 뒤에는 긍정형으로, No 뒤에는 부정형으로 대답한다. 내용상 배가 고프지만 지금 다이어트 중이라는 말이 되어야 하므로 긍정형(Yes)으로 대답해야 한다. Yes, I am. (= Yes, I am hungry.)

50 ⑤ Where are my socks?

51 3형식 문장에서 동사 give, teach, tell, show가 오면 간접목적어 앞에 전치사 to를 쓰고, make가 오면 for를 쓴다.

52 감탄문의 어순 「How+형용사/부사(+주어+동사)!」 또는 「What(+a/an)+형용사+명사(+주어+동사)!」

53 ③ Sumi likes dancing, doesn't she?

54 ② What a wonderful gift this is!
③ What nice pants these are!
④ How smart your dog is!
⑤ What a cloudy day it is!

55 ⑤ look like 다음에는 명사를 쓴다. (looks like → looks)

③ taste like(~와 같은 맛이 나다) 뒤에는 명사가 오므로 명사 chicken이 온 것이 적절하다. chicken이 '닭고기'의 의미로 쓰일 때는 셀 수 없는 명사로서 관사 없이 쓰인다. '음식이 아닌 닭'의 의미로 쓰일 때는 셀 수 있는 명사로서 관사 a를 사용할 수 있다. 여기서는 '닭고기'를 의미하는 It tastes like chicken.이 적절하다.

56 (1) be동사 의문문 「Be동사+주어~?」
(2) 일반동사 부정의문문 「Don't[Doesn't, Didn't]+주어+동사원형~?」
(3) 일반동사 의문문 「Do[Does, Did]+주어+동사원형~?」

57 ③ They made some soup for me.

58 ① 부정명령문 「Do not[Don't]+동사원형」
② 4형식: My father gave me the guitar.
3형식: My father gave the guitar to me.
③ 부정문(aren't) 뒤에는 긍정(are)의 부가의문문이 와야 한다.
⑤ 주어가 3인칭 단수일 때 일반동사의 부정문은 동사원형 앞에 does not[doesn't]를 쓴다.

CHAPTER 2 시제 Tense

본문 _ p.38

PRACTICE 1

1	stands	2	reaches	3	impresses
4	reads	5	begins	6	wishes
7	pushes	8	spends	9	sends
10	misses	11	wakes	12	meets
13	teaches	14	solves	15	wears
16	catches	17	sounds	18	goes
19	mixes	20	finds	21	passes
22	finishes	23	rides	24	watches
25	washes	26	sits	27	throws
28	burns	29	climbs	30	crosses

PRACTICE 2

1	drinks	2	buys	3	studies
4	hurries	5	discusses	6	draws
7	lays	8	sells	9	has
10	pays	11	says	12	cries
13	copies	14	puts	15	closes
16	enjoys	17	touches	18	tries
19	believes	20	loses	21	tells
22	carries	23	repeats	24	grows
25	plays	26	makes	27	costs
28	judges	29	cheers	30	uses
31	brings	32	thinks	33	means
34	breaks	35	shows	36	flies
37	visits	38	feels	39	sings
40	turns	41	harms	42	wins
43	falls	44	builds	45	stays
46	sets	47	sees	48	envies
49	dreams	50	speaks	51	eats
52	leaves	53	gets	54	understands
55	worries	56	keeps	57	gives
58	laughs	59	holds	60	hears

PRACTICE 3

1	iz	2	z	3	z	4	z
5	z	6	s	7	iz	8	s
9	z	10	s	11	iz	12	s
13	z	14	s	15	iz	16	z
17	z	18	s	19	s	20	z
21	s	22	iz	23	iz	24	s
25	z	26	iz	27	s	28	iz
29	z	30	z	31	iz	32	s
33	iz	34	iz	35	s	36	iz
37	z	38	iz	39	iz	40	z
41	s	42	z	43	s	44	iz
45	s						

PRACTICE 4

1	am	2	plays	3	leaves
4	are	5	goes	6	are
7	likes	8	is	9	look
10	are	11	watches	12	are
13	studies	14	is	15	rises
16	gets	17	has	18	drinks
19	make				

CHAPTER 2

> **19** 이 문장에서 hands는 '일손, 일꾼'이란 뜻이며, '일손이 많으면 일이 수월해진다'는 문장으로 우리나라 속담 '백짓장도 맞들면 낫다'와 비슷하다.

PRACTICE 5

1	shopped	**2**	agreed	**3**	called		
4	wished	**5**	invented	**6**	believed		
7	crossed	**8**	rained	**9**	saved		
10	worked	**11**	started	**12**	turned		
13	lived	**14**	planned	**15**	raised		
16	happened	**17**	wanted	**18**	moved		
19	improved	**20**	loved	**21**	walked		
22	jumped	**23**	visited	**24**	arrived		
25	pushed	**26**	covered	**27**	placed		
28	stopped	**29**	learned	**30**	opened		

PRACTICE 6

1 closed	**2** guided	**3** worried
4 used	**5** repeated	**6** waited
7 stayed	**8** joined	**9** wondered
10 ended	**11** studied	**12** surprised
13 added	**14** connected	**15** dropped
16 played	**17** tried	**18** spoiled
19 baked	**20** suggested	**21** rolled
22 tied	**23** collected	**24** carried
25 entered	**26** obeyed	**27** discussed
28 answered	**29** touched	**30** solved
31 enjoyed	**32** helped	**33** married
34 served	**35** listened	**36** wasted
37 watched	**38** sounded	**39** shared
40 trained	**41** hurried	**42** poured
43 cheered	**44** danced	**45** returned
46 missed	**47** locked	**48** laughed
49 hated	**50** typed	**51** seemed
52 failed	**53** looked	**54** decided
55 practiced	**56** kicked	**57** guessed
58 changed	**59** reached	**60** swallowed

PRACTICE 7

1 t	**2** d	**3** t	**4** d
5 t	**6** id	**7** d	**8** d
9 id	**10** d	**11** id	**12** d
13 t	**14** d	**15** t	**16** d
17 d	**18** t	**19** id	**20** d
21 t	**22** d	**23** d	**24** t
25 d	**26** t	**27** id	**28** t
29 t	**30** id	**31** d	**32** d
33 t	**34** t	**35** id	**36** t
37 d	**38** d	**39** t	**40** id
41 t	**42** d	**43** d	**44** id
45 d							

PRACTICE 8

1 set, set	**2** held, held
3 became, become	**4** smelled/smelt, smelled/smelt
5 bore, borne/born	**6** broke, broken
7 cost, cost	**8** meant, meant
9 stayed, stayed	**10** dreamed/dreamt, dreamed/dreamt
11 ran, run	**12** blew, blown
13 fed, fed	**14** drove, driven
15 put, put	**16** understood, understood
17 came, come	**18** chose, chosen
19 drank, drunk	**20** drew, drawn
21 read, read	**22** shopped, shopped
23 fought, fought	**24** stood, stood
25 wore, worn	**26** bit, bitten
27 sang, sung	**28** let, let
29 won, won	**30** hit, hit
31 told, told	**32** wrote, written
33 sold, sold	**34** slid, slid
35 took, taken	**36** woke, woken
37 flew, flown	**38** carried, carried
39 tried, tried	**40** swam, swum
41 felt, felt	**42** showed, shown
43 burned/burnt, burned/burnt	**44** kept, kept
45 forgot, forgotten	**46** rang, rung
47 sent, sent	**48** heard, heard
49 built, built	**50** hurt, hurt
51 rose, risen	**52** caught, caught
53 brought, brought	**54** spread, spread
55 lent, lent	**56** grew, grown

57 began, begun	58 threw, thrown		
59 bought, bought	60 enjoyed, enjoyed		
61 sat, sat	62 was/were, been		
63 played, played	64 found, found		
65 went, gone	66 gave, given		
67 planned, planned	68 ate, eaten		
69 rode, ridden	70 knew, known		
71 spent, spent	72 closed, closed		
73 spoke, spoken	74 got, got(ten)		
75 taught, taught	76 saw, seen		
77 led, led	78 studied, studied		
79 made, made	80 had, had		
81 fell, fallen	82 said, said		
83 lost, lost	84 left, left		
85 slept, slept	86 did, done		
87 met, met	88 thought, thought		
89 laid, laid	90 paid, paid		

PRACTICE 9

1 was	2 am	3 wasn't			
4 was	5 were	6 were			
7 weren't	8 is	9 are			
10 weren't					

PRACTICE 10

1 bought	2 eat	3 went			
4 wears	5 built	6 began			
7 read	8 found	9 finished			
10 practices					

PRACTICE 11

1 is going to get	2 are going to go	
3 are going to get	4 is going to visit	
5 is going to make	6 are going to paint	

PRACTICE 12

1 spend	2 Is	3 will	
4 went	5 make	6 Will	
7 be	8 gets	9 stayed	
10 are			

PRACTICE 13

1 am going to paint		2 will travel	
3 is going to study		4 will have	
5 are going to buy			

PRACTICE 14

1 living	2 leaving	3 sleeping			
4 holding	5 drawing	6 playing			
7 carrying	8 believing	9 writing			
10 saying	11 buying	12 spending			
13 losing	14 waking	15 checking			
16 bringing	17 looking	18 diving			
19 joining	20 smoking	21 doing			
22 blowing	23 making	24 choosing			
25 adding	26 selling	27 giving			
28 having	29 taking	30 meeting			

PRACTICE 15

1 getting	2 lying	3 changing			
4 opening	5 parking	6 pushing			
7 reading	8 wearing	9 putting			
10 calling	11 finding	12 biking			
13 burning	14 setting	15 coming			
16 respecting	17 winning	18 seeing			
19 closing	20 beginning	21 tying			
22 growing	23 keeping	24 drinking			
25 swimming	26 helping	27 climbing			
28 entering	29 singing	30 going			
31 jumping	32 shopping	33 lending			
34 catching	35 collecting	36 sending			
37 staying	38 riding	39 falling			
40 flying	41 teaching	42 dreaming			
43 sitting	44 driving	45 planting			
46 turning	47 standing	48 starting			
49 floating	50 breaking	51 telling			
52 eating	53 speaking	54 running			
55 arriving	56 building	57 asking			
58 camping	59 cheering	60 walking			

PRACTICE 16

1 It is snowing.
2 I am cleaning my room.

3 Sumi is making a card.
4 He is wearing blue jeans.
5 It was flying over the tree.
6 We were enjoying the holiday.
7 They are doing their best.
8 My grandparents were smiling at us.
9 A man was standing in front of the door.
10 I was playing basketball with my friends.

PRACTICE 17

2 am reading a book
3 is visiting her aunt
4 are eating out with their family
5 are going to church

PRACTICE 18

1 is writing
2 went
3 am going to climb
4 will paint
5 was reading

PRACTICE 19

2 has driven
3 haven't heard
4 Has, met
5 has had
6 Have, visited
7 haven't seen
8 has taught
9 Have, studied

PRACTICE 20

2 Has she watched
3 haven't left
4 have fed
5 has had
6 hasn't gone
7 has found
8 has he been
9 have never read
10 has grown

2 현재완료시제 의문문은 「Have/Has+주어+과거분사」로 나타낸다. 동사 watch의 과거분사형은 watched이다.
3, 6 현재완료시제 부정문은 「haven't/hasn't+과거분사」로 나타낸다. leave의 과거분사형은 left, go의 과거분사형은 gone이다.
4, 7, 10 현재완료시제는 「have/has+과거분사」로 나타낸다. feed의 과거분사는 fed, find의 과거분사는 found, grow의 과거분사는 grown이다.
5 세연이가 작년부터 계속 휴대전화를 가지고 있다는 의미의 문장이므로 과거시제가 아닌 현재완료시제로 나타내야 한다.
8 문장의 주어 he가 3인칭 단수이므로 has를 써서 현재완료시제를 나타낸다.
9 살아오면서 한 번도 <Harry Potter>를 읽은 적이 없다는 경험을 나타내고 있으므로 현재완료시제를 쓴다.

PRACTICE 21

1 Have
2 has lived
3 brushed
4 did
5 left
6 have been
7 known
8 played
9 met
10 has
11 have studied
12 watched
13 has worked
14 went
15 ended
16 has rained
17 had
18 listened
19 threw
20 made
21 Did
22 won
23 visited
24 has played
25 snowed
26 Have
27 was

1, 26 현재완료시제의 의문문은 「Have/Has+주어+과거분사~?」 형태로 쓴다.
2, 6, 7, 8, 10, 11, 13, 16, 18, 20, 24 기간을 나타내는 부사(구)가 있으므로 현재완료시제를 쓴다. 'since+시점' 또는 'for+기간'과 함께 쓰여 현재완료 용법 중 '계속'을 나타낸다.
3, 5, 9, 14, 15, 17, 22, 23, 27 명백한 과거 시점을 나타내는 부사(구)가 있으므로 과거시제를 쓴다.
4, 21 괄호 뒤에 동사원형이 쓰였으므로 현재완료시제(have[has]+과거분사)가 될 수 없다. 따라서 과거시제가 적합하며, 과거시제의 의문문은 「Did+주어+동사원형~?」 형태로 쓴다. 4번은 의문사가 포함된 의문문으로 「의문사+did[does, do]+주어+동사원형~?」 형태로 쓴다.
12, 19, 25 ago는 명백한 과거 시점을 나타내는 부사이므로 항상 과거시제와 함께 쓰인다.

Chapter Review Test 정답 본문_p.63

1 ④ **2** ⓐ decorates → decorated ⓑ come → came ⓒ sing → sang **3** ② **4** builded → built **5** ⑤ **6** does **7** ① **8** was **9** is leaving **10** ⓐ has ⓑ brings ⓒ helps ⓓ saves
11 ①,④ **12** ② **13** ⑤ **14** ③ **15** ②
16 ① **17** ⑤ **18** ② **19** ③,④ **20** ④
21 ② **22** ② **23** Is she watering the plant?
24 (1) Yumi is singing a song. (2) Mike is swimming in the pool. **25** ⑤ **26** ② **27** ④
28 (1) She is taking a picture[pictures]. (2) They are riding bicycles. **29** He will be a scientist.
30 ③ **31** am washing, is reading **32** ②,⑤

> 33 ④ 34 ⑤ 35 opens 36 is going to go swimming (on Thursday) 37 ② 38 get → gets, go → goes 39 ② 40 ③ 41 ④ 42 ① 43 ② 44 ⑤ 45 ⑤ 46 ate 47 ④ 48 ① 49 ② 50 ② 51 ⑤ 52 ⑤ 53 (1) are going to play the guitar (2) is going to make spaghetti 54 ③ 55 ④ 56 ⑤

Chapter Review Test 해설

1. ④ 주어가 3인칭 단수인 현재시제 문장이므로 동사는 teaches가 와야 한다. (teach → teaches)

2. 어제 있었던 일로 과거시제로 통일한다. decorate의 과거형은 decorated, come의 과거형은 came, sing의 과거형은 sang이다.

3. ② 현재진행형(is moving)이 미래를 의미하는 부사구(next month)와 쓰여서 미래를 나타낼 수 있다.
   ① 과거를 나타내는 부사(yesterday)가 나왔으므로 과거시제로 써야 한다. (Does → Did)
   ③ '그녀가 그 집을 작년부터 계속 가지고 있다.'는 의미로 기간을 나타내는 부사구(since last year)가 쓰였으므로 과거부터 현재까지 계속되는 상태를 의미하는 현재완료를 써야 한다. (had → has had)
   ④ '내가 이미 나의 일을 끝냈다.'는 문장으로 앞에 have가 나온 것으로 보아 현재완료 시제를 쓰는 것이 적절하다. (finish → finished)
   ⑤ 현재를 나타내는 부사 now가 쓰였으므로 과거진행형이 아닌 현재진행형이 적절하다. (was walking → is walking)

4. 첫 문장의 동사 liked로 보아 이 글의 시제는 과거이다. build의 과거형은 built이다.

5. 주어진 문장의 동사(go)의 형태로 보아 3인칭 단수인 주어는 올 수 없다.
   ⑤ 3인칭 단수 ① 1인칭 복수 ②③④ 3인칭 복수

6. 주어(She)가 3인칭 단수이므로 do를 does로 바꾸어 쓴다.

7. '~하는 중이었다/~하고 있었다'는 과거진행시제이므로 「was/were+~ing」를 써야 하는데, 주어가 We이므로 be동사는 were이 와야 한다.

8. 주어가 3인칭 단수이고, 과거를 나타내는 부사(yesterday)가 있으므로 be동사로 was가 와야 한다.

9. 미래를 나타내는 부사와 함께 현재진행형으로 미래를 나타낼 수 있다.

10. 주어인 Homemade food, It(it)이 3인칭 단수이고, 동명사 주어(Cooking) 또한 3인칭 단수 취급을 하므로 빈칸에는 3인칭 단수형을 쓴다.

11. ride-rode-ridden   draw-drew-drawn
    bear-bore-born   begin-began-begun

12. ③ ~하기 위해서'라는 의미를 나타내기 위해 to부정사를 쓰는 것은 적절하다.
    ① yesterday는 과거를 나타내므로 동사의 시제는 과거형이어야 한다. (take → took)
    ② 동사 do를 수식해야 하므로 '잘'이라는 의미의 부사 well로 고쳐야 한다. (very good → very well)
    ④ 특정한 날짜 앞에 전치사는 in이 아닌 on을 쓴다. (in → on)
    ⑤ '~할 예정이다'를 나타내는 be going to 뒤에는 동사원형을 써야 한다. (studying → study)

13. did로 물었으므로 과거를 나타내는 부사(구)가 와야 한다. next Saturday는 미래를 나타내는 부사구이다.

14. 1인칭 복수 주어(We)에 알맞은 be동사 과거형은 were이다.
    ③ We were making a chair.

15. 의문사로 시작하는 의문문은 Yes나 No로 대답할 수 없으며, be going to로 묻는 질문에 대해 be going to로 답한 ②번이 가장 적절하다.

16. ① 「be going to+장소」 '~에 가고 있다(진행시제)'
    ②③④⑤ 「be going to+동사원형」 '~하려고 하다(미래시제)'

17. 주어(he and his family와 they)가 복수이므로 have가 와야 한다.

18. 모음+y로 끝나는 동사의 3인칭 단수형은 -s를 붙여서 나타낸다.
    ② She plays the violin with her mother.

19. 미래를 나타내는 부사구(next weekend)가 있으므로 미래시제가 와야 한다. 또한 현재진행시제도 미래를 나타내는 부사구와 함께 가까운 미래를 나타낸다.

20. 과거에 일어난 일을 현재와 연관지어 표현할 때 「have/has+과거분사」의 형태인 현재완료시제를 쓴다. 주어(Susan)가 3인칭 단수이므로 has가 와야 한다.

21. ⓒ read-read-read
    ⓓ 주어가 복수(Mr. and Mrs. Cheney)이므로 be동사는 are가 적절하다.
    ⓐ This is는 This's로 줄여 쓸 수 없다.
    ⓑ will을 사용한 미래시제는 「will+동사원형」으로 나타낸다.
    ⓔ 주어(Jane and I)가 복수이므로 be동사는 are가

적절하다.
22 과거를 나타내는 부사구(A few years ago)가 있으므로 과거형(made)이 와야 한다.
23 현재진행형의 의문문 「be동사+주어+-ing~?」
24 「am/is/are+-ing」 '~하고 있다'
25 ⑤ 진행을 나타내는 현재진행형
①②③④ 미래를 나타내는 현재진행형
26 ⓐⓒⓔ「be going to+동사원형」 '~하려고 하다' (미래시제)
ⓑⓓ「be going to+장소」 '~에 가고 있다' (진행시제)
27 첫 번째 빈칸이 포함된 문장은 문맥상 '너는 농담을 하고 있는 게 틀림없어.'라는 의미가 되어야 한다. 조동사 must(~임에 틀림없다) 뒤에 「be동사+동사원형ing」를 써서 '~하고 있음에 틀림없다'는 의미를 나타낼 수 있다. 두 번째 빈칸이 포함된 문장은 '하지만 나는 농담하고 있는 게 아니야.'라는 내용이 오는 게 적절하다. 진행 시제는 「be동사+동사원형ing」를 써서 '~하고 있다'는 의미를 나타낸다.
28 현재진행시제 「am/is/are+-ing」 '~하고 있다'
29 will 다음에는 동사원형이 온다. be동사 is의 동사원형은 be이다.
30 미래시제는 「will+동사원형」으로 나타낸다.
③ She will play the piano.
31 현재진행시제 「am/is/are+-ing」 '~하고 있다'
32 ② 과거를 나타내는 부사구(last week)가 있으므로 시제를 과거로 일치시킨다. (go → went)
⑤ She의 소유격은 Her이다. (She's → Her)
33 ④ make - made - made
34 ⑤ 동명사, ①②③④ 현재진행형
35 현재의 습관, 반복적인 일은 현재시제로 표현한다. 주어(It)가 3인칭 단수이므로 opens를 쓴다.
36 그녀는 (목요일에) 수영을 하러 갈 예정이다.
「be going to+동사원형」의 형태로 나타낸다.
37 last year는 과거, now는 현재, next year는 미래를 나타내는 부사구이다.
38 주어가 3인칭 단수인 현재시제 문장이므로 get은 gets로, go는 goes로 고쳐 쓴다.
39 -ie로 끝나는 동사의 -ing형은 ie를 y로 바꾸고 ing를 붙여서 만든다.
② She is lying on the floor.
40 ⓐ 주어가 3인칭 단수(Bora)이므로 was가 와야 한다.
ⓑ 두 번째 문장의 동사(saw)로 이 글의 시제가 과거임을 알 수 있다. 따라서 시제를 일치시키기 위해 asked가 와야 한다.

ⓒ 빈칸 앞에 be동사(were)가 있어서 과거진행시제가 되는 것이 자연스러우므로 looking이 적절하다. be동사(were)와 일반동사(look)를 동시에 같이 쓰는 것은 어법에 맞지 않다.
41 be동사(am)가 있으므로 talk의 진행형인 talking을 써야 한다.
42 ① cleanned → cleaned
43 미래시제는 「will+동사원형」으로 나타낸다.
① I will be a good designer.
② I will visit my grandmother tomorrow.
④ Mr. Park will be busy tomorrow.
현재진행시제의 부정문은 「be동사+not+-ing」의 어순으로 나타낸다.
⑤ He was not playing basketball this morning.
44 과거시제로 묻는 질문에 과거시제로 대답한다. 무슨 일이 있었는데? – 내 아기 여동생이 밤새 울었어.
45 ⑤ 자음+y로 끝나는 동사의 3인칭 단수형은 y를 i로 바꾸고 -es를 붙여서 나타낸다. (flys → flies)
46 과거시제로 묻는 질문에 과거시제로 대답한다. eat의 과거형은 ate이다.
47 Minho는 3인칭 단수 주어이므로, 동사로 goes가 온다.
48 미래시제는 「be going to+동사원형」이므로, Mike is going to be busy next week.로 써야 한다.
49 ② B는 'Sunny와 그녀의 이모가 지금 막 점심식사를 끝냈다.'라는 의미로 지금은 이미 밥을 다 먹은 상태를 나타낸다. 그러므로 '지금도 먹고 있다'라고 현재진행형을 쓸 수 없다.
① A는 '나는 2년 동안 변호사로 일해오고 있다.'는 의미로 '2년 전에 변호사로서 일을 시작했고 지금도 여전히 변호사이다'는 의미이다.
③ C는 'Kate와 미나가 아기였을 때부터 서울에서 살아왔다.'라는 의미로 '그들이 지금도 서울에서 살고 있다'는 의미이다.
④ D는 '지아가 그녀의 가족과 함께 호주로 갔다.'라는 의미로 '지아가 호주에서 현재에도 살고 있어서 지금 여기에는 없다'라는 의미이다.
⑤ E는 '준호는 이 애니메이션을 일곱 살 때부터 줄곧 좋아했다.'라는 의미로 '준호가 이 애니메이션을 좋아했고 지금도 여전히 좋아한다'라는 의미이다.
50 ① now는 현재를 나타내므로 과거진행인 「were+-ing」와 쓸 수 없다. (were → are)
③ tomorrow는 미래를 나타내므로 과거형인 learned와 쓸 수 없다. (learned → will learn)
④ a few minutes ago는 과거를 나타내므로 미래시

제인 will과 쓸 수 없다. (will finish → finished)
⑤ last week는 과거를 나타내므로 미래를 나타내는 be going to와 쓸 수 없다. (We're going to have → We had)

51 ⑤ 감사의 표현으로 화요일에 점심을 사겠다는 의미가 되어야 하므로 동사는 과거가 아닌 미래형을 쓰는 것이 적절하다. (was → will be)
④ 시간의 부사절 'until ~ office?'에서는 현재시제가 미래시제를 대신하므로(Ch.13 PSS 5 참조) 현재형 동사 am이 쓰인 것이 적절하다.

52 미래시제를 나타내는 의문문은 「Will+주어+동사원형 ~?」 또는 「Be동사+주어+going to+동사원형 ~?」으로 쓴다. (Will you visit Paris this summer?/Are you going to visit Paris this summer?)

53 「be going to+동사원형」 형태를 활용하여 미래에 있을 일에 대하여 영작하는 문제이다.
(1) 주어가 3인칭 복수(Mina and Suji)이므로 be동사도 복수형(are)으로 씀에 유의한다.
(2) 주어가 3인칭 단수(Jieun)이므로 be동사도 3인칭 단수형(is)으로 써야 한다.

54 ㉠ 기간을 나타내는 부사구 since last year가 쓰여, 작년부터 지금까지 지속해서 중국어를 공부하고 있는 상황을 나타내므로, 현재완료 시제를 사용한다. They have studied Chinese since last year.
㉡ 과거 특정한 시점을 나타내는 부사구 last weekend가 사용되었으므로, 과거시제를 사용한다. Tony visited his parents last weekend.
㉢ 부사구 for the past 3 years가 쓰여, 과거부터 현재까지 계속되는 상태를 나타내므로, 현재완료 시제를 사용한다. She has taught English in this school for the past 3 years.

55 과거를 나타내는 부사구(last winter vacation)가 쓰였으므로 be동사의 과거형이 와야 한다. 주어(Nami와 She)가 3인칭 단수이므로 was를 쓴다.

56 B가 '이번 토요일에 조부모님 댁에 방문할 예정이야.'라고 대답했으므로 '이번 토요일에 무엇을 할 예정이니?'라고 물어야 한다.
① 너희 조부모님 댁에 어떻게 방문할 거니?
② 너는 매주 너희 조부모님 댁에 방문하니?
③ 너는 무엇 때문에 너희 조부모님 댁을 방문하니?
④ 너는 왜 조부모님 댁 방문을 계획했니?

CHAPTER 3 조동사
Modals

본문 _ p.72

PRACTICE 1

1	watch	2	swim	3	be able to
4	see	5	leaves	6	come
7	be	8	wants	9	wash
10	have	11	writes	12	bite

> 1, 2, 4, 6, 7, 9, 10, 12 「조동사+동사원형」 형태로 쓴다.
> 3 조동사는 겹쳐 쓰지 않으므로 will 뒤에 can을 쓸 수 없다.
> 5, 8, 11 주어-동사 수일치를 하여 3인칭 주어인 경우 동사에 '-(e)s'를 붙인다.

PRACTICE 2

1 Jane will not[won't] use your desk.
2 You must not[mustn't] take this ball.
3 She cannot[can't] play the guitar.
4 He should not[shouldn't] break the promise.
5 It might not[mightn't] be true.
6 Minsu could not[couldn't] dance last night.
7 I knew she would not[wouldn't] come here.
8 You may not like the movie.
9 You had better not['d better not] stay here.

PRACTICE 3

1 Will they get there by subway?
2 Should we take a bus?
3 Can he play the violin?
4 Will Jenny move to London?
5 Should I buy this shirt?
6 Can Minsu cook Chinese food?
7 Will the movie start at 11:20?
8 Can this elephant draw pictures?

CHAPTER 3

PRACTICE 4

1 Can you use chopsticks?
2 Would you like some coffee?
3 Should I invite Minsu to dinner?
4 May I use your phone?
5 Could you carry my bag?
6 Will you go there with me?
7 Must I recycle these bottles?
8 May I speak to Bill?

PRACTICE 5

1 is able to
2 am not able to
3 Are, able to
4 was able to
5 were not[weren't] able to
6 Are, able to

PRACTICE 6

1 can
2 can't
3 can[could]
4 Can[Could]
5 can[could]
6 can't
7 Can[Could]
8 can't
9 Can[Could]
10 can

> 1 목말라 보이시네요. 당신은 거기서 주스를 마셔도 됩니다. (허가)
> 2 당신은 밤에 혼자 나가서는 안 됩니다. 그건 위험합니다. (금지)
> 3 Jane, 내가 너의 펜을 빌려도 될까? (허가)
> 4 값을 조금만 깎아 주시겠어요? (요청)
> 5 여보세요, Tom과 통화할 수 있을까요? (허가)
> 6 그녀는 그를 사랑하지만, 그녀는 그와 결혼할 수 없어. (능력)
> 7 저를 좀 도와주시겠어요? (요청)
> 8 여기 주차해서는 안 돼요. 차를 옮겨주세요. (금지)
> 9 나의 부탁을 들어주겠니? (요청)
> 10 네가 원한다면 너도 와도 돼. (허가)

PRACTICE 7

1 허가
2 허가
3 추측
4 추측
5 추측
6 허가
7 허가
8 추측
9 추측
10 추측
11 허가
12 추측
13 허가
14 허가

> 1 안녕하세요, 제가 도와드려도 괜찮을까요? (허가)
> 2 너는 나의 연필을 써도 좋아. (허가)
> 3 그녀는 아프지 않을지도 몰라. (추측)
> 4 그것은 사실일지도 몰라. (추측)
> 5 그들은 바쁠지도 몰라. (추측)
> 6 제가 질문을 해도 될까요? (허가)
> 7 여보세요, Smith 씨랑 통화해도 될까요? (허가)
> 8 그녀는 우리를 보고 싶지 않을지도 몰라. (추측)
> 9 그 버스가 5분 후에 올지도 몰라. (추측)
> 10 Jenny는 목이 마를지도 몰라. (추측)
> 11 너는 내일 그것을 돌려줘도 좋아. (허가)
> 12 그녀는 마흔두 살일지도 몰라. (추측)
> 13 내가 그 차를 빌려도 될까? (허가)
> 14 너는 자리에 앉아도 좋아. (허가)

PRACTICE 8

1 may[can]
2 not
3 you
4 course
5 not
6 Sure[Okay]
7 may[must]
8 Why

PRACTICE 9

1 Will you stay here?
2 Would you help me?
3 Would you turn off the radio?
4 Will you send me a letter?
5 Will you wake me up at 7 a.m. tomorrow?
6 Would you tell me your phone number?
7 Would you show me your ID card?

PRACTICE 10

1 would like
2 Would, like to
3 would like to
4 would like to
5 Would, like
6 would, like to, would like to

PRACTICE 11

1 Could
2 could
3 Can
4 will
5 may
6 Would
7 Will
8 Can

> 1 could가 허가를 나타낸다.
> 2 '문제를 풀지 못했다'고 했으므로 능력의 can을 과거시제로 맞추어 could를 써야 한다.
> 3 can이 능력을 나타낸다.
> 4 will+동사원형: ~할 것이다
> 5 may가 추측을 나타낸다.
> 6 would like+(대)명사: ~을 원하다
> 7 'Will(Would) you ~?' 구문이 요청을 나타낸다.
> 8 can이 요청을 나타낸다.

PRACTICE 12

1	의무	2	강한 추측	3	의무
4	의무	5	강한 추측	6	강한 추측
7	의무	8	의무	9	강한 추측
10	강한 추측	11	의무	12	강한 추측

1 차들이 이 거리에서 매우 빨리 다닌다. 우리는 조심해야 한다. (의무)
2 그녀는 하루 종일 아무것도 먹지 않았다. 그녀는 배가 고픔에 틀림없다. (강한 추측)
3 군인들은 군복을 입어야 한다. 그들은 평상복을 입을 수 없다. (의무)
4 나는 내일 회의가 있다. 나는 내 발표를 준비해야 한다. (의무)
5 죄송합니다. 제가 전화를 잘못 건 것이 분명합니다. (강한 추측)
6 아기가 울고 있다. 그녀는 졸림에 틀림없다. (강한 추측)
7 그것에 대해 아무 말도 하지 마세요. 당신은 그것을 비밀로 해야 합니다. (의무)
8 불이 났다. 우리는 소방서에 전화해야 한다. (의무)
9 나리는 매일 핑크색 옷을 입는다. 그녀는 그 색깔을 좋아함에 틀림없다. (강한 추측)
10 민호는 어려 보인다. 그는 학생임에 틀림없다. (강한 추측)
11 나는 밖에 나갈 수 없다. 나는 집에서 엄마를 도와드려야 한다. (의무)
12 그는 밤을 새웠다. 그는 피곤함에 틀림없다. (강한 추측)

PRACTICE 13

1	have to	2	has to	3	has to
4	have to	5	have to	6	have to

PRACTICE 14

1	had to	2	has to	3	have to
4	had to	5	have to	6	has to
7	had to	8	have to	9	had to
10	had to				

PRACTICE 15

1	doesn't have to	2	must not
3	don't have to	4	must not
5	must not	6	don't have to

PRACTICE 16

1	should make	2	had better put
3	should not throw	4	had better wear
5	should not play	6	had better not go
7	should change	8	had better not walk
9	should not steal	10	had better not stay

1 make a good impression on: ~에게 좋은 인상을 주다
2 put on: ~을 입다
6 go outside: 밖에 나가다
7 change clothes: 옷을 갈아입다
9 steal: 훔치다, 도둑질하다
10 stay out: 밖에 나가 있다

PRACTICE 17

1	must	2	don't have to
3	cannot	4	Would
5	could	6	may
7	may, had better	8	have to
9	Would	10	should not
11	Can	12	should
13	must not	14	had better
15	Could	16	should not
17	had to	18	will

1 must가 강한 추측을 나타낸다.
2 don't have to가 불필요를 나타낸다.
3, 5 cannot, could가 능력을 나타낸다.
4 'Would you ~?'가 요청을 나타낸다.
6 may가 추측을 나타낸다.
7 may가 추측, had better가 강한 충고나 권유를 나타낸다.
8, 17 have to(=must), had to가 의무를 나타낸다.
9 would like+(대)명사: ~을 원하다
10, 16 should not(~하면 안 된다)이 금지를 나타낸다.
11 can이 허가를 나타낸다.
12 should가 의무를 나타낸다.
13 must not이 강한 금지를 나타낸다.
14 had better가 강한 충고나 권유를 나타낸다.
15 could가 요청을 나타낸다.
18 will not+동사원형: ~하지 않을 것이다

Chapter Review Test 정답   본문 _ p.88

1 ① 2 ① 3 is able to 4 ③ 5 ⑤ 6 had better 7 (1) are → be (2) borrowing → borrow 8 ⑤ 9 ④ 10 Do I have to go home now? 11 are able to 12 ④ 13 Will he meet his friends tomorrow? 14 ④ 15 ③ 16 (1) She will not[won't] listen to pop songs. (2) Will you be quiet in the library? 17 ③ 18 ④ 19 ① 20 ③ 21 ① 22 ③ 23 ③ 24 ④ 25 ③ 26 You must not carry a balloon here. 27 ④ 28 Can you play the violin? 29 like to 30 ⑤ 31 ③ 32 ① 33 ② 34 ② 35 ②

36 ①	37 ⑤	38 ①	39 ③	40 ①	41 ④
42 ④	43 You had better go to bed			44 ②	
45 ②	46 ③	47 ④	48 ⑤	49 ②	

Chapter Review Test 해설

1 조동사(may) 뒤에는 동사원형이 와야 한다.
2 '~해야 한다'의 뜻을 나타내는 조동사 must는 의무를 나타내는 have/has to와 바꾸어 쓸 수 있는데, 주어가 You이므로 have to가 가장 적절하다.
3 능력을 나타내는 can은 be able to와 바꾸어 쓸 수 있는데, 주어가 She이므로 is able to가 와야 한다.
4 would like to '~하고 싶다'
5 Yes나 sure 뒤에는 긍정형이, No 뒤에는 부정형이 와야 한다. 조동사는 인칭에 관계없이 항상 형태가 같다.
6 had better '~하는 게 낫다'
7 (1) 조동사(will) 뒤에는 동사원형이 와야 한다. are의 동사원형은 be이다.
   (2) 조동사로 시작하는 의문문 「조동사+주어+동사원형 ~?」
8 접속사 But으로 시작하는 두 번째 문장은 앞 문장과 반대의 의미를 나타내므로 조동사의 부정형 can't가 들어가야 한다. 우리는 돈으로 무엇이든 살 수 있다. 그러나 그것(돈)으로 건강을 살 수는 없다.
9 빈칸 이후 이어지는 말에 '주차금지' 표지판이 언급되었으므로 '~해서는 안 된다'는 거절의 답이 와야 한다. May I ~?에 대한 거절의 표현으로 No, you must not.을 쓸 수 있다. 제가 여기에 주차를 해도 되나요? – 아니요, 안 됩니다. '주차금지' 표지판이 있어요.
10 have to는 do[does]를 써서 의문문을 만든다.
11 능력을 나타내는 can은 be able to와 바꾸어 쓸 수 있다. 주어(Humans)가 복수이므로 are able to로 쓴다.
12 강한 추측을 나타내는 must '~임에 틀림없다'
13 '~할 것이다'라는 의미가 되려면 will 또는 be going to가 와야 한다. 조건에서 6단어로 쓰라고 했으므로 will을 쓰는 것이 적절하다.
14 ④ don't have to '~할 필요가 없다'
15 ③ don't have to '~할 필요가 없다'
    ①②④⑤ '~해서는 안 된다'
16 will not[won't] '~하지 않을 것이다'
    Will[Would] you ~? '~해 줄래요?'
17 would like to = want to '~하고 싶다'
18 should는 '~해야 한다'의 뜻이므로 너는 도서관에서 떠들어야 한다.는 어색하다.
    (should → should not[shouldn't])
19 may '~일지도 모른다' 만약 창문을 열어 놓고 잠들면, 너는 감기에 걸릴지도 모른다.
20 ⓐⓓ 허가의 can '~해도 된다'
    ⓑⓒⓔ 능력의 can '~할 수 있다'
21 Can I ~? '~해도 될까(요)?' 내가 햄버거 좀 먹어도 될까? – 물론이지. 여기 있어.
22 • May I ~? '~해도 될까(요)?'
    • must '~해야 한다' 엄마, 친구들이랑 야구해도 되나요? – 안 돼! 너는 먼저 숙제를 끝내야 해.
23 have to의 의문문 「Do[Does]+주어+have to+동사원형 ~?」
24 you로 물었으므로 I로 대답하는 것이 적절하다.
    ④ Yes, I can.
25 ③ had better+동사원형
    (had better to go → had better go)
26 「must not+동사원형」 '~해서는 안 된다'
27 ④ 허가의 may '~해도 좋다'
    ①②③⑤ 추측의 may '~일지도 모른다'
28 조동사로 시작하는 의문문은 「조동사+주어+동사원형 ~?」의 어순으로 나타낸다. 할 수 있는지 능력을 묻고 있으므로 조동사 can을 쓴다.
29 want to는 would like to와 바꾸어 쓸 수 있다.
30 뒤에 동사원형이 나오므로 조동사가 와야 한다. 빈칸에는 의무를 나타내는 조동사가 들어가야 의미상 자연스럽다. should는 '~해야 한다'는 뜻이다.
31 조동사 may를 사용해 허가를 묻는 문장이므로 may, can/can't, should와 같은 조동사를 사용하여 승낙 또는 거절의 표현으로 대답한다. 주어를 I로 물었으므로 대답으로는 you가 오는 것이 적절하다.
32 숙제를 해야 하므로 함께 갈 수 없다는 거절의 표현이 와야 한다.
33 • This work may be easy for you.
    • You don't have to bring your library card.
    • He must practice English every day.
34 will의 부정형의 축약형은 won't이다.
    ② willn't → won't
35 ② 주어가 3인칭 단수(Mr. Brown)이므로 has to로 써야 한다.
36 could '~할 수 있었다'
37 May I ~? '~해도 될까(요)?'

38 Will you ~? '~해줄래요?' 문 좀 닫아 줄래요?
– 알겠어요.

39 조동사가 있는 의문문은 「(의문사+)조동사+주어+동사원형 ~?」의 형태로 나타낸다.

40 must는 인칭에 관계없이 항상 형태가 같다.
 cf. have[has] to는 인칭에 따라 다르게 쓰인다.
  You have to get there before dark.
  She has to buy a new book.

41 had to '~해야 했다'
 cf. 과거의 의무를 나타낼 때는 must를 쓸 수 없고 반드시 had to로만 쓴다.

42 should '~해야 한다' 나는 네가 치과에 가봐야 한다고 생각해.

43 「had better+동사원형」 '~하는 게 낫다' 너는 오늘 밤 일찍 잠자리에 드는 게 낫다.

44 What would you like to eat for lunch? 너는 점심으로 무엇을 먹고 싶니?

45 ② 허가의 may '~해도 좋다'
 ①③④⑤ 추측의 may '~일지도 모른다'

46 ③ 너는 식사를 걸러야 한다.
  (should → should not[shouldn't])
 ① 너는 매일 운동해야 한다.
 ② 너는 정크 푸드를 먹지 말아야 한다.
 ④ 너는 늦게 잠자리에 들지 말아야 한다.
 ⑤ 너는 채소를 많이 먹어야 한다.

47 ① You had better see a doctor.
 ② She can be a nice teacher.
 ③ I'd like to drink some ice tea.
 ⑤ You must not talk on the phone here.

48 보기 중 May I ~?에 대한 거절의 표현으로 may not[must not/cannot]을 쓸 수 있으며 금지의 표현으로 must not, may not, cannot을 쓸 수 있다.

49 must not '~해서는 안 된다'
 don't have to '~할 필요가 없다'

CHAPTER 4 수동태
Passive Voice

본문 _ p.96

PRACTICE 1

1	① him	② He
2	① They	② them
3	① Sumi	② Sumi
4	① It	② it
5	① We	② us
6	① my family	② My family
7	① I	② me
8	① You	② you
9	① The bird	② the bird
10	① her	② She
11	① Your brother	② your brother
12	① Their parents	② their parents

9 wore, worn
10 blew, blown
11 read, read
12 built, built
13 flew, flown
14 killed, killed
15 lost, lost
16 woke, woken
17 took, taken
18 cleaned, cleaned
19 bore, borne/born
20 said, said
21 answered, answered
22 found, found
23 caught, caught
24 knew, known
25 invited, invited
26 stole, stolen
27 thought, thought
28 wrote, written
29 rode, ridden
30 opened, opened
31 spent, spent
32 was/were, been
33 bought, bought
34 stopped, stopped
35 used, used
36 spoke, spoken
37 bit, bitten
38 put, put
39 got, got(ten)
40 did, done
41 collected, collected
42 laid, laid
43 understood, understood
44 drank, drunk

PRACTICE 2

1	threw, thrown	2	cooked, cooked
3	made, made	4	brought, brought
5	began, begun	6	called, called
7	invented, invented	8	held, held

CHAPTER 4

45	broke, broken	46	kept, kept
47	sold, sold	48	forgot, forgotten
49	carried, carried	50	ate, eaten
51	sent, sent	52	saw, seen
53	sang, sung	54	set, set
55	tried, tried	56	drew, drawn
57	gave, given	58	told, told
59	dropped, dropped	60	taught, taught

PRACTICE 3

1 A letter is written by David.
2 An e-mail is sent by me.
3 Eggs are laid by chickens.
4 Foreign coins are collected by me.
5 The steaks are cooked by my mother.
6 They are taught by their father.
7 The book is read by my brother.
8 This expression is used by most people.
9 They are called by the principal.
10 These bags are made by her.
11 Those pictures are painted by her.
12 The questions are answered by the teacher.
13 The trash in the river is picked up by Jacob.

PRACTICE 4

1	were opened	2	is played
3	were broken	4	is used
5	are washed	6	was bitten
7	is sung	8	was invented
9	are grown	10	was delivered

PRACTICE 5

1 A lot of letters are written (by us).
2 Groceries are bought here.
3 Shorts are worn in summer (by you).
4 My son was killed during the war (by them).
5 Smartphones are used every day (by us).
6 My bicycle was stolen (by someone).
7 The memories were forgotten.
8 This wine was made in 1970 (by someone).
9 Fresh fruit is sold in the store (by us).
10 These buildings were built (by them) 20 years ago.

PRACTICE 6

1 The story is found interesting by some readers.
2 He was elected president.
3 A lion is called the king of the jungle.
4 People are made happy by good paintings.
5 The rabbit was found dead by Mira.
6 I was called a princess by my parents.

> 5형식 문장을 수동태로 전환할 때는 능동태의 목적어와 목적격 보어가 각각 주어, 주격 보어가 된다. 능동태의 동사를 'be동사+과거분사' 형태로 바꾸고, be동사는 바뀐 주어의 인칭과 수, 원래 능동태 문장의 동사의 시제에 일치시킨다. 능동태의 주어는 'by+목적격' 형태로 행위자를 나타낸다.
>
>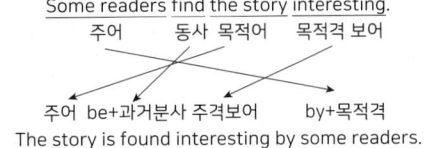
>
> 1, 3 수동태의 주어가 3인칭 단수이고, 원래 문장의 시제가 현재이므로 be동사의 형태는 is가 적절하다. 3번의 people은 일반 사람을 나타내기 때문에 'by+목적격'을 생략한다.
> 2, 5, 6 원래 문장의 시제가 과거이고, 수동태 문장의 주어가 단수이므로 수동태 문장의 동사는 'was+과거분사' 형태가 적절하다. 2번의 we는 일반 사람을 가리키므로 'by+목적격'을 생략한다.
> 4 수동태의 주어 people이 복수이고, 원래 문장의 시제가 현재이므로 be동사의 형태는 are가 적절하다.

PRACTICE 7

1 She is respected by her children.
2 His sister was made angry by him.
3 We were helped by the teacher.
4 Their village is kept clean.
5 Those dresses were designed by Andre Kim.
6 This work was finished by Ms. Smith.
7 Many languages are spoken in Switzerland.
8 TV programs are watched by a lot of teenagers.
9 Mozart and Beethoven are called great musicians.
10 The magazine was published in 1997 by the company.

> 3형식 문장을 수동태로 전환할 때는 능동태의 목적어가 주어가 된다. 능동태의 동사를 'be동사+과거분사' 형태로 바꾸고, be동사는 바뀐 주어의 인칭과 수, 원래 능동태 문장의 동사의 시제에 일치시킨다. 능동태의 주어는 'by+목적격' 형태로 행위자를 나타낸다. 5형식 문장의 수동태에서는 추가적으로 능동태의 목적격 보어가 주격 보어가 되며, 나머지는 3형식과 동일하다.

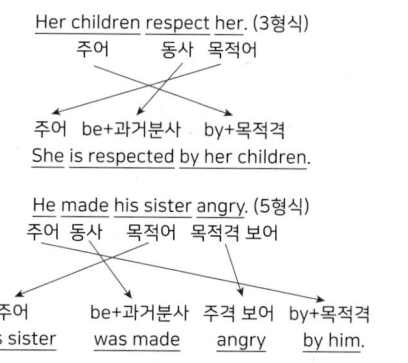

1, 4 수동태의 주어가 3인칭 단수이고, 원래 문장의 시제가 현재이므로 be동사의 형태는 is가 적절하다. 4번의 they처럼 행위자가 분명하지 않거나 나타낼 필요가 없을 때에는 「by+목적격」을 생략한다.
2, 6, 10 수동태의 주어가 3인칭 단수이고, 원래 문장의 시제가 과거이므로 be동사의 형태는 was가 적절하다.
3, 5 수동태의 주어가 복수이고, 원래 문장의 시제가 과거이므로 be동사의 형태는 were가 적절하다.
7, 8, 9 수동태의 주어가 복수이고, 원래 문장의 시제가 현재이므로 be동사의 형태는 are가 적절하다. 7번과 9번의 we는 일반 사람을 가리키므로 「by+목적격」을 생략한다.

Chapter Review Test 정답 본문 _ p.104

1 ③   2 We, invited   3 by people   4 ②
5 ⑤   6 ①   7 ③   8 was written   9 am made happy   10 ③   11 was washed by her
12 ④   13 (1) English is taught by Mr. Kim.
(2) Her handbag was stolen by the thief.
14 ④   15 ⑤   16 The house was built by my grandfather.   17 is visited   18 ③
19 ② is → was   20 ③   21 ③   22 (1) was bought by Jake (2) broke the desk

Chapter Review Test 해설

1 주어(Honey)가 동작의 대상이 되므로 「be동사+과거분사」의 형태인 수동태가 되어야 한다. 주어(Honey)가 3인칭 단수이므로 is가 온다.
cf. make - made - made

2 주어진 문장의 목적어 us가 주어 We가 되고, 수동태는 「be동사+과거분사」의 형태이므로 invite의 과거분사형인 invited를 쓴다.

3 행위자가 일반 사람을 나타낼 경우 「by+목적격」을 생략할 수 있다.

4 주어(The World Cup)가 동작의 대상이 되므로 「be동사+과거분사」의 형태인 수동태가 되어야 한다.
cf. hold - held - held

5 능동태의 동사(broke)를 「be동사+과거분사」의 형태로 바꾼다. 동사가 과거형이므로 be동사의 과거형(was)이 와야 한다.
cf. break - broke - broken

6 주어(gimchi)가 동작의 대상이 되므로 「be동사+과거분사」의 형태인 수동태가 되어야 한다.

7 (A) 수동태의 부정문은 be동사에 not을 붙여서 「주어+be동사+not+과거분사 ~.」로 나타낸다.
(B) 수동태 문장의 의문문은 주어와 be동사의 위치를 바꾸어 「be동사+주어+과거분사 ~?」로 나타낸다.

8 주어(Romeo and Juliet)가 동작의 대상이 되므로 「be동사+과거분사」의 형태인 수동태가 되어야 한다. Romeo and Juliet은 작품명이므로 단수이고, 이미 끝난 과거의 일이므로 be동사는 was를 쓴다.
cf. write - wrote - written

9 5형식 문장의 수동태 전환은 능동태의 동사(makes)를 「be동사+과거분사」의 형태로 바꾸고, 그 뒤에 보어(happy)를 쓴다.

10 수동태의 동사는 「be동사+과거분사」의 형태로 나타낸다.
③ My bicycle was fixed by Tom.

11 능동태를 수동태로 바꾸기 위해서는 능동태 문장의 목적어가 수동태의 주어 자리로 가고 능동태의 동사는 시제를 맞추어 「be동사+과거분사」의 형태로 바꾸어 쓴다. 능동태의 주어는 「by+목적격」의 형태로 바꾸어 수동태 문장 마지막에 쓴다.

12 능동태의 동사(invented)가 「be동사+과거분사」의 형태가 되어야 하며, be동사는 바뀐 주어(The airplane)의 수와 일치시켜 was가 와야 한다. 능동태의 주어는 「by+목적격」의 형태로 바꾸어 수동태 문장 마지막에 쓴다.

13 (1) English를 주어로 하는 수동태 문장으로 써야 한다. 주어가 3인칭 단수이고 현재시제이므로 be동사는 is를 쓴다.
(2) Her handbag을 주어로 하는 수동태 문장으로 써야 한다. 주어가 3인칭 단수이고 과거시제이므로 be동사는 was를 쓴다.

14 5형식 문장에서 능동태의 목적어(her)는 수동태의 주어(She)로, 동사는 「be동사+과거분사」의 형태로 쓰고, 그 뒤에 보어(Big Mouth)를 쓴다. 능동태의 동사

(call)가 현재형이므로 be동사는 is가 와야 한다
cf. 능동태의 주어(People)가 일반 사람을 나타내므로 「by+목적격」은 생략한다.

15 ⑤ 주어진 우리말에서 주어인 거울이 '다루어져야 한다'고 했으므로 수동태 문장으로 영작해야 한다.
(handle → be handled)

16 수동태의 어순 「주어+be동사+과거분사+by+목적격」

17 능동태의 동사(visit)를 「be동사+과거분사」의 형태로 바꾼다. 수동태의 주어(The museum)가 단수이므로 be동사는 is를 쓴다.

18 It은 picture를 가리키며, 이는 동작의 대상이 되므로 「be동사+과거분사」의 형태인 수동태가 되어야 한다. 지금 보는 사진의 촬영 시점은 과거일 수 밖에 없으므로 be동사는 과거형(was)이어야 한다.

19 과거를 나타내는 부사구(a week ago)가 있으므로 be동사의 과거형(was)이 와야 한다.

20 수동태의 동사는 「be동사+과거분사」의 형태로 나타낸다.
③ He was bitten by my dog.

21 • Some cookies were maden by her.
   → Some cookies were made by her.
   • The cartoons were drawing by us.
   → The cartoons were drawn by us.

22 (1) 문장의 목적어(the wallet)가 주어가 되었으므로 「be동사+과거분사+by 행위자」 형태의 수동태 문장을 써야 한다.
(2) 수동태 문장의 행위자(my brother)가 주어이므로 능동태 문장을 써야 한다.

CHAPTER 5 명사와 관사
Nouns and Articles

본문 _ p.108

PRACTICE 1

1	③	2	②	3	⑤	4	④
5	②	6	①	7	⑤	8	②
9	③	10	④				

1 coffee는 물질명사고 나머지는 보통명사다.
2 Becky는 고유명사고 나머지는 보통명사다.
3 dictionary는 보통명사고 나머지는 집합명사다.
4 club은 집합명사고 나머지는 고유명사다.
5 dish는 보통명사고 나머지는 추상명사다.
6 class는 집합명사고 나머지는 물질명사다.
7 family는 집합명사고 나머지는 추상명사다.
8 Mt. Halla는 고유명사고 나머지는 물질명사다.
9 smoke는 물질명사고 나머지는 보통명사다.
10 snow는 물질명사고 나머지는 추상명사다. 두 종류 다 셀 수 없는 명사지만, 물질명사는 실존하는 반면 추상명사는 형태 없이 개념이나 감정을 나타내는 명사다.

PRACTICE 2

1	Water	2	a child	3	family
4	sugar	5	Korea	6	Friendship
7	class	8	freedom	9	Mike
10	a flower	11	butter	12	Love

1, 4, 11 water, sugar, butter는 물질명사로, 부정관사 a와 함께 사용할 수 없다.
2, 10 child, flower는 셀 수 있는 명사로, 부정관사 a와 함께 쓰는 것이 적절하다.
3, 7 family, class와 같은 명사는 해당 집합을 개개인의 모임으로 볼 때는 복수 취급하지만, 단일한 한 개의 집단으로 볼 때는 단수 취급한다. is에 수를 일치시키려면 family, class가 적절하다.
5, 9 Korea, Mike는 고유명사로, 부정관사 a와 함께 사용할 수 없다.
6, 8, 12 friendship, freedom, love는 추상명사로, 부정관사 a와 함께 사용할 수 없다.

PRACTICE 3

1	eggs	2	buses	3	addresses
4	stars	5	days	6	presents
7	photos	8	umbrellas	9	sports
10	cups	11	beaches	12	friends
13	cats	14	problems	15	tomatoes
16	shirts	17	boxes	18	maps
19	zoos	20	baths	21	cookies
22	boats	23	flowers	24	watches
25	radios	26	mosquito(e)s		

27	passports	28	tests	29	brushes	10	sheep	11	oxen	12 deer
30	potatoes					13	teeth	14	slices	

PRACTICE 4

1 candies	2 songs	3 days
4 ideas	5 knives	6 bodies
7 cows	8 classes	9 shelves
10 factories	11 wives	12 ladies
13 buildings	14 animals	15 mistakes
16 doors	17 families	18 safes
19 pencils	20 stories	21 dishes
22 pictures	23 audios	24 dolls
25 toys	26 keys	27 wolves
28 foxes	29 boys	30 sandwiches
31 ships	32 videos	33 monkeys
34 leaves	35 letters	36 bananas
37 pianos	38 computers	39 babies
40 notes	41 towns	42 parties
43 blouses	44 questions	45 pigs
46 doughnuts	47 cards	48 holidays
49 cities	50 farmers	51 headaches
52 bottles	53 houses	54 countries
55 posters	56 roofs	57 blocks
58 diaries	59 churches	60 selves

PRACTICE 5

1 ducks	2 hobbies	3 oxen
4 festivals	5 scarves/scarfs	6 deer
7 rooms	8 students	9 sheep
10 men	11 candles	12 months
13 mice	14 feet	15 teams
16 subjects	17 snowmen	18 neighbors
19 geese	20 hours	21 fish
22 women	23 sweaters	24 bags
25 children	26 seats	27 benches
28 habits	29 teeth	30 thieves

PRACTICE 6

1 knives	2 Mice	3 church
4 children	5 room	6 feet
7 leaves	8 fish	9 women

PRACTICE 7

1 glasses of milk	2 pieces of furniture
3 bottles of juice	4 pieces of chalk
5 glasses of water	6 slices of bread
7 pairs of scissors	8 pounds of sugar
9 cups of tea	10 pieces of news
11 slices of pizza	12 pairs of socks
13 pieces of paper	14 bottles of ink
15 pounds of flour	

PRACTICE 8

1 pair	2 pair
3 piece[slice]	4 pieces[slices]
5 glass[bottle/cup]	6 cups
7 pair	8 slices[pounds]
9 glasses[bottles]	10 piece

> 1, 2, 7 scissors, jeans, glasses와 같이 두 개의 짝으로 이루어져 복수형으로 쓰는 명사의 수량을 나타낼 때에는 단위명사 pair를 사용한다.

PRACTICE 9

2 boys' middle school
3 Ted's birthday
4 dog's name
5 women's university
6 women's apparel
7 Mr. Kim's son
8 parents' photo album
9 people's ideas
10 children's bookstore
11 dogs' houses
12 Ana and Hailey's restaurant
13 Andy's job
14 Richard's voice

> 2, 8, 11 -s로 끝나는 복수명사는 어퍼스트로피(')만을 붙여 소유격을 표현한다.
> 3, 4, 7, 13, 14 -s로 끝나지 않는 단수명사는 's를 붙여 소유격을 표현한다.
> 5, 6, 9, 10, 12 -s로 끝나지 않는 복수명사는 's를 붙여 소유격을 표현한다.

CHAPTER 5

PRACTICE 10

2 the end of this city
3 the door of the room
4 sense of smell
5 The people of the village
6 the color of your shoes
7 the list of the classes
8 the middle of the table
9 The future of the company
10 the name of the mountain

> 2~10 무생물을 나타내는 명사는 of를 이용하여 소유격을 만든다.

PRACTICE 11

1 umbrella, Mira's
2 voice, my daughter's
3 puppy, her brother's
4 house, Mr. Felini's
5 books, Peter's
6 arm, a robot's
7 painting, Mr. Smith's
8 room, Yumi's
9 jacket, my friend's
10 toys, the children's

PRACTICE 12

1 four-leaf
2 five-week
3 one hundred-page
4 three-year-old
5 ten-story
6 eight-year-old
7 two-month
8 two-meter-long
9 five-dollar
10 ten-minute

> 1 복수형인 leaves를 단수형 leaf로 바꿔 four와 하이픈으로 연결한다.
> 5 복수형인 stories를 단수형 story로 바꿔 ten과 하이픈으로 연결한다. 여기에서 story는 '(건물의) 층'을 의미한다.

PRACTICE 13

1 an	2 a	3 an	4 a
5 a	6 an	7 an	8 a
9 an	10 a	11 an	12 a
13 an	14 an	15 a	16 an
17 a	18 a	19 a	20 an

> 1, 3, 6, 7, 11, 13, 16, 20 첫소리가 모음으로 시작하기 때문에 부정관사 an을 사용한다.
> 2, 4, 5, 10 철자는 모음으로 시작하지만, 첫소리가 자음 '[ju]'로 시작하기 때문에 부정관사 a를 사용한다.
> 8, 12, 15, 17, 19 첫소리가 자음으로 시작하기 때문에 부정관사 a를 사용한다.
> 9, 14 첫 글자인 'h'가 묵음 처리되어 첫소리가 모음이기 때문에 부정관사 an을 사용한다.
> 18 철자는 모음으로 시작하지만, 첫소리가 자음 '[ji]'로 시작하기 때문에 부정관사 a를 사용한다.

PRACTICE 14

1 ①   2 ③   3 ②   4 ①
5 ②   6 ③   7 ③   8 ①
9 ②

> [보기]
> ① 그는 아들 하나와 딸 둘이 있다. (하나의)
> ② 나는 한 달에 한 번 그를 만났다. (~에, ~마다)
> ③ 물고기는 물 없이는 살 수 없다. (종족 전체를 대표)
>
> 1 그들은 한 시간 동안 달리고 있었다. (①하나의)
> 2 학은 긴 다리를 가졌다. (③종족 전체를 대표)
> 3 그녀는 일주일에 수업이 세 개밖에 없다. (②~마다)
> 4 우리는 하나의 팀을 위해 열한 명의 선수가 필요하다. (①하나의)
> 5 나는 주로 하루에 여덟 시간 공부한다. (②~마다)
> 6 뱀은 겨울 동안 잠을 잔다. (③종족 전체를 대표)
> 7 코끼리는 긴 코를 가지고 있다. (③종족 전체를 대표)
> 8 로마는 하루아침에 이루어지지 않았다. (①하나의)
> 9 민수는 일 년에 두 번 그의 조부모님을 방문한다. (②~마다)

PRACTICE 15

1 ④   2 ⑤   3 ⑦   4 ③
5 ⑥   6 ①   7 ②

> [보기]의 밑줄 친 the의 용법은 다음과 같다.
> ① 앞에 나온 명사가 다시 반복될 때
> ② 문맥이나 상황으로 보아 무엇을 가리키는지 알 수 있을 때
> ③ 구나 절에 의해 수식을 받아 가리키는 대상이 분명할 때 (the rooms in the house)
> ④ 일반적으로 유일한 것을 말할 때 (the sky)
> ⑤ 최상급 앞
> ⑥ 악기 이름 앞
> ⑦ 종족 전체를 대표
> 4 'of France(프랑스의)'라는 구에 의해 수식을 받아 어떤 수도(capital)인지 의미가 분명해진다.
> 7 행인에게 길을 물어보는 상황을 고려했을 때 근처에 있는 우체국의 위치를 물어보는 점이 분명하다.

PRACTICE 16

1 the   2 the   3 the
4 a   5 The   6 A

CHAPTER 5

7	an	8	the	9	a
10	The	11	the	12	the
13	The				

> 1 악기 앞에는 정관사 the를 사용한다.
> 2, 8, 12 서수, same, last 앞에는 정관사 the를 사용한다.
> 3 '저 신호등을 봐'라는 뜻으로, 청자와 화자가 한 자리에 있어서 상황상 가리키는 대상이 분명하기 때문에 정관사 the를 사용하는 것이 적절하다.
> 4 '그들은 하루에 9시간을 학교에서 보낸다'는 뜻으로, '~마다'의 의미를 가진 부정관사 a를 사용하는 것이 적절하다.
> 5 태양은 세상에서 유일한 것이기 때문에 정관사 the를 사용한다.
> 6, 7, 9 '하나의'를 의미하는 부정관사 a/an을 사용하는 것이 적절하다.
> 10, 11 각각 'of the station'과 'in the door'의 수식을 받고 있기 때문에 정관사 the를 사용하는 것이 적절하다.
> 13 앞서 쓰인 명사 boy를 다시 언급하고 있으므로 정관사 the를 사용하는 것이 적절하다.

PRACTICE 17

1	an	2	X	3	the
4	X	5	X	6	the
7	the	8	a	9	X
10	X	11	the	12	X
13	a	14	X	15	the

> 1 'F'의 첫소리가 모음 [e]로 시작하므로 부정관사 an을 사용한다.
> 2, 5, 9, 12 식사, 운동, 질병의 이름 앞에 관사를 사용하지 않는다.
> 3 최상급 tallest 앞에 정관사 the를 사용한다.
> 4, 10 건물이 본래의 목적으로 쓰일 때 건물을 나타내는 명사 앞에 관사를 사용하지 않는다.
> 6 '내 딸을 (차에) 태우기 위해' 가는 것이므로 학교의 본래 목적으로 쓰이지 않았기 때문에 관사를 생략할 수 없다.
> 7 악기 이름 앞에 정관사 the를 사용한다.
> 8 '하나의'의 의미를 가진 부정관사 a를 쓰는 것이 적절하다.
> 11 same 앞에 정관사 the를 사용한다.
> 13 '한 달에 3번'이라는 빈도를 나타내기 위해 '~마다'를 의미하는 a를 사용한다.
> 14 기구가 본래의 목적(잠을 자는 것)대로 언급되고 있기 때문에 관사를 사용하지 않는다.
> 15 '문 좀 닫아줄래?'와 같은 명령문의 경우, 일반적으로 청자와 화자가 한 공간에 있어야 발화가 가능하다. 따라서 상황상 가리키는 대상이 분명하기 때문에 정관사 the를 사용할 수 있다.

PRACTICE 18

1	is	2	Are	3	is
4	Are	5	Is	6	are
7	are	8	Is	9	are
10	is				

> 3, 8, 10 money, sugar, water는 셀 수 없는 물질명사이므로 단수 취급한다.

PRACTICE 19

1	there is	2	Was there
3	are there	4	there weren't
5	How many, There are		
6	Are, there are	7	There are
8	Is, there is	9	How much, There is

> 5 대답이 Yes/No가 아닌 의문문은 의문사로 시작한다. 대답에 학생의 인원수가 언급되었고, student는 셀 수 있는 명사이므로 how many로 질문한다.
> 9 대답이 Yes/No가 아니고, 대답에서 구체적인 우유의 양이 언급되었으므로 의문사로 시작하는 의문문으로 질문했음을 알 수 있다. milk는 셀 수 없는 물질명사이기 때문에 how much로 질문한다.

PRACTICE 20

1	X	2	X	3	O	4	O
5	X	6	O	7	X	8	O
9	X	10	X	11	O	12	X
13	O	14	X				

> 2 콤마가 day를 수식하는 형용사 hot, humid, airless를 나열하기 위해 사용되었다.

Chapter Review Test 정답 본문 _ p.128

1 ② 2 ③ 3 ② 4 air, furniture, money, milk 5 ② 6 ⑤ 7 ② 8 ② 9 ⓐ deer ⓑ feet ⓒ Men 10 ① 11 (1) Jane's jacket (2) father's building (3) my friend's 12 ④ 13 ⓐ are ⓑ Is ⓒ is 14 ③,④,⑤ 15 ⓐ I am playing basketball with my friends. 16 ⑤ 17 ⑤ 18 ③ 19 ④ 20 ① 21 ③ 22 ④ 23 ② 24 ① 25 ⓐ an ⓑ an ⓒ a 26 ⑤ 27 ② 28 ⑤ 29 ⑤ 30 uncle's 31 ④ 32 the Earth 33 (1) How many books are there on the desk? (2) They are Jane's books [Jane's]. 34 ④ 35 (1) There is a cat on the bed. (2) There are two balls on the floor. 36 ③ 37 ① 38 ② 39 ④ 40 ③ 41 ② 42 ③ 43 (1) the school → school (2) ten-minutes → ten-minute (3) the lunch → lunch 44 ④ 45 ⑤ 46 Sungmin, the leader of our volunteer club, is kind to everyone. 47 ② 48 ⑤ 49 ② 50 ③ 51 ④ 52 ③

Chapter Review Test 해설

1 water는 셀 수 없는 명사이므로 a를 붙일 수 없다.
2 주어진 문장에 many가 있으므로 셀 수 있는 명사 복수형이 와야 한다. sheep은 단수형과 복수형이 같다.
3 umbrella의 첫소리는 모음으로 시작하므로 an을 붙인다.
   cf. umbrella가 단수형이므로 many나 lots of는 올 수 없다.
4 air, money, milk: 셀 수 없는 물질명사
   furniture: 집합명사의 의미를 가진 셀 수 없는 명사
5 ② 소유격 's, ①③④⑤ is의 축약형
6 '~가 있니?'의 뜻인 Is there ~?의 질문에 대해 Yes, there is. 또는 No, there isn't.로 대답한다.
7 milk는 셀 수 없는 명사이므로 five 뒤에 올 수 없다.
8 주어진 문장의 주어(five beds and two desks)가 복수형이므로 be동사의 수도 복수형(are)으로 맞춰야 한다.
   ② is → are
9 deer의 복수형은 'deer', foot의 복수형은 'feet', Man의 복수형은 'Men'이다.
10 ① hour는 철자가 자음으로 시작하지만, h가 묵음이기 때문에 발음은 모음으로 시작한다. 철자가 자음으로 시작하더라도 발음이 모음으로 시작하는 경우에는 부정관사 an을 쓴다.
   ② spoon은 자음으로 시작하므로, 앞에 부정관사 a를 쓴다.
   ③ 명사 앞에 명사를 수식하는 형용사가 있을 경우, 형용사에 맞춰 부정관사 a/an을 쓴다. interesting은 모음으로 시작하므로, 부정관사 an을 쓴다.
   ④ office worker는 모음으로 시작하므로, 부정관사 an을 쓴다.
   ⑤ uniform은 철자는 모음으로 시작하지만 u가 발음상 자음 '[ju:]'로 시작하기 때문에 부정관사 a를 씀에 유의한다.
11 's를 이용하여 명사의 소유격(~의)이나 소유대명사(~의 것)를 표현할 수 있다.
12 ① Gooses → Geese
   ② lifes → lives
   ③ child → children
   ⑤ hobbys → hobbies
13 첫 번째 문장의 주어는 many beautiful fish(복수)이므로 ⓐ에는 복수동사 are, 두 번째 문장의 주어(salt)와 세 번째 문장의 주어(juice)는 모두 물질명사로 단수 취급하므로 ⓑ, ⓒ에는 단수동사 is가 온다.
14 ③ is → are
   ④ women → woman
   ⑤ window → windows
15 운동을 나타내는 명사 앞에는 the를 붙이지 않는다.
16 명사나 대명사의 동격을 나타낼 때는 그 뒤에 콤마(,)를 덧붙여 다른 명사(구)를 쓴다.
17 셀 수 없는 명사(juice)는 단수 취급한다.
   ⑤ There is a lot of juice in the bottle.
18 ③ one '하나의' ①②④⑤ per '~마다'
19 ④ My hobby is playing the guitar. 악기 이름 앞에는 the를 쓴다.
20 ① is ②③④⑤ are
21 useful의 첫소리는 자음 [ju:]로 시작하므로 a를, office의 첫소리는 모음으로 시작하므로 an을 쓴다.
22 • There are+복수 명사(some shoes)
   • There are+복수 명사(jeans)
   • There is+단수 명사(a clock)
23 child의 복수형은 children이다.
   ② childrens → children
24 ② two mouses → two mice
   ③ four wolfs → four wolves
   ④ three benchs → three benches
   ⑤ five foxs → five foxes
25 ⓐ umbrella의 첫소리는 모음으로 시작하므로 an을 쓴다.
   ⓑ hour는 h로 시작하지만 h가 묵음으로 첫소리가 모음으로 시작하므로 an을 쓴다.
   ⓒ uniform은 u로 시작하는 단어이므로 관사 an이 올 것이라 생각하기 쉽지만 첫소리가 [ju:]로 자음이므로 a를 쓴다.
26 ① We had a nice dinner.
   ② I will see you at noon. (the 삭제)
   ③ My father is very fat. (a 삭제)
   ④ Do you play the piano?
27 물질명사의 수량을 나타낼 때는 물질명사는 그대로 두고 단위를 나타내는 명사에 -(e)s를 붙인다.
28 There are+복수 명사(many old buildings)
29 hair는 셀 수 없는 물질명사로 단수 취급한다.
   ⑤ red hairs → red hair
30 사람을 나타내는 명사(uncle)의 소유격은 's를 붙인다.
31 ① She likes to wear a uniform. uniform의 첫 소리는 자음[ju:]으로 시작한다.

② My son is a middle school student.
③ Your father is a taxi driver.
⑤ Are you a nurse?

32 일반적으로 유일한 것 앞에는 the를 붙인다.

33 (1) '~가 몇 개 있니?'의 표현으로 How many ~ are there?를 쓴다.
(2) 's를 이용하여 명사의 소유격(~의)이나 소유대명사(~의 것)를 표현할 수 있다.

34 보기와 ④ per '~마다'
① one '하나의'
② 종족 전체를 대표
③⑤ 막연한 하나

35 There is/are는 '~가 있다'의 뜻이며, 고양이는 한 마리이므로 There is를, 공은 두 개이므로 There are를 써서 문장을 완성한다.

36 물질명사의 수량을 나타낼 때에는 물질명사는 그대로 두고 단위를 나타내는 명사를 복수형으로 나타낸다.
① pairs → pair
② glass → glasses
④ two bottle of juices → two bottles of juice
⑤ papers → paper

37 per의 의미로 day 앞에 a를 쓰고, 서수(third) 앞에는 the를 쓴다.

38 ① Is John a student?
③ Today is the second day of the festival.
④ My wife is from Busan. (a 삭제)
⑤ She looks very honest. (a 삭제)

39 무생물의 소유격은 of로 나타낸다.
④ The color of the door is yellow.

40 ③ 운동 이름 앞에는 관사를 쓰지 않는다.

41 문장의 주어(many famous buildings)가 복수이므로 be동사 복수형(were)을 쓴다.
② was → were

42 두 개의 짝으로 이루어진 명사는 복수형으로 나타낸다.
① I'm wearing glasses.
② What kind of pants do you want?
④ Miki likes these jeans.
⑤ Did you find your scissors?

43 (1) 건물이 본래의 목적으로 쓰일 때는 건물 앞에 관사를 쓰지 않는다.
(2) 숫자와 명사가 하이픈(-)으로 연결되어 형용사처럼 쓰일 때는 「숫자+단수 명사」의 형태로 쓴다.
(3) 식사 앞에 관사를 쓰지 않는다.

44 a pair of는 jeans, shoes, scissors, glasses와 같이 두 개의 짝으로 이루어져 항상 복수형으로 쓰는 명사와 함께 쓸 수 있다.

45 How much is it?의 it은 단수이므로 복수형인 tomatoes는 올 수 없다.

46 명사나 대명사의 동격을 나타낼 때는 그 뒤에 콤마(,)를 덧붙여 다른 명사(구)를 쓴다.

47 '~가 몇 개 있니?'의 표현으로 How many ~ are there?를 쓴다. 대답으로 단수 명사(one orange)가 나왔으므로 There is가 와야 한다.

48 ⑤ is의 축약형 's, ①②③④ 명사의 소유격 's

49 ② there '거기에', ①③④⑤ there is/are '~가 있다'

50 숫자와 명사가 하이픈(-)으로 연결되어 형용사처럼 쓰일 때는 「숫자+단수 명사」의 형태가 와야 한다.

51 advice는 셀 수 없는 명사로 단수형으로 쓴다.
④ advices → advice

52 ③의 콤마(,)는 열거를 나타내고 ①②④⑤의 콤마(,)는 동격을 나타낸다.

CHAPTER 6 대명사
Pronouns

본문 _ p.136

PRACTICE 1

1	his	**2**	It	**3**	mine
4	theirs	**5**	She	**6**	hers
7	We	**8**	He	**9**	Its
10	us	**11**	Our	**12**	It
13	her	**14**	them[yours]	**15**	Their
16	yours				

> [보기]
> I don't want grapes. → I don't want them.
> grapes는 복수명사이고 문장 내에서 목적어에 해당하기 때문에 목적인 them으로 바꾸는 것이 적절하다.
> 1, 3, 4, 6, 16 빈칸에 밑줄 친 명사구를 그대로 쓸 경우, 문장 내에 같은 명사가 반복되기 때문에 소유대명사를 사용하는 것이 적절하다.

PRACTICE 2

1	your	**2**	them	**3**	his
4	me	**5**	his	**6**	yours
7	my	**8**	Her	**9**	him
10	ours	**11**	It	**12**	theirs
13	us	**14**	you	**15**	our
16	her	**17**	its	**18**	mine
19	hers	**20**	their		

> 1, 5, 7, 8, 15, 17, 20 명사 앞에서 명사를 꾸며주려면 소유격 인칭대명사가 와야 한다.
> 2, 9 전치사 뒤에는 목적격 인칭대명사가 오는 것이 적절하다.
> 3, 10, 12, 18, 19 주어로 쓰인 어떤 사물에 대한 설명을 보충해주는 내용이 필요하므로 의미상 '~의 것'을 의미하는 소유대명사가 알맞다.
> 4, 13, 14, 16 타동사의 목적어 자리에는 목적격 인칭대명사가 오는 것이 적절하다.
> 6 전치사 뒤에 목적격 인칭대명사가 올 수 있지만, 이 문장에서는 비교 대상이 culture이므로 your culture를 의미하는 yours를 쓰는 것이 적절하다.
> 11 주어 자리에는 주격 인칭대명사를 써준다.

PRACTICE 3

1	myself	**2**	themselves	**3**	itself
4	myself	**5**	himself	**6**	yourself
7	himself	**8**	itself	**9**	herself
10	themselves	**11**	myself	**12**	ourselves
13	yourself	**14**	himself	**15**	themselves

> 1, 9, 11, 15 행위 주체와 같은 개체이며 전치사의 목적어 자리에 쓰였으므로 생략이 불가능한 재귀 용법이다.
> 2, 5, 6, 8 생략해도 완벽한 문장이 되며, 문장 구조가 변하지 않으므로 생략 가능한 강조 용법이다.
> 3, 4, 14 행위 주체와 같은 개체이며 동사의 목적어 자리에 쓰였으므로 생략이 불가능한 재귀 용법이다.
> 7 think to oneself: 조용히 생각하다, 마음속으로 생각하다
> 전치사의 목적어 자리에 쓰였으므로 생략이 불가능한 재귀 용법이다.
> 10, 12 enjoy oneself: 즐거운 시간을 보내다
> 동사의 목적어 자리에 쓰였으므로 생략이 불가능한 재귀 용법이다.
> 13 help oneself to: ~을 마음껏 먹다, 자유로이 먹다
> 동사의 목적어 자리에 쓰였으므로 생략이 불가능한 재귀 용법이다.

PRACTICE 4

1	O	**2**	X	**3**	X	**4**	O
5	O	**6**	O	**7**	X	**8**	X
9	O	**10**	X				

> 1, 5, 9 생략해도 완전한 문장이므로 강조 용법의 재귀대명사. 문장의 맨 끝에 위치해 주어를 강조하고 있다.
> 2, 3, 10 전치사의 목적어로 쓰인 재귀 용법의 재귀대명사. 생략 시 불완전한 문장이 되기 때문에 생략할 수 없다.
> 4, 6 생략해도 완전한 문장이므로 강조 용법의 재귀대명사. 주어의 바로 뒤에서 주어를 강조하고 있다.
> 7 타동사의 목적어로 쓰인 재귀대명사. 생략 시 불완전한 문장이 되기 때문에 생략할 수 없다.
> 8 '역사는 스스로를 반복한다.'는 뜻으로, 역사 속에서 비슷한 일이 계속해서 일어난다는 의미이다. itself가 타동사 repeat의 목적어로 쓰였으므로 재귀 용법이고, 생략할 수 없다.

PRACTICE 5

1	B	**2**	A	**3**	A	**4**	B
5	A	**6**	A	**7**	A	**8**	A
9	B	**10**	A	**11**	A	**12**	B
13	A	**14**	B	**15**	B	**16**	A

> [보기]
> A. It is Saturday. → 요일을 나타내는 비인칭 주어 it ('그것'이라고 해석하지 않는다.)
> B. I'll bring it tomorrow. → 가리키는 것이 분명한 대명사 it ('그것'이라고 해석한다.)
> 1, 4, 9, 12, 14, 15 가리키는 것이 문장 내에 명시되어 있거나 그 대상을 화자-청자가 모두 알고 있어서 분명한 경우이므로 대명사 it이다.
> 2, 5, 13 비인칭 주어 it이 시간을 나타낸다
> 3, 7 비인칭 주어 it이 계절(summer, spring)을 나타낸다.
> 6 비인칭 주어 it이 요일을 나타낸다.
> 8 비인칭 주어 it이 날씨를 나타낸다.
> 10 비인칭 주어 it이 날짜를 나타낸다.
> 11 비인칭 주어 it이 명암을 나타낸다.
> 16 비인칭 주어 it이 거리를 나타낸다.

PRACTICE 6

1	This	2	that	3	those
4	This	5	these	6	That
7	those	8	These		

PRACTICE 7

1	ones	2	it	3	one
4	It	5	one	6	ones

> 1 그녀가 구매한 엽서들과 같은 종류지만 다른 개체이기 때문에 부정대명사를 사용한다. 복수형 명사 postcards가 언급되었기 때문에 ones를 사용한다.
> 2, 4 앞서 언급한 명사(paper, London)를 지칭하고 있기 때문에 대명사 it을 사용한다.
> 3 의문문에서 umbrella 앞에 부정관사 an을 썼으므로 특정하지 않은 아무 우산(단수)을 나타낼 수 있는 부정대명사 one을 사용하는 것이 적절하다.
> 5 내 가방은 이미 잃어버렸으므로 동일 개체를 가리킬 수 없다. 같은 종류(가방)의 다른 대상을 나타내는 부정대명사 one을 사용하는 것이 적절하다.
> 6 앞의 문장에서 노란색 장미를 언급하였는데, 화자는 그것과 같은 종류(장미)지만 다른(빨간색) 것을 구매할 것이므로 부정대명사를 사용하는 것이 적절하다. roses가 복수형이므로 ones를 사용한다.

PRACTICE 8

1	others	2	another	3	Some
4	the other	5	other	6	another
7	the other	8	the others	9	One
10	another				

> 1 괄호 뒤에 복수형 동사(are)가 오므로 others가 적절하다. 한편 other는 단독으로 대명사 역할을 할 수 없다.
> 2, 6 another+단수명사
> 3 여자가 많은 과일들을 갖고 있는데 그들 중 몇몇(some of them)은 오렌지이고, 나머지 것들(the others)은 사과라고 하고 있으므로 some이 적절하다.
> 4, 7, 9 문장의 앞에서 전체 수량이 2개임이 언급되었다. 처음 한 개는 둘 중 어느 것을 가리켜도 one으로 부를 수 있다. 첫 번째 것을 고르고 난 뒤에는 한 개만 남아 대상이 특정되므로 '나머지 하나'를 가리키는 the other를 사용한다.
> 5 앞서 나온 some과 짝을 이루고, courses를 꾸밀 수 있는 형용사여야 하므로 other가 적절하다.
> 8 드레스들 중 몇몇은 깨끗하고, 나머지 전부는 더럽다고 하는 것이므로 the others가 적절하다. 한편 other는 단독으로 대명사 역할을 할 수 없다.
> 10 부러진 펜 대신 다른 것을 갖고 있는지 묻는 것이므로 another가 적절하다.

PRACTICE 9

1	man	2	present	3	has
4	is	5	year		

PRACTICE 10

1	Whom	2	Who	3	Whose
4	Who	5	Whom	6	Whom
7	Whose	8	Who	9	Whose
10	Who				

> 1, 5, 6 평서문으로 바꾸면
> 1 They helped _____.
> 5 He visited _____.
> 6 She talks to _____.
> 의 형태가 되는데, 빈칸의 위치가 타동사나 전치사의 목적어 자리이므로 목적격인 whom이 적절하다. 의문문에서 whom 대신 who를 쓰는 것도 가능하다.
> 2, 4, 8, 10 사람의 이름이나 관계를 묻고 있으므로 who가 적절하다.
> 3, 9 평서문으로 바꾸면
> 3 This watch is _____.
> 9 Those clothes are _____.
> 의 형태가 되는데, 빈칸에 소유대명사(~의 것)를 넣어 보어로 사용하는 것이 적절하다. 목적격을 사용할 경우, 사물이 사람(whom)과 같다는 의미가 되어서 어색하다.
> 7 명사 book을 앞에서 꾸며줄 수 있어야 하므로, 소유격이 적절하다.

PRACTICE 11

1	What	2	Whom	3	Whose
4	Who	5	What	6	Whose
7	Which	8	Which		

> 1 선택의 범위가 제한되지 않은 상태에서 사람이 아닌 것(your favorite song)에 대해 질문하려고 하므로 what이 적절하다.
> 2 평서문으로 바꾸면 'He met _____ last night.'가 되는데, 목적어 자리가 비게 되므로 목적격 의문대명사 whom이 적절하다.
> 3, 6 who와 whose 중 명사 앞에서 명사를 꾸며줄 수 있는 것은 소유격인 whose이다.
> 4 사람의 이름이나 관계에 대한 질문이므로 who가 적절하다.
> 5 명사 size 앞에서 명사를 꾸며주면서, 선택의 범위가 제한되지 않은 질문을 하려면 what을 사용하는 것이 적절하다. 여기서 what은 의문형용사로 사용되어 size를 꾸며주고 있고, what size는 '어떤 사이즈'를 의미한다.
> 7 Canada와 Australia로 선택의 범위가 제한되어 있으므로 what이 아닌 which가 적절하다.
> 8 dog과 cat으로 선택의 범위가 제한되어 있으므로 what이 아닌 which가 적절하다. 여기서 which는 pet을 꾸며주는 의문형용사로 사용되었고, which pet은 '어느 반려동물'을 의미한다.

PRACTICE 12

1	ⓓ	2	ⓐ	3	ⓒ	4	ⓑ

5 ⓕ　**6** ⓗ　**7** ⓔ　**8** ⓖ

PRACTICE 13

1 I don't think so.
2 They don't look the same.
3 He has the same opinion as you.
4 I like bright colors such as yellow.
5 These shoes are the same size.

> 1 앞서 나온 긍정의 문장을 대신하기 위해서 think의 목적어 자리에 so가 와야 한다.
> 2 '같아 보이다'라는 뜻과 일치하게 만들려면 look 다음에 the same을 배열해야 한다.
> 3, 5 '같은 의견', '사이즈가 같다'라는 뜻과 일치하게 만들기 위해서 the same이 각각 opinion과 size를 꾸며줘야 한다.
> 4 '노란색과 같은' = such as yellow

Chapter Review Test 정답 본문 _ p.148

1 ⑤　**2** this　**3** ③　**4** (1) One (2) the other
5 ④　**6** ①　**7** Which　**8** ④　**9** ②　**10** ①
11 ③　**12** ③　**13** ⑤　**14** my watch　**15** It
16 himself　**17** ③　**18** ①　**19** ④　**20** herself
21 ③　**22** not the same as the ostrich
23 ④　**24** This is　**25** ②　**26** ③　**27** ①
28 ①　**29** ②　**30** Does everybody like your paintings?　**31** ④　**32** Which season do you like the most?　**33** ②　**34** ①　**35** ④　**36** ③,⑤　**37** ①　**38** ③　**39** ②

Chapter Review Test 해설

1 pop songs는 복수이고, 동사 like의 목적어이므로 목적격 형태인 them이 들어가야 한다.

2 지시대명사 this는 가까이에 있는 사람이나 사물을 가리킬 때, 그리고 전화상에서 전화를 건 사람과 받는 사람을 가리킬 때 쓰인다.

3 질문에 대한 대답이 '나의 아버지의 것이야.'이므로, '누구의'라는 의미로 명사 camera를 꾸며줄 수 있는 소유격 Whose가 적절하다. What과 Which도 명사를 꾸며줄 수 있지만, 각각 '무엇'과 '어느 것'이라는 의미이므로 여기에서는 적절하지 않다.

4 두 번째 문장에서 영화의 수량이 두 개임이(two different movies) 언급되었다. 두 개 중 처음 영화 한 개를 가리킬 때는 one, 한 개를 고르고 난 뒤 나머지 하나를 가리킬 때는 the other를 사용한다.

5 (A) 1인칭 단수를 나타내며 주어자리에 들어갈 인칭대명사는 I이고, (B) 나와 나의 가족들이 가장 좋아하는 나라이므로 We의 소유격인 Our를 쓴다. (C) 단수 명사인 Korea는 대명사 It으로 받는다.

6 사람의 이름이나 관계 등을 물을 때 who를 쓴다.

7 제한된 선택(a chocolate cake or a cheesecake)의 범위 내에서 '어느 것'인지를 물을 때 which를 쓴다.

8 ⓐ 빨간 것이 아닌 또 다른 하나를 보여달라는 의미이므로 '또 다른 하나'라는 의미의 another를 쓰는 것이 적절하다.
ⓑ 여러 개 중 일부를 나타낼 때는 some을 쓴다.
ⓒⓓ 개가 두 마리라고 언급되었다. 둘 중 처음 하나를 가리킬 때는 one, 나머지 하나를 가리킬 때는 the other를 사용한다.

9 •「what+명사」의 형태로 명사를 수식하는 의문형용사 What이 와야 한다. which도 명사를 수식하지만 선택의 범위가 제한되어 있지 않으므로 빈칸에 들어갈 수 없다. What time is it? 몇 시니?
• What's the weather like? 날씨가 어때?는 날씨가 어떤지 묻는 표현이다. How's the weather?과 바꾸어 쓸 수 있다.

10 the same ~ as … '…와 같은 ~'
Sora has the same bag as Jinhee.

11 • 빈칸은 주격 보어의 자리이다. '이 집은 ~의 것이다'라는 뜻이 적절하므로 보어의 자리에서 '~의 것'이라는 뜻을 나타내는 소유대명사 mine이나 theirs가 들어가는 것이 알맞다.
This house is mine[theirs].
• 전치사 to의 목적어 자리이다. 따라서 목적어로 쓰이는 목적격 대명사 you나 us가 들어가는 것이 알맞다.
This house belongs to you[us].
• 주어의 자리이고 동사가 own(복수형)이므로 주격 대명사 you가 들어가는 것이 알맞다.
You own this house.
cf. belong to '~의 소유물이다'

12 Seho and I(세호와 나)는 We(우리)로 쓸 수 있다.

13 • 감탄문의 어순「What(+a/an)+형용사+명사(+주어+동사)!」

- '무엇'의 의미로 의문대명사 What이 들어가야 한다.
  너는 주말마다 무엇을 하니?
14 소유대명사는 「소유격+명사」로 표현할 수 있다.
15 시간이나 날씨를 나타낼 때 비인칭 주어 it을 쓴다.
16 문장의 주어(He)와 목적어가 같을 때 재귀대명사(himself)를 쓴다.
17 ③ 앞에서 언급한 특정한 명사(the red one)를 가리킬 때는 it을 쓴다.
18 사물을 물을 때는 what을, 사람을 물을 때는 who를 쓴다.
19 ④ It's는 It is의 줄임말이므로 명사(tail)를 꾸며줄 수 있는 It의 소유격인 Its를 써야 한다.(It's → Its)
20 • She에 대한 재귀대명사로 herself를 쓴다. 의미상, 주어와 목적어가 같으므로 재귀 용법으로 쓰였다.
   • 주어(My mom)를 강조하기 위해 문장 맨 끝에 강조 용법의 재귀대명사(herself)를 쓸 수 있다.
   • 전치사의 목적어 자리이므로 재귀 용법으로 재귀대명사 herself를 쓴다.
   cf. say to oneself '혼잣말을 하다'
21 보기와 ⓐⓒⓔ 비인칭 주어 it ⓑⓓ 대명사 it
22 A is[are] not the same as B 'A는 B와 같지 않다'
23 its는 it의 소유격을 나타내므로 it is의 줄임말인 it's를 써야 한다.(its → it's)
24 전화상에서 전화를 건 사람과 받는 사람을 가리킬 때 this를 쓴다.
25 여러 대상 중 몇몇을 나타낼 때는 some을 사용한다. 복수 명사 people을 수식해야 하므로 복수 명사를 수식하는 other이 적절하다. Others와 The others는 대명사이므로 명사를 수식할 수 없다. Another은 단수 명사를 수식한다.
26 앞에서 언급한 명사(backpack)와 종류는 같지만, 다른 성질의 개체(yellow backpack)에 대해 말할 때 one을 쓴다.

27 사람의 직업을 물을 때 「What+do[does]+주어+do (for a living)?」 표현을 쓴다.
   cf. What do you do? 당신은 무엇을 합니까?(당신의 직업은 무엇입니까?)
28 재귀대명사는 재귀 용법으로 쓰였을 때는 생략이 불가능하며, 강조 용법으로 쓰였을 때 생략이 가능하다. ①은 introduce의 목적어로 쓰인 재귀 용법이므로 생략이 불가능하다.
29 Everyone은 '모든 사람'을 뜻하지만 단수 취급하므로 3인칭 단수 동사인 plays를 쓴다.
30 everybody는 단수 취급하므로 「Does+주어+동사원형~?」의 의문문으로 써야 한다.
31 ④ 대명사 it ①②③⑤ 비인칭 주어 it
32 which는 「which+명사」의 형태로 명사를 수식하는 의문형용사로 쓰이므로 'Which+명사+do+주어+동사원형~?'의 어순으로 쓴다.
33 지하철 노선이라는 제한된 선택의 범위 내에서 '어느 것'인지를 물을 때 which를 쓴다.
34 so는 '그렇게'라는 뜻으로 think의 목적어로 쓰여 앞에 나온 긍정의 문장을 대신한다.
35 we의 소유대명사는 ours이다.
   ④ This is our car. = This car is ours.
   cf. us는 we의 목적격 대명사이다.
36 ③ every는 단수 명사를 수식하므로 children이 아닌 child를 써야 한다.(children → child)
   ⑤ Everything은 단수 취급하므로, 동사는 3인칭 단수의 형태로 looks를 써야 한다.(look → looks)
37 One ~ the other … '하나는 ~, 다른 사람[것]은 …'
38 ③ Spanish and French는 복수이므로 3인칭 복수형 목적격 대명사 them으로 바꿔야 한다.
   (it → them)
39 • such as ~ '~와 같은 그런'
   • the same ~ '같은 ~'

CHAPTER 7 부정사
Infinitives

본문 _ p.154

PRACTICE 1

1 to visit a historic place
2 It is a farmer's work
3 to make good friends
4 It was my plan
5 to get enough sleep
6 It was very dangerous

> 1~6 to부정사가 주어인 경우에는 주어 자리에 it을 쓰고 to부정사구를 뒤로 보낼 수 있다. to부정사로 시작하는 문장보다 「It~to부정사」구문이 보다 자연스러운 문장이다. 이때 쓰인 it을 가주어라고 하고, to부정사구를 진주어라고 한다.

PRACTICE 2

1 (1) to go   (2) go
2 (1) to learn   (2) learn
3 (1) to visit   (2) visit

> 1 (1) want의 목적어로 명사 역할을 하는 to부정사 to go를 쓴다.
> (2) go가 동사로 쓰였으며 조동사 should가 있으므로 동사원형으로 쓴다.
> 2 (1) 주격 보어로 명사 역할을 하는 to부정사 to learn을 쓴다.
> (2) learn이 동사로 쓰인 문장이고, 주어가 We all이므로 동사의 형태는 원형으로 쓴다.
> 3 (1) 주격 보어로 명사 역할을 하는 to부정사 to visit을 쓴다.
> (2) visit이 동사로 쓰였으며, 주어가 I이므로 동사의 형태는 원형으로 쓴다.

PRACTICE 3

1 to start   2 to buy
3 to live   4 to meet
5 to watch   6 to come

> plan, need, want, hope, love, like는 to부정사를 목적어로 가질 수 있다.
> 1 start jogging: 조깅을 시작하다
> 2 buy a book: 책을 사다
> 3 live in+장소: ~에 살다
> 4 meet+사람: ~를 만나다
> 5 watch the stars: 별을 보다
> 6 come to dinner: 저녁 식사에 오다

PRACTICE 4

1 began to fall

2 expected to stay
3 how to use
4 decided to meet him
5 started to grow tomatoes
6 what to buy
7 tries to keep
8 how to get

> 3 how to use: 어떻게 쓰는지, 사용하는 법
> 6 「what+to부정사」는 '무엇을 ~할지'라는 뜻을 나타낸다.
> 7 try+to부정사: ~하려고 노력하다
> 8 「how+to부정사」는 '~하는 법'이라는 뜻으로 문장 내에서 목적어 역할을 하고 있다.

PRACTICE 5

1 chores to do
2 turn to introduce
3 place to visit
4 chance to talk
5 time to exercise
6 ship to sail
7 something to put on
8 time to say
9 air to breathe
10 anything to read

> 1~10 to부정사가 명사나 대명사를 뒤에서 꾸며주는 형용사의 역할을 할 때는 '~할, ~해야 할'로 해석된다. 형용사는 보통 수식하는 명사 앞에 쓰이지만, to부정사는 명사 뒤에서 수식한다.
> 1 chores to do 할 집안일
> 2 turn to introduce 소개할 차례
> 3 place to visit 방문할 곳
> 4 chance to talk 말할 기회
> 5 time to exercise 운동할 시간
> 6 ship to sail 항해할 배
> 7 something to put on 입을 만한 무엇(어떤 것)
> 8 time to say 말할 시간
> 9 air to breathe 숨 쉴 공기
> 10 anything to read 읽을 만한 어떤 것

PRACTICE 6

1. time to go back
2. something to eat
3. city to visit
4. shirt to wear
5. test to take
6. bill to pay

> 1~6 to부정사의 형용사적 용법은 명사를 뒤에서 수식하며 '~할, ~해야 할'로 해석된다.
> 1 time to go back 돌아갈 시간
> 2 something to eat 먹을 것
> 3 city to visit 방문할 도시
> 4 shirt to wear 입을 셔츠
> 5 test to take 치를 시험
> 6 bill to pay 지불해야 할 청구서

PRACTICE 7

1. to be a famous painter
2. to hear the bad news
3. to make cookies
4. to be 100 years old
5. to find a new cure
6. to watch with children
7. to understand without a dictionary
8. to play soccer

> 1 (결국) 유명한 화가가 되었다 (부사적 용법 중 결과)
> 2 나쁜 소식을 들어서 (부사적 용법 중 감정의 원인)
> 3 쿠키를 만들기 위해서 (부사적 용법 중 목적)
> 4 100세까지 (부사적 용법 중 결과)
> 5 새로운 치료제를 발견해서 (부사적 용법 중 감정의 원인)
> 6 아이들과 함께 보기에 (부사적 용법 중 형용사 수식)
> 7 사전 없이 이해하기에 (부사적 용법 중 형용사 수식)
> 8 축구를 하기 위해서 (부사적 용법 중 목적)

PRACTICE 8

1. 너는 무엇을 사기를 원하니?
2. 목표를 설정하는 것은 중요하다.
3. 일어날 시간이다.
4. 우리는 종이를 만들기 위해 나무를 베어 넘어뜨린다.
5. 우리는 살을 빼기 위해 무엇을 할 수 있을까?
6. 그의 소설은 읽기에 쉬웠다.
7. 보는 것이 믿는 것이다.
8. 그녀는 80세까지 살았다.

> 1, 2, 7 to부정사가 명사의 역할을 하므로 '~하는 것'으로 해석한다.
> 3 to부정사가 time을 뒤에서 수식하며 형용사의 역할을 하고 있으므로 '~할'로 해석한다.
> 4, 5 to부정사가 목적을 나타내는 부사의 역할을 하고 있으므로 '~하기 위해'로 해석한다.
> 6 to부정사가 형용사 easy를 뒤에서 수식하며 부사의 역할을 하고 있으므로 '~하기에'로 해석한다.
> 8 to부정사가 결과를 나타내는 부사의 역할을 하고 있으므로 '(결국) ~하다'로 해석한다.

PRACTICE 9

1. Let me hold
2. make people feel good
3. help us chat with others
4. make weeds die
5. let me stay
6. had my sister read books

> 1 Let me+동사원형: 내가 ~하게 해 줘, 내가 ~해 줄게
> 2, 4, 5, 6 「사역동사+목적어+목적격 보어」 순서로 배열할 수 있으며 목적격 보어로 원형부정사를 사용한다.
> 3 준사역동사 help는 「help+목적어+목적격 보어」 순서로 배열할 수 있으며 목적격 보어로 원형부정사나 to부정사를 사용한다.

PRACTICE 10

1	to solve	2	play	3	coming
4	cross	5	show	6	clean
7	selling	8	run	9	calling
10	know				

> 1 help는 목적격 보어로 원형부정사뿐 아니라 to부정사도 사용 가능하다.
> 2, 4 지각동사 saw, watched의 목적격 보어로 원형부정사를 사용한다.
> 3, 7, 9 현재 진행 중인 상황을 강조하기 위해 지각동사 felt, saw, heard의 목적격 보어로 현재분사를 사용하기도 한다.
> 5 Let me+동사원형: 내가 ~하게 해 줘, 내가 ~해 줄게
> 6, 8, 10 사역동사 made, had, let의 목적격 보어로 원형부정사를 사용한다.

PRACTICE 11

| 1 | go(ing) | 2 | bring | 3 | shout(ing) |
| 4 | wait | 5 | run(ning) | 6 | swim |

> 1 go out: 밖으로 나가다
> 4 wait for+시간: ~동안 기다리다
> 5 run after+(대)명사: ~를 뒤쫓다

PRACTICE 12

1 write	2 to swim	3 go
4 study	5 wait	6 fly
7 talk	8 to use	9 find
10 walking	11 looking	12 to get

> 1 Let me+동사원형: 내가 ~하게 해 줘, 내가 ~해 줄게
> 2, 8, 12 how와 to부정사가 결합되어 '~하는 방법'이라는 뜻이다. 문장에서 동사의 목적어로 쓰였다.
> 3, 4, 5, 9 (준)사역동사의 목적격 보어로 원형부정사를 사용한다.
> 6, 7 지각동사의 목적격 보어로 원형부정사를 사용한다.
> 10, 11 지각동사(saw, feel)의 목적격 보어로 현재분사를 사용하여 진행 중인 일을 강조할 수 있다.

Chapter Review Test 정답 본문 _ p.163

1 ③ 2 ② 3 ④ 4 ③ 5 to do 6 ⑤
7 ④ 8 inviting → to invite 9 (1) how to ride (2) how to get[go] 10 ④ 11 ① 12 ⑤
13 ①,④ 14 ② 15 ② 16 ② 17 ①
18 ⑤ 19 It is dangerous to walk alone at night. 20 ② 21 ⑤ 22 ⑤ 23 ⑤ 24 ③
25 ③ 26 ② 27 (1) to borrow a book (2) to send a letter

Chapter Review Test 해설

1 and에 의해 (to) hear과 연결된 병렬구조이고, hope는 to부정사를 목적어로 쓰는 동사이므로 「to+동사원형」 또는 to가 생략된 동사원형의 형태가 와야 한다.

2 ② 명사처럼 쓰이는 to부정사의 용법 중 주격 보어의 역할 (go → to go)
cf. 보어의 역할을 하는 동명사(going)로도 표현할 수 있다.

3 want는 to부정사를 목적어로 쓰는 동사이므로 to buy가 뒤따라와야 하고, 의문문의 어순을 고려하여 do가 주어(they) 앞에 위치해야 한다.

4 ③ love의 목적어로 to부정사(to go) 또는 동명사(going)가 와야 한다.(go → to go/going)

5 명사(much work)를 꾸미는 to부정사의 형용사적 용법으로 to do를 써야 한다.

6 보기와 ⑤ 가주어 it
①② 비인칭 주어 it ③④ 인칭대명사 it

7 사역동사(Let)는 to가 없는 원형부정사(close)를 목적격 보어로 쓴다.(closes → close)

8 decide는 to부정사를 목적어로 쓰는 동사이므로 「to+동사원형」의 형태가 와야 한다.

9 「how+to부정사」는 '~하는 방법'으로 해석된다. '~에 가다'라는 의미는 go to 외에도 get to를 써서 나타낼 수 있다.

10 감정을 나타내는 형용사(happy)를 꾸미는 to부정사는 부사처럼 쓰여 감정의 원인을 나타낸다.
미라는 그녀의 친구들을 다시 보게 되어 행복하다.

11 사역동사(made)는 to가 없는 원형부정사(paint)를 목적격 보어로 쓴다.

12 명사(주어)처럼 쓰인 to부정사
①②③④ 명사(주어)처럼 쓰인 to부정사
⑤ 부사처럼 쓰인 to부정사의 용법 중 목적

13 지각동사(saw)는 to가 없는 원형부정사(swim)나 현재분사(swimming)를 목적격 보어로 쓴다.

14 보기와 ② 부사처럼 쓰인 to부정사의 용법 중 목적
①④ 명사(목적어)처럼 쓰인 to부정사
③ 형용사처럼 쓰인 to부정사
⑤ 명사(주어)처럼 쓰인 to부정사

15 enjoy는 동명사를 목적어로 쓰는 동사이다.

16 ①③④⑤ 지각동사와 사역동사는 목적격 보어로 to가 없는 원형부정사를 쓴다.
② help는 목적격 보어로 원형부정사 대신 to부정사를 쓰기도 한다.

17 보기와 ②③④⑤ 형용사처럼 쓰인 to부정사
① 명사(목적어)처럼 쓰인 to부정사

18 보기와 ⑤ 「to+동사원형」to부정사
①②③④ 「to+명사」 전치사 to '~에게, ~로'
cf. from side to side '좌우로 (흔들리는)'

19 주어로 쓰인 to부정사의 길이가 길 경우 주어 자리에 가주어 It을 쓰고 to부정사를 뒤로 보낸다.

20 「how+to부정사」 '~하는 방법'
그녀는 이번 겨울에 스키 타는 법을 배울 것이다.

21 ① 사역동사 let은 목적격 보어로 원형부정사를 쓴다.
「Let me+동사원형」 '내가 ~하게 해줘, 내가 ~해 줄게' (to show → show)
② want는 목적어로 to부정사를 쓰는 동사이다. (going → to go)
③ 지각동사 hear은 목적격 보어로 원형부정사나 현재분사를 쓴다. (to bark → bark/barking)
④ decide는 목적어로 to부정사를 쓰는 동사이다.

22 ⑤ (staying → stay)
「to+장소」방향을 나타내는 전치사 to '~에게, ~로'
①②③④ 「to+동사원형」to부정사

23 '~하기 위해서'라는 뜻의 목적을 나타내는 표현으로는 「to+동사원형」, 「in order to+동사원형」, 「so that+주어+동사」, 「in order that+주어+동사」가 있다.

24 be going to '~할 예정이다' have to '~해야 한다' try to '~하려 노력하다' decide to '~하기로 결정하다'

25 '~하는 방법'이라는 뜻의 「how to+동사원형」은 「how+주어+should+동사원형」으로 바꿔 쓸 수 있다.

26 지문의 밑줄 친 부분과 ② 부사처럼 쓰인 to부정사
①③④⑤ 명사처럼 쓰인 to부정사
①⑤ 목적어 자리
③ 목적격보어 자리
④ 진주어 자리

27 「to+동사원형」 형태의 to부정사가 부사적 용법으로 목적을 나타낸다. Jim은 도서관에 책을 빌리기 위해 (to borrow a book) 갔으며 우체국에 편지를 부치기 위해(to send a letter) 갔다.

CHAPTER 8 동명사
Gerunds

본문 _ p.168

PRACTICE 1

1 reading
2 keeping
3 Exercising
4 coming
5 playing
6 taking
7 drawing
8 joining
9 becoming
10 Buying

1 read a magazine: 잡지를 읽다
2 keep a diary: 일기를 쓰다
3 exercise regularly: 규칙적으로 운동하다
4 come to see: 보러 오다
5 play the piano: 피아노를 치다
6 take the subway: 지하철을 타다
7 draw cartoons: 만화를 그리다
8 join a club: 동아리에 가입하다
9 become a teacher: 교사가 되다
10 buy ~ through the Internet: 인터넷으로 ~을 사다

PRACTICE 2

1	①	2	③	3	①	4	④
5	②	6	③	7	②	8	③
9	④	10	①	11	④	12	②

[보기]
① 그와 이야기하는 것은 지루하다. (주어 역할)
② 우리의 목표는 상을 타는 것이다. (보어 역할)
③ 그녀는 보고서 쓰는 것을 끝냈다. (타동사의 목적어 역할)
④ 고양이들은 오르는 것을 잘한다. (전치사의 목적어 역할)

1, 3, 10 동명사가 문장의 주어로 쓰였다.
2, 6, 8 동명사가 각각 타동사 love, practice, enjoy의 목적어로 쓰였다.
4, 9, 11 동명사가 각각 전치사 for, in, for의 목적어로 쓰였다.
5, 7, 12 동명사가 주어에 대해 설명하는 보어로 쓰였다.

PRACTICE 3

1 travel(l)ing, to travel
2 opening
3 studying, to study
4 to watch
5 waiting
6 to go
7 trying
8 falling, to fall
9 eating
10 to visit
11 going
12 sneezing
13 to stay
14 to exercise
15 washing, to wash
16 to obey
17 seeing, to see
18 singing

19 playing, to play **20** to drive
21 shopping, to shop **22** to leave

> **1, 3, 8, 15, 17, 19, 21** love, continue, start, begin, hate, like, prefer는 동명사와 to부정사 모두를 목적어로 쓰는 동사들이다.
> **2, 7, 9, 11, 12, 18** mind, give up, finish, enjoy, stop, practice는 동명사만 목적어로 쓰는 동사이다.
> **4, 6, 10, 13, 14, 16, 20, 22** would like, decide, hope, expect, need, want, plan은 to부정사를 목적어로 쓰는 동사들이다.
> **5** 「keep+-ing」 계속해서 ~ 하다

PRACTICE 4

1 go swimming **2** went skating
3 go fishing **4** goes surfing
5 went shopping **6** go skiing
7 went sailing **8** go hiking
9 go driving **10** went dancing
11 go riding **12** went hunting
13 went jogging

> 1 stay at: ~에 머물다
> 2 visit+장소 명사: ~에 방문하다
> 3 take a picture: 사진을 찍다
> 4 go to the movie theater: 영화를 보러 가다
> 5 write a letter: 편지를 쓰다
> 6 talk about: ~에 대해 얘기하다
> 7 try on: ~을 입어[신어]보다
> 8 do one's homework: 숙제를 하다
> 9 play basketball: 농구를 하다
> 10 eat ~ for lunch: 점심으로 ~을 먹다

PRACTICE 5

1 staying **2** visiting **3** taking
4 going **5** writing **6** talking
7 trying **8** doing **9** playing
10 eating

PRACTICE 6

1 How[What] about helping each other?
2 How[What] about getting some rest?
3 How[What] about keeping the promise?
4 How[What] about having lunch together?
5 How[What] about going out for some fresh air?
6 How[What] about drinking a cup of coffee?
7 How[What] about studying Spanish?
8 How[What] about reading the newspaper?

9 How[What] about buying some fruit?
10 How[What] about sitting down on the bench?

PRACTICE 7

1 stopped, from sleeping
2 spent, buying
3 kept, from going out
4 is spending, talking
5 spent, eating out
6 keep, from leaving
7 stopped, from fighting
8 keep, from coming out
9 spend, talking
10 stopped, from biting
11 keep, from becoming
12 spend, using

> **1, 3, 6, 7, 8, 10, 11** 'keep/stop … from -ing'는 '… 가 ~하는 것을 막다[방지하다]'라는 의미로 쓰인다.
> **2, 4, 5, 9, 12** 'spend+시간/돈+-ing'는 '~하는 데 시간/돈을 쓰다'라는 의미로 쓰인다.

Chapter Review Test 정답 본문_p.176

1 ② **2** swimming **3** ② **4** ④ **5** ⑤ **6** ②
7 How about listening to music? **8** ④ **9** ③
10 ⑤ **11** going **12** ③ **13** ② **14** (1) learn → learning (2) overcome → overcoming[to overcome] **15** ② **16** ③ **17** ①,④ **18** ①
19 ⑤ **20** ② **21** ③ **22** ③ **23** ⑤ **24** ③
25 (A) from (B) planting **26** ① **27** ①
28 gave up exercising **29** ③,⑤ **30** ②,⑤
31 ② **32** ②

Chapter Review Test 해설

1 ⓐ 동사 like는 to부정사와 동명사 모두 목적어로 쓸 수 있다.
ⓑ 동사 plan은 to부정사만 목적어로 쓸 수 있다.
ⓒ 목적어절의 주어는 'talking with people from different countries'로 동명사구이다. 동명사구가 주어로 쓰일 때는 항상 단수 취급한다.
(are → is)

ⓓ practice는 동명사를 목적어로 쓰는 동사이다.
(speak → speaking)
ⓔ 등위접속사 and가 조동사(will) 뒤에서 동사원형으로 쓰인 go와 밑줄 친 단어를 병렬 구조로 연결하므로, tries를 동사원형인 try로 고쳐야 한다.
(tries → try)

2 go -ing '~하러 가다'
3 want는 to부정사(to read)를 목적어로 쓰는 동사이다.
4 ① 동사 keep의 뒤에 동사가 오면 -ing형으로 쓴다.
「keep ~ing」 '계속 ~하다' (to draw → drawing)
② 접속사가 없이 한 개의 문장에서 동사가 두 개 나올 수 없다. 따라서 밑줄 친 부분을 주어의 역할을 할 수 있는 동명사나 to부정사로 바꿔야 한다.
(Protect → Protecting/To protect)
③ 전치사의 목적어로 동사가 올 때는 동명사의 형태로 쓴다. (help → helping)
⑤ 「How about -ing?」는 '~하는 것이 어떠니?'라는 의미의 동명사를 사용한 관용표현이다. (play → playing)
5 전치사(at)와 stop은 동명사(singing)를 목적어로 쓴다.
cf. stop의 뒤에 to부정사가 올 때는 목적을 나타내는 부사적 용법이다.
「stop+to부정사」 '~를 하기 위해 멈추다'
6 expect는 to부정사(to go)를, enjoy는 동명사(taking)를 목적어로 쓰는 동사이다.
7 「how about+동명사 ~?」는 '~하는 게 어때?'라는 뜻이다.
8 ⓐ '~하는 데 어려움을 겪다'는 뜻의 표현은 「have trouble+동명사」로 나타낸다.
(study → studying)
ⓑ '~을 잘하다'는 「be good at+동명사」로 나타낸다.
(listen → listening)
ⓒ 문장의 주어가 동명사일 경우 단수 취급한다.
(are → is)
ⓔ 사역동사 let의 목적격 보어 자리에는 원형부정사가 온다. (knowing → know)
9 What about -ing? '~하는 것이 어떠니?'
10 • keep … from ~ing '…가 ~하는 것을 막다'
• spend … ~ing '~하는 데 …를 소비하다'
11 「keep+-ing」계속해서 ~ 하다
12 give up은 동명사를 목적어로 가진다.
③ He gave up climbing a tree.

13 「stop+동명사」 '~하는 것을 멈추다'(동사의 목적어)
cf. 「stop+to부정사」 '~하기 위해 멈추다'
(to부정사의 부사적 용법)
14 (1) 첫 번째 줄 끝의 give up은 '포기하다'라는 뜻으로 동명사를 목적어로 쓴다.
(2) 밑에서 두 번째 줄의 continue는 동명사와 to부정사 모두를 목적어로 쓸 수 있는 동사이다. 접속사 없이 동사가 연달아 나올 수 없으므로 overcome을 목적어 역할을 할 수 있는 동명사나 to부정사로 고쳐야 한다.
15 (A) 전치사 뒤에는 동명사(flying)가 목적어로 나온다.
(B) want는 to부정사(to become)를 목적어로 취한다.
16 practice는 동명사를 목적어로 쓰는 동사이며 Let's는 「Let's+동사원형」의 형태로 권유나 제안을 나타낸다.
17 빈칸은 주격보어의 자리이다. 동명사와 to부정사는 명사처럼 쓰여 문장 내에서 보어 역할을 한다.
② ate → eating[to eat]
③ recycled → recycling[to recycle]
⑤ do → doing[to do]
18 ① 문장의 주어가 동명사일 경우 단수 취급한다.
(are → is)
19 plan은 to부정사를 목적어로 가진다.
⑤ staying → to stay
20 보기와 ①③④⑤ 동명사 ② 현재분사
21 • spend … ~ing '~하는 데 …를 소비하다'
• enjoy는 동명사를 목적어로 쓰는 동사이다.
• 전치사(on)의 목적어로 동명사가 와야 한다.
22 ①②④⑤ 주어의 역할을 하는 동명사
③ 보어의 역할을 하는 동명사
23 stop은 동명사를 목적어로 쓰는 동사이다. stop의 뒤에 오는 to부정사는 부사적 용법으로 목적을 나타낸다.
「stop+동명사」 '~하는 것을 멈추다'
「stop+to부정사」 '~하기 위해 멈추다'
24 ① 의문사가 있는 일반동사의 의문문은 「의문사+do(es)+주어+동사원형 ~?」의 어순으로 쓴다.
(wants to do → want to do)
② 주어(He)가 3인칭 단수일 때, 일반동사의 현재형은 「동사원형+-s」로 나타낸다. (want to → wants to)
④ 미래 시제는 'be going to'를 사용하여 표현할 수 있다. be going to의 의문문은 「의문사+be+주어+going to+동사원형 ~?」으로 쓴다. (does → is)

⑤ 미래 시제를 나타내는 표현 'be going to'의 뒤에는 동사원형을 쓴다. (went → go)

25 (A) keep … from ~ing '…가 ~하는 것을 막다'
(B) spend … ~ing '~하는 데 …를 소비하다'.

26 (a)의 빈칸 뒤에 to부정사가 오므로, 동명사를 목적어로 쓰는 ③의 kept와 ⑤의 gave up은 올 수 없다.
(b)의 빈칸 뒤에는 동명사가 오므로, to부정사를 목적어로 쓰는 ②의 decided와 ④의 wants는 올 수 없다.
(a) expected
(b) enjoys

27 love는 동명사와 to부정사 모두를 목적어로 쓰는 동사이며, finish는 동명사를 목적어로 쓰는 동사이다.

28 「give up+-ing」 '~하는 것을 포기하다'

29 ⓒⓔ 동명사   ⓐⓑⓓ 현재분사

30 ② practice는 동명사를 목적어로 쓰는 동사이므로 playing을 써야 한다.
⑤ 동명사는 단수 취급을 하므로 is를 써야 한다.

31 (A) finish는 동명사를 목적어로 쓰는 동사이므로 cleaning이다.
(B) want는 to부정사를 목적어로 쓰는 동사이므로 to play이다.
(C) spend … ~ing '~하는 데 …를 소비하다'

32 ② 현재분사 ①③④⑤ 동명사

CHAPTER 9 분사 (Participles)

본문 _ p.182

PRACTICE 1

1	dying	2	lost
3	ringing	4	forgotten
5	sleeping	6	given
7	baked	8	rolling
9	used	10	rising
11	smiling	12	broken

1, 3, 5, 8, 10, 11 빈칸 뒤의 명사와 '능동/진행'의 의미 관계를 이루므로 '동사원형+-ing' 형태인 현재분사가 알맞다.
2, 4, 6, 7, 9, 12 빈칸 뒤의 명사와 '수동/완료'의 의미관계를 이루므로 과거분사 형태가 알맞다. 일반적으로 과거분사는 '동사원형+-ed'의 형태이지만, lose-lost-lost, forget-forgot-forgotten, give-gave-given, break-broke-broken처럼 불규칙 동사들은 과거/과거분사 형태가 불규칙하게 변화한다.

PRACTICE 2

1	broken	2	flying
3	dancing	4	burning
5	used	6	built

1, 5, 6 수식받는 명사와 '수동/완료'의 의미 관계를 이루므로 과거분사가 알맞다.
2, 3, 4 수식받는 명사와 '능동/진행'의 의미 관계를 이루므로 현재분사가 알맞다.

1 부서진 의자 (break-broke-broken)
2 하늘을 날고 있는 연
3 춤추고 있는 소녀
4 타고 있는 두 개의 초
5 사용된(중고) 자전거
6 붉은 벽돌로 지어진 집 (build-built-built)

PRACTICE 3

1	singing	2	surprising
3	picking	4	spent
5	walking	6	borrowed
7	dying	8	written
9	born	10	crossing
11	coming	12	lost
13	listening	14	painted
15	finished	16	crossed

CHAPTER 9

> 1, 2, 3, 5, 7, 10, 11, 13 수식받는 명사와 '능동/진행'의 의미 관계를 이루므로 현재분사가 알맞다.
> 4, 6, 8, 9, 12, 14, 15 수식받는 명사와 '수동/완료'의 의미 관계를 이루므로 과거분사가 알맞다.
> 1 노래하는 새
> 2 놀라게 하는(놀라운) 소식
> 3 쓰레기를 줍고 있는 소년
> 4 쓰여진 돈 (spend-spent-spent)
> 5 걸어 다니는 사전
> *a walking dictionary: '걸어 다니는 사전'은 비유적으로 '박학다식한 사람'을 의미한다.
> 6 빌려진(빌린) 펜
> 7 죽어가는 개
> 8 영어로 쓰여진 책 (write-wrote-written)
> 9 유럽에서 태어난 사람 (bear-bore-born/borne)
> 10 길을 건너는 남자
> 11 공장에서 나오는 물
> 12 잃어버려진(잃어버린) 딸 (lose-lost-lost)
> 13 음악을 듣고 있는 소녀
> 14 유미에 의해 그려진(유미가 그린) 그림
> 15 완성된 제품(완제품)
> 16 목적격 보어로 과거분사(crossed)를 사용하여 목적어(my fingers)가 당하는 행위나 상태를 서술한다.
> *keep[have] one's fingers crossed: '행운을 빌다, 좋은 결과가 나오기를 빌다'라는 의미이다. 세 번째 손가락을 두 번째 손가락 위에 포개는 손동작을 묘사한 것으로, 이러한 손동작이 행운을 가져온다는 믿음에서 유래한 표현이다.

PRACTICE 4

1	broken	2	been
3	living	4	planted
5	eating	6	practicing
7	called	8	stolen
9	worked	10	made
11	flooded	12	ridden
13	making	14	done
15	walking		

> 1, 4, 7, 8, 11 be동사와 과거분사가 결합하여 수동태 구문을 이루어야 알맞다.
> 2, 9, 10, 12, 14 have/has와 과거분사가 결합된 완료형 구문이 알맞다.
> 3, 5, 6, 13, 15 be동사와 현재분사가 결합된 진행형이 되어야 알맞다.

PRACTICE 5

1	현재분사	2	동명사	3	현재분사
4	동명사	5	동명사	6	현재분사
7	동명사	8	현재분사	9	현재분사
10	동명사	11	현재분사	12	동명사

> 1, 8, 11 '~하는 중이다/중이었다'라는 뜻으로 진행을 나타내는 현재분사로 쓰였다.
> 2, 4, 10 밑줄 친 부분이 뒤에 오는 명사의 용도나 목적을 나타내므로 동명사로 쓰였다.
> 3, 6 밑줄 친 부분이 뒤에 오는 명사를 꾸며주어 능동의 의미 (interesting)나 현재 상태(living)를 나타내므로 현재분사로 쓰였다.
> 5, 7, 9, 12 '~하는 것이다'라는 뜻으로, 밑줄 친 부분이 주격 보어 역할을 하므로 동명사로 쓰였다.

PRACTICE 6

1	① interesting	② interested
2	① pleased	② pleasing
3	① shocking	② shocked
4	① moved	② moving
5	① exciting	② excited
6	① disappointing	② disappointed

> 1 ① interesting stories: 흥미로운 이야기
> ② be interested in: ~에 흥미를 느끼다
> 2 ① be pleased with: ~에 만족하다
> ② pleasing: 기분 좋게 하는
> 3 ① shocking: 놀라게 하는
> ② be shocked at: ~에 충격을 받다
> 4 ① be moved by: ~에 감동을 받다
> ② moving: 감동을 주는
> 5 ① exciting: 흥분하게 하는
> ② be excited about: ~에 대해 흥분하다, 들뜨다
> 6 ① disappointing: 실망시키는
> ② be disappointed (with): (~에) 실망하다, 낙담하다

PRACTICE 7

1	tired	2	surprised
3	amazing	4	satisfying
5	depressed	6	boring

> 1 feel tired: 피로를 느끼다
> 2 be surprised by: ~에 놀라다
> 3 amazing powers: 놀라운 힘
> 4 a satisfying result: 만족스러운 결과
> 5 be depressed: 우울해하다
> 6 boring: 지루한

PRACTICE 8

1	interesting	2	tired
3	amazing	4	surprised
5	moved	6	shocking
7	satisfying	8	disappointing

| 9 | confusing | 10 | bored |
| 11 | pleased | 12 | frustrating |

1, 3, 6, 7, 8, 9, 12 주어 또는 수식받는 명사가 감정을 일으키는 주체이므로 감정을 나타내는 동사의 -ing 형태가 알맞다.
2, 4, 5, 10, 11 주어가 감정을 느끼는 주체이므로 감정을 나타내는 동사의 -ed 형태가 알맞다.

Chapter Review Test 정답 본문 _ p.190

1 ② 2 ⑤ 3 ③ 4 ② 5 ③ 6 ② 7 ②
8 ② 9 ④ 10 standing 11 ⑤ 12 pleased
13 ④ 14 ③ 15 ③ 16 ⑤ 17 written
18 ④ 19 ② 20 (1) The girl sitting on the bench is my sister. (2) Look at that nice sports car parked under the tree. 21 ①

Chapter Review Test 해설

1 '깨진'은 수동·완료의 의미이므로 window를 수식하는 과거분사(broken)가 와야 한다.

2 • 「be동사+현재분사」는 진행시제를 나타낸다.
 • 지각동사(heard)의 목적격 보어로 원형부정사(ring)나 현재분사(ringing)를 쓴다.

3 스포츠를 좋아한다고 대답하였으므로 boring(지루한)은 문맥상 어울리지 않는다.

4 ② 진행을 나타내는 현재분사
 ①④⑤ 보어의 역할을 하는 동명사
 ③ 주어 역할을 하는 동명사

5 명사(a girl)를 수식하는 분사로, '쓰고 있는'은 능동·진행의 의미이므로 현재분사(wearing)를 쓴다. 동사 enjoy는 동명사(looking)를 목적어로 쓴다.

6 식물이 음악을 좋아한다는 사실이 감정을 일으키는 주체이므로 현재분사(surprising)가 와야 한다.

7 두 번째 문장의 주어 The weather는 감정을 일으키는 주체이므로 현재분사(amazing)가 와야 하며, 마지막 문장의 주어 We는 감정을 느끼는 대상이므로 과거분사(disappointed)가 와야 한다.

8 주어 She는 감정을 느끼는 대상이므로 과거분사(interested)가 와야 한다.
 cf. be interested in '~에 흥미가 있다'

9 보기와 ④ 명사의 역할을 하는 동명사
 ①②③⑤ 진행을 나타내는 현재분사

10 앞 명사 the boy를 수식하는 것으로 진행을 나타내는 현재분사(standing)가 와야 한다.

11 ⑤ 현재분사   ①②③④ 동명사

12 주어 She는 감정을 느끼는 대상이므로 과거분사(pleased)가 와야 한다.

13 주어 He는 감정을 느끼는 대상이므로 과거분사(tired)가 적절하다.
 ④ He feels tired.

14 ⓐⓒⓔ 현재분사   ⓑⓓ 동명사

15 • 진행을 나타내는 현재분사(Sleeping '자고 있는')가 와야 한다.
 • 명사(leaves)를 수식할 수 있는 분사가 적절하다. 진행을 나타내는 현재분사(falling '떨어지고 있는') 또는 완료를 나타내는 과거분사(fallen '떨어진')가 올 수 있다.

16 ⑤ 현재분사   ①②③④ 동명사

17 명사 a novel이 스스로 쓴 것이 아니라 쓰여진 것이므로 수동 의미의 과거분사(written)가 들어간다.

18 ④ 목적어 people은 감정을 느끼는 대상이므로 과거분사(depressed)가 와야 한다.

19 • 뒤에 나온 명사 car를 수식하는 것으로 수동·완료의 의미를 갖는 과거분사(used)가 와야 한다.
 cf. a used car 중고차
 • 「have/has+과거분사」는 현재완료 시제를 나타낸다.

20 (1) 현재분사(sitting)가 부사구(on the bench)의 수식을 받는 경우에는 뒤에서 명사(The girl)를 수식한다.
 (2) 과거분사(parked)가 부사구(under the tree)의 수식을 받는 경우에는 뒤에서 명사(that nice sports car)를 수식한다.

21 ⓑ 접속사 없이 동사가 연달아 나올 수 없다. 동사 cook을 목적어 역할을 할 수 있는 동명사나 to부정사로 바꿔야 한다. like는 동명사와 to부정사 모두를 목적어로 취하는 동사이다. (cook → cooking[to cook])
 ⓒ 앞에 나온 meat를 수식하는 것으로 수동·완료의 의미인 과거분사(roasted '구워진')가 와야 한다.
 ⓓ Everybody가 감정을 느끼는 대상이므로 과거분사(surprised)가 와야 한다.

CHAPTER 10 형용사 Adjectives

본문 _ p.194

PRACTICE 1

1 special   2 careful   3 wonderful
4 dangerous   5 helpful   6 ready
7 good   8 hungry   9 sick
10 curious

> 1, 3, 7 명사를 앞에서 꾸며주는 자리이므로 형용사가 알맞다.
> 2, 4, 5, 6, 8, 9, 10 be동사 뒤에서 주어의 상태나 성질을 나타내는 주격 보어가 들어갈 자리이므로 형용사가 알맞다.

PRACTICE 2

1 B, A   2 A, B   3 B, A
4 A, B   5 A, B   6 A, B
7 B, A   8 A, B   9 A, B
10 A, B

> [보기]
> A. 좋은(잘한) 일 → 명사를 앞에서 꾸며주는 한정적 용법
> B. 수학을 잘한다 → 주어의 상태나 모습을 설명하는 서술적 용법
>
> 1 과목이 어렵다 (서술) / 어려운 퍼즐 (한정)
> 2 아름다운 목걸이 (한정) / 날씨가 아름답다[좋다] (서술)
> 3 시장이 혼잡하다 (서술) / 혼잡한 장소 (한정)
> 4 완벽한 사람 (한정) / 그는 완벽하다 (서술)
> 5 좋은 기억력 (한정) / 맛이 좋다 (서술)
> 6 다른 수업 (한정) / 민수는 다르다 (서술)
> 7 케이크가 달다 (서술) / 달콤한 것 (한정)
> 8 거대한 장소 (한정) / 궁전이 거대하다 (서술)
> 9 맛있는 음식 (한정) / 샌드위치가 맛있게 보인다 (서술)
> 10 전혀 흥미롭지 (않은) 것 (한정) / 게임이 흥미진진하다 (서술)

PRACTICE 3

1 something sweet   2 anything else
3 Everything delicious   4 something cold
5 anything interesting   6 nobody special
7 something important   8 anything slow
9 nothing wrong   10 everything necessary
11 something useful   12 anyone famous
13 anything sharp   14 new thing
15 something old   16 nothing cheap

> 1, 2, 3, 4, 5, 7, 8, 9, 10, 11, 13, 15, 16 -thing으로 끝나는 대명사를 꾸미는 형용사는 항상 대명사 뒤에 온다.
> 6, 12 -body 또는 -one으로 끝나는 대명사를 꾸미는 형용사는 항상 대명사의 뒤에 온다.
> 14 thing이 단독으로 쓰일 때는 형용사 new가 thing을 앞에서 꾸며준다.

PRACTICE 4

2 two, second   3 three, third
4 four, fourth   5 five, fifth
6 six, sixth   7 seven, seventh
8 eight, eighth   9 nine, ninth
10 ten, tenth   11 eleven, eleventh
12 twelve, twelfth   13 thirteen, thirteenth
14 fourteen, fourteenth   15 fifteen, fifteenth
16 sixteen, sixteenth
17 seventeen, seventeenth
18 eighteen, eighteenth
19 nineteen, nineteenth
20 twenty, twentieth
21 twenty-one, twenty-first
22 twenty-two, twenty-second
23 thirty, thirtieth   24 forty, fortieth
25 fifty, fiftieth   26 fifty-five, fifty-fifth
27 sixty, sixtieth   28 seventy, seventieth
29 eighty, eightieth   30 ninety, ninetieth
31 a[one] hundred, one hundredth
32 a[one] thousand, one thousandth
33 a[one] million, one millionth
34 a[one] billion, one billionth

PRACTICE 5

1 second   2 ninth   3 twelfth
4 first   5 eighth   6 fortieth
7 third   8 thirtieth   9 fifth
10 twentieth

PRACTICE 6

1 four thousand, two hundred (and) fifty-six
2 thirty-six
3 fifty-seven thousand, four hundred (and) three
4 a[one] thousand, fifty-two
5 five hundred (and) thirty
6 eight thousand, eight hundred (and) twenty-six
7 seventy-two
8 six hundred (and) one
9 seventy-five thousand, four hundred (and)

nineteen
10 twelve million
11 five thousand, five hundred
12 seven hundred (and) thirteen
13 two hundred (and) twenty-three thousand, six hundred
14 four hundred (and) eleven
15 two thousand, seven hundred (and) eighty
16 a[one] hundred (and) thirty-one
17 six thousand, two hundred (and) thirty-eight
18 two hundred (and) fifty-six
19 ninety-nine
20 three hundred (and) two

PRACTICE 7

1 eight four six, o two three six
2 three o six, four four[double four] o o[double o]
3 area code zero two, four two eight, five five [double five] nine seven
4 three one nine, two seven one three
5 zero one eight, two eight one eight, three seven one o
6 two seven four, five five[double five] one five
7 area code zero three one, eight six five, eight four three eight
8 one one[double one] nine
9 two o six o, four three six two
10 nine six three, five nine o eight
11 019-1792-0012
12 (064) 440-3318
13 594-3386
14 (042) 754-3892
15 296-4300
16 1-677-820-3322
17 114
18 646-5958
19 (051) 755-0081
20 010-535-7587

PRACTICE 8

1 three-fourths[three-quarters]
2 a quarter[one-quarter]
3 two point five

4 (zero) point three one
5 two point zero nine
6 twenty and a third[one-third]
7 two-sevenths
8 two-ninths
9 one and a half[one-half]
10 five and three-tenths
11 (zero) point nine nine
12 one point two seven two
13 7/15
14 4/11
15 3 6/7
16 6 1/5
17 0.6
18 34.9
19 3.126
20 5 5/6

PRACTICE 9

1 nine twenty
2 three-(o)-five
3 eight twenty-five
4 five (o'clock)
5 ten thirty
6 one thirty-seven
7 six fifteen
8 eleven (o'clock)
9 twelve-(o)-eight
10 four fifty

PRACTICE 10

1 (a) quarter to ten
2 (a) quarter after[past] one
3 five to twelve
4 twenty after four
5 (a) quarter after[past] seven
6 twenty-five to eight
7 ten to nine
8 ten after three
9 (a) quarter to six
10 five to two
11 (a) quarter after[past] three
12 ten to six
13 half past three
14 five after six
15 twenty-five after two
16 half past eleven
17 ten after nine

18 twenty to five
19 twenty after ten
20 half past seven

PRACTICE 11

1 October (the) thirteenth[the thirteenth of October]
2 two thousand (and) twenty[twenty twenty]
3 fifteen ninety-two
4 February (the) twentieth[the twentieth of February]
5 four (hundred and) fifty-two
6 July (the) first[the first of July]
7 nineteen eighty
8 March (the) thirty-first[the thirty-first of March]
9 nineteen ten
10 December (the) fifteenth[the fifteenth of December]
11 April (the) eighth[the eighth of April]
12 September (the) twenty-sixth[the twenty-sixth of September]
13 nineteen ninety-nine
14 May (the) fifth[the fifth of May]
15 two thousand
16 November (the) tenth[the tenth of November]
17 twelve thirty-eight
18 June (the) seventeenth[the seventeenth of June]
19 sixteen hundred
20 nineteen seventy

PRACTICE 12

1 a[one] dollar (and) twenty-five cents
2 five thousand two hundred won
3 ten dollars (and) ten cents
4 twelve thousand won
5 a[one] thousand eight hundred (and) fifty won
6 seventy-five cents
7 twelve dollars (and) thirty cents
8 four hundred won
9 three dollars (and) fifty cents
10 four thousand nine hundred won

PRACTICE 13

1 twenty-three degrees Celsius
2 fifty degrees Fahrenheit
3 a[one] hundred (and) fifty degrees Celsius
4 seventy-five degrees Fahrenheit
5 three hundred (and) fifty degrees Fahrenheit
6 two hundred (and) seventy-five degrees Celsius
7 a[one] hundred (and) eighty degrees Celsius
8 a[one] hundred (and) sixteen point six degrees Fahrenheit
9 two hundred (and) seventy-three point one five degrees Celsius
10 four hundred (and) twenty degrees Fahrenheit

PRACTICE 14

1 Add, a, quarter
2 invented, fourteen, forty, three
3 costs, four, thousand, nine, hundred
4 sold, eighteen, dollars, ninety, cents
5 arrived, the, first, March
6 rose, eighty, point, seven
7 received, four, fifths
8 get, up, quarter, after[past], seven
9 was, born, November, fourth, two, thousand
10 collected, four, thousand, seven, hundred, seventy, four
11 starts, one, hundred, Celsius
12 is, area, code, zero, two, four, three, six, seven
13 reached, eighty, six, degrees
14 is, zero, one, zero, double[nine], nine, eight
15 saved, million, two, hundred, twenty, nine, thousand, nine, hundred

PRACTICE 15

1 millions of
2 tens[dozens] of
3 four hundred
4 Hundreds of
5 five hundred
6 Thousands of
7 Millions of
8 tens[dozens] of
9 a[one] thousand
10 Three million

PRACTICE 16

1 every five days
2 every two weeks

3	every three days	4	every fourth week
5	every ten years	6	every seven days
7	every fifteen days	8	every four years
9	every second day	10	every ninth day

PRACTICE 17

1	many flowers	2	much water
3	many dishes	4	many clubs
5	much soup	6	many dreams
7	many kites	8	much juice
9	many planets	10	many jobs
11	much rain	12	many places
13	much sleep	14	many Korean friends
15	many courses	16	much pleasure
17	much snow	18	many sports activities
19	many interesting sites		
20	much interest	21	much experience
22	many people		

> 1, 3, 4, 6, 7, 9, 10, 12, 14, 15, 18, 19, 22 셀 수 있는 명사 앞에 와서 '많은, 다수의'라는 의미로 쓰이는 many가 알맞고, 이때 수식을 받는 명사는 복수 형태로 써야 한다.
> 2, 5, 8, 11, 13, 16, 17, 20, 21 셀 수 없는 명사 앞에 와서 '많은'이라는 의미로 쓰이는 much가 알맞다.

PRACTICE 18

2	much time	3	many apple pies
4	many schools	5	much money
6	many pictures	7	much courage
8	many animals	9	much coffee
10	many things	11	many insects
12	much fun	13	many children
14	Many people	15	much oil
16	many questions	17	much information
18	many different countries		
19	many rules	20	much sleep

> 1, 3, 4, 6, 8, 10, 11, 13, 14, 16, 18, 19 괄호 안의 명사가 셀 수 있는 명사이므로 a lot of나 lots of 대신 many로 바꿔 쓸 수 있다. 이때 명사는 -(e)s를 붙인 복수 명사 형태가 되어야 한다.
> 2, 5, 7, 9, 12, 15, 17, 20 괄호 안의 명사가 셀 수 없는 명사이므로 a lot of나 lots of 대신 much로 바꿔 쓸 수 있다.

PRACTICE 19

1	few	2	little	3	A few
4	little	5	a few	6	few
7	little	8	a little	9	little
10	A few	11	A little	12	A little
13	a few	14	little	15	a few
16	Few				

> 1, 6, 16 셀 수 있는 명사 앞에 쓰이며 '거의 없는'이라는 의미를 나타내는 few가 알맞다.
> 2, 4, 7, 9, 14 셀 수 없는 명사 앞에 쓰이며 '거의 없는'이라는 의미를 나타내는 little이 알맞다.
> 3, 5, 10, 13, 15 셀 수 있는 명사 앞에 쓰이며 '약간의'라는 의미를 나타내는 a few가 알맞다.
> 8, 11, 12 셀 수 없는 명사 앞에 쓰이며 '약간의'라는 의미를 나타내는 a little이 알맞다.

PRACTICE 20

1	some	2	some	3	any	4	any
5	some	6	any	7	any	8	any
9	any	10	some	11	some	12	some
13	any	14	any	15	some	16	some

> 1, 2, 5, 11, 12, 16 셀 수 있는 명사와 셀 수 없는 명사 앞에 모두 와서 '약간의'라는 의미로 쓰이는 some이 알맞다.
> 3, 4, 6, 9, 13 부정문에서 '조금도[전혀] ~ 없는[아닌]'이라는 의미로 쓰이는 any가 알맞다.
> 7, 8, 14 의문문에서 '어떤/약간의'라는 의미로 쓰이는 any가 알맞다.
> 10, 15 '~해주시겠어요?' 또는 '~하시겠어요?'라는 의미로 권유/부탁을 하는 의문문이므로 some이 알맞다.

PRACTICE 21

1	no	2	nobody	3	nothing
4	no one	5	nowhere	6	no
7	nobody	8	nothing	9	nowhere
10	no				

Chapter Review Test 정답 본문 _ p.215

1 ⑤ 2 ③ 3 ④ 4 ② 5 ④ 6 a very pretty girl 7 ③ 8 ④ 9 ninth 10 ③
11 ② 12 ⑤ 13 ② 14 ③ 15 ③
16 I want something delicious for lunch.
17 Hundreds of 18 ⓐ sixth ⓑ six 19 ③
20 three → third 21 ⑤ some → any 22 ③
23 ② 24 no 25 second 26 ⑤ 27 ⑤
28 ⑤ 29 ④ 30 ③ 31 ④ 32 It's a quarter to four. 33 ② 34 ② 35 ③ 36 ④ 37 ④
38 ③ 39 have no houses 40 ③ 41 ③

42 (1) ⓑ There are many[a lot of/lots of] pencils on the desk. (2) ⓒ There's too much garbage in the park. **43** ③ **44** (1) two[week] → second[weeks] (2) hundreds → hundred (3) three-forth → three-fourths

Chapter Review Test 해설

1 ⑤ 형용사 - 부사
①②③④ 명사 - 형용사

2 ③ '매우'라는 뜻의 부사
①②④⑤ 명사(boy)를 꾸며줄 수 있는 형용사

3 ④ twelveth → twelfth

4 much는 셀 수 없는 명사 앞에 쓰는 형용사

5 ④ 보어로 쓰인 형용사의 서술적 용법
①②③⑤ 명사를 수식하는 형용사의 한정적 용법

6 서술적 용법의 형용사를 명사(girl)를 꾸미는 한정적 용법의 형용사로 바꾸어 쓸 수 있다.

7 ③ four - fourth

8 ④ 연도는 보통 두 자리씩 끊어서 읽는다.
1871년 = eighteen seventy-one

9 ninth '아홉 번째'

10 ③ 정수는 세 자리씩 끊어서 천 단위로 읽으며, hundred 뒤의 and는 생략 가능하다.
1,251 = a[one] thousand, two hundred (and) fifty-one

11 셀 수 없는 명사(coffee) 앞에 '많은'의 의미로 much를 쓴다.

12 ⑤ '~을 지나서'를 뜻하는 after[past]를 사용하여 읽는다. to는 '~전에'라는 뜻이다.
1:10 = ten after[past] one

13 날짜는 서수를 이용하여 읽는다.
cf. June '6월'   July '7월'

14 날짜는 서수를 이용하여 읽는다.

15 11시 15분 전 = 10시 45분
cf. (a) quarter '15분'   to '~ 전에'

16 -thing으로 끝나는 대명사(something)를 꾸미는 형용사(delicious)는 항상 뒤에 위치한다.

17 hundreds of '수백의'
cf. tens[dozens] of '수십의'
   thousands of '수천의' millions of '수백만의'

18 「every+서수+단수 명사」=「every+기수+복수 명사」 '매~, ~마다'

19 셀 수 있는 명사(animals) 앞에 '많은'의 의미로 many를 쓴다.

20 순서를 나타내는 서수(third)로 바꾸어야 한다. (three → third)

21 ⑤ 일반적으로 부정문과 의문문에서는 any를 쓴다.

22 ③ A lots of → A lot of[Lots of]

23 ② 6시 45분 ≠ 6시 15분 전(=5시 45분)
It is fifteen to six.의 six를 seven으로 바꿔야 한다.

24 not ~ any는 no로 바꾸어 쓸 수 있다.

25 학년을 나타낼 때는 순서를 나타내는 서수(second)를 써야 한다.

26 ⑤ feel은 '~하게 느끼다'라는 뜻의 감각동사이므로, 보어로 형용사를 쓴다. softly는 '부드럽게'라는 뜻의 부사이다. (softly → soft)
① smell은 '~한 냄새가 나다'라는 뜻의 감각동사이므로, 보어로 형용사를 쓴다.
② sound는 '~하게 들리다'라는 뜻의 감각동사이므로, 보어로 형용사를 쓴다. silly는 뒤에 -ly가 붙지만 부사가 아닌 '어리석은'이라는 뜻의 형용사이다.
③ taste는 '~한 맛이 나다'라는 뜻의 감각동사이므로, 보어로 형용사를 쓴다.
④ look은 '~하게 보이다'라는 뜻의 감각동사이므로, 보어로 형용사를 쓴다. lovely는 -ly가 붙지만, 부사가 아닌 '사랑스러운'이라는 뜻의 형용사이다.

27 부정문에서는 일반적으로 any를 쓴다.
⑤ We don't need any special ideas.

28 부정문에서는 any를 쓰며 의미상 anything이 와야 한다. 민지는 지난밤에 열심히 공부했지만 지금 아무것도 기억할 수가 없다.
cf. anyone '누구, 아무'

29 미국의 화폐 단위인 dollar와 cent는 1보다 클 경우 복수형으로 쓴다.
④ $2.39 = two dollars and thirty-nine cents

30 분자는 기수로, 분모는 서수로 읽으며 분자를 먼저 읽는다. 분자가 2 이상인 경우 분모에 -s를 붙인다.
① 1/5 = one-fifth[a fifth]
② 3/5 = three-fifths
④ 5/6 = five-sixths
⑤ 3 1/8 = three and one-eighth[an eighth]

31 (A) 명사 doctor를 앞에서 수식하는 형용사 successful이 적절하다.
(B) 관사 a와 빈칸 앞에 위치한 형용사 great로 보아 빈칸에는 명사 success가 들어가는 것이 적절하다.

great가 앞에서 명사를 수식하고 있다.

32 a quarter는 15분이라는 뜻이고, to는 '~전에'라는 뜻이다. 이를 이용해 4시 15분 전이라는 뜻으로 만든다.
4시 15분 전이다.

33 일반적으로 의문문에는 any를, 긍정문에는 some을 쓴다.

34 '~을 지나서'를 뜻하는 past가 와야 한다.

35 ① 밑줄 친 우리말과 같은 뜻이 아니므로 빈칸에 적절하지 않다. 'I don't know.'는 모른다는 뜻이다.
② Nothing처럼 -thing으로 끝나는 대명사는 형용사(special)가 뒤에서 수식한다.
④ something은 긍정문에서 '어떤 것, 무엇'이라는 뜻으로 쓰이는 부정대명사이다. 특별한 일이 없다고 했으므로 '특별한 일이 있어'라는 뜻으로 해석되는 ④번 보기는 적절하지 않다.
⑤ nothing은 「not ~ anything」과 바꾸어 쓸 수 있다. 이미 문장에 not이 포함되어 있으므로 nothing이 쓰이는 것은 적절하지 않다. 또한 특별한 일이 없다고 했으므로 '특별한'이라는 뜻의 형용사 special도 함께 써야 한다. 따라서 I don't have anything special이 적절한 표현이다.

36 ④ a little은 셀 수 없는 명사 앞에 쓴다.

37 그 젊은 남자는 건전한 정신을 가지고 있다.(형용사)
① 교회 종이 11시에 울렸다.(동사)
② 그것은 매우 흥미롭게 들린다.(감각동사 sound)
③ 바이올린은 여러 가지 소리들을 낼 수 있다.(명사)
④ 그는 심신이 건강하다.(형용사)
⑤ 우리는 옆 방에서 이상한 소리를 들었다.(명사)
cf. sound 명 소리 동 소리가 나다, ~하게 들리다
형 건전한, 건강한

38 ① soup는 셀 수 없는 명사이므로 복수형으로 쓸 수 없다. (soups → soup)
② coffee는 셀 수 없는 명사이므로 복수형으로 쓸 수 없다. (coffees → coffee)

④ many는 셀 수 있는 명사의 복수형 앞에서 명사를 수식하는 형용사이다. 따라서 셀 수 있는 명사인 book은 복수형으로 써야 한다. (book → books)
⑤ money는 셀 수 없는 명사이므로 복수형으로 쓸 수 없다. (moneys → money)

39 not ~ any는 no로 바꾸어 쓸 수 있다.

40 '많은'의 의미로 셀 수 있는 명사 앞에는 many를 쓰고 셀 수 없는 명사 앞에는 much를 쓴다. few는 '거의 없는'의 뜻으로 셀 수 있는 명사 앞에 쓴다.

41 ③ many는 셀 수 있는 명사의 복수형 앞에서 명사를 수식한다. 동사(are)와 빈칸 뒤의 명사가 복수형(cafeterias)인 것으로 보아 빈칸에는 many가 들어갈 수 있다.
①②④⑤ milk, water, money, trash는 셀 수 없는 명사이다. 셀 수 없는 명사의 앞에는 much가 들어간다.

42 ⓑ '많은'의 의미을 가지는 many[a lot of/lots of]는 셀 수 있는 명사(pencils) 앞에 쓴다.
ⓒ too much는 셀 수 없는 명사 앞에 쓰여 '과도하게'라는 뜻을 가진다.

43 ⓐ 일반적으로 긍정문에 some을 쓴다.
ⓑ '많은'의 의미로 셀 수 있는 명사(things) 앞에는 many를 쓴다.
ⓒ '거의 없는'의 의미로 셀 수 없는 명사(snow) 앞에는 little을 쓴다.

44 (1) 두 번째 줄에서 '매~, ~마다'라는 뜻으로 쓰이는 every는 「every+기수+복수명사」나 「every+서수+단수명사」로 써야 한다.
(2) 4번째 줄에서 500이라는 정수를 표현할 때는, hundred에 -s를 붙이지 않고 「기수+hundred」로 나타낸다.
(3) 밑에서 두 번째 줄에서 3/4라는 분수를 표현할 때는 분자가 2 이상이기 때문에 분모에 -s를 붙여야 한다.

CHAPTER 11 부사
Adverbs

본문 _ p.222

PRACTICE 1

1	kind	2	gladly
3	loud	4	proudly, new
5	terribly	6	quietly
7	Luckily, easily	8	carefully
9	beautiful	10	Suddenly, heavily

1 명사 nurse의 앞에서 수식하는 형용사 kind가 알맞다.
2 동사 opened를 수식하는 부사 gladly가 알맞다.
3 '(소리가) 큰'이라는 뜻의 형용사 loud가 알맞다.
4 동사 showed를 수식하는 부사 proudly와 명사 smartphone을 수식하는 형용사 new가 알맞다.
5 형용사 sick을 수식하는 부사 terribly가 알맞다.
6 동사 opened를 수식하는 부사 quietly가 알맞다.
7 문장 전체를 수식하는 부사 Luckily와 동사 win을 수식하는 부사 easily가 알맞다.
8 동사 listened를 수식하는 부사 carefully가 알맞다.
9 명사 flower를 수식하는 형용사 beautiful이 알맞다.
10 문장 전체를 수식하는 부사 Suddenly와 동사 rain을 수식하는 부사 heavily가 알맞다.

PRACTICE 2

1	nicely	2	beautifully
3	happily	4	clearly
5	differently	6	kindly
7	carefully	8	heavily
9	usually	10	really
11	quickly	12	gladly
13	luckily	14	surprisingly
15	prettily	16	strongly
17	dangerously	18	noisily
19	loudly	20	easily
21	newly	22	regularly
23	slowly	24	sadly
25	bravely	26	greatly
27	specially	28	quietly
29	similarly	30	badly

PRACTICE 3

1	happy	2	usually
3	great	4	really
5	easy	6	suddenly
7	safe	8	surprisingly
9	important	10	quietly

| 11 | sadly | 12 | bravely |

1, 3 feel, taste와 같은 감각 동사 뒤에는 보어로 형용사가 와야 한다.
2, 4, 6, 8, 10, 11, 12 의미상 동사를 수식할 수 있는 부사가 들어가는 것이 알맞다.
5, 7 주어의 성질이나 상태를 나타내는 주격 보어의 자리이므로 형용사가 알맞다.
9 명사를 수식하므로 형용사가 와야 한다.

PRACTICE 4

1	A, B	2	B, A	3	B, A
4	B, A	5	A, B	6	B, A
7	B, A	8	A, B		

[보기]
A. fast food: 빠른 음식(패스트푸드) → 형용사
B. go very fast: 아주 빠르게 가다 → 부사

1 be late: 늦다, 지각하다 → 형용사
　too late: 너무 늦게 → 부사
2 open early: 일찍 열다 → 부사
　be too early: 너무 이르다 → 형용사
3 live long: 오래 살다 → 부사
　long line: 긴 줄 → 형용사
4 study very hard: 아주 열심히 공부하다 → 부사
　be hard: 힘들다 → 형용사
5 low price: 낮은 가격 → 형용사
　fly low: 낮게 날다 → 부사
6 drive fast: 빠르게 운전하다 → 부사
　fast runner: 빠른 달리기 주자 → 형용사
7 come daily: 날마다 오다 → 부사
　daily paper: 매일 나오는 신문(일간지) → 형용사
8 high fever: 높은 열 → 형용사
　fly high: 높이 날다 → 부사

PRACTICE 5

1	never	2	always
3	often	4	never
5	usually	6	often
7	sometimes	8	always
9	usually	10	sometimes
11	always	12	never
13	usually	14	sometimes

PRACTICE 6

1 Mrs. Kim is always kind.
2 Do you often surf the Internet?

CHAPTER 11

3 Shelly always tries to smile.
4 I have never taken an airplane.
5 This street is sometimes crowded.
6 Tom is never at home after 8 o'clock.
7 It is often foggy in London.
8 He has often made mistakes.
9 He never finishes his work on time.
10 I often go to the French restaurant.
11 My work usually starts at 8:30.
12 What do you usually do on weekends?
13 She has always been nice to others.
14 She sometimes walks to her office.
15 The newspaper is usually delivered at 7.
16 You can always count on me.

> 1, 5, 6, 7, 15 빈도부사는 be동사 뒤에 온다.
> 2, 3, 9, 10, 11, 12, 14 빈도부사는 일반동사 앞에 온다.
> 4, 8, 13, 16 빈도부사는 have, can, will과 같은 조동사 뒤에 온다.

PRACTICE 7

1	either	2	too	3	either
4	too	5	too	6	either
7	too	8	either	9	either
10	either	11	too	12	too
13	either	14	too	15	either
16	too	17	either	18	too

PRACTICE 8

1	well	2	good	3	well
4	good	5	well	6	well
7	good	8	good	9	good
10	well	11	well	12	good
13	good	14	well		

> 1, 3, 6, 10, 11, 14 동사를 수식하는 부사가 필요한 자리이므로 well이 알맞다.
> 1 sleep well: 잘 자다
> 3 eat well: 잘 먹다
> 6 know well: 잘 알다
> 10 do well: 잘 하다 *do well on: ~을 잘하다, 잘 보다
> 11 speak well: 잘 말하다
> 14 read well: 잘 읽다
> 2, 4, 9, 12 be동사 뒤 주격 보어 자리이므로 형용사 good이 알맞다.
> 5 get well은 '병이 나아지다'라는 뜻이다. 이때의 get은 '~한 상태로 변하다, ~한 상태가 되다'라는 뜻의 상태 변화를 나타내는 2형식 동사이므로 뒤에 형용사가 와야 한다. 따라서 get well의 well은 feel well에서처럼 '건강한, 몸이 좋은'이라는 뜻의 형용사로 쓰인 것이다.
> 7, 8 명사를 수식하는 형용사 자리이므로 good이 알맞다.
> 7 good place: 좋은 장소
> 8 good painter: 훌륭한 화가(그림을 잘 그리는 사람)
> 13 '감각동사 look+형용사'는 '~하게 보이다, ~처럼 보이다'라는 의미로, 형용사가 주격 보어 역할을 하므로 good이 알맞다.
> * look good on: ~에게 잘 어울리다

PRACTICE 9

1	on	2	off	3	on
4	away	5	up	6	back
7	off	8	on	9	back
10	on				

> 1 put on: 입다[쓰다/끼다]
> 2 turn off: (전원을) 끄다
> 3, 8 try on: 입어[신어]보다
> 4 throw away: 버리다
> 5 pick up: (차로) 데리러 가다
> 6, 9 bring back: 돌려주다
> 7 take off: 벗다
> 10 turn on: (전원을) 켜다

PRACTICE 10

1	turn on the radio	2	try them on
3	turn off the alarm	4	picked up Bob
5	threw away her hat	6	took his raincoat off
7	bring them back	8	put on her necklace
9	turn it on	10	throw them away
11	give him up	12	write her name down

> 1~12 turn on, try on, turn off, pick up, throw away, take off, bring back, put on, give up, write down은 모두 「타동사+부사」로 이루어진 동사구이다. 「타동사+부사」로 이루어진 동사구의 목적어로 일반명사가 올 때는 「타동사+명사+부사」와 「타동사+부사+명사」의 어순이 모두 가능하지만, 목적어가 대명사인 경우에는 반드시 「타동사+대명사+부사」 어순으로 써야 한다.

PRACTICE 11

1 Where is my bag?
2 How do you like this food?
3 When is her birthday?
4 Why did you call me?
5 How is the weather in Seoul?
6 When did Minsu finish the work?
7 Why doesn't he like the book?

8 Where are you going to travel?
9 Where did you eat lunch?
10 Why were you running?

> 1, 8, 9 장소/지역을 나타내는 표현으로 답하고 있으므로 의문부사 Where로 시작하는 의문문을 쓴다.
> 2 How do you like 표현을 사용하여 '~는 어때?'라는 뜻의 질문을 한다.
> 3, 6 시간을 나타내는 표현으로 답하고 있으므로 When으로 시작하는 의문문을 쓴다.
> 4, 7, 10 Because로 시작하는 '왜냐하면 ~이다'라고 답하고 있으므로 Why로 시작하는 의문문을 만든다.
> 5 How is the weather 표현을 사용하여 날씨를 묻는 질문을 한다.

PRACTICE 12

1	long	2	old	3	much
4	often	5	far	6	much
7	tall	8	many	9	many
10	long	11	old	12	long
13	far	14	tall	15	often

> 1, 10, 12 소요 시간/기간으로 답하고 있으므로 How long(얼마나 오래)이 알맞다.
> 2 나이로 답하고 있으므로 How old(몇 살)가 알맞다.
> 3, 6 금액으로 답하고 있으므로 How much(금액이 얼마인지)가 알맞다.
> 4, 15 every day(매일), once a month(한 달에 한 번) 같은 빈도 표현으로 답하고 있으므로 How often(얼마나 자주)이 알맞다.
> 5, 13 거리로 답하고 있으므로 How far(얼마나 먼)가 알맞다.
> 7 사람의 키로 답하고 있으므로 How tall(얼마나 큰)이 알맞다.
> 8, 9 셀 수 있는 명사(shoes, dog, cat)의 수량으로 답하고 있으므로 How many(얼마나 많은)가 알맞다.
> 11 B: About ten years old.(약 10년 정도 되었어.)라고 답하고 있으므로 질문은 '이 탁자가 얼마나 오래 되었니?'가 되는 것이 적절하다. How old는 '얼마나 오래 되었는지'의 뜻도 가지고 있다.
> 14 B: It has 27 stories.(그것은 27층이야.)라고 답하고 있으므로 질문은 '건물이 얼마나 높니?'가 되는 것이 적합하다. story는 명사로 '(건물의) 층'이라는 뜻도 갖고 있다.

PRACTICE 13

| 1 | ⓓ | 2 | ⓒ | 3 | ⓐ |
| 4 | ⓔ | 5 | ⓑ | | |

> 1 When 의문문이므로 시점을 밝힌 응답이 알맞다. → ⓓ 3일 후에
> 2 Why 의문문이므로 이유를 밝힌 응답이 알맞다. → ⓒ 병원에 가야 하기 때문에
> 3 How often 의문문이므로 빈도를 제시한 응답이 알맞다. → ⓐ 하루에 세 번
> 4 Where 의문문이므로 장소나 위치를 제시한 응답이 알맞다. → ⓔ 소파 뒤에
> 5 How old 의문문이므로 나이를 제시한 응답이 알맞다. → ⓑ 세 살이다

Chapter Review Test 정답 본문 _ p.236

1 ① 2 ① 3 ④ 4 ④ 5 ⑤ 6 ②
7 well 8 he never drinks coffee at night
9 ② 10 ④ 11 ⑤ 12 ② 13 ⑤
14 (1) Why did you go there (2) How long did you stay there 15 ③ 16 ① 17 ⑤ 18 ②
19 ⑤ 20 too 21 ④ 22 How 23 ③
24 ⑤ 25 ① 26 ② 27 (1) often (2) usually (3) sometimes (4) never (5) always 28 ②
29 ② 30 (L)uckily 31 ③ 32 ⑤ 33 ④
34 ⑤

Chapter Review Test 해설

1 빈도부사는 일반동사(dream) 앞에 위치한다.
2 교통수단으로 대답하고 있으므로 방법/수단을 묻는 의문부사 How가 와야 한다.
3 Ⓐ many는 셀 수 있는 명사의 복수형을 수식한다. 셀 수 있는 명사일 때 time은 '횟수, ~번'이라는 뜻이다. (time → times)
  Ⓑ 한 문장에서 접속사 없이 동사가 연달아 올 수 없다. 밑줄 친 부분은 동사의 목적어 자리이므로 like의 목적어가 될 수 있는 to부정사나 동명사로 써야 한다. like는 to부정사와 동명사 모두 목적어로 쓸 수 있는 동사이다. (play → to play[playing])
  Ⓒ water는 셀 수 없는 명사이다. 셀 수 없는 명사의 앞에는 부정관사를 쓰지 않는다. (drink a water → drink water)
  Ⓔ '시간이 있다'는 뜻은 정관사를 쓰지 않고 「have time」으로 쓴다. (have the time → have time)
4 try on '입어보다'   turn on '켜다'
5 장소로 대답하고 있으므로 장소를 묻는 의문부사 Where가 와야 한다.
6 too와 either는 '또한, 역시'의 뜻이며, either는 부정문에, too는 긍정문에 쓴다. also도 '역시'라는 뜻이지만 부정문에 쓰지 않고, 보통 be동사와 조동사 뒤, 일반동사 앞에 온다.
7 '잘, 훌륭하게'의 뜻을 나타내는 부사 well은 동사(cooks)를 수식한다.
8 빈도부사 never(절대로 ~않다)를 넣어 영작하는 문제이다. 빈도부사는 조동사 뒤, 일반동사 앞에 쓴다.
9 nice-nicely는 형용사-부사의 관계이다. '멋진-멋지

게'
① 명사-형용사: friend '친구'- friendly '친근한'
② 형용사-부사: careful '주의 깊은'- carefully '주의 깊게'
③ 형용사-형용사: elder '나이가 더 많은'- elderly '연세가 드신'
④ 명사-형용사: week '주'- weekly '매주의'
⑤ 명사-부사: luck '행운'- luckily '운 좋게'

10 25달러라는 가격으로 답하고 있으므로 가격을 묻는 표현 How much ~?가 적절하다.

11 Why don't we ~?는 '~하는 게 어때?'라는 뜻으로 쓰이는 관용표현이며, 장소를 물을 때는 의문부사 Where를 쓴다.

12 turn off '끄다'   take off '벗다'

13 ⑤ 빈도부사는 be동사 뒤에 위치한다.
(always is → is always)

14 (1) 이유를 대답하고 있으므로 이유를 묻는 의문부사 Why를 쓴다.
(2) 머문 기간을 대답하고 있으므로 기간을 묻는 How long을 쓴다.

15 ③ too와 either는 '또한, 역시'라는 뜻을 가지고 있지만 too는 긍정문에서, either는 부정문에서 쓰인다. (too → either)

16 한 달에 세 번이라는 빈도로 답하고 있으므로 빈도를 묻는 표현 How often ~?이 적절하다.

17 ⑤ look at은 '~를 보다'라는 뜻의 「자동사+전치사」로 이루어진 동사구이다. 전치사의 목적어는 항상 전치사의 뒤에 써야 한다. (looked it at → looked at it)

18 ② How long ~?은 기간 또는 걸리는 시간을 묻는 표현이므로 거리를 나타내는 It is 530km.와 어울리지 않는다. 거리를 묻는 표현은 How far ~?이다.

19 What time은 때를 묻는 의문부사 When과 바꾸어 쓸 수 있다.

20 also는 '또한, 역시'의 뜻으로 긍정문의 문장의 끝에 나오는 too와 같은 의미로 쓰인다.

21 ⓐ violin과 같은 악기명의 앞에는 정관사를 써야 한다. (violin → the violin)
ⓑ 주어(Mom and my sister)가 복수이므로 동사에 -s를 붙이지 않는다. (plays → play)
ⓒ 빈도부사는 일반동사의 앞에 쓴다. (goes often → often goes)
ⓔ hope는 목적어로 to부정사를 쓰는 동사이다. (having → to have)

22 • How long은 기간이나 걸린 시간을 묻는 표현이다.
• 방법을 묻는 의문부사 How가 와야 한다.

23 How often ~?은 빈도를 묻는 표현이므로 시간의 길이를 나타내는 An hour.는 적절하지 않다.

24 의문사로 시작하는 의문문은 Yes나 No로 대답할 수 없으며, 방법을 묻는 How에 어울리는 대답은 by train으로 답한 ⑤번이다.

25 ① '아침에 버스가 매우 늦게 도착했다'라는 의미가 되어야 하므로 '늦게'라는 뜻의 부사 late를 써야 한다. lately는 '최근에'라는 뜻의 부사이다. (lately → late)

26 뉴욕이라는 장소로 대답했으므로 장소를 묻는 의문부사 Where가 와야 한다.

27 일주일에 세 번은 often(종종), 일주일에 다섯 번은 usually(대개), 일주일에 한 번은 sometimes(때때로), 전혀 하지 않는 것은 never(결코 ~않는), 늘 하는 것은 always(항상)의 빈도부사를 쓴다.

28 보기의 단어는 형용사와, 형용사에 -ly가 붙어 만들어지는 부사로, 형용사-부사의 관계이다.
② 형용사-부사(시끄러운-시끄럽게)
① 동사-명사(놀다-선수)
③ 동사-형용사(말하다-수다스러운)
④ 동사원형-과거형(잡다-잡았다)
⑤ 명사-형용사(친구-친절한)

29 either는 부정문에 쓰여 '또한, 역시'의 뜻으로 앞 문장에 대한 동의를 나타낸다. A가 공포 영화를 보는 것을 좋아하지 않는다는 말에 B도 동의하고 있으므로 I don't, either.는 I don't like watching horror movies.를 나타낸다.

30 lucky의 부사형은 luckily이다.

31 기차역이라는 장소로 답했으므로 장소를 나타내는 의문부사 where가 와야 한다.

32 ⑤ fast는 형용사와 부사의 형태가 같다.
(fastly → fast)

33 (A) It's not 뒤에는 주격 보어로 명사나 형용사가 올 수 있다. 문맥상 쉽지 않다는 내용이 들어가야 하므로 형용사인 easy가 와야 한다.
(B) 문맥상 올해 말쯤 자신이 제일 좋아하는 곡을 '아름답게' 연주할 수 있기를 바란다는 내용이 와야 하므로 동사를 수식하는 부사 beautifully가 답이다.

34 ⑤ Lucy는 목요일에 버스를 타고 직장에 가므로 'Lucy는 결코 직장에 버스를 타고 가지 않는다.'는 표의 내용과 다르다.

CHAPTER 12 비교구문 Comparisons

본문 _ p.242

PRACTICE 1

1 kinder, kindest
2 larger, largest
3 taller, tallest
4 louder, loudest
5 safer, safest
6 weaker, weakest
7 greater, greatest
8 softer, softest
9 lower, lowest
10 huger, hugest
11 smarter, smartest
12 cheaper, cheapest
13 nicer, nicest
14 stronger, strongest
15 cleaner, cleanest
16 faster, fastest
17 poorer, poorest
18 braver, bravest
19 sweeter, sweetest
20 fresher, freshest

PRACTICE 2

1 hotter, hottest
2 lighter, lightest
3 milder, mildest
4 noisier, noisiest
5 heavier, heaviest
6 fatter, fattest
7 wiser, wisest
8 sunnier, sunniest
9 dirtier, dirtiest
10 cooler, coolest
11 warmer, warmest
12 happier, happiest
13 hungrier, hungriest
14 bigger, biggest
15 wetter, wettest
16 tastier, tastiest
17 stricter, strictest
18 uglier, ugliest
19 prettier, prettiest
20 harder, hardest

PRACTICE 3

1 busier, busiest
2 more interesting, most interesting
3 more beautiful, most beautiful
4 brighter, brightest
5 more seriously, most seriously
6 more careful, most careful
7 friendlier, friendliest
8 more important, most important
9 gladder, gladdest
10 more expensive, most expensive
11 lovelier, loveliest
12 more quickly, most quickly
13 more useful, most useful
14 quieter, quietest
15 more exciting, most exciting
16 more special, most special
17 sooner, soonest
18 more difficult, most difficult
19 closer, closest
20 more helpful, most helpful
21 more popular, most popular
22 easier, easiest
23 more colorful, most colorful
24 tougher, toughest
25 more curious, most curious
26 more delicious, most delicious
27 nearer, nearest
28 more dangerous, most dangerous
29 more diligent, most diligent
30 luckier, luckiest

PRACTICE 4

1 darker, darkest
2 older, oldest
3 more boring, most boring
4 slower, slowest
5 more terrible, most terrible
6 more tired, most tired
7 more various, most various
8 smaller, smallest
9 worse, worst
10 more wonderful, most wonderful
11 better, best
12 costlier, costliest
13 more similar, most similar
14 later, latest
15 richer, richest
16 further, furthest
17 cuter, cutest
18 younger, youngest
19 farther/further, farthest/furthest
20 more famous, most famous
21 thinner, thinnest
22 more faithful, most faithful
23 slimmer, slimmest
24 worse, worst

CHAPTER 12

25 more patient, most patient
26 thicker, thickest
27 more useless, most useless
28 more handsome[handsomer], most handsome[handsomest]
29 thirstier, thirstiest
30 worse, worst
31 more heavily, most heavily
32 deeper, deepest
33 angrier, angriest
34 latter, last
35 elder, eldest
36 colder, coldest
37 more, most
38 more different, most different
39 more foolish, most foolish
40 less, least
41 more easily, most easily
42 more peaceful, most peaceful
43 more, most
44 more generous, most generous
45 higher, highest
46 more crowded, most crowded
47 funnier, funniest
48 more comfortable, most comfortable
49 better, best
50 more hopeless, most hopeless
51 longer, longest

PRACTICE 5

1 as well as
2 as small as
3 not as[so] tall as
4 as interesting as
5 not as[so] angry as
6 as clever as
7 not as[so] slow as
8 as cold as
9 as simple as
10 not as[so] loud as

PRACTICE 6

1 isn't as[so] old as
2 is as expensive as
3 isn't as[so] long as
4 is as high as
5 don't clean my room as[so] often as
6 is as huge as

7 can't go as[so] fast as
8 is as honest as
9 isn't as[so] thick as
10 doesn't look as[so] fresh as

> 1, 3, 5, 7, 9, 10 비교하는 두 대상의 정도에 차이가 있으므로 '~만큼 …하지 않은'이라는 뜻이 되도록 「not as[so]+원급+as」 구문을 사용한다.
> not as[so] old as: ~만큼 나이가 많지 않은
> not as[so] long as: ~만큼 길지 않은
> not as[so] often as: ~만큼 자주는 아닌
> not as[so] fast as: ~만큼 빨리는 아닌
> not as[so] thick as: ~만큼 두껍지 않은
> not as[so] fresh as: ~만큼 신선하지 않은
> 2, 4, 6, 8 비교하는 두 대상의 정도가 같으므로 '~만큼 …한'이라는 뜻이 되도록 「as+원급+as」를 사용한다.
> as expensive as: ~만큼 비싼
> as high as: ~만큼 높은
> as huge as: ~만큼 거대한
> as honest as: ~만큼 정직한

PRACTICE 7

2 heavier than
3 better than
4 cooler than
5 more careful than
6 younger than
7 more interesting than
8 more beautiful than
9 more quickly than
10 brighter than
11 newer than
12 more modern than
13 higher than
14 more difficult than
15 more useful than
16 quieter than
17 more intelligent than
18 worse than

> 2 heavier than yours: 네 것보다 무거운
> 3 better than hers: 그녀의 것보다 더 나은
> (good-better-best)
> 4 cooler than this week: 이번 주보다 더 시원한
> 5 more careful than her sister: 그녀의 언니보다 더 주의 깊은
> 6 younger than Minho: 민호보다 더 어린
> 7 more interesting than the play: 그 연극보다 더 흥미로운
> 8 more beautiful than Mr. Kim's: 김 선생님의 것보다 더 아름다운
> 9 more quickly than Miss Ford: Ford 씨보다 더 빠르게
> 10 brighter than before: 이전보다 더 밝은
> 11 newer than mine: 내 것보다 더 새로운
> 12 more modern than that one: 저것보다 더 현대적인
> 13 higher than our voices: 우리의 목소리보다 더 높은
> 14 more difficult than eating: 먹는 것보다 더 어려운
> 15 more useful than butterflies: 나비보다 더 유용한
> 16 quieter than the cafeteria: 구내식당보다 더 조용한
> 17 more intelligent than dogs: 개보다 더 지적인
> 18 worse than no excuse: 변명을 안 하는 것보다 더 나쁜
> (bad-worse-worst)

CHAPTER **14**

18 • walk around '~ 주위를 걷다'
 • work for '~에서 일하다'
19 on+요일
 ① There are no classes on Saturday and Sunday.
20 ⓐ spend ~ on … '…에 ~를 소비하다[쓰다]'
 ⓑ like '~처럼, ~같이'
 ⓒ for '~을 위해' (for future purposes '미래의 목적을 위해')
21 across '~건너편에, 맞은편에'
22 in+마을, 도시, 국가와 같은 넓은 장소
 at+구체적인 시각
 on+특정한 날
23 조깅하면서 영어 팟캐스트를 듣는다는 내용, 집에 돌아오는 길에 차에 기름을 넣고 세탁소도 들를 것이라는 내용, 출장차 런던에 가 있는 동안 친척 집도 방문했다는 내용은 모두 일석이조의 상황을 가리키므로 Kill two birds with one stone. 이 적절하다.
24 on the[one's] way home '집에 가는 길에'
25 은행을 기준으로 타임스퀘어의 위치를 나타낼 때 빈칸에 위치나 방향을 나타내는 전치사가 들어가야 한다.
 ④ looking for는 '~를 찾는'이라는 뜻으로 빈칸에 들어갈 수 없다.
26 ③ on foot '걸어서'
 ①②④⑤ by+교통수단 '~을 타고'
27 to는 go, come과 같은 동사와 함께 쓰여 도착 지점을 나타낸다.
 on a subway '지하철을 타고'
 cf. 교통수단 앞에 관사가 없는 경우에는 by를 쓴다.
 by subway '지하철을 타고'
28 like '~처럼, ~같이'
29 ① Yesterday라는 과거를 나타내는 부사가 쓰였으므로, 동사도 과거시제로 써야 한다. (take → took)
 ② '강을 따라서 걷고 있었다'라는 해석이 자연스러우므로, '~을 따라서'라는 뜻의 전치사 along을 써야 한다. on은 표면 상에 맞닿은 것을 말한다. (on → along)
 ④ 개가 세 마리 있다고 언급되어 있으므로 '(셋 이상의) ~ 사이에'라는 뜻의 전치사 among을 써야 한다. between은 두 개의 대상 사이를 지칭한다. (between → among)
 ⑤ 완료형 시제와 함께 쓰였으므로 과거부터 시작한 일이 현재까지 지속되는 것을 나타내는 전치사 since를 써야 한다. from은 완료형 이외의 시제들과 함께 쓰인다. (from → since)
30 ② '좋아하다' (동사)
 ①③④⑤ '~처럼, ~같이' (전치사)
31 without '~ 없이'
32 be full of '~로 가득 차다' be good for '~에 좋다'
33 • 그녀는 꽃에 관한 책을 읽었다.
 • 아이들은 그들 주위에 있는 모든 것에 호기심을 갖는다.
 ⑤ write about '~대해 글을 쓰다'
 ① look at '~을 보다'
 ② be afraid of '~을 두려워하다'
 ③ be famous for '~으로 유명하다'
 ④ be interested in '~에 흥미[관심]가 있다'
34 be different from '~와 다르다'
 different를 수식하는 quite는 different 앞에 쓴다.
35 ④ 동사 like '좋아하다'
 ①②③⑤ 전치사 like '~처럼, ~같이'
36 ④ look at '~을 보다'
 ① arrive at '~에 도착하다'
 ② by+교통수단 '~를 타고'
 ③ into '~ 안으로'
 ⑤ from '~로부터'
37 전치사 in은 우주나 하늘을 나타내는 표현과 함께 쓴다.
 ② Look at the beautiful kites in the sky.
 ④ '해변에서'라는 뜻은 on the beach로 나타낸다.
 ⑤ be on a diet '식이요법 중이다'
38 (1) buy … for ~ '~에게 …을 사주다'
 (2) about '~에 대해'
39 각 나라에 맞는 식사 예절을 지키라는 내용이므로 '로마에 가면 로마의 법을 따르라.'는 뜻의 When in Rome, do as the Romans do.가 적절하다.
40 • 하나의 지점을 나타낼 때는 at을 쓴다.
  그 버스는 광화문에서 선다.
 • 도구와 함께 쓰이는 with는 '~을 가지고'의 뜻을 나타낸다. 그녀는 그녀의 엄지 손가락과 검지 손가락으로 원을 만들었다.
 • 길을 말할 때는 on을 쓴다. 5번가에 백화점이 있다.
41 look for '~을 찾다'
 look at '~을 보다'
42 특정한 시점 앞에는 at을 쓴다.

CHAPTER 12

25 more patient, most patient
26 thicker, thickest
27 more useless, most useless
28 more handsome[handsomer], most handsome[handsomest]
29 thirstier, thirstiest
30 worse, worst
31 more heavily, most heavily
32 deeper, deepest
33 angrier, angriest
34 latter, last
35 elder, eldest
36 colder, coldest
37 more, most
38 more different, most different
39 more foolish, most foolish
40 less, least
41 more easily, most easily
42 more peaceful, most peaceful
43 more, most
44 more generous, most generous
45 higher, highest
46 more crowded, most crowded
47 funnier, funniest
48 more comfortable, most comfortable
49 better, best
50 more hopeless, most hopeless
51 longer, longest

PRACTICE 5

1 as well as
2 as small as
3 not as[so] tall as
4 as interesting as
5 not as[so] angry as
6 as clever as
7 not as[so] slow as
8 as cold as
9 as simple as
10 not as[so] loud as

PRACTICE 6

1 isn't as[so] old as
2 is as expensive as
3 isn't as[so] long as
4 is as high as
5 don't clean my room as[so] often as
6 is as huge as
7 can't go as[so] fast as
8 is as honest as
9 isn't as[so] thick as
10 doesn't look as[so] fresh as

1, 3, 5, 7, 9, 10 비교하는 두 대상의 정도에 차이가 있으므로 '~만큼 …하지 않은'이라는 뜻이 되도록 「not as[so]+원급+as」 구문을 사용한다.
not as[so] old as: ~만큼 나이가 많지 않은
not as[so] long as: ~만큼 길지 않은
not as[so] often as: ~만큼 자주는 아닌
not as[so] fast as: ~만큼 빠르는 아닌
not as[so] thick as: ~만큼 두껍지 않은
not as[so] fresh as: ~만큼 신선하지 않은
2, 4, 6, 8 비교하는 두 대상의 정도가 같으므로 '~만큼 …한'이라는 뜻이 되도록 「as+원급+as」를 사용한다.
as expensive as: ~만큼 비싼
as high as: ~만큼 높은
as huge as: ~만큼 거대한
as honest as: ~만큼 정직한

PRACTICE 7

2 heavier than
3 better than
4 cooler than
5 more careful than
6 younger than
7 more interesting than
8 more beautiful than
9 more quickly than
10 brighter than
11 newer than
12 more modern than
13 higher than
14 more difficult than
15 more useful than
16 quieter than
17 more intelligent than
18 worse than

2 heavier than yours: 네 것보다 무거운
3 better than hers: 그녀의 것보다 더 나은 (good-better-best)
4 cooler than this week: 이번 주보다 더 시원한
5 more careful than her sister: 그녀의 언니보다 더 주의 깊은
6 younger than Minho: 민호보다 더 어린
7 more interesting than the play: 그 연극보다 더 흥미로운
8 more beautiful than Mr. Kim's: 김 선생님의 것보다 더 아름다운
9 more quickly than Miss Ford: Ford 씨보다 더 빠르게
10 brighter than before: 이전보다 더 밝은
11 newer than mine: 내 것보다 더 새로운
12 more modern than that one: 저것보다 더 현대적인
13 higher than our voices: 우리의 목소리보다 더 높은
14 more difficult than eating: 먹는 것보다 더 어려운
15 more useful than butterflies: 나비보다 더 유용한
16 quieter than the cafeteria: 구내식당보다 더 조용한
17 more intelligent than dogs: 개보다 더 지적인
18 worse than no excuse: 변명을 안 하는 것보다 더 나쁜 (bad-worse-worst)

PRACTICE 8

1	more beautiful	2	kind
3	smaller	4	much
5	popular	6	slower
7	busy	8	less
9	cheaper	10	cute
11	older	12	farther
13	often	14	easier
15	cleaner	16	brave
17	dirtier		

> 1, 3, 6, 8, 9, 11, 12, 14, 15, 17 괄호 뒤에 'than+비교 대상'이 왔으므로 「-er than」 또는 「more+원급+than」 형태의 비교급 구문이 되어야 한다. 8번의 little(little-less-least)과 12번의 far(far-farther-farthest)는 불규칙 변화하는 단어들이다.
> 2, 4, 5, 7, 10, 13, 16 괄호 앞뒤에 as가 왔으므로 「as+원급+as」 구문이 되어야 한다. 4번의 much의 비교급은 more, 최상급은 most이다.

PRACTICE 9

1 poorer and poorer
2 more and more handsome
  [handsomer and handsomer]
3 redder and redder
4 more and more boring
5 better and better
6 worse and worse
7 quieter and quieter
8 fatter and fatter
9 more and more heavily
10 cheaper and cheaper
11 whiter and whiter
12 warmer and warmer

> 1 become poorer and poorer: 점점 더 가난해지다
> 2 become more and more handsome: 점점 더 잘생겨지다
> 3 turn redder and redder: 점점 더 빨갛게 변하다
> 4 get more and more boring: 점점 더 지루해지다
> 5 get better and better: 점점 더 나아지다
> 6 get worse and worse: 점점 더 나빠지다
> 7 become quieter and quieter: 점점 더 조용해지다
> 8 grow fatter and fatter: 점점 더 살이 찌다
> 9 rain more and more heavily: 점점 더 비가 심하게 오다
> 10 become cheaper and cheaper: 점점 더 싸지다
> 11 turn whiter and whiter: 점점 더 하얘지다
> 12 get warmer and warmer: 점점 더 따뜻해지다
> *become/turn/get/grow+형용사: ~해지다, (~한 상태로) 변하다

PRACTICE 10

1	far more important	2	a lot better
3	much stricter	4	even harder
5	much more helpful	6	still thinner
7	even stronger	8	far more convenient
9	still safer	10	a lot more

> 1 far more important than money: 돈보다 훨씬 더 중요한
> 2 a lot better than her sister's: 그녀의 언니의 것보다 훨씬 더 나은
> 3 much stricter rules than his: 그의 것보다 훨씬 더 엄격한 규칙
> 4 even harder than he did: 그가 했던 것보다 훨씬 더 열심히
> 5 much more helpful to me than they were: 나에게 그들보다 훨씬 더 도움이 되는
> 6 still thinner than his: 그의 것보다 훨씬 더 얇은
> 7 even stronger than lions: 사자들보다 훨씬 더 힘이 센
> 8 far more convenient than air mail: 항공우편보다 훨씬 더 편리한
> 9 still safer than that one: 저것보다 훨씬 더 안전한
> 10 a lot more rain than Rome: 로마보다 훨씬 더 많은 비

PRACTICE 11

1	O	2	X	3	O	4	X
5	X	6	O	7	O	8	O
9	O	10	X	11	X	12	X
13	X	14	O	15	O		

> 2, 5, 10, 12 even, a lot, much, far 같은 부사는 비교급 앞에서 '훨씬, 더욱'의 뜻으로 쓰여 비교급을 강조한다. 따라서 밑줄 친 부분을 원급을 수식하는 very로 바꿔야 한다.
> 4, 11, 13 very는 '매우'의 뜻으로 형용사나 부사의 원급을 수식한다. 따라서 비교급 앞에서 '훨씬'의 뜻으로 쓰여 비교급을 강조하는 even, much, still, far, a lot 같은 부사로 바꿔야 한다.

PRACTICE 12

2	the most important	3	the youngest
4	the happiest	5	the worst
6	the heaviest	7	the brightest
8	the poorest	9	the highest
10	the best	11	the least
12	the fastest	13	the most interesting
14	the latest	15	the thickest

> 최상급 뒤에 in이나 of가 이끄는 전치사구가 와서 비교의 대상을 한정하는 경우가 많은데, 앞뒤 문맥상으로 그 내용을 미루어 짐작할 수 있는 경우에는 'the+최상급' 뒤에 오는 명사를 생략하기도 한다.
> 1 the coldest day of the year: 일 년 중 가장 추운 날

2 the most important person in the group: 그 집단에서 가장 중요한 사람
3 the youngest (child) of his brothers: 그의 형제들 중에서 가장 막내 (아이)
4 the happiest day of his life: 그의 인생에서 가장 행복한 날
5 the worst choice of my life: 내 인생에서 가장 나쁜 선택
6 the heaviest (bag) of them all: 그것들 모두 중에서 가장 무거운 (가방)
7 the brightest (room) in this house: 이 집에서 가장 밝은 (방)
8 the poorest people in the village: 그 마을에서 가장 가난한 사람들
9 the highest mountain in the world: 세계에서 가장 높은 산
10 the best singer of pop music: 팝음악에서 가장 우수한 가수
11 the least work in the team: 그 팀에서 가장 적은 일
12 the fastest (animal) of all animals: 모든 동물 중에서 가장 빠른 (동물)
13 the most interesting (picture) of them all: 그것들 모두 중에서 가장 흥미로운 (그림)
14 the latest news: 최신 뉴스(late-later-latest)
15 the thickest tree in the garden: 정원에서 가장 굵은 나무

PRACTICE 13

1 one of the most exciting festivals
2 one of the nicest restaurants
3 one of the highest scores
4 one of the most beautiful cities
5 one of the biggest animals
6 one of the most handsome[the handsomest] actors
7 one of the most pleasant[the pleasantest] presents
8 one of the most expensive things
9 one of the strongest boys
10 one of the most faithful animals

「one of the+최상급」 뒤에는 복수 명사가 와서 '가장 ~한 것들 중의 하나'라는 뜻을 나타낸다.
1 one of the most exciting festivals: 가장 신나는 축제들 중의 하나
2 one of the nicest restaurants: 가장 멋진 식당들 중의 하나
3 one of the highest scores: 가장 높은 점수들 중의 하나
4 one of the most beautiful cities: 가장 아름다운 도시들 중의 하나
5 one of the biggest animals: 가장 큰 동물들 중의 하나
6 one of the most handsome actors: 가장 잘생긴 배우들 중의 하나
7 one of the most pleasant presents: 가장 기분 좋은 선물들 중의 하나
8 one of the most expensive things: 가장 비싼 것들 중의 하나
9 one of the strongest boys: 가장 강한 소년들 중의 하나
10 one of the most faithful animals: 가장 충직한 동물들 중의 하나

PRACTICE 14

1 Ted 2 Cathy 3 John
4 Cathy 5 John

1 원급 as tall as(~만큼 키가 큰)로 비교하고 있으므로 빈칸에는 John과 키가 같은 Ted가 알맞다.
2 비교급 taller than(~보다 키가 큰)으로 비교하고 있으므로 빈칸에는 John보다 키가 작은 Cathy가 알맞다.
3 not as old as(~만큼 나이가 많지 않은)가 쓰였다. 즉, 'Ted는 _____만큼 나이가 많지 않다'는 뜻이므로 빈칸에는 John(25세)이 와야 한다.
4 비교급 younger than(~보다 어린)으로 비교하고 있으므로 빈칸에는 Ted보다 어린 Cathy가 알맞다.
5 최상급 the oldest of(~ 중에서 가장 나이가 든)를 이용해 비교하고 있으므로 빈칸에는 셋 중 나이가 가장 많은 John이 알맞다.

PRACTICE 15

1 fattest 2 brightest 3 smarter
4 difficult 5 cool 6 much
7 babies 8 biggest 9 quieter
10 men 11 healthy 12 even
13 sports 14 more 15 much

1, 2, 8 the의 수식을 받으며, 뒤에 비교의 대상을 한정하는 in, of가 이끄는 전치사구가 왔으므로 최상급이 알맞다.
the fattest of them all: 그들 모두 중에서 가장 뚱뚱한
the brightest star in the sky: 하늘에서 가장 밝은 별
the biggest of all the bees: 모든 벌들 중에서 가장 큰
3, 9 뒤에 비교 대상을 나타내는 than이 왔으므로 비교급이 알맞다.
smarter than dogs: 개들보다 더 똑똑한
quieter than her sister: 그녀의 여동생보다 더 조용한
4, 5, 6 앞뒤에 as가 왔으므로 as ~ as …(…만큼 ~한) 구문을 이루는 원급이 알맞다.
as difficult as that one: 저것만큼 어려운
not as cool as that one: 저것만큼 시원하지 않은
not as much money as her friends did: 그녀의 친구만큼 많지 않은 돈
7, 10, 13 「one of the+최상급」 뒤에는 복수 명사가 와서 '가장 ~한 것들 중의 하나'라는 뜻을 나타낸다.
one of the loveliest babies: 가장 사랑스러운 아기들 중 하나
one of the happiest men at the party: 파티에서 가장 행복한 남자들 중 하나
one of the most exciting sports: 가장 신나는 스포츠들 중 하나
11 very는 '매우'의 뜻으로 형용사나 부사의 원급을 수식한다.
very healthy food: 매우 건강에 좋은 음식
12, 15 비교급 앞에는 부사인 even, much, still, far, a lot가 와서 '훨씬, 더욱'의 뜻으로 비교급을 강조한다.
even worse than before: 이전보다 훨씬 나쁜
much smaller than my house: 우리 집보다 훨씬 더 작은
14 「비교급+and+비교급」은 get, become, grow, turn과 같은 동사들과 함께 쓰여 '점점 더 ~하다'라는 뜻을 나타낸다.
become more and more famous: 점점 더 유명해지다

Chapter Review Test 정답 본문 _ p.258

1 ③ **2** ② **3** ⑤ **4** one of the most famous musicians **5** ⑤ **6** Dogs are not so big as bears. **7** (1) as old as (2) as early as **8** animals in **9** ④ **10** more difficult than **11** ① **12** ④ **13** (1) taller (2) younger (3) the oldest (4) the heaviest **14** longer and longer **15** ⑤ **16** ②,⑤ **17** ⑤ **18** ④ **19** (1) the most expensive (2) the largest (3) the most delicious **20** the cheapest **21** ② **22** ② **23** ⑤ **24** ⑤ **25** ④ **26** (1) better (2) better **27** ④ **28** ④,⑤ **29** ② **30** ⑤ **31** ①

Chapter Review Test 해설

1 ⓐ의 앞에 the가 있는 것으로 보아 ⓐ에는 최상급인 largest가 들어가고, ⓑ의 뒤에는 than이 있으므로 ⓑ에는 비교급인 larger가 들어간다.

2 funny의 비교급은 funnier이므로 more와 함께 쓸 수 없다.

3 「as+원급+as」 '~만큼 …한'
원급의 형태로 '잘, 훌륭하게'라는 뜻의 부사 well이 들어가야 한다.

4 「one of the+최상급+복수명사」 '가장 ~한 것들 중에 하나'
famous는 앞에 most를 붙여 최상급을 만든다.

5 ⑤ brave의 비교급은 braver이다.
(more brave → braver)

6 「not so[as]+원급+as」 '~만큼 …하지 않은'

7 「as+원급+as」 '~만큼 …한'
cf. 원급은 형용사나 부사의 원형을 말한다.

8 「one of the+최상급+복수명사+in+장소, 범위」

9 like A better than B 'B보다 A를 더 좋아한다'

10 비교급을 이용한 비교는 「비교급+than」으로 나타낸다. 2음절 이상인 difficult의 비교급은 more difficult이다.

11 ① beautiful은 2음절 이상이므로 앞에 most를 붙여 최상급을 만든다. (beautifulest → most beautiful)

12 ④ Cheese burger가 $3.99로 메뉴 중에서 가장 저렴하다.

13 (1),(2) 비교급+than
(3),(4) the+최상급+(명사)+of+복수명사

14 '점점 더 ~한'은 「비교급+and+비교급」의 형태로 표현한다.

15 ① 가장 인기가 없는 것은 농구이다.
(Soccer → Basketball)
② 야구가 농구보다 인기가 많다. (Basketball is more popular than baseball. → Baseball is more popular than basketball.)
③ 축구가 농구보다 인기가 많다. (less → more)
④ 야구는 축구보다 인기가 많다. (Baseball is as popular as soccer. → Baseball is more popular than soccer.)

16 ① 비교급은 even/much/still/far/a lot으로 강조한다. (very → even[much/still/far/a lot])
③ '점점 더 ~한'은 「비교급+and+비교급」으로 나타내는데 dark의 비교급은 darker이다.
(more and more dark → darker and darker)
④ 비교급을 이용한 비교는 「비교급+than」으로 쓴다. 정관사는 쓰지 않는다. (the heavier → heavier)

17 ① good의 최상급은 best이다. (the bestest → the best)
② '가장 ~한 것들 중의 하나'라는 의미를 나타낼 때에는 「one of the+최상급+복수명사」의 문형으로 쓴다. (activity → activities)
③ strong의 최상급은 strongest이다. (the most strongest → the strongest)
④ difficult의 최상급은 most difficult이다. (the difficultest → the most difficult)

18 • '~보다'의 뜻인 than이 있으므로 비교급의 형태 (longer)가 와야 한다.
cf. a lot은 비교급을 강조하는 부사
• 「the+최상급+(명사)+of/in」은 '~중에서 가장 …한' 의 표현으로 최상급의 형태(longest)가 와야 한다.

19 「the+최상급+(명사)」 '가장 …한'

20 cheap(싼)의 최상급은 the cheapest(가장 싼)이다.

21 분홍색과 파란색 중 더 좋아하는 색에 대해 물었으므로 대답도 둘 중 더 좋아하는 것으로 답해야 한다. ② 번은 파란색이 더 어둡다는 것이므로 대답으로 적절하지 않다.
분홍색과 파란색 중 어느 색을 더 좋아하니?
② 파란색이 분홍색보다 더 어둡다.

22 ② latter: (순서가) 나중의, 후자의 (latter → later)

23 ① 최상급 뒤에 '~중에서 가장 ...한'의 뜻으로 비교의 대상을 한정해 주려면 전치사 of를 사용하여 「the+최상급+(명사)+of+복수명사」의 어순으로 써야 한다. (all movies → of all movies)
② hot의 올바른 비교급은 hotter이다. 단모음+단자음으로 끝나는 1음절 단어이므로 마지막 자음을 하나 더 씀에 유의한다. (more hot → hotter)
③ 원급 비교는 「as+원급+as」의 어순으로 쓴다. (long as → as long as)
④ '가장 ~한 것들 중의 하나'라는 의미는 「one of the+최상급+복수명사」의 어순으로 쓴다. funny의 최상급은 funniest이다. 자음+y로 끝나는 경우 y를 i로 바꾸고 -est를 붙임에 유의한다. (funny → funniest)

24 비교급은 even/much/still/far/a lot으로 강조한다.
⑤ My car is even[much/still/far/a lot] bigger than your brother's.

25 Sena의 수면 시간은 8시간 30분, Yumi의 수면 시간은 8시간으로 Sena가 더 오래 잔다.
④ Sena sleeps longer than Yumi.

26 well과 good의 비교급은 better이다.

27 표에 따르면 C의 용량은 20,000mAh, B의 용량은 10,000mAh이므로, 「비교급+than」을 써서 C의 용량이 더 크다는 사실을 옳게 나타낸 ④가 정답이다.

28 ④ '~보다'의 뜻인 than이 있으므로 비교급의 형태 (earlier)가 와야 한다. (early → earlier)
⑤ 「one of the+최상급+복수명사」 '가장 ~한 것들 중의 하나'
cheap의 최상급은 cheapest로 쓴다.
(most cheap steak → cheapest steaks)

29 (1) 세 번째 줄의 pretty는 최상급을 prettiest로 쓴다. 자음+y로 끝나는 경우 y를 i로 바꾸고 -est를 붙임에 유의한다. (most pretty → prettiest)
(2) 마지막에서 두 번째 줄의 very cheaper에서, 비교급을 수식할 수 있는 것은 even, much, still, far, a lot이다. very는 형용사나 부사의 원급만을 수식한다. (very →even/much/still/far/a lot)

30 ⑤ 나의 방이 너의 방보다 깨끗하지 않다고 했으므로 같은 의미의 문장은 '너의 방이 나의 방보다 깨끗하다'라는 뜻의 'Your room is cleaner than my room.'이 되어야 한다.
나의 방은 너의 방보다 깨끗하지 않다.
≠ 너의 방은 나의 방만큼 깨끗하다.

31 ② '가장 ~한 것들 중의 하나'라는 의미는 「one of the+최상급+복수명사」의 어순으로 쓴다.
(team → teams)
③ 형용사의 뒤에 than이 나오므로 비교급으로 써야 한다. comfortable은 2음절 이상의 단어이므로 앞에 more를 붙여서 비교급을 만든다. 이때 정관사는 쓰지 않는다. (the most comfortable → more comfortable)
④ 최상급 뒤에 '~중에서 가장 ...한'의 뜻으로 비교의 대상을 한정해 주려면 전치사 of를 사용하여 「the+최상급+(명사)+of+복수명사」의 어순으로 써야 한다. (at → of)
⑤ 비교의 대상이 My hair이므로 yours 또는 your hair로 받아야 한다. (you → yours[your hair])

CHAPTER 13 접속사
Conjunctions

본문 _ p.264

PRACTICE 1

1 but	2 and	3 and
4 but	5 and	6 but
7 and	8 but	9 but
10 and	11 but	12 and

1, 4, 6, 8, 9, 11 앞의 내용과 반대되거나 대조되는 내용을 연결할 때는 접속사 but을 사용한다.
2, 3, 5, 7, 10, 12 앞의 내용과 비슷하거나 대등한 내용을 연결할 때는 접속사 and를 사용한다.

PRACTICE 2

1 or	2 but	3 and
4 or	5 or	6 and
7 or	8 and	9 or
10 or	11 and	12 or

1, 4, 9 명령문 다음에 접속사 or를 사용하면 '~해라 그렇지 않으면 ~'이라는 뜻을 나타낸다.
2 앞의 내용과 반대되는 내용을 연결할 때는 접속사 but을 사용한다.
3, 6, 11 명령문 다음에 접속사 and를 사용하면 '~해라 그러면~'이라는 뜻을 나타낸다.
*succeed: 성공하다
*put on: ~을 입다
5, 7, 10, 12 '둘 중 하나'의 뜻을 표현할 때는 접속사 or를 사용한다.
8 앞의 내용과 대등한 내용을 연결할 때는 접속사 and를 사용한다.

PRACTICE 3

1 Turn right, and you will see the post office.
2 Put salt on your hamburger, or it won't taste good.
3 Call him, and he will help you.
4 Take the medicine, or you won't feel better.
5 Eat all your dinner, and you can have some ice cream.
6 Go now, or you can't avoid traffic jams.
7 Wait a moment, and I'll come and open the door.
8 Get up early, or you won't see the sunrise.

1, 3, 5, 7 If 조건절은 '만약 ~한다면, ~할 것이다.'라는 뜻이기 때문에 주절의 조동사를 그대로 사용하여 '명령문, and~'구문으로 바꾸면 된다.
2, 4, 6, 8 명령문+or 구문을 사용하여 '~해라, 그렇지 않으면~'으로 표현해야 하는데, If 조건절이 '만약 ~한다면, ~할 것이다.'라는 뜻이기 때문에 주절의 조동사를 반대로 (긍정 → 부정, 부정 → 긍정) 쓰면 된다.
2 햄버거에 소금을 넣어라, 그렇지 않으면 맛이 없을 것이다.
4 약을 먹어라, 그렇지 않으면 (몸 상태가) 더 나아지지 않을 것이다.
6 지금 가라, 그렇지 않으면 교통 체증을 피할 수 없을 것이다.
8 일찍 일어나라, 그렇지 않으면 해가 뜨는 것을 볼 수 없을 것이다.

PRACTICE 4

1 but	2 but	3 and	4 so
5 so	6 and	7 so	8 or
9 so	10 or		

PRACTICE 5

1 Minji believes √ there is a God.
2 The doctor says √ I have a cold.
3 I don't think √ it is a nice restaurant.
4 They wish √ they weren't late.
5 Do you believe √ she is kind?
6 Kate thinks √ there is no one at home now.
7 I wish √ I could meet your family soon.
8 Sumi hopes √ she can speak English well.
9 Did you know √ the dolphin is very clever?
10 People say √ only the strongest man survives.

PRACTICE 6

1 that it is a nice building
2 that we will stay there for two days
3 that the weather would be fine
4 that Mary is the prettiest girl
5 that he could do well on his test

PRACTICE 7

1 If it snows, we will go skiing.
We will go skiing if it snows.
2 Because she got up late, she took a taxi.
She took a taxi because she got up late.

3 When I took a walk, I met my best friend.
I met my best friend when I took a walk.

4 Because there are no traffic lights, this road is dangerous.
This road is dangerous because there are no traffic lights.

5 When it rains hard, my uncle usually listens to music.
My uncle usually listens to music when it rains hard.

6 If you go to the supermarket, buy some milk for me.
Buy some milk for me if you go to the supermarket.

7 Because I was tired, I went home early.
I went home early because I was tired.

8 When he heard the news, he cried.
He cried when he heard the news.

9 If you ask Ms. Han about the problem, you'll get the answer.
You'll get the answer if you ask Ms. Han about the problem.

10 Because I didn't dress warmly, I have a cold.
I have a cold because I didn't dress warmly.

PRACTICE 8

1	A	2	C	3	B	4	C
5	B	6	C	7	B	8	A
9	A	10	C				

[보기]
(A) As the days get long, the nights get short. (~함에 따라, ~할수록)
낮이 길어질수록, 밤은 짧아진다.
(B) As I said before, it's all about me. (~처럼, ~대로)
내가 전에 말했던 것처럼, 그것은 모두 나에 대한 것이다.
(C) As the book was so sad, he was crying. (~때문에)
책이 너무 슬펐기 때문에, 그는 울고 있었다.

1, 8, 9 문장에서 as가 '~함에 따라, ~할수록'이라는 뜻으로 사용되었다.
*grow darker: 어두워지다 *get brighter: 밝아지다
2, 4, 6, 10 문장에서 as가 '~때문에'라는 뜻으로 사용되었다.
* snow heavily: 눈이 많이 내리다
3, 5, 7 문장에서 as가 '~처럼, ~대로'라는 뜻으로 사용되었다.
3 (속담) 로마에 가면 로마법을 따르라.

PRACTICE 9

1	However	2	Therefore
3	Therefore	4	For example
5	However	6	Therefore
7	However	8	Therefore
9	For example	10	For example
11	However	12	For example

1 날씨가 화창한 것(It is sunny.)과 약간 추운 것(it is a little cold.)은 반대되는 내용이므로 역접, 대조를 나타낼 때 쓰는 접속부사 However가 와야 한다.
2 매우 피곤했기 때문에(She was very tired.) 일찍 잠자리에 든 것(she went to bed early.)이므로 인과를 나타내는 접속부사 Therefore가 와야 한다.
3 돈이 없어서(We didn't have any money.) 집에 걸어가야 했던 것(we had to walk home.)이므로 인과를 나타내는 접속부사 Therefore가 와야 한다.
4 그녀가 항상 미소 짓고 그녀의 이웃을 돕는다는(she always smiles and helps her neighbors.) 내용은 Barbara가 친절하다(Barbara is kind.)는 말의 구체적인 사례이기 때문에 '예를 들어'를 뜻하는 접속부사 For example이 와야 한다.
5 시험이 어려웠지만(Jenny's test was difficult.) 그럼에도 불구하고 시험을 잘 봤다(she did very well.)는 의미이므로 역접, 대조를 의미하는 접속부사 However가 와야 한다.
6 내가 사용된 것들을 버리지 않기 때문에(I don't throw away used things.) 내 방이 오래된 것들로 가득 찬 것(my room is full of old things.)이므로 인과를 나타내는 접속부사 Therefore가 와야 한다.
7 그가 새로운 컴퓨터를 샀지만(He bought a new computer.) 그럼에도 불구하고 그것이 그의 일에 도움이 되지 못했다(it didn't help him with his work.)는 의미이므로 역접, 대조를 의미하는 접속부사 However가 와야 한다.
8 많은 이들이 장미를 좋아하기 때문에(Many people like roses.) 내가 그녀에게 장미를 사준 것(I bought some for her.)이므로 인과를 나타내는 접속부사 Therefore가 와야 한다.
9 인터넷에서 책과 옷을 살 수 있다(you can order books and clothes on it.)는 것은 인터넷에서 쇼핑을 할 수 있다(You can shop on the Internet.)는 말의 구체적 예시이므로 '예를 들어'를 뜻하는 접속부사 For example이 와야 한다.
10 그가 주말에 테니스, 축구 그리고 그 외 여러 운동들을 한다(he plays tennis, soccer, and many other sports on weekends.)는 것은 그가 운동을 좋아한다(He likes sports.)는 말의 구체적 예시이므로 '예를 들어'를 뜻하는 For example이 와야 한다.
11 내가 매우 피곤했지만(I was very tired.) 그럼에도 불구하고 회의를 위한 발표를 준비하기 위해 밤새 깨어 있었다(I stayed up all night preparing my presentation for the meeting.)는 내용이므로 역접, 대조를 나타내는 However가 와야 한다.
12 흰 티셔츠와 파란 치마(a white T-shirt and a blue skirt)는 내가 필요로 하는 옷(I need some clothes.)의 구체적 예시이므로 '예를 들어'를 뜻하는 For example이 와야 한다.

Chapter Review Test 정답 본문 _ p.272

1 ②   2 ③   3 ③   4 ②   5 ④   6 ③   7 ①
8 ⑤   9 ③   10 ④   11 ③   12 ④   13 ④
14 ④   15 ②   16 when[as]   17 ①   18 ⑤
19 I do not believe that he told a lie.
20 (1) like dogs (2) but, doesn't like   21 ⑤
22 ③   23 because[as, since]   24 ②
25 ③   26 ④   27 ③   28 ④   29 ④
30 ⑤   31 I couldn't sleep at all because it was noisy outside.[Because it was noisy outside, I couldn't sleep at all.]   32 ④

Chapter Review Test 해설

1 명령문 뒤에 and가 쓰이면 '그러면'의 뜻을 나타낸다.
   - 지금 일어나라, 그러면 너는 아침을 먹을 수 있다.
   - 채소를 더 먹어라, 그러면 너는 건강해질 것이다.

2 반대 혹은 대조되는 내용을 연결하는 but이 와야 한다. 그것은 힘든 일이었지만, 우리는 우리 자신을 자랑스럽게 느꼈다.

3 ③ 빠르게 달리지 않으면 늦을 것이라는 해석이 적절하므로, 명령문 뒤에서 '그렇지 않으면'의 뜻을 나타내는 or이 들어가야 한다.
   Run fast, or you'll be late.
   빠르게 달려라, 그렇지 않으면 너는 늦을 것이다.

4 타동사(think) 뒤에 목적어절을 이끄는 that을 쓸 수 있다.

5 반대 혹은 대조되는 내용을 말할 때는 But을, 둘 중 하나를 선택하여 말할 때는 or를 쓴다.

6 원인이나 이유를 나타내는 접속사 as, because, since가 와야 한다.

7 - 때를 나타내는 접속사 when
   - 시간을 묻는 의문부사 when

8 원인이나 이유를 나타내는 because가 와야 한다.

9 부사 so는 '그만큼, 그렇게'의 뜻을 나타낸다.
   왜 너는 어제 그렇게 일찍 잠자리에 들었니?
   접속사 so 앞의 절은 원인을, 뒤의 절은 결과를 나타낸다. 나는 피곤해서 일찍 잠자리에 들었어.

10 명령문 뒤의 and는 '그러면', or은 '그렇지 않으면'의 뜻이다.
    ④ Get up now, and you won't be late for school. 지금 일어나, 그러면 너는 학교에 늦지 않을 거야.

11 인과를 나타내는 Therefore가 와야 한다.
    더러운 환경은 우리의 몸에 해롭다. 그러므로, 우리는 환경에 대해 더 관심을 가져야 한다.

12 ③ 지시형용사 that   ①②④⑤ 접속사 that

13 - 빈칸의 뒤에 명사구(the Dragon team)가 나오므로 '~와 함께'라는 뜻의 전치사 with을 쓰는 것이 적절하다.
    - 게임에서 졌지만 실망하지 않았다는 역접의 내용이 이어지므로 접속부사 However가 들어가는 것이 적절하다.
    - 빈칸의 뒤에 '최선을 다했기 때문에'라는 이유가 나오므로 이유나 원인을 나타내는 접속사 because가 들어가야 한다. 접속사 because는 뒤에 주어와 동사로 이루어진 절이 오는 반면, because of 뒤에는 명사(구)가 이어진다. 주어진 빈칸의 뒤에는 절(we did our best)이 오므로 접속사 because가 적절하다.
    - '지는 것으로부터 배운다'는 뜻이 되어야 하고 뒤에 losing이라는 동명사가 오므로, '~부터'라는 뜻의 전치사 from이 적절하다.
    - 노력하는 것을 멈추지 않을 것이라는 절과 다음에는 이길 수 있도록 계속할 것이라는 비슷한 내용의 절이 이어지므로 접속사 and가 적절하다.
    우리는 지난 화요일에 Dragon 팀과 함께 야구를 했다. 우리는 그 경기에서 졌다. 하지만, 우리는 우리의 최선을 다했기 때문에 실망하지 않았다. 우리는 때때로 승리에서보다 패배에서 더 많이 배운다는 것을 안다. 우리는 노력을 멈추지 않고, 다음번에 이기기 위해 계속 나아갈 것이다.

14 ④ she is 뒤에 이어지는 자리는 주격 보어의 자리이다. 부사는 보어가 될 수 없으므로 kind가 주격 보어로 쓰여야 한다. (kindly → kind)

15 '만약 ~라면'의 조건을 나타내는 if가 와야 한다. 만약 당신이 영국 사람들에게 혀를 내민다면 그들은 화가 날 것인데, 왜냐하면 영국에서 그것은 "나는 당신을 존경하지 않아요."를 뜻하기 때문이다.

16 때를 나타내는 접속사 when[as]을 써야 한다. 내가 Katie를 불렀을 때 그녀는 길고양이에게 먹이를 주고 있었다.

17 인과를 나타내는 Therefore가 와야 한다.
    서울의 지하철 체계는 매우 잘 조직되어 있어서 원하는 곳 어디든지 갈 수 있다. 그러므로 서울에 오는 방문객들은 대개 지하철을 타고 이동한다.

18 앞 문장에 대한 예시를 나타내므로 For example이 와야 한다. 수미는 외국어에 능하다. 예를 들어, 그녀는 영어, 중국어, 일본어를 잘 말할 수 있다.

19 타동사(believe) 뒤에 목적어절을 이끄는 that을 쓴다.

20 (1) Minwoo and Dana는 복수 주어이고 둘은 모두 개를 좋아하므로 답은 like dogs이다.
(2) 표에 따르면 Minwoo는 컴퓨터 게임을 좋아하는데, Dana는 좋아하지 않는다(doesn't like). 서로 반대되는 의미의 두 문장을 연결하기 위해 접속사 but을 쓴다. (1) 민우와 Dana는 개를 좋아한다. (2) 민우는 컴퓨터 게임을 좋아하지만, Dana는 컴퓨터 게임을 좋아하지 않는다.

21 보기와 ⑤ '~처럼, ~대로' (접속사)
①②③ '~할수록' (접속사)
④ '~로서' (전치사)

22 조건을 나타내는 부사절에서는 현재시제가 미래시제를 대신하므로 미래의 의미를 나타내더라도 현재시제로 써야 한다.

23 이유, 원인을 나타내는 because나 as, since가 와야 한다. 나는 감기에 걸려서 캠핑을 갈 수 없었다.

24 ⓐⓑ 대등한 내용을 연결하고 있으므로 and가 적합하다.
ⓒ 둘 중 하나를 선택하여 말할 때는 or를 쓴다.
몸매를 가꾸고 건강해지기를 원하십니까? 오셔서 Fitness Gym에 가입하세요! 그룹 요가부터 사이클링까지 다양한 프로그램이 있습니다. 자세한 내용을 알려면 체육관을 방문하시거나 808-524-8425로 전화하십시오.

25 ③ 의문사 when '언제'
①②④⑤ 접속사 when '~할 때'

26 「because+절」, 「because of+명사(구)」
④ because of
①②③⑤ because

27 보기와 ①②④⑤ 접속사 that
③ 지시형용사 that

28 보기와 ①②③⑤ '~ 때문에'
④ '~함에 따라'

29 ⓐ 전화기의 발명 전의 상황을 언급한 후, 전화기의 발명으로 그 상황이 바뀌었음을 말하고 있으므로 역접, 대조를 나타내는 접속부사 however가 적절하다.
ⓑ 전화기의 발명이 사회에 지대한 영향을 끼쳤고 특히 사업에 유용했다고 말한 이후, 마지막 문장에서 그 결과가 어떠했는지를 설명하고 있으므로 '그러므로'라는 뜻의 접속부사 Therefore가 적절하다.
전화기가 발명되기 전에는 먼 거리에 있는 다른 사람들과 직접 연락하는 것이 불가능했다. 그러나 전화기가 그것을 가능하게 했다. 그것은 사회에 지대한 영향을 끼쳤다. 그것은 메시지를 보내는 데 걸리는 시간을 줄여주었기 때문에 특히 사업에 유용했다. 그 결과, 사업 성장이 가속화되었고 사회가 빠르게 발전했다.

30 ① 조건을 나타내는 if절에서는 미래를 나타내더라도, 현재시제로 미래시제를 나타낸다.
(will clean → clean)
② '비가 내리지 않았기 때문에 현장학습을 갔다'는 해석이 자연스러우므로, 주절의 시제도 부사절의 시제에 맞게 과거시제를 쓰는 것이 적절하다. (go → went)
③ because of는 전치사로 뒤에 명사(구)를 쓴다. 주어진 문장에서는 절(he got up early)이 이어지므로 접속사 because를 쓰는 것이 적절하다. (because of → because)
④ '좋은 몸 상태를 유지하고 싶어서 매일 아침 운동한다'는 해석이 적절하므로 결과를 나타내는 접속사 so를 써야 한다. (but → so)

31 because 다음에는 주절의 원인이나 이유가 되는 절을 쓴다. 바깥이 시끄러웠다는 절이 원인인 것이 자연스러우므로 because의 뒤에 쓴다.

32 ⓐ 시간을 나타내는 부사절에서는 현재시제가 미래시제를 대신한다. I'll call you when she <u>comes</u> back.
ⓔ 부사절의 시제는 주절의 시제(was)와 맞춰야 한다. He was tired because he <u>got</u> up early.

CHAPTER 14 전치사 & 속담
Prepositions & Proverbs

본문 _ p.278

PRACTICE 1

1	at	2	on	3	at	4	on
5	in	6	in	7	on	8	at
9	at	10	on				

> 1 at+구체적인 시각
> 2 on+요일
> 3, 8, 9 at+특정한 시점
> *at this time tomorrow: 내일 이맘때에
> 4, 7 on+특정한 날
> *on New Year's Day: 새해 첫날
> 5 in+아침
> 6 in+연도
> 10 on+날짜

PRACTICE 2

1	After the meeting	2	before six
3	Before lunch	4	After work
5	Before twelve	6	after school

PRACTICE 3

1	for	2	during	3	for
4	during	5	during	6	for
7	during	8	during		

> 1, 3, 6 for+시간의 길이를 나타내는 표현
> 2, 4, 5, 7, 8 during+숫자가 없는(명사로 된) 특정 기간을 나타내는 표현

PRACTICE 4

1	since	2	since	3	from
4	since	5	From	6	from

> 1, 2, 4 전치사 since는 '~이래로'라는 뜻으로 과거에 시작된 일이 현재까지 지속되는 것을 나타내며 주로 완료형 시제와 함께 쓰인다.
> 3, 5, 6 전치사 from은 '~부터'라는 뜻으로, 시작된 시점만 나타내며 완료형 이외의 시제들과 함께 쓰인다.

PRACTICE 5

1 from eight to four
2 From morning to afternoon
3 from March to June
4 from 12:00 to 12:40
5 from late fall to early spring
6 from 2003 to 2005

PRACTICE 6

1	at	2	on	3	After
4	since	5	In	6	at
7	before	8	since	9	for
10	to	11	at	12	from
13	in	14	from	15	after

> 1, 6, 11 at+특정한 시점, 구체적인 시각
> 2 on+특정한 날의 아침/저녁
> 3, 15 '~후에'라는 뜻의 after가 적절하다.
> 4,8 동사가 현재완료시제이므로 since가 적절하다.
> 5, 13 연도, 월 앞에는 전치사 in을 쓴다.
> 7 동사가 현재시제이므로, '~이래로'라는 뜻을 가진 since보다는 '~전에'라는 뜻의 before가 적절하다.
> 9 for+숫자가 들어간 시간의 길이를 나타내는 표현
> 10, 12 'A에서 B까지'라는 뜻의 'from A to B'를 써야 한다.
> 14 동사가 미래 시제이므로, '~부터'라는 뜻의 from이 적절하다.

PRACTICE 7

1	at	2	in	3	on
4	at	5	on	6	in
7	at	8	at	9	on
10	at	11	on	12	on
13	in	14	on	15	in
16	in	17	on, on[in]	18	at
19	In, in, in	20	on	21	on
22	in				

> 1, 4 at+하나의 지점
> 2, 13, 15 in+건물, 탈것, 용기 등의 내부
> 3, 9, 11 on+교통수단, 통신수단
> *on foot: 걸어서, 도보로
> 5, 14, 21 표면상에 맞닿은 것을 말할 때 전치사 on을 사용한다.
> 6 in+국가, 비교적 넓은 장소
> 7, 18 at+행사, 모임
> 8, 10 건물의 용도에 맞는 일을 하고 있을 때 전치사 at을 사용한다.
> 12, 20 길을 말할 때 전치사 on을 사용한다.
> 16, 22 in+우주, 하늘
> 17 첫 번째 빈칸에는 통신수단과 함께 쓰이는 전치사 on을 사용한다. 두 번째 빈칸에는 교통수단과 함께 쓰이는 전치사 on이나 탈 것의 내부를 뜻하는 전치사 in을 써야 한다.
> 19 첫 번째 빈칸에는 국가와 함께 쓰이는 전치사 in을 사용한다. 두 번째와 세 번째 빈칸에는 'come in: (물품이나 상품이) 나오다'라는 표현에 쓰이는 in을 사용한다.
> * carton: (음식이나 음료를 담는) 갑, 상자

CHAPTER 14

PRACTICE 8

1	under	2	over	3	over
4	under	5	over	6	under

PRACTICE 9

1	in front of	2	Minji
3	behind[in back of]	4	Yunsu
5	next to[beside/by]	6	Minji
7	Nami	8	behind[in back of]

PRACTICE 10

1	between	2	between	3	among
4	among	5	between	6	among
7	among	8	between		

PRACTICE 11

1	in	2	between	3	at
4	to	5	under	6	in
7	on	8	in	9	on
10	over	11	on	12	behind
13	in	14	among	15	in front of

> 1, 8 in+도시, 국가와 같은 비교적 넓은 장소
> 2 between: ~사이에(둘 사이)
> 3 at+하나의 지점
> 4 next to: ~ 옆에
> 5 '바다 아래에는 많은 식물들이 있다.'라는 표현이 적절하므로, '~아래에'라는 뜻의 under를 써야 한다.
> 6, 13 in+건물의 내부
> 7, 9 표면상에 맞닿은 것을 말할 때는 전치사 on을 사용한다.
> 10 '그녀는 벽 위로 공을 던졌다.'라는 표현이 적절하므로, '~위에'라는 뜻의 over를 써야 한다.
> 11 on+통신수단
> 12 behind: ~뒤에
> 14 among: ~사이에(셋 이상)
> 15 '3시에 역 앞에서 만나자'라는 표현이 적절하므로, '~앞에'라는 뜻의 in front of를 써야 한다.

PRACTICE 12

1	up	2	into	3	down
4	out of	5	into	6	up

PRACTICE 13

1	around	2	across	3	through
4	around	5	along	6	through

> 1 지구는 태양 주위를 돈다.
> 2 사람들은 초록 불일 때 길을 가로질러 간다.
> 3 도둑이 창문을 통하여 집으로 들어왔다.
> 4 박물관 주위에 높은 건물들이 많이 있다.
> 5 우리는 강을 따라서 산책했다.
> 6 기차는 터널을 통과하여 지나가고 있다.

PRACTICE 14

1	to	2	for	3	to
4	from	5	for	6	from, to
7	from	8	for[to]		

> 8 head for[to]: ~로 향하다

PRACTICE 15

1	to	2	for	3	after
4	around	5	into	6	down
7	for	8	across	9	in
10	by	11	up	12	on
13	at	14	along	15	into

> 1 to는 '~에, ~으로'라는 뜻으로 come과 함께 쓰여 도착 지점을 나타낸다.
> 2 전치사 for는 '~을 향하여'라는 뜻으로 start와 함께 쓰여 방향을 나타낸다.
> *start for: ~을 향해 출발하다
> 3 '~이래로'라는 뜻의 since보다는 '~후에'라는 뜻의 after가 적절하다.
> 4 '달은 지구 주위를 돈다'라는 표현이 적절하므로, '~을 통하여'라는 뜻의 through보다는 '~주위에'라는 뜻의 around를 써야 한다.
> 5 between(~사이에)은 뒤에 복수명사가 나와야 하므로, '~안으로'라는 뜻의 into를 써야 한다.
> *walk into: ~로 들어가다
> 6 '눈물이 그녀의 볼 아래로 흘러내렸다.'라는 표현이 적절하므로, '~안으로'라는 뜻의 into보다는 '~아래로'라는 뜻의 down을 써야 한다.
> 7 for+숫자가 들어간 시간의 길이를 나타내는 표현
> 8 '~위에'라는 뜻의 over보다는 '~을 가로질러'라는 뜻의 across가 적절하다.
> 9 in+연도
> 10 among(~사이에)은 뒤에 복수명사가 나와야 하므로, '~옆에'라는 뜻의 by를 써야 한다.
> 11 '원숭이들이 나무 위로 올라갔다.'라는 표현이 적절하므로, '~사이에(둘 사이)'라는 뜻의 between보다는 '~위로'라는 뜻의 up을 써야 한다.
> 12 표면상에 맞닿은 것을 말할 때는 전치사 on을 사용한다.
> 13 at+구체적인 시간
> 14 '~ 보다 위에'라는 뜻의 above보다는 '~을 따라서'라는 뜻의 along이 적절하다.
> 15 '아이들이 물 안으로 뛰어들었다'라는 표현이 적절하므로 '~사이에(셋 이상)'라는 뜻의 among보다는 '~안으로'라는 뜻의 into가 적절하다.

CHAPTER 14

PRACTICE 16

1	by	2	on	3	with
4	by	5	by	6	with
7	by				

PRACTICE 17

1	without	2	about	3	like
4	like	5	about	6	without
7	like	8	Without		

PRACTICE 18

1	by	2	like	3	with
4	without	5	on	6	without
7	with	8	by	9	by
10	with				

> 1, 8, 9 by+교통수단: ~을 타고
> 2 look like+명사: ~처럼 보이다
> 3, 7, 10 with+도구: ~을 가지고
> 4, 6 문맥상 '~없이'라는 뜻의 전치사 without을 쓰는 것이 적절하다.
> 5 on foot: 걸어서

PRACTICE 19

1	in	2	for
3	for	4	about
5	for	6	of
7	from	8	of
9	at	10	for
11	from	12	for[about]
13	of	14	for

PRACTICE 20

1	at	2	for
3	for	4	for
5	to	6	for
7	on	8	in
9	into	10	After
11	without	12	to
13	on	14	from
15	out of	16	for

17	on	18	on
19	before	20	at
21	for	22	at
23	in	24	during
25	with	26	at
27	of	28	by
29	in	30	around

> 1 look at: ~을 보다
> 2 wait for: ~을 기다리다
> 3 thank A for B: A에게 B에 대해 고맙게 여기다
> 4 buy A for B: B에게 A를 사주다
> 5 give A to B: B에게 A를 주다
> 6 look for: ~를 찾다
> 7 표면상에 맞닿은 것을 말할 때 전치사 on을 사용한다.
> 8 in+계절
> 9 throw A into B: A를 B로 던지다
> 10 '점심식사를 하고 난 후에, 그들은 소풍 장소를 청소했다.'라는 표현이 적절하므로 '~후에'라는 뜻의 after를 써야 한다.
> 11 '한국인들은 김치 없이는 살 수 없다.'라는 표현이 적절하므로, '~옆에'라는 뜻의 by보다는 '~없이'라는 뜻의 without을 써야 한다.
> 12 전치사 to는 '~에', '~으로'라는 뜻으로 도착 지점을 나타낸다.
> 13 on+날짜
> 14 동사가 과거 시제이므로, from이 적절하다.
> 15 'Susan은 상자 밖으로 그녀의 선물을 꺼냈다'라는 표현이 적절하므로, '~안으로'라는 뜻의 into보다는 '~밖으로'라는 뜻의 out of를 써야 한다.
> 16 for+시간의 길이를 나타내는 표현
> 17 on+통신수단
> 18 on+요일
> 19 여름은 가을보다 먼저 오기 때문에 '~전에'라는 뜻의 before가 적절하다.
> 20 at+구체적인 시간
> 21 leave for: ~로 떠나다
> 22 be good at: ~을 잘하다
> 23 in+월
> 24 during+숫자가 없는(명사로 된) 특정 기간을 나타내는 표현
> 25 '그녀는 비누를 가지고 그녀의 머리를 감았다'라는 표현이 적절하므로 '~옆에'라는 뜻의 by보다는 '~을 가지고'라는 뜻의 with를 써야 한다.
> 26 at+특정한 시점
> *at this time yesterday: 어제 이 시간에
> 27 be full of: ~으로 가득 차다
> 28 교통수단은 전치사 by, on[in] 모두 사용하여 표현할 수 있는데, 'by+교통수단', 'on[in]+관사+교통수단' 형태로 써야 한다. boat 앞에 관사가 없으므로 by가 적절하다.
> 29 in+도시
> 30 '해변가 주위에 아무도 없었다'라는 표현이 적절하므로, '~을 통하여'라는 뜻의 through보다는 '~주위에'라는 뜻의 around를 써야 한다.

PRACTICE 21

2	⑦, Fine clothes make the man.
3	⑥, Don't judge a book by its cover.
4	⑨, Go home and kick the dog.

5 ④, Even a worm will turn.
6 ②, Small drops make a shower.
7 ③, A good medicine tastes bitter.
8 ①, Two heads are better than one.
9 ⑧, Too many cooks spoil the broth.
10 ⑤, A journey of 1000 miles begins with a single step.

PRACTICE 22

1 blames his tools		**2**	the best
3 The early bird		**4**	Practice, perfect
5 without fire		**6**	men, minds
7 dog, day		**8**	as the Romans do
9 pain, gain		**10**	sight, mind
11 barking, bites		**12**	second nature
13 Honesty, policy		**14**	leap
15 haste, speed			

PRACTICE 23

1 with	**2**	to	**3**	until	
4 with	**5**	from	**6**	over	

Chapter Review Test 정답   본문 _ p.303

1 ③   2 ③   3 on   4 ④   5 (1) behind (2) in
6 ④   7 at   8 ③   9 ②   10 ②   11 ①
12 ④   13 ②   14 on   15 I felt sorry for her
16 ⑤   17 ③   18 ④   19 ①   20 ③
21 across   22 ④   23 ④   24 ③   25 ④
26 ③   27 ②   28 ②   29 ③   30 ②
31 without   32 ⑤   33 ⑤   34 Our customs are quite different from yours.   35 ④   36 ④
37 ②   38 (1) for (2) about   39 ③   40 ①
41 for, at   42 at   43 for   44 (1) on (2) under (3) in front of   45 ⑤   46 ④   47 ②   48 ③
49 ③   50 ③   51 (1) in (2) in (3) for   52 ④
53 (1) There are books on the table. (2) There is a dog under the table.   54 (1) by foot → on foot (2) on nature → in nature (3) go in → go into[go to]   55 ③   56 ④   57 ④

Chapter Review Test 해설

1 on+요일
2 in+월
3 on+날짜
4 for a minute '잠시 동안'
 cf. wait a minute '잠깐 기다리다'
    in a minute '곧, 즉시'
5 (1) behind '~ 뒤에'
 (2) live in '~에 살다'
 cf. 마을, 도시, 국가와 같은 비교적 넓은 장소 앞에 in 을 쓴다.
6 도구와 함께 쓰이는 with는 '~을 가지고'의 뜻을 나타낸다. 이 사과 좀 칼로 잘라줄 수 있니?
7 be good at '~을 잘하다'
8 • from A to B 'A에서 B까지'
 • be[come] from '~로부터 오다, ~ 출신이다'
9 ② after '~ 후에'
 ① before '~ 전에'
 ③ at '~에'
 ④ during '~ 동안'
 ⑤ for '~ 동안'
10 be ready for '~을 준비하다'
11 농장의 땅에 맞닿아 작물이 자라는 것이므로 전치사 on이 적절하다.
 look at '~을 보다'
12 • be late for '~에 늦다'
 • without '~ 없이'
 • 「for+시간의 길이를 나타내는 표현」 '~ 동안에'
13 시계는 책상 위에 있으므로 on을 써야 한다.
 ② There is a clock on the desk.
 cf. next to '~옆에'
14 통신수단을 말할 때는 on을 쓴다.
 on channel 9 '9번 채널에서' on TV 'TV에서'
15 feel sorry for '~를 안쓰럽게 여기다'
16 • in+계절
 • 건물의 내부를 말할 때는 in을 쓴다.
17 • 빵집은 우체국의 옆에 있으므로 '~ 옆에'라는 뜻의 전치사 next to를 쓴다. in front of는 '~ 앞에'라는 뜻이다.
 • 빵집은 우체국과 은행의 사이에 위치해 있다. 따라서 '(둘) ~ 사이에'라는 뜻의 between이 적절하다. among도 '~ 사이에'라는 뜻이지만 세 개 이상의 대상들 사이를 지칭할 때 쓴다.

18
- walk around '~ 주위를 걷다'
- work for '~에서 일하다'

19 on+요일
① There are no classes on Saturday and Sunday.

20 ⓐ spend ~ on … '…에 ~를 소비하다[쓰다]'
ⓑ like '~처럼, ~같이'
ⓒ for '~을 위해' (for future purposes '미래의 목적을 위해')

21 across '~건너편에, 맞은편에'

22 in+마을, 도시, 국가와 같은 넓은 장소
at+구체적인 시각
on+특정한 날

23 조깅하면서 영어 팟캐스트를 듣는다는 내용, 집에 돌아오는 길에 차에 기름을 넣고 세탁소도 들를 것이라는 내용, 출장차 런던에 가 있는 동안 친척 집도 방문했다는 내용은 모두 일석이조의 상황을 가리키므로 Kill two birds with one stone. 이 적절하다.

24 on the[one's] way home '집에 가는 길에'

25 은행을 기준으로 타임스퀘어의 위치를 나타낼 때 빈칸에 위치나 방향을 나타내는 전치사가 들어가야 한다.
④ looking for는 '~를 찾는'이라는 뜻으로 빈칸에 들어갈 수 없다.

26 ③ on foot '걸어서'
①②④⑤ by+교통수단 '~을 타고'

27 to는 go, come과 같은 동사와 함께 쓰여 도착 지점을 나타낸다.
on a subway '지하철을 타고'
cf. 교통수단 앞에 관사가 없는 경우에는 by를 쓴다.
 by subway '지하철을 타고'

28 like '~처럼, ~같이'

29 ① Yesterday라는 과거를 나타내는 부사가 쓰였으므로, 동사도 과거시제로 써야 한다. (take → took)
② '강을 따라서 걷고 있었다'라는 해석이 자연스러우므로, '~을 따라서'라는 뜻의 전치사 along을 써야 한다. on은 표면 상에 맞닿은 것을 말한다. (on → along)
④ 개가 세 마리 있다고 언급되어 있으므로 '(셋 이상의) ~ 사이에'라는 뜻의 전치사 among을 써야 한다. between은 두 개의 대상 사이를 지칭한다. (between → among)
⑤ 완료형 시제와 함께 쓰였으므로 과거부터 시작한 일이 현재까지 지속되는 것을 나타내는 전치사 since를 써야 한다. from은 완료형 이외의 시제들과 함께 쓰인다. (from → since)

30 ② '좋아하다' (동사)
①③④⑤ '~처럼, ~같이' (전치사)

31 without '~ 없이'

32 be full of '~로 가득 차다' be good for '~에 좋다'

33
- 그녀는 꽃에 관한 책을 읽었다.
- 아이들은 그들 주위에 있는 모든 것에 호기심을 갖는다.

⑤ write about '~대해 글을 쓰다'
① look at '~을 보다'
② be afraid of '~을 두려워하다'
③ be famous for '~으로 유명하다'
④ be interested in '~에 흥미[관심]가 있다'

34 be different from '~와 다르다'
different를 수식하는 quite는 different 앞에 쓴다.

35 ④ 동사 like '좋아하다'
①②③⑤ 전치사 like '~처럼, ~같이'

36 ④ look at '~을 보다'
① arrive at '~에 도착하다'
② by+교통수단 '~를 타고'
③ into '~ 안으로'
⑤ from '~로부터'

37 전치사 in은 우주나 하늘을 나타내는 표현과 함께 쓴다.
② Look at the beautiful kites in the sky.
④ '해변에서'라는 뜻은 on the beach로 나타낸다.
⑤ be on a diet '식이요법 중이다'

38 (1) buy … for ~ '~에게 …을 사주다'
(2) about '~에 대해'

39 각 나라에 맞는 식사 예절을 지키라는 내용이므로 '로마에 가면 로마의 법을 따르라.'는 뜻의 When in Rome, do as the Romans do.가 적절하다.

40
- 하나의 지점을 나타낼 때는 at을 쓴다.
 그 버스는 광화문에서 선다.
- 도구와 함께 쓰이는 with는 '~을 가지고'의 뜻을 나타낸다. 그녀는 그녀의 엄지 손가락과 검지 손가락으로 원을 만들었다.
- 길을 말할 때는 on을 쓴다. 5번가에 백화점이 있다.

41 look for '~을 찾다'
look at '~을 보다'

42 특정한 시점 앞에는 at을 쓴다.

at noon '정오에'
at the end of this year '올 연말에'

43 for는 '~ 동안'의 의미로 구체적인 시간의 길이를 나타내는 말과 함께 쓴다.
cf. during은 특정 기간을 나타내는 말과 함께 쓴다.

44 (1) 그림에서 바지는 탁자 위에 있으므로, '~위에'라는 뜻으로 표면에 맞닿아 있는 것을 나타내는 전치사 on을 사용한다.
(2) 양말은 탁자의 아래에 있으므로, '~아래에'라는 뜻의 전치사 under을 사용한다.
(3) 상자는 침대의 앞에 있으므로, '~ 앞에'라는 뜻의 전치사 in front of를 사용한다.
Jason에게, 네 방을 좀 보렴. 네 바지는 탁자 위에 있구나. 네 양말 한 짝은 탁자 아래에 있어. 상자를 보렴. 그것은 네 침대 앞에 있구나. 제발, 네 방 청소하는 걸 잊지 마라! 엄마가.

45 be absent from '~에 결석하다'
be good for '~에 좋다, 유익하다'

46 세호가 적은 돈을 아껴서 원하는 물건을 사려 한다는 내용이므로 '티끌 모아 태산'이라는 뜻의 Small drops make a shower.가 적절하다.

47 for '~으로, ~로서(속성, 자격)'
후식으로 어떤 음식을 원하니?
① be late for '~에 늦다' 그는 항상 학교에 늦는다.
② for '~으로, ~로서(속성, 자격)'
   우리는 저녁으로 스테이크를 먹었다.
③ look for '~을 찾다'
   그녀는 그녀의 가방을 찾고 있다.
④ for '~ 동안'
   나는 2주 동안 여기에 머물기로 계획했다.
⑤ thank ~ for … '~에게 …에 대해 고맙게 여기다'
   너의 편지에 대해 고마워.

48 • next to '~ 옆에'
• write … to ~ '~에게 …을 쓰다'
• go to see a doctor '병원에 가다'

49 Thomas의 이웃은 Thomas의 옷만 중요시 했으므로 '겉모습보단 내면이 중요하다.'라는 뜻의 속담 Don't judge a book by its cover.가 적절하다.

50 ③ suffer from '~으로부터 고통 받다'
① in the world '세계에'
② in danger '위험에 처해서'
④ in one's life/lives '~의 삶[인생]에'
⑤ in need '어려움에 처한'
이 세상의 많은 아이들이 지금 위험에 처해 있다. 그들은 배고픔과 질병으로 고통 받고 있다. 그들은 당신의 도움이 필요하다. 당신은 그들을 위해서 돈을 기부할 수 있다. 당신은 한 달에 3000원으로 시작할 수 있다! 당신의 작은 도움이 그들의 삶에 큰 변화를 만들 수 있다. 어려움에 처한 아이들을 위해 당신의 돈을 모아라.

51 (1) 도시, 국가와 같은 넓은 장소일 때 전치사 in을 쓴다.
(2) in the morning '아침에'
(3) 구체적인 시간의 길이를 나타낼 때 전치사 for를 쓴다.
보령은 세계적인 머드(진흙) 축제로 유명하다. 그것은 한국에서 가장 유명한 축제들 중 하나다. 그것(축제)은 갯벌에서 열린다. 그것(축제)은 보통 매우 이른 아침에 시작한다. 그것(축제)은 11일간 지속된다.

52 「during+특정 기간」, 「for+구체적인 시간의 길이」

53 (1) 책은 탁자의 위에 있으므로, '~위에'라는 뜻으로 표면에 맞닿은 것을 나타내는 전치사 on을 사용하는 것이 적절하다.
(2) 개는 탁자의 아래에 있으므로 '~아래에'라는 뜻의 전치사 under을 사용한다.

54 (1) 두 번째 줄: '걸어서'라는 뜻은 전치사 on을 사용해 나타낸다.
(2) 세 번째 줄: '자연 안에서 시간을 보내는 것을 좋아한다'라는 해석이 자연스러우므로 내부를 뜻하는 전치사 in을 사용하는 것이 적절하다. on은 표면에 맞닿은 것을 나타낸다.
(3) 밑에서 두 번째 줄: '숲의 안으로 들어간다'는 뜻이 되어야 하므로 '~ 안으로'의 뜻으로 방향성을 나타내는 전치사 into[to]를 사용하는 것이 적절하다. in은 '~안에'라는 뜻으로 이미 완료된 동작을 나타낸다.
주말에 Maria의 가족은 캠핑을 간다. 그들은 걸어서 그곳으로 간다. 그들은 대개 통나무집에서 머문다. 그들은 자연 속에서 시간 보내는 걸 좋아한다. 날씨가 맑은 날에 Maria와 그녀의 동생 Anna는 야생 과일을 따기 위해 숲 속으로 간다.

55 ⓐ give동사는 3형식 문장에서 간접목적어 앞에 전치사 to를 쓴다.
ⓑ 하나의 지점을 말하고 있으므로 at을 쓴다.
ⓒ 길을 말할 때는 on을 쓴다.
ⓓ 크레용을 가지고 색칠을 하는 것이므로 도구를 나타내는 with를 쓴다.
ⓐ 그녀는 그녀의 어머니에게 초콜릿을 드렸다.

ⓑ 나는 병원에서 봉사활동을 하고 싶다.
ⓒ 길가에 길 잃은 강아지가 있었다.
ⓓ 그는 갈색 크레용으로 벽을 칠했다.

56 <보기> 강의 위에 다리가 지어진 것이므로 '~ 위에'를 뜻하는 전치사 over이 들어간다. on은 표면에 맞닿아 있는 것을 나타내므로 여기에서는 적절하지 않다.
① 동사 come과 함께 쓰여 도착 지점을 나타낼 때는 전치사 to를 사용한다.
② 입으로 집어 넣은 것이므로 '~ 안으로'라는 뜻의 방향을 나타내는 전치사 into 또는 in을 쓸 수 있다.
③ 필리핀에서 왔다는 뜻이므로 '~ 부터'를 나타내는 전치사 from이 들어간다. be from은 국적이나 고향을 나타내는 관용표현이다.
④ '강의 위로 새가 날아가는 중이다'라는 해석이 자연스러우므로 '~ 위에'를 뜻하는 전치사 over이 들어간다.
⑤ 디지털 카메라로 영화를 만든다는 뜻이므로, 도구를 나타내는 전치사 with을 사용한다.

57 ⓐ 건물의 용도에 맞는 일을 하고 있을 때 전치사 at 또는 in을 쓸 수 있다.
ⓑ 표면상에 맞닿은 것을 말할 때 전치사 on을 쓴다.
ⓒ 교통수단과 함께 쓰이는 전치사 by를 쓴다. on은 교통수단의 앞에 관사가 올 때 쓸 수 있다.

탄탄한 영어 실력을 위한 영문법의 시작

마더텅
영문법 3800제
단어·표현 암기장

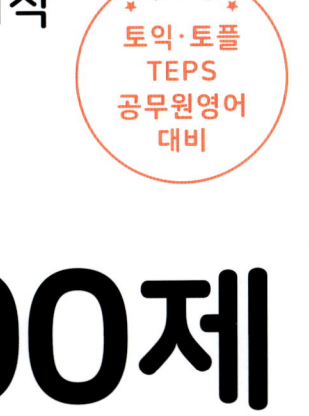

BASIC 1

마더텅 영문법 3800제 단어·표현 암기장 활용법

1 마더텅 영문법 3800제 단어·표현 암기장은 한 달 학습 계획(총 31일)으로 구성되어 있습니다.

2 오늘 외울 단어를 원어민 녹음 MP3파일을 활용하여 암기합니다.

3 세트로 구성된 Word Test를 스스로 풀어 본 후 단어·표현 암기장을 확인하며 채점합니다.
(정답표가 필요하신 경우 마더텅 홈페이지를 통해 다운로드 받으실 수 있습니다.
www.toptutor.co.kr)

4 [오늘 외울 단어]로 제공되는 단어들은 마더텅 영문법 3800제 본문에서 선정된 필수 암기 영단어입니다.

5 교재와 함께 시작하여 매일 학습 단어를 암기해 나가면, 한 달(31일)이면 주요 단어를 모두 학습할 수 있습니다.

마더텅 영문법 3800제 1
BASIC

단어·표현 암기장
Problem Solving Skill

마더텅

Day 01

오늘 외울 단어 **35**개

Chapter 1 문장의 기초
PSS & PRACTICE

- 001 **bicycle** [báisikl] 명 자전거
- 002 **pretty** [príti] 형 예쁜 부 꽤, 매우
- 003 **police officer** [pəlíːs ɔ́(ː)fisər] 명 경찰관
- 004 **excited** [iksáitid] 형 신이 난, 들뜬
- 005 **wonderful** [wʌ́ndərfəl] 형 아주 멋진, 훌륭한
- 006 **tired** [taiərd] 형 피곤한, 지친
- 007 **parents** [pɛ́ːərənts] 명 부모
- 008 **angry** [ǽŋgri] 형 화난
- 009 **visitor** [vízitər] 명 방문객
- 010 **warm** [wɔːrm] 형 따뜻한
- 011 **busy** [bízi] 형 바쁜
- 012 **friendly** [fréndli] 형 다정한
- 013 **be afraid of** ~을 두려워하다
- 014 **late** [leit] 형 늦은
- 015 **rain** [rein] 동 비가 오다
- 016 **drink** [driŋk] 동 마시다
- 017 **newspaper** [njúːzpèipər] 명 신문
- 018 **happen** [hǽpən] 동 (일, 사건 등이) 일어나다
- 019 **work** [wəːrk] 동 일하다
- 020 **player** [pléiər] 명 선수, 경기자
- 021 **go to the cinema** 영화 보러 가다
- 022 **have breakfast** 아침식사를 하다
- 023 **hungry** [hʌ́ŋgri] 형 배고픈
- 024 **near** [niər] 전 ~의 가까이(에) 부 가까이
- 025 **photograph** [fóutəgrǽf] 명 사진
- 026 **hospital** [háspitl] 명 병원
- 027 **interesting** [íntərəstiŋ] 형 흥미있는, 재미있는
- 028 **use the Internet** 인터넷을 이용하다
- 029 **married** [mǽrid] 형 결혼한
- 030 **speak** [spiːk] 동 말하다
- 031 **enjoy** [indʒɔ́i] 동 즐기다
- 032 **draw** [drɔː] 동 (그림을) 그리다
- 033 **free** [friː] 형 한가한, 자유로운
- 034 **movie** [múːvi] 명 영화
- 035 **go jogging** 조깅하러 가다

Day 02

오늘 외울 단어 36개

☐ 036 **absent** [ǽbsnt]	형 결석한	☐ 054 **helmet** [hélmit]	명 헬멧, 안전모
☐ 037 **vacation** [veikéiʃən]	명 휴가, 방학	☐ 055 **enter** [éntər]	동 들어가다
☐ 038 **great** [greit]	형 훌륭한	☐ 056 **worry** [wə́:ri]	동 걱정하다
☐ 039 **buy** [bai]	동 사다	☐ 057 **careful** [kέərfəl]	형 조심스러운
☐ 040 **grade** [greid]	명 성적	☐ 058 **upset** [ʌpsét]	형 속상한, 마음이 상한
☐ 041 **writer** [ráitər]	명 작가	☐ 059 **ready** [rédi]	형 준비가 된
☐ 042 **corner** [kɔ́:rnər]	명 모퉁이	☐ 060 **turn on**	켜다
☐ 043 **clean** [kli:n]	동 청소하다 형 깨끗한	☐ 061 **introduce** [intrədjú:s]	동 소개하다
☐ 044 **prepared** [pripέərd]	형 준비가 되어 있는	☐ 062 **keep in touch**	연락하고 지내다, 연락하다
☐ 045 **study** [stʌ́di]	동 공부하다	☐ 063 **take a break**	휴식을 취하다
☐ 046 **swim** [swim]	동 수영하다	☐ 064 **hurry** [hə́:ri]	동 서두르다
☐ 047 **gym** [dʒim]	명 체육관	☐ 065 **from now on**	지금부터
☐ 048 **fast** [fæst]	형 빠른 부 빨리	☐ 066 **ride** [raid]	동 (탈것에) 타다
☐ 049 **sleep** [sli:p]	동 잠자다	☐ 067 **go climbing**	등산하러 가다
☐ 050 **quiet** [kwaiət]	형 조용한	☐ 068 **daughter** [dɔ́:tər]	명 딸
☐ 051 **classroom** [klǽsrù:m]	명 교실	☐ 069 **really** [rí:əli]	부 정말로, 실제로
☐ 052 **make a noise**	시끄럽게 하다	☐ 070 **amazing** [əméiziŋ]	형 놀라운
☐ 053 **wear** [wεər]	동 (옷을) 입다, (모자 등을) 쓰다	☐ 071 **huge** [hju:dʒ]	형 거대한

Day 03

오늘 외울 단어 **36개**

- 072 **waterfall** [wɔ́:tərfɔ̀:l] 명 폭포
- 073 **handsome** [hǽnsəm] 형 잘생긴
- 074 **move** [mu:v] 동 움직이다
- 075 **liar** [laiər] 명 거짓말쟁이
- 076 **mountain** [máuntn] 명 산
- 077 **museum** [mju:zí:əm] 명 박물관
- 078 **dictionary** [díkʃənèri] 명 사전
- 079 **delicious** [dilíʃəs] 형 맛있는
- 080 **paint** [peint] 동 페인트를 칠하다
- 081 **boring** [bɔ́:riŋ] 형 지루한
- 082 **favorite** [féivərit] 형 매우 좋아하는
- 083 **subject** [sʌ́bdʒikt] 명 과목
- 084 **believe** [bilíːv] 동 믿다
- 085 **keep a diary** 일기를 쓰다
- 086 **healthy** [hélθi] 형 건강한
- 087 **make a mistake** 실수를 하다
- 088 **plant** [plænt] 동 심다
- 089 **honest** [ánist] 형 정직한, 솔직한
- 090 **exciting** [iksáitiŋ] 형 신나는, 흥미진진한
- 091 **become** [bikʌ́m] 동 ~이 되다
- 092 **cook** [kuk] 명 요리사
- 093 **wash the dishes** 설거지하다
- 094 **shine** [ʃain] 동 빛나다
- 095 **article** [á:rtikl] 명 기사
- 096 **engineer** [èndʒiníər] 명 기술자
- 097 **sweet** [swi:t] 형 달콤한, 감미로운
- 098 **strange** [streindʒ] 형 이상한
- 099 **terrible** [térəbl] 형 끔찍한, 심한
- 100 **sour** [sauər] 형 신, 시큼한
- 101 **ask** [æsk] 동 묻다
- 102 **question** [kwéstʃən] 명 질문
- 103 **secret** [sí:krit] 명 비밀
- 104 **favor** [féivər] 명 호의
- 105 **cousin** [kʌ́zn] 명 사촌
- 106 **math** [mæθ] 명 수학
- 107 **storybook** [stɔ́:ribùk] 명 동화책

Day 04

오늘 외울 단어 **35개**

- ☐ 108 **information** [ìnfərméiʃən] 명 정보
- ☐ 109 **senior citizen** [síːnjər sítəzən] 명 노인, 고령자
- ☐ 110 **fairy tale** [fɛ́(ː)əri teil] 명 동화, 옛날 이야기
- ☐ 111 **report card** [ripɔ́ːrt kɑːrd] 명 성적표
- ☐ 112 **sand castle** [sænd kǽsl] 명 모래성

Chapter Review Test

- ☐ 113 **television** [téləvìʒən] 명 텔레비전
- ☐ 114 **farmer** [fɑ́ːrmər] 명 농부
- ☐ 115 **umbrella** [ʌmbrélə] 명 우산
- ☐ 116 **swimmer** [swímər] 명 수영 선수
- ☐ 117 **classmate** [klǽsmèit] 명 동급생, 반 친구
- ☐ 118 **play computer games** 컴퓨터 게임을 하다
- ☐ 119 **history** [hístəri] 명 역사
- ☐ 120 **practice** [prǽktis] 동 연습하다
- ☐ 121 **hometown** [hóumtáun] 명 고향
- ☐ 122 **far** [fɑːr] 형 먼
- ☐ 123 **present** [prézənt] 명 선물
- ☐ 124 **beautiful** [bjúːtəfəl] 형 아름다운
- ☐ 125 **evening** [íːvniŋ] 명 저녁
- ☐ 126 **watch** [watʃ] 동 보다, 지켜보다
- ☐ 127 **lady** [léidi] 명 숙녀, 여성
- ☐ 128 **bring** [briŋ] 동 가져오다
- ☐ 129 **yesterday** [jéstərdei] 부 어제
- ☐ 130 **event** [ivént] 명 행사, 사건
- ☐ 131 **bookstore** [búkstɔ̀ːr] 명 서점
- ☐ 132 **badminton** [bǽdmintn] 명 배드민턴
- ☐ 133 **often** [ɔ́ːfən] 부 종종, 자주
- ☐ 134 **office worker** [ɔ́ːfis wə́ːrkər] 명 회사원
- ☐ 135 **lazy** [léizi] 형 게으른
- ☐ 136 **sweater** [swétər] 명 스웨터
- ☐ 137 **vegetable** [védʒtəbl] 명 채소
- ☐ 138 **guitar** [gitɑ́ːr] 명 기타
- ☐ 139 **cloudy** [kláudi] 형 (날씨가) 흐린
- ☐ 140 **scarf** [skɑːrf] 명 스카프, 목도리
- ☐ 141 **soup** [suːp] 명 수프
- ☐ 142 **nonsense** [nánsèns] 명 허튼소리

Day 05

오늘 외울 단어 **35개**

Chapter 2 시제
PSS & PRACTICE

- ☐ 143 **get** [get] 동 얻다
- ☐ 144 **know** [nou] 동 알다
- ☐ 145 **walk** [wɔːk] 동 걷다
- ☐ 146 **pass** [pæs] 동 지나가다, (시험 등을) 통과하다
- ☐ 147 **mix** [miks] 동 섞다
- ☐ 148 **finish** [fíniʃ] 동 끝내다
- ☐ 149 **stand** [stænd] 동 서다, 서 있다
- ☐ 150 **reach** [riːtʃ] 동 도착하다
- ☐ 151 **impress** [imprés] 동 감명을 주다
- ☐ 152 **sing** [siŋ] 동 노래하다
- ☐ 153 **wish** [wiʃ] 동 바라다
- ☐ 154 **push** [puʃ] 동 밀다
- ☐ 155 **spend** [spend] 동 쓰다, 소비하다
- ☐ 156 **send** [send] 동 보내다
- ☐ 157 **miss** [mis] 동 놓치다, 그리워하다
- ☐ 158 **wake** [weik] 동 잠이 깨다
- ☐ 159 **teach** [tiːtʃ] 동 가르치다
- ☐ 160 **solve** [sɑlv] 동 풀다, 해결하다
- ☐ 161 **catch** [kætʃ] 동 붙잡다
- ☐ 162 **sound** [saund] 동 소리가 나다
- ☐ 163 **throw** [θrou] 동 던지다
- ☐ 164 **burn** [bəːrn] 동 불타다
- ☐ 165 **cross** [krɔːs] 동 교차하다, 건너가다
- ☐ 166 **copy** [kápi] 동 복사하다
- ☐ 167 **grandmother** [grǽnmʌðər] 명 할머니
- ☐ 168 **try** [trai] 동 노력하다, 시도하다
- ☐ 169 **pay** [pei] 동 지불하다
- ☐ 170 **say** [sei] 동 말하다
- ☐ 171 **help** [help] 동 돕다, 거들다
- ☐ 172 **lay** [lei] 동 놓다, 두다
- ☐ 173 **sell** [sel] 동 팔다
- ☐ 174 **kick** [kik] 동 발로 차다
- ☐ 175 **put** [put] 동 놓다, 두다
- ☐ 176 **touch** [tʌtʃ] 동 만지다, 접촉하다, 닿다
- ☐ 177 **lose** [luːz] 동 잃다

Day 06

오늘 외울 단어 **36개**

- ☐ 178 **tell** [tel] — 동 말하다
- ☐ 179 **carry** [kǽri] — 동 나르다, 운반하다
- ☐ 180 **repeat** [ripíːt] — 동 반복하다
- ☐ 181 **grow** [grou] — 동 성장하다, 기르다
- ☐ 182 **cost** [kɔːst] — 동 비용이 들다
- ☐ 183 **judge** [dʒʌdʒ] — 동 판단하다
- ☐ 184 **cheer** [tʃiər] — 동 갈채하다, 응원하다
- ☐ 185 **use** [juːz] — 동 사용하다
- ☐ 186 **think** [θiŋk] — 동 생각하다
- ☐ 187 **mean** [miːn] — 동 의미하다
- ☐ 188 **break** [breik] — 동 깨뜨리다
- ☐ 189 **show** [ʃou] — 동 보여주다
- ☐ 190 **fly** [flai] — 동 날다
- ☐ 191 **turn** [təːrn] — 동 돌다
- ☐ 192 **harm** [hɑːrm] — 동 해치다
- ☐ 193 **win** [win] — 동 이기다
- ☐ 194 **fall** [fɔːl] — 동 떨어지다
- ☐ 195 **build** [bild] — 동 (건물 등을) 짓다
- ☐ 196 **stay** [stei] — 동 머무르다
- ☐ 197 **set** [set] — 동 놓다, 설정하다, (시계 등을) 맞추다
- ☐ 198 **see** [siː] — 동 보다, 이해하다
- ☐ 199 **envy** [énvi] — 동 부러워하다
- ☐ 200 **dream** [driːm] — 동 꿈꾸다
- ☐ 201 **live** [liv] — 동 살다
- ☐ 202 **leave** [liːv] — 동 떠나다
- ☐ 203 **understand** [ʌ̀ndərstǽnd] — 동 이해하다
- ☐ 204 **keep** [kiːp] — 동 계속하다, 유지하다
- ☐ 205 **give** [giv] — 동 주다
- ☐ 206 **laugh** [læf] — 동 웃다
- ☐ 207 **hear** [hiər] — 동 듣다
- ☐ 208 **stop** [stɑp] — 동 멈추다
- ☐ 209 **forget** [fərgét] — 동 잊다
- ☐ 210 **lend** [lend] — 동 빌려주다
- ☐ 211 **hug** [hʌg] — 동 껴안다
- ☐ 212 **arrive** [əráiv] — 동 도착하다
- ☐ 213 **seem** [siːm] — 동 ~처럼 보이다

Day 07

오늘 외울 단어 **36**개

- 214 **agree** [əgríː] 동 동의하다
- 215 **change** [tʃeindʒ] 동 바꾸다
- 216 **call** [kɔːl] 동 부르다, 전화하다, 이름을 지어주다
- 217 **check** [tʃek] 동 확인하다
- 218 **decorate** [dékərèit] 동 장식하다
- 219 **order** [ɔ́ːrdər] 동 명령하다, 주문하다
- 220 **beat** [biːt] 동 이기다, 때리다
- 221 **attack** [ətǽk] 동 공격하다
- 222 **sneeze** [sniːz] 동 재채기하다
- 223 **suggest** [səgdʒést] 동 제안하다
- 224 **place** [pleis] 동 두다, 놓다
- 225 **guess** [ges] 동 추측하다
- 226 **bless** [bles] 동 축복하다
- 227 **escape** [iskéip] 동 달아나다, 탈출하다
- 228 **raise** [reiz] 동 기르다, (들어) 올리다
- 229 **brush** [brʌʃ] 동 솔질하다
- 230 **cause** [kɔːz] 동 ~을 야기시키다, 초래하다
- 231 **dance** [dæns] 동 춤추다 / 명 춤
- 232 **gather** [gǽðər] 동 모으다
- 233 **moss** [mɔːs] 명 이끼
- 234 **sick** [sik] 형 병든, 아픈
- 235 **earth** [əːrθ] 명 지구
- 236 **capital** [kǽpitl] 명 수도
- 237 **east** [iːst] 명 동쪽
- 238 **in the morning** 아침에, 오전에
- 239 **drop** [drɑp] 동 떨어지다
- 240 **plan** [plæn] 동 계획하다
- 241 **invent** [invént] 동 발명하다
- 242 **save** [seiv] 동 구하다, 절약하다, 저축하다
- 243 **improve** [imprúːv] 동 개선하다, 나아지다
- 244 **jump** [dʒʌmp] 동 뛰다, 뛰어넘다
- 245 **cover** [kʌ́vər] 동 덮다
- 246 **learn** [ləːrn] 동 배우다
- 247 **obey** [oubéi] 동 준수하다, 따르다
- 248 **guide** [gaid] 동 안내하다
- 249 **join** [dʒɔin] 동 가입하다, 합류하다

Day 08

오늘 외울 단어 **35개**

☐ 250 **wonder** [wʌ́ndər]	동 궁금해 하다, ~에 놀라다	☐ 268 **lock** [lɑk]	동 (자물쇠로) 잠그다
☐ 251 **end** [end]	동 끝내다	☐ 269 **hate** [heit]	동 미워하다
☐ 252 **surprise** [sərpráiz]	동 놀라게 하다	☐ 270 **type** [taip]	동 타자를 치다
☐ 253 **add** [æd]	동 더하다	☐ 271 **fail** [feil]	동 실패하다
☐ 254 **connect** [kənékt]	동 연결하다	☐ 272 **decide** [disáid]	동 결정하다
☐ 255 **spoil** [spɔil]	동 망치다	☐ 273 **swallow** [swálou]	동 삼키다
☐ 256 **bake** [beik]	동 (빵 등을) 굽다	☐ 274 **shout** [ʃaut]	동 외치다
☐ 257 **roll** [roul]	동 구르다	☐ 275 **spell** [spel]	동 철자를 말하다
☐ 258 **tie** [tai]	동 묶다	☐ 276 **hurt** [həːrt]	동 다치다, 다치게 하다
☐ 259 **collect** [kəlékt]	동 모으다, 수집하다	☐ 277 **let** [let]	동 ~하게 하다
☐ 260 **answer** [ǽnsər]	동 대답하다	☐ 278 **spread** [spred]	동 퍼지다, 펼치다
☐ 261 **marry** [mǽri]	동 결혼하다	☐ 279 **feed** [fiːd]	동 먹이다 명 먹이
☐ 262 **serve** [səːrv]	동 (음식을) 차려주다, 제공하다	☐ 280 **fight** [fait]	동 싸우다
☐ 263 **waste** [weist]	동 낭비하다	☐ 281 **have** [hæv]	동 가지다, 먹다
☐ 264 **share** [ʃɛər]	동 공유하다	☐ 282 **lead** [liːd]	동 인도하다
☐ 265 **train** [trein]	동 훈련하다	☐ 283 **slide** [slaid]	동 미끄러지다
☐ 266 **pour** [pɔːr]	동 따르다, 붓다	☐ 284 **smell** [smel]	동 냄새 맡다, 냄새가 나다
☐ 267 **return** [ritə́ːrn]	동 돌아오다[가다]		

Day 09

오늘 외울 단어 **32개**

- ☐ 285 **bear** [bɛər] 통 낳다
- ☐ 286 **bite** [bait] 통 물다
- ☐ 287 **blow** [blou] 통 불다
- ☐ 288 **choose** [tʃu:z] 통 선택하다
- ☐ 289 **ring** [riŋ] 통 (종, 벨이) 울리다
- ☐ 290 **rise** [raiz] 통 오르다
- ☐ 291 **take** [teik] 통 가지고 가다
- ☐ 292 **break out** 일어나다, 발발하다
- ☐ 293 **restaurant** [réstərənt] 명 식당
- ☐ 294 **skip** [skip] 통 건너뛰다
- ☐ 295 **novel** [návəl] 명 소설
- ☐ 296 **exam** [igzǽm] 명 시험
- ☐ 297 **grandparent** [grǽndpɛ̀ərənt] 명 조부, 조모
- ☐ 298 **make dinner** 저녁식사를 준비하다
- ☐ 299 **make time** 시간을 만들다, 시간을 내다
- ☐ 300 **during** [djúəriŋ] 전 ~ 동안
- ☐ 301 **dive** [daiv] 통 (물속으로) 뛰어들다
- ☐ 302 **have lunch** 점심을 먹다
- ☐ 303 **together** [təgéðər] 부 함께
- ☐ 304 **holiday** [hálədèi] 명 휴가, 휴일
- ☐ 305 **smile** [smail] 통 미소 짓다
- ☐ 306 **library** [láibrèri] 명 도서관
- ☐ 307 **eat out** 외식하다
- ☐ 308 **ill** [il] 형 병든
- ☐ 309 **sunrise** [sʌ́nràiz] 명 일출
- ☐ 310 **project** [prɑ́dʒekt] 명 계획, 기획, 프로젝트
- ☐ 311 **actor** [ǽktər] 명 (남자)배우
- ☐ 312 **role** [roul] 명 역할, 배역
- ☐ 313 **heavily** [hévili] 부 심하게, 아주 많이
- ☐ 314 **snow** [snou] 통 눈이 내리다
- ☐ 315 **ago** [əgóu] 부 ~ 전에
- ☐ 316 **midnight** [mídnàit] 명 자정

Day 10

오늘 외울 단어 **34개**

- ☐ 317 **throw away** — 버리다
- ☐ 318 **carpet** [ká:rpit] — 명 카펫, 깔개

Chapter Review Test

- ☐ 319 **pick** [pik] — 동 고르다, 선택하다
- ☐ 320 **write** [rait] — 동 쓰다, 집필하다
- ☐ 321 **hide** [haid] — 동 감추다, 숨기다
- ☐ 322 **thank** [θæŋk] — 동 고마워하다
- ☐ 323 **explain** [ikspléin] — 동 설명하다
- ☐ 324 **climb** [klaim] — 동 오르다, 등반하다
- ☐ 325 **table tennis** [téibl tènis] — 명 탁구
- ☐ 326 **weather** [wéðər] — 명 날씨
- ☐ 327 **tropical** [trápikəl] — 형 열대의
- ☐ 328 **visit** [vízit] — 동 방문하다
- ☐ 329 **weekend** [wí:kènd] — 명 주말
- ☐ 330 **kite** [kait] — 명 연
- ☐ 331 **listen to** — ~을 듣다
- ☐ 332 **have a barbecue** — 바비큐 파티를 하다
- ☐ 333 **concert** [kánsə(:)rt] — 명 콘서트, 음악회
- ☐ 334 **review** [rivjú:] — 동 복습하다
- ☐ 335 **take a picture** — 사진을 찍다
- ☐ 336 **future** [fjú:tʃər] — 명 미래
- ☐ 337 **begin** [bigín] — 동 시작하다
- ☐ 338 **discuss** [diskʌ́s] — 동 상의하다, 논의하다
- ☐ 339 **last year** — 작년(에)
- ☐ 340 **get up** — (잠자리에서) 일어나다
- ☐ 341 **daily** [déili] — 형 매일 일어나는
- ☐ 342 **foreigner** [fɔ́(:)rinər] — 명 외국인
- ☐ 343 **designer** [dizáinər] — 명 디자이너
- ☐ 344 **loudly** [láudli] — 부 큰 소리로, 시끄럽게
- ☐ 345 **aunt** [ænt] — 명 이모, 고모
- ☐ 346 **field trip** [fí:ld trìp] — 명 현장학습
- ☐ 347 **these days** — 요즘에는
- ☐ 348 **spaghetti** [spəgéti] — 명 스파게티
- ☐ 349 **play baseball** — 야구를 하다
- ☐ 350 **headset** [hédsèt] — 명 헤드폰

Day 11

오늘 외울 단어 **35개**

Chapter 3 조동사

PSS & PRACTICE

- 351 **something** [sʌ́mθiŋ] — 대 무엇인가, 어떤 것
- 352 **right** [rait] — 형 옳은, 오른쪽의
- 353 **match** [mætʃ] — 명 경기, 시합
- 354 **break off** — 꺾어버리다
- 355 **branch** [bræntʃ] — 명 나뭇가지
- 356 **promise** [prάmis] — 명 약속
- 357 **true** [truː] — 형 진실의, 참된
- 358 **bill** [bil] — 명 지폐
- 359 **chopstick** [tʃάpstìk] — 명 젓가락
- 360 **invite** [inváit] — 동 초대하다
- 361 **recycle** [rìːsáikl] — 동 재활용하다
- 362 **for a while** — 잠시 동안
- 363 **lecture** [léktʃər] — 명 강의
- 364 **find** [faind] — 동 찾다, 알아내다
- 365 **exit** [égzit] — 명 출구
- 366 **make it** — 성공하다, 해내다
- 367 **thirsty** [θə́ːrsti] — 형 목마른
- 368 **alone** [əlóun] — 부 홀로
- 369 **dangerous** [déindʒərəs] — 형 위험한
- 370 **minute** [mínit] — 명 (시간 단위) 분
- 371 **have a seat** — 앉다
- 372 **go out** — 외출하다, 나가다
- 373 **tomorrow** [təmɔ́ːrou] — 부 내일
- 374 **phone number** [fóun nʌ̀mbər] — 명 전화번호
- 375 **tonight** [tənáit] — 부 오늘밤에
- 376 **try on** — 입어 보다
- 377 **problem** [prάbləm] — 명 문제
- 378 **casual** [kǽʒuəl] — 형 평상복의
- 379 **clothes** [klouz] — 명 옷, 의복
- 380 **follow** [fάlou] — 동 따르다
- 381 **law** [lɔː] — 명 법
- 382 **outside** [áutsàid] — 부 바깥에
- 383 **elevator** [éləvèitər] — 명 엘리베이터
- 384 **stair** [stɛər] — 명 계단
- 385 **traffic** [trǽfik] — 명 교통

Day 12

오늘 외울 단어 33개

- ☐ 386 **dentist** [déntist] 명 치과 의사
- ☐ 387 **protect** [prətékt] 동 보호하다
- ☐ 388 **tell a lie** 거짓말하다
- ☐ 389 **exercise** [éksərsàiz] 동 운동하다
- ☐ 390 **straight** [streit] 부 똑바로, 일직선으로
- ☐ 391 **take off** 벗다

Chapter Review Test

- ☐ 392 **be interested in** ~에 관심이 있다
- ☐ 393 **take care of** ~을 돌보다
- ☐ 394 **anything** [éniθiŋ] 대 무엇, 아무것
- ☐ 395 **park** [pɑːrk] 동 주차하다
- ☐ 396 **human** [hjúːmən] 명 사람, 인간
- ☐ 397 **fall asleep** 잠들다
- ☐ 398 **turn off** 끄다
- ☐ 399 **theater** [θíːətər] 명 극장
- ☐ 400 **contest** [kάntest] 명 대회, 시합
- ☐ 401 **post office** [póust ɔ́ːfis] 명 우체국
- ☐ 402 **succeed** [səksíːd] 동 성공하다
- ☐ 403 **balloon** [bəlúːn] 명 풍선
- ☐ 404 **clean up** 청소하다
- ☐ 405 **matter** [mǽtər] 명 문제
- ☐ 406 **toothache** [túːθèik] 명 치통
- ☐ 407 **be late for school** 학교에 지각하다
- ☐ 408 **squirrel** [skwə́ːrəl] 명 다람쥐
- ☐ 409 **lie** [lai] 동 거짓말하다 명 거짓말

Chapter 4 수동태

PSS & PRACTICE

- ☐ 410 **foreign** [fɔ́ːrin] 형 외국의
- ☐ 411 **pick up** ~을 집다, 들어올리다
- ☐ 412 **expression** [ikspréʃən] 명 표현
- ☐ 413 **principal** [prínsəpəl] 명 교장 선생님
- ☐ 414 **president** [prézidənt] 명 대통령, 사장
- ☐ 415 **deliver** [dilívər] 동 배달하다
- ☐ 416 **speech** [spiːtʃ] 명 연설
- ☐ 417 **kill** [kil] 동 죽이다
- ☐ 418 **war** [wɔːr] 명 전쟁

Day 13

오늘 외울 단어 **33**개

- 419 **once** [wʌns] — 부 한 번
- 420 **memory** [méməri] — 명 기억
- 421 **someone** [sʌ́mwÀn] — 대 누군가
- 422 **fresh** [freʃ] — 형 신선한
- 423 **building** [bíldiŋ] — 명 건물
- 424 **refrigerator** [rifrídʒərèitər] — 명 냉장고
- 425 **reader** [ríːdər] — 명 독자
- 426 **elect** [ilékt] — 동 선출하다
- 427 **jungle** [dʒʌ́ŋgl] — 명 밀림지대, 정글
- 428 **painting** [péintiŋ] — 명 그림, 회화
- 429 **dead** [ded] — 형 죽은
- 430 **princess** [prínses] — 명 공주
- 431 **respect** [rispékt] — 동 존경하다
- 432 **village** [vílidʒ] — 명 마을
- 433 **design** [dizáin] — 동 디자인하다
- 434 **language** [lǽŋgwidʒ] — 명 언어
- 435 **teenager** [tíːnèidʒər] — 명 10대의 청소년
- 436 **musician** [mjuːzíʃən] — 명 음악가
- 437 **publish** [pʌ́bliʃ] — 동 출판하다
- 438 **magazine** [mæ̀gəzíːn] — 명 잡지

Chapter Review Test

- 439 **bee** [biː] — 명 벌
- 440 **be born** — 태어나다
- 441 **crowd** [kraud] — 동 모여들다, 붐비다
- 442 **fix** [fiks] — 동 고치다, 수리하다
- 443 **make** [meik] — 동 ~하게 하다
- 444 **found** [faund] — 동 설립하다, 세우다
- 445 **robber** [rábər] — 명 도둑, 강도
- 446 **steal** [stiːl] — 동 훔치다
- 447 **somebody** [sʌ́mbÀdi] — 대 어떤 사람, 누군가

Chapter 5 명사와 관사

PSS & PRACTICE

- 448 **audience** [ɔ́ːdiəns] — 명 청중, 관중
- 449 **beauty** [bjúːti] — 명 아름다움, 미(美)
- 450 **truth** [truːθ] — 명 진실
- 451 **freedom** [fríːdəm] — 명 자유

Day 14

오늘 외울 단어 **36개**

- ☐ 452 **peace** [piːs] 명 평화
- ☐ 453 **flour** [flauər] 명 밀가루
- ☐ 454 **wealth** [welθ] 명 부, 재산
- ☐ 455 **kindness** [káindnis] 명 친절함
- ☐ 456 **pity** [píti] 명 동정, 연민
- ☐ 457 **pleasure** [pléʒər] 명 즐거움, 기쁨
- ☐ 458 **lesson** [lésn] 명 수업, 교훈
- ☐ 459 **smoke** [smouk] 명 연기
- ☐ 460 **happiness** [hǽpinis] 명 행복
- ☐ 461 **form** [fɔːrm] 명 모양, 형상
- ☐ 462 **friendship** [fréndʃip] 명 우정
- ☐ 463 **mosquito** [məskíːtou] 명 모기
- ☐ 464 **address** [ədrés] 명 주소
- ☐ 465 **passport** [pǽspɔ̀ːrt] 명 여권
- ☐ 466 **bath** [bæθ] 명 목욕
- ☐ 467 **brush** [brʌʃ] 명 솔
- ☐ 468 **shelf** [ʃelf] 명 선반
- ☐ 469 **wife** [waif] 명 부인, 아내
- ☐ 470 **safe** [seif] 명 금고 / 형 안전한
- ☐ 471 **roof** [ruːf] 명 지붕
- ☐ 472 **country** [kʌ́ntri] 명 나라, 국가
- ☐ 473 **factory** [fǽktəri] 명 공장
- ☐ 474 **idea** [aidíː(ː)ə] 명 생각, 아이디어
- ☐ 475 **headache** [hédèik] 명 두통
- ☐ 476 **bottle** [bάtl] 명 병
- ☐ 477 **poster** [póustər] 명 포스터, 전단 광고
- ☐ 478 **block** [blɑk] 명 나무 조각, 구역
- ☐ 479 **deer** [diər] 명 사슴
- ☐ 480 **sheep** [ʃiːp] 명 양
- ☐ 481 **goose** [guːs] 명 거위, 기러기
- ☐ 482 **mouse** [maus] 명 생쥐
- ☐ 483 **ox** [ɑks] 명 황소
- ☐ 484 **festival** [féstəvəl] 명 축제
- ☐ 485 **candle** [kǽndl] 명 양초
- ☐ 486 **month** [mʌnθ] 명 달, 개월
- ☐ 487 **wagon** [wǽgən] 명 수레, 짐마차

Day 15

오늘 외울 단어 36개

- 488 **thief** [θiːf] 명 도둑
- 489 **autumn** [ɔ́ːtəm] 명 가을
- 490 **chalk** [tʃɔːk] 명 분필, 초크
- 491 **advice** [ədváis] 명 충고
- 492 **furniture** [fə́ːrnitʃər] 명 가구
- 493 **university** [jùːnəvə́ːrsəti] 명 대학교
- 494 **famous** [féiməs] 형 유명한
- 495 **be known for** ~로 알려져 있다
- 496 **sense** [sens] 명 감각
- 497 **special** [spéʃəl] 형 특별한
- 498 **story** [stɔ́ːri] 명 (건물의) 층
- 499 **break** [breik] 명 잠깐의 휴식
- 500 **European** [jùərəpíːən] 명 유럽 사람 형 유럽의
- 501 **elementary** [èləméntəri] 형 초급의, 초등의
- 502 **downtown** [dáuntáun] 명 도심지, 상업 지구
- 503 **crane** [krein] 명 학, 두루미
- 504 **snake** [sneik] 명 뱀
- 505 **floor** [flɔːr] 명 마루, 층
- 506 **clear** [kliər] 형 맑은
- 507 **imagine** [imǽdʒin] 동 상상하다
- 508 **insect** [ínsekt] 명 곤충
- 509 **faithful** [féiθfəl] 형 충실한
- 510 **bathroom** [bǽθrùː(ː)m] 명 화장실
- 511 **station** [stéiʃən] 명 역
- 512 **airplane** [ɛ́ərplèin] 명 비행기
- 513 **cancer** [kǽnsər] 명 암
- 514 **same** [seim] 형 같은
- 515 **another** [ənʌ́ðər] 대 또 하나, 다른 것
- 516 **seat** [siːt] 명 좌석
- 517 **pocket** [pákit] 명 호주머니
- 518 **bowl** [boul] 명 사발
- 519 **armchair** [áːrmtʃɛ̀ər] 명 안락의자
- 520 **mug** [mʌg] 명 컵, 머그잔
- 521 **popular** [pápjulər] 형 인기 있는
- 522 **humid** [hjúmid] 형 습한
- 523 **airless** [ɛ́ərlis] 형 숨막히는, 공기가 안 통하는

Day 16

오늘 외울 단어 **33개**

- ☐ 524 **turkey** [tə́:rki] 명 칠면조
- ☐ 525 **recognize** [rékəgnàiz] 동 알아보다
- ☐ 526 **come into** ~에 들어가다

Chapter Review Test

- ☐ 527 **blackboard** [blǽkbɔ̀:rd] 명 칠판
- ☐ 528 **plate** [pleit] 명 접시, 그릇
- ☐ 529 **play** [plei] 명 연극, 놀이
- ☐ 530 **dessert** [dizə́:rt] 명 후식, 디저트
- ☐ 531 **at the end of** ~의 끝에
- ☐ 532 **wolf** [wulf] 명 늑대
- ☐ 533 **uncle** [ʌ́ŋkl] 명 (외)삼촌, 이모[고모]부
- ☐ 534 **uniform** [jú:nəfɔ̀:rm] 명 제복, 교복
- ☐ 535 **in front of** ~의 앞에
- ☐ 536 **several** [sévərəl] 대 몇몇 / 형 각각의, 몇몇의
- ☐ 537 **useful** [jú:sfəl] 형 유용한
- ☐ 538 **pair** [pɛər] 명 한 쌍[벌]
- ☐ 539 **slice** [slais] 명 (음식을 얇게 썬) 조각
- ☐ 540 **sightseeing** [sáitsì:iŋ] 명 관광, 구경

- ☐ 541 **jeans** [dʒi:nz] 명 청바지
- ☐ 542 **look for** ~을 찾다
- ☐ 543 **scissors** [sízərz] 명 가위
- ☐ 544 **cent** [sent] 명 (화폐 단위) 센트
- ☐ 545 **volunteer** [vàləntíər] 명 지원자, 자원 봉사자
- ☐ 546 **necklace** [néklis] 명 목걸이
- ☐ 547 **oak tree** [óuk trì:] 명 오크나무
- ☐ 548 **leaf** [li:f] 명 (나무) 잎
- ☐ 549 **clover** [klóuvər] 명 클로버, 토끼풀
- ☐ 550 **always** [ɔ́:lweiz] 부 항상
- ☐ 551 **human being** [hjú:mən bí:iŋ] 명 인간, 사람
- ☐ 552 **each other** [i:tʃ ʌ́ðər] 대 서로

Chapter 6 대명사

PSS & PRACTICE

- ☐ 553 **bakery** [béikəri] 명 빵집, 제과점
- ☐ 554 **rest** [rest] 동 쉬다, 휴식하다
- ☐ 555 **tail** [teil] 명 꼬리
- ☐ 556 **be full of** ~로 가득차다

Day 17

오늘 외울 단어 35개

- 557 **still** [stil] 부 여전히
- 558 **journey** [dʒə́ːrni] 명 여행, 여정
- 559 **tough** [tʌf] 형 힘든
- 560 **prize** [praiz] 명 상
- 561 **culture** [kʌ́ltʃər] 명 문화
- 562 **similar** [símələr] 형 유사한
- 563 **important** [impɔ́ːrtənt] 형 중요한
- 564 **textbook** [tékstbùk] 명 교과서
- 565 **color** [kʌ́lər] 동 색을 칠하다 / 명 색
- 566 **kill oneself** 자살하다
- 567 **pay for** ~에 대해 돈을 지불하다
- 568 **catch[have] a cold** 감기에 걸리다
- 569 **dark** [dɑːrk] 형 어두운
- 570 **turtle** [tə́ːrtl] 명 거북
- 571 **between** [bitwíːn] 전 ~ 사이에
- 572 **fault** [fɔːlt] 명 잘못, 실수
- 573 **pine tree** [páin triː] 명 소나무
- 574 **dishonest** [disánist] 형 부정직한
- 575 **course** [kɔːrs] 명 교과과정, 과목
- 576 **example** [igzǽmpl] 명 예, 실례
- 577 **weigh** [wei] 동 무게가 나가다
- 578 **wrap** [ræp] 동 싸다, 포장하다
- 579 **pound** [paund] 명 (중량의 단위) 파운드
- 580 **science** [sáiəns] 명 과학
- 581 **homeroom teacher** [hóumrùːm tíːtʃər] 명 담임 선생님
- 582 **backpack** [bǽkpæ̀k] 명 배낭
- 583 **no way** 절대로 아니다, 절대로 안 되다

Chapter Review Test

- 584 **science fiction** [sáiəns fíkʃən] 명 공상 과학 영화[소설]
- 585 **horror** [hɔ́ːrər] 명 공포 영화, 공포
- 586 **after school** 방과 후에
- 587 **rotten** [rátən] 형 썩은
- 588 **belong to** ~에 속하다, ~의 소유이다
- 589 **own** [oun] 동 소유하다
- 590 **proud** [praud] 형 자랑스러운
- 591 **fall** [fɔːl] 명 가을

Day 18

오늘 외울 단어 **34개**

- □ 592 **season** [síːzən] 명 계절
- □ 593 **mirror** [mírər] 명 거울
- □ 594 **need** [niːd] 명 필요한 것
- □ 595 **fur** [fəːr] 명 모피, 털
- □ 596 **hamster** [hǽmstər] 명 햄스터
- □ 597 **on the Internet** 인터넷(상)에서
- □ 598 **musical instrument** [mjúːzikəl ínstrəmənt] 명 악기
- □ 599 **knife** [naif] 명 칼
- □ 600 **pilot** [páilət] 명 조종사
- □ 601 **each** [iːtʃ] 형 각각의

Chapter 7 부정사
PSS & PRACTICE

- □ 602 **easy** [íːzi] 형 쉬운
- □ 603 **goal** [goul] 명 목표
- □ 604 **get lost** 행방불명이 되다
- □ 605 **simple** [símpl] 형 간단한, 단순한
- □ 606 **historic** [histɔ́ːrik] 형 역사상 중요한
- □ 607 **place** [pleis] 명 장소

- □ 608 **helpful** [hélpfəl] 형 도움이 되는
- □ 609 **soon** [suːn] 부 곧, 이내
- □ 610 **expect** [ikspékt] 동 기대하다
- □ 611 **scientist** [sáiəntist] 명 과학자
- □ 612 **peaceful** [píːsfəl] 형 평화로운
- □ 613 **get to** ~에 도착하다
- □ 614 **turn** [təːrn] 명 순번, 차례
- □ 615 **ask for** ~을 요청하다
- □ 616 **sail** [seil] 동 항해하다
- □ 617 **breathe** [briːð] 동 숨쉬다
- □ 618 **go back** 되돌아가다
- □ 619 **bill** [bil] 명 청구서
- □ 620 **pleased** [pliːzd] 형 기뻐하는
- □ 621 **surprised** [sərpráizd] 형 놀란
- □ 622 **deaf** [def] 형 귀가 먼
- □ 623 **grow up** 자라다, 성장하다
- □ 624 **cure** [kjuər] 명 치료
- □ 625 **lose weight** 살을 빼다

Day 19

오늘 외울 단어 **35개**

- 626 **cut down** 베다, 줄이다
- 627 **one's school days** ~의 학창 시절
- 628 **plant** [plænt] 명 식물
- 629 **chat** [tʃæt] 동 잡담하다, 채팅하다
- 630 **chemical** [kémikəl] 명 화학 물질
- 631 **weed** [wiːd] 명 잡초
- 632 **whole** [houl] 형 전체의
- 633 **blind** [blaind] 형 눈이 먼, 맹인의
- 634 **football** [fútbɔ̀ːl] 명 미식축구
- 635 **storm** [stɔːrm] 명 폭풍
- 636 **run after** 뒤쫓다

Chapter Review Test

- 637 **hear from** ~에게서 소식을 듣다
- 638 **do volunteer work** 자원봉사를 하다
- 639 **hobby** [hábi] 명 취미
- 640 **focus on** ~에 집중하다
- 641 **blouse** [blaus] 명 블라우스
- 642 **pool** [puːl] 명 수영장
- 643 **close** [klouz] 동 닫다, 막다, (눈을) 감다
- 644 **travel** [trævl] 동 여행하다
- 645 **abroad** [əbrɔ́ːd] 부 해외에, 외국에
- 646 **habit** [hǽbit] 명 습관, 버릇
- 647 **save time** 시간을 아끼다
- 648 **mascot** [mǽskət] 명 마스코트
- 649 **race** [reis] 명 경주, 경기
- 650 **shake** [ʃeik] 동 흔들(리)다, 떨다
- 651 **pencil case** [pénsl kèis] 명 필통
- 652 **from side to side** 좌우로 (흔들리는)
- 653 **campaign** [kæmpéin] 명 캠페인
- 654 **painter** [péintər] 명 화가
- 655 **take part in** ~에 참가하다
- 656 **early** [ə́ːrli] 부 일찍
- 657 **see a doctor** 의사에게 진찰을 받다
- 658 **take a walk** 산책하다
- 659 **talk about** ~에 대해 얘기하다
- 660 **nursing home** [nə́ːrsiŋ houm] 명 요양원

Day 20

오늘 외울 단어 **33개**

661 **elderly** [éldərli]	형 나이가 지긋한	677 **tear** [tiər]	명 눈물
		678 **come out**	나오다
Chapter 8 동명사		679 **anyone** [éniwʌ̀n]	대 아무나, 누구나
PSS & PRACTICE		**Chapter Review Test**	
662 **activity** [æktívəti]	명 활동	680 **thank for**	~에 대해 감사하다
663 **farm** [fáːrm]	동 농사를 짓다	681 **nature** [néitʃər]	명 자연
664 **regularly** [régjulərli]	부 규칙적으로	682 **be good at**	~를 잘하다
665 **health** [helθ]	명 건강	683 **suddenly** [sʌ́dnli]	부 갑자기, 불현듯
666 **mind** [maind]	동 꺼려하다	684 **stadium** [stéidiəm]	명 경기장
667 **cartoon** [kɑːrtúːn]	명 (시사 풍자) 만화	685 **meal** [miːl]	명 식사
668 **through** [θru]	전 ~을 통하여	686 **noise** [nɔiz]	명 소음
669 **win a prize**	상을 타다	687 **keep ~ from …**	~가 …하지 못하게 하다
670 **continue** [kəntínjuː]	동 계속하다	688 **give up**	포기하다
671 **someday (= some day)** [sʌ́mdèi]	부 언젠가, 머지않아	689 **disabled** [diséibld]	형 신체장애가 있는
672 **go for a walk**	산책하러 가다	690 **play the violin**	바이올린 연주를 하다
673 **rule** [ruːl]	명 규칙	691 **overcome** [òuvərkʌ́m]	동 극복하다
674 **go on a picnic**	소풍 가다	692 **limitation** [lìmitéiʃən]	명 한계
675 **take a test**	테스트[검사]를 받다, 시험을 보다	693 **astronaut** [æstrənɔ̀ːt]	명 우주 비행사
676 **bench** [bentʃ]	명 벤치, 긴 의자		

Day 21

오늘 외울 단어 **34개**

- ☐ 694 **give a hand** — 도움을 주다
- ☐ 695 **ride a bicycle** — 자전거를 타다
- ☐ 696 **be good for** — ~에 좋다, 유익하다
- ☐ 697 **strength** [streŋθ] — 명 힘, 기운, 강점
- ☐ 698 **be bad for** — ~에 나쁘다
- ☐ 699 **hold** [hould] — 동 잡고 있다, 개최하다
- ☐ 700 **fishing** [fíʃiŋ] — 명 낚시, 어업
- ☐ 701 **in-line skating** [ínlaɪn skéitiŋ] — 명 인라인 스케이팅
- ☐ 702 **get rid of** — 제거하다
- ☐ 703 **overflow** [òuvərflóu] — 동 넘치다
- ☐ 704 **gas** [gæs] — 명 기체
- ☐ 705 **little by little** — 조금씩, 차츰
- ☐ 706 **therefore** [ðɛ́ərfɔ̀ːr] — 부 그러므로
- ☐ 707 **avoid** [əvɔ́id] — 동 피하다, 막다
- ☐ 708 **beach** [biːtʃ] — 명 해변
- ☐ 709 **apologize** [əpálədʒàiz] — 동 사과하다
- ☐ 710 **along** [əlɔ́(ː)ŋ] — 전 ~을 따라
- ☐ 711 **take the stairs** — 계단을 이용하다
- ☐ 712 **be tired of** — 싫증이 나다

Chapter 9 분사

PSS & PRACTICE

- ☐ 713 **gate** [geit] — 명 정문, (대)문
- ☐ 714 **actress** [ǽktris] — 명 여배우
- ☐ 715 **garage sale** [gərάːʒ seil] — 명 차고 세일
- ☐ 716 **brick** [brik] — 명 벽돌
- ☐ 717 **sparrow** [spǽrou] — 명 참새
- ☐ 718 **trash** [træʃ] — 명 쓰레기
- ☐ 719 **person** [pə́ːrsən] — 명 사람
- ☐ 720 **remember** [rimémbər] — 동 기억하다
- ☐ 721 **product** [prάdʌkt] — 명 생산품
- ☐ 722 **company** [kʌ́mpəni] — 명 회사
- ☐ 723 **flood** [flʌd] — 동 범람하다 / 명 홍수
- ☐ 724 **film** [film] — 명 영화
- ☐ 725 **death** [deθ] — 명 죽음
- ☐ 726 **result** [rizʌ́lt] — 명 결과
- ☐ 727 **behavior** [bihéivjər] — 명 행동

Day 22

오늘 외울 단어 **33개**

- ☐ 728 **accident** [ǽksidənt] 명 사고
- ☐ 729 **performance** [pərfɔ́ːrməns] 명 공연

Chapter Review Test

- ☐ 730 **look at** ~을 보다
- ☐ 731 **broken** [bróukən] 형 부서진, 망가진
- ☐ 732 **cell phone** [sel foun] 명 휴대폰
- ☐ 733 **enjoyable** [indʒɔ́iəbl] 형 즐길 수 있는
- ☐ 734 **fluently** [flúːəntli] 부 유창하게
- ☐ 735 **topic** [tápik] 명 주제
- ☐ 736 **full moon** [ful muːn] 명 보름달
- ☐ 737 **hesitant** [hézitənt] 형 주저하는, 망설이는
- ☐ 738 **set up** 세우다
- ☐ 739 **key** [kiː] 명 비결, 열쇠
- ☐ 740 **disappointed** [dìsəpɔ́intid] 형 실망한
- ☐ 741 **wild flower** [wáild flàuər] 명 들꽃, 야생초
- ☐ 742 **shocking** [ʃáːkiŋ] 형 충격적인
- ☐ 743 **tiring** [táiəriŋ] 형 피곤하게 만드는
- ☐ 744 **stage** [steidʒ] 명 무대
- ☐ 745 **carnation** [kɑːrnéiʃən] 명 카네이션
- ☐ 746 **compete** [kəmpíːt] 동 경쟁하다, ~와 겨루다
- ☐ 747 **situation** [sìtʃuéiʃən] 명 상황, 환경
- ☐ 748 **show up** 나타나다, 눈에 띄다
- ☐ 749 **roast** [roust] 동 (불에) 굽다
- ☐ 750 **garlic** [gáːrlik] 명 마늘
- ☐ 751 **onion** [ʌ́njən] 명 양파
- ☐ 752 **satisfied** [sǽtisfàid] 형 만족하는

Chapter 10 형용사

PSS & PRACTICE

- ☐ 753 **field** [fiːld] 명 들판
- ☐ 754 **poor** [puər] 형 가난한
- ☐ 755 **talent** [tǽlənt] 명 재능
- ☐ 756 **piece** [piːs] 명 조각
- ☐ 757 **glass** [glæs] 명 유리
- ☐ 758 **danger** [déindʒər] 명 위험
- ☐ 759 **readily** [rédili] 부 손쉽게, 기꺼이
- ☐ 760 **hunger** [hʌ́ŋgər] 명 굶주림, 기아

Day 23

오늘 외울 단어 35개

- 761 **sickness** [síknis] 몡 병
- 762 **curious** [kjúriəs] 혱 궁금한, 호기심이 많은
- 763 **class** [klæs] 몡 학급, 수업
- 764 **crowded** [kráudid] 혱 붐비는
- 765 **perfect** [pə́ːrfikt] 혱 완벽한
- 766 **palace** [pǽlis] 몡 궁전
- 767 **else** [els] 혱 그 밖의 다른 / 부 그 밖에 달리
- 768 **be sold out** 품절되다
- 769 **discover** [diskʌ́vər] 동 발견하다
- 770 **wrong** [rɔːŋ] 혱 틀린
- 771 **necessary** [nésəsèri] 혱 필요한
- 772 **clever** [klévər] 혱 영리한
- 773 **bride** [braid] 몡 신부
- 774 **reporter** [ripɔ́ːrtər] 몡 기자
- 775 **temple** [témpl] 몡 사원
- 776 **planet** [plǽnit] 몡 행성
- 777 **rock** [rɑk] 몡 바위
- 778 **courage** [kə́ːridʒ] 몡 용기
- 779 **French** [frentʃ] 혱 프랑스의 / 몡 프랑스어
- 780 **trouble** [trʌ́bl] 몡 불편, 문제점
- 781 **luck** [lʌk] 몡 운, 행운
- 782 **wallet** [wɑ́lit] 몡 지갑
- 783 **medicine** [médsn] 몡 약
- 784 **without** [wiðáut] 전 ~이 없이
- 785 **chance** [tʃæns] 몡 기회

Chapter Review Test

- 786 **basket** [bǽskit] 몡 바구니
- 787 **century** [séntʃəri] 몡 100년, 세기
- 788 **past** [pæst] 혱 지난, 지나간, 이전의
- 789 **vote** [vout] 몡 표, 투표
- 790 **boil** [bɔil] 동 끓다, 끓이다
- 791 **degree** [digríː] 몡 (온도 단위) 도
- 792 **animal** [ǽniml] 몡 동물
- 793 **butter** [bʌ́tər] 몡 버터
- 794 **grade** [greid] 몡 학년
- 795 **roommate** [rúːmmèit] 몡 룸메이트

Day 24

오늘 외울 단어 **34**개

- 796 **church** [tʃəːrtʃ] — 명 교회
- 797 **quarter** [kwɔːrtər] — 명 4분의 1, 15분
- 798 **nothing special** — 특별한 일이 없다
- 799 **sound** [saund] — 형 건전한
- 800 **spirit** [spírit] — 명 정신
- 801 **temperature** [témpərətʃər] — 명 온도
- 802 **sand** [sænd] — 명 모래
- 803 **playground** [pléigràund] — 명 놀이터, 운동장
- 804 **bobsled** [bábslèd] — 명 봅슬레이
- 805 **difficulty** [dífikʌlti] — 명 어려움, 고난
- 806 **cafeteria** [kæ̀fətíriə] — 명 식당, 구내식당
- 807 **experience** [ikspí(ː)əriəns] — 명 경험
- 808 **effort** [éfərt] — 명 노력, 공
- 809 **neighborhood** [néibərhùd] — 명 인근, 이웃
- 810 **half** [hæf] — 명 절반, 30분
- 811 **until** [əntíl] — 전 ~까지
- 812 **before** [bifɔ́ːr] — 전 ~전에

Chapter 11 부사

🎧 PSS & PRACTICE

- 813 **quick** [kwik] — 형 빠른
- 814 **large** [lɑːrdʒ] — 형 큰, 넓은
- 815 **lucky** [lʌ́ki] — 형 운 좋은
- 816 **wise** [waiz] — 형 현명한
- 817 **usual** [júːʒuəl] — 형 보통의
- 818 **real** [ríːəl] — 형 진짜의
- 819 **surprising** [sərpráiziŋ] — 형 놀라운
- 820 **sincere** [sinsíər] — 형 진실된, 진정한, 진심어린
- 821 **silent** [sáilənt] — 형 조용한
- 822 **noisy** [nɔ́izi] — 형 시끄러운
- 823 **loud** [laud] — 형 소리가 큰
- 824 **sudden** [sʌ́dən] — 형 갑작스러운
- 825 **regular** [régjulər] — 형 정기적인
- 826 **serious** [síəriəs] — 형 심각한, 진지한
- 827 **brave** [breiv] — 형 용감한
- 828 **various** [vɛ́əriəs] — 형 여러 가지의, 다양한
- 829 **main** [mein] — 형 주된, 주요한

Day 25

오늘 외울 단어 **35**개

- 830 **graceful** [gréisfəl] — 형 우아한
- 831 **dear** [diər] — 형 친애하는
- 832 **act** [ækt] — 동 행동하다
- 833 **appear** [əpíər] — 동 나타나다
- 834 **worm** [wəːrm] — 명 벌레
- 835 **everybody** [évribàdi] — 대 각자 모두, 누구든지
- 836 **price** [prais] — 명 가격
- 837 **fever** [fíːvər] — 명 열
- 838 **depend on** — ~에 의지하다, ~에 달려 있다
- 839 **never** [névər] — 부 결코 ~ 않다
- 840 **plastic bag** [plǽstik bǽg] — 명 비닐봉지
- 841 **foggy** [fɔ́ːgi] — 형 안개 낀
- 842 **deliver** [dilívər] — 동 배달하다
- 843 **meeting** [míːtiŋ] — 명 회의
- 844 **dish** [diʃ] — 명 요리
- 845 **count on** — ~을 믿다
- 846 **hope** [houp] — 동 바라다, 희망하다
- 847 **glasses** [glǽsiːz] — 명 안경
- 848 **jacket** [dʒǽkit] — 명 재킷
- 849 **suit** [suːt] — 명 수트, 정장 한 벌
- 850 **garbage** [gáːrbidʒ] — 명 쓰레기
- 851 **alarm** [əláːrm] — 명 자명종
- 852 **put on** — (옷 따위를) 입다, 쓰다
- 853 **twice** [twais] — 부 두 번
- 854 **behind** [biháind] — 전 ~ 뒤에

Chapter Review Test

- 855 **carrot** [kǽrət] — 명 당근
- 856 **work out** — 운동하다
- 857 **flash** [flæʃ] — 명 플래시, 번득임, 섬광
- 858 **dancer** [dǽnsər] — 명 댄서, 무용수
- 859 **junk food** [dʒʌŋk fuːd] — 명 정크 푸드
- 860 **quickly** [kwíkli] — 부 빨리, 빠르게
- 861 **weekly** [wíːkli] — 형 매주의, 주간의
- 862 **look around** — 둘러보다
- 863 **pack** [pæk] — 동 (짐을) 싸다
- 864 **stuff** [stʌf] — 명 물건

Day 26

오늘 외울 단어 **34개**

- 865 **lately** [léitli] — 부 최근에, 얼마 전에
- 866 **happily** [hǽpili] — 부 행복하게
- 867 **carefully** [kɛ́ərfəli] — 부 주의하여, 조심스럽게
- 868 **scary** [skɛ́:ri] — 형 무서운
- 869 **well** [wel] — 부 잘, 좋게

Chapter 12 비교구문
PSS & PRACTICE

- 870 **hard** [hɑ:rd] — 형 힘든 부 열심히
- 871 **weak** [wi:k] — 형 약한
- 872 **smart** [smɑ:rt] — 형 영리한
- 873 **fat** [fæt] — 형 뚱뚱한
- 874 **light** [lait] — 형 가벼운
- 875 **mild** [maild] — 형 온화한
- 876 **tasty** [téisti] — 형 맛좋은
- 877 **strict** [strikt] — 형 엄격한
- 878 **hopeless** [hóuplis] — 형 가망 없는, 절망적인
- 879 **foolish** [fú:liʃ] — 형 어리석은
- 880 **patient** [péiʃənt] — 형 인내심 있는
- 881 **bright** [brait] — 형 밝은
- 882 **lovely** [lʌ́vli] — 형 사랑스러운
- 883 **close** [klous] — 형 가까운
- 884 **badly** [bǽdli] — 부 나쁘게
- 885 **colorful** [kʌ́lərfəl] — 형 다채로운, 형형색색의
- 886 **diligent** [dílədʒənt] — 형 근면한
- 887 **costly** [kɔ́:stli] — 형 값비싼
- 888 **thin** [θin] — 형 가는, 야윈
- 889 **slim** [slim] — 형 가는, 날씬한
- 890 **thick** [θik] — 형 두꺼운
- 891 **useless** [jú:slis] — 형 쓸모없는
- 892 **deep** [di:p] — 형 깊은
- 893 **generous** [dʒénərəs] — 형 관대한
- 894 **comfortable** [kʌ́mfərtəbl] — 형 편안한
- 895 **husband** [hʌ́zbənd] — 명 남편
- 896 **other** [ʌ́ðər] — 형 다른 대 다른 것
- 897 **modern** [mɑ́dərn] — 형 현대적인
- 898 **butterfly** [bʌ́tərflài] — 명 나비

Day 27

오늘 외울 단어 33개

- 899 **public** [pʌ́blik] 형 공공의
- 900 **air mail** [ɛər meil] 명 항공 우편
- 901 **drugstore** [drʌ́gstɔ̀ːr] 명 약국
- 902 **intelligent** [intélədʒənt] 형 지적인, 총명한
- 903 **excuse** [ikskjúːz] 명 변명, 이유
- 904 **clothing** [klóuðiŋ] 명 의류
- 905 **choice** [tʃɔis] 명 선택
- 906 **cheetah** [tʃíːtə] 명 치타
- 907 **bridge** [bridʒ] 명 다리, 교량
- 908 **score** [skɔːr] 명 점수
- 909 **dinosaur** [dáinəsɔ̀ːr] 명 공룡
- 910 **pleasant** [plézənt] 형 즐거운
- 911 **illness** [ílnis] 명 병

Chapter Review Test

- 912 **moment** [móumənt] 명 순간
- 913 **Antarctica** [æntɑ́ːrktikə] 명 남극대륙
- 914 **elephant** [éləfənt] 명 코끼리
- 915 **shrimp** [ʃrimp] 명 새우
- 916 **daytime** [déitàim] 명 낮
- 917 **zebra** [zíːbrə] 명 얼룩말
- 918 **opinion** [əpínjən] 명 의견
- 919 **entire** [intáiər] 형 전체의
- 920 **giraffe** [dʒərǽf] 명 기린

Chapter 13 접속사

PSS & PRACTICE

- 921 **subway** [sʌ́bwèi] 명 지하철
- 922 **unhealthy** [ʌnhélθi] 형 건강하지 않은
- 923 **garden** [gɑ́ːrdən] 명 정원
- 924 **be good with** ~에 밝다, 능숙하다
- 925 **work on** ~을 열심히 하다, ~에 애쓰다
- 926 **Japanese** [dʒæ̀pəníːz] 명 일본어, 일본인
- 927 **Chinese** [tʃàiníːz] 명 중국어, 중국인
- 928 **machine** [məʃíːn] 명 기계
- 929 **round** [raund] 형 둥근
- 930 **survive** [sərváiv] 동 살아남다
- 931 **traffic light** [træfik lait] 명 교통 신호(등)

Day 28

오늘 외울 단어 **33**개

- ☐ 932 **supermarket** [súːpərmàːrkit] — 명 슈퍼마켓
- ☐ 933 **dress** [dres] — 동 옷을 입다 / 명 옷
- ☐ 934 **warmly** [wɔ́ːrmli] — 부 따뜻하게
- ☐ 935 **Italian** [itǽljən] — 형 이탈리아의
- ☐ 936 **art** [ɑːrt] — 명 예술
- ☐ 937 **a little** — 조금, 약간
- ☐ 938 **mark** [mɑːrk] — 명 점수
- ☐ 939 **neighbor** [néibər] — 명 이웃

Chapter Review Test

- ☐ 940 **rest** [rest] — 명 휴식
- ☐ 941 **environment** [inváiərənmənt] — 명 환경
- ☐ 942 **curly** [kə́ːrli] — 형 머리칼이 곱슬곱슬한
- ☐ 943 **in time** — 제시간에, 늦지 않게
- ☐ 944 **harmful** [hɑ́ːrmfəl] — 형 해로운
- ☐ 945 **care about** — ~를 걱정하다, 신경을 쓰다
- ☐ 946 **work** [wəːrk] — 동 일하다, 작동되다
- ☐ 947 **tell the truth** — 사실을 말하다
- ☐ 948 **presentation** [prèzəntéiʃən] — 명 발표
- ☐ 949 **anywhere** [énihwɛ̀ər] — 부 어디든지
- ☐ 950 **stick out** — ~를 내밀다, 눈에 띄다
- ☐ 951 **tongue** [tʌŋ] — 명 혀
- ☐ 952 **organized** [ɔ́ːrgənàizd] — 형 정리된
- ☐ 953 **volleyball** [válibɔ̀ːl] — 명 배구
- ☐ 954 **raincoat** [réinkout] — 명 우의, 비옷
- ☐ 955 **go on a field trip** — 현장학습을 가다
- ☐ 956 **shape** [ʃeip] — 명 모양
- ☐ 957 **be in shape** — 건강한 상태다, 몸매가 좋다

Chapter 14 전치사&속담

PSS & PRACTICE

- ☐ 958 **dawn** [dɔːn] — 명 새벽
- ☐ 959 **lunchtime** [lʌ́ntʃtàim] — 명 점심시간
- ☐ 960 **move** [muːv] — 동 이사하다
- ☐ 961 **take a rest** — 휴식을 취하다
- ☐ 962 **violin** [vàiəlín] — 명 바이올린
- ☐ 963 **everything** [évriθìŋ] — 대 모두, 모든 것
- ☐ 964 **all day** — 하루 종일

Day 29

오늘 외울 단어 **36**개

- 965 **stay out of** ~을 피하다
- 966 **mealtime** [míːltàim] 명 식사 시간
- 967 **repair** [ripέər] 동 수리하다
- 968 **need** [niːd] 동 필요로 하다
- 969 **west** [west] 부 서쪽으로 / 명 서쪽
- 970 **sunset** [sʌ́nsèt] 명 일몰
- 971 **spring** [spriŋ] 명 봄
- 972 **airport** [έərpɔ̀ːrt] 명 공항
- 973 **wedding** [wédiŋ] 명 결혼식
- 974 **among** [əmʌ́ŋ] 전 ~사이에
- 975 **space** [speis] 명 우주, 공간
- 976 **ground** [graund] 명 땅바닥, 지면
- 977 **island** [áilənd] 명 섬
- 978 **drawer** [drɔ́ːər] 명 서랍
- 979 **plane** [plein] 명 비행기
- 980 **rainbow** [réinbòu] 명 무지개
- 981 **boat** [bout] 명 보트
- 982 **department store** [dipάːrtmənt stɔːr] 명 백화점
- 983 **toyshop** [tɔ́iʃὰp] 명 장난감 가게
- 984 **difference** [dífərəns] 명 차이점
- 985 **finger** [fíŋgər] 명 손가락
- 986 **wall** [wɔːl] 명 벽
- 987 **hill** [hil] 명 언덕
- 988 **envelope** [énvəlòup] 명 봉투
- 989 **step** [step] 명 (발)걸음
- 990 **gift shop** [gift ʃɑp] 명 선물 가게
- 991 **salmon** [sǽmən] 명 연어
- 992 **stream** [striːm] 명 흐름, 시내
- 993 **river** [rívər] 명 강
- 994 **tunnel** [tʌ́nəl] 명 터널
- 995 **town** [taun] 명 읍, (소)도시
- 996 **dinner** [dínər] 명 저녁식사, 정찬
- 997 **head for** ~로 향하다
- 998 **land** [lænd] 동 착륙하다, 도착하다
- 999 **fence** [fens] 명 울타리
- 1000 **spacecraft** [spéiskrὰft] 명 우주선

Day 30

오늘 외울 단어 **35**개

- ☐ 1001 **get well** — 병이 나아지다
- ☐ 1002 **coupon** [kú:pɑn] — 명 쿠폰, 할인권
- ☐ 1003 **enough** [inʌ́f] — 형 충분한
- ☐ 1004 **ID card(= identification card)** [aidèntəfikéiʃən kɑ:rd] — 명 신분증
- ☐ 1005 **crayon** [kréian] — 명 크레용
- ☐ 1006 **gargle** [gá:rgl] — 동 양치질하다
- ☐ 1007 **traditional** [trədíʃənl] — 형 전통의
- ☐ 1008 **jazz music** [dʒæz mjú:zik] — 명 재즈 음악
- ☐ 1009 **area** [ɛ́əriə] — 명 지역, 구역
- ☐ 1010 **middle-aged** [mídl-éidʒid] — 형 중년의
- ☐ 1011 **treasure** [tréʒər] — 명 보물
- ☐ 1012 **drama** [drɑ́:mə] — 명 연극
- ☐ 1013 **leap** [li:p] — 동 뛰어오르다, 도약하다
- ☐ 1014 **haste** [heist] — 명 서두름
- ☐ 1015 **bark** [bɑ:rk] — 동 짖다
- ☐ 1016 **shower** [ʃáuər] — 명 소나기
- ☐ 1017 **spill** [spil] — 동 엎지르다, 쏟다
- ☐ 1018 **policy** [pɑ́ləsi] — 명 수단, 정책
- ☐ 1019 **bitter** [bítər] — 형 쓴
- ☐ 1020 **sight** [sait] — 명 시야
- ☐ 1021 **broth** [brɔ:θ] — 명 수프, 국
- ☐ 1022 **lead to** — ~로 이어지다
- ☐ 1023 **blame** [bleim] — 동 ~를 탓하다, 비난하다
- ☐ 1024 **tool** [tu:l] — 명 연장
- ☐ 1025 **workman** [wə́:rkmən] — 명 일꾼
- ☐ 1026 **put off** — 미루다

Chapter Review Test

- ☐ 1027 **comedian** [kəmí:diən] — 명 코미디언, 희극배우
- ☐ 1028 **do the dishes** — 설거지하다
- ☐ 1029 **rainy** [réini] — 형 비가 오는
- ☐ 1030 **for a minute** — 잠시 동안
- ☐ 1031 **bungee jumping** [bʌ́ndʒi dʒʌ́mpiŋ] — 명 번지점프
- ☐ 1032 **calendar** [kǽlindər] — 명 달력
- ☐ 1033 **turn right** — 오른쪽으로 돌다
- ☐ 1034 **allowance** [əláuəns] — 명 용돈
- ☐ 1035 **wisely** [wáizli] — 부 현명하게

Day 31

오늘 외울 단어 **36개**

☐ 1036 **as a result**	결과적으로	☐ 1054 **polite** [pəláit]	형 예의바른, 공손한
☐ 1037 **hang out**	어울려 놀다	☐ 1055 **etiquette** [étikit]	명 예의, 에티켓
☐ 1038 **achieve** [ətʃíːv]	동 달성하다, 성취하다	☐ 1056 **circle** [sə́ːrkl]	명 원, 동그라미
☐ 1039 **pain** [pein]	명 고통, 아픔	☐ 1057 **thumb** [θʌm]	명 엄지
☐ 1040 **monthly** [mʌ́nθli]	형 매달의 부 달마다	☐ 1058 **forefinger** [fɔ́ːrfiŋɡər]	명 검지
☐ 1041 **come across**	우연히 만나다	☐ 1059 **sore** [sɔːr]	형 아픈
☐ 1042 **throat** [θrout]	명 목, 목구멍	☐ 1060 **earn** [əːrn]	동 (돈을) 벌다
☐ 1043 **look like**	~처럼 생기다, ~와 닮다	☐ 1061 **about** [əbáut]	전 ~에 대한 부 약, ~쯤
☐ 1044 **spaceship** [spéisʃip]	명 우주선	☐ 1062 **moreover** [mɔːróuvər]	부 게다가
☐ 1045 **bazaar** [bəzáːr]	명 바자회, 특매장	☐ 1063 **suffer** [sʌ́fər]	동 고통을 받다
☐ 1046 **bacteria** [bæktíːəriə]	명 박테리아	☐ 1064 **welcome** [wélkəm]	동 환영하다
☐ 1047 **custom** [kʌ́stəm]	명 관습, 풍습	☐ 1065 **donate** [dóuneit]	동 기부하다
☐ 1048 **different from**	~와 다른	☐ 1066 **in need**	어려움에 처한, 궁핍한
☐ 1049 **bagel** [béigəl]	명 베이글	☐ 1067 **mud flat** [mʌd flæt]	명 개펄
☐ 1050 **come from**	~에서 오다, ~ 출신이다	☐ 1068 **take place**	일어나다, 발생하다
☐ 1051 **treat** [triːt]	동 대우하다	☐ 1069 **last** [læst]	동 지속되다
☐ 1052 **on a diet**	다이어트 중인	☐ 1070 **lost** [lɔːst]	형 잃어버린, 분실된
☐ 1053 **rude** [ruːd]	형 무례한	☐ 1071 **guesthouse** [ɡésthàus]	명 관광객용 숙소

마더텅 영문법 3800제 1
BASIC

Word Test

Problem Solving Skill

마더텅

Word Test 001-035　　　　　Day 01

날짜:　　　　　점수　　/35

● 영어를 우리말로 쓰세요.

01 | player
02 | parents
03 | speak
04 | be afraid of
05 | newspaper
06 | pretty
07 | warm
08 | go to the cinema
09 | photograph
10 | angry
11 | happen
12 | have breakfast
13 | movie
14 | friendly
15 | interesting
16 | draw
17 | wonderful
18 | go jogging

● 우리말을 영어로 쓰세요.

19 | 즐기다
20 | 일하다
21 | 경찰관
22 | 늦은
23 | 결혼한
24 | 자전거
25 | 병원
26 | 한가한, 자유로운
27 | 신이 난, 들뜬
28 | 비가 오다
29 | 배고픈
30 | 인터넷을 이용하다
31 | ~의 가까이(에), 가까이
32 | 마시다
33 | 피곤한, 지친
34 | 바쁜
35 | 방문객

Word Test 036-071　　　　　Day 02

날짜:　　　　점수　　/36

● 영어를 우리말로 쓰세요.

01 | amazing
02 | fast
03 | careful
04 | vacation
05 | enter
06 | sleep
07 | take a break
08 | wear
09 | turn on
10 | prepared
11 | go climbing
12 | grade
13 | keep in touch
14 | really
15 | great
16 | make a noise
17 | from now on
18 | ready

● 우리말을 영어로 쓰세요.

19 | 사다
20 | 작가
21 | 조용한
22 | 딸
23 | 교실
24 | 속상한, 마음이 상한
25 | 결석한
26 | 소개하다
27 | 거대한
28 | 공부하다
29 | 헬멧, 안전모
30 | 모퉁이
31 | (탈것에) 타다
32 | 수영하다
33 | 서두르다
34 | 체육관
35 | 청소하다, 깨끗한
36 | 걱정하다

Word Test 072-107 — Day 03

날짜: 점수   /36

●영어를 우리말로 쓰세요.

01	sweet	10	terrible
02	make a mistake	11	believe
03	cook	12	article
04	handsome	13	keep a diary
05	ask	14	strange
06	shine	15	engineer
07	delicious	16	subject
08	exciting	17	wash the dishes
09	storybook	18	healthy

●우리말을 영어로 쓰세요.

19	심다	28	호의
20	~이 되다	29	지루한
21	신, 시큼한 (맛의)	30	질문
22	페인트를 칠하다	31	사전
23	거짓말쟁이	32	수학
24	비밀	33	폭포
25	산	34	매우 좋아하는
26	사촌	35	움직이다
27	정직한, 솔직한	36	박물관

Word Test 108-142　　　　　　　　　　Day 04

날짜:　　　　　　점수　　/35

● 영어를 우리말로 쓰세요.

01 | umbrella
02 | sweater
03 | senior citizen
04 | hometown
05 | play computer games
06 | practice
07 | classmate
08 | guitar
09 | present
10 | often
11 | watch
12 | bring
13 | event
14 | report card
15 | cloudy
16 | far
17 | office worker

● 우리말을 영어로 쓰세요.

18 | 모래성
19 | 수프
20 | 동화, 옛날 이야기
21 | 역사
22 | 저녁
23 | 수영 선수
24 | 스카프, 목도리
25 | 서점
26 | 아름다운
27 | 허튼소리
28 | 텔레비전
29 | 숙녀, 여성
30 | 게으른
31 | 배드민턴
32 | 어제
33 | 정보
34 | 농부
35 | 채소

Word Test 143-177

Day 05

날짜: 점수   / 35

● 영어를 우리말로 쓰세요.

01 | lose
02 | lay
03 | send
04 | reach
05 | copy
06 | wish
07 | kick
08 | know
09 | get
10 | teach
11 | pay
12 | catch
13 | say
14 | finish
15 | push
16 | impress
17 | touch
18 | wake

● 우리말을 영어로 쓰세요.

19 | 놓치다, 그리워하다
20 | 노래하다
21 | 섞다
22 | 팔다
23 | 지나가다, (시험 등을) 통과하다
24 | 돕다, 거들다
25 | 걷다
26 | 노력하다, 시도하다
27 | 서다, 서 있다
28 | 교차하다, 건너가다
29 | 할머니
30 | 던지다
31 | 놓다, 두다
32 | 불타다
33 | 풀다, 해결하다
34 | 쓰다, 소비하다
35 | 소리가 나다

Word Test 178-213　　　Day 06

날짜:　　　점수　　/36

● 영어를 우리말로 쓰세요.

01 | understand
02 | grow
03 | live
04 | laugh
05 | arrive
06 | turn
07 | set
08 | keep
09 | dream
10 | cost
11 | leave
12 | seem
13 | envy
14 | give
15 | see
16 | tell
17 | hear
18 | think

● 우리말을 영어로 쓰세요.

19 | 해치다
20 | 껴안다
21 | 머무르다
22 | 갈채하다, 응원하다
23 | 깨뜨리다
24 | 이기다
25 | 반복하다
26 | 보여주다
27 | 의미하다
28 | 나르다, 운반하다
29 | 날다
30 | 떨어지다
31 | 잊다
32 | 판단하다
33 | 멈추다
34 | (건물 등을) 짓다
35 | 빌려주다
36 | 사용하다

Word Test 214-249 Day 07

● 영어를 우리말로 쓰세요.

01 | agree
02 | in the morning
03 | call
04 | check
05 | dance
06 | cover
07 | plan
08 | guess
09 | guide
10 | raise
11 | order
12 | change
13 | drop
14 | place
15 | improve
16 | suggest
17 | invent
18 | escape

● 우리말을 영어로 쓰세요.

19 | 가입하다, 합류하다
20 | 배우다
21 | 뛰다, 뛰어넘다
22 | 준수하다, 따르다
23 | 동쪽
24 | 솔질하다
25 | 병든, 아픈
26 | 공격하다
27 | 수도
28 | 축복하다
29 | 구하다, 절약하다, 저축하다
30 | ~을 야기시키다, 초래하다
31 | 모으다
32 | 재채기하다
33 | 이끼
34 | 이기다, 때리다
35 | 지구
36 | 장식하다

Word Test 250-284　　　　　Day 08

날짜:　　　　점수　/35

● 영어를 우리말로 쓰세요.

01 | shout
02 | return
03 | hurt
04 | lead
05 | smell
06 | marry
07 | collect
08 | end
09 | have
10 | let
11 | hate
12 | fight
13 | connect
14 | spread
15 | slide
16 | add
17 | train

● 우리말을 영어로 쓰세요.

18 | 실패하다
19 | 삼키다
20 | 망치다
21 | 먹이다, 먹이
22 | 공유하다
23 | 결정하다
24 | 궁금해 하다, ~에 놀라다
25 | 놀라게 하다
26 | 낭비하다
27 | 구르다
28 | 따르다, 붓다
29 | (자물쇠로) 잠그다
30 | 타자를 치다
31 | 대답하다
32 | 묶다
33 | (음식을) 차려주다, 제공하다
34 | 철자를 말하다
35 | (빵 등을) 굽다

Word Test 285 - 316 — Day 09

●영어를 우리말로 쓰세요.

01 | make dinner
02 | holiday
03 | actor
04 | take
05 | restaurant
06 | role
07 | ill
08 | bear
09 | ago
10 | have lunch
11 | exam
12 | smile
13 | heavily
14 | rise
15 | choose
16 | during

●우리말을 영어로 쓰세요.

17 | 시간을 만들다, 시간을 내다
18 | 도서관
19 | 불다
20 | 소설
21 | 눈이 내리다
22 | (종, 벨이) 울리다
23 | 물다
24 | 함께
25 | 외식하다
26 | 일어나다, 발발하다
27 | 일출
28 | 자정
29 | 건너뛰다
30 | 계획, 기획, 프로젝트
31 | 조부, 조모
32 | (물속으로) 뛰어들다

Word Test 317-350　　　Day 10

날짜:　　　점수　　/34

● 영어를 우리말로 쓰세요.

01 | take a picture
02 | visit
03 | begin
04 | hide
05 | these days
06 | explain
07 | review
08 | throw away
09 | climb
10 | get up
11 | pick
12 | discuss
13 | listen to
14 | loudly
15 | last year
16 | thank
17 | field trip

● 우리말을 영어로 쓰세요.

18 | 매일 일어나는
19 | 탁구
20 | 미래
21 | 스파게티
22 | 연
23 | 야구를 하다
24 | 날씨
25 | 외국인
26 | 콘서트, 음악회
27 | 디자이너
28 | 카펫, 깔개
29 | 헤드폰
30 | 열대의
31 | 이모, 고모
32 | 쓰다, 집필하다
33 | 주말
34 | 바비큐 파티를 하다

Word Test 351-385 — Day 11

●영어를 우리말로 쓰세요.

01 | have a seat
02 | bill
03 | find
04 | try on
05 | alone
06 | make it
07 | outside
08 | break off
09 | casual
10 | go out
11 | lecture
12 | stair
13 | match
14 | clothes
15 | exit
16 | for a while
17 | dangerous
18 | traffic

●우리말을 영어로 쓰세요.

19 | 나뭇가지
20 | 전화번호
21 | 젓가락
22 | 재활용하다
23 | 따르다
24 | 옳은, 오른쪽의
25 | 내일
26 | 진실의, 참된
27 | 초대하다
28 | 법
29 | 목마른
30 | (시간 단위) 분
31 | 무엇인가, 어떤 것
32 | 문제
33 | 오늘밤에
34 | 엘리베이터
35 | 약속

Word Test 386-418 — Day 12

날짜: 점수   /33

● 영어를 우리말로 쓰세요.

01 | clean up
02 | human
03 | speech
04 | be late for school
05 | tell a lie
06 | dentist
07 | balloon
08 | protect
09 | pick up
10 | kill
11 | theater
12 | lie
13 | matter
14 | contest
15 | take care of
16 | expression

● 우리말을 영어로 쓰세요.

17 | ~에 관심이 있다
18 | 전쟁
19 | 끄다
20 | 치통
21 | 우체국
22 | 배달하다
23 | 성공하다
24 | 운동하다
25 | 벗다
26 | 다람쥐
27 | 무엇, 아무것
28 | 교장 선생님
29 | 잠들다
30 | 대통령, 사장
31 | 주차하다
32 | 외국의
33 | 똑바로, 일직선으로

Word Test 419-451 — Day 13

날짜: 점수   /33

●영어를 우리말로 쓰세요.

01 | fresh
02 | found
03 | building
04 | language
05 | robber
06 | dead
07 | audience
08 | village
09 | truth
10 | refrigerator
11 | painting
12 | teenager
13 | princess
14 | beauty
15 | fix
16 | someone

●우리말을 영어로 쓰세요.

17 | 모여들다, 붐비다
18 | 자유
19 | 디자인하다
20 | 기억
21 | 밀림지대, 정글
22 | 태어나다
23 | 출판하다
24 | 벌
25 | 잡지
26 | 존경하다
27 | 한 번
28 | 훔치다
29 | 어떤 사람, 누군가
30 | 선출하다
31 | 음악가
32 | 독자
33 | ~하게 하다

Word Test 452 - 487　　　Day 14

●영어를 우리말로 쓰세요.

01 | brush
02 | wealth
03 | safe
04 | bottle
05 | wagon
06 | bath
07 | festival
08 | peace
09 | wife
10 | candle
11 | sheep
12 | kindness
13 | happiness
14 | country
15 | mouse
16 | pleasure
17 | factory
18 | deer

●우리말을 영어로 쓰세요.

19 | 거위, 기러기
20 | 두통
21 | 동정, 연민
22 | 선반
23 | 연기
24 | 황소
25 | 지붕
26 | 여권
27 | 포스터, 전단 광고
28 | 우정
29 | 밀가루
30 | 주소
31 | 달, 개월
32 | 모양, 형상
33 | 나무 조각, 구역
34 | 수업, 교훈
35 | 생각, 아이디어
36 | 모기

Word Test 488-523 — Day 15

날짜:　　　　　점수　　　/36

● 영어를 우리말로 쓰세요.

01 | another
02 | faithful
03 | popular
04 | station
05 | floor
06 | airless
07 | seat
08 | special
09 | snake
10 | thief
11 | clear
12 | university
13 | autumn
14 | same
15 | bathroom
16 | European
17 | armchair
18 | imagine

● 우리말을 영어로 쓰세요.

19 | 곤충
20 | 가구
21 | ~로 알려져 있다
22 | 도심지, 상업 지구
23 | (건물의) 층
24 | 충고
25 | 호주머니
26 | 습한
27 | 유명한
28 | 컵, 머그잔
29 | 학, 두루미
30 | 암
31 | 사발
32 | 분필, 초크
33 | 초급의, 초등의
34 | 감각
35 | 잠깐의 휴식
36 | 비행기

Word Test 524-556　　Day 16

날짜:　　　　점수　/33

● 영어를 우리말로 쓰세요.

01 | each other
02 | blackboard
03 | be full of
04 | always
05 | leaf
06 | uncle
07 | in front of
08 | look for
09 | recognize
10 | volunteer
11 | clover
12 | useful
13 | at the end of
14 | pair
15 | cent
16 | several

● 우리말을 영어로 쓰세요.

17 | (음식을 얇게 썬) 조각
18 | 청바지
19 | 꼬리
20 | 오크나무
21 | 빵집, 제과점
22 | ~에 들어가다
23 | 늑대
24 | 가위
25 | 접시, 그릇
26 | 쉬다, 휴식하다
27 | 인간, 사람
28 | 제복, 교복
29 | 관광, 구경
30 | 칠면조
31 | 후식, 디저트
32 | 연극, 놀이
33 | 목걸이

Word Test 557-591 — Day 17

●영어를 우리말로 쓰세요.

01 | between
02 | example
03 | horror
04 | course
05 | culture
06 | still
07 | pay for
08 | dark
09 | no way
10 | belong to
11 | journey
12 | weigh
13 | tough
14 | science fiction
15 | prize
16 | fault
17 | important

●우리말을 영어로 쓰세요.

18 | 거북
19 | 소나무
20 | 담임 선생님
21 | 유사한
22 | 감기에 걸리다
23 | 썩은
24 | 과학
25 | 소유하다
26 | 싸다, 포장하다
27 | 자살하다
28 | 방과 후에
29 | 가을
30 | 교과서
31 | 배낭
32 | 부정직한
33 | 자랑스러운
34 | (중량의 단위) 파운드
35 | 색을 칠하다, 색

Word Test 592-625　　　　　Day 18

날짜:　　　　　점수　　/34

● 영어를 우리말로 쓰세요.

01 | historic
02 | surprised
03 | each
04 | soon
05 | go back
06 | turn
07 | place
08 | easy
09 | expect
10 | on the Internet
11 | grow up
12 | ask for
13 | musical instrument
14 | get to
15 | hamster
16 | pleased
17 | goal

● 우리말을 영어로 쓰세요.

18 | 청구서
19 | 필요한 것
20 | 평화로운
21 | 거울
22 | 칼
23 | 치료
24 | 숨쉬다
25 | 계절
26 | 도움이 되는
27 | 귀가 먼
28 | 항해하다
29 | 행방불명이 되다
30 | 조종사
31 | 간단한, 단순한
32 | 살을 빼다
33 | 과학자
34 | 모피, 털

Word Test 626-660 — Day 19

● 영어를 우리말로 쓰세요.

01 | talk about
02 | hobby
03 | race
04 | early
05 | cut down
06 | storm
07 | abroad
08 | see a doctor
09 | pool
10 | travel
11 | do volunteer work
12 | chemical
13 | campaign
14 | take part in
15 | whole
16 | one's school days
17 | blind

● 우리말을 영어로 쓰세요.

18 | ~에게서 소식을 듣다
19 | 좌우로 (흔들리는)
20 | 요양원
21 | 마스코트
22 | 흔들(리)다, 떨리다
23 | 블라우스
24 | 식물
25 | 필통
26 | 잡담하다, 채팅하다
27 | 뒤쫓다
28 | 화가
29 | 잡초
30 | 산책하다
31 | 습관, 버릇
32 | 닫다, 막다, (눈을) 감다
33 | ~에 집중하다
34 | 미식축구
35 | 시간을 아끼다

Word Test 661-693 — Day 20

날짜:　　　　　점수　　/33

● 영어를 우리말로 쓰세요.

01 | stadium
02 | take a test
03 | come out
04 | play the violin
05 | keep ~ from …
06 | disabled
07 | win a prize
08 | suddenly
09 | continue
10 | cartoon
11 | bench
12 | through
13 | go on a picnic
14 | give up
15 | thank for
16 | go for a walk
17 | mind

● 우리말을 영어로 쓰세요.

18 | 자연
19 | 소음
20 | 우주 비행사
21 | 식사
22 | ~를 잘하다
23 | 규칙
24 | 극복하다
25 | 언젠가, 머지않아
26 | 건강
27 | 아무나, 누구나
28 | 눈물
29 | 나이가 지긋한
30 | 농사를 짓다
31 | 한계
32 | 활동
33 | 규칙적으로

Word Test 694 - 727 — Day 21

● 영어를 우리말로 쓰세요.

01 | apologize
02 | ride a bicycle
03 | avoid
04 | overflow
05 | in-line skating
06 | be bad for
07 | result
08 | get rid of
09 | fishing
10 | gas
11 | person
12 | hold
13 | along
14 | be good for
15 | remember
16 | little by little
17 | trash

● 우리말을 영어로 쓰세요.

18 | 생산품
19 | 범람하다, 홍수
20 | 행동
21 | 차고 세일
22 | 영화
23 | 벽돌
24 | 힘, 기운, 강점
25 | 참새
26 | 정문, (대)문
27 | 계단을 이용하다
28 | 싫증이 나다
29 | 도움을 주다
30 | 해변
31 | 회사
32 | 여배우
33 | 죽음
34 | 그러므로

Word Test 728-760 — Day 22

날짜: 점수   / 33

● 영어를 우리말로 쓰세요.

01 | topic
02 | enjoyable
03 | look at
04 | disappointed
05 | show up
06 | readily
07 | key
08 | piece
09 | danger
10 | accident
11 | set up
12 | satisfied
13 | poor
14 | broken
15 | situation
16 | performance

● 우리말을 영어로 쓰세요.

17 | 휴대폰
18 | 재능
19 | 경쟁하다, ~와 겨루다
20 | 마늘
21 | 무대
22 | 유창하게
23 | 굶주림, 기아
24 | 카네이션
25 | (불에) 굽다
26 | 양파
27 | 들꽃, 야생초
28 | 보름달
29 | 유리
30 | 피곤하게 만드는
31 | 들판
32 | 충격적인
33 | 주저하는, 망설이는

Word Test 761-795 — Day 23

● 영어를 우리말로 쓰세요.

01 | trouble
02 | be sold out
03 | past
04 | planet
05 | grade
06 | discover
07 | medicine
08 | degree
09 | rock
10 | else
11 | boil
12 | chance
13 | crowded
14 | luck
15 | bride
16 | sickness
17 | clever
18 | courage

● 우리말을 영어로 쓰세요.

19 | ~이 없이
20 | 틀린
21 | 프랑스의, 프랑스어
22 | 동물
23 | 표, 투표
24 | 지갑
25 | 학급, 수업
26 | 바구니
27 | 사원
28 | 버터
29 | 필요한
30 | 100년, 세기
31 | 궁금한, 호기심이 많은
32 | 궁전
33 | 룸메이트
34 | 기자
35 | 완벽한

Word Test 796-829 Day 24

날짜:　　　　　점수　　/34

● 영어를 우리말로 쓰세요.

01 | until
02 | spirit
03 | noisy
04 | nothing special
05 | regular
06 | experience
07 | difficulty
08 | quick
09 | cafeteria
10 | various
11 | wise
12 | silent
13 | before
14 | surprising
15 | sound
16 | sincere

● 우리말을 영어로 쓰세요.

17 | 보통의
18 | 용감한
19 | 절반, 30분
20 | 큰, 넓은
21 | 4분의 1, 15분
22 | 진짜의
23 | 노력, 공
24 | 갑작스러운
25 | 놀이터, 운동장
26 | 주된, 주요한
27 | 운 좋은
28 | 소리가 큰
29 | 모래
30 | 교회
31 | 인근, 이웃
32 | 심각한, 진지한
33 | 봅슬레이
34 | 온도

Word Test 830-864 — Day 25

● 영어를 우리말로 쓰세요.

01 | put on
02 | worm
03 | garbage
04 | foggy
05 | quickly
06 | twice
07 | dear
08 | depend on
09 | work out
10 | meeting
11 | act
12 | dish
13 | stuff
14 | hope
15 | appear
16 | never
17 | graceful
18 | price

● 우리말을 영어로 쓰세요.

19 | 비닐봉지
20 | 댄서, 무용수
21 | 안경
22 | 매주의, 주간의
23 | ~ 뒤에
24 | 각자 모두, 누구든지
25 | 당근
26 | 둘러보다
27 | ~을 믿다
28 | 플래시, 번득임, 섬광
29 | 배달하다
30 | 재킷
31 | 열
32 | 자명종
33 | (짐을) 싸다
34 | 수트, 정장 한 벌
35 | 정크 푸드

Word Test 865 - 898　　　　　　　Day 26

날짜:　　　　　점수　　/34

● 영어를 우리말로 쓰세요.

01 | well

02 | useless

03 | scary

04 | mild

05 | other

06 | lately

07 | badly

08 | smart

09 | costly

10 | patient

11 | happily

12 | thin

13 | tasty

14 | hard

15 | colorful

16 | foolish

17 | light

● 우리말을 영어로 쓰세요.

18 | 두꺼운

19 | 엄격한

20 | 깊은

21 | 주의하여, 조심스럽게

22 | 가는, 날씬한

23 | 뚱뚱한

24 | 남편

25 | 나비

26 | 근면한

27 | 밝은

28 | 편안한

29 | 가망 없는, 절망적인

30 | 사랑스러운

31 | 약한

32 | 관대한

33 | 가까운

34 | 현대적인

Word Test 899-931 — Day 27

●영어를 우리말로 쓰세요.

01 | opinion
02 | choice
03 | be good with
04 | pleasant
05 | survive
06 | public
07 | daytime
08 | clothing
09 | illness
10 | unhealthy
11 | drugstore
12 | machine
13 | work on
14 | round
15 | moment
16 | score
17 | entire

●우리말을 영어로 쓰세요.

18 | 변명, 이유
19 | 기린
20 | 남극대륙
21 | 항공 우편
22 | 공룡
23 | 교통 신호(등)
24 | 새우
25 | 치타
26 | 얼룩말
27 | 다리, 교량
28 | 중국어, 중국인
29 | 코끼리
30 | 정원
31 | 지적인, 총명한
32 | 지하철
33 | 일본어, 일본인

Word Test 932 - 964 — Day 28

날짜: 점수   / 33

● 영어를 우리말로 쓰세요.

01 | take a rest
02 | care about
03 | stick out
04 | warmly
05 | dawn
06 | neighbor
07 | go on a field trip
08 | volleyball
09 | anywhere
10 | mark
11 | be in shape
12 | environment
13 | supermarket
14 | move
15 | harmful
16 | organized
17 | in time

● 우리말을 영어로 쓰세요.

18 | 혀
19 | 이탈리아의
20 | 점심시간
21 | 일하다, 작동되다
22 | 발표
23 | 옷을 입다
24 | 우의, 비옷
25 | 하루 종일
26 | 휴식
27 | 사실을 말하다
28 | 조금, 약간
29 | 예술
30 | 바이올린
31 | 머리칼이 곱슬곱슬한
32 | 모두, 모든 것
33 | 모양

Word Test 965 - 1000 — Day 29

날짜: 점수   /36

● 영어를 우리말로 쓰세요.

01 | difference
02 | among
03 | stream
04 | repair
05 | plane
06 | dinner
07 | envelope
08 | mealtime
09 | step
10 | land
11 | drawer
12 | spacecraft
13 | stay out of
14 | gift shop
15 | space
16 | fence
17 | ground
18 | town

● 우리말을 영어로 쓰세요.

19 | 벽
20 | 공항
21 | 강
22 | 보트
23 | 터널
24 | 서쪽으로, 서쪽
25 | 언덕
26 | 무지개
27 | ~로 향하다
28 | 필요로 하다
29 | 장난감 가게
30 | 연어
31 | 백화점
32 | 봄
33 | 섬
34 | 손가락
35 | 일몰
36 | 결혼식

Word Test 1001-1035　　Day 30

날짜:　　　점수　/35

● 영어를 우리말로 쓰세요.

01 | treasure
02 | wisely
03 | get well
04 | broth
05 | gargle
06 | leap
07 | enough
08 | lead to
09 | haste
10 | do the dishes
11 | ID card
12 | area
13 | tool
14 | traditional
15 | for a minute
16 | put off
17 | policy
18 | workman

● 우리말을 영어로 쓰세요.

19 | 시야
20 | 중년의
21 | 달력
22 | 소나기
23 | ~를 탓하다, 비난하다
24 | 크레용
25 | 쓴
26 | 엎지르다, 쏟다
27 | 오른쪽으로 돌다
28 | 연극
29 | 비가 오는
30 | 짖다
31 | 코미디언, 희극배우
32 | 번지점프
33 | 쿠폰, 할인권
34 | 용돈
35 | 재즈 음악

Word Test 1036-1071 — Day 31

날짜:　　　　점수　　/36

● 영어를 우리말로 쓰세요.

01	take place
02	come across
03	forefinger
04	spaceship
05	earn
06	bazaar
07	as a result
08	sore
09	treat
10	donate
11	hang out
12	about
13	look like
14	welcome
15	in need
16	come from
17	moreover
18	achieve

● 우리말을 영어로 쓰세요.

19	원, 동그라미
20	박테리아
21	갯벌
22	~와 다른
23	지속되다
24	다이어트 중인
25	엄지
26	고통, 아픔
27	예의바른, 공손한
28	잃어버린, 분실된
29	무례한
30	베이글
31	예의, 에티켓
32	매달의, 달마다
33	관광객용 숙소
34	관습, 풍습
35	고통을 받다
36	목, 목구멍

마더텅 영문법 3800제 1 BASIC 학습계획표

DAY	Ch	학습내용	학습날짜
DAY 1	1	PSS 1-1 ~ 1-4	월 일
DAY 2		PSS 1-5 ~ 1-9	월 일
DAY 3		PSS 1-10 ~ 1-13	월 일
DAY 4		PSS 2-1 ~ 2-5	월 일
DAY 5		Chapter Review Test	월 일
DAY 6	2	PSS 1-1 ~ 2-5	월 일
DAY 7		PSS 3 ~ 4-4	월 일
DAY 8		PSS 5-1 ~ 5-2	월 일
DAY 9		Chapter Review Test	월 일
DAY 10	3	PSS 1 ~ 4-2	월 일
DAY 11		PSS 4-3 ~ 4-6	월 일
DAY 12		PSS 4-7 ~ 4-10	월 일
DAY 13		Chapter Review Test	월 일
DAY 14	4	PSS 1 ~ 2	월 일
DAY 15		PSS 3 ~ 4	월 일
DAY 16		PSS 5 ~ 6	월 일
DAY 17		Chapter Review Test	월 일
DAY 18		Chapter 1 ~ 4 Review	월 일
DAY 19	5	PSS 1 ~ 2-3	월 일
DAY 20		PSS 3 ~ 5	월 일
DAY 21		PSS 6 ~ 11	월 일
DAY 22		Chapter Review Test	월 일
DAY 23	6	PSS 1 ~ 3	월 일
DAY 24		PSS 4 ~ 5-3	월 일
DAY 25		PSS 6-1 ~ 7	월 일
DAY 26		Chapter Review Test	월 일
DAY 27	7	PSS 1-1 ~ 1-2	월 일
DAY 28		PSS 2 ~ 3	월 일
DAY 29		PSS 4-1 ~ 4-2	월 일
DAY 30		Chapter Review Test	월 일
DAY 31	8	PSS 1 ~ 2	월 일
DAY 32		PSS 3-1 ~ 3-3	월 일
DAY 33		Chapter Review Test	월 일
DAY 34	9	PSS 1 ~ 3	월 일
DAY 35		PSS 4 ~ 5	월 일
DAY 36		Chapter Review Test	월 일
DAY 37		Chapter 5 ~ 9 Review	월 일
DAY 38	10	PSS 1 ~ 4-2	월 일
DAY 39		PSS 4-3 ~ 4-9	월 일
DAY 40		PSS 5-1 ~ 6-4	월 일
DAY 41		Chapter Review Test	월 일
DAY 42	11	PSS 1-1 ~ 2-2	월 일
DAY 43		PSS 3 ~ 4	월 일
DAY 44		PSS 5-1 ~ 6-2	월 일
DAY 45		Chapter Review Test	월 일
DAY 46	12	PSS 1-1 ~ 1-4	월 일
DAY 47		PSS 2 ~ 3-3	월 일
DAY 48		PSS 4-1 ~ 4-2	월 일
DAY 49		Chapter Review Test	월 일
DAY 50	13	PSS 1 ~ 2	월 일
DAY 51		PSS 3 ~ 4	월 일
DAY 52		PSS 5 ~ 7	월 일
DAY 53		Chapter Review Test	월 일
DAY 54	14	PSS 1-1 ~ 1-4	월 일
DAY 55		PSS 2-1 ~ 2-4	월 일
DAY 56		PSS 3-1 ~ 3-3	월 일
DAY 57		PSS 4 ~ 6-2	월 일
DAY 58		PSS 7	월 일
DAY 59		Chapter Review Test	월 일
DAY 60		Chapter 10 ~ 14 Review	월 일

학습계획표 작성하고, 선물 받으세요! 참여해 주신 모든 분께 선물을 드립니다.

책을 다 풀고, SNS 또는 온라인 커뮤니티에 작성한 학습계획표 사진을 업로드

좌측 QR코드를 스캔하여 작성한 게시물의 URL 인증

참여자 전원 증정!

1천 원권 + 2천 점

필수 태그 #마더텅 #마더텅영문법3800제 #학습계획표 #공스타그램
SNS / 온라인 커뮤니티 페이스북, 인스타그램, 블로그, 네이버/다음 카페 등

※ 상품은 이벤트 참여일로부터 2~3일(영업일 기준) 내에 발송됩니다.
※ 동일한 교재의 학습계획표로 중복 참여시 이벤트 대상에서 제외됩니다.
※ 자세한 사항은 왼쪽 QR 코드를 스캔하시거나 또는 홈페이지 이벤트 공지글을 참고해 주세요.
※ 만 14세 미만은 부모님께서 신청해 주셔야 합니다.
※ 이벤트 기간: 2023년 12월 31일까지 (※ 해당 이벤트는 당사 사정에 따라 조기 종료될 수 있습니다.)

B Book 포인트란? 마더텅 인터넷 서점(http://book.toptutor.co.kr)에서 교재 구매 시 현금처럼 사용할 수 있는 포인트입니다.

필수암기 동사구

단어	뜻	예시
bring up	~을 기르다, 양육하다	She brought up five children. 그녀는 다섯 명의 아이를 길렀다.
carry out	~을 수행하다	They will carry out their duties. 그들은 그들의 임무를 수행할 것이다.
catch up with	~을 따라잡다	James started pedalling faster, and within seconds caught up with her. James는 더 빨리 페달을 밟기 시작했고, 수 초 이내에 그녀를 따라잡았다.
call off	~을 취소하다	I have to call off the meeting. 나는 회의를 취소해야겠어요.
deal with	~을 처리하다	There are important matters to deal with. 처리해야 할 중요한 사안들이 있다.
get rid of	~을 없애다, 처분하다	I am going to get rid of my old car. 나는 낡은 차를 처분하려고 한다.
knock down	~을 치다, 때려눕히다	He knocked his opponent down three times. 그는 상대를 세 번 때려눕혔다.
laugh at	~을 비웃다	Amy thinks people will laugh at her if she sings. Amy는 만약 그녀가 노래를 한다면 사람들이 그녀를 비웃을 것이라고 생각한다.
look after	~을 돌보다	I need someone to look after my dog. 내 애완견을 돌봐줄 사람이 필요하다.
look down on	~을 낮춰보다(얕보다)	Don't look down on me because I'm young. 내가 어리다고 얕보지 마세요.
look up to	~을 존경하다	I look up to my parents. 나는 우리 부모님을 존경한다.
take advantage of	~을 이용하다	We took full advantage of the school facilities. 우리는 학교 시설을 최대한 이용했다.
pay attention to	~에 주의를 기울이다	Pay attention to what I'm saying! 제 말에 귀 기울여 주세요!
pick up	~을 줍다/(차에) 태우다	They picked up garbage on the street. 그들은 거리에서 쓰레기를 주웠다.
put off	~을 연기하다	Never put off till tomorrow what you can do today. 오늘 할 수 있는 일을 내일로 미루지 마라.
refer to A as B	A를 B라고 부르다/일컫다	Mark refers to him as a dear friend. Mark는 그를 소중한 친구라고 부른다.
speak ill of	~에 대해 안 좋게 말하다	Don't speak ill of others behind their backs. 뒤에서 남의 욕을 하지 마라.
take care of	~을 돌보다/처리하다	Please take care of my son. 제 아들을 돌봐 주세요.
throw away	~을 버리다	We throw away paper and plastic. 우리는 종이와 플라스틱을 버린다.
turn down	~을 거절하다	He asked her to marry him but she turned him down. 그가 그녀에게 청혼을 했지만 그녀가 거절했다.
turn off	~을 끄다	Please turn the television off before you go to bed. 잠자리에 들기 전에 텔레비전을 꺼 주세요.
turn on	~을 켜다	I'll turn on the air conditioner. 제가 에어컨을 켤게요.

필수문법용어

용어	설명	예문
동명사	동사를 동사원형+~ing의 형태로 변형하여 명사처럼 쓸 수 있도록 한 말 문장에서 주어, 보어, 목적어의 역할을 함	I enjoyed **playing** baseball last summer. 나는 지난여름 야구 하는 것을 즐겼다.
분사	동사가 변형되어 형용사 역할을 하는 말 예 현재분사, 과거분사	I found a big **melting** ice. 나는 녹고 있는 큰 얼음을 찾았다. There were a lot of **fallen** leaves. 떨어진 잎이 많이 있었다.
현재분사	'~하고 있는, ~하는'의 의미로 진행이나 능동을 나타내는 분사	It is an **interesting** story. 그것은 흥미로운 이야기이다.
과거분사	'~한, ~된, ~당한'의 의미로 완료나 수동을 나타내는 분사	It was just a **broken** radio. 그것은 단지 고장 난 라디오였다.
가정법	실제로 일어나지 않은 상황을 가정할 때 쓰는 동사의 형태	If I **were** rich, I **could buy** the house. 내가 부자라면, 그 집을 살 수 있을 텐데.
관계대명사 관계부사	두 개의 문장을 연결하여 두 문장의 관계를 나타내는 말 접속사+대명사[부사]의 역할을 함	This is the letter **which** was written by her. 이것은 그녀에 의해 쓰여진 편지다. I remember the day **when** he left. 나는 그가 떠났던 날을 기억한다.
선행사	관계사 앞에 오는 말로 관계사가 수식하는 명사, 구, 절을 의미함	Once there lived **a farmer** who was diligent. 옛날에 부지런한 한 농부가 살았다.

필수문법용어

		예문
직접목적어	4형식 문장에서 **동작의 대상**이 되는 목적어 '~을[를]'이라고 해석	I gave him **a piece of advice**. 나는 그에게 조언을 해 주었다.
간접목적어	4형식 문장에서 직접목적어를 받는 사람(사물) '~에게'라고 해석	I gave **him** a piece of advice. 나는 그에게 조언을 해 주었다.
대과거	과거 시점보다 **더 앞선 과거**, had+과거분사의 형태로 나타냄	He lost the pen he **had bought** the day before. 그는 전날 산 펜을 잃어버렸다.
시제	사건이나 사실이 **언제 일어난** 것인지 표시하는 문법 요소 현재, 과거, 미래, 진행 시제, 완료 시제 등을 포함한 12시제가 있음	He **teaches** English to us. 그는 우리에게 영어를 가르친다. World War II **ended** in 1945. 세계 2차 대전은 1945년에 끝났다.
격	명사, 대명사가 문장 안에서 갖는 자격 예) 주격, 목적격, 소유격	I know **a girl**. **Her** eyes are very big. 나는 한 소녀를 안다. 그녀의 눈은 매우 크다.
조동사	동사 앞에서 의무, 추측, 가능, 요청, 허가, 제안 등의 의미를 더하는 말	You **must** stay awake. 너는 깨어 있어야 한다.
태	주어와 동사와의 관계 - 능동태: 주어가 동작을 스스로 할 경우 - 수동태: 주어가 동작을 받는 경우	She **built** this house. 그녀는 이 집을 지었다. This house **was built** by her. 이 집은 그녀에 의해 지어졌다.

인칭대명사 CHAPTER 1 PSS 1 & CHAPTER 6 PSS 1

수	인칭	주격	소유격	목적격	소유대명사
단수	1	I	my	me	mine
	2	you	your	you	yours
	3	he	his	him	his
	3	she	her	her	hers
	3	it	its	it	–
복수	1	we	our	us	ours
	2	you	your	you	yours
	3	they	their	them	theirs

명사의 복수형 CHAPTER 5 PSS 2

규칙 복수형 I	대부분의 경우	-s	pencil – pencils, sport – sports
	-s, -x, -ch, -sh로 끝날 때	-es	bus - buses, box - boxes, church - churches, dish - dishes
	자음 +o로 끝날 때	-es	potato - potatoes, tomato - tomatoes *cf.* piano - pianos, photo - photos
	모음 +o로 끝날 때	-s	radio - radios, audio - audios
규칙 복수형 II	자음 +y로 끝날 때	y를 i로 바꾸고 -es	candy - candies, country - countries
	모음 +y로 끝날 때	-s	day - days, boy - boys
	-f, -fe로 끝날 때	f / fe를 v로 바꾸고 -es	leaf - leaves, wolf - wolves knife - knives *cf.* roof - roofs
불규칙 복수형	단수형과 복수형이 같은 명사		deer - deer, fish - fish, sheep - sheep
	그 밖의 명사의 불규칙 복수형		foot - feet, tooth - teeth, man - men, woman - women, goose - geese, mouse - mice

spend	spent	spent	소비하다
teach	taught	taught	가르치다
tell	told	told	말하다
think	thought	thought	생각하다
understand	understood	understood	이해하다
win	won	won	이기다

3. ABC형 (원형, 과거형, 과거분사형이 다른 형)

원형	과거형	과거분사형	뜻
be	was / were	been	~이다, 있다
begin	began	begun	시작하다
break	broke	broken	깨뜨리다
choose	chose	chosen	선택하다
do	did	done	하다
drive	drove	driven	운전하다
eat	ate	eaten	먹다
fall	fell	fallen	떨어지다
forget	forgot	forgotten	잊다
give	gave	given	주다
go	went	gone	가다
know	knew	known	알다
see	saw	seen	보다
sing	sang	sung	노래하다
speak	spoke	spoken	말하다
swim	swam	swum	수영하다
take	took	taken	가지고 가다
throw	threw	thrown	던지다
wear	wore	worn	입다
write	wrote	written	쓰다

4. ABA형 (원형과 과거분사형이 같은 형)

원형	과거형	과거분사형	뜻
become	became	become	되다
come	came	come	오다
run	ran	run	달리다

원급, 비교급, 최상급 CHAPTER 12 PSS 1

1. 규칙 변화형

	원급	비교급	최상급
대부분의 경우: -er/-est	tall	tall**er**	tall**est**
-e로 끝나는 경우: -r/-st	nice	nic**er**	nic**est**
단모음 + 단자음으로 끝나는 경우 : 마지막 자음 하나 더 쓰고 -er/-est	fat	fat**ter**	fat**test**
자음 +y로 끝나는 경우 : y를 i로 바꾸고 -er/-est	pretty	prett**ier**	prett**iest**
대부분의 2음절 이상 형용사	useful	**more** useful	**most** useful
	famous	**more** famous	**most** famous
분사 형태 형용사	excited	**more** excited	**most** excited
[형용사 + ly] 형태의 부사	quickly	**more** quickly	**most** quickly

2. 불규칙 변화형

원급	비교급	최상급
good / well	better	best
bad / badly / ill	worse	worst
many / much	more	most
little	less	least
old	older (나이 든)	oldest
	elder (연상의)	eldest
late	later (늦은)	latest
	latter (나중인)	last
far	farther (먼)	farthest
	further (더욱)	furthest

일반동사의 불규칙 변화형 CHAPTER 2 PSS 2-4

1. AAA형 (원형, 과거형, 과거분사형이 같은 형)

원형	과거형	과거분사형	뜻
cost	cost	cost	비용이 들다
hit	hit	hit	치다
let	let	let	~하게 하다
put	put	put	놓다
read [riːd]	read [red]	read [red]	읽다
set	set	set	놓다

2. ABB형 (과거형과 과거분사형이 같은 형)

원형	과거형	과거분사형	뜻
bring	brought	brought	가져오다
build	built	built	짓다
buy	bought	bought	사다
catch	caught	caught	잡다
feel	felt	felt	느끼다
fight	fought	fought	싸우다
find	found	found	발견하다
get	got	got(ten)	얻다
have	had	had	가지다, 먹다
hear	heard [həːrd]	heard [həːrd]	듣다
hold	held	held	지니다
keep	kept	kept	유지하다
lead	led	led	인도하다
leave	left	left	떠나다
lose	lost	lost	잃어버리다
make	made	made	만들다
meet	met	met	만나다
pay	paid	paid	지불하다
say	said [sed]	said [sed]	말하다
sell	sold	sold	팔다
send	sent	sent	보내다
sit	sat	sat	앉다

마더텅 영문법 3800제 1 BASIC 학습진도표

CHAPTER 1 문장의 기초

PSS		체크	학습날짜
PSS 1	1-1	☐	/
	1-2	☐	/
	1-3	☐	/
	1-4	☐	/
	1-5	☐	/
	1-6	☐	/
	1-7	☐	/
	1-8	☐	/
	1-9	☐	/
	1-10	☐	/
	1-11	☐	/
	1-12	☐	/
	1-13	☐	/
PSS 2	2-1	☐	/
	2-2	☐	/
	2-3	☐	/
	2-4	☐	/
	2-5	☐	/
Chapter Review Test		☐	/

CHAPTER 2 시제

PSS		체크	학습날짜
PSS 1	1-1	☐	/
	1-2	☐	/
	1-3	☐	/
	1-4	☐	/
PSS 2	2-1	☐	/
	2-2	☐	/
	2-3	☐	/
	2-4	☐	/
	2-5	☐	/
PSS 3		☐	/
PSS 4	4-1	☐	/
	4-2	☐	/
	4-3	☐	/
	4-4	☐	/
PSS 5	5-1	☐	/
	5-2	☐	/
Chapter Review Test		☐	/

CHAPTER 3 조동사

PSS		체크	학습날짜
PSS 1		☐	/
PSS 2		☐	/
PSS 3		☐	/
PSS 4	4-1	☐	/
	4-2	☐	/
	4-3	☐	/
	4-4	☐	/
	4-5	☐	/
	4-6	☐	/
	4-7	☐	/
	4-8	☐	/
	4-9	☐	/
	4-10	☐	/
Chapter Review Test		☐	/

CHAPTER 4 수동태

PSS	체크	학습날짜
PSS 1	☐	/
PSS 2	☐	/
PSS 3	☐	/
PSS 4	☐	/
PSS 5	☐	/
PSS 6	☐	/
Chapter Review Test	☐	/

CHAPTER 5 명사와 관사

PSS		체크	학습날짜
PSS 1		☐	/
PSS 2	2-1	☐	/
	2-2	☐	/
	2-3	☐	/
PSS 3		☐	/
PSS 4		☐	/
PSS 5		☐	/
PSS 6		☐	/
PSS 7		☐	/
PSS 8		☐	/
PSS 9		☐	/
PSS 10		☐	/
PSS 11		☐	/
Chapter Review Test		☐	/

CHAPTER 6 대명사

PSS		체크	학습날짜
PSS 1		☐	/
PSS 2		☐	/
PSS 3		☐	/
PSS 4		☐	/
PSS 5	5-1	☐	/
	5-2	☐	/
	5-3	☐	/
PSS 6	6-1	☐	/
	6-2	☐	/
PSS 7		☐	/
Chapter Review Test		☐	/

마더텅 영문법 3800제 1 BASIC 학습진도표

CHAPTER 7 부정사

PSS		체크	학습날짜
PSS 1	1-1	☐	/
	1-2	☐	/
PSS 2		☐	/
PSS 3		☐	/
PSS 4	4-1	☐	/
	4-2	☐	/
Chapter Review Test		☐	/

CHAPTER 8 동명사

PSS		체크	학습날짜
PSS 1		☐	/
PSS 2		☐	/
PSS 3	3-1	☐	/
	3-2	☐	/
	3-3	☐	/
Chapter Review Test		☐	/

CHAPTER 9 분사

PSS	체크	학습날짜
PSS 1	☐	/
PSS 2	☐	/
PSS 3	☐	/
PSS 4	☐	/
PSS 5	☐	/
Chapter Review Test	☐	/

CHAPTER 10 형용사

PSS		체크	학습날짜
PSS 1		☐	/
PSS 2		☐	/
PSS 3		☐	/
PSS 4	4-1	☐	/
	4-2	☐	/
	4-3	☐	/
	4-4	☐	/
	4-5	☐	/
	4-6	☐	/
	4-7	☐	/
	4-8	☐	/
	4-9	☐	/
PSS 5	5-1	☐	/
	5-2	☐	/
PSS 6	6-1	☐	/
	6-2	☐	/
	6-3	☐	/
	6-4	☐	/
Chapter Review Test		☐	/

CHAPTER 11 부사

PSS		체크	학습날짜
PSS 1	1-1	☐	/
	1-2	☐	/
PSS 2	2-1	☐	/
	2-2	☐	/
PSS 3		☐	/
PSS 4		☐	/
PSS 5	5-1	☐	/
	5-2	☐	/
PSS 6	6-1	☐	/
	6-2	☐	/
Chapter Review Test		☐	/

CHAPTER 12 비교구문

PSS		체크	학습날짜
PSS 1	1-1	☐	/
	1-2	☐	/
	1-3	☐	/
	1-4	☐	/
PSS 2		☐	/
PSS 3	3-1	☐	/
	3-2	☐	/
	3-3	☐	/
PSS 4	4-1	☐	/
	4-2	☐	/
Chapter Review Test		☐	/

CHAPTER 13 접속사

PSS	체크	학습날짜
PSS 1	☐	/
PSS 2	☐	/
PSS 3	☐	/
PSS 4	☐	/
PSS 5	☐	/
PSS 6	☐	/
PSS 7	☐	/
Chapter Review Test	☐	/

CHAPTER 14 전치사 & 속담

PSS		체크	학습날짜
PSS 1	1-1	☐	/
	1-2	☐	/
	1-3	☐	/
	1-4	☐	/
PSS 2	2-1	☐	/
	2-2	☐	/
	2-3	☐	/
	2-4	☐	/
PSS 3	3-1	☐	/
	3-2	☐	/
	3-3	☐	/
PSS 4		☐	/
PSS 5		☐	/
PSS 6	6-1	☐	/
	6-2	☐	/
PSS 7		☐	/
Chapter Review Test		☐	/

PROBLEM SOLVING SKILL

www.toptutor.co.kr